YO-BRX-344

LIFE AND TIMES OF
BENJAMIN FRANKLIN

Volume II

A Da Capo Press Reprint Series

THE AMERICAN SCENE
Comments and Commentators

GENERAL EDITOR: WALLACE D. FARNHAM
University of Illinois

LIFE AND TIMES OF
BENJAMIN FRANKLIN

By James Parton

Volume II

DA CAPO PRESS • NEW YORK • 1971

Chadron State College Library

Chadron, Nebr.

A Da Capo Press Reprint Edition

This Da Capo Press edition of the
Life and Times of Benjamin Franklin
is an unabridged republication of the first
edition published in 1864.

Library of Congress Catalog Card Number 72-126603

SBN 306-70048-4

Published by Da Capo Press
A Division of Plenum Publishing Corporation
227 West 17th Street, New York, N.Y. 10011

All Rights Reserved

Manufactured in the United States of America

R
F85p
v. 2

LIFE AND TIMES OF
BENJAMIN FRANKLIN

Volume II

H.B.Hall.

MRS. SARAH BACHE.

DAUGHTER OF FRANKLIN.

H. B. Hall.

FRANKLIN IN PARIS.

AGED 71.

LIFE AND TIMES

OF

BENJAMIN FRANKLIN.

BY

JAMES PARTON,

AUTHOR OF "LIFE AND TIMES OF AARON BURR," "LIFE OF ANDREW JACKSON,"
"GENERAL BUTLER IN NEW ORLEANS," ETC.

"I will follow the right cause even to the stake: but without the
stake if I can."—MONTAIGNE.

VOL. II.

NEW YORK:
MASON BROTHERS, NO. 7 MERCER ST.
BOSTON: MASON & HAMLIN; PHILADELPHIA: J. B. LIPPINCOTT & CO.;
CHICAGO: S. C. GRIGGS & CO.
LONDON: TRUBNER & CO., 60 PATERNOSTER ROW.
1864.

Entered according to Act of Congress, in the year 1864,

By MASON BROTHERS,

In the Clerk's Office of the District Court of the United States for the
Southern District of New York.

C. A. ALVORD, STEREOTYPER AND PRINTER.

CONTENTS OF VOL II.

PART IV.—Continued.

CONTENTS.

LIFE AND TIMES OF BENJAMIN FRANKLIN.

CHAPTER IX.

THE TORIES RAGE, AND THE WHIGS IMAGINE A VAIN THING.

ENGLAND had lost her colonies, though no one yet suspected it. Madness now seized both parties; only there was method in the madness of the colonists. It is not ours to relate the public events which accompanied and followed the scenes just described : such as the destruction of the tea in Boston harbor; the passage of Lord North's avenging measure, called the Boston Port Bill; the adoption of the cause of Boston as their own by the other colonies; six regiments of British troops posted in Boston; the calm protests of Washington, Lee, and Jefferson; the wild eloquence of Patrick Henry; the passage of the bill transferring political offenders to England for trial, with their train of witnesses and advocates; the torrents of petitions against these measures; the haughty rejection of these petitions; the tumults in America; the exasperating insolence of the king's speeches to Parliament; and, above all, the meeting of the Continental Congress at Philadelphia. All these things have been eloquently told by Mr. Bancroft, and are familiar to decently informed persons in every land. America became the universal topic, France appearing to be more interested in it than England, though there were in Parliament fifty "field-night" debates upon America during the next three or four years.

How the tories raved against America! "Sir," Dr. Johnson would say, "the Americans are a race of convicts, and ought to be thankful for any thing we can give them." At this crisis he wrote his extravagant pamphlet, "Taxation no Tyranny," a production which the ministry instigated and revised. The old tory followed the custom of his employers in styling Franklin the "master of mischief," who taught Congress "to put in motion the engine of electricity, and give the great stroke by the name of Boston." Johnson could not even be witty in this cause, so bitter was his malevolence. Indeed, his animosity against the Americans was such that his friends often sat confounded at the spectacle of his wrath. Talking pleasantly, one day, with Miss Sewall and other ladies, upon the universal benevolence enjoined by Christianity, he chanced to say, "I am willing to love all mankind except an American." Instantly, says Boswell, "his inflammable corruption bursting into horrid fire, he breathed out threatenings and slaughter, calling them rascals, robbers, pirates, and exclaiming he'd burn and destroy them." The lady gave him a mild but cutting rebuke. "Sir," said she, "this is an instance that we are always most violent against those whom we have injured." At which, says Bozzy, "he roared out another tremendous volley, which, one might fancy, could be heard across the Atlantic." On another occasion Boswell ventured the audacity of praising Dr. Franklin's famous definition of Man: "A tool-making animal." Johnson was upon him straight. "Many a man," said he, "never made a tool; and suppose a man without arms, he could not make a tool." Such poor nonsense could this wittiest of savages utter when an American was the object of attack. The tories in Parliament, in the cabinet, in the palace, were less savage than their pamphleteer, but they were not less arrogant, ignorant, and infatuated.

And the men of liberal minds, unhappily, were dissolute. The errors of virtuous men tend to bring virtue itself into disrepute. Perhaps a man like George III., who possessed and represented such virtue as there then was in England, makes more roués and debauchees than such a king as George IV., who was himself a roué and debauchee; for the one renders virtue odious, and the other renders vice odious. However that may be, it is certain that the younger men of that day, who might have rescued their country from the king, were dissipated beyond all English parallel. There was Charles James Fox, for example, the gallant Prince Hal of politics, he could have saved his country, with Burke's mighty help, if he had been as virtuous as Burke. It was at this very time that he and his comrades were running that course of dissipation which posterity will never read of without amazement. They had a club at Almacks, Horace Walpole records, " where they played only for rouleaux of £50 each, and generally there was £10,000 in specie on the table. Lord Holland had paid above £20,000 for his two sons. Nor were the manners of the gamesters, or even their dresses for play, undeserving notice. They began by pulling off their embroidered clothes and put on frieze greatcoats, or turned their coats inside outwards for luck. They put on pieces of leather (such as are worn by footmen when they clean the knives) to save their laced ruffles; and to guard their eyes from the light and to prevent tumbling their hair, wore high-crowned straw hats with broad brims, and adorned with flowers and ribbons; masks to conceal their emotions when they played at quinze. Each gamester had a small neat stand by him, to hold their tea, or a wooden bowl with an edge of ormolu to hold their rouleaux. They borrowed great sums of Jews at exorbitant premiums. Charles Fox called his outward room, where those Jews waited till he rose, his Jerusalem Chamber."

Consider the scene, also, which occurred on the night of an illumination in London : " It happened at three in the morning, that Charles Fox, Lord Derby and his brother, Major Stanley, and two or three more young men of quality, having been drinking at Almack's, suddenly thought of making a tour of the streets, and were joined by the Duke of Ancaster, who was very drunk, and, what showed it was no premeditated scheme, the latter was a courtier, and had actually been breaking windows. Finding the mob before Palliser's house, some of the young lords said: ' Why don't you break Lord G. Germaine's windows ?' The populace had been so little tutored that they asked who he was, and being encouraged, broke his windows. The mischief pleasing the juvenile leaders, they marched to the Admiralty, forced the gates, and demolished Palliser's and Lord Lisburne's windows. Lord Sandwich, exceedingly terrified, escaped through the garden, with his mistress, Miss Ray, to the Horse Guards, and there betrayed most manifest panic."

Burke alone, among the leaders of the Opposition, added the great weight of character to the force of illustrious talents. But Burke had no influential family connections, little fortune, an imperfect temper, and no tact. He always astonished, often charmed, sometimes electrified, frequently fatigued, seldom convinced the House of Commons. The Opposition, moreover, were divided into two factions, who could unite to oppose, but not to govern— *one*, while the victory was doubtful; *two*, on the question of the spoils.

And what a prize England was trifling with! In 1774 Great Britain exported to North America nearly the whole of the surplus products of her industry. Since 1704, the American trade had grown from half a million sterling a year to six millions and a half; a trade which had started Scotland upon its prosperous career, enriched the English seaports, and stimulated the industry of the country. Boston and New England, which made so much noise in the world, were far from being then the most important portion of the continent. Philadelphia had become a city of forty thousand inhabitants. The great colony of Virginia, abounding in able and valiant men, exerted an almost overshadowing influence. Bostonians who visited Charleston, saw there evidences of wealth, commerce, and refinement, which their native town had never exhibited. Josiah Quincy, of Boston, who was at Charleston in 1773, wrote:

"The number of shipping far surpassed any thing I had ever seen in Boston. * * * This town makes a most beautiful appearance as you come up to it, and in many respects a magnificent one. * * I can only say in general, that in grandeur, splendor of buildings, decorations, equipages, numbers, commerce, shipping, and, indeed, in almost every thing, it far surpasses all I ever saw, or ever expected to see in America. * * All seems at present to be trade, riches, magnificence, and great state in every thing; much gayety and dissipation." He mentions that the fashionable musical society of the city paid their first violin a salary of five hundred guineas per annum, and that the concerts of the society were attended by two hundred and fifty ladies in great costume. True to their blood, the "flaming tories" of Charleston (as mad then as now) regarded the late events at the north as certain proofs that "Boston aims at nothing less than the sovereignty of the whole continent." "I KNOW it," roared one of these intelligent gentlemen, after dinner.

Through such a country, inhabited by nearly three millions of people, of whom a respectable number had seen service in the field, and a vast multitude were familiar with arms and hardship, a British general said, in Franklin's presence, that he could lead a thousand British grenadiers, and inflict upon every male the last indignity.

Mr. Burke complained, too, that the English people, even the classes most interested in commerce, were strangely apathetic with regard to America. In September, 1774, he writes to the Marquis of Rockingham : " I agree with your lordship entirely ; the American and foreign affairs will not come to any crisis sufficient to rouse the public from its present stupefaction during the course of the next session. I have my doubts whether those, at least of America, will do it *for some years to come*. It is evident, from the spirit of the Pennsylvania instructions, as well as the measure of a congress, and consequent embassy, that the affair will draw out into great length. If it does, I look upon it as next to impossible that the present temper and unanimity of America can be kept up ; popular remedies must be quick and sharp, or they are very ineffectual. The people there can only work on ministry through the people here, and the people here will be little affected by the sight of half a dozen gentlemen from America dangling at the levees of Lord Dartmouth and Lord North, or negotiating with Mr. Pownall. If they had chosen the non-importation measure as the leading card, they would have put themselves on a par with us ; and we should be in as much haste to negotiate ourselves out of our commercial, as they out of their constitutional difficulties. But in the present temper of the nation, and with the character of the present administration, the disorder and discontent of all America, and the more remote future mischiefs which may arise from those causes, operate as little as the division of Poland. The insensibility of the merchants of London is of a degree and kind scarcely to be conceived. Even those who are most likely to be overwhelmed by any real American confusion are amongst the most supine. The character of the ministry either produces or perfectly coincides with the disposition of the public."*

These sentences were penned six months before the battle of Lexington. The Duke of Richmond's remark in the House of Lords, a little later, may partly explain the apathy of liberal men :

* Burke's Works and Correspondence, vol. i., page 285.

" I confess I feel very languid about this American business. The only thing that can restore common sense to this country is feeling the dreadful consequences which must soon follow such diabolical measures."

CHAPTER X.

WAITING FOR THE CONGRESS.

FRANKLIN'S official life in London appeared to be ended. He went to court no more, nor to the levees of ministers, nor dangled about the office of Lord Dartmouth. He was a marked man, whom it was a point of party discipline for the tories to defame and the whigs to praise. The royal governors in America interposed obstacles to the payment of his salaries, and tory organs in England advised his arrest as the prime mover of the colonial discontents. His liberal friends were more attentive to him than before, and he continued to frequent his clubs and the circles of the Opposition. Resuming his preparations to return to Philadelphia, the great news that Massachusetts had come into the proposed measure of a general congress induced him to pause. Friends on both sides of the ocean entreated him to wait a little longer, since the congress might agree upon measures which his presence in Europe could materially forward. He consented to delay his departure the more willingly because Arthur Lee, who was to succeed him as agent for Massachusetts, was on the continent making the tour of Europe.

His pen and his influence were still actively employed in behalf of his country. He published, this year, a thick pamphlet, the joint production of himself and Arthur Lee, which gave a complete and passionless history of the whole controversy between the ministry and Massachusetts, with all the important documents and correspondence relating to it. Nothing could have been more convincing than this naked statement of facts. He gave to the *Public Advertiser* several Essays of his own; one entitled The Rise and Progress of the Differences between Great Britain and her Colo-

nies, and others of a more humorous turn ; all published with fictitious signatures. He concluded one of these little pieces with two
questions : " Did ever any tradesman succeed who attempted to
drub customers into his shop ?   And will honest JOHN BULL, the
farmer, be long satisfied with servants that before his face attempt
to kill his *plow-horses*."

On another occasion he discoursed as follows : " Your correspondent Brittannicus inveighs violently against Dr. Franklin, for his
ingratitude to the ministry of this nation, who have conferred upon
him so many favors.   They gave him the post-office of America ;
they made his son a governor ; and they offered him a post of five
hundred a year in the salt-office, if he would relinquish the interests
of his country ; but he has had the wickedness to continue true to
it, and is as much an American as ever.   As it is a settled point in
government here, that every man has his price, it is plain they are
bunglers in their business, and have not given him enough.   Their
master has as much reason to be angry with them, as Rodrigue in
the play with his apothecary for not effectually poisoning Pandolpho, and they must probably make use of the apothecary's justification, viz. :

" *Rodrigue.* ' You promised to have this Pandolpho upon his
bier in less than a week ; 'tis more than a month since, and he still
walks and stares me in the face.'

" *Fell.* ' True ; and yet I have done my best endeavors.   In
various ways I have given the miscreant as much poison as would
have killed an elephant.   He has swallowed dose after dose ; far
from hurting him, he seems the better for it.   He hath a wonderfully strong constitution.   I find I cannot kill him but by cutting
his throat, and that, as I take it, is not my business.'

" *Rodrigue.* ' Then it must be mine.' "

At the same time he read in a Boston paper that he had been
restored to the favor of the king, and was about to be employed in
an office superior to that from which he had been dismissed.   This
announcement he had the amusement of reading when he was in
some fear of arrest.   " My situation here," he wrote in October,
" is thought by many to be a little hazardous ; for if, by some accident, the troops and people of New England should come to blows,
I should probably be taken up ; the ministerial people affecting
everywhere to represent me as the cause of all the misunderstand-

ing ; and I have been frequently cautioned to secure my papers, and by some advised to withdraw. But I venture to stay, in compliance with the wish of others, till the result of the Congress arrives, since they suppose my being here might on that occasion be of use; and I confide in my innocence, that the worst which can happen to me will be an imprisonment upon suspicion, though that is a thing I should much desire to avoid, as it may be expensive and vexatious, as well as dangerous to my health."

It afterward appeared that his apprehensions of arrest were not groundless. Copies of some of his late letters to Boston, and of Arthur Lee's, having been transmitted to England, secret orders were sent out to General Gage to procure the originals, which the ministry intended to use as the basis of a prosecution for treason. Some old letters of Franklin's were afterward found in Boston and laid before the king, which happened to contain warm expressions of loyalty to the monarch and of affection for the mother country.

It must not be concealed from the reader that there were persons in Massachusetts who entertained suspicions of Dr. Franklin's fidelity to the cause of his country. No public man who deserves praise escapes censure. It may be comforting to some calumniated servants of the public to know that Benjamin Franklin, with all his merit and all his prudence, had to encounter his share of misrepresentation, not merely from the enemies of his country, but from its friends also. We must now expend a little space in pointing out the source and motive of the calumnies which, during the next ten years of his life, sometimes disturbed his peace, and sometimes lessened his influence.

Arthur Lee was the source, and desire of Franklin's place was the motive.

Many persons have gained immortal fame by being the friends of great men. Of Arthur Lee posterity will know little more than that he was the enemy of Franklin. Unless the reader of these lines is an exceptionally well-informed or an exceptionally ill-informed person, there is in his mind, at this moment, a lurking distrust of Franklin's absolute sincerity which could be traced back, through various channels of calumny, to the peculiarly constituted brain of Arthur Lee.

Yet Arthur Lee was long supposed to be an honest man and a fervent patriot !

He was of that family in Virginia which furnished three brothers
to the civil service of the country during the revolutionary period:
Richard Henry Lee, the well-known orator and member of Congress ; Arthur Lee, noted in the diplomatic service ; William Lee,
first a merchant and alderman of London, afterward American
minister to the courts of Frederick the Great and Maria Theresa.
The two volumes of the Life and Letters of Arthur Lee contain
seven lines of real biography. They are these: " Arthur was the
youngest son of the family ; and, according to the customs of that
day in regard to the youngest sons, was left, until an advanced
period of boyhood, with the children of his father's slaves ; to partake of their fare, and to participate in their hardy sports and toils.
Hence his body was early inured to hardship, and his mind accustomed to unrestrained exercise and bold adventures." That is to
say : Arthur Lee spent the first fourteen years of his life in the
closest contact and most intimate association with servile barbarians ;
whom he could insult without receiving a word in reply ; whom
he could strike without being struck back ; who were obliged to
humor, obey, and flatter him ; nourishing his worst propensities,
and walling him in against the influences he needed most. It is
one of the direst of the dire results of slavery, that it renders manly
education hopelessly impossible ; for that requires equality among
playmates and subordination in the school-room.* Perhaps Arthur

* " Watch the children play together; the young master romps with his dark-colored subjects ;
if they play 'horse' they are driven, he the driver; they must not contend with him for a point
at marbles, or a right to be equal in a game; if they play at battles it is theirs to take, not to return blows; childhood does not make them equals in childhood's plays, and one gleam of independence on their, or assertion of unfairness on master's part, makes them liable to his complaint, and the angry touch of his mother's heavy hand. I have seen a little girl of ten years of
age order a colored lad of eighteen to be flogged for simply mistaking upon which pony she had
ordered the side-saddle to be placed for her lesson in equestrianship. In our latitude a smiling
request to have the mistake rectified would have followed, but the pretty, spoiled daughter of the
South lost her tiny temper, and her doting uncle, angry at her annoyance, confirmed her repulsive
fiat. The writer was little beyond childhood herself at the time, and well remembers pleading for
the remission of a like sentence passed upon a slave girl who had forgotten to obey some one of
her trivial requests. To have such an offense heavily punished was intended as a mark of respect
to the youthful guest.
" The lady of this mansion, who was a confirmed invalid, always had a small hide whip in her
work-basket; when this whip was occasionally hidden by some one of the horde of fearful little
negroes, I have known her to send them to cut fresh switches and fetch them to be used upon
their own trembling, ill-covered shoulders and arms. As to boxed-ears and most energetic
slaps administered to govern house servants, they were too frequent to be instanced. Their own
excuse, when any remark was hazarded upon this common practice was, that by no other means
could slaves be 'kept under;' that they were too stupid, too obstinate, to be reasoned with ; that
to abolish frequent and instant punishment for even trivial errors, would be to render them un-

Lee was aware of this truth ; he was a frequent declaimer against slavery, though he could not outlive its effects upon his own character. Nearly every Virginian, however, was then a hater of slavery. Three or four generations of Saxon men must live and die among slaves, and the race must get down to the very dregs of its pristine intelligence and virtue, before it can produce human creatures capable of saying that slavery is not wrong. *Believe it*, no one ever did ; no, not the most unrelenting overseer of Alabama ; not the abjectest priest in either Carolina ; not the fiercest editor in New Orleans ; not the bloodiest Legree of Arkansas ; not the silliest woman in Virginia.

Arthur Lee had the opportunity of correcting his plantation habits on the free play-grounds of English Eton. He studied medicine at Edinburgh, graduating from the University there with distinction. He practiced his profession in Virginia, but abandoned it soon, returned to London, studied law, was admitted to the bar, and was getting into business of some emolument in London, when the controversy with the colonies drew him into politics. From the beginning to the end of that controversy he was a consistent and most earnest advocate of his country's cause.

The great defect of his character was an extreme and morbid propensity to think ill of other men's motives. He was one of those unhappy persons who are ceaselessly haunted with distrust, credulous of evil, incredulous of good. Even John Adams, his particular friend, himself too prone to suspicion, admitted that Arthur Lee " had confidence in nobody, believed all men selfish, and no man honest or sincere." " This," adds Mr. Adams, " I fear is his creed, from what I have heard him say ; I have often disputed with him on this point."* We need no testimony upon this unfortunate trait except his own letters, which teem with expressions of distrust. He thought Dr. Bancroft corrupt ; he could not " implicitly confide in" Lord Shelburne ; Lord North he pronounced in one letter to be " nothing," and in another " plausible, deep, and treacherous." Lord

controllable. No assertion can be falser than this ; upon the pliant, child-like mind of the colored race, kindness works like magic ; their devotion and attachment to homes wherein they have been made to drink many a bitter cup, speaks loudly of their wonderful capacity of affection.

"But with such influence molding the young character, is it to be wondered at that pride, impatience, and love of aristocratic, unjust power, grow with the growth, and strengthen with the strength of this people, and that young men of the South are haughty, arrogant, and self-willed, or the young women high-tempered, hasty, and often cruel ?—*N. Y. Tribune*, Jan. 17th, 1862,

* Life and Works of John Adams, iii., 188.

Dartmouth he considered " insignificant ;" nay, he was " even ad-
dicted to methodism ;" which " argued a weak mind or a hipo-
critical heart." John Jay he thought was a man who required
watching. Indeed, he scarcely mentions a man but to assert or insinuate evil of him. So credulous of evil was he, that he would
send to America such tales as this : " The Highlanders are all sworn
under their colors never to give quarter to an American," and had
already hanged many prisoners in their belts. Nothing was too
absurd for him to believe, provided it were only as wicked as it was
absurd. How he revelled in the sounding malignancy of Junius.
Junius was his model; the only writer in England, he thought,
who was worth attending to. He even adopted the name, and obtained considerable celebrity on both sides of the Atlantic by a series of papers, signed Junius Americanus.

It is common to say that a man who is prone to assign to innocent actions corrupt motives, convicts himself of corruptibleness.
This opinion does not appear to be correct, for some of the most
honest of men have labored under this infirmity ; John Adams and
John Jay, for examples. I think it is always a sign of a limited
understanding ; sometimes of morbid vanity ; sometimes of envy
and bad temper. In Arthur Lee it seems to have resulted from
limitedness, conceit, and envy. He had a very high opinion of the
great Junius Americanus ; he thought him capable of the greatest
employments ; he had not understanding enough to perceive the
immeasurable superiority of Dr. Franklin's airy, unpretending
sense to the ponderous, declamatory nothingness of the American
Junius.

Thrown into the society of Dr. Franklin, he was alternately attracted and repelled by him. He could neither resist the charm of
Franklin's wit and good nature, nor avoid coveting his place ; and,
consequently, his letters to Boston contain high encomiums upon the
conduct and character of Franklin, as well as the most gross and scandalous insinuations respecting his motives. At the time when Franklin was at open war with Lord Hillsborough, and was refused admittance to his presence, Arthur Lee regarded him as a tool of that nobleman, and an anonymous letter to that effect was sent to the Speaker
of the Massachusetts Assembly. If this letter was not written by
Arthur Lee, it certainly expressed his opinion ; for, at the same
time, June, 1771, he wrote to Samuel Adams in the terms follow-

ing : " I have read lately in your papers an assurance from Dr. Franklin, that all designs against the charter of the colony are laid aside. This is just what I expected from him ; and, if it be true, the Doctor is not the dupe but the instrument of Lord Hillsborough's treachery. That Lord Hillsborough gives out this assurance is certain ; but notorious as he is for ill faith and fraud, his duplicity would not impose on one possessed of half Dr. Franklin's sagacity. The possession of a profitable office at will, the having a son in a high post at pleasure, the grand purpose of his residence here being to effect a change in the government of Pennsylvania, for which administration must be cultivated and courted, are circumstances which, joined with the temporizing conduct he has always 'held in American affairs, preclude every rational hope, that in an open contest between an oppressive administration and a free people, Dr. Franklin can be a faithful advocate for the latter ; or oppose and expose the former with a spirit and integrity, which alone can, in times like these, be of any service. By temporizing I mean, consulting the inclination of ministers, and acting conformably to that, not to the interests of the province." And much more of the same purport.

Eager for place, he sent home charges against the agent for Virginia, and added that he should be happy to serve his native province in the capacity of agent. To Boston he wrote in June, 1773, when the affair of the Hutchinson Letters was in progress : " Dr. Franklin frequently assures me that he shall sail for Philadelphia in a few weeks, but I believe he will not quit us till he is gathered to his fathers." In another communication he strongly intimates a suspicion that Dr. Franklin had been " bribed to betray his trust ;" or, if not bribed, that his conduct was directed with a single eye to the retention of his office. Yet, in writing an account of the outrage in the Privy Council, he said that Dr. Franklin bore the assaults of Wedderburn " with a calmness and equanimity which conscious integrity alone can inspire." He added, that the same cause which rendered him obnoxious to the ministry must endear him to his countrymen ; and that his dismissal from an office which had been made valuable by his own wisdom and industry, was a damage to the government rather than to him.

That this tardy justice did not obliterate the impressions produced by years of misrepresentation, we have abundant proofs, but

they need not be detailed.   It is painful to know that such men as
Samuel Adams, John Adams, Josiah Quincy, and many kindred
spirits in Boston, should have been obliged, for some years, to entertain doubts of the fidelity of a man who did more than all others
together to generate the spirit, and disseminate the knowledge,
which prepared the colonists to maintain their rights.

In November of this year came to London Josiah Quincy, a
brilliant member of the Boston bar, a patriot surcharged with zeal
for his country's cause.   It is too probable, from the Diary of this
noble young man, that part of his errand to London was to ascertain whether Dr. Franklin was indeed an American at heart.   All
doubts were quickly dispelled from his generous soul.   His first
entry is this: "Waited upon Dr. Franklin and drank tea with him.
He appears to be in good health and spirits, and *seems* warm in our
cause, and confident of success."   On the same day, he writes:
"Dr. Franklin *appears* the staunch friend of our cause."   A week
later, he diarizes thus: "Dr. Franklin took me to the Club of the
Friends of Liberty at the London Coffee-House," where he met Dr.
Price, Alderman Oliver, Mr. Vaughan, and "eight or nine dissenting clergymen."   Three days later: "Dr. Franklin is an American, heart and soul.   You may trust him.   * * He is explicit
and bold.   * * Two worthy Norfolk farmers sailed to settle in
America, under the auspices of the great Dr. Franklin."   Ten days
after: "In the House of Lords, last week, when the address to the
king was in debate, Lord Hillsborough said that there were then
men walking in the streets of London who ought to be in Newgate
or at Tyburn.   The Duke of Richmond demanded explanation,
saying, if that was the case, the ministry was grossly to blame for
not arresting them."   Lord Hillsborough replied evasively, but
made it sufficiently plain that the persons to whom he referred
were Dr. Franklin and Josiah Quincy.   Again, January 17th, 1775:
"Dined with Mrs. Stevenson, with a number of ladies and gentlemen, in celebration of Dr. Franklin's birthday, who made one of
the festive company, although he this day enters the seventieth
year of his age."

His last London entry, dated March 3d, 1775, is interesting in
view of the succeeding catastrophe: "This being the day before
my departure, I dined with Dr. Franklin, and had three hours private conversation with him.   Dissuades from France or Spain.   In-

timate with both the Spanish and French embassadors; the latter a shrewd, great man. By no means take any step of great consequence, unless upon a sudden emergency, without advice of the Continental Congress. Explicitly, and in so many words, said, that New England alone could hold out for ages against this country, and if they were firm and united, in *seven years* would conquer them. Said he had the best intelligence that the manufacturers were feeling bitterly, and loudly complaining of the loss of the American trade. Let your adherence be to the non-importation and non-exportation agreement, a year from next December or to the next session of Parliament, and the day is won."

Mr. Quincy was far gone in consumption when he sailed. The doctors advised him to defer his departure, particularly Dr. Fothergill, " who would take no fee of an American." It was so desirable, however, to transmit to Boston intelligence which could not be trusted to writing, that he insisted on going, content if he could just reach his native shore, and gasp the information with which he was charged with his dying breath. The voyage was rough, wet, cold, and long. He grew worse and weaker, as the slow weeks rolled miserably by; until, in the seventh week, the agonizing truth was revealed to him that he could not live to tread again the land he loved. There was no one on board whom he could trust. To a sailor who had befriended him in his sickness, he dictated a last message to his family, apologizing to them, as it were, for undertaking the voyage : " The most weighty motive of all that determined my conduct, was the extreme urgency of about fifteen or twenty most stanch friends of America, and many of them the most learned and respectable characters in the kingdom, for my immediately proceeding to Boston. * * To commit their sentiments to writing was neither practicable nor prudent at this time. To the bosom of a friend they could intrust what might be of great advantage to my country. To me that trust was committed, and I was, immediately upon my arrival, to assemble certain persons to whom I was to communicate my trust, and, had God spared my life, it seems it would have been of great service to my country."

He could speak no more. Five days longer he lingered, and breathed his last when the shores of New England had just been descried. Few young men have been so mourned. Franklin was touched with his devotion to his country, and his frank, cordial de-

meanor, and foresaw that his zeal for the cause would consume him.
It fell to the lot of Mrs. Adams to console the widow of the young
patriot. "Poor afflicted woman," she wrote, "my heart was
wounded for her." The heart of New England was wounded for
her.

The purport of Mr. Quincy's message has not transpired, but we
can infer its substance from what is now known of the state of
things in England in the spring of 1775. He was probably commissioned to inform his fellow patriots, that the KING was the
great obstacle to the redress of their wrongs; that the premier
was reluctant to push the colonies to extremities ; that the opposition, comprising the ablest orators and statesmen of England, could
not but prevail at length; that the great body of dissenters sympathized with America ; that the manufacturers and merchants, who
were already restive, would be clamorous for a change in the colonial policy, if the colonists strictly adhered to their agreement to
suspend all business relations with the mother country ; that a single
year of non-importation, with a total abstinence from political movement and agitation, would insure the triumph of America, as
every nobleman and member of Parliament would feel the consequences of the king's infatuation in a reduced or suspended income.
Such may have been the substance of Mr. Quincy's message.
Whether it could have restrained the impetuosity of Samuel Adams and his party ; whether the people could have been induced to
endure in silence for twelve months more the insulting presence
of a British army, the closing of their harbor, and the suspension
of their rights, are questions no one need essay to answer. It is probable the attempt would have been made if the young messenger had
arrived in time. Dr. Franklin, we know, was convinced that the
ministry, in one year more, *must* have yielded or resigned, if the
colonists consumed no British goods, and performed no political
act; since the sudden and total loss of the trade with America would
have quickly brought the active capitalists of England, Ireland, and
Scotland, to bankruptcy, and a million laborers to beggary.

Another remarkable person presented himself, in 1774, to the
notice of Dr. Franklin—Thomas Paine, then among the obscurest
of the obscure, destined to sudden and long celebrity. Paine had
reached the age of thirty-seven, and was still a homeless wanderer.
He had been a staymaker in a country town, like his father before

him. He had served as a sailor on board a privateer. He resumed
staymaking and married. He relinquished that business again, and
obtained a small office in the excise. He was removed for cause
unknown ; lost his wife ; married again ; set up a little tobacco-
nist's shop, and became a bankrupt. He separated himself from his
second wife, with her consent, and went to London to see what
fortune would send him in that great resort of Britons who knew
not where else to go. He had picked up a little knowledge in his
devious course through life, and had written a pamphlet to show
that the salaries of excise officers ought to be raised. " My father,"
he says, " being of the Quaker profession, it was my good fortune
to have an exceeding good moral education, and a tolerable stock
of useful learning. Though I went to the grammar school, I did
not learn Latin, not only because I had no inclination to learn languages, but because of the objection the Quakers have against the
books in which the language is taught. But this did not prevent
me from being acquainted with the subjects of all the Latin books
used in the school. The natural bent of my mind was to science.
I had some turn, and I believe some talent for poetry ; but this I
rather repressed than encouraged, as leading too much into the
field of imagination. As soon as I was able, I purchased a pair of
globes, and attended the philosophical lectures of Martin and Fer-
guson, and became afterwards acquainted with Dr. Bevis, of the
society called the Royal Society, then living in the Temple, and an
excellent astronomer. I had no disposition for what is called politics. It presented to my mind no other idea than is contained in
the word Jockeyship. When, therefore, I turned my thoughts
towards matters of government, I had to form a system for myself, that accorded with the moral and philosophic principles in
which I had been educated." *

In the summer of 1774, he made his way to Dr. Franklin, and,
soon after, set sail for America, bearing a letter of introduction
from Dr. Franklin to his son-in-law, Mr. Bache. The letter shows
the modesty of Paine's pretensions at this time : "The bearer, Mr.
Thomas Paine, is very well recommended to me, as an ingenious,
worthy young man. He goes to Pennsylvania with a view of settling there. I request you to give him your best advice and coun-

* Age of Reason, Part i.

tenance, as he is quite a stranger there.   If you can put him in a
way of obtaining employment as a clerk, or assistant tutor in a
school, or assistant surveyor, (of all which I think him very capable,) so that he may procure a subsistence at least, till he can make
acquaintance and obtain a knowledge of the country, you will do
well, and much oblige your affectionate father."

Mr Bache immediately procured him several pupils, and he was
soon engaged to assist in conducting a magazine just started in
Philadelphia. He wrote back to Franklin, with expressions of
gratitude, that he owed his good fortune in Philadelphia to the letter he had brought with him.   He continued to labor in moder-
ately prosperous obscurity for a year after his arrival in Pennsylvania, no one suspecting, least of all himself, the work he was destined
to do for his adopted country.

One public act remained for Franklin to do in England, this year.
The Congress had met.   A new Parliament had been elected, in
which the ministry were stronger than in the old.   America was
more determined, England more infatuated, than before.   Congress,
yearning for reconciliation with the mother country, resolved to
make one united, solemn appeal to the justice of the king, whom
from childhood they had been taught to revere ; and to address
the People of England, whom they had been proud to regard as
elder and honored brethren.   The dignity, the moderation, and
the pathos of these great documents, no writings have surpassed ;
every liberal mind in Europe admired them ; they would have
melted any thing but a stone or a prejudice-hardened heart.   The
petition to the king enumerated the wrongs of the colonies, but
contained not a resentful word.   It declared, that the councils of
America had been influenced by no other motive than a dread of
impending destruction, and concluded with these affecting sentences :

"Permit us, then, most gracious sovereign, in the name of all your
faithful people in America, with the utmost humility to implore
you, for the honor of Almighty God, whose pure religion our
enemies are undermining; for the glory, which can be advanced
only by rendering your subjects happy, and keeping them united ;
for the interests of your family, depending on an adherence to the
principle that enthroned it; for the safety and welfare of your kingdoms and dominions, threatened with almost unavoidable dangers

and distresses; that your majesty, as the loving father of your whole people, connected by the same bands of law, loyalty, faith, and blood, though dwelling in various countries, will not suffer the transcendent relation formed by these ties, to be further violated in uncertain expectation of effects, which, if attained, never can compensate for the calamities through which they must be gained.

"We therefore most earnestly beseech your majesty, that your royal authority and interposition may be used for our relief, and that a gracious answer may be given to this petition.

"That your majesty may enjoy every felicity through a long and glorious reign over loyal and happy subjects, and that your descendants may inherit your prosperity and dominions till time shall be no more, is, and always will be our sincere and fervent prayer."

The petition having been agreed upon in the Congress, it was further resolved, that it should be sent to the "several colony agents, in order that the same may be by them presented to his Majesty; and that the agents be requested to call in the aid of such noblemen and gentlemen as are esteemed firm friends to American liberty." The agents were also instructed, after presenting the petition to the king, to cause it to be published in the newspapers, and to give the address to the people of England as extensive a dissemination as possible in the seaport and manufacturing towns. Dr. Franklin received the petition in December, and immediately invited all the colonial agents in London to join him in presenting it to the king. All declined except the gentlemen representing Massachusetts, Arthur Lee and Mr. Bollan; the others excusing themselves on the ground that they had received no instructions from the colonies which they served. Dr. Franklin, Mr. Lee, and Mr. Bollan went together to the official residence of Lord Dartmouth, handed him the petition, and requested him to present it to the king. That timid, well-intending minister would not consent to deliver it, until he had first ascertained whether it contained matter improper for the king's perusal. The petition was left with him for examination. A few days after he sent for the three agents, and informed them that he had laid the petition before the king, who had received it graciously, and commanded the secretary to inform the gentlemen who had brought it, that it contained matters of so much importance that he would submit it to the consideration of Parliament. "We then," adds Franklin, "consulted on the publication, and were advised by wise and able men, friends of America, whose names it will not be proper to mention, by no means to publish it till it should be before Parliament, as it would be deemed disrespectful to the king. We flattered ourselves, from the answer given by Lord Dartmouth, that the king would have been pleased to recommend it to the consideration of Parliament by some message; but we were mistaken. It came down among a great heap of letters of intelligence from governors and officers in America, newspapers, pamphlets, and handbills, from that country, the last in the list, and was laid upon the table with them, undistinguished by any particular recommendation of it to the notice of either House."

It remained unnoticed for several days. To compel attention to it, the three gentlemen asked to be heard on the subject by counsel at the bar of the House of Commons. The request was refused. The petition became at length the topic of debate, when it was assailed with contemptuous violence by the tory orators, and dismissed from further consideration by an immense majority. "Petitions," wrote Franklin, "are odious here, and petitioning is far from being a probable means of obtaining redress." Nothing could exceed the vulgarity of the abuse which some of the ministerial leaders heaped upon the colonists in this debate. They spoke of the Americans with just that curious blending of bitterness and scorn with which southern plantationists, in these modern days, are wont to amuse us when they discourse on northern men and things. Lord Sandwich said that the colonists were such arrant cowards that the more there were of them the more easily they would be defeated ; the very sound of a cannon would scatter them. This is quite in the plantation style. The same spirit—the same object— the same language.

While Dr. Franklin, in December, 1774, was busied about the petitions, a melancholy scene was transpiring at his home in Philadelphia. His fond and faithful wife was dying. She had attained nearly to the age of threescore and ten, and still enjoyed good health; her old age cheered by her daughter, and her grandchildren. But she longed continually for the return of her husband, now ten .years absent from her, and yet every summer expected. She had said at the beginning of the year, that if her husband did not return in the autumn, she should never see him again. A paralytic stroke hastened her departure; she lingered five days, scarcely conscious, and died without a struggle or a groan. Governor Franklin came from the capital of his province to follow her remains to the grave; himself and Mr. Bache being the chief mourners. The coffin was borne by some of Dr. Franklin's oldest friends, who had known him when, fifty-four years before, he and his young wife began house-keeping in the printing house, and ate their breakfast of bread and milk from bowls of delf. A large concourse of citizens followed the corpse to its resting place in the burial-ground of Christ Church; where lay the dust of her father, her mother, and her infant son.

In the varied circumstances of their lot, in a lowly station and in a high one, she had been a faithful and able helpmeet to her hus-band. She assisted him to acquire the priceless possession of leisure, and, then, by wisely administering his fortune, enabled him to de-vote that leisure to the pursuit of science and the service of his country. It is mournful to think that, for so many years, she should have been deprived of her husband's society. The very qualities which made her so good a wife, rendered it possible for him to re-main absent from his affairs. She lost her husband by deserving him.

That Franklin was constantly sensible of her worth, and of his obligations to her, his and her letters equally attest. They ex-changed letters and gifts by every ship; but the fine apparel which he sent her she kept to wear after his return, saying that she could not find it in her heart to go gayly dressed while her husband was away. He made friends for her in England, who joined him in en-deavoring to overcome her repugnance to the sea. A sea voyage at that time, when the smallness of the ships made privacy on board almost impossible, was terrible indeed to ladies, and they seldom crossed the ocean except from necessity. Dr. Franklin, too, was always on the point of returning. There was no spring, during the whole of his ten years' absence, when he did not expect to go home before the autumn, and no autumn in which he did not count upon setting sail in the spring. And so it was, that their parting in 1765 for a few months' separation, proved a separation for ever.

The Governor of New Jersey, in the letter which communicated the sad intelligence, entreated his father to lose no time in coming home. This letter shows how little Governor Franklin compre-hended the state of things, and how widely father and son were diverging. "If there was any prospect," wrote the governor, " of your being able to bring the people in power to your way of thinking, or those of your way of thinking being brought into power, I should not think so much of your stay. But as you have had by this time pretty strong proofs that neither can be reasonably expected, and that you are looked upon with an evil eye in that country, and are in no small danger of being brought into trouble for your political conduct, you had certainly better return while you are able to bear the fatigues of the voyage, to a country where the people revere you, and are inclined to pay a deference to your opinions. I wonder none of them, as you say, requested your attendance at the late Congress, for I heard from all quarters that your return was ardently wished for at that time, and I have since heard it lamented by many that you were not at that meeting ; as they imagined, had you been there, you would have framed some plan for an accommodation of our differences that would have met with the approbation of a majority of the delegates, though it would not have coincided with the deep designs of those who influenced that majority. However mad you may think the measures of the ministry are, yet I trust you have candor enough to acknowledge that we are no ways behindhand with them in madness on this side of the water. However, it is a disagreeable subject, and I'll drop it."*

In the same letter he expresses a wish to have his son, William Temple Franklin, bred to the law, and sent to King's College at New York for a year or two. That young gentleman still lived with his grandfather in London, and was beginning to be useful to him as his secretary. The governor concluded by saying, that he was very happily settled in a very good house at Perth Amboy, where he hoped to see both his father and his son in the spring, and where an apartment should always be at his father's service. It was very far from William Franklin's anticipations, that his father's mad friends would be under the necessity, by and by, of providing an apartment for the last royal governor of New Jersey.

* Letters to Dr. Franklin, p 60.

CHAPTER XI.

DR. FRANKLIN AND LORD CHATHAM.

THE Earl of Chatham came forward at this crisis to attempt to save England her American colonies. Aged and infirm, long withdrawn from official life, attached to no party, and out of favor at court, he was still the greatest name in England. He was, indeed, a great man, but great after an antique pattern. From the utterances of ruling spirits we can frequently select a single word, or phrase, which seems to contain a summary of their policy or their character. In discoursing of the leading nations of the historic world, Lord Chatham, with lofty mien and imperial gesture, would speak of them as MASTER-STATES: an expression which revealed what he chiefly wished for England. It is now confessed that a policy founded upon such an aim is barbarous and heathen, worthy of pagan Rome, or of dissolute France under Louis XIV., but not of modern, industrial, Christian England. For if there are master-states, there must be subject-states also; and it is now an admitted, fundamental truth of statesmanship, that no nation gains any thing by another nation's loss or degradation. As it is every man's interest that every other man should be prosperous and happy, so it is the interest of every nation that every other nation should be great, flourishing, and satisfied.

Lord Chatham had fed his growing country with victories; which is like bringing up a bull-dog upon blood. Those victories, necessary at the time, inflamed the pride of the English people, and helped to render them capable of sustaining George III. against America. Lord Chatham, also, had a strange weakness with regard to the king and the king's closet; he seemed spell-bound in the presence of the monarch, and addressed him as though he really was the vicegerent of God. His letters to the king teem with expressions which read to us like the most abject flattery, but which he considered merely as the "technical respect due to royalty." Unhappily, George III. was not man enough to take such language in a technical sense. I suppose that Lord Chatham's extreme respect for a king was owing, not to any thing servile in his mind, but merely to the power of his imagination, which often tyrannized over him, and "carried him away."

Nevertheless, he was a great, brilliant, noble being, who hated injustice, meanness, and blundering ; a true, though elder brother of the wiser men his country has since produced.   He was not more illustrious in the Senate than he was amiable at his home.   No one can read his family letters without loving his memory.

From first to last, he opposed the king's mad policy respecting America.   When the Stamp Act was about to be repealed, as he was so debilitated by his disease, that he could not stand to speak, he asked and received permission to speak sitting ; and remained in the House all night, till the vote was taken which decided the question.   In 1770, when the bloody affray took place in Boston between the citizens and the troops, he felt that the colonies were lost unless the king receded.   He wondered if " this wretched isl-.and was still to be called by the once respected name of England." " I think," he wrote to Lord Shelburne, " all is ruined, and I am determined to be found at my post when destruction falls upon us. The times are pollution in the very quintessence."   Again : " I think the infatuation of St. James unexampled, and I look upon the day of destruction as near at hand."   The labors of Franklin and his friends, in these years, had his warm approval.   In 1773, he wrote to Lord Shelburne : "Mr. Franklin's preface (to the Boston pamphlet) is important, considering the sobriety and worthiness of that gentleman's character."   * * *   " I am charmed and edified by the sermon on America, preached by the Bishop of St. Asaph.   This noble discourse speaks the preacher, not only fit to bear rule in the church, but in the State ; indeed, it does honor to the right-reverend bench."

In August. 1774, the Earl of Chatham, whose presence Franklin had vainly striven to reach fourteen years before, sought an interview with Franklin for the purpose of consulting him upon American affairs.   The Earl then lived at Hayes in Kent, two hours' ride from London.   He called upon Dr. Franklin, who was visiting a friend's house in the neighborhood, and took him home in his carriage.   Of the interview which followed, Dr. Franklin has left us a particular and interesting account :

" That truly great man," he wrote, " received me with abundance of civility, inquired particularly into the situation of affairs in America, spoke feelingly of the severity of the late laws against the Massachusetts, gave me some account of his speech in opposing

them, and expressed great regard and esteem for the people of
that country, who he hoped would continue firm and united in defending by all peaceable and legal means their constitutional rights.
I assured him that I made no doubt they would do so; which he
said he was pleased to hear from me, as he was sensible I must be
well acquainted with them.

" I then took occasion to remark to him, that in former cases
great empires had crumbled first at their extremities, from this
cause: that countries remote from the seat and eye of government,
which therefore could not well understand their affairs for want of
full and true information, had never been well governed, but had
been oppressed by bad governors, on presumption that complaint was
difficult to be made and supported against them at such a distance.
Hence, such governors had been encouraged to go on, till their op-
pressions became intolerable. But that this empire had happily
found, and long been in the practice of, a method, whereby every
province was well governed, being trusted in a great measure with
the government of itself; and that hence had arisen such satisfaction in the subjects, and such encouragement to new settlements,
that, had it not been for the late wrong politics (which would have
Parliament to be *omnipotent*, though it ought not to be so unless it
could at the same time be *omniscient*), we might have gone on extending our western empire, adding province to province, as far as
the South Sea. That I lamented the ruin which seemed impending
over so fine a plan, so well adapted to make all the subjects of the
greatest empire happy; and I hoped that, if his Lordship, with the
other great and wise men of the British nation, would unite and
exert themselves, it might yet be rescued out of the mangling hands
of the present set of blundering ministers; and that the union and
harmony between Britain and her colonies, so necessary to the welfare of both, might be restored.

" He replied, with great politeness, that my idea of extending our
empire in that manner was a sound one, worthy of a great, benevolent, and comprehensive mind. He wished with me for a good
understanding among the different parts of the opposition here, as
a means of restoring the ancient harmony of the two countries,
which he most earnestly desired; but he spoke of the coalition of
our domestic parties as attended with difficulty, and rather to be
desired than expected. He mentioned an opinion prevailing here,

that America aimed at setting up for itself as an *independent state;* or, at least, to get rid of the *Navigation Acts.* I assured him, that having more than once traveled almost from one end of the continent to the other, and kept a great variety of company, eating, drinking, and conversing with them freely, I never had heard in any conversation from any person, drunk or sober, the least expression of a wish for a separation, or hint that such a thing would be advantageous to America. And as to the Navigation Act, the main, material part of it, that of carrying on trade in British or plantation bottoms, excluding foreign ships from our ports, and navigating with three quarters British seamen, was as acceptable to us as it could be to Britain. That we were even not against regulations of the general commerce by Parliament, provided such regulations were *bonâ fide* for the benefit of the *whole empire,* not for the small advantage of one part to the great injury of another, such as the obliging our ships to call in England with our wine and fruit, from Portugal or Spain; the restraints on our manufactures, in the woolen and hat-making branches, the prohibiting of slitting-mills, steelworks, &c. He allowed that some amendment might be made in those acts; but said those relating to the slitting-mills, trip-hammers, and steel-works, were agreed to by our agents, in a compromise on the opposition made here to abating the duty.

"In fine, he expressed much satisfaction in my having called upon him, and particularly in the assurances I had given him, that America did not aim at *independence ;* adding, that he should be glad to see me again as often as might be. I said, I should not fail to avail myself of the permission he was pleased to give me of waiting upon his Lordship occasionally, being very sensible of the honor, and of the great advantages and improvement I should reap from his instructive conversation ; which indeed was not a mere compliment."

Before leaving Hayes, Dr. Franklin promised to keep Lord Chatham advised of any important intelligence which might arrive from America. Four months passed away before they met again. In December came the Petition and the Address from Congress; and as soon as the Petition had been presented to Lord Dartmouth, Dr. Franklin rode out to Hayes to submit copies of both docu ments to the perusal of Lord Chatham.

"He received me," continues Franklin, "with an affectionate

kind of respect, that from so great a man was extremely engaging; but the opinion he expressed of the Congress was still more so. They had acted, he said, with so much temper, moderation, and wisdom, that he thought it the most honorable assembly of statesmen since those of the ancient Greeks and Romans, in the most virtuous times. That there were not in their whole proceedings above one or two things he could have wished otherwise; perhaps but one, and that was their assertion, that the keeping up a standing army in the colonies in time of peace, without consent of their legislatures, was against law. He doubted that was not well founded, and that the law alluded to did not extend to the colonies. The rest he admired and honored. He thought the petition decent, manly, and properly expressed. He inquired much and particularly concerning the state of America, the probability of their perseverance, the difficulties they must meet with in adhering for any long time to their resolutions, the resources they might have to supply the deficiency of commerce ; to all which I gave him answers with which he seemed well satisfied. He expressed a great regard and warm affection for that country, with hearty wishes for their prosperity ; and that government here might soon come to see its mistakes, and rectify them ; and intimated that possibly he might, if his health permitted, prepare something for its consideration, when the Parliament should meet after the holidays; on which he should wish to have previously my sentiments.

"I mentioned to him the very hazardous state I conceived we were in, by the continuance of the army in Boston; that, whatever disposition there might be in the inhabitants to give no just cause of offense to the troops, or in the general to preserve order among them, an unpremeditated, unforeseen quarrel might happen between perhaps a drunken porter and a soldier, that might bring on a riot, tumult, and bloodshed, and in its consequences produce a breach impossible to be healed ; that the army could not possibly answer any good purpose *there*, and might be infinitely mischievous; that no accommodation could properly be proposed and entered into by the Americans while the bayonet was at their hearts ; that, to have any agreement binding all force should be withdrawn. His lordship seemed to think these sentiments had something in them that was reasonable."

The result of these interviews was, that Lord Chatham determined, if his gout would permit, to appear in the House of Lords, and move the immediate and unconditional withdrawal of the troops from Boston. Lady Chatham preceded him to London. His daily notes to her show how full his heart was of the business in hand. The House was to convene on the nineteenth or twentieth of January. On the sixteenth he wrote to her: "I beg you will send positive and certain information if the House of Lords meets on Thursday, or not till Friday. I fear jockeyship, am resolved to be there on the first day of meeting, and wish you would tell Lord Stanhope that I shall propose something relative to America on the first day." January the 18th, she wrote to her lord: "I think it important you should know what infinite pains are taken to circulate an authoritative report, that you are *determined* to give yourself no trouble upon American affairs, and that, for certain, you do not mean to come to town. It is so strong that it proves how much there is to be afraid of jockeyship, and whatever is bad." He replied on the same day: "Don't disquiet yourself about the impudent and ridiculous lie of the hour. The plot does not lie very deep. It is only a pitiful device of fear; court fear and faction fear. If gout does not put in a veto, which I trust in heaven it will not, I will be in the House of Lords on Friday, then and there to make a motion relative to America. Be of good cheer, noble love.

"'Yes, I am proud—I must be proud—to see
Men, not afraid of God, afraid of me.'"

The next day he wrote to Lord Stanhope: "I mean to-morrow to touch only the threshold of American business, and knock at the minister's door to wake him, as well as show I attend to America. I shall move for an address to send orders immediately for removing the forces from the town of Boston as soon as practicable. Be so good as not to communicate what my intended motion is to any one whatever; but the more it is known and propagated that I am to make a motion *relative to America*, the better. Adieu till to-morrow, my dear lord. I greatly wish Dr. Franklin may be in the House, if the House is open to others than members of Parliament." The next day Lady Chatham wrote to the Earl: "Duchesses, grandees, and others have dropped their cards of visits to me in every street, I think." [It was not known where she was stopping.] "This seeking so much about, to be civil, is flattering at least." To which he replied, (transmuting by a touch her prose into poetry) : "Your duchesses and archbishops *littering all the streets with cards to catch you in your passage*, is, indeed, flattering enough.'"

Lord Stanhope sent Dr. Franklin the required notification, and added, that Lord Chatham himself would introduce him into the House. "I attended," Franklin records, "and met him accordingly. On my mentioning to him what Lord Stanhope had written to me, he said, 'Certainly; and I shall do it with the more pleasure, as I am sure your being present at this day's debate will be of more service to America than mine;' and so taking me by the arm, was leading me along the passage to the door that enters near the throne, when one of the door-keepers followed, and acquainted him that, by the order, none were to be carried in at that door but the eldest sons or brothers of peers; on which he limped back with me to the door near the bar, where were standing a number of gentlemen, waiting for the peers who were to introduce them, and some peers waiting for friends they expected to introduce; among whom he delivered me to the door-keepers, saying aloud, 'This is Dr. Franklin, whom I would have admitted into the House;' when they readily opened the door for me accordingly.

"As it had not been publicly known, that there was any communication between his Lordship and me, this I found occasioned some speculation. His appearance in the House, I observed, caused a kind of bustle among the officers, who were hurried in sending messengers for members, I suppose those in connection with the ministry, something of importance being expected when that great man appears; it being but seldom that his infirmities permit his attendance."

Besides a great concourse of lords, the House was attended by large numbers of the Commons, and by as many Americans as could contrive to procure admission. William Pitt, a *man* of seventeen, the heir of the great orator's fame and mind, was present. Dr. Franklin enjoyed this day the true ecstacy of a civilized being: which is, to hear deeply cherished convictions glorified in the language of genius; to behold our plain, dusty, Cinderella thoughts alight upon us, transformed into princesses dazzling with beauty and diamonds.

We have but a shadow of this great speech. Lord Chatham began by remarking upon the dilatoriness of the administration in

dealing with the affairs of America; and that was the apology for
his own interference. " But," said he, " as I have not the honor of
access to his majesty, I will endeavor to transmit to him, through
the constitutional channel of this House, my ideas of America, to
rescue him from the misadvice of his present ministers." Congratulating the House, that the business was at last entered upon, he
read the motion which he had carefully studied for many previous
days. The motion proposed to ask the king to send immediate
orders to General Gage to remove the troops from Boston as soon
as the rigor of the season had abated, and proper provision could
be made for their accommodation elsewhere. This he proposed
only as a preliminary measure, to open the way toward reconciliation, by allaying tumults and softening animosities. On the present occasion, he said, he designed merely to knock at the door
of a sleeping and confounded ministry, and rouse them to a sense
of impending danger. What he demanded for America was not
pardon, not indulgence, but justice. America, he admitted, owed
to the mother country a limited obedience; but he added, " let
the sacredness of their property remain inviolate, let it be taxable
only by their own consent, *or it ceases to be property !*" He dwelt
very happily upon the ludicrous and pitiable situation of General
Gage and the troops under his command; penned up, as they
were, in a hostile town; pining in inglorious inactivity; an army
of impotence, whose only policy was to suffer disgrace; who were
necessitated to be contemptible; who could triumph only by the
ruin of their cause and country.

This, indeed, was the burden of his speech—the impossibility
of conquering America by force of arms; a truth which Dr. Franklin had uniformly asserted ever since the first agitation of the stamp
act. " I remember," said he, " some years ago, when the repeal of
the stamp act was in agitation, in a friendly conference with a person of undoubted respect and authenticity on that subject, he assured me, that you might destroy their towns, and cut them off
from the superfluities, perhaps the conveniences of life, but that
they were prepared to despise your power, and would not lament
their loss, whilst they had—what, my lords ?—*their woods and their
liberty !* The spirit," continued the speaker, " which now resists
taxation in America, is that which formerly opposed ship-money in
England, the spirit which effected the establishment of the basis

of British liberty; which is, that no subject of England shall be taxed, but by his own consent."

The orator soon broke into that noble and just eulogium of the proceedings of the legislative bodies of America, which posterity, in all countries, has ratified, and which America still loves to repeat. "When your lordships look at the papers transmitted us from America; when you consider their decency, firmness, and wisdom, you cannot but respect their cause, and wish to make it your own. For myself, I must declare and avow, that in all my reading and observation—and it has been my favorite study—I have read Thucydides, and have studied and admired the master-states of the world—that for solidity of reasoning, force of sagacity, and wisdom of conclusion, under such a complication of difficult circumstances, no nation or body of men can stand in preference to the General Congress at Philadelphia." From the lofty character and calm resolution of the Congress, he drew the certain inference, that the people they represented could not be reduced to submission. "We shall be forced," exclaimed the orator, "ultimately to retract; let us retract while we can, not when we must. I say we must necessarily, undo these violent oppressive acts. They *must* be repealed. You *will* repeal them; I pledge myself for it, that you will, in the end, repeal them; I stake my reputation on it. I will consent to be taken for an idiot, if they are not finally repealed." Besides this prophecy, so soon fulfilled, he foretold the alliance between France and America—France "watching your conduct, and waiting for the maturity of your errors." These ideas the speaker enforced and illustrated with a fluency and originality worthy of his great powers, and his great cause. The mere outline of his speech, that was preserved is all point and fire. He concluded with the well-known words : "If the ministers persevere in misadvising and misleading the king, I will not say that they can alienate the affections of his subjects from his crown; but I will affirm, that they will make the crown not worth his wearing. I will not say that the king is betrayed, but I will pronounce that the kingdom is undone."

Lord Chatham's motion was most ably supported by Lord Camden, and others; but "all availed," said Franklin, "no more than the whistling of the winds. The motion was rejected. Sixteen Scotch peers, and twenty-four bishops, with all the lords in posses-

sion or expectation of places, when they vote together unanimously, as they generally do for ministerial measures, make a dead
majority, that renders all debating ridiculous in itself, since it can
answer no end."

William Pitt wrote to his mother the next morning: "Nothing
prevented his speech from being the most forcible that can be imagined, and the administration fully felt it. The matter and the
manner, both were striking, far beyond what I can express. It was
every thing that was superior; and though it had not the desired
effect upon an obdurate House of Lords, it must have an infinite
effect without doors; the bar being crowded with Americans."
The ministry, he added, were "violent beyond description, almost to
madness;" and, so far from being disposed to withdraw the troops,
they were inclined to send more.

Having received from Lord Stanhope a copy of the motion, Dr.
Franklin acknowledged that courtesy in noble language: "Dr.
Franklin presents his best respects to Lord Stanhope, with many
thanks to his Lordship and Lord Chatham, for the communication
of so authentic a copy of the motion. Dr. F. is filled with admiration of that truly great man. He has seen, in the course of life,
sometimes eloquence without wisdom, and often wisdom without
eloquence; in the present instance he sees both united, and both,
as he thinks, in the highest degree possible."

The motion for the withdrawal of the troops, as we have seen,
was designed by the mover as a preliminary measure only—a knocking at the door of the cabinet. The violent rejection of the motion
did not prevent Lord Chatham from introducing the more extensive scheme which he had announced. A very few days after the
debate, Lord Mahon called at Craven Street to say that the Earl of
Chatham desired again to consult with Dr. Franklin; who, accordingly, rode out to Hayes on the twenty-seventh of January. Dr.
Franklin records the interview and its results:

"I took a post-chaise about nine o'clock, and got to Hayes about
eleven; but my attention being engaged in reading a new pamphlet,
the post-boy drove me a mile or two beyond the gate. His Lordship, being out on an airing in his chariot, had met me before I
reached Hayes, unobserved by me, turned and followed me, and
not finding me there, concluded, as he had seen me reading, that I
had passed by mistake, and sent a servant after me. He expressed

great pleasure at my coming, and acquainted me in a long conversation with the outlines of his plan, parts of which he read to me. He said he had communicated it only to Lord Camden, whose advice he much relied on, particularly in the law part; and that he would, as soon as he could, get it transcribed, put it into my hands for my opinion and advice, but should show it to no other person before he presented it to the House; and he requested me to make no mention of it, otherwise parts might be misunderstood and blown upon beforehand, and others perhaps adopted and produced by ministers as their own. I promised the closest secrecy, and kept my word, not even mentioning to any one that I had seen him. I dined with him, his family only present, and returned to town in the evening.

"On the Sunday following, being the 29th, his Lordship came to town, and called upon me in Craven Street. He brought with him his plan transcribed, in the form of an act of Parliament, which he put into my hands, requesting me to consider it carefully, and communicate to him such remarks upon it as should occur to me. His reason for desiring to give me that trouble was, as he was pleased to say, that he knew no man so thoroughly acquainted with the subject, or so capable of giving advice upon it; that he thought the errors of ministers in American affairs had been often owing to their not obtaining the best information; that, therefore, though he had considered the business thoroughly in all its parts, he was not so confident of his own judgment, but that he came to set it right by mine, as men set their watches by a regulator. He had not determined when he should produce it in the House of Lords; but in the course of our conversation, considering the precarious situation of his health, and that if presenting it was delayed, some intelligence might arrive which would make it seem less seasonable, or in all parts not so proper; or the ministry might engage in different measures, and then say, 'If you had produced your plan sooner, we might have attended to it;' he concluded to offer it the Wednesday following; and therefore wished to see me upon it the preceding Tuesday, when he would again call upon me, unless I could conveniently come to Hayes. I chose the latter, in respect to his Lordship, and because there was less likelihood of interruptions; and I promised to be with him early, that we might have more time. He stayed with me near two hours, his equipage waiting at the door;

and being there while people were coming from church, it was much taken notice of, and talked of, as at that time was every little circumstance that men thought might possibly any way affect American affairs. Such a visit from so great a man, on so important a business, flattered not a little my vanity ; and the honor of it gave me the more pleasure, as it happened on the very day twelve months that the ministry had taken so much pains to disgrace me before the Privy Council."

Dr. Franklin scanned the bill with the closest attention. He found that it conceded much that his countrymen claimed, contained some good points, some objectionable ones, and was far in advance of any plan previously proposed by an English statesman. With all its defects, it provided for the immediate and total repeal of the offensive acts enumerated in the petition of the Congress. Having noted down his objections to the bill, and a number of suggestions for its improvement, he went to Hayes again, two days after his conference with Lord Chatham in London.

" We entered," he continues, " into consideration of the plan ; but, though I stayed near four hours, his Lordship, in the manner of, I think, all eloquent persons, was so full and diffuse in supporting every particular I questioned, that there was not time to go through half my memorandums. He is not easily interrupted ; and I had such pleasure in hearing him, that I found little inclination to interrupt him. Therefore, considering that neither of us had much expectation, that the plan would be adopted entirely as it stood ; that, in the course of its consideration, if it should be received, proper alterations might be introduced ; that, before it would be settled, America should have opportunity to make her objections and propositions of amendment; that, to have it received at all here, it must seem to comply a little with some of the prevailing prejudices of the legislature ; that, if it was not so perfect as might be wished, it would at least serve as a basis for treaty, and in the mean time prevent mischiefs ; and that, as his Lordship had determined to offer it the next day, there was not time to make changes and another fair copy ; I therefore ceased my querying ; and, though afterwards many people were pleased to do me the honor of supposing I had a considerable share in composing it, I assure you that the addition of a single word only was made at my instance, viz.: ' *constitutions*' after ' charters ;' for my filling up, at his request, a blank with the titles of acts proper to be repealed, which I took from the proceedings of the Congress, was no more than might have been done by any copying clerk.

" On Wednesday, Lord Stanhope, at Lord Chatham's request, called upon me, and carried me down to the House of Lords, which was very soon full. Lord Chatham, in a most excellent speech, introduced, explained, and supported his plan. When he sat down, Lord Dartmouth rose, and very properly said, it contained matter of such weight and magnitude, as to require much consideration; and he therefore hoped the noble Earl did not expect their Lordships to decide upon it by an immediate vote, but would be willing it should lie upon the table for consideration. Lord Chatham answered readily, that he expected nothing more.

" But Lord Sandwich rose, and in a petulant, vehement speech, opposed its being received at all, and gave his opinion, that it ought to be immediately *rejected*, with the contempt it deserved. That he could never believe it to be the production of any British Peer. That it appeared to him rather the work of some American; and, turning his face towards me, who was leaning on the bar, said, he fancied he had in his eye the person who drew it up, one of the bitterest and most mischievous enemies this country had ever known. This drew the eyes of many Lords upon me; but, as I had no inducement to take it to myself, I kept my countenance as immovable as if my features had been made of wood. Then several other Lords of the administration gave their sentiments also for rejecting it, of which opinion also was strongly the *wise* Lord Hillsborough. But the Dukes of Richmond and Manchester, Lord Shelburne, Lord Camden, Lord Temple, Lord Lyttleton, and others, were for receiving it, some through approbation, and others for the character and dignity of the House. One Lord mentioning with applause the candid proposal of one of the ministers, Lord Dartmouth, his Lordship rose again and said, that having since heard the opinions of so many Lords against receiving it, to lie upon the table for consideration, he had altered his mind, could not accept the praise offered him for a candor of which he was now ashamed, and should therefore give his voice for rejecting the plan immediately.

" I am the more particular in this, as it is a trait of that nobleman's character, who from his office is supposed to have so great a share in American affairs, but who has in reality no will or judgment of his own, being, with dispositions for the best measures, easily prevailed with to join in the worst.

"Lord Chatham, in his reply to Lord Sandwich, took notice of his illiberal insinuation, that the plan was not the person's who proposed it; declared that it was entirely his own; a declaration he thought himself the more obliged to make, as many of their Lordships appeared to have so mean an opinion of it; for if it was so weak or so bad a thing, it was proper in him to take care that no other person should unjustly share in the censure it deserved. That it had been heretofore reckoned his vice, not to be apt to take advice; but he made no scruple to declare, that, if he were the first minister of this country, and had the care of settling this momentous business, he should not be ashamed of publicly calling to his assistance a person so perfectly acquainted with the whole of American affairs as the gentleman alluded to, and so injuriously reflected on; one, he was pleased to say, whom all Europe held in high estimation for his knowledge and wisdom, and ranked with our Boyles and Newtons; who was an honor, not to the English nation only, but to human nature! I found it harder to stand this extravagant compliment than the preceding equally extravagant abuse; but kept as well as I could an unconcerned countenance, as not conceiving it to relate to me.

"To hear so many of these *hereditary* legislators declaiming so vehemently against, not the adopting merely, but even the *consideration* of a proposal so important in its nature, offered by a person of so weighty a character, one of the first statesmen of the age, who had taken up this country when in the lowest despondency, and conducted it to victory and glory, through a war with two of the mightiest kingdoms in Europe; to hear them censuring his plan, not only for their own misunderstandings of what was in it, but for their imaginations of what was not in it, which they would not give themselves an opportunity of rectifying by a second reading; to perceive the total ignorance of the subject in some, the prejudice and passion of others, and the willful perversion of plain truth in several of the ministers; and, upon the whole, to see it so ignominiously rejected by so great a majority, and so hastily too, in breach of all decency, and prudent regard to the character and dignity of their body, as a third part of the national legislature, gave me an exceeding mean opinion of their abilities,

and made their claim of sovereignty over three millions of virtuous, sensible people in America seem the greatest of absurdities,
since they appeared to have scarce discretion enough to govern a
herd of swine. *Hereditary legislators!* thought I. There would
be more propriety, because less hazard of mischief, in having (as
in some university of Germany) *hereditary professors of mathematics!* But this was a hasty reflection; for the *elected* House of
Commons is no better, nor ever will be while the electors receive
money for their votes, and pay money wherewith ministers may
bribe their representatives when chosen."

Thus ended, for the time, Lord Chatham's endeavor to stay the
blundering career of the king's advisers. He continued, however,
to denounce the ministerial measures, and to defend the American
people against their senseless vituperation. He told ministers, on
one occasion, that the people of the large American towns were as
"learned and polite, and understood the Constitution of the empire
as well as the noble lords now in office," which was *meant* as a
compliment to the Americans. When, at last, hostilities began,
Lord Pitt, the eldest son of the Earl of Chatham, chanced to be
serving as aid-de-camp to General Sir Guy Carleton, then commanding the British troops in Canada. The young soldier was
fond and proud of his profession, which he had just entered under
auspices that secured his rapid advancement. His noble mother
wrote to him, urging him, if he thought with his father, to resign
his commission rather than draw his sword in so unnatural a contest. To the great contentment of his parents, Lord Pitt returned
to England, and resigned.

A year later, in that month when America was thrilled with the
Declaration of Independence, the Earl of Chatham being very sick,
and not expecting to recover, solemnly charged his physician, Dr.
Addington, to bear testimony that he died with his opinions respecting America unchanged. He renewed, also, his prediction,
that unless England changed her policy, France would espouse
the cause of the Americans. France, he said, waited only till England was more deeply engaged "in this ruining war against herself
in America, as well as to prove how far the Americans, abetted by
France indirectly, may be able to make a stand, before she takes
an open part by declaring war upon England."[*]

* Correspondence of the Earl of Chatham, iv., 424.

CHAPTER XII.

SECRET NEGOTIATIONS WITH AGENTS OF THE MINISTRY.

MINISTERS had assumed a bold front in these debates. We could hardly believe, if Dr. Franklin had not minutely recorded the facts, that during this whole period, from October to March, agents of the ministry were secretly negotiating, or, at least, tampering with Franklin, with a view, real or pretended, to effect an amicable arrangement of the dispute with the colonies.

Lord North was troubled with a commodity of brains; and *brains enough* are always on the side of honor, justice, truth, and freedom. Like Launcelot Gobbo in the play, he was pulled two ways at once; his intellect inclined him to the side of the Americans; his good nature and his fondness for the king made him a reluctant instrument of oppression. There was probably no hour from 1775 to 1783, in which he would not have preferred to resign rather than continue to carry out the king's designs. But the spell of the royal closet enthralled him ; the seductive, flattering appeals of the king to the soft places in his heart subdued him, and the glories of his great place had their effect upon him. He is one among the thousand examples which prove that, let a man possess all good gifts and graces, talent, knowledge, good nature, and good intentions, and all in high degree, and yet lack firmness of purpose, he is of no avail in the strife of Right against Wrong. The unflinching king, whose inferior endowments made him the natural foe of freedom, subdued to his purposes, *because* he was unflinching, the witty and yielding Lord North, whose intellect impelled him to defend the liberties of man. It was to Lord North's reluctance and hesitation, that the events are to be, in part, attributed, which we are now to relate.

One evening, about the beginning of November, 1774, at the rooms of the Royal Society, Mr. Raper, one of the members, told Dr. Franklin there was a great lady in London who had a particular desire to play at chess with him, as she thought she could beat him. It was Mrs. Howe, sister of Admiral Lord Howe, a name honored in America, for the gallant conduct of General.Viscount Howe during the Seven Years' war. Massachusetts had erected a monument in Westminster Abbey to that General, who fell in the attack upon Ticonderoga in 1758. At this time, both Lord Howe and General Howe voted with ministers, and expected employment from them. Dr. Franklin endeavored to evade the challenge, but Mr. Raper being urgent, he consented at length to call upon the lady and test her ability in a few games. However, feeling the awkwardness of waiting upon a lady with whom he was unacquainted, he deferred his visit from week to week. At the end of the month, being again at the Royal Society, Mr. Raper reminded him of his promise, insisted on his naming a day, and offered to accompany him to the lady's house. Franklin complied. He was struck with the excellent sense and agreeable manners of Mrs. Howe, played several games with her, and very readily accepted her invitation to a second encounter.

A day or two after this interview, David Barclay, a member of Parliament, a person of great note among the Quakers on both sides of the ocean, called upon Dr. Franklin to converse with him upon American affairs. The present measures, Mr. Barclay averred, threatened nothing less than civil war, and immense would be the merit of that man who should avert the immeasurable calamity. Dr. Franklin, he added, was the man who, from his knowledge of both countries, his great influence in America, and his known abilities, could do more than any one else to effect a reconciliation. Franklin replied, that he should be very happy to aid in so good a work, but he saw no prospect of effecting it. The Americans desired nothing so much as a just and friendly accommodation; but the ministry, so far from wishing a peaceful solution, seemed resolved upon forcing the colonists into rebellion, that they might have an excuse for wreaking a bloody vengeance upon them. Mr. Barclay thought he judged ministers too hardly; he felt sure that, at least, some of them would be exceedingly glad to be extricated from the American difficulty on any terms that should save the honor and dignity of government. He requested Dr. Franklin to reflect on the subject, and he would call again in a few days to converse further upon it. Franklin had no difficulty in promising to reflect upon a topic which had become the sole occupant of his mind. He again, however, expressed the opinion that no reflections of his could then be of any use.

Two days after, he received a note from Mr. Barclay; who said, that on his way home from Craven Street, he had met their common friend, Dr. Fothergill, to whom he had communicated the substance of their conversation. Dr. Fothergill, he added, wished to join in their next conference, and desired it might take place at his house the next evening at five. The day named by Mr. Barclay was the one appointed for the chess party at Mrs. Howe's, but as the lady had invited him for the afternoon, he proposed to comply with both invitations.

He attended Mrs. Howe in the afternoon of December 3d. After playing," he records, " as long as we liked, we fell into a little chat, partly on a mathematical problem, and partly about the new Parliament, then just met, when she said, ' And what is to be done with this dispute between Great Britain and the colonies ? I hope we are not to have a civil war.' ' They should kiss and be friends,' said I; ' what can they do better? Quarreling can be of service to neither, but is ruin to both.' ' I have often said,' replied she, ' that I wished government would employ you to settle the dispute for them; I am sure nobody could do it so well. Do not you think that the thing is practicable?' ' Undoubtedly, Madam, if the parties are disposed to reconciliation; for the two countries have really no clashing interests to differ about. It is rather a matter of punctilio, which two or three reasonable people might settle in half an hour. I thank you for the good opinion you are pleased to express of me; but the ministers will never think of employing me in that good work; they choose rather to abuse me.' ' Ay,' said she, ' they have behaved shamefully to you. And indeed some of them are now ashamed of it themselves.'

" I looked upon this as accidental conversation, thought no more of it, and went in the evening to the appointed meeting at Dr. Fothergill's, where I found Mr. Barclay with him.

" The Doctor expatiated feelingly on the mischiefs likely to ensue from the present difference, the necessity of accommodating it, and the great merit of being instrumental in so good a work; concluding with some compliments to me; that nobody understood the subject so thoroughly, and had a better head for business of the kind; that it seemed therefore a duty incumbent on me, to do every thing I could to accomplish a reconciliation; and that, as he had with pleasure heard from David Barclay, that I had promised to think of it, he hoped I had put pen to paper, and formed some

plan for consideration, and brought it with me.   I answered, that
I had formed no plan; as the more I thought of the proceedings
against the colonies, the more satisfied I was, that there did not
exist the least disposition in the ministry to an accommodation;
that therefore all plans must be useless.   He said, I might be mistaken; that, whatever was the violence of some, he had reason,
good reason, to believe others were differently disposed; and that,
if I would draw a plan, which we three upon considering should
judge reasonable, it might be made use of, and answer some good
purpose, since he believed that either himself or David Barclay
could get it communicated to some of the most moderate among
the ministers, who would consider it with attention; and what appeared reasonable to us, two of us being Englishmen, might appear
so to them.

   "As they both urged this with great earnestness, and when I
mentioned the impropriety of my doing any thing of the kind at
the time we were in daily expectation of hearing from the Congress, who undoubtedly would be explicit on the means of restoring a good understanding, they seemed impatient, alleging, that it
was uncertain when we should receive the result of the Congress,
and what it would be; that the least delay might be dangerous;
that additional punishments for New England were in contemplation, and accidents might widen the breach, and make it irreparable; therefore, something preventive could not be too soon
thought of and applied.   I was therefore finally prevailed with to
promise doing what they desired, and to meet them again on Tuesday evening at the same place, and bring with me something for
their consideration."

   He met them, accordingly, and took with him a paper containing
a series of "Hints for conversation" upon the terms which would
probably produce a durable union between Great Britain and the
colonies.   These Hints embraced the points following: The tea
destroyed in Boston Harbor to be paid for by Massachusetts; the
tea duty to be repealed, and all duties received under it to be refunded; the ancient commercial system to be re-established; the
colonies to be permitted to manufacture without restriction; all duties collected in the colonies to be paid into their own treasuries;
custom-house officers to be appointed by the colonial governors,
not sent from England; the colonies to grant no supplies to the

king in time of peace, and, in time of war, each colony to raise and grant its just proportion; no troops to enter any colony but with the consent of its legislature; Castle William in Boston harbor to be given up to the province, and no fortress to be built in any province but with the consent of its legislature; the oppressive acts relating to Boston harbor to be repealed, and a free government granted to Canada; judges to hold their offices during good behavior, and to be paid by the assemblies; governors to be appointed by the king, but paid by the assemblies; all power of internal legislation in the colonies to be disclaimed by Parliament; the late acts respecting the transportation of offenders to England for trial, to be repealed. In a word, Dr. Franklin demanded that Englishmen in America should enjoy the essential rights and privileges which Englishmen in England claimed as their birthright; claimed them both because they were just in themselves, and because they formed part of the compact between their fathers and the reigning family.

The three gentlemen conversed long upon the Hints; the Englishmen objecting to some of them, not as unjust, but as not likely to be conceded; Franklin demonstrating the necessity of each.

"Having gone through the whole," continues Dr. Franklin, "I was desired to make a fair copy for Dr. Fothergill, who now informed us that, having an opportunity of seeing daily Lord Dartmouth, of whose good disposition he had a high opinion, he would communicate the paper to him, as the sentiments of considerate persons, who wished the welfare of both countries. 'Suppose,' said Mr. Barclay, 'I were to show this paper to Lord Hyde; would there be any thing amiss in so doing? He is a very knowing man; and, though not in the ministry, properly speaking, he is a good deal attended to by them. I have some acquaintance with him; we converse freely sometimes; and perhaps, if he and I were to talk these articles over, and I should communicate to him our conversation upon them, some good might arise out of it.' Dr. Fothergill had no objection, and I said I could have none. I knew Lord Hyde a little, and had an esteem for him. I had drawn the paper at their request, and it was now theirs to do with it what they pleased. Mr. Barclay then proposed that I should send the fair copy to him, which, after making one for Dr. Fothergill and one for himself, he would return to me. Another question then arose, whether I had any objection to their mentioning that I had been consulted. I said, none that related to myself; but it was my opinion, if they wished any attention paid to the propositions, it would be better not to mention me; the ministry having, as I conceived, a prejudice against me, and every thing that came from me. They said, on that consideration it might be best not to mention me; and so it was concluded. For my own part, I kept this whole proceeding a profound secret; but I soon after discovered, that it had taken air by some means or other.

"Being much interrupted the day following, I did not copy and send the paper. The next morning I received a note from Mr. Barclay, pressing to have it before twelve o'clock. I accordingly sent it to him."

He soon received intimations that the paper had found its way to Lord Hyde, Lord Dartmouth, and, probably, Lord North. A rumor too was started in the city, that Dr. Franklin and Lord North had agreed upon terms of accommodation; which had the effect of recovering the public stocks three or four per cent. The proceedings of the Congress arrived, and they, too, greatly encouraged all reasonable men in the hope of speedy adjustment.

In the evening of Christmas day, he called again upon his friend Mrs. Howe. He relates the unexpected events which occurred on this festive occasion : " She told me as soon as I went in, that her brother, Lord Howe, wished to be acquainted with me; that he was a very good man, and she was sure we should like each other. I said, I had always heard a good character of Lord Howe, and should be proud of the honor of being known to him. ' He is but just by,' said she; ' will you give me leave to send for him ?' ' By all means, Madam, if you think proper.' She rang for a servant, wrote a note, and Lord Howe came in a few minutes.

"After some extremely polite compliments as to the general motives for his desiring an acquaintance with me, he said he had a particular one at this time, which was the alarming situation of our affairs with America, which no one, he was persuaded, understood better than myself; that it was the opinion of some friends of his, that no man could do more towards reconciling our differences than I could, if I would undertake it; that he was sensible I had been very ill treated by the ministry, but he hoped that would not be considered by me in the present case; that he, himself, though not in opposition, had much disapproved of their con-

duct towards me; that some of them, he was sure, were ashamed
of it, and sorry it had happened; which he supposed must be sufficient to abate resentment in a great and generous mind; that, if
he were himself in administration, he should be ready to make me
ample satisfaction, which, he was persuaded, would one day or
other be done; that he was unconnected with the ministry, except
by some personal friendships; wished well, however, to government;
was anxious for the general welfare of the whole empire, and had
a particular regard for New England, which had shown a very en-
dearing respect to his family; that he was merely an independent
member of Parliament, desirous of doing what good he could,
agreeably to his duty in that station; that he therefore had wished
for an opportunity of obtaining my sentiments on the means of
reconciling our differences, which he saw must be attended with
the most mischievous consequences, if not speedily accommodated;
that he hoped his zeal for the public welfare would, with me, excuse the impertinence of a mere stranger, who could have otherwise no reason to expect, or right to request, me to open my mind
to him on these topics; but he did conceive, that, if I would indulge him with my ideas of the means proper to bring about a
reconciliation, it might be of some use; that perhaps I might not
be willing myself to have any *direct* communication with this ministry on this occasion; that I might likewise not care to have it
known, that I had any *indirect* communication with them, till I
could be well assured of their good dispositions; that, being himself upon no ill terms with them, he thought it not impossible that
he might, by conveying my sentiments to them and theirs to me,
be a means of bringing on a good understanding, without committing either them or me, if his negotiation should not succeed; and
that I might rely on his keeping perfectly secret every thing I
should wish to remain so.

" Mrs. Howe here offering to withdraw, whether of herself, or
from any sign from him, I know not, I begged she might stay, as
I should have no secret in a business of this nature, that I could
not freely confide to her prudence : which was truth; for I had
not conceived a higher opinion of the discretion and excellent understanding of any woman on so short an acquaintance. I added,
that, though I had never before the honor of being in his lordship's
company, his manner was such as had already engaged my confi-

dence, and would make me perfectly easy and free in communicating myself to him.

" I begged him, in the first place, to give me credit for a sincere desire of healing the breach between the two countries ; that I would cheerfully and heartily do every thing in my small power to accomplish it ; but that I apprehended from the king's speech, and from the measures talked of, as well as those already determined on, no intention or disposition of the kind existed in the present ministry, and therefore no accommodation could be expected till we saw a change. That, as to what his lordship mentioned of the *personal injuries* done me, those done my country were so much greater, that I did not think the other, at this time, worth mentioning ; that, besides, it was a fixed rule with me, not to mix my private affairs with those of the public ; that I could join with my personal enemy in serving the public, or, when it was for its interest, with the public in serving that enemy ; these being my sentiments, his lordship might be assured, that no private considerations of the kind should prevent my being as useful in the present case as my small ability would permit.

" He appeared satisfied and pleased with these declarations, and gave it me as his sincere opinion, that some of the ministry were extremely well disposed to any reasonable accommodation, preserving only the dignity of government ; and he wished me to draw up in writing some propositions containing the terms on which I conceived a good understanding might be obtained and established, and the mode of proceeding to accomplish it ; which propositions, as soon as prepared, we might meet to consider, either at his house, or at mine, or where I pleased ; but, as his being seen at my house, or me at his, might, he thought, occasion some speculation, it was concluded to be best to meet at his sister's, who readily offered her house for the purpose, and where there was a good pretense with her family and friends for my being often seen, as it was known we played together at chess. I undertook, accordingly, to draw up something of the kind ; and so for that time we parted, agreeing to meet at the same place on the Wednesday following."

Dr. Franklin was punctual to his appointment, but, having been detained longer than usual at Lord Chatham's, he had not been able to prepare the promised paper. His interview, however, was

of the most interesting character.   Lord Howe began by saying,
that he could now positively affirm that both Lord North and
Lord Dartmouth had a sincere desire to accommodate the differences, and were prepared to listen favorably to any reasonable proposition.   Dr. Franklin had already received assurances to the same
effect from his old friend, Governor Pownall, who was then verg-
ing toward the ministerial side.   Hearing the same positive assurances from so important a person as Lord Howe, he could not conceal his joy; tears rolled down his cheeks.   But the opening prospect was soon clouded over.   "Lord Howe asked me," he relates,
"what I thought of sending some person or persons over, commissioned to inquire into the grievances of America upon the spot,
converse with the leading people, and endeavor with them to agree
upon some means of composing our differences.   I said, that a person of rank and dignity, who had a character of candor, integrity,
and wisdom, might possibly, if employed· in that service, be of
great use.

"He seemed to be of the same opinion, and that whoever was
employed should go with a hearty desire of promoting a sincere
reconciliation, on the foundation of mutual interests and mutual
good-will; that he should endeavor, not only to remove their prejudices against government, but equally the prejudices of government against them, and bring on a perfect good understanding.
Mrs. Howe said, 'I wish, brother, you were to be sent thither on
such a service; I should like that much better than General
Howe's going to command the army there.'   'I think, madam,'
said I, 'they ought to provide for General Howe some more honorable employment.'   Lord Howe here took out of his pocket a
paper, and offering it to me said, smiling, 'If it is not an unfair
question, may I ask whether you know any thing of this paper?'
Upon looking at it, I saw it was a copy, in David Barclay's hand,
of the 'HINTS' before recited; and said, that I had seen it; adding,
a little after that, since I perceived his Lordship was acquainted
with a transaction, my concern in which I had understood was to
have been kept a secret, I should make no difficulty in owning to
him that I had been consulted on the subject, and had drawn up
that paper.   He said, he was rather sorry to find that the sentiments expressed in it were mine, as it gave him less hopes of promoting, by my assistance, the wished for reconciliation; since he

had reason to think there was no likelihood of the admission of those propositions. He hoped, however, that I would reconsider the subject, and form some plan that would be acceptable here. He expatiated on the infinite service it would be to the nation, and the great merit in being instrumental in so good a work; that he should not think of influencing me by any selfish motive, but certainly I might with reason expect any reward in the power of government to bestow.

"This to me was what the French vulgarly called *spitting in the soup.* However, I promised to draw some sketch of a plan, at his request, though I much doubted, I said, whether it would be thought preferable to that he had in his hand. But he was willing to hope that it would; and, as he considered my situation, that I had friends here and constituents in America to keep well with, that I might possibly propose something improper to be seen in my handwriting; therefore, it would be better to send it to Mrs. Howe, who would copy it, send the copy to him to be communicated to the ministry, and return me the original. This I agreed to, though I did not apprehend the inconvenience he mentioned. In general, I liked much his manner, and found myself disposed to place great confidence in him on occasion; but in this particular the secrecy he proposed seemed not of much importance."

Dr. Franklin drew up the proposed paper, which contained a series of propositions similar to those which he had given to Mr. Barclay and Dr. Fothergill. The government, he maintained, should first withdraw the troops, and repeal the oppressive acts; then send a commissioner of rank and dignity to preside over a general congress, and unite with the members in framing a plan of permanent union with the mother country. He sent the paper to Mrs. Howe, who copied it, and forwarded it to her brother. She acknowledged the receipt of the paper in mysterious language:

"Mrs. Howe's compliments to Dr. Franklin; she incloses him a letter she received last night, and returns him many thanks for his very obliging present, which has already given her great entertainment. If the Doctor has any spare time for chess, she will be exceedingly glad to see him any morning this week, and as often as will be agreeable to him, and rejoices in having so good an excuse for asking the favor of his company."

The inclosed letter proved to be one from Lord Howe to his

sister, in which he intimated that the Paper contained propositions which, he feared, the ministry would consider inadmissible.
Nevertheless, he would forward them. He did forward them, and
they were considered by ministers.

Parliament met on the nineteenth of January, and Lord Howe
returned to town to attend. "We had another meeting," Franklin
records, "at which he lamented, that my propositions were not such
as probably could be accepted; intimated, that it was thought I
had powers or instructions from the Congress to make concessions
on occasion, that would be more satisfactory. I disclaimed the
having any of any kind, but what related to the presenting of their
petition. We talked over all the particulars in my paper, which I
supported with reasons; and finally said, that, if what I had proposed would not do, I should be glad to hear what *would* do; I
wished to see some propositions from the ministers themselves.
His Lordship was not, he said, as yet fully acquainted with their
sentiments, but should learn more in a few days."

Weeks passed by before he heard another word from Lord Howe.
He learned, meanwhile, from Dr. Fothergill, that Lord Dartmouth
and the speaker of the House of Commons had deliberated upon
the paper of Hints, and agreed, that while some of them were
reasonable, others could not be accepted by government without
deep humiliation. The worthy Doctor reminded them that the
humiliation which comes from the acknowledgment of error and
the reparation of wrong is just and noble; the pill might be bitter,
said he, but it would be salutary. He told Dr. Franklin that both
the Secretary of State and the Speaker were extremely anxious for
reconciliation with the colonies, and he still hoped that peaceful
counsels would prevail.

Then followed the summary rejection by the House of Lords of
Lord Chatham's scheme; after which Dr. Franklin expected to hear
no more of amicable negotiation. He was surprised, however, a
day or two after that explosion of ministerial wrath, to receive
from Mr. Barclay an invitation to meet him once more at Dr.
Fothergill's. Still more surprised was he, on meeting the gentleman, to hear that the ministry were extremely well-disposed toward
the Hints, and thought they might, if slightly amended, be accepted
as the basis of an accommodation. "Dr. Fothergill," adds Franklin, "with his usual philanthropy, expatiated on the miseries of

war; that even a bad peace was preferable to the most successful war; that America was growing in strength; and, whatever she might be obliged to submit to at present, she would in a few years be in a condition to make her own terms."

Mr. Barclay proceeded to quench the enthusiasm of Fothergills and the hopes of Franklin: "He hinted how much it was in my power to promote an agreement; how much it would be to my honor to effect it; and that I might expect, not only restoration of my old place, but almost any other I could wish for. I need not tell you, who know me so well, how improper and disgusting this language was to me. The Doctor's was more suitable. Him I answered, that we did not wish for war, and desired nothing but what was reasonable and necessary for our security and well-being. To Mr. Barclay I replied, that the ministry, I was sure, would rather give me a place in a cart to Tyburn, than any other place whatever; and to both, that I sincerely wished to be serviceable; that I needed no other inducement than to be shown how I might be so; but saw they imagined more to be in my power than really was. I was then told again, that conferences had been held upon the 'Hints;' and the paper being produced was read, that I might hear the observations that had been made upon them."

He soon learned from Mr. Barclay's report of the ministerial comments, that the government was not inclined to concede points which the Congress deemed essential. It would not withdraw the troops; nor refund the tea duties; nor permit the governors to appoint officers of the customs; nor relinquish the building of fortresses; nor grant a free government to Canada; nor repeal any of the most offensive acts except the Boston Port Bill; nor renounce the claim of Parliament to legislate for the colonies. "I shortened the conversation upon these points," adds Franklin, "by observing that, while the Parliament claimed and exercised a power of altering our constitutions at pleasure, there could be no agreement; for we were rendered unsafe in every privilege we had a right to, and were secure in nothing. And, it being hinted how necessary an agreement was for America, since it was so easy for Britain to burn all our seaport towns, I grew warm; said that the chief part of my little property consisted of houses in those towns; that they might make bonfires of them whenever they pleased; that the fear of losing them would never alter my resolution to re-

sist to the last that claim of Parliament; and that it behooved this
country to take care what mischief it did us; for that sooner or
later it would certainly be obliged to make good all damages with
interest! The Doctor smiled, as I thought, with some approbation
of my discourse, passionate as it was, and said, he would certainly
repeat it to-morrow to Lord Dartmouth.

"In the discourse concerning the 'HINTS,' Mr. Barclay happened
to mention, that, going to Lord Hyde's, he found Lord Howe with
him; and that Lord Hyde had said to him, 'You may speak any
thing before Lord Howe that you have to say to me, for he is a
friend in whom I confide;' upon which he accordingly had spoken
with the same freedom as usual. By this I collected how Lord
Howe came by the paper of 'HINTS,' which he had shown me.
And, it being mentioned as a measure thought of, to send over a
commissioner with powers to inquire into grievances, and give
redress on certain conditions, but that it was difficult to find a
proper person, I said, 'Why not Lord Hyde? He is a man of
prudence and temper, a person of dignity, and, I should think,
very suitable for such an employment; or, if he would not go,
there is the other person you just mentioned, Lord Howe, who
would, in my opinion, do excellently well.' This passed as mere
conversation, and we parted."

A week later, the three friends conferred again. On this occasion, Mr. Barclay produced a paper containing a series of Articles
which, he was authorized to say, expressed the utmost that the
ministry could then concede. Several of the specific demands of
the colonies were granted in this scheme. So much was granted,
that, had the concessions been made a year before, the colonies
would probably have been conciliated by them, if not satisfied.
But times had changed. The scheme was fatally defective; since
the troops were not to be withdrawn; the authority of Parliament
over the colonies was not limited; even the Boston Port Bill was
only to be suspended; Massachusetts was to pay for the destroyed
tea; but the tea duties were not to be refunded. What Mr. Barclay said, however, was more important than the written paper
which he presented. He declared that the ministry were so
anxious for an accommodation, that all they asked was a decent
excuse for making concessions. Let the colonial agents in London
merely petition the king for redress, and, in that petition, *engage*

that the tea should be paid for, and they would find ministers eager to comply with all reasonable demands. More troops were preparing to embark, said Barclay, and such a petition would prevent their being dispatched.

" I was therefore urged," says Franklin, " to engage the colony agents to join with me in such a petition. My answer was, that no agent had any thing to do with the tea business, but those for Massachusetts Bay, who were Mr. Bollan for the Council, myself for the Assembly, and Mr. Lee, appointed to succeed me when I should leave England; that the latter, therefore, could hardly yet be considered as an agent; and that the former was a cautious, exact man, and not easily persuaded to take steps of such importance without instructions or authority; that, therefore, if such a step were to be taken, it would lie chiefly on me to take it ; that, indeed, if there were, as they supposed, a clear probability of good to be done by it, I should make no scruple of hazarding myself in it : but I thought the empowering a commissioner to suspend the Boston Port Act was a method too dilatory, and a mere suspension would not be satisfactory ; that, if such an engagement were entered into, all the Massachusetts acts should be immediately repealed.

" They laid hold of the readiness I had expressed to petition on a probability of doing good, applauded it, and urged me to draw up a petition immediately. I said it was a matter of importance, and with their leave I would take home the paper, consider the propositions as they now stood, and give them my opinion to-morrow evening. This was agreed to, and for that time we parted.

" Weighing now the present dangerous situation of affairs in America, and the daily hazard of widening the breach there irreparably, I embraced the idea proposed in the paper of sending over a commissioner, as it might be a means of suspending military operations and bring on a treaty, whereby mischief would be prevented, and an agreement by degrees be formed and established. I also concluded to do what had been desired of me as to the engagement, and essayed a draft of a memorial to Lord Dartmouth for that purpose simply, to be signed only by myself. As to the sending of a commissioner, a measure which I was desired likewise to propose, and express my sentiments of its utility, I appre-

hended my colleagues in the agency might be justly displeased if
I took a step of such importance without consulting them, and
therefore I sketched a joint petition to that purpose, for them to
sign with me if they pleased ; but, apprehending that would meet
with difficulty, I drew up a letter to Lord Dartmouth, containing the
same proposition, with the reasons for it, to be sent from me only."

The letter to Lord Dartmouth was drawn up in the following
terms : " My Lord : Being deeply apprehensive of the impending
calamities that threaten the nation and its colonies through the
present unhappy dissensions, I have attentively considered by
what possible means those calamities may be prevented. The
great importance of a business which concerns us all, will, I hope,
in some degree excuse me to your Lordship, if I presume unasked
to offer my humble opinion, that, should his Majesty think fit to
authorize delegates from the several provinces to meet at such
convenient time and place, as in his wisdom shall seem meet, then
and there to confer with a commissioner or commissioners to be
appointed and empowered by his Majesty, on the means of establishing a firm and lasting union between Britain and the American provinces, such a measure might be effectual for that purpose. I cannot therefore but wish it may be adopted, as no one
can more ardently and sincerely desire the general prosperity of
the British dominions, than, my Lord, your Lordship's most obedient, &c."

This letter, with the draft of the proposed petition to the king,
and a paper of Remarks upon the ministerial propositions, he submitted to Dr. Fothergill and Mr. Barclay at their next meeting.
Dr. Franklin, in one of these papers, risked his whole fortune for
his country ; and this was not the first occasion on which he had
done so. With admirable magnanimity he offered to *engage personally* to pay for the destroyed tea, valued at fifteen thousand
pounds, provided the offensive acts of Parliament were repealed.
The two gentlemen, having heard the papers read, expressed the
opinion that the paper of Remarks contained a fatal objection.
Dr. Franklin proposed to pay for the tea if an assurance were
given that *all* the acts enumerated by Congress should be repealed ; whereas the ministry were disposed to consider the repeal
of the Boston Port Bill alone a full equivalent for that concession.
Upon learning this, Dr. Franklin pocketed his drafts, and only

gave his Remarks to be submitted to the ministry. Mr. Barclay engaged to present these, and ascertain if the government were inclined to yield any thing further.

The next movement on the part of the ministry, was an attempt to bribe Dr. Franklin. I will not abridge this part of the narrative—so fraught with interest—so full of biography—so honorable to Franklin!

"The next morning," he continues, "I met Lord Howe, according to appointment. He seemed very cheerful, having, as I imagine, heard from Lord Hyde what that Lord might have heard from Mr. Barclay the evening of the 16th, viz., that I had consented to petition, and engage payment for the tea; whence it was hoped, the ministerial terms of accommodation might take place. He let me know, that *he was thought of to be sent commissioner for settling the differences in America;* adding, with an excess of politeness, that, sensible of his own unacquaintedness of the business, and of my knowledge and abilities, he could not think of undertaking it without me; but, with me, he should do it most readily; for he should found his expectation of success on my assistance. He therefore had desired this meeting, to know my mind upon a proposition of my going with him in some shape or other, as a friend, an assistant, or secretary; that he was very sensible, if he should be so happy as to effect any thing valuable, it must be wholly owing to the advice and assistance I should afford him; that he should therefore make no scruple of giving me upon all occasions the full honor of it; that he had declared to the ministers his opinion of my good dispositions towards peace, and what he now wished was to be authorized by me to say, that I consented to accompany him, and would co-operate with him in the great work of reconciliation. That the influence I had over the minds of people in America was known to be very extensive; and that I could, if any man could, prevail with them to comply with reasonable propositions.

"I replied, that I was obliged to his Lordship for the favorable opinion he had of me, and for the honor he did me in proposing to make use of my assistance; that I wished to know what propositions were intended for America; that, if they were reasonable ones in themselves, possibly I might be able to make them appear such to my countrymen; but, if they were otherwise, I doubted whether that could be done by any man, and certainly I should not undertake it.

" His Lordship then said, that he should not expect my *assistance* without a *proper consideration*. That the business was of great importance ; and, if he undertook it, he should insist on being enabled to make *generous* and *ample* appointments for those he took with him, particularly for me ; as well as a firm promise of *subsequent rewards*. ' And,' said he, ' that the ministry may have an opportunity of showing their good disposition towards yourself, will you give me leave, Mr. Franklin, to procure for you previously some mark of it ; suppose the payment here of the arrears of your salary, as agent for New England, which I understand they have stopped for some time past ?'

" 'My Lord,' said I, ' I shall deem it a great honor to be in any shape joined with your Lordship in so good a work ; but, if you hope service from any influence I may be supposed to have, drop all thoughts of procuring me any previous favors from ministers ; my accepting them would destroy the very influence you propose to make use of ; they would be considered as so many bribes to betray the interest of my country ; but only let me see the *propositions*, and, if I approve of them, I shall not hesitate a moment, but will hold myself ready to accompany your Lordship at an hour's warning.' He then said, he wished I would discourse with Lord Hyde upon the business, and asked if I had any objection to meet his Lordship. I answered, none, not the least ; that I had a great respect for Lord Hyde, and would wait upon him whenever he should please to permit it. He said he would speak to Lord Hyde and send me word.

" On the Monday following, I received a letter from Lord Howe. To understand it better, it is necessary to reflect, that in the mean time there was opportunity for Mr. Barclay to communicate to that nobleman the ' REMARKS ' I had made on the Plan, the sight of which had probably changed the purpose of making any use of me on the occasion. The letter follows :

" 'Not having had a convenient opportunity to talk with Lord Hyde until this morning, on the subject I mentioned when I had, my worthy friend, the pleasure to see you last, I now give you the earliest information of his Lordship's sentiments upon my proposition.

" 'He declares he has no personal objection, and that he is always
desirous of the conversation of men of knowledge, consequently,
in that respect, would have a pleasure in yours. But he appre-
hends, that on the present American contest your principles and
his, or rather those of Parliament, are as yet so wide from each
other, that a meeting merely to discuss them might give you unnecessary trouble. Should you think otherwise, or should any propitious circumstances approximate such distant sentiments, he
would be happy to be used as a channel to convey what might tend
to harmony from a person of credit to those in power. And I will
venture to advance, from my knowledge of his Lordship's opinion
of men and things, that nothing of that nature would suffer in the
passage.'

"As I had no desire of obtruding myself upon Lord Hyde, though
a little piqued at his declining to see me, I thought it best to show
a decent indifference, which I endeavored in the following answer :

" 'Having nothing to offer on the American business in addition
to what Lord Hyde is already acquainted with from the papers
that have passed, it seems most respectful not to give his Lordship
the trouble of a visit; since a mere discussion of the sentiments
contained in those papers is not, in his opinion, likely to produce
any good effect. I am thankful, however, to his Lordship for the
permission of waiting on him, which I shall use if any thing occurs, that may give a chance of utility in such an interview.'

" On the morning of the same day, February 20th, it was currently and industriously reported all over the town, that Lord
North would that day make a pacific motion in the House of Commons for healing all differences between Britain and America. The
House was accordingly very full, and the members full of expectation. The Bedford party, inimical to America, and who had urged
severe measures, were alarmed, and began to exclaim against the
minister for his timidity, and the fluctuation of his *politics ;* they
even began to count voices, to see if they could not, by negativing
his motion, at once unhorse him, and throw him out of administration. His friends were therefore alarmed for him, and there was
much caballing and whispering. At length a motion, as one had
been promised, was made, but whether that originally intended, is
with me very doubtful. I suspect, from its imperfect composition,
from its inadequateness to answer the purpose previously professed,

and from some other circumstances, that, when first drawn, it contained more of Mr. Barclay's plan, but was curtailed by advice, just before it was delivered. My old proposition of giving up the regulating duties to the colonies was in part to be found in it; and many, who knew nothing of that transaction, said it was the best part of the motion. It was as follows:

"'That it is the opinion of this committee, that, when the Governor, Council, and Assembly, or General Court of his Majesty's provinces or colonies shall propose to make provision according to their respective conditions, circumstances, and situations, for contributing their proportion to the common defense, such proportion to be raised under the authority of the General Court or General Assembly of such province or colony, and disposable by Parliament, and shall engage to make provision also for the support of the civil government and the administration of justice in such province or colony, it will be proper, if such proposal shall be approved by his Majesty in Parliament, and for so long as such provision shall be made accordingly, to forbear, in respect of such province or colony, to levy any duties, tax, or assessment, or to impose any further duty, tax, or assessment, except only such duties as it may be expedient to impose for the regulation of commerce; the net produce of the duties last mentioned to be carried to the account of such province, colony, or plantation, exclusively.'

"After a good deal of wild debate, in which this motion was supported upon various and inconsistent principles by the ministerial people, and even met with an opposition from some of them, which showed a want of concert, probably from the suddenness of the alterations above supposed, they all agreed at length, as usual, in voting it by a large majority.

"Hearing nothing during all the following week from Messrs. Barclay and Fothergill, (except that Lord Hyde, when acquainted with my willingness to engage for the payment of the tea, had said it gave him *new life,*) nor any thing from Lord Howe, I mentioned his silence occasionally to his sister, adding, that I supposed it owing to his finding what he had proposed to me was not likely to take place; and I wished her to desire him, if that was the case, to let me know it by a line, that I might be at liberty to take other measures. She did so as soon as he returned from the country, where he had been for a day or two; and I received from her the following note:

"Mrs. Howe's compliments to Dr. Franklin; Lord Howe not quite understanding the message received from her, will be very glad to have the pleasure of seeing him, either between twelve and one this morning, (the only hour he is at liberty this day,) at her house, or at any other hour to-morrow most convenient to him.'

"I met his Lordship at the hour appointed. He said, that he had not seen me lately, as he expected daily to have something more material to say to me than had yet occurred; and hoped that I would have called on Lord Hyde, as I had intimated I should do when I apprehended it might be useful, which he was sorry to find I had not done. That there was something in my verbal message by Mrs. Howe, which, perhaps she had apprehended imperfectly; it was the hint of my purpose to take other measures. I answered, that having, since I had last seen his Lordship, heard of the death of my wife at Philadelphia, in whose hands I had left the care of my affairs there, it was become necessary for me to return thither as soon as conveniently might be; that what his Lordship had proposed of my accompanying him to America might, if likely to take place, postpone my voyage to suit his conveniency; otherwise I should proceed by the first ship; that I did suppose by not hearing from him, and by Lord North's motion, all thoughts of that kind were laid aside, which was what I only desired to know from him.

"He said, my last paper of 'REMARKS' by Mr. Barclay, wherein I had made the indemnification of Boston for the injury of stopping its port, a condition of my engaging to pay for the tea (a condition impossible to be complied with), had discouraged further proceeding on that idea. Having a copy of that paper in my pocket, I showed his Lordship that I had proposed no such condition, nor any other than the repeal of all the Massachusetts acts. That what followed relating to the indemnification was only expressing my private opinion, that it would be just, but by no means insisting upon it. He said the arrangements were not yet determined on; that, as I now explained myself, it appeared I had been much misapprehended, and he wished of all things I would see Lord Hyde, and asked if I would choose to meet him there (at Mrs. Howe's), or that he should call upon me. I said, that I would by no means give Lord Hyde that trouble. That, since he (Lord Howe) seemed to think it might be of use, and wished it done soon, I would wait upon Lord Hyde. I knew him to be an early riser, and would be with him at eight o'clock the next morning; which Lord Howe undertook to acquaint him with. But I added, that, from what circumstances I could collect of the disposition of ministry, I apprehended my visit would answer no material purpose. He was of a different opinion ; to which I submitted.

"The next morning, March 1st, I accordingly was early with Lord Hyde, who received me with his usual politeness. We talked over a great part of the dispute between the countries. I found him ready with all the newspaper and pamphlet topics; of the expense of settling our colonies, the protection afforded them, the heavy debt under which Britain labored, the equity of our contributing to its alleviation ; that many people in England were no more represented than we were, yet all were taxed and governed by Parliament, &c., &c. I answered all, but with little effect; for, though his Lordship seemed civilly to hear what I said, I had reason to believe he attended very little to the purport of it, his mind being employed the while in thinking on what he himself purposed to say next.

"He had hoped, he said, that Lord North's motion would have been satisfactory ; and asked what could be objected to it. I replied, the terms of it were, that we should grant money till Parliament had agreed we had given enough, without having the least share in judging of the propriety of the measure for which it was to be granted, or of our own abilities to grant ; that these grants were also to be made under a threat of exercising a claimed right of taxing us at pleasure, and compelling such taxes by an armed force, if we did not give till it should be thought we had given enough; that the proposition was similar to no mode of obtaining aids that ever existed, except that of a highwayman, who presents his pistol and hat at a coach window, demanding no specific sum, but, if you will give all your money, or what he is pleased to think sufficient, he will civilly omit putting his own hand into your pockets ; if not, there is his pistol. That the mode of raising contributions in an enemy's country was fairer than this, since there an explicit sum was demanded, and the people who were raising it knew what they were about, and when they should have done; and that, in short, no free people could ever think of beginning to grant upon such terms. That, besides, a new dispute had now been raised, by the Parliament's pretending to a power of altering our

charters and established laws, which was of still more importance
to us than their claim of taxation, as it set us all adrift, and left us
without a privilege we could depend upon, but at their pleasure;
this was a situation we could not possibly be in; and as Lord
North's proposition had no relation to this matter, if the other had
been such as we could have agreed to, we should still be far from a
reconciliation.

"His Lordship thought I misunderstood the proposition; on
which I took it out and read it. He then waved that point, and
said he should be glad to know from me, what would produce a
reconciliation. I said, that his Lordship, I imagined, had seen
several proposals of mine for that purpose. He said he had; but
some of my articles were such as would never be agreed to. That
it was apprehended I had several instructions and powers to offer
more acceptable terms, but was extremely reserved, and perhaps
from a desire he did not blame, of doing better for my constituents;
but my expectations might deceive me; and he did think I might
be assured I should never obtain better terms than what were now
offered by Lord North. That administration had a sincere desire
of restoring harmony with America; and it was thought, if I would
co-operate with them, the business would be easy. That he hoped
I was above retaining resentment against them for what nobody
now approved, and for which satisfaction might be made me; that
I was, as he understood, in high esteem among the Americans;
that, if I would bring about a reconciliation on terms suitable to
the dignity of government, I might be as highly and generally esteemed here, and be honored and *rewarded*, perhaps, *beyond my
expectation*.

"I replied, that I thought I had given a convincing proof of my
sincere desire of promoting peace, when, on being informed that
all wanted for the honor of government was, to obtain payment
for the tea, I offered, without any instruction to warrant my so doing, or assurance that I should be reimbursed, or my conduct approved, to engage for that payment, if the Massachusetts acts were
to be repealed; an engagement in which I must have risked my
whole fortune, which I thought few besides me would have done.
That, in truth, private resentments had no weight with me in public business; that I was not the reserved man imagined, having
really no secret instructions to act upon. That I was certainly

willing to do every thing that could reasonably be expected of me. But, if any supposed I could prevail with my countrymen to take black for white, and wrong for right, it was not knowing either them or me; they were not capable of being so imposed on, nor was I capable of attempting it.

"He then asked my opinion of sending over a commissioner, for the purpose mentioned in a preceding part of this account, and my answer was to the same effect. By the way, I apprehend, that to give me an opportunity of discoursing with Lord Hyde on that point, was a principal motive with Lord Howe for urging me to make this visit. His Lordship did not express his own sentiments upon it. And thus ended this conversation.

"Three or four days after, I received the following note from Mrs. Howe: 'Mrs. Howe's compliments to Dr. Franklin; Lord Howe begs to have the pleasure of meeting him once more before he goes at her house; he is at present out of town, but returns on Monday; and any day or hour after that, that the Doctor will name, he will be very glad to attend him.'

"I answered, that I would do myself the honor of waiting on Lord Howe, at her house, the Tuesday following, at eleven o'clock. We met accordingly. He began by saying, that I had been a better prophet than himself, in foreseeing that my interview with Lord Hyde would be of no great use; and then said, that he hoped I would excuse the trouble he had given me, as his intentions had been good both towards me and the public. He was sorry, that at present there was no appearance of things going into the train he had wished, but that possibly they might yet take a more favorable turn; and, as he understood I was going soon to America, if he should chance to be sent thither on that important business, he hoped he might still expect my assistance. I assured him of my readiness at all times of co-operating with him in so good a work; and so, taking my leave, and receiving his good wishes, ended the negotiation with Lord Howe. And I heard no more of that with Messrs. Fothergill and Barclay. I could only gather, from some hints in their conversation, that neither of them were well pleased with the conduct of the ministers respecting these transactions. And, a few days before I left London, I met them by their desire, at the Doctor's house, when they desired me to assure their friends from them, that it was now their fixed opinion, that nothing could secure the privileges of America, but a firm, sober adherence to the terms of the association made at the Congress, and that the salvation of English liberty depended now on the perseverance and virtue of America.

"During the whole, my time was otherwise much taken up, by friends calling continually to inquire news from America; members of both Houses of Parliament, to inform me what passed in the Houses, and discourse with me on the debate, and on motions made, or to be made; merchants of London and of the manufacturing and port towns, on their petitions; the Quakers, upon theirs, &c., &c.; so that I had no time to take notes of almost any thing. This account is therefore chiefly from recollection, in which doubtless much must have been omitted, from deficiency of memory; but what there is, I believe to be pretty exact; except that, discoursing with so many different persons about the same time, on the same subject, I may possibly have put down some things as said by or to one person, which passed in conversation with another."

A few days after the close of these negotiations, Dr. Franklin attended, for the last time, the House of Lords, and heard there such wild vituperation of his countrymen as moved even his placid mind to rage. American courage, American religion, American intellect, became by turns the theme of lordly denunciation. "We were treated," says Franklin, "with the utmost contempt, as the lowest of mankind, and almost of a different species from the English of Britain; but particularly, American honesty was abused by some of the lords, who asserted that we were all knaves, and wanted only by this dispute to avoid paying our debts." Burning with indignation, he hurried home, and drew up a Protest against the proceedings of the government, in the form of a memorial to the Earl of Dartmouth:

"Whereas, an injury done can only give the party injured a right to full reparation; or, in case that be refused, a right to return an equal injury; and whereas, the blockade of Boston, now continued nine months, hath every week of its continuance done damage to that town, equal to what was suffered there by the India Company; it follows that such *exceeding* damage is an *injury* done by this government, for which reparation ought to be made; and whereas, reparation of injuries ought always (agreeably to the custom of all nations, savage as well as civilized) to be first required, before satisfaction is taken by a return of damage to the aggressors; which was not done by Great Britain in the instance above mentioned; I, the underwritten, do therefore, as their agent, in the behalf of my country and the said town of Boston, protest against the continuance of the said blockade; and I do hereby solemnly demand satisfaction for the accumulated injury done them, beyond the value of the India Company's tea destroyed.

"And whereas, the conquest of the Gulf of St. Lawrence, the coasts of Labrador and Nova Scotia, and the fisheries possessed by the French there and on the Banks of Newfoundland, so far as they were more extended than at present, was made by the *joint forces* of Britain and the colonies, the latter having nearly an equal number of men in that service with the former; it follows, that the colonies have an equitable and just right to participate in the advantage of those fisheries; I do, therefore, in behalf of the colony of the Massachusetts Bay, protest against the act now under consideration in Parliament, for depriving that province, with others, of that fishery, (on pretense of their refusing to purchase British commodities,) as an act highly unjust and injurious; and I give notice, that satisfaction will probably one day be demanded for all the injury that may be done and suffered in the execution of such act; and that the injustice of the proceeding is likely to give such umbrage to *all the colonies*, that in no future war, wherein other conquests may be meditated, either a man or a shilling will be obtained from any of them to aid such conquests, till full satisfaction be made as aforesaid."

When he had finished the draft of this Protest, he showed it to his friend, Thomas Walpole, a liberal member of Parliament. "He looked at it," says Franklin, "and at me several times alternately, as if he apprehended me a little out of my senses." Walpole strongly advised the indignant agent not to present the memorial, as it would certainly exasperate the nation, and probably lead to the arrest of the author. "I had no desire," Franklin adds, "to make matters worse, and being grown cooler, took the advice so kindly given me."

Thus ended his connection with the governing powers of England. Down to the packing of his last trunk, he had still striven with all the might of his genius, his wisdom, his patience, and his wrath, to save entire the great Empire of his pride and love.

Nothing could ever long suspend the fruitful gayety of Franklin's mind. It was during these last exciting weeks, that he conceived that peerless fable of the Eagle and the Cat, which John Adams was good enough to record, after hearing the story from Franklin's own lips. At a nobleman's house, one evening, the conversation having turned upon fables, a gentleman expressed the opinion that Æsop, La Fontaine, Gay, and the rest, had exhausted that mine of illustration. No man, he continued, could now find an animal, bird, fish, or reptile which could be worked into an original fable. The company appeared to concur in this remark. Franklin mused upon the subject, but said nothing; until, his silence being noticed, the gentleman asked his opinion. He replied, that he considered fables an inexhaustible resource, and he believed that many new and instructive ones could be invented. " Can you think of one now ?" asked a lord. Franklin answered, that if he was furnished with pen and paper, he could produce one on the spot. The articles were brought, and he began to write. In a few minutes he had given inimitable expression, in the form of a fable, to the political situation of England and America:

" Once upon a time, an eagle, scaling round a farmer's barn, and espying a hare, darted down upon him like a sunbeam, seized him in his claws, and remounted with him to the air. He soon found, that he had a creature of more courage and strength than a hare ; for which, notwithstanding the keenness of his eyesight, he had mistaken a cat. The snarling and scrambling of his prey were very inconvenient; and, what was worse, she had disengaged herself from his talons, grasped his body with her four limbs, so as to stop his breath, and seized fast hold of his throat with her teeth. ' Pray,' said the eagle, ' let go your hold, and I will release you.' ' Very fine,' said the cat ; ' I have no fancy to fall from this hight, and be crushed to death. You have taken me up, and you shall stoop, and let me down.' The eagle thought it necessary to stoop accordingly."*

* Life and Works of John Adams, ix., 268.

CHAPTER XIII.

RETURN TO AMERICA.

FRANKLIN took leave of his London friends. He did not think it a final farewell, for he said, in a letter, written three days before his departure, that he left his affairs in the hands of Mrs. Stevenson, and purposed, God willing, to return to England in October. He, probably, hoped to come back to London charged with proposals from the Congress, which the ministry, after six months' observation of the determination of America, and six months' experience of the commercial consequences of that determination, might be willing to accept. He still felt, with George Washington, John Adams, John Jay, and Henry Laurens, that he would give every thing he possessed to restore the relations of the colonies and the mother country, to the state in which they were before the passage of the Stamp Act.

M. Garnier, the French Minister, sought a last interview with him. They had often conferred before on the great topic, each having a sincere esteem for the other. On this occasion M. Garnier reminded Franklin of the aid which French genius, in the time of Henry IV., had contributed to the United Provinces in their struggle for independence. Franklin noted well the prophetic hint. It occurred, however, to Garnier, that the American colonies had no navy, no allies, no Prince of Orange. But they had Franklin. M. Garnier told the French Minister for Foreign Affairs, that Franklin, when he reached home, would cut out work enough for the English cabinet.

The day before his last in London, he spent several hours with Edmund Burke. Again, he recalled the happy days when the British Empire presented the only instance in history of a great empire as well governed in its distant members as at the metropolis. Again, he justified the resistance of his countrymen, and lamented the infatuation of the blunderers who had provoked it. The old friends parted, never to meet again.

Three days after, Mr. Burke pronounced that fine eulogium of the colonies, in his place in the House of Commons, which was a stock piece for declamation in the schools of the last generation. Doubtless, his long conversation with Franklin suggested some of the happy points of this splendid oration. "Look," exclaimed Mr. Burke, " at the manner in which the people of New England have, of late, carried on the whale fishery! Whilst we follow them among the tumbling mountains of ice, and behold them penetrating into the deepest frozen recesses of Hudson's Bay and Davis's Straits; whilst we are looking for them beneath the arctic circle, we hear they have pierced into the opposite region of polar cold, that they are at the antipodes, and engaged under the frozen serpent of the south. Falkland Island, which seemed too remote and romantic an object for the grasp of national ambition, is but a stage and resting-place in the progress of their victorious industry. Nor is the equinoctial heat more discouraging to them, than the accumulated winter of both the poles. We know that, whilst some of them draw the line and strike the harpoon on the coast of Africa, others run the longitude, and pursue their gigantic game along the coast of Brazil. No sea but what is vexed by their fisheries; no climate that is not witness of their toils. Neither the perseverance of Holland, nor the activity of France, nor the dexterous and firm sagacity of English enterprise, ever carried this most perilous mode of hard industry to the extent to which it has been pushed by this recent people; a people who are still, as it were, but in the gristle, and not yet hardened into the bone of manhood."

Again, in speaking of the education of the colonists : " I have been told by an eminent bookseller, that in no branch of his business, after tracts of popular devotion, were so many books as those on the law exported to the plantations. The colonists have now fallen into the way of printing them for their own use. I hear that they have sold nearly as many of 'Blackstone's Commentaries' in America as in England. General Gage marks out this disposition very particularly in a letter on your table. He states, that all the people in his government are lawyers, or smatterers in law; and that in Boston they have been enabled, by successful chicane, wholly to evade many parts of one of your capital penal constitutions. * * * This study renders men acute, inquisitive, dexterous, prompt in attack, ready in defense, full of resources. In other countries, the people, more simple, and of a less mercurial cast, judge of an ill principle in government only by an actual grievance; here they anticipate the evil, and judge of the pressure of the grievance by the badness of the principle. They augur misgovernment at

a distance, and snuff the approach of tyranny in every tainted
breeze."

If the reader will turn to this great speech, one of the greatest
ever delivered, he will perceive, I think, many traces of Franklin in
it. Its effect in America upon the minds of some members of Congress was almost sufficient to neutralize for a time that of General
Gage's bloody acts in Massachusetts.

Franklin's last day of all in London, he spent with Dr. Priestley.
Worse news appears to have arrived from America, and they sat
long together reading American newspapers. Dr. Priestley relates
some particulars of the interview :

"It is probable that no person now living was better acquainted
with Dr. Franklin and his sentiments on all subjects of importance,
than myself for several years before the American war. I think I
knew him as well as one man can generally know another. At that
time I spent the winters in London, in the family of the Marquis
of Lansdowne, and few days passed without my seeing more or less
of Dr. Franklin ; and the last day that he passed in England, having
given out that he should depart the day before, we spent together,
without any interruption, from morning until night."   *   *   *

"It was at his request, enforced by that of Dr. Fothergill, that I
wrote an anonymous pamphlet, calculated to show the injustice
and impolicy of a war with the colonies, previous to the meeting
of a new Parliament. As I then lived at Leeds, he corrected the
press himself ; and to a passage in which I lamented the attempt to
establish arbitrary power in so large a part of the British empire,
he added the following clause: 'To the imminent hazard of our
most valuable commerce, and of that national strength, security,
and felicity, which depend on union and on liberty.'

"The unity of the British empire in all its parts was a favorite
idea of his. He used to compare it to a beautiful china vase, which,
if ever broken, could never be put together again ; and so great
an admirer was he of the British constitution, that he said he saw
no inconvenience from its being extended over a great part of the
globe. With these sentiments he left England."   *   *   *

"By many persons Dr. Franklin is considered as having been a
cold-hearted man ; so callous to every feeling of humanity, that the
prospect of all the horrors of a civil war could not affect him. This
was far from being the case. A great part of the day above-men-

tioned that we spent together, he was looking over a number of American newspapers, directing me what to extract from them for the English ones; and in reading them, he was frequently not able to proceed for the tears literally running down his cheeks. To strangers he was cold and reserved; but where he was intimate, no man indulged more in pleasantry and good humor. By this he was the delight of a club, to which he alludes in one of his letters, called the Whig Club, that met at the London Coffee-House, of which Dr. Price, Dr. Kippis, Mr. John Lee, and others of the same stamp were members."*

In the evening of that day, he received a note from the good Dr. Fothergill, with a packet of letters for America. Even the charitable and benevolent Fothergill gave up the ministers as incurable. He advised Dr. Franklin, as soon as he reached Philadelphia, " to get his friends together, and inform them that whatever specious pretenses are offered, they are all hollow; and that to get a larger field on which to fatten a host of worthless parasites is all that is regarded. Perhaps it may be proper to acquaint them with David Barclay's and our united endeavors, and the effects. They will stun, at least, if not convince, the most worthy, that nothing very favorable is intended." " The doctor," adds Franklin, " in the course of his daily visits among the great, in the practice of his profession, had full oportunity of being acquainted with their sentiments, the conversation everywhere turning upon the subject of America." Dr. Fothergill had great reputation in America, particularly among the Quakers, many of whom had crossed the Atlantic on purpose to consult him.

Franklin left to Arthur Lee the agency which that gentleman had coveted so long. He told Mr. Lee that, though he might return to London in a few months, he could not again undertake the agency. It fell to the lot of Arthur Lee, after the departure of Dr. Franklin, to render service to the colonies.

Franklin remained to the last under apprehensions that he would not be permitted to embark; and it is now known that Governor Hutchinson, who still had the king's ear, avowed the opinion that he ought to be arrested. He posted rapidly, and with precautions, to Portsmouth, accompanied by his grandson, and embarked,

* " Life of Dr. Priestley," i., 448.

without molestation, on board the Pennsylvania packet on the twenty-first of March. He had left his man-servant with Dr. Priestley, for he was going to a country which could then find better than menial labor for all its men. His attentive grandson gave him all the little aid his vigorous age required.

The voyage, which was of six weeks' duration, was singularly tranquil and pleasant; so that he could employ the whole time in useful and interesting labors. Franklin once said (after he had crossed the ocean eight times), that he had never in his life made a voyage without having firmly resolved never, for any reason, or any combination of reasons, to go to sea again. Yet the records of his various voyages show that he was alive to all the wonders of the sea, and full of curiosity with regard to its sublime phenomena and their causes. None of his voyages was richer in results than this one. His first labor was to write, in the form of a letter to his son, a full account of his late interviews and negotiations with Lord Chatham, Mrs. Howe, Lord Howe, Lord Hyde, Mr. Barclay, and Dr. Fothergill. The material parts of this narrative have been embodied in the last two chapters of this work, but the whole must have filled about two hundred and fifty pages of foolscap ; a severe task for a man of sixty-nine, in the cabin of a small ship.

I may remark here, that the copy of this paper which was given to the world by William Temple Franklin, appears to have been subjected to a process of expurgation. Mr. Jefferson received a copy from Franklin's own hands, which, soon after Franklin's death, he gave to his grandson, to whom the departed philosopher had bequeathed his papers. In writing of this narrative twenty years later, Mr. Jefferson quoted a sentence from it which is not to be found in the version published by William Temple Franklin. " I remember," he says, " that Lord North's answers were dry, unyielding, in the spirit of unconditional submission, and betrayed an absolute indifference to the occurrence of a rupture ; and he said to the mediators distinctly, at last, that ' a rebellion was not to be deprecated on the part of Great Britain ; that the confiscations it would produce, would provide for many of their friends.' This expression was reported by the mediators to Dr. Franklin, and indicated so cool and calculated a purpose in the ministry, as to render compromise hopeless, and the negotiation was discontinued." * * " The paper certainly established views so atrocious in the

British government, that its suppression would, to them, be worth a great price. But could the grandson of Dr. Franklin be, in such degree, an accomplice in the parricide of the memory of his immortal grandfather?"*

Mr. Jefferson's memory was not perfectly trustworthy, as has frequently been shown. It is possible, however, that William Temple Franklin, an Englishman born and bred, and living on terms of intimacy with his father's friends, may have suppressed the most odious passages of the narrative.

On this voyage, the diligent use of his thermometer led Dr. Franklin to the discovery that the Gulf Stream is warmer than the surrounding ocean; and from this fact he inferred the tropical source of that current, and its cause, the trade winds. His observations confirmed, too, a previous impression, that by shaping a vessel's course so as not to stem the Gulf Stream, the voyage from Europe to America might be shortened. He conceived an idea still more practically useful, which has since given rise to a little library of nautical works, and conferred unmerited honor upon a naval charlatan—Maury. This idea was, that by studying the form and motions of the earth and directing a ship's course so that it shall *partake* of the earth's diurnal motion, a voyage may be materially shortened. Besides these observations, he made suggestions, some valuable, all ingenious, respecting the form of ships, their sails, anchors, and rigging. He kept a record of the weather, temperature of the sea, color of the water, soundings, phosphorescence, and floating weeds. He was the first to note that the water of the Gulf Stream is not phosphorescent.

The packet dropped anchor in the Delaware opposite Philadelphia on the fifth of May, in the evening. What news greeted his return! He heard it, probably, before leaving the ship. Farewell philosophy, its peaceful implements, its careful, exact records! The sea had been tranquil, but the land was heaving; tempests had forsaken their proper domain, and raged on shore. He heard, and heard, doubtless, with bated breath and dilated eyes, that General Gage, after having summoned the Legislature of Massachusetts to meet for the purpose of considering Lord North's peace-inviting Resolution, had precipitated war by sending a body of troops to

* Works of Jefferson, i., 108.

destroy the colonial stores.   The affairs of Lexington and Concord
had been the result.   Forty-nine Americans killed and thirty-four
wounded ; avenged by a British loss, in killed, wounded, and missing, of two hundred and seventy-three !   These great events, decisive of the course of colonial history, had occurred sixteen days
before ; and the news, fresh in Pennsylvania, was speeding its electric way southward, calling each colony to arms as it passed.
Franklin heard it undismayed.   He had hoped for other tidings,
but no man was better prepared than he for the last resort.

Going on shore in the evening, he went quietly to his house in
Market street, which he had never before seen, though it was then
nine years old.   He found his daughter and her family well.   In
all suitable ways, America welcomed home her faithful champion,
then incomparably her foremost man; the heroes of the coming
war being still in obscurity, and the great men of Congress not yet
of eminent renown.   His return at such a moment was felt to be
most opportune, the time having come when the colonists needed
all that they could command of knowledge, experience, talent, and
courage.   The Assembly of Pennsylvania, with which Franklin
had then been connected, in various ways, for a quarter of a century, was in session.   The morning after his arrival, they unanimously resolved, "that Benjamin Franklin, Honorable Thomas
Willing, and James Wilson, Esquires, be, and they are hereby,
added to the deputies appointed by this House on the part of
Pennsylvania, to attend the Continental Congress expected to meet
on the 10th instant in this city."

The press of the city noticed his arrival in the flowery manner
of the time.   In the *Pennsylvania Packet* of May 8th, we find it
thus announced :

"MAY 5th.   This evening arrived at Philadelphia, Captain Os-
borne, from London, with whom came passenger the worthy Dr.
Benjamin Franklin, Agent for Massachusetts government and the
province of Pennsylvania."

In another column of the same paper the following appears :

"To THE FRIEND OF HIS COUNTRY AND MANKIND, DOCTOR
BENJAMIN FRANKLIN, ON HIS RETURN FROM ENGLAND, May 6th,
1775 :

"Welcome !   Once more
To these fair western plains—thy native shore.

Here-live beloved, and leave the tools at home
To run their length, and finish out their doom.
Here lend thine aid to quench their brutal fires,
Or fan the flame which Liberty inspires,
Or fix the grand conductor, that shall guide
The tempest back, and 'lectrify their pride.
Rewarding Heaven will bless thy cares at last,
And future glories glorify the past.

" Why stayed the apostate, Wedderburn, behind,
The scum—the scorn—the scoundrel of mankind ?
Whose heart at large to every vice is known,
And every devil claims him for his own ;
Why came he not to take the large amount
Of all we owe him, due on thine account ?"

To one of such strong local attachments, it must have been a pleasure to walk again the streets of Philadelphia, and observe with what rapidity it had advanced during his absence. The city had become the recognized metropolis of the country, and exhibited, within and without, the signs of an ancient prosperity : plain, but spacious mansions, agreeable country-seats, abundant shipping, busy wharves, and extensive stores. Among the trifling changes which Franklin may have noted in his first walks, perhaps, he observed, with a smile, the new " Franklin Inn," at the corner of Fifth Street and Walnut ; the first of the many hundreds of taverns which have since taken the name.

The political condition of Pennsylvania was such as to render his return, just then, peculiarly welcome to the liberal party. During his long absence from the scene, his old antagonist, John Dickinson, had gained a predominant influence in the Assembly, in which the proprietary party had long been in the majority. That body, it appears, had fallen into contempt among the people. Josiah Quincy, who visited Philadelphia in 1773, wrote thus of Pennsylvania politics : "There is a proprietary influence in this province, destructive of a liberal conduct in the legislative branch, and in the executive authority. The House of Representatives are but thirty-six in number ; as a body, held in great and remarkable contempt ; much despised for their acquiescence with the views and measures of the proprietary party, and singularly odious for certain provincial maneuvres."* He adds, that the Assembly of Pennsylvania was as completely under the influence of the proprietary, as the British Parliament was under that of Lord Bute.

When a community is divided into a war party and a peace party—resistants and submissionists—the first blood that is shed practically annihilates the peace party. To the moment of actual collision, a pacific solution of the difficulty seems possible; after that moment, it is generally impossible. The news of Lexington and Concord changed thousands of minds in Pennsylvania, and confirmed in warlike sentiments thousands more who had been undecided. Joseph Reed, a friend of Lord Dartmouth, and a leader of the proprietary party, now "banished from his mind all anxiety or hope for a compromise."† Old Christopher Marshall, a retired druggist of Philadelphia, a Quaker expelled for taking an active part against the king, wrote in his diary on the seventh of May, 1775 : "It is admirable to see the alteration of the tory class in this place since the account of the engagement in New England ; their language is quite softened, and many of them have so far renounced their former sentiments, as that they have taken in arms and are joined in the associations ; nay, even many of the stiff Quakers, some even of those who drew up the Testimony, are ashamed of their proceedings. The Friends held a meeting last Fifth day afternoon, in order to consider how to send a supply to the Bostonians, it being a matter they had before treated with contempt and ridicule." The people, he adds, were signing petitions to the Assembly asking them to raise fifty thousand pounds for the defense of the province, and to obstruct the navigation of the river by sinking ships. Military companies, organized on Franklin's system, were exercising in every public ground in and about the city ; while the Philosophical Society was searching its books to discover the process of making saltpeter. Soon, the bold conception was promulgated that, perhaps, by the favor of Heaven and the wit of patriots, even cannon might be cast in Philadelphia.

At such a time, stepped on shore the long exiled chief of the

---

* "Life of Josiah Quincy, jun.," p. 185.   † "Life of Joseph Reed," i., 100.

liberals; "to the satisfaction of his friends and of the lovers of liberty," says Christopher Marshall. Party discipline and governmental patronage might still prevent the voice of Pennsylvania from being full and clear for resistance; but, the people being sound and Franklin at home, there could be no doubt of the result of the controversy. If the proprietary government made common cause with the king, the proprietary government must prepare for departure.

Franklin heartily accepted the new posture of affairs. He expressed an honest exultation in the gallantry of his New England countrymen. To Mr. Burke he wrote: "Gen. Gage's troops made a most vigorous retreat—twenty miles in three hours—scarce to be paralleled in history; the feeble Americans, who pelted them all the way, could scarce keep up with them." To Dr. Priestley, by the same ship: "You will have heard, before this reaches you, of a march stolen by the regulars into the country by night, and of their *expedition* back again. They retreated twenty miles in six hours. The governor had called the Assembly to propose Lord North's pacific plan, but before the time of their meeting, began cutting of throats. You know it was said he carried the sword in one hand, and the olive branch in the other; and it seems he chose to give them a taste of the sword first." To one who said, that the firing from behind stone walls proved the cowardice of the Americans, he replied: "I beg to inquire if those same walls had not two sides to them?"

Anxious for the safety of his sister, Jane Mecom, and other relatives, whom he supposed to be shut up in beleaguered Boston, he wrote to her, inviting her to come and live with him in Philadelphia, and asking her to make known their situation and wants. She replied that she had escaped from the city with some of her effects, and locked up the rest in her house. "Your care for me at this time," she wrote, "added to the innumerable instances of your goodness to me, gives me great comfort under the difficulties I feel with others, but not in a greater degree, for I am in want of nothing, having money sufficient to support me some time, if I should go to board, and I have with me most of the things I had to sell, and now and then sell some small matter." She entreated him not to think of crossing the Atlantic again: "As your talents are superior to most other men's, I can't help requiring your country should enjoy the benefit of them while you live, but can't bear the thought of your going to England again, as has been suggested here, and one sentence in your letter seems to favor. You positively must not go; you have served the public in that way beyond what any other man can boast till you are now come to a good old age, and some younger men must now take that painful service upon them. Don't go, pray, don't go; you certainly may do as much good here as circumstances are at present, and possibly the Congress may not think it proper to send since those late transactions of the army."*

To appreciate properly the labors of Dr. Franklin during the next two years, we must not lose sight of the fact, that he had reached that period of life when most men find it necessary, and all men find it pleasant, to desist from toil. But he was an old man only in years. His mind never grew old; and his body, at this time, was not perceptibly impaired. Writers of the period describe him as having grown portly, and he himself frequently alludes, in jocular exaggeration, to his great bulk. He had now discarded the cumbersome wig of his earlier portraits, and wore his own hair, thin and gray, without powder or pigtail. His head being remarkably large and massive, the increased size of his body was thought to have given proportion as well as dignity to his frame. His face was ruddy, and indicated vigorous health. His countenance expressed serenity, firmness, benevolence; and easily assumed a certain look of comic shrewdness, as if waiting to see whether his companion had "taken" a joke. Some of his portraits preserve this expression. In conversation, he excelled greatly in the rare art of listening, and seemed devoid of the least taint of a desire to shine. His was a weighty and expressive silence, which elicited talk, not quelled it; and his taciturnity gave to his utterances, when he did speak, the character of events to be remembered and reported. Hence, anecdotes of Franklin were among the current coin of conversation in Philadelphia, and the staple of editorial paragraphs throughout the colonies.

* "Letters to Franklin," p. 62.

PART V.

MEMBER OF THE CONGRESS.

PART V.

CHAPTER I.

DELEGATES to the Congress began to reach Philadelphia soon after Franklin's arrival. May the ninth, the four members from South Carolina landed from the Charleston packet, and had joyful welcome. The next day, approached in a body the delegates from Virginia, North Carolina, Maryland, and Delaware; George Washington and Patrick Henry among them. There was no drilling in the public grounds of Philadelphia on that day. The officers of all the city companies, and nearly every gentleman who could get a horse, five hundred mounted men in all, rode six miles out of town to meet the coming members and escort them to the city. At the distance of two miles the cavalcade was met by the companies of foot and a band of music. All Philadelphia gathered in the streets, at the windows, on the housetops, to see the procession pass, and salute the delegates with cheers.* The day after, arrived the members from New England, New York, and New Jersey, whose whole journey had been an ovation. In the friendly manner of the time, the members all dined together a day or two after assembling. "Your health, was among the foremost," wrote Franklin to Burke.

Congress met on the tenth of May; nearly the whole of its sixty-three delegates present. Few readers need to be reminded of the proceedings of that immortal body which adopted the New England army as its own; which elected George Washington commander-in-chief; which heard the news of the battle of Bunker Hill; which issued continental money; which accepted the supreme direction of colonial resistance. Most worthily has Mr. Bancroft

* Diary of Christopher Marshall, p. 28.

related its first unanimity, its subsequent hesitation, its firm determination to resist the ministerial measures, its reluctance to sever
the tie which had bound the parts of the empire together, its extreme caution, its practical wisdom. We have to do with little
more than Franklin's part in its deliberations and resolves.

It soon appeared that the proprietary party of Pennsylvania,
represented by Mr. John Dickinson, was the clog upon the wheel,
and that John Adams was the propelling force. Mr. Dickinson,
besides possessing a great fortune, was subjected (so says John
Adams) to domestic influences which amiable and timid men do
not resist. The Quakers, Mr. Adams reports, had intimidated Mr.
Dickinson's wife and mother, who continually distressed him with
remonstrances. His mother said to him, " Johnny, you will be
hanged; your estate will-be forfeited and confiscated; you will
leave your excellent wife a widow, and your charming children or-
phans, beggars, and infamous." Mr. Adams comments upon this
with his usual robust candor : " From my soul I pitied Mr. Dickinson. I made his case my own. If my mother and my wife had
expressed such sentiments to me, I am certain that, if they did not
wholly unman me, and make me an apostate, they would make me
the most miserable man alive."

Mr. Dickinson accordingly favored what his impetuous opponent
styled " that measure of imbecility," a second petition to the king,
to be conveyed to England by Governor Richard Penn. This was
the first dividing question that came before Congress. Mr. Adams,
and all the more ardent spirits opposed it as useless, and worse
than useless. One day, after Mr. Adams had spoken against the
petition, he met Mr. Dickinson in the State House yard, when a
very disagreeable scene occurred. " He broke out upon me," Mr.
Adams relates, " in a most abrupt and extraordinary manner, in as
violent a passion as he was capable of feeling, and with an air, countenance, and gestures, as rough and haughty as though I had been
a schoolboy and he the master : ' What is the reason, Mr. Adams,
that you New England men oppose our measures of reconciliation?
There now is Sullivan, in a long harangue, following you in a determined opposition to our petition to the king. Look ye! if you don't
concur with us in our peaceful system, I and a number of us will
break off from you in New England, and we will carry on the op
position in our own way.' I own I was shocked with this magis-

terial salutation. I know of no pretensions Mr. Dickinson had to dictate to me more than I had to catechise him. I was, however, as it happened at that moment, in a very happy temper, and I answered him very coolly : Mr. Dickinson, there are many things I can very cheerfully sacrifice to harmony, and even to unanimity, but I am not to be threatened into an express adoption or approbation of measures which my judgment reprobates. Congress must judge, and if they pronounce against me, I must submit ; or, if they determine against you, you ought to acquiesce.' "* Upon this they parted, never again to hold private converse together. The Pennsylvania lord appears to have presumed upon his wealth and importance, and upon the imagined insignificance of the Massachusetts lawyer.

This collision between the two extremes of Congress enables us to show in a word the position of Dr. Franklin on the question. He knew the petition to be useless, and opposed it; but believing it to be comparatively harmless, he opposed it without vehemence. It was, moreover, of the greatest possible importance to humor and conciliate Mr. Dickinson and his friends, so that the colonies might present to the ministry an unbroken front, and combine all their powers to resist. The petition was voted, therefore, and Dr. Franklin was one of the committee of five appointed to prepare the first draft. Upon Mr. Dickinson, who was chairman of the committee, the congenial task of writing it devolved.

The other work of this Congress was chiefly practical; it made a beginning of organizing the army and organizing the country; to both of which tasks Dr. Franklin lent an able, a willing, a most diligent hand.

One of the first measures was to appoint a committee of six, Franklin chairman, to "consider the best means of establishing posts for conveying letters and intelligence throughout this continent." Franklin was at home in this employment, and soon sketched a plan which is, essentially, the same as that upon which the post-office of America has ever since been conducted. The committee recommended, "that a postmaster-general be appointed for the united colonies, who shall hold his office at Philadelphia, and shall be allowed a salary of 1,000 dollars per annum, for himself,

---

* Life and Works of John Adams, ii., 409.

and 340 dollars per annum for a secretary and comptroller, with
power to appoint such and so many deputies as to him may seem
proper and necessary. That a line of posts be appointed under the
direction of the postmaster-general, from Falmouth, in New England, to Savannah, in Georgia, with as many cross posts as he shall
think fit. That the allowance to the deputies, in lieu of salary and
all contingent expenses, shall be 20 per cent. on the sums they collect and pay into the general post-office annually, when the whole
is under or not exceeding 1,000 dollars, and ten per cent. for all
sums above 1,000 dollars a year. That the several deputies account
quarterly with the general post-office, and the postmaster-general
annually with the Continental treasurers, when he shall pay into the
receipt of the said treasurers the profits of the post-office; and if the
necessary expense of this establishment should exceed the produce
of it, the deficiency shall be made good by the united colonies, and
paid to the postmaster-general by the Continental treasurers."

Congress adopted the plan; and mindful, we may presume, of
the Wedderburn scene in the privy council, unanimously elected
"Benjamin Franklin, Esq., postmaster-general for one year, and
until another is appointed by a future Congress." Thus, eighteen
months after his dismissal, he found himself, in a manner most unexpected, reinstated in office, with higher rank and augmented
authority. He had the pleasure of appointing his son-in-law, Mr.
Bache, his deputy. In franking letters at this time, instead of
writing "Free, B. Franklin," as he had formerly done, he used to
write,

"B free Franklin."

After the election of General Washington, Dr. Franklin was
appointed one of a committee to draw up a Declaration to be published by the general on taking command of the army. Franklin
wrote the draft of a Declaration, which was a vigorous refutation
of tory calumnies. To show that the resistance of the colonies to
lawless taxation did not proceed from an unwillingness to share the
general burden, he proposed to declare, "that whenever England
shall think fit to abolish her monopoly, and give us the same privileges of trade as Scotland received at the union, and allow us a free
commerce with all the rest of the world, we shall willingly agree to
give and pay into the sinking fund one hundred thousand pounds

sterling per annum for the term of one hundred years; which duly faithfully, and inviolably applied to that purpose, is demonstrably more than sufficient to extinguish all her present national debt; since it will in that time amount, at legal British interest, to more than two hundred and thirty millions of pounds."

Ill news from England arrived to prevent the adoption of any such proffer as this; and, probably, the draft was not even presented to Congress, as no mention of it appears in the journal. We must confess, indeed, that Franklin's Declaration was not such a paper as a grave and earnest body of men would have chosen to present to the world; for Franklin, remembering his burlesque of the Edict of the King of Prussia, concluded the Declaration with a repetition of that joke. He retorted the well-worn charge of "ingratitude" upon the mother country; "who, not only never contributes any aid, nor affords, by an exclusive commerce, any advantages to Saxony, her mother country; but no longer since than in the last war, without the least provocation, subsidized the King of Prussia while he ravaged that *mother country*, and carried fire and sword into its capital, the fine city of Dresden! An example we hope no provocation will induce us to imitate."

General Washington would have relished the fun of this conclusion, but would certainly have objected to publishing it as the deliberate utterance of his country. And here, perhaps, we have one of the reasons why Dr. Franklin, who was universally confessed to be the ablest pen in America, was not always asked to write the great documents of the revolution. He would have put a joke into the Declaration of Independence, if it had fallen to him to write it. At this time, he was a humorist of fifty years standing, and had become fixed in the habit of illustrating great truths by grotesque and familiar similes. His jokes, the circulating medium of Congress, were as helpful to the cause as Jay's conscience or Adams's fire; they restored good humor, and relieved the tedium of delay, but were out of place in formal, exact, and authoritative papers.

In the course of the session, Dr. Franklin served on not less than ten committees. He was on the committee to investigate the sources of saltpeter; he served on one of the committees to negotiate with the Indians; he was one of the committee to get the Continental money engraved and printed, and obtained the work for his son-in-law, Mr. Bache; he was on the committee appointed to consider Lord North's conciliatory Resolution; on the salt and lead committee; and on that appointed to bring in a plan for regulating and protecting the commerce of the colonies.

At the first outpouring of that mighty torrent of paper money, in which Congress, the country, and the cause were nearly overwhelmed, he gave sound advice to the Congress. He proposed, first, that the bills should bear interest. That suggestion having been rejected, and the first issue exhausted, he then advised that the bills should be borrowed back upon interest, instead of issuing more. This measure was afterwards adopted, but not in time to prevent over-issue and depreciation. Finally, to stay the downward rush of the bills, he proposed to pay the interest in hard money. Congress, in the course of the war, approved that expedient also; but, by that time, the vice of over-issue was past remedy.

Active as Franklin was in the practical business of the Congress, he took no prominent part, during the first two months, in originating or debating measures. He gave free play to Mr. Dickinson and his friends, believing it right and necessary to concede a great deal to men of tender consciences and cautious habits, who had much to lose. Late in July, however, the petition being at last agreed to and engrossed, he struck the great blow of the session by bringing forward a Plan for the permanent union and efficient government of the colonies. His plan was exceedingly simple; it proposed little more than to make the existing state of things perpetual; each colony to retain its internal independence, but to confide to a Congress, annually elected, its external affairs, particularly the measures of resistance to ministerial oppression. The supreme executive authority of the confederacy, he proposed, should be vested in a council of twelve, elected by the Congress. All the British colonies, including *Ireland*, Canada, the West Indies, Bermuda, Nova Scotia, Florida, and the thirteen already represented, should be invited to join. The Union to last until Great Britain should cease to oppress, and make restitution for past injuries; failing which, it should endure for ever. This Plan of Union, it appears, was referred to a Committee, and it may have been discussed by the House. It was not acted upon; the time was not ripe for it, and the conservative members were aware that the very idea of a union of the colonies was, of all things, the most abominable in the eyes of George III., whom the House had just humbly petitioned.

It is easy to see that this placid Franklin was deeply moved by the sufferings of his friends, relatives, and countrymen in Massachusetts; and moved to wrath more than pity. The insertion of the word, *Ireland* in his Plan of Union, was spirited, but, perhaps, not wise; it was the act of a man who had just heard of the burning of Charlestown, a place familiar to him as the pleasant residence of many whom he loved. The news of this burning, and of the battle of Bunker Hill seems to have destroyed the last vestige of his hope for reconciliation.

It was at this time that he wrote his celebrated note to Mr. Strahan, which has been erroneously supposed to have terminated their ancient friendship. It had not that effect. It was the outcry of wounded patriotism only.

To Dr. Priestley, a day or two after, he wrote : " I conclude that England has lost her colonies forever. She has begun to burn our seaport towns; secure, I suppose, that we shall never be able to return the outrage in kind. She may doubtless destroy them all; but, if she wishes to recover our commerce, are these the probable means ? She must certainly be distracted ; for no tradesman out of Bedlam ever thought of increasing the number of his customers, by knocking them on the head ; or of enabling them to pay their debts by burning their houses. If she wishes to have us subjects, and that we should submit to her as our compound sovereign, she is now giving us such miserable specimens of her government, that we shall ever detest and avoid it, as a complication of robbery, murder, famine, fire, and pestilence."

The Plan of Union, I notice, was soon published in England. The reader may find it in the Annual Register for 1775, though with an important omission. Either the cooler reflection of Franklin or the prudence of the editor had erased Ireland from the list of colonies. The editor gave the Plan, not as proposed, but as adopted ; an error well calculated to banish from the king's mind the last relenting thought, and turn his wooden head to stone.

While attending the Congress, Dr. Franklin was assiduously employed in the service of Pennsylvania. He was elected, soon after his return from England, chairman of the provincial Committee of Safety, which consisted of twenty-five members. The duty assigned this Committee was to arm and defend Pennsylvania; to call out, drill, and organize the militia, provide supplies and ammunition, and

Philad.ª July 5. 1775

Mr Strahan,

You are a Member of Parliament, and one of that Majority which has doomed my Country to Destruction.—You have begun to burn our Towns, and murder our People.—Look upon your Hands!—They are stained with the Blood of your Relations!—You and I were long Friends:—You are now my Enemy,—and

I am,

Yours,

B Franklin

issue bills of credit to pay for them. Before the year ended, the Delaware was so protected by forts, batteries, and a chevaux-de-frise, that when, in 1777, a British fleet essayed to ascend the river, it was retarded for two months by these works. Mr. Henry Laurens assigns to Dr. Franklin all the credit of the chevaux-de-frise. A letter from Mr. Laurens to Major Huger, written while the fleet was engaged in reducing the defenses of the river, contains this sentence : " Forts Mifflin and Mercer, together with some of our armed vessels, have performed such acts of defense against the attempts of a British fleet and army, as will unite the commanders in future history with the name of Franklin, when that valuable man shall be celebrated for his construction of the marine chevaux-de-frise."*

Josiah Quincy writes to General Washington, October 31st, 1775 : " Dr. Franklin's row-galleys are in great forwardness; seven of them are completely manned, armed, etc. I went down the river the other day with all of them. I have as much confidence in them as you have. But the people here have made machines to be sunk in the channel of Delaware River. Three rows of them are placed in the river, with timbers, barbed with iron. They are frames of timber sunk with stone ; machines very proper for our channel in the Narrows. Dr. Franklin says they may be made in the form of a chevaux-de-frise, and used to great advantage."†

It was a busy summer with him. " In the morning at six," he wrote to Priestley, July 7th, "I am at the Committee of Safety, which committee holds till near nine, when I am at the Congress, and that sits till after four in the afternoon. Both these bodies proceed with the greatest unanimity, and their meetings are well attended. It will scarce be credited in Britain, that men can be as diligent with us from zeal for the public good, as with you for thousands per annum. Such is the difference between uncorrupted new states, and corrupted old ones. Great frugality and great industry are now become fashionable here. Gentlemen, who used to entertain with two or three courses, pride themselves now in treating with simple beef and pudding. By these means, and the stoppage of our consumptive trade with Britain, we shall be better able to pay our voluntary taxes for the support of our troops. Our savings in the article of trade amount to near five millions sterling per annum."

Franklin's grandson has preserved a dateless anecdote, which may

* " Materials for History," p. 61.   † " Letters to Washington," i., 75.

be in place here.   Some of the more strenuous patriots of Pennsylvania desired the Committee of Safety, most of whom were dissenters, to require the Episcopal clergy to refrain from praying for the King. Dr. Franklin, foreseeing that such an injunction would create more disturbance than the matter was worth, quenched the proposal in laughter.   " The measure," said he, " is quite unnecessary ; for the Episcopal clergy, to my certain knowledge, have been constantly praying, these twenty years, that ' *God would give to the king and his council wisdom ;*' and we all know that not the least notice has ever been taken of that prayer.   So, it is plain, the gentlemen have no interest in the court of Heaven."   The Committee laughed, and the motion was dropped.

August 1st, Congress adjourned to meet again on the 5th of September ; having been in session two months and twenty days.

CHAPTER II.

FATHER AND SON LOSE A SON.

" THE gods are just, and of our pleasant vices make instruments to scourge us."

The law of nature, thus expressed by Shakspeare, Dr. Franklin was about to exemplify, after having escaped it for the long period of forty-five years.   All the atonement to society for the error of his youth which was possible, he had made, in giving to his illegitimate son the advantages of education, and of his own position in the world.   Yet from the very completeness of that atonement sprang the bitterest mortification of his whole life.   The father's justice and liberality had raised the son to a hight whence he could wound that father's pride, affection and patriotism ; and all the world witness the stroke.

Soon after his return from England, Dr. Franklin sent his grandson to pay his duty to his father at Perth Amboy, the capital of New Jersey at that time.   Governor Franklin, who had not seen his son since he was an infant, gave him a paternal welcome, it appears ; for Dr. Franklin wrote, soon after. that the young gentleman "was very happy" at Perth Amboy with his father, and was coming back in September to enter the college at Philadelphia. When Congress adjourned, Dr. Franklin himself went to Perth Amboy, and remained for several days at his son's house; but was, probably, *not* "very happy" there.

William Franklin had long ago lived down the early prejudice entertained against him on account of his birth and inexperience He had been an active, just, and courteous governor, and became, at length, a popular one. Besides being efficient and enterprising as a magistrate, he was a handsome and extremely agreeable man, as abounding in facetious anecdote, almost, as his father. Like his father, too, he had become correct in his habits, after his marriage with Miss Downs, to whom he was devotedly attached. A tradition of this lady's gentleness and unobtrusive worth still lives in the minds of aged Jerseymen in the neighborhood of Perth Amboy. Governor Franklin, as the ancient records show, promoted the improvement of roads in his province, induced the Assembly to offer bounties to successful farmers, and was among the earliest advocates of a mitigation of the laws relating to the imprisonment of debtors. He invested the surplus of his salary in a tract of land on the banks of the Rancocus, near Burlington, which he converted into what we should now call a model farm. He imported from England such agricultural implements as the skill of Jersey artisans was not then competent to produce, renowned as their success in this branch of manufacture has since become. Like Washington and Jefferson, he was learned in plows, and could talk of crops and beeves with the best farmers going. His library was, probably, the best in the province, and he still exhibited his tact in performing electrical experiments. Happy in his home, useful and honored as governor and as citizen, he seemed destined to pass and end his days in dignified and prosperous tranquillity.

Another destiny, however, awaited him. Without supporting, or expressly approving the earlier measures of the ministry against the freedom of the colonies, he could not forget that he was a royal governor; he remained, as we have seen, "a thorough government man," and deemed the opposition of the colonists, more "mad" than the measures of the ministry. He only did what nearly all the king's servants in America did; what all men, except the strongest and the noblest, will do in similar circumstances, *i. e.*, he sympathized with the power which had given and could take away his place. This, too, is a law of nature for seven-tenths of the family of man. All that an average man hath will he give for his life; and most men, in critical circumstances, appear to be of Shylock's opinion, that he takes a man's life who takes away his means of living. Let us allow, also, that the law of nature is beneficent which impels a man to cling most tenaciously to the nest which warms and shelters those whom he should love better than himself. And this does but enhance the merit of those superior men, who know when a truer regard for the nestlings requires the brave abandonment of the nest and the familiar sources that supplied it with food.

During this visit of Dr. Franklin to his son, the last visit he ever made him, father and son discussed the controversy between the mother country and the colonies. Tradition reports that their conversations on this exciting topic were frequent and very warm; each trying his utmost, and each failing utterly, to convince the other. No man in the colonies, not John or Samuel Adams, nor Jefferson, nor Patrick Henry, was more perfectly resolved upon resistance than Dr. Franklin. All his familiar letters of this year show it. Probably, to his son, he said in substance, what he had written : " The eyes of all Christendom are now upon us, and our honor as a people is become a matter of the utmost consequence to be taken care of. If we tamely give up our rights in this contest, a century to come will not restore us in the opinion of the world; we shall be stamped with the character of dastards, poltroons, and fools; and be despised and trampled upon, not by this haughty, insolent nation only, but by all mankind."

On one point only, father and son appear to have agreed : both blamed General Gage for precipitating hostilities. But, widely as they differed on the grounds of the dispute, they separated amicably on this occasion. At least, Dr. Franklin wrote his son a friendly letter six weeks after, telling him with what willingness the people submitted to the losses and hardships of the war, and how unfaltering was the resolution even of those whom the burning of Charlestown and the siege of Boston had driven homeless and beggared upon the world. "I am not terrified," said he, "by the *expense of this war, should it continue ever so long.* A little more frugality or a little more industry in individuals will with ease defray it. Suppose it a £100,000 a month, or £1,200,000 a year. If 500,000 families will each spend a shilling a week less or earn a shilling a week more; or if they will spend sixpence a week less, and earn sixpence a week more, they may pay the whole sum without otherwise feeling it. Forbearing to drink tea saves three-fourths of the money; and 500,000 women doing each threepence worth of spinning or knitting in a week, will pay the rest. I wish, nevertheless, most earnestly for peace, this war being a truly unnatural and mischievous one; but we have nothing to expect from submission but slavery and contempt."*

When Dr. Franklin wrote at the end of this letter, "Your affectionate father," he was not yet aware that his son had ceased to be a passive opponent of the popular movement. In less than a month after his father left him, Governor Franklin performed an act which placed him in clear opposition to the people and the Assembly of New Jersey, and reduced him to isolated impotence. Lord Stirling, a member of the Council of New Jersey, a friend and correspondent of Dr. Franklin, having accepted a military commission from the Congress, Governor Franklin declared him suspended from his seat in the council. The province, keenly resenting the act, became totally estranged from the governor, and only hostile communication took place between them. The province was, in effect, without a government, and so remained for some months, neither party seeing a way to escape the imbroglio. Governor Franklin explained his position in a dispatch to Lord Dartmouth, and explained it in language natural to a royal governor. He told the Secretary of State, that his situation was embarrassing in the extreme, as there were but one or two among the principal officers of government to whom he could even speak confidentially on public affairs. He renewed his declarations of unalterable attachment to the throne, and expressed the most decided opposition to the patriotic measures of the colonists. This dispatch was intercepted by Lord Stirling, who promptly laid it before the Assembly. A guard of soldiers was stationed about the governor's house, to prevent his escape. He remonstrated against the indignity as needless, since he had already given the Assembly a solemn assurance that he would not leave the province, unless ordered away by

---

* N. Y. Historical Magazine for October, 1861.

the king, or taken away by violence. His parole was at length accepted, the guard was removed, and he remained at his house,
harmless and unmolested, for five months. In June, 1776, he received dispatches from England, directing him how to proceed;
and, in obedience to these, he summoned the Assembly of his province. By that time, however, Congress had abolished all the
royal governments, and forbidden the exercise of any authority not
derived from the people or their representatives. The Congress
forthwith pronounced the proclamation of Governor Franklin to be
in contempt of their order, declared that no obedience was due to
it, and recommended that no further payments be made to Mr.
Franklin on account of salary. Before these resolves of Congress
were known at Perth Amboy, the Assembly ordered the arrest of
their late governor, " with all the delicacy and tenderness the service
can possibly admit of." A company of militia executed the order,
and the governor again found himself a prisoner in his own house,
guarded by sixty men. The Assembly continued to behave towards him with " all the delicacy and tenderness" which the circumstances admitted. They offered to withdraw the guard on the
simple condition of his engaging his honor as a gentleman to leave
Perth Amboy within two days, and go directly to Princeton, Bor-
dertown, or his own farm at Rancocus, there remain to the end of
the war, and perform no act calculated to help the royal, or harm
the patriotic cause. Governor Franklin indignantly refused to sign
the reasonable parole presented to him, and addressed a very vigorous remonstrance to the legislature. A few days after, he was
taken from his home and from his distracted wife, and conveyed,
under guard, to Burlington, whence he again sent an indignant remonstrance against the " independent republican tyranny" which
held him captive. He said he could account for the treatment he
had received only by supposing that " by tearing one in my station
from his wife and family," the party in power meant " to intimidate
every man in the province from giving any opposition to their iniquitous course." He declared that he had spirit enough to face
the danger that threatened him. "*For King and Country* was the
motto I assumed when I first commenced my political life, and I
am resolved to retain it till death shall put an end to my mortal
existence."

He was contumacious to the last. Congress having ordered him into confinement, he was removed to Connecticut,* to the sore distress of his wife. In this sad extremity, Dr. Franklin, who could do nothing to save his son from the just consequences of his own ill-timed obduracy, sent his grandson to Perth Amboy to aid and console his afflicted daughter-in-law. He also sent her a little money—sixty dollars—of which, it appears, she was in pressing need. She wrote him (Aug. 6th, 1776), an affecting letter of thanks and entreaty: " My troubles do, indeed, lie heavy on my mind, and though many people may suffer still more than I do, yet that does not lessen the weight of mine, which are really more than so weak a frame is able to support. I will not distress you by enumerating all my afflictions, but allow me, dear sir, to mention that it is greatly in your power to relieve them. Suppose that Mr. Franklin would sign a parole not dishonorable to himself and satisfactory to Governor Trumbull, of Connecticut, why may he not be permitted to return into this province and to his family? Many of the officers that have been taken during the war, have had that indulgence shown them, and why should it be denied to him? His private affairs are unsettled, his family distressed, and he is living very uncomfortably and at a great expense, which he can very ill afford at present. Consider, my dear and honored sir, that I am now pleading the cause of your son and my beloved husband. If I have said or done any thing wrong, I beg to be forgiven. I am with great respect, honored sir, your dutiful and affectionate daughter, ELIZA FRANKLIN."

It is not known what answer Franklin made to this letter, nor whether he interceded with Congress on his son's behalf. This we know, that Congress was disposed to treat Governor Franklin with the utmost consideration and leniency. They permitted him to reside at Middletown, in Connecticut, on parole, and in November, 1776, ordered General Washington to offer him in exchange

---

* One of the newspaper notices of this event is as follows: "Day before yesterday, Governor Franklin, of New Jersey, passed through Hartford, in Connecticut, on his way to Governor Trumbull at Lebanon. Mr. Franklin is a noted tory and ministerial tool, and has been exceedingly busy in perplexing the cause of liberty, and in serving the designs of the British king and his ministers. The people of the Jerseys, on account of his abilities, connections, principles and address, viewed him as a mischievous and dangerous enemy in that province, and consequently thought it expedient to remove him, under a strong guard, to Connecticut. He is safely arrived, and will probably have leisure to reconnoiter his past life. He is son to Dr. Benjamin Franklin, the genius of the day, and the great patron of American liberty. If his Excellency escapes the vengeance of the people, due to the enormity of his crimes, his redemption will flow, not from his personal merit, but from the high esteem and veneration which the country entertains for his honored father.—*Constitutional Gazette*, July 13, 1776.

for General Thomson. Before General Washington had executed
this order, the deposed governor and his royalist friends in Middletown were guilty of a gross and stupid indiscretion, which compelled Congress to countermand their order. The royalists met
for an evening's entertainment; in the course of which they sang
songs in honor of King George and General Howe, the whole company joining in the chorus. As the wine flowed in, the wit ran
out, and the choruses became, at length, so wild and loud, that the
military watch gathered about the house and heard the royalists
chanting treason. About midnight, the company sallied forth,
roaring drunk, and made night hideous to the patriotic citizens of
Middletown. The watch respectfully remonstrated. The royalists
retorted with riotous abuse, and Governor Franklin called one of
them a damned villain, and threatened him with vengeance. The
next day the gentlemen composing the watch drew up a statement of these proceedings, and Congress promptly resolved that
it was inexpedient to exchange Governor Franklin.

But this was not the end of his contumacy. It was discovered,
that he had been very busy in circulating Lord Howe's offer of
pardon; that he was, in fact, and meant to continue, an active
agent for the British ministry in the heart of a patriotic province.
He was then confined in Litchfield jail; denied, for a while, the
use of pen, ink, and paper; and his tory allies were not permitted
to converse with him, except in the hearing of an officer. He
remained in confinement for the greater part of two years.

Mrs. Franklin could not join her husband in his prison, and she
never saw him again. She died in the city of New York in July,
1778, before Governor Franklin had been exchanged. Her remains were placed within the chancel of St. Paul's Church, on a
wall of which edifice may still be seen the tablet which her husband, after the close of the war, caused to be erected to her memory. It bears the following inscription :

" Beneath the altar of this Church are deposited the remains of
Mrs. ELIZABETH FRANKLIN, wife of His Excellency,
WILLIAM FRANKLIN, Esq., late Governor under
His Britannick Majesty, of the *Province of New Jersey*.
Compelled by the adverse circumstances of the times to
part from the husband she loved, and, at length,
deprived of the soothing hope of his speedy return,

she sank under accumulated distresses, and departed this
life on the 28th day of July, 1778, in the 49th year of her age.

SINCERITY and SENSIBILITY,
POLITENESS and AFFABILITY,
GODLINESS and CHARITY,
were
with SENSE refined and PERSON elegant, in her UNITED.
From a grateful remembrance of her affectionate tenderness
and constant performance of all the duties of a GOOD WIFE
This monument is erected, in the year 1787,
By him who knew her worth, and still laments her loss."

Released after a detention of two years and four months, William
Franklin came to New York, where he resided four years, an
active and zealous royalist. We catch glimpses of him in the
royalist letters of the time, founding and presiding over the Refugee Club, which met twice a month at Hie's tavern; writing
long letters to the administration; recommending a vigorous prosecution of the war; getting a grant of fifty guineas each for the
royalists who had been driven from their estates; always "in high
spirits, though reduced in flesh."[*] We have even one of his own
letters, written at New York in 1779, which breathes the warmest
devotion to the royal cause. "The glorious successes of His Majesty's arms in the West Indies and Georgia," he wrote, "have
put us all in high spirits, as you may imagine. If the Blow is properly follow'd by Prevost, it will soon be all over with Congressional Power in the Southern colonies. Everything is going on
exceedingly well on this side the water, and if Great Britain is not
wanting to herself, all may be easily settled to her Satisfaction in
a few months. I am promoting an Association among the Refugees, and under my Patronage several Companies are already completed. If they meet with that Encouragement from Head Quarters, which I have at present Reason to expect, I shall soon fill
the Rebel adjacent Country with Partisan Parties, that must distress them to a very great degree."[†]
He appears to have had abundant "encouragement from head-
quarters." At least, we find Governor Tryon writing home to
Lord George Germain, one of the Secretaries of State, that "he

* N. Y. Historical Magazine for November and December, 1861.
† N. Y. Historical Magazine, June, 1862.

conceived it would be good policy, and attended with advantage to the king's cause, to set Governor Franklin forward in contrast to his father's conduct," and this, thought the astute governor, "would have its weight in Europe." It had its weight with Lord George Germain; for Governor Franklin, when his cause was lost, went to England with the other tories, and the Government gave him eighteen hundred pounds in partial compensation for his losses, and settled upon him for life a pension of eight hundred pounds a year.*

How keenly Dr. Franklin felt this defection of his son, we could infer, if he had not recorded it. At this time, he was occasionally styled the Father of his Country, and few would have been then inclined to dispute his right to the title. Even Arthur Lee spoke of him as "our Pater Patriæ," in a letter to Lord Shelburne, written in 1776. That he should not have been able to bring his only son over to the side of his country, could not but have been deeply mortifying to his pride. Nine years after, he wrote, that "nothing had ever affected him with such keen sensations as to find himself deserted in his old age by his only son; and not only deserted, but to find him taking up arms against him in a cause wherein his good fame, fortune, and life were all at stake." "You conceived, you say," continued Franklin, "that your duty to your king and regard for your country required this. I ought not to blame you for differing in sentiment with me in public affairs. We are men, all subject to errors. Our opinions are not in our own power; they are formed and governed much by circumstances, that are often as inexplicable as they are irresistible. Your situation was such that few would have censured your remaining neuter, though there are natural duties which precede political ones, and cannot be extinguished by them."

The truth of this last observation is self-evident, but it may well be doubted whether it was applicable to the case in question. Governor Franklin was forty-five years of age, and had a clear right to decide upon his own course.

In 1776, Henry Laurens, of South Carolina, not certain whether his son, John, was prepared to accept the extreme measure of declaring independence, wrote to him these words:

---

* Whitehead's History of East Jersey, pp. 185 to 207.

"Remember you are of full age, entitled to judge for yourself; pin not your faith upon my sleeve, but act the part which an honest heart after mature deliberation shall dictate, and your services on the side which you may take, because you think it the right side, will be the more valuable. I cannot rejoice in the downfall of an old friend, of a parent from whose nurturing breasts I have drawn my support and strength; every evil which befalls old England grieves me. Would to God she had listened in time to the cries of her children, and had checked the insidious slanders of those who call themselves the king's servants and the king's friends, especially such of them as had been transported to America in the character of civil officers. If my own interests, if my own rights alone had been concerned, I would most freely have given the whole to the demands and disposal of her ministers in preference to a separation; but the rights of posterity were involved in the question. I happened to stand as one of their representatives, and dared not betray my trust."*

It was easy for Mr. Laurens to write this passage, because he had no serious apprehension that his son would forsake the side of his country, and because his own heart had not been weaned from England, as Franklin's had, by personal observation of the arrogance and ignorance of her ruling class. James Otis, on the other hand, could not, to his dying hour, forgive one of his daughters for marrying a British officer, and marked his resentment in his will by leaving her five shillings. It is idle to demand of human nature that which it is not capable of yielding. When men have staked their lives, their fortunes, and their sacred honors upon an issue; the risk being real, not a flight of Fourth-of-July rhetoric; when, in the event of defeat, they will, in very truth, lose their lives, their fortunes, and their good name; they cannot regard with philosophic toleration one of their own blood who throws the weight of his influence and his talents upon the adverse side; least of all, when that adverse side is supposed to be infinitely the stronger, and his own motives do not appear to be disinterested.

The son of William Franklin adhered to his grandfather, and saw his father no more until the great controversy had been decided by arms. Thus was the strange coincidence made complete;

---

* "Materials for History," part i., p. 88.

Dr. Franklin lost his son ; that son lost his ; both sons were born just before their fathers' marriage ; both were reared and educated in disregard of that circumstance ; both abandoned their fathers at the same time and for the same cause. We shall see, also, that both were reconciled to their fathers at about the same time, and in about the same imperfect degree.

"The gods are just, and of our pleasant vices make instruments to scourge us."

CHAPTER III.

IN CONGRESS AGAIN.

DR. FRANKLIN returned from Perth Amboy to Philadelphia, and resumed his duties in Congress, a quorum of which assembled on the thirteenth of September. The city was all astir with war-like preparations. Twice a day the most zealous of the military companies drilled in the square. The saltpeter works were beginning to produce a little of that anxiously-sought commodity. Of six powder-mills designed, two were nearly ready to go into operation ; which, in the following spring, delivered twenty-five hundred pounds of powder a week. A manufactory of muskets was about to open, and turn out twenty-five muskets a day, with all the appendages complete. The fortifications upon the Delaware were advancing toward completion. Congress, the Committee of Safety, and numerous subordinate bodies, were in session every day. Arrests of suspected persons were frequent, and Sub-Committees of Safety boarded arriving vessels, to pick out treason from the letter-bags. Occasionally, there was tarring and feathering of tories ; but oftener, the obnoxious person chose the alternative of mounting a cart, "publicly acknowledging his errors, and asking pardon of the crowd." The ladies, of course, were scraping lint and preparing bandages, in compliance with the published request of the Committee of Safety : Mrs. Bache among the busiest. Exciting news from Boston every week : the enemy re-enforced ; General Washington strangely inactive ; New England still unanimous for resistance.

Again Dr. Franklin was chosen to serve on most of the working committees of Congress. He was a member who wrote little, spoke less, and worked always. We find him very busy this autumn at such employments as arranging a system of posts and expresses for the swift conveyance of dispatches; forming a line of packet vessels to sail between Europe and America; promoting the circulation of the Continental money, and drafting instructions for the generals in the field. He was still an active member of the Committee of Safety; and, as if these duties were not enough for an old man, he was elected in October a member of the Assembly of Pennsylvania. He was then a member of three bodies, each of which was in session daily, and upon each devolved duties which were novel, difficult, and absorbing.

Ill news from General Washington reached Congress a few days after the session opened. His extemporized army was falling to pieces; terms of enlistment were expiring, and most of the men were mad to get home; winter approaching, and no proper shelter for the troops; no winter clothing, no fuel, no money, small supply of provisions, scarcely any gunpowder; no adequate system of discipline, no provision made for raising new regiments, no well-defined limits to the authority of the governors of colonies; the entire system in need of revision and exact regulation. Glad, indeed, would the timid Dickinsonians have been to make no further hostile movement until news arrived of the effect upon a gracious king of that second petition which Richard Penn had carried to England. But General Washington's dispatch, written from the midst of an agonizing chaos, could not be disregarded. On the last day of September Congress elected a committee of three: Benjamin Franklin, of Pennsylvania, Thomas Lynch, of South Carolina, and Benjamin Harrison, of Virginia, to go to Cambridge, and there confer with General Washington, and with delegates from the New England colonies, and arrange a plan for raising, supplying, and governing the Continental Army.

Before setting out upon this important mission Dr. Franklin resigned his seat in the Assembly, and asked to be excused from further attendance upon the Committee of Safety. "It would be a happiness to me," he wrote, "if I could serve the public duly in all those stations; but, aged as I now am, I feel myself unequal to so much business, and on that account think it my duty to decline a

Chadron State College Library
Chadron, Nebraska

part of it." The day before his departure for the camp he wrote to Dr. Priestley that humorous summing up of the grand result of the first campaign, the substance of which was a standing paragraph in the liberal newspapers during the early years of the war : " Britain, at the expense of three millions, has killed one hundred and fifty Yankees this campaign, which is twenty thousand pounds a head; and at Bunker's Hill she gained a mile of ground, half of which she lost again by our taking post on Ploughed Hill. During the same time sixty thousand children have been born in America. From these *data* Dr. Price's mathematical head will easily calculate the time and expense necessary to kill us all, and conquer our whole territory."

The commissioners left Philadelphia on the fourth of October, and reached Cambridge after a ride of thirteen days. Franklin trod once more his native soil, and saw, but only saw, the city in which he was born. Joyful, indeed, was the meeting with his sister, his nephews, nieces and old friends : of whom there were many near Cambridge. The army and its chiefs, the people and their leaders, welcomed, with peculiar respect, their venerable and illustrious countryman. A single sentence from a letter of General Greene flashes light upon an evening scene at head-quarters. Greene, too, had the blood of blacksmiths in his veins. He had been one of those book-devouring boys of New England, who eat their dinner in ten minutes in order to get the other fifty for reading; who secrete candle-ends for a midnight debauch upon Euclid ; who hoard their pence to buy an old Latin dictionary, and their minutes, to study it ; who play deep tricks to balk the paternal dunce who does not mean to be put out of countenance by a son knowing more than himself; who work their way to education against every conceivable adverse influence ; and astonish their relations, who foretold ruin from such wasting of time, by becoming the great men of their families before they are thirty-five. General Greene had now the felicity of seeing the founder of that noble New England Order—the first and greatest of the candle-end stealers and furtive book-absorbents. The young enthusiast gazed with rapture upon his aged chief. " During the whole evening," he wrote, " I viewed that very great man with silent admiration."*

* Bancroft's " History of the United States," viii., 112.

Mrs. John Adams now saw Dr. Franklin for the first time, and recorded, but too briefly, her impressions: "I had the pleasure of dining with Dr. Franklin, and of admiring him, whose character from my infancy I had been taught to venerate. I found him social but not talkative; and, when he spoke, something useful dropped from his tongue. He was grave, yet pleasant and affable. You know I make some pretensions to physiognomy, and I thought I could read in his countenance the virtues of his heart, among which, patriotism shone in its full luster: and with that is blended every virtue of a Christian."

The Council met at head-quarters on the eighteenth of October, and sat four days, General Washington presiding. The conference was harmonious and successful, and the colonies, from that time, began to have a military system. It was agreed that a new army of twenty-six regiments should be raised; that officers should be immediately required to report whether they intended to retire at the end of the year, or not; that preparations should at once be made for recruiting. The articles of war were revised. Rules for the exchange of prisoners and for the disposal of sea prizes were drawn up. A plan was settled for the employment of the Indians. The wants of the army were ascertained, and arrangements planned for its supply. And, above all, General Washington and the New England delegates acquired an additional assurance that America adopted and would sustain the forces employed about Boston; and that the colonies most remote from the scene, charged themselves willingly with their share of the burden. The Council over, Dr. Franklin remained a few days longer in the camp, conversing continually with General Washington, and confirming that mutual regard begun, long ago, in the camp of General Braddock. The commissioners returned to Philadelphia, after an absence of about six weeks. The reader may be amused to learn, that the whole expense of the long journey of the three members and their three servants, was $581 90.

Dr. Franklin returned to Philadelphia in an altered mood. Bitterness was in his heart, and words of fury on his tongue. It was long before he could pen any more jokes upon the war. As he was about to leave camp, news had arrived of the wanton bombardment and burning of defenseless Falmouth (now Portland), by a British man-of-war. The church, the public buildings, the ships, and one hundred and thirty houses were consumed; the rest were half destroyed by shot and shell. On the edge of a Maine winter, which is polar in every thing but length, this dastardly deed was done; and done with every aggravation which the evil genius of the captain could devise. Marines landed to fire the buildings which the shells could not ignite, and the complete destruction of the vessels deprived the homeless people of occupation, and placed them a month further from effective succor. As this news spread over the continent, *then* it was that that abhorrence of England struck to the heart of America, which it required two entire generations to eradicate. A dark shade falls upon the letters of the period after the burning of Falmouth. " I could not join to day," wrote Mrs. Adams, a few days after, " in the petitions of our worthy pastor for a reconciliation between our no longer parent, but tyrant state, and these colonies. Let us separate; they are not worthy to be our brethren. Let us renounce them, and instead of supplications, as formerly, for their prosperity and happiness, let us beseech the Almighty to blast their counsels, and bring to naught all their devices." These words, penned by the most gifted woman of the revolutionary period, expressed the heart of America in November, 1775.

The news from England was worse and worse, after Franklin's return to Congress. Richard Penn and Arthur Lee conveyed the Dickinson petition to Lord Dartmouth, who returned the brief reply that no answer to it would be given. But an answer was given; for, two days after, appeared a royal Proclamation declaring the colonies to be in rebellion, and pledging all the power and resources of the kingdom for its suppression. Lord North's prohibitory bill soon followed, which legalized whatever warlike acts had been, or might be done against the colonies on land and sea.

Franklin, who was now prepared to go all lengths in opposition to the king, drew up a series of resolves, to shut up the British custom-houses, and open the ports of America to the commerce of all the world except Great Britain. These resolves concluded with this truly revolutionary paragraph:

"And whereas, whenever kings, instead of protecting the lives and properties of their subjects, as is their bounden duty, do endeavor to perpetrate the destruction of either, they thereby cease to be kings, become tyrants, and dissolve all ties of allegiance be-

tween themselves and their people; we hereby further solemnly declare, that, whenever it shall appear clearly to us, that the king's
troops and ships now in America, or hereafter to be brought there,
do, *by his Majesty's orders*, destroy any town or the inhabitants of
any town or place in America, or that the savages have been by the
same orders hired to assassinate our poor out-settlers and their
families, we will from that time renounce all allegiance to Great
Britain, so long as that kingdom shall submit to him, or any of his
descendants, as its sovereign."

Whether these resolutions were introduced or not is unknown;
they were found among Franklin's papers in his own hand-writing.

Another undated fragment in his hand-writing was, probably,
elicited by the Prohibitory Bill. Mr. Dickinson, I trust, heard it
read in the House; Mr. Adams would have enjoyed seeing him
wince under it:

"Whereas, the British nation, through great corruption of
manners and extreme dissipation and profusion, both private and
public, have found all honest resources insufficient to supply their
excessive luxury and prodigality, and thereby have been driven to
the practice of every injustice which avarice could dictate or ra-
pacity execute; And whereas, not satisfied with the immense plunder of the East, obtained by sacrificing millions of the human species, they have lately turned their eyes to the West, and grudging
us the peaceable enjoyment of the fruits of our hard labor and
virtuous industry, have for years past been endeavoring to extort
the same from us, under color of laws regulating trade, and have
thereby actually succeeded in draining us of large sums, to our
great loss and detriment; And whereas, impatient to seize the
whole, they have at length proceeded to open robbery, declaring
by a solemn act of Parliament that all our estates are theirs, and
all our property found upon the sea divisible among such of their
armed plunderers as shall take the same; and have even dared in
the same act to declare, that all the spoilings, thefts, burnings of
houses and towns, and murders of innocent people, perpetrated by
their wicked and inhuman corsairs on our coasts, previous to any
war declared against us, were just actions, and shall be so deemed,
contrary to several of the commandments of God (which by this
act they presume to repeal), and to all the principles of right, and
all the ideas of justice, entertained heretofore by every other na-

tion, savage as well as civilized; thereby manifesting themselves
to be *hostes humani generis;* And whereas it is not possible for
the people of America to subsist under such continual ravages
without making some reprisals; Therefore, RESOLVED"—no man
will ever know *what;* for at this point the writer paused, and
concluded to waste no more labor. Several persons this winter
applied to Congress for letters of marque and reprisal; but " Congress could not feel bold enough" to grant them, wrote Joseph
Reed to General Washington.

Franklin would no longer, even as a formality, acknowledge
allegiance to the king. He had been elected, as we have seen,
a member of the Pennsylvania Assembly, a body of which Mr. Dickinson was still the lord paramount. From of old, it had been
required of members, on taking their seats, that they should
promise allegiance to the king, and this odious preliminary Mr.
Dickinson's majority refused to abolish. Dr. Franklin, consequently,
would not take his seat in the House; and this was probably the
true reason of his resigning his seat. Not the less, however, did
the inconsistent Assembly re-elect him to Congress; he alone of
their nine delegates being decided for Independence.

It now appeared that Pennsylvania was to be the battle-ground
of Independence; since, not the insolent rejection of the petition,
nor the king's insulting proclamation, nor the vindictive acts of
Parliament, nor the burning of Falmouth, had produced a practicable breach in the dense prejudices of the Dickinsonians. In
these circumstances, the liberal party fell back upon Franklin's old
expedient, an appeal to the People through the printing press.
Overwhelmed with a multiplicity of business, Dr. Franklin did not
attempt the execution of the task himself. His protégé, Thomas
Paine, was at hand to undertake it; a man who wrote in epigrams,
and went to the root of a matter. The pamphlet which he now
produced was an attack upon the prejudices, and a reply to the
arguments of the proprietary party of Pennsylvania. It had little
to say of the colonial grievances; that topic had been exhausted,
and there was no difference of opinion upon it. Paine's object was
to break the spell of the name of England, to destroy the preposterous veneration for the person and throne of the king, and expose
the imperfections of the idolized British Constitution. Grievances
or no grievances, the time had come, he maintained, when an

island should cease the attempt to govern a continent. The best government was but a necessary evil, and monarchy was a very bad government by necessity. The absurdity and the evil of hereditary succession was the subject of one section of the pamphlet; in which he expressed what two-thirds of the colonists were prepared to accept. *Now* was the priceless moment to cut the tie which bound the young and vigorous communities of America to the cumbrous, trammeling, corrupt institutions of the past. "Now is the seed-time of continental union, faith, and honor. The least fracture now will be like a name engraved with the point of a pin on the tender rind of a young oak : the wound will enlarge with the tree, and posterity read it in full-grown characters. By referring the matter from argument to arms, a new era for politics is struck, a new method of thinking hath arisen. All plans, proposals, prior to the nineteenth of April, *i. e.*, to the commencement of hostilities, are like the almanacks of the last year; which, though proper then, are superseded and useless now." England, he declared, was *not* the mother-country of America; not more than a third of the people even of Pennsylvania were of English lineage; the mother-country of America was EUROPE! "To be always running three or four thousand miles with a tale or a petition, waiting four or five months for an answer, which, when obtained, requires five or six more to explain it in, will in a few years be looked upon as folly and childishness—there was a time when it was proper, and there is a proper time for it to cease."

Paine assailed with great effect the Dickinsonian idea that the connection with England was a source of security to the colonies: "Europe is too thickly planted with kingdoms to be long at peace, and whenever a war breaks out between England and any foreign power, the trade of America goes to ruin, *because of her connection with Britain.* The next war may not turn out like the last; and should it not, the advocates for reconciliation now, will be wishing for separation then, because neutrality in the case would be a safer convoy than a man of war. Every thing that is right or natural pleads for separation. The blood of the slain, the weeping voice of nature cries, IT IS TIME TO PART." There never was a better pamphlet. Nothing was omitted that could help the argument, and not a line was really superfluous, considering all the circumstances. It expressed with such simple exactness the opinions and wishes of the liberal party, that Dr. Rush, of Philadelphia, after he had read the still unnamed production, advised the author to entitle it COMMON SENSE.*

Every one knows what a startling success it had with the public; what editions were sold; what converts it made; what replies it provoked. The letters of the time contain numberless allusions to it, all tending to show that the staymaker's son had spoken the word which America had been longing to hear. After reading Common Sense (borrowing for the purpose eyes of 1776) we see why it was that General Washington cherished to the last a tender respect for Thomas Paine, and why President Jefferson thought it due to him to bring him back from France in a national ship. But for that short tract upon Miracles (Age of Reason) which he afterwards wrote to relieve the tedium of a French exile, the man would have been held in only honorable remembrance who had the genius to put into a pamphlet of thirty pages the quintessence of George Fox, Turgot, Adam Smith, Franklin, Jefferson, and Thomas Paine, and give the whole such compact and vivid expression as to thrill a continent, and quicken the march of events. It is not dull reading now, though it convinced us all years before we were born. America has absorbed and incorporated the doctrines of this pamphlet. At the present day it is like a battering-ram, which, having battered down the enemy's wall, still swings in the air, the victors no longer regarding the mighty engine which let them in to conquest and to glory.†

* The following is the original advertisement of this celebrated pamphlet in the *Pennsylvania Journal* for January 10th, 1776:

"This day was published, and is now selling by Robert Bell, in Third Street (price two shillings),

"COMMON SENSE,

"ADDRESSED TO THE INHABITANTS OF AMERICA,

" On the following interesting subjects:

" I. Of the origin and design of Government in general, with certain remarks on the English Constitution.

"II. Of Monarchy and hereditary succession.

"III. Thoughts on the present state of American Affairs.

"IV. Of the present ability of America, with some miscellaneous Reflections.

"'Man knows no MASTER save creating Heaven,
Or those whom choice and common good ordain.'—THOMSON."

† Theodore Parker has a good word for 'poor Tom': "I see some one has written a paper on Thomas Paine, in the *Atlantic*, which excites the wrath of the men who are not worthy to stoop down and untie the latchet of his shoes, or to black his shoes, or even to bring them home to him from the shoe-blacks. Yet Paine was no man for my fancying—in the latter years of his life

The representatives of a people are more slowly convinced than the people themselves, and ought to be. The conservatives in Congress still shrank with terror from the brink of independence, and proposed to unite in a formal declaration that independence was *not* their aim. A resolution to this effect was carried by the aid of members from New England. At this unexpected and disheartening crisis, Samuel Adams sought consolation and counsel from Dr. Franklin. They were both of opinion that the colonies should be united in a confederacy without delay, even if some of them should refuse to concur. Mr. Adams went so far as to say, that, though none of the other colonies should join, he would endeavor to form the New England provinces into a confederacy. " I approve your proposal," said Franklin, " and if you succeed I will cast in my lot among you." Happily this extreme measure was not necessary. The leaven of Common Sense was working among the people; its effect quickened by the king's speeches to Parliament and by the progress of events at the seat of war. Mr. Dickinson's majority dwindled, and some of the Pennsylvania members of Congress began to waver. It was in January, 1776, that Samuel Adams proposed this desperate measure to Franklin; only six months before the Fourth of July.

A strange incident had occurred in November, 1775, which led to consequences of the utmost importance. A message was conveyed to Congress, that a foreign gentleman had arrived at Philadelphia, who desired to make to Congress a confidential communication. No notice being taken of the message, it was repeated several times. A committee was, at length, appointed, consisting of John Jay, Dr. Franklin, and Thomas Jefferson, to meet the mysterious foreigner, and hear what he had to offer. At an appointed time the committee met in one of the rooms of Carpenters' Hall, where they found waiting for them a lame, elderly man of dignified

---

he was filthy in his personal habits; there seems to me a tinge of lowness about him. But it must not be denied that he had less than the average amount of selfishness or vanity; his instincts were human and elevated, and his life mainly devoted to the great purposes of humanity. His political writings fell into my hands in my early boyhood, and still I think they were of immense service to the country. His theological works I know less of, chiefly from his enemies; they are not always in good taste, nor does he always understand the scriptures of Old and New Testaments he comments upon. But I think he did more to promote piety and morality among men than a hundred ministers of that age in America. He did it by showing that religion is not responsible for the absurd doctrines taught in its name. For this reason honest but bigoted ministers oppose him. They had a right to; but they misrepresented his doctrines."—*Life and Correspondence*, ii., 425.

military bearing, whose accent was that of a Frenchman, and who had the appearance of a retired French officer. He received the committee with the politeness of his profession; and they informed him that they were authorized to receive his communication. He then said that his most Christian majesty, THE KING OF FRANCE, had heard with pleasure of the exertions made by the American colonies in defense of their rights and privileges; that his majesty wished them success, and would, whenever it should become necessary, manifest more openly his friendly sentiments toward them. The committee desired to know his authority for giving them these assurances. He replied by drawing his hand across his throat, and saying, "Gentlemen, I shall take care of my head." The committee inquired what evidences of the friendship of the king Congress might expect. The stranger answered: "Gentlemen, if you want arms, you shall have them; if you want ammunition, you shall have it; if you want money, you shall have it." The committee remarked that these offers were, indeed, most important, but it was not less important that they should know by what authority they were made. Again the wary old gentlemen drew his hand across his throat, and said, "Gentlemen, I shall take care of my head." No other answer could be got from him. The conference ended, the stranger retired, and was seen in Philadelphia no more.*

The manner and aspect of the man went far toward convincing the committee that he really was an emissary from the French government, and the general expectation of such offers from France strengthened the impression. Among the leaders of the revolutionary movement, it had been some time a familiar opinion, that the allied governments of France and Spain would not fail to embrace the coming opportunity of undoing some of the work of the Seven Years' War, and weakening the Power which they supposed to be their "natural enemy." Mr. Wirt relates that Patrick Henry, in 1774, being asked whether he thought an infant nation like America could wage a successful war against the fleets and armies of Great Britain, made this reply: "I doubt whether we shall be able, alone, to cope with so powerful a nation. But (rising from his chair with great animation) where is France? Where is

* Related on the authority of John Jay.—*Life of John Jay*, i., 89.

Spain? Where is Holland?—the natural enemies of Great Britain. Do you suppose they will stand by idle and indifferent spectators to the contest? Will Louis XVI. be asleep all this time? Believe me, No. When Louis XVI. shall be satisfied of our serious opposition, and by our Declaration of Independence, that all prospect of a reconciliation is gone, then, and not till then, will he furnish us with arms, ammunition, and clothing; and not with these only, but he will send his fleets and armies to fight our battles for us; he will form with us a treaty, offensive and defensive, against our unnatural mother. Spain and Holland will join the confederation. Our independence will be established, and we shall take our stand among the nations of the earth!"* This prophecy was, perhaps, improved after the war by mingling a little history with it; nevertheless, it was like Patrick Henry to have performed a flight of that kind, in a group of admiring friends.

Upon hearing the report of the committee, Congress acted with its usual caution. A motion to send envoys to France was made and lost. On the twenty-ninth of November a committee was appointed "to correspond secretly with friends in Great Britain, Ireland, *and other parts of the world.*" The committee consisted of five members, Benjamin Franklin, Benjamin Harrison, John Dickinson, Thomas Johnson, and John Jay. They were empowered to take confidential agents into their pay in foreign countries, and to send agents abroad. To Dr. Franklin, from his extensive acquaintance with Europe and its diplomacy, fell the greater part of the first labors of this committee; and he entered upon those labors without delay.

During one of his visits to Holland, he had become acquainted with Professor Charles W. F. Dumas, a native of Switzerland, who had long resided at the Hague, and much frequented the circle of diplomatists who dawdled away existence at that sedate capital. Mr. Dumas, who had made international law his specialty, recalled himself very acceptably to Dr. Franklin in the autumn of 1775, by sending him copies of Vatel, edited and annotated by himself; a most timely gift, which was pounced upon by studious members of Congress, groping their way without the light of precedents. To him

---

* "It is actually whispered that the King of Prussia has been secretly tampering with the Bostonians, but with what success has not transpired."—*Rivington's New York* (tory) *Gazette*, March, 1774, under head of London News.

Dr. Franklin addressed the first letter authorized by the ·Committee of Secret Correspondence. Mr. Dumas was requested to sound the embassadors residing at the Hague, and ascertain if any of the powers were inclined to assist the colonies, or form an alliance with them. "We only recommend to your discretion," wrote Franklin, "that you proceed therein with such caution, as to keep the same from the knowledge of the English embassador, and prevent any public appearance, at present, of your being employed in any such business." Mr. Dumas was desired to suggest confidentially to merchants that arms, gunpowder, and saltpeter were in active demand in the colonies, and brought very high prices. He was requested also to send to America two engineer officers competent to direct sieges, construct forts and field-works, and command artillery. Finally, Mr. Dumas was to be the channel through which the European friends and agents of America were to correspond with the Secret Committee. To compensate Mr. Dumas, who was not a man of fortune, for his services, the committee enclosed him a draft for one hundred pounds sterling, and gave him an assurance that his labors in behalf of America would be "considered and honorably rewarded by Congress." Mr. Dumas accepted the appointment, and served Congress with zeal and ability to the end of the war. "I shall die content," he wrote in his first letter, "if the remainder of my life can be devoted to the service of so glorious and just a cause."

A letter of similar purport was sent to Mr. Arthur Lee in London : " It would be agreeable to Congress to know the disposition of foreign powers towards us," and, " we remit you for the present two hundred pounds."

By the same ship Dr. Franklin wrote to a Spanish prince, Don Gabriel de Bourbon, who had lately sent him a copy of the splendid Sallust, printed at the royal press of Madrid, in 1772. In this letter Franklin blended thanksgiving and diplomacy very neatly : " I am extremely sensible of the honor done me, and beg you would accept my thankful acknowledgments. I wish I could send hence any American literary production worthy of your perusal ; but as yet the Muses have scarcely visited these remote regions. Perhaps, however, the proceedings of our American Congress, just published, may be a subject of some curiosity at your court. I, therefore, take the liberty of sending your Highness a copy, with some other papers, which contain accounts of the successes where-

with Providence has lately favored us. Therein your wise politicians may contemplate the first efforts of a rising state, which seems
likely soon to act a part of some importance on the stage of human
affairs, and furnish materials for a future Sallust. I am very old,
and can scarce hope to see the event of this great contest; but,
looking forward, I think I see a powerful dominion growing up
here, whose interest it will be to form a firm and close alliance
with Spain (their territories bordering), and who, being united, will
be able, not only to preserve their own people in peace, but to repel the force of all the other powers in Europe. It seems, therefore, prudent on both sides to cultivate a good understanding, that
may hereafter be so useful to both; towards which a fair foundation is already laid in our minds, by the well-founded popular opinion entertained here of Spanish integrity and honor. I hope my
presumption in hinting this will be pardoned. If in any thing on
this side the globe I can render either service or pleasure to your
Royal Highness, your commands will make me happy."

Nothing could be better of its kind than this. The mode in
which the change of topic is effected from Sallust to Congress, without absolutely losing sight of Sallust, is very happy.

These important dispatches were not intrusted to any of the
ordinary modes of conveyance. A special messenger was employed, Mr. Thomas Story, who was ordered to visit London, Holland, and Paris, deliver to Mr. Lee and Mr. Dumas their letters,
and receive their replies, forward the Spanish dispatch, confer
with certain friends of Dr. Franklin in Paris, and return to America with all speed. Soon after the departure of Mr. Story, a M.
Penet left Philadelphia for France, carrying with him from the
committee a large contract for supplying arms, ammunition, and
clothing for the American army. M. Penet was a merchant of
Nantes in France, a man zealous to serve the colonies, but not of
great capital or great connections. To him, also, Dr. Franklin intrusted letters to his friends in France, particularly to Dr. Dubourg,
of Paris, the translator of his works, his fond and enthusiastic disciple.

Early in 1776, long before the Secret Committee had received
any reply from Dr. Dubourg, Mr. Dumas, or Mr. Lee, they resolved upon the bolder measure of sending an agent to France,
authorized to treat with the French ministry. Perhaps, as John

Adams intimates, the committee were the more easily induced to do this, because a person of some importance happened, just then, to want the employment. Mr. Silas Deane, of Connecticut, a member of the first and second Congresses, had lost his election to the third; but, instead of going home, remained in Philadelphia, and (so says jealous and suspicious John Adams) applied to the Secret Committee for an appointment abroad. Mr. Adams, I should observe, was not well pleased with being left out of so important a committee. It appears that Arthur Lee, true to his character, had sent over a letter to a member of Congress, advising him to look well to John Jay, for he was not to be trusted. This ridiculous letter, having been too freely handed about by Mr. Adams's friends, seems to have been among the causes which led to the selection of John Jay for one of the Secret Committee; also, one of the causes of John Adams's exclusion. Be that as it may, Mr. John Adams's comments upon the committee, their proceedings and their servants, are tinged with ill humor, and are not to be taken as absolute gospel.

Silas Deane was a native of Connecticut and a graduate of Yale College, who began life in the usual New England way, by keeping school; and afterwards subsided from his school to a law office. He practiced law and carried on trade, acquired some property and some consideration in his province. As a member of Congress he appears to have been assiduous and well esteemed, and it was natural the committee should incline to employ one who had become perfectly informed of American affairs by a year's attendance in Congress, and by serving on many leading committees. Congress, also, stood high in the esteem of mankind; there were few circles in Europe (and none worth entering) in which a member of the Congress of 1774 and 1775 would not have been received with homage and enthusiasm. Mr. Deane, we are assured, was a man of somewhat striking manners and good appearance, accustomed to live and entertain in liberal style, and fond of showy equipage and appointment. With the usual ignorance of college-bred men at that day, he could not speak French with any fluency, nor write it at all. Of course not. How should he, who had spent his early years in adding the ignorance of the ancients to the ignorance he was born with? The only man of the leading diplomatic agents sent by Congress to Europe during the revolution

who could speak French on reaching Paris, was the only man
among them who had never been at college.

For the guidance of Mr. Deane, Dr. Franklin prepared a letter
of minute instructions; and gave him letters of introduction to
several of his own friends in Paris. He was to assume in France
the character of a merchant, and actually purchase goods for the
Indian trade. On reaching Paris, he was to deliver his letters,
which would at once introduce him to a set, all of whom were
friends to the Americans, and among whom the true Parisian accent could be acquired. In particular, he was charged to cultivate
the acquaintance of M. Dubourg, "a man prudent, faithful, secret,
intelligent in affairs, and capable of giving you very sage advice."
M. Dubourg, who spoke English, would put him in a way of procuring access to M. de Vergennes, the French minister for foreign
affairs. On attaining the presence of the minister, Mr. Deane was
to show him his letter of credence, and say that Congress, being
unable to procure in America the requisite munitions of war, had
dispatched him to apply to some European power for a supply.
Of all the nations in Europe, he was to say, Congress preferred the
friendship and alliance of France; and to France, therefore, he had
come. By granting aid to the struggling colonies, their friendship
would be secured, and they would gladly transfer the bulk of their
trade from England to France. He was to ask for clothing and
arms for twenty-five thousand men, a quantity of ammunition, and
one hundred pieces of field artillery; all of which Congress would
pay for soon after the resumption of commerce. He was to ask
convoy, also, for these articles, as well as for the Indian merchandise which he was to purchase. If he found M. de Vergennes reserved, he should shorten his visit, ask him to consider the matter,
leave his address, and say that he would not presume to ask another audience; but if M. de Vergennes should at any time have
any commands for him, he would promptly present himself on the
slightest notification. At a second audience, if the minister should
appear more inclined to listen, he should ask him, with the customary circumlocution, whether, in case the colonies should form
themselves into an independent State, France would acknowledge
them, receive embassadors from them, and form treaties with
them; and if she would, on what conditions. Finally, he was to
consult and correspond with Mr. Dumas, Arthur Lee, Dr. Bancroft,

M. Garnier, and keep Congress constantly informed of his movements.

For the purchase of the Indian goods Mr. Deane would require money. Cargoes of tobacco and rice, to the value of forty thousand pounds, were to be at once dispatched, so as to begin to arrive at French ports soon after his own arrival. For his present subsistence, he was supplied with a few hundred pounds in gold. Every precaution was taken to conceal the object of Mr. Deane's mission. Mr. Jay busied himself with providing a quantity of invisible ink, and prepared paper for the correspondence of the emissary, who was to sign his letters "Timothy Jones," and write a common business letter with common ink on part of the sheet, and cover all the rest with the real dispatch written with the invisible fluid. He sailed in April, and reached France in June, having stopped on the way at the Bermudas. As he retained in France his proper name, which had been published in most of the capitals in Europe among the signatures appended to Congressional documents, his mission was soon guessed. He had not been in Paris many weeks before he was spoken of in the English newspapers as "the plenipotentiary of the American Congress."

While the Secret Committee was employed in dispatching Silas Deane, the public mind was occupied with affairs in Canada. News had reached Congress that the assault upon Quebec on the thirty-first of December, 1775, had failed; that General Montgomery had been left dead on the snowy hights, and General Benedict Arnold borne wounded from the field; that cold, small-pox, and hunger were wasting the army; that discipline was forgotten, the credit of Congress diminished, and the people indifferent or inimical. On this occasion Congress resorted to the expedient which had answered so well in the case of General Washington and the chaos around Boston; they appointed three commissioners to go to Montreal, confer with General Arnold, and arrange a plan for the rectification of Canadian affairs. The commissioners selected were Dr. Franklin, Samuel Chase, of Maryland, and Charles Carroll of Carrollton, in the same province. Mr. Carroll was requested by Congress to endeavor to prevail upon his brother John, a Catholic priest, who had been educated in France, and spoke French like a native, to accompany the commissioners, for the purpose of bringing over the clergy of Canada to the side of Congress. The worthy

priest consented to go.   The sending of this gentleman was regarded as "a master-stroke of policy," Mrs. Adams records.   But the
policy of selecting an old man of seventy to head the commission,
was open to objection, in view of the journey to be made before the
commissioners could begin the execution of their task.   The other
commissioners were in the prime of life, and were all destined to
rise high in the service and estimation of their country.
The commissioners were clothed with extraordinary powers.   They
were authorized to receive Canada into the union of colonies, and
organize their government on the republican system of the thirteen ;
they were empowered to suspend military officers, decide disputes
between the civil and military authorities, vote at councils of war,
draw upon Congress to the amount of one hundred thousand dollars,
raise additional troops, and issue military commissions.   Whatever
authority Congress itself could be supposed to exercise over Canada
was conferred upon the three commissioners.   Chiefly, however,
they were charged to convince, conciliate, and win the Canadians
by appeals to their reason and interest ; in aid of which, they were
to take measures for establishing a newspaper to be conducted by
a friend to Congress.

Fully equipped for a journey of five hundred miles, the commissioners, their priestly companion, and their servants, left Philadelphia at the end of March, and reached in two days the city of New
York.   "It was no more," wrote Mr. John Carroll to his mother,
"the gay, polite place it used to be esteemed, but it was become
almost a desert, unless for the troops.   The people were expecting
a bombardment, and had therefore removed themselves out of town ;
and on the other side the troops were working on the fortifications
with the utmost activity."*   The commissioners spent "some disagreeable days" at the deserted town.   On the second of April, at
five in the afternoon, they all embarked on board the sloop engaged
for them by Lord Stirling, and sailed towards Albany ; they made
thirteen miles in the course of the evening, and then comfortably
dropped anchor for the night.   At one o'clock in the morning, an
alarm!   A great fire in the harbor, off New York; perhaps on
Bedloe's Island, from which "our generals" had determined to
drive the British.   Dr. Franklin came on deck, and thought "our

* "American Archives," Fourth Series, vol. v., p. 1160.

generals" had made the attempt, as the flashes of light looked like musketry. The next day a northeast storm of wind and rain kept the sloop at anchor till five in the afternoon, when " the wind breezed up from the south," and bore the vessel on to the beginning of the Highlands, forty miles from the city. Now behold the perils of river navigation! " The river here," journalized Mr. Charles Carroll,* " is greatly contracted, and the lands on each side very lofty. When we got into this strait the wind increased and blew in violent flaws; in doubling one of these steep, craggy points, we were in danger of running on the rocks : endeavored to double the cape called St. Anthony's Nose, but all our efforts proved ineffectual; obliged to return some way back in the straits to seek shelter ; in doing which, our mainsail was split to pieces by a sudden and most violent blast of wind off the mountains. Came to anchor." Let us no longer discourse lightly of the "raging canal."

All that night and all the next day the storm continued, and the sloop remained at anchor ; the crew mending the mainsail, and the commissioners marveling at the scene around them, as hundreds of thousands of us have since marveled. " St. Anthony's Nose is said to be full of sulphur," wrote our journalizer. At noon of the third day of the voyage, the mainsail being repaired, the anchor was heaved, and the sloop slowly wound its way through the sublime defile. Mr. Chase and Mr. Charles Carroll rowed ashore to examine a waterfall, leaving a leg of mutton boiling in the galley for the commissioners' dinner. " Mr. Chase, very apprehensive of the leg of mutton being boiled too much, was impatient to get on board," and so the waterfall was not examined with the attention which Mr. Carroll desired. At five that afternoon the sloop anchored off West Point, and the two younger commissioners went to the opposite shore and inspected Constitution Fort, upon which Congress relied for the defense of the river. Finding it inadequate for the purpose, and having heard of the arrival of the British fleet at Sandy Hook, the commissioners sent an express to Congress, telling them that the Hudson River was open to the ascent of a vigorous enemy. " In the Highlands," remarked Mr. Charles Carroll, " are many convenient spots to construct batteries on ; but in order to make them answer the intended purpose,

---

* " Journal of Charles Carroll of Carrollton," published by Maryland Historical Society.

weighty metal should be placed on those batteries, and skillful gun-
ners should be engaged to serve the artillery." Congress will
look to the Highlands.

Weighing anchor at seven in the morning of the fourth day,
their luck turned, and they had a splendid run of ninety miles,
which brought them within four miles of Albany; and there they
cast anchor for the night. At half-past seven the next morning
the commissioners stepped on shore at Albany. General Schuyler met them at the landing "to receive us and invite us to dine
with him; he behaved to us with great civility; lives in pretty
style; has two daughters (Betsey and Peggy), lively, agreeable,
black-eyed gals." Two days at Albany, conferring with General
Schuyler and General Thomas, and chatting with the good Mrs.
Schuyler and her lively black-eyed girls. "General Schuyler informed me," records Mr. Carroll, "that an uninterrupted water-
carriage between New York and Quebec might be perfected at
fifty thousand pounds sterling expense."

April 9th. The commissioners, the priest, Mrs. Schuyler, her
two daughters, General Schuyler, and General Thomas, all set off
together for Saratoga, thirty-two miles from Albany, where General Schuyler had a country seat. A rough ride over muddy, bad
roads, in a large country wagon, added to the extreme fatigue and
constant exposure of the river voyage, was almost too much for
Dr. Franklin. "At Saratoga," he wrote, "I begin to apprehend
that I have undertaken a fatigue, which, at my time of life, may
prove too much for me; so I sit down to write to a few friends by
way of farewell." They had caught up, too, with retreating
winter; the ice in the lakes had not budged, and six inches of
snow lay upon the ground as late as the thirteenth of April. A
week's rest at the hospitable and well-appointed abode of General
Schuyler, with such nursing and attendance as the noble lady of
that noble mansion knew how to bestow upon an aged philosopher,
brought him round again, and he was ready to start before the
ice had started. The commissioners moved towards Lake George
on the sixteenth—snow still on the ground. "I parted with regret," wrote Mr. Carroll, "from the amiable family of General
Schuyler; the ease and affability with which we were treated, and
the lively behavior of the young ladies, made Saratoga a most pleasing *séjour*, the remembrance of which will long remain with me."

Two days and a half of hard traveling brought them to that pleasing and now familiar spot, the southern end of Lake George. The ice had broken up, and they determined to make an effort the next day to push their way through the floating masses. General Schuyler, who had gone before them to prepare the means of transportation, had a batteau ready for them, thirty-six feet long, eight broad, and one deep, with a mast, a blanket-sail, and awning, in lieu of a cabin. At one o'clock in the afternoon of April 19th they embarked, accompanied by the indefatigable Schuyler. When they had accomplished four miles, they went ashore to take tea and rearrange their boat; after which they again embarked, and made three or four miles more. And so they pushed their way, often delayed by the ice, and achieved the thirty-six miles of Lake George in about thirty-six hours. Mr. Carroll regretted that the earliness of the season prevented their catching any of the famous fish of this translucent lake ; and the more, " as one of our company is so excellent a judge in the science of good eating ;" a hit for the gentleman who thought more of his leg of mutton than of Mr. Carroll's waterfall. Six yoke of oxen drew their batteau on wheels across the four-mile neck of land which separates the two lakes; and, after a delay of five days, they were afloat on Lake Champlain. Sailing when they could, rowing when they must, hauling up at night, and generally stopping for breakfast, dinner, and tea, delayed sometimes by ice and sometimes by head winds, they reached St. John's, near the upper end of the lake, in three days and a half, and thought they had done very well. Another day of most laborious travel brought them to Montreal, half dead with fatigue. No wonder; for they performed the last day's journey in Montreal caleches, which appear to have been similar to the torturing vehicles which swarm still in Montreal, and are called by the same name.

The commissioners were received with distinction. Mr. John Carroll reports: " We were received at the landing by General Arnold, and a great body of officers and gentry, and saluted by the firing of cannon, and other military honors. Being conducted to the General's house, we were served with a glass of wine; while people were crowding in to pay their compliments; which ceremony being over, we were shown into another apartment, and, unexpectedly, met in it a large number of ladies, most of them French.

After drinking tea, and sitting some time, we went to an elegant supper, which was followed with the singing of the ladies, which proved very agreeable, and would have been more so if we had not been so much fatigued with our journey. The next day we spent in receiving visits, and dining with a large company." Mr. John Carroll may have spent the next day in that manner, but not the three commissioners; for whom there was sterner work. They sat at a council of war, of which General Arnold was president, and heard the whole of the dismal truth with regard to the affairs of Congress in Canada.

Canada was lost. The first dispatch of the commissioners informed Congress that their credit in Canada was not merely impaired, but destroyed. "Not the most trifling service can be procured without an assurance of instant pay in silver or gold. The express we sent from St. Johns, to inform the General of our arrival there, and to request carriages for La Prairie, was stopped at the ferry, till a friend passing changed a dollar bill for him, into silver ; and we are obliged to that friend for his engagement to pay the calashes, or they would not have come for us." Disasters in the field, violated promises to pay, depreciated paper, and the expectation of a British army, had caused , this deplorable state of things.

The commissioners were plunged into a fathomless sea of embarrassment. "We have tried in vain," they wrote to Congress, at the end of their first week, "to borrow some hard money here, for the immediate occasion of the army, either on the public, or on our own private credit. We cannot even sell sterling bills of exchange, which some of us have offered to draw. It seems it had been expected, and given out by our friends, that we should bring money with us. The disappointment has discouraged everybody, and established an opinion that none is to be had, or that the Congress has not credit enough in their own colonies to procure it. Many of our friends are drained dry ; others say they are so, fearing, perhaps, we shall never be able to reimburse them. They show us long accounts, no part of which we are able to discharge, of the supplies they have furnished to our army, and declare that they have borrowed and taken up on credit so long for our service, that they can now be trusted no longer, even for what they want themselves. The tories will not trust us a farthing, and some who, perhaps, wish us well, conceiving that we shall, through our own poverty, or from superior forces, be soon obliged to abandon the country, are afraid to have any dealings with us, lest they should hereafter be called to account for abetting our cause. Our enemies take the advantage of this distress to make us look contemptible in the eyes of the Canadians, who have been provoked by the violence of our military in exacting provisions and services from them without pay, which makes them wish our departure; and, accordingly, we have daily intimations of plots hatching, and insurrections intended, for expelling us, on the first news of the arrival of the British Army.

" You will see from hence, that your commissioners themselves are in a critical and most irksome situation, pestered hourly with demands, great and small, that they cannot answer, in a place where our cause has a majority of enemies, the garrison weak, and a greater would, without money, increase our difficulties. In short, if money cannot be had to support your army here with honor, so as to be respected, instead of being hated by the people, we report it, as our firm and unanimous opinion, that it is better immediately to withdraw it. The fact before your eyes, that the powerful British nation cannot keep an army in a country where the inhabitants are become enemies, must convince you of the necessity of enabling us immediately to make this people our friends. Exclusive of a sum of money to discharge the debts already contracted, which General Arnold informs us amounts to fourteen thousand pounds, besides the account laid before Congress by Mr. Price, a further sum of hard money, not less than six thousand pounds, will be necessary to re-establish our credit in this colony. With this supply, and a little success, it may be possible to regain the affections of the people, to attach them firmly to our cause, and induce them to accept a free government, perhaps to enter into the Union; in which case the currency of our paper money, we think, follows as a certain consequence."

Two days after this letter was written, a messenger reached Montreal with the news that a British fleet with troops on board had arrived at Quebec, had landed a large force which had attacked the little disheartened American army, and put it to flight. A council of war, attended by the commissioners, at once decided that nothing remained but to withdraw the troops to St. John's; fortify, supply, and re-enforce them there; and there endeavor to stay the south-ward progress of the British army. The requisite orders were issued immediately. The next morning Dr. Franklin, accompanied by Mr. John Caroll, set out on his return homeward, to expedite the necessary measures, and give Congress complete information respecting their affairs in the north. He left his brother commissioners to superintend the retreat and the erection of the defensive works at the head of Lake Champlain.

General Schuyler assisted the travelers on their way down the lakes, entertained them again at his house, and lent them his own chariot and driver for the journey from Albany to New York. From New York, Dr. Franklin wrote back to the other commissioners: " We met yesterday two officers from Philadelphia, with a letter from the Congress to the commissioners, and a sum of hard money. I opened the letter, and sealed it again, directing them to carry it forward to you. I congratulate you on the great prize carried into Boston. Seventy-five tons of gunpowder are an excellent supply, and the thousand carbines with bayonets, another fine article. The German auxiliaries are certainly coming. It is our business to prevent their returning. I shall be glad to hear of your welfare. As to myself, I find I grow daily more feeble, and think I could hardly have got along so far, but for Mr. Carroll's friendly assistance and tender care of me. Some symptoms of the gout now appear, which makes me think my indisposition has been a smothered fit of that disorder, which my constitution wanted strength to form completely."

He reached Philadelphia early in June, having been absent about ten weeks. For the lovers of detail, I will mention that the account presented by Dr. Franklin to Congress of money expended on this journey, showed that he had advanced the sum of $1,221 ;* of which $560 was to be charged to General Arnold, and $124 to Mr. Charles Carroll. The beds and outfits of the party cost $164. The whole expense incurred by Dr. Franklin and his priestly comrade, was $372.

These two, the philosopher and the priest, men most dissimilar in

---

* Dr. Franklin himself says, that while in Canada he "advanced to General Arnold, and other servants of Congress, then in extreme necessity, £358, in gold, out of his own pocket, on the credit of Congress, which was of great service at that juncture, in procuring provisions for our army.' *Sparks,* x., 373.

age, vocation, belief, and experience, conceived for each other, during this toilsome journey, a warm regard which they always cherished. A few years later, Dr. Franklin embraced an opportunity of testifying his esteem for Mr. John Carroll in a signal manner. In the quiet of his own home Dr. Franklin recovered his health, and soon renewed his labors, in Congress and elsewhere, with all his accustomed ardor. The timely arrival of powder relieved his mind from one source of anxiety. The scarcity of this article before his departure for Canada had been such, that he seriously proposed arming some of the troops with bows and arrows. "I still wish with you," he wrote to General Charles Lee, "that pikes could be introduced, and I would add bows and arrows. These were good weapons, not wisely laid aside; 1st. Because a man may shoot as truly with a bow as with a common musket. 2dly. He can discharge four arrows in the time of charging and discharging one bullet. 3dly. His object is not taken from his view by the smoke of his own side. 4thly. A flight of arrows, seen coming upon them, terrifies and disturbs the enemies' attention to their business. 5thly. An arrow striking in any part of a man puts him *hors de combat* till it is extracted. 6thly. Bows and arrows are more easily provided everywhere than muskets and ammunition.

"Polydore Virgil, speaking of one of our battles against the French in Edward the Third's reign, mentions the great confusion the enemy was thrown into, *sagittarum* nube, from the English; and concludes, *Est res profecto† dictu mirabilis, ut tantus ac potens exercitus a solis fere Anglicis sagittariis victus fuerit ; adeo Anglus est sagittipotens, et id genus armorum valet.* If so much execution was done by arrows when men wore some defensive armor, how much more might be done now that it is out of use."

Not against troops armed with modern muskets, Doctor.

A letter from Dr. Priestley, received soon after his return from Canada, concluded with some pleasant items: "The club of *honest Whigs*, as you justly call them, think themselves much honored by your having been one of them, and also by your kind remembrance of them. Our zeal in the good cause is not abated ; you are often the subject of our conversation. Lord Shelburne and Colonel Barré

---

* "By the cloud of arrows."

† "It is indeed a thing wonderful to be related, that an army so great and powerful should have been vanquished almost alone by the English bowmen ; truly your Englishman is mighty with the bow, and of a puissant stock."

were pleased with your remembrance of them, and desire their best respects and good wishes in return. Your old servant, Fevre, often mentions you with affection and respect. He is, in all respects, an excellent servant. I value him much, both on his own account and yours. He seems to be very happy. Mrs. Stévenson is much as usual. She can talk about nothing but you."

CHAPTER IV.

JULY, 1776.

PHILADELPHIA had been the scene of the keenest party strife during the absence of Dr. Franklin in Canada. After a series of elections most warmly contested, in which all the old electioneering artifices were employed, the party for Independence stormed the citadel of the Assembly, and deprived Mr. Dickinson of his ancient, compact majority. Then the doom of the Proprietary Government was sealed, and it only remained to execute the sentence. Yet it died hard. When Congress had decreed the extinction of all authority derived from the king of England, the Assembly still hesitated, adjourned from day to day, knew not what to do, until the will of the people was manifested in ways so various and unequivocal, that they could not disregard it. The struggle was given up at length; the government of Pennsylvania was declared to be dissolved; and the Assembly melted away.

For four months the great and populous province of Pennsylvania was without any thing that even pretended to be a government. There was no authority vested in any one to arrest a malefactor, suppress a riot, or compel the payment of debt. Franklin assured Sir Samuel Romilly that, during that long period, public order was perfectly preserved in every part of the State, and that no man who should have attempted to take advantage of the circumstances to evade the payment of a debt, could have borne the contempt in which he would have been held.* The easy, simple manner in

* Life of Sir Samuel Romilly, Appendix.

which the people extricated themselves from a dilemma so unprecedented was still more remarkable. The process seems to have been
this : The Committee of Safety recommended the people of Pennsylvania to elect delegates to a CONFERENCE. The people proceeded to elect delegates—Philadelphia choosing twenty-five, of
whom Franklin was one. On the eighteenth June the Conference
met at Philadelphia, sat five days, including a Sunday, renounced
allegiance to the king, swore obedience to Congress, and called
upon the people to elect delegates—-eight from Philadelphia and
eight from each county—to meet in CONVENTION, and form a constitution. The elections were held accordingly, and Dr. Franklin
was one of the eight chosen by Philadelphia. All this was done,
and the Convention actually assembled, in thirty-one days.

The great event of the contest had taken place, meanwhile, in
Congress ; where still sat seven Pennsylvanians, though the body
which had elected them had, in effect, ceased to exist. Of these
seven, four were opposed to the Declaration of Independence, and
their leader, Mr. Dickinson, stated his objections in a last speech of
much force, which would have carried conviction to the minds of
most men of large property and no enthusiasm. A man standing
upon the bank of a river, in which a child was struggling for life,
could make an argument against jumping in to save it, which the
soundest logician in the world would pronounce unanswerable.
But if he jumps in and saves the child, and bears it limp and drip-
ping to its mother's arms, what does the sound logician say then ?
He says nothing. He rushes up to the wet hero, clasps him to his
breast, tries to speak his love and admiration, but chokes, and cannot, and has to content himself with wringing his hand and garments, running a mile to the nearest brandy bottle, and doing
the distance in twelve minutes. Great is prudence. Every great
man is greatly prudent. But there come times in the lives of men
and nations when the true prudence is to risk *all* for the sake of
securing that which, being lost, nothing is worth having. A nation's freedom, a man's self-respect, when they are irrecoverably
gone, every thing else may as well go.

Franklin's part in the Declaration of Independence was not important. A committee of five was elected by ballot to draft the
declaration: Thomas Jefferson, Benjamin Franklin, John Adams,
Robert R. Livingston, and Roger Sherman. Mr. Jefferson, as we

all know, was pressed by his colleagues to write the draft, and yielded to their solicitations. When he had finished it he showed it to Dr. Franklin and Mr. Adams, neither of whom suggested any alterations except very few verbal ones quite unimportant. Approved unanimously by the committee, it was submitted to the House, where it was subjected to sharp criticism, and where John Adams, " the colossus of this debate," " the Atlas of the Declaration," defended it with consummate ability. Two anecdotes of Dr. Franklin, both extremely well worn, are all that we possess of him in connection with these memorable days. Mr. Jefferson relates one of them :

" When the Declaration of Independence was under the consideration of Congress, there were two or three unlucky expressions in it which gave offense to some members. The words ' Scotch and other foreign auxiliaries,' excited the ire of a gentleman or two of that country. Severe strictures on the conduct of the British king, in negativing our repeated repeals of the law which permitted the importation of slaves, were disapproved by some southern gentlemen whose reflections were not yet matured to the full abhorrence of that traffic. Although the offensive expressions were immediately yielded, these gentlemen continued their depredations on other parts of the instrument. I was sitting by Dr. Franklin, who perceived that I was not insensible to (' *that I was writhing under*,' he says elsewhere) these mutilations.

" ' I have made it a rule,' said he, ' whenever in my power, to avoid becoming the draftsman of papers to be reviewed by a public body. I took my lesson from an incident which I will relate to you. When I was a journeyman printer, one of my companions, an apprenticed hatter, having served out his time, was about to open shop for himself. His first concern was to have a handsome signboard, with a proper inscription. He composed it in these words, *John Thompson, Hatter, makes and sells Hats for ready Money*, with a figure of a hat subjoined. But he thought he would submit it to his friends for their amendments. The first he showed it to thought the word *hatter* tautologous, because followed by the words *makes hats*, which showed he was a hatter. It was struck out. The next observed that the word *makes* might as well be omitted, because his customers would not care who made the hats; if good and to their mind they would buy, by whomsoever made. He struck it out. A third said he thought the words *for ready money* were useless, as it was not the custom of the place to sell on credit. Every one who purchased expected to pay. They were parted with ; and the inscription now stood, ' John Thompson sells hats.' '*Sells* hats ?' says his next friend ; ' why, nobody will expect you to give them away. What, then, is the use of that word ?' It was stricken out, and *hats* followed, the rather as there was one painted on the board. So his inscription was reduced ultimately to *John Thompson*, with the figure of a hat subjoined.' "

When the members were about to sign the document, Mr. Hancock is reported to have said : " We must be unanimous; there must be no pulling different ways ; we must all hang together." Tradition assigns to Franklin the well-known, witty reply : " Yes ; we must, indeed, all hang together, or, most assuredly, we shall all hang separately."

Franklin's signature to the Declaration has the exuberant flourish under it with which he was accustomed to decorate his name. He had the gratification, at length, of seeing the vote of Pennsylvania cast for the Declaration ; but it was only because Mr. Dickinson and Robert Morris chose to avoid taking their seats that day, though present in the House.

The people of Pennsylvania instantly swept aside the relics of the old proprietary party. Four days after the Fourth of July, the elections for delegates to the Constitutional Convention occurred. The result of the election in the city and county of Philadelphia, John Adams dashed off to his wife : " Dr. Franklin will be governor of Pennsylvania ! The new members from this city are all in this taste—chosen because of their inflexible zeal for Independence. All the old members left out because they opposed Independence, or were lukewarm about it, Dickinson, Morris, and Allen, all fallen like grass before the scythe, notwithstanding all their vast advantages in point of fortune, family, and abilities." In the evening of this great day, the triumph of the liberal party was celebrated in Philadelphia by " bonfires, bells, and other great demonstrations of joy," reports Christopher Marshall. July 20th, the Convention elected nine members of Congress, of whom Dr. Franklin received the highest number of votes.

When Congress had completed the great affair of the Declaration, the next business in order was to form the thirteen States into a confederacy, and to settle the terms of union. The debates on the several articles proposed were long, and, not unfrequently, warm and acrimonious, but we know little of the details, and only catch glimpses of the leading performers on the scene. Mr. Adams and Mr. Jefferson, in their diaries and correspondence, rescue from oblivion a few words of Franklin uttered in these important discussions.

The most perplexing difficulty was to arrange a plan of voting in Congress which would give the large States their just weight, and, at the same time, afford the small States a share of real sovereignty. This is managed in our present Constitution by assigning to each State two senators, but admitting to the other House a number of representatives proportioned to population. Thus, the big brother is still the big brother, but the little brother is always a *brother*, equal to the biggest in every thing but inches. The old Congress could agree upon no better way than to vote on all questions by States, and to give to every State, great or small, one vote. To Franklin this system seemed equally absurd and dangerous; he thought that Virginia and Pennsylvania could not long be content to exert no more influence in the counsels of the Union than Delaware and Rhode Island; and that, in attempting to change the system to one more just, extreme danger to the Union would arise. He never opposed any thing with more vehemence than he did the adoption of this plan of voting. There was, indeed, one short period of this summer, when he meditated advising his State not to come into the confederation unless this article was changed, and nothing but the absolute necessity of immediate union prevented his doing so.

Mr. Adams records this remark of Franklin—a speech in two sentences : " Let the smaller colonies give equal money and men, and then have an equal vote. But if they have an equal vote without bearing equal burdens, a confederation upon such iniquitous principles will never last long." Again : " If we had been born and bred under an unequal representation, we might bear it ; but to set out with an unequal representation is unreasonable. It is said the great colonies will swallow up the less. Scotland said the same thing at the union." Here comes in a passage from Mr. Jefferson to complete the illustration. Dr. Franklin observed, that " at the time of the union of England and Scotland, the Duke of Argyle was most violently opposed to that measure, and among other things predicted that, as the whale had swallowed Jonah, so Scotland would be swallowed by England. "However," said the Doctor, " when Lord Bute came into the government, he soon brought into its administration so many of his countrymen, that it was found, in event, that Jonah had swallowed the whale." This little story produced a general laugh, and restored good humor.

In the course of the same debate, one of the Southern members spoke of slaves and sheep as property equally liable to taxation. To this Dr. Franklin made a reply, which Mr. Adams condenses into a sentence : " Slaves rather weaken than strengthen the state, and there is, therefore, some difference between them and sheep; sheep will never make any insurrections." In the conversation that arose on this subject, the Southern members gave free utterance to the self-evident proposition, that slavery is monstrous policy.

I should add, perhaps, that this subject of representation was one which Dr. Franklin had well considered, and upon which, while still residing in England, he had reached opinions one hundred years in advance of England. Among his papers was found a printed sheet upon which he had written, as descriptive of its contents, " Some good Whig Principles." The paper was entitled, " Declaration of those Rights of the Commonalty of Great Britain without which they cannot be free." The leading propositions were these three : " That *every man* of the commonalty (excepting infants, insane persons, and criminals) is, of common right, and by the laws of God, *a freeman*, and entitled to the free enjoyment of *liberty*. That liberty, or freedom, consists in having *an actual share* in the appointment of those who frame the laws, and who are to be the guardians of every man's life, property, and peace; for the *all* of one man is as dear to him as the *all* of another; and the poor man has an *equal* right, but *more* need, to have representatives in the Legislature than the rich one. That they who have *no* voice nor vote in the electing of representatives, *do not enjoy* liberty; but are absolutely *enslaved* to those who *have* votes, and to their representatives; for to be enslaved is to have governors whom *other men have set over us*, and be subject to laws *made by the representatives of others*, without having had representatives of our own to give consent in *our* behalf."

These principles so familiar to us now, and so obviously just,

were startling and incredible novelties in 1770; abhorrent to nearly
all Englishmen, and to great numbers of Americans. They serve
to show us why Franklin should have opposed, with such unusual
pertinacity, a plan of voting which gave to the smallest States as
much weight in Congress as the largest. It savored of the injustice which gave to a borough of twenty cottages as many members
of Parliament as a great manufacturing town of a hundred thousand
inhabitants, abounding in talent, intelligence, and capital.

In this memorable month of July, 1776, Congress appointed
Franklin, Jefferson, and John Adams a committee to prepare a de-
vice for the seal of the Confederacy. Each of the committee, as we
learn from one of Mr. Adams's letters to his wife, had an idea : " * *
Dr. Franklin proposes, Moses lifting up his wand, and dividing the
Red Sea, and *Pharaoh* in his chariot overwhelmed with the waters.
This motto, 'Rebellion to Tyrants is obedience to *God*.' Mr.
Jefferson has proposed, The children of Israel in the wilderness ;
led by a cloud by day, and a pillar of fire by night ; and on the
other side, Hengist and Horsa, the Saxon Chiefs, from whom we
claim the honor of being descended, and whose political principles
and form of government we have assumed. I proposed, The choice
of Hercules, as engraved by *Gribelin*, in some editions of Lord
Shaftesbury's works. The hero resting on his club ; VIRTUE pointing to her rugged mountain on one hand, and persuading him to
ascend ; SLOTH, glancing at her flowery paths of pleasure, wantonly reclining on the ground, displaying the charms both of her
eloquence and person, to seduce him into vice."*   *   *

The committee deliberated on the matter for nearly six weeks,
not reporting until the tenth of August. They then recommended
that the Great Seal of the United States should have on one side
the national arms ; which arms they proposed should contain
something emblematic of each of the nations from which America
had been peopled ; a rose for England, a thistle for Scotland, a
harp for Ireland, a fleur-de-lis for France, a black eagle for Germany, a lion for the low countries. The border should consist of
the arms and initials of each of the United States. For support-
ers, the committee recommended the goddess of Liberty in armor, holding in her right hand the spear and cap, and with her left

* "American Archives," Fifth Series, i., 944.

supporting a shield; also, a figure of Justice bearing the sword and balance. Crest: " The eye of Providence in a radiant triangle, whose glory extends over the shield and beyond the figures." Motto : *E Pluribus Unum.* Legend round the whole: " Seal of the United States of America, MDCCLXXVI." For the other side of the seal the committee adopted Franklin's device: " Pharaoh sitting in an open chariot, a crown on his head and a sword in his hand, passing through the divided waters of the Red Sea in pursuit of the Israelites. Rays from a pillar of fire in the cloud, expressive of the Divine presence and command, beaming on Moses, who stands on the shore, and extending his hand over the sea, causes it to overflow Pharaoh. Motto: ' Rebellion to tyrants is obedience to God.' "

Congress appears not to have approved of this elaborate design. It was ordered to lie on the table, where it remained until Dr. Franklin was gone from the country. Other committees took the seal in hand, and suppressed, at length, all of the original design except that most felicitous of mottoes, *E Pluribus Unum*, and the Eye of Providence.

On the arrival of the Hessians this summer, Franklin was active in carrying out the plans of Congress for their seduction. A short address was drawn up, and translated into German, offering, in the name of Congress, a tract of land to every Hessian soldier who should abandon the ignominious service to which his sovereign had sold him. Some of these addresses were printed on such paper as was commonly used for tobacco at that time ; the design being to put up tobacco in them and distribute the packets among the Hessians. Another address was prepared for circulation among the officers. Whether Dr. Franklin was the originator of these devices, or only assisted in giving them effect, does not appear; nor are we informed as to their success. A few months later, if Dr. Franklin had been in Philadelphia, he would have had the delight of seeing nine hundred of the Hessian soldiers marching through the streets as prisoners of war.

The convention elected to form a Constitution and frame a government for the State of Pennsylvania, met at Philadelphia on the sixteenth of July, and sat until the twenty-eighth of September. Dr. Franklin was unanimously chosen president of the convention. Although his occupations as a member of Congress prevented him from attending regularly the sittings of this body, yet he was present during the more important debates, and exerted a controlling influence over some of its conclusions. The system of government finally adopted by the convention had the peculiarity of providing for only one House of Representatives; and in this Franklin concurred. He had seen the ill effects of a divided authority in the old proprietary government, and he had come to regard the British House of Lords in the light of an obstructive nuisance merely. He was of opinion that a single representative body would be more effective in promoting good measures, and less liable to intrigue and corruption than two bodies. He afterwards defended this feature of the Constitution of Pennsylvania in these terms:

"The wisdom of a few members in one single legislative body, may it not frequently stifle bad motions in their infancy, and so prevent their being adopted? whereas, if those wise men, in case of a double legislature, should happen to be in that branch wherein the motion did not arise, may it not, after being adopted by the other, occasion long disputes and contentions between the two bodies, expensive to the public, obstructing the public business, and promoting factions among the people, many tempers naturally adhering obstinately to measures they have once publicly adopted? Have we not seen, in one of our neighboring States, a bad measure adopted by one branch of the legislature for want of the assistance of some more intelligent members who had been packed into the other, occasion many debates, conducted with much asperity, which could not be settled but by an expensive general appeal to the public? * * * The division of the legislature into two or three branches in England, was it the product of wisdom, or the effect of necessity, arising from the pre-existing prevalence of an odious feudal system? which government, notwithstanding this division, is now become, in fact, an absolute monarchy; since the king, by bribing the representatives with the people's money, carries, by his ministers, all the measures that please him; which is equivalent to governing without a Parliament, and renders the machine of government much more complex and expensive, and, from its being more complex, more easily put out of order. Has not the famous political fable of the snake, with two heads and one body, some useful instruction contained in it? She was going to a brook to drink, and in her way was to pass through a hedge, a twig of which opposed her direct course; one head chose to go on the right side of the twig, the other on the left; so that time was spent in the contest, and, before the decision was completed, the poor snake died with thirst."

If Dr. Franklin had lived to our day, he might have drawn a different inference from the example of the English House of Lords. He would, perhaps, have pointed to Great Britain, and said : " Behold, my Pennsylvanians, a vast empire governed by a single House, namely, the House of Commons! The House of Lords as a governing power, is so nearly extinct, that if it were to vanish entirely, the chief practical effect of the event would be to give the *Times* a little more room for the debates of the other House." Perhaps, too, he would have made some observations upon the long periods when the Senate of the United States seemed the impregnable stronghold of every thing that was false, corrupt, and reactionary; and shown how, between the two houses, the most indubitably just measures have often been slipped into oblivion. He might have quoted, with very good effect, a remark made by the late Senator Douglas to Mr. Horace Greeley, when the latter gentleman was a member of the House of Representatives : " If the House does not stop passing retrenchment bills for Buncombe, and then running to the Senate and begging Senators to stop them there, I, for one, will vote to put through the next mileage-reduction bill that comes to the Senate, just to punish members for their hypocrisy." However, this is a great question, and much may be said on both sides. Experience, not argument, will settle it.

The last act of the Constitutional Convention of Pennsylvania was to pass the following Resolution : " *Resolved unanimously*, That the thanks of this Convention be given to the President for the honor he has done it by filling the chair during the debates on the most important parts of the Bill of Rights and frame of Government, and for his able and disinterested advice thereon."

Such are the slight, occasional traces of Franklin, in these summer weeks of 1776, which the writings of the time afford us. How inadequate they are! How little they reveal to us of the mighty stir and ferment of the period! The chroniclers of those important days tell us scarcely any thing of what they felt; their drawing is mostly in outline, without color or shading. For example, when a British fleet in the Delaware brought the war within hearing of the Philadelphians, Christopher Marshall begins the entry in his diary for that day with the business-like expression, that "*Sundry pieces of news are circulated about town;*" one of which was the arrival of the British fleet. The worthy druggist catalogued the most startling items of intelligence as he would a new invoice of herbs. Other sundries of the same day were, the arrival off Sandy Hook of a prodigious British fleet and army; the conveyance to Connecticut of Governor Franklin; and the total ruin of the patriot cause in Canada. Think what must have been the effect, as the tidings flew from street to street, from house to house, from room to room, of sedate, domestic Philadelphia; neighbor hurrying with it to neighbor, the well whispering it to the sick, Committees of Safety gathering, and all the streets in the warm evenings filled with knots and groups of anxious men. Awful rumors were in the air. July the first, Mr. Marshall records that information had been brought in to the Committee of Safety by a combmaker, that "not less than four different clubs of Tories" were in the habit of meeting in Philadelphia: and that frequently! At such a time as this! Under the very nose of Congress!

In those first days of July down came all the King's Arms, from court rooms, from taverns, from government houses and pretentious shops; those of the State House being taken down with ceremony in the presence of thousands of people, placed upon the top of a vast heap of tar barrels, and gloriously burnt. All this, while a British fleet of a hundred and twenty sail lay in New York harbor. What a hurrying forward of troops, too, as the greatness of Lord Howe's fleet, and the number of the troops in it, became known! Six thousand Pennsylvanians, encamped at Lancaster, were ordered to make all speed to Brunswick, in New Jersey, the rendezvous of the troops of both provinces; and Christopher Marshall went about the streets of Philadelphia collecting awnings to make tents for them. Troops passed through the city nearly every day on their way to New York. July 14th, "sixteen shallops with Maryland troops going to Trenton, amounting, it is said, to eleven hundred." Same day, two or three companies from Cumberland County came in; they stay all night; to Trenton on the morrow: "the whole, it is said, in high spirits."

August 28th, Dr. Franklin concluded one of his letters to General Gates with these words: "While I am writing comes an account that the armies were engaged on Long Island, the event unknown, which throws us into anxious suspense. God grant success." It was three days before the people of Philadelphia knew all the extent of the disaster, including the retreat from Long Island.

Mr. Marshall, in his diary for August 31st, gives informanion to posterity of two events. One was, that the said Christopher, on that day, got in his winter's wood, eleven cords and a half, price £10, and for hauling, carrying, and piling, £2 2s. 10d. Having recorded this always cheering circumstance, he proceeded to state, in the same number of lines, namely six, that Gen. Washington had got his army safely and in good order over the East River to New York, with all his field-pieces and stores; and that, while General Sullivan and Lord Stirling were prisoners in the enemy's hands, it was rumored that " our people" had killed two of the British generals. Still the troops went forward. Three thousand left Philadelphia within two days after the news came of the defeat upon Long Island.

Amid such scenes and such events, Dr. Franklin lived and labored during the summer of 1776.

CHAPTER V.

THE CONFERENCE WITH LORD HOWE.

LORD HOWE reappears in our narrative. From the chapter in which that nobleman has already figured, some irreverent readers may have derived the impression that his zeal in behalf of America, and his sister's also, was owing, in part, to his wish for an advantageous appointment. That virtuous desire was gratified one year after the discontinuance of the negotiations with Dr. Franklin; when he was appointed admiral of the king's naval forces in America, and joint commissioner with his brother, General William Howe, to grant pardons to such of the American rebels as should lay down their arms and renew their allegiance to the king.

He arrived off Sandy Hook on the twelfth of July, with the great fleet to which allusion has just been made. He sent on shore a packet addressed to each of the royal governors, containing a copy of a document which, being addressed to no one in particular, he styled a Declaration. This was nothing more than an announcement, that himself and his brother had been endowed by a gracious king with power to grant pardons both to individuals and to whole colonies. This Declaration the royal governors were commanded to distribute as widely as possible among a deluded people. The worthy admiral (a great sailor, though an unskillful politician), who was sincerely desirous of restoring peace to his country, cherished the expectation of being aided in the work of pacification by his old friend, Dr. Franklin. The English friends of Franklin had availed themselves of the opportunity afforded by Lord Howe's appointment, to send over to him letters, parcels, and books, which the admiral dispatched on shore by the boat which conveyed his Declaration, and, at the same time, sent to Dr. Franklin a very civil letter :

"I cannot, my worthy friend," wrote the admiral, "permit the letters and parcels (which I have sent in the state I received them) to be landed, without adding a word upon the subject of the injurious extremities in which our unhappy differences have engaged us. You will learn the nature of my mission from the official dispatches, which I have recommended to be forwarded by the same conveyance. Retaining all the earnestness I ever expressed to see our differences accommodated, I shall conceive, if I meet with the disposition in the colonies I was once taught to expect, the most flattering hopes of proving serviceable in the objects of the king's paternal solicitude, by promoting the establishment of lasting peace and union with the colonies. But, if the deep-rooted prejudices of America, and the necessity for preventing her trade from passing into foreign channels, must keep us still a divided people, I shall, from every private as well as public motive, most heartily lament that this is not the moment wherein those great objects of my ambition are to be attained; and that I am to be longer deprived of an opportunity to assure you personally of the regard with which I am your sincere and faithful humble servant."

Congress received Lord Howe's Declaration, and Dr. Franklin received his letter, by the same carrier. The retort of Congress to the Declaration was spirited and wise; they merely ordered the publication of the document in the newspapers, "that the few who still remain suspended by a hope founded either in the justice or moderation of their late king, may now at length be convinced that the valor alone of their country is to save its liberties." Dr. Franklin submitted his letter to Congress, who, after a day's deliberation, "Resolved, that Dr. Franklin may, if he thinks proper, return a reply to the letter he received from Lord Howe." He did think proper. Having written a reply, he either read it to Congress, or showed it to so many of the members, that the whole body was perfectly acquainted with its contents. The more decided patriots appear to have relished it exceedingly, and even Mr. Joseph Reed thought it "most excellent," and wished it had been in his power to take a copy of it. This letter, once so celebrated throughout Europe and America, ought, I think, to have place here:

"My Lord: I received safe the letters your lordship so kindly forwarded to me, and beg you to accept my thanks.

"The official dispatches, to which you refer me, contain nothing more than what we had seen in the act of Parliament, viz., offers of pardon upon submission, which I am sorry to find, as it must give your lordship pain to be sent so far on so hopeless a business.

"Directing pardons to be offered the colonies, who are the very parties injured, expresses indeed that opinion of our ignorance, baseness, and insensibility, which your uninformed and proud nation has long been pleased to entertain of us; but it can have no other effect than that of increasing our resentment. It is impossible we should think of submission to a government that has with the most wanton barbarity and cruelty burnt our defenseless towns in the midst of winter, excited the savages to massacre our farmers, and our slaves to murder their masters, and is even now bringing foreign mercenaries to deluge our settlements with blood. These atrocious injuries have extinguished every remaining spark of affection for that parent country we once held so dear; but, were it possible for *us* to forget and forgive them, it is not possible for *you* (I mean the British nation) to forgive the people you have so heavily injured. You can never confide again in those as fellow subjects, and permit them to enjoy equal freedom, to whom you know you have given such just cause of lasting enmity. And this must impel you, were we again under your government, to endeavor the breaking our spirit by the severest tyranny, and obstructing, by every means in your power, our growing strength and prosperity.

"But your lordship mentions 'The king's paternal solicitude for promoting the establishment of lasting *peace* and union with the colonies.' If by peace is here meant a peace to be entered into between Britain and America, as distinct states now at war, and his majesty has given your lordship powers to treat with us of such a peace, I may venture to say, though without authority, that I think a treaty for that purpose not yet quite impracticable, before we enter into foreign alliances. But I am persuaded you have no such powers. Your nation, though, by punishing *those American governors* who have created and fomented the discord, rebuilding our burnt towns, and repairing as far as possible the mischiefs done us, might yet recover a great share of our regard, and the greatest part of our growing commerce, with all the advantage of that additional strength to be derived from a friendship with us; but I know too well her abounding pride and deficient wisdom, to believe she will ever take such salutary measures. Her fondness for conquest, as a warlike nation, her lust of dominion, as an ambitious one, and her thirst for a gainful monopoly, as a commercial one (none of them legitimate causes of war), will all join to hide from her eyes every view of her true interests, and continually goad her on in those ruinous distant expeditions, so destructive both of lives and treasure, that must prove as pernicious to her in the end, as the crusades formerly were to most of the nations of Europe.

"I have not the vanity, my lord, to think of intimidating by thus predicting the effects of this war; for I know it will in England have the fate of all my former predictions, not to be believed till the event shall verify it.

"Long did I endeavor, with unfeigned and unwearied zeal, to preserve from breaking that fine and noble China vase, the British empire; for I knew that, being once broken, the separate parts could not retain even their share of the strength or value that existed in the whole, and that a perfect reunion of those parts could scarce ever be hoped for. Your lordship may possibly remember the tears of joy that wet my cheek, when, at your good sister's in London, you once gave me expectations that a reconciliation might soon take place. I had the misfortune to find those expectations disappointed, and to be treated as the cause of the mischief I was laboring to prevent. My consolation under that groundless and malevolent treatment was, that I retained the friendship of many

wise and good men in that country, and among the rest, some share
in the regard of Lord Howe.

"The well-founded esteem, and permit me to say, affection,
which I shall always have for your lordship, makes it painful to
me to see you engaged in conducting a war, the great ground of
which, as expressed in your letter, is 'the necessity of preventing
the American trade from passing into foreign channels.' To me it
seems, that neither the obtaining or retaining of any trade, how
valuable soever, is an object for which men may justly spill each
other's blood; that the true and sure means of extending and securing commerce, is the goodness and cheapness of commodities;
and that the profit of no trade can ever be equal to the expense of
compelling it, and of holding it, by fleets and armies.

"I consider this war against us, therefore, as both unjust and
unwise; and I am persuaded that cool, dispassionate posterity will
condemn to infamy those who advised it; and that even success
will not save from some degree of dishonor those who voluntarily
engaged to conduct it. I know your great motive in coming hither
was the hope of being instrumental in a reconciliation: and I believe, when you find *that* impossible on any terms given you to
propose, you will relinquish so odious a command, and return to a
more honorable private station."

This letter was delivered to Lord Howe ten days after its date,
on board his flag ship in the harbor of New York, by Colonel Palfrey of the American army, who went on board to arrange a plan
for the exchange of naval prisoners. Colonel Palfrey saw the good-
natured Admiral read the letter. "I watched his countenance,"
he wrote the next day to Mr. Hancock, "and observed him often
to exhibit marks of surprise. When he had finished reading it he
said his old friend had expressed himself very warmly; that when
he had the pleasure of seeing him in England, he made him acquainted with his sentiments respecting the dispute between Great
Britain and the colonies, and with his earnest desire that a reconciliation might take place, equally honorable and advantageous to
both. Possessed of these sentiments, and the most ardent desire
to be the means of effecting this union, he had accepted the honor
the king had done him in appointing him one of the commissioners;
and that unfortunately a long passage prevented his arriving here
before the Declaration of Independence. I told him he had now a

fair opportunity to mention to his friend, Dr. Franklin, in a private letter, his design in coming out, and what his expectations from America were. This he declined, saying that the Doctor had grown too warm, and if he expressed his sentiments fully to him, he should only give him pain, which he would wish to avoid."

Three weeks later Lord Howe wrote again to Dr. Franklin, on terms of perfect civility, regretting that he was not to have the advantage of Dr. Franklin's assistance, and professing for him an unabated esteem. To this letter it was not the intention of Franklin to reply, since some members of Congress did not approve his corresponding with a public enemy. Events went their course, meanwhile. The battle of Long Island was fought, and the result was discouraging to the Americans, though far from being decisive of the campaign. If the American army had suffered a partial defeat, its honor had been saved by the gallantry of some of the regiments, and the skillful retreat to New York, where it was still formidable. The moment was deemed by Lord Howe extremely favorable for negotiation, since both sides were still powerful, and either of them could concede much without the concession seeming to be the result of intimidation. He, therefore, paroled General Sullivan, one of the prisoners of war, and sent him to Philadelphia, charged with a verbal message to Congress.

September the second, Congress having been notified of General Sullivan's arrival and errand, ordered him to appear before them and deliver his message. He obeyed both commands. Congress then ordered him to reduce the message to writing, which he did, and presented it on the following day; to this effect :

"Lord Howe could not at present treat with Congress, as such; yet he desired to confer with some of its members, whom he would regard as private gentlemen, and meet at any place they might appoint. He and his brother had full powers to arrange an accommodation on terms advantageous to both countries, the obtaining of which had detained him in England two months, so that he did not arrive in America until after the Declaration of Independence. Nevertheless, if Congress were disposed to treat, many things which they had not yet even asked might and ought to be granted them, and the authority of Congress itself recognized."

Such was the purport of the message brought by General Sullivan. Warm and long debates followed its delivery. John Adams

was of opinion, to use his own language, " that the whole affair of the
commission was a bubble, an ambuscade, a mere insidious maneuver, calculated only to decoy and deceive,", and that no notice whatever ought to be taken of it. After a debate which occupied parts
of three days, Congress agreed to the following : "*Resolved*, That
General Sullivan be requested to inform Lord Howe, that this Congress, being the representatives of the free and independent States of
America, cannot, with propriety, send any of its members to confer
with his lordship in their private characters, but that, ever desirous
of establishing peace on reasonable terms, they will send a committee of their body to know whether he has any authority to treat
with persons authorized by Congress for that purpose on behalf of
America, and what that authority is, and to hear such propositions
as he shall think fit to make respecting the same."

Dr. Franklin, John Adams, and Edward Rutledge were elected
the Committee. Mr. Adams wrote to one of his friends : " All
sides agreed in sending me ;" both the stanch and intrepid friends
of Independence, and his own political opponents, all " pushed for
me, that as little evil might come of it as possible." Dr. Franklin
now answered Lord Howe's last letter, and named " the governor's
house at Amboy, or the house on Staten Island, opposite to Amboy," as places suitable for the conference. Lord Howe preferred
the house on Staten Island, and agreed to send a boat to Amboy
with a flag of truce, and convey the committee to the island.

What a graphic and entertaining narrative Mr. Adams has given
us of the two days' journey of the committee from Philadelphia to
Amboy—himself on horseback, and his companions in chairs! The
second night they lodged at an inn in New Brunswick, whither
were marching bodies of troops for General Washington's army, to
help hold New York. " On the road," says Mr. Adams, " and at
all the public houses, we saw such numbers of officers and soldiers
straggling and and loitering, as gave me, at least, but a poor opinion of the discipline of our forces, and excited as much indignation
as anxiety. Such thoughtless dissipation at a time so critical, was
not calculated to inspire very sanguine hopes, or give great courage
to embassadors. I was, nevertheless, determined that it should not
dishearten me. I saw that we must, and had no doubts but we
should, be chastised into order in time." Mr. Adams remembered
what he had seen.

Owing to the rush of soldiery, the taverns on the way were so full that the committee could scarcely find admission, much less accommodation. At New Brunswick Dr. Franklin and Mr. Adams were compelled to share one bed; of which adventure Mr. Adams has left us a delicious account. " The chamber," he says, " was little larger than the bed, without a chimney, and with only one small window. The window was open, and I, who was an invalid, and afraid of the air of the night, shut it close. ' Oh!' says Franklin, ' don't shut the window, we shall be suffocated.' I answered I was afraid of the evening air. Dr. Franklin replied, ' The air within the chamber will soon be, and indeed is now, worse than that without doors. Come, open the window and come to bed, and I will convince you. I believe you are not acquainted with my theory of colds.' Opening the window and leaping into bed, I said I had read his letters to Dr. Cooper, in which he had advanced that nobody ever got cold by going into a cold church or any other cold air, but the theory was so little consistent with my experience, that I thought it a paradox. However, I had so much curiosity to hear his reasons, that I would run the risk of a cold. The Doctor then began a harangue upon air and cold, and respiration and perspiration, with which I was so much amused that I soon fell asleep, and left him and his philosophy together; but I believe they were equally sound and insensible within a few minutes after me, for the last words I heard pronounced were more than half asleep. I remember little of the lecture, except that the human body, by respiration and perspiration, destroys a gallon of air per minute; that two such persons as were now in that chamber would consume all the air in it in an hour or two; that by breathing over again the matter thrown off by the lungs and skin, we should imbibe the real cause of colds, not from abroad, but from within. I am not inclined to introduce here a dissertation on this subject. There is much truth, I believe, in some things he advanced, but they warrant not the assertion that a cold is never taken from cold air. I have often conversed with him since on the same subject, and I believe with him, that colds are often taken in foul air in close rooms, but they are often taken from cold air abroad, too. I have often asked him whether a person heated with exercise going suddenly into cold air, or standing still in a current of it, might not have his pores suddenly contracted, his perspiration stopped, and that matter thrown into the circulation or cast upon the lungs, which he acknowledged was the cause of colds. To this he could never give me a satisfactory answer."

Resuming their journey the next morning, a ride of a few miles brought them to the beautiful shore opposite Staten Island. Lord Howe's boat was there at the appointed time. In it came over an officer, who informed the committee that he was ordered to remain subject to their orders, a hostage for their safe return. Mr. Adams turned to Dr. Franklin, and said it would be childish in them to depend upon such a pledge, and proposed taking back the officer in the barge. "My colleagues," says our high-minded chronicler, "exulted in the proposition, and agreed to it instantly." The hostage was, accordingly, notified, that if he held himself under their direction, he must go back with them in the boat; to which he bowed assent, and they all embarked.

Lord Howe had made hasty preparations for the entertainment of his expected guests. The house appointed for the interview was a rather large, plain, old-fashioned house of stone, with a veranda in front; the residence of a man of wealth; but, of late, it had been occupied by soldiers, and had become dilapidated and dirty. The house was standing and inhabited as late as 1858, though it was an old house in 1776. One large apartment Lord Howe had caused to be strewn and hung with moss and branches, till he had made it, says Mr. Adams, "not only wholesome, but romantically elegant." In this delightful bower the hospitable representative of the majesty of Britain had ordered to be spread a collation, which consisted, as Mr. Adams records, of "good claret, good bread, cold ham, tongues, and mutton." His preparations complete, the Admiral saw the barges approaching, and walked toward the shore to meet the committee, while the colonel of the Hessian regiment in attendance drew up his men in two lines, so as to form a lane of soldiers from the beach to the house. The barge reached the shore. Lord Howe perceiving his officer with the committee, cried out, "Gentlemen, you make me a very high compliment, and you may depend upon it I will consider it the most sacred of things." He shook hands very cordially with Dr. Franklin, who introduced his companions, and they all moved towards the house conversing pleasantly together. The sight of the Hessians appears to have stirred the wrath of John Adams a little, for he says : " We walked up to the house between lines of guards of grenadiers, looking fierce as ten Furies, making all the grimaces, and gestures, and motions of their muskets with bayonets fixed, which, I suppose, military etiquette requires, but which we neither understood nor regarded." After reaching the apartment prepared, Lord Howe, his secretary, Mr. Henry Strachey, the committee, and the Hessian colonel, all sat down to the collation, and spent an agreeable half hour in discussing the good claret, the good bread, the cold ham, the tongues, and the mutton. The colonel then withdrew, the table was cleared, and the conference began.

Of the conversation which followed we have unusually full information. Besides the report of the interview given to Congress by the committee, and several narratives, more or less complete, from the vivacious pen of John Adams, we now have in New York the minutes of the conversation taken down at the time by Mr. Strachey; whose manuscript, with notes in pencil by Lord Howe himself, is the property of one of our eminent historical collectors.* From all these sources we can now reproduce the conversation with sufficient exactness.

Lord Howe. " Long ago, gentlemen, I entertained the opinion that the differences between the mother-country and her colonies might be accommodated to the satisfaction of both. I was known in England to be a well-wisher to America—particularly to the province of Massachusetts Bay, which had endeared itself to me by the very high honor it had bestowed upon my eldest brother. I assure you, gentlemen, that I esteem that honor to my family above all things in this world. Such is my gratitude and affection to this country on that account, that I feel for America as for a brother, and if America should fall, I should feel and lament it like the loss of a brother."

Dr. Franklin. (" *With an easy air, a collected countenance, a bow, a smile, and all that naiveté which sometimes appeared in his conversation and often in his writings.*"†) " My lord, we will use our utmost endeavors to save your lordship that mortification."

Lord Howe. (*Taking the joke too seriously, but suppressing his feelings.*) " I suppose you will endeavor to give us employment in

---

* MR. GEORGE H. MOORE, Secretary and Librarian of the New York Historical Society, who obligingly gave me a copy of this most interesting relic.
† John Adams.

Europe." (*Dead silence on the part of the committee, and counte-nances blank. Lord Howe recovers from the digression.*) "My going out as commissioner from the king was talked of long ago, as Dr. Franklin is aware. After his departure, I heard no more of it for a long time. Then an idea arose of sending over several commissioners, but to this I objected, for my plan was to go alone, with only a civil commission, and proceed straight to Philadelphia, and meet the Congress face to face. I objected even to my brother's being in the commission, from the delicacy of the employment, and from my desire to take upon myself all the reproach that might be the consequence of it. It was thought best, however, that General Howe, being in command of the army in America, should be joined in the commission, and that I should have the naval command; since, in that case, the two commissioners would control the move-ments of both forces. I acquiesced in this arrangement. I hoped to reach America before the army had made a movement to begin the campaign, and had no doubt that if the disposition of Congress remained the same as expressed in their last petition to the king, I should be able to bring about an accommodation. That petition, I thought, was a sufficient basis to confer upon; as it contained matter which, with candor and discussion, might be wrought into a permanent system. True, the Address to the People, which ac-companied the petition to his majesty, had injured the effect of the petition. Nevertheless, to the moment of my arrival in America, I flattered myself that, taking the petition as a basis, I should be able to do some good. But since I left England, you have your-selves changed your ground by the Declaration of Independency. That act, gentlemen, if it cannot be got over, precludes all treaty-making; for, as you are aware, I have not, nor do I expect ever to have, powers to consider the colonies in the light of independent States. You must be sensible, also, that I cannot confer with Con-gress. I cannot acknowledge a body which is not acknowledged by the king, whose delegate I am, and, for the same reason, I can-not confer with you, gentlemen, as a committee of the Congress. If you are unwilling to lay aside that distinction, it will be im-proper for me to proceed. That, however, I trust, you will regard as an unessential form, which may for a moment lie dormant, and give me leave to consider you merely as gentlemen of great ability and influence in the country, who have met here to converse with me, and try if we can devise the outline of a plan to stay the calamities of war.   I beg you to consider the delicacy of my situation, and the reproach I should be liable to if I should be understood, by any act of mine, to have treated with the Congress or acknowledged its authority. I hope you will not, by any implication, commit me upon that point. Even in the present meeting I have gone rather beyond my powers."

Dr. Franklin. "You may depend upon our taking care of that, my lord."

Lord Howe. "I think the idea of a Congress may easily be thrown out at present; because, if matters can be so settled that the king's government is re-established, the Congress would of course cease to exist. And if you really mean an accommodation of that kind, you must see how unnecessary it is to stand upon a form which you are negotiating to give up."

Dr. Franklin. "Your lordship may consider us in any view you think proper. We, on our part, are at liberty to consider ourselves in our real character. But there is, really, no necessity on this occasion to distinguish between members of Congress and individuals. The conversation may be held as among friends."

Mr. Adams. "Your lordship may consider *me* in what light you please. Indeed, I should be willing to consider myself for a few moments in any character which would be agreeable to your lordship, *except that* of a *British subject*."

Lord Howe. (*With gravity.*) "Mr. Adams is a decided character."

Mr. Rutledge. "I think, with Dr. Franklin, that the conversation may be as among friends."

Lord Howe. "On my arrival in this country, gentlemen, I thought it expedient to issue a Declaration, which one of you has done me the honor to comment upon. I endeavored to couch it in such terms as would be least exceptionable, and I conclude you must have supposed I did not express in it all I had to offer. I thought, however, that I said enough to bring on a discussion which might lead the way to accommodation. But the Declaration of Independency has since rendered me more cautious of opening myself, for it is absolutely impossible for me to treat, or even confer upon that ground, or to admit the idea in the smallest degree. If that is given up, I flatter myself there is still room for me to effect the king's purpose.   His majesty's most earnest desire is to make his American subjects happy, to cause a reform in whatever affected the freedom of their legislation, and to concur with his Parliament in the redress of any real grievances.   My powers are, speaking generally, to restore peace and grant pardons, to attend to complaints and representations, and to confer upon the means of a reunion upon terms honorable and advantageous to the colonies and to Great Britain.   You know, gentlemen, that we expect aid from America; our dispute seems only to be concerning the mode of obtaining it."

Dr. Franklin. " Aid we never refused upon *requisition*."

Lord Howe. " Your money, let me assure you, is the smallest consideration.   America can confer upon Great Britain more solid advantages; it is her commerce, her strength, her men, that we chiefly want."

Dr. Franklin. " Ay, my lord, we have in America a pretty considerable manufactory of *men*."*

Lord Howe. " It is desirable to put a stop to these ruinous extremities, as well for the sake of our country as yours.   When an American falls, England feels it.   The question is: Is there no way of treating back of this step of Independency, and thus opening the door to a full discussion?   Now, gentlemen, having opened to you the general purport of my commission, and the king's disposition to a permanent peace, I must stop to hear what you may choose to observe."

Dr. Franklin. " I suppose your lordship has seen the Resolution of the Congress which has sent us hither.   It authorizes us to inquire what authority your lordship bears, and what propositions you have to offer for the consideration of the Congress.   That Resolution contains the whole of our commission.   Nevertheless, this conversation, if productive of no immediate good effect, may be of service at a future time.   I will therefore say, that America considered the Prohibitory Act as the answer to her last petition to the king.   Forces have been sent out, and towns have been burnt. We cannot now expect happiness under the domination of Great Britain.   All former attachments are obliterated.   America cannot

---

* Mr. Strachey, misunderstanding this remark, added these words: "alluding as should seem to their numerous army." Lord Howe, more used to Dr. Franklin's manner, corrected his secretary by penciling on the margin: "No; their increasing population."

return to the domination of Great Britain, and I imagine that Great Britain means to rest it upon force. The other gentlemen will doubtless deliver their sentiments."

Mr. Adams. "The resolution of the Congress which declared Independency was not taken up upon its own authority. Congress had been instructed so to do by all the colonies. It is not in our power, therefore, my lord, to treat otherwise than as independent states, and, for my own part, I avow my determination never to depart from the idea of Independency."

Mr. Rutledge. "I am one of the oldest members of the Congress, my lord, having been a member from the beginning. I think it is worth the consideration of Great Britain whether she would not derive greater advantages from an alliance with the colonies as independent states than she has hitherto done. England may still enjoy a great share of the American commerce, and so procure raw materials for her manufactures. Besides: the United States can protect the West India Islands more effectually and more easily than England can, to say nothing of the New Foundland fishery; while the products both of the West Indies and of New Foundland would continue to enrich the merchants of England. I am glad this conversation has occurred, as it will be the occasion of opening to Great Britain the consideration of the advantages she may derive from an alliance with America before any thing is settled with *other* foreign powers. With regard to the people consenting to come again under the English government, it is impossible. I can answer for South Carolina. The royal government there was very oppressive. The officers of the crown claimed 'privilege,' and confined people for breaches of 'privilege.' At last we took the government into our own hands, and the people are now settled and happy under that government. They would not, even if the Congress should desire it, return to the king's government."

Lord Howe. "If such are your sentiments, gentlemen, I can only lament that it is not in my power to bring about the accommodation I wish. I have not authority, nor do I ever expect to have, to treat with the colonies as states independent of the crown of Great Britain. I am sorry, gentlemen, that you have had the trouble of coming so far to so little purpose. If the colonies will not give up the system of independency, it is impossible for me to enter into any negotiation."

Dr. Franklin. "It would take as much time for us to refer to and and get answers from our constituents, as it would the royal com¹ missioners to get fresh instructions from home, which, I suppose, might be about three months."

Lord Howe. "It is in vain to think of my receiving instructions to treat upon that ground."

Dr. Franklin. (*After a pause.*) "Well, my lord, as America is to expect nothing but upon unconditional submission"—

Lord Howe. (*Interrupting him.*) "No, Dr. Franklin. Great Britain does not require unconditional submission. I think that what I have already said proves the contrary, and I desire, gentlemen, that you will not go away with such an idea."

Dr. Franklin. "As your lordship has no proposition to make to us, give me leave to ask whether, if *we* should make propositions to Great Britain (not that I know, or am authorized to say we shall), you would receive and transmit them?"

Lord Howe. "I do not know that I could avoid receiving any papers that should be put into my hands, though I am doubtful of the propriety of transmitting them home. Still, I do not say that I would decline doing so."

The conference ended. Lord Howe politely attended the committee to the barge, which bore them, in a few minutes, to the shore of New Jersey. Two days after the committee gave to Congress a brief account of the conversation, and reported that, "upon the whole, it did not appear that his lordship's commission contained any other authority than that expressed in the act of Parliament, namely, that of granting pardons, with such exceptions as the commissioners should think proper to make, and of declaring America, or any part of it, to be in the king's peace, upon submission." Congress, therefore, ordered the committee to publish their report in the newspapers, and took no further action upon it. The practical result of the affair was the furnishing of a new topic for the oratory of Mr. John Adams. He tells us, in his Autobiography, that during his journey to Amboy, he observed such dissipation and idleness, such confusion and distraction among officers and soldiers, as astonished, grieved, and alarmed him. Hitherto his incessant cry had been Independence, Independence, Independence! Henceforward it was Discipline, Discipline, Discipline! The reward of his exertions was the adoption by Congress of the British Discipline and articles of war, which, to this hour, constitute the substance of the military system of the United States.

The conference with Lord Howe closed the ancient account between the thirteen colonies and Great Britain. England would not treat with independent America. It was now to be ascertained whether there was, in any part of the world, a Power that would.

CHAPTER VI.

A LONG LETTER ARRIVES FROM FRANCE.

No news yet from over the sea. Mr. Thomas Story had been gone eight months; M. Penet, seven months; Mr. Silas Deane, five months, and no letters from them had reached the Committee of Secret Correspondence, except, perhaps, one from Mr. Deane written at the Bermudas, recommending Congress to seize and fortify that convenient little group. From Arthur Lee, not a word. Nothing from the zealous Dumas. From the enthusiastic Dubourg, nothing. No whisper from the mysterious French officer who was so solicitous for the safety of his head.

This was not very surprising, for, even in peaceful years, an answer could seldom be obtained from Europe in less than four or five months; and now, to all the usual perils and delays, were added those arising from the cruisers of the first naval power in the world. During the first three years of the revolutionary war, it was only with the greatest difficulty that Congress maintained any communication at all with their servants in Europe. When Congress had as many as twelve paid agents on that continent, all of whom wrote by every opportunity, and some of whom were authorized to make opportunities, and actually did attempt to start a packet once a month, there was one period of eleven months during which Congress had not a line from one of them. Silas Deane, too, was in Europe five months before he received a letter from the Committee which employed him.

And so the whole summer of 1776 passed away, and Congress knew not whether their infant nation had, or had not, a friend on the other side of the ocean. The campaign had been disastrous. The battle of Long Island had been followed by the loss of the city of New York, which involved the evacuation of Manhattan Island, and the retreat into Westchester. Some instances of bad behavior on the part of the troops had occurred during these operations, and some invaluable officers had fallen. These events, it must be owned, had cast a gloom over the country, and had made many men seriously doubt whether, after all, the thirteen states had not undertaken a task which was beyond their unassisted strength. Judge, then, with what a longing anxiety the Secret Committee, Congress, General Washington, and all well-informed men, waited to hear from the old world during these two months of calamity, August and September. It is often said that the path of virtue is one of pleasantness and peace, and there is, doubtless, a certain truth in the remark. Nevertheless, it often happens, both in the lives of men and of nations, that a great step in the right direction, a great, valiant, virtuous RESOLVE, is quickly followed by disaster. Long the colonies lingered on the brink of Independence. After they had taken the plunge, they experienced little but discouragement and calamity for many months. The true path *leads* to peace and pleasantness, but it is itself steep, narrow, obstructed, and thorny.

At length, however, the painful suspense was relieved by an arrival from France with most cheering intelligence. It came in the form of an astonishingly long letter from Dr. Dubourg to Dr. Franklin; who hastened to communicate its contents to Congress, and caused a translation of it to be instantly dispatched to General Washington, to encourage him in his unequal strife with the armies and fleets of Britain. Even now, this long letter entertains the reader. With what intensity of interest must it have been read in September, 1776! In no way, perhaps, can the reader of these pages begin to be informed more agreeably of the state of things in France, than by the perusal of this lively epistle. Dr. Dubourg, it will be easily perceived, was engaged in affairs to which he was unaccustomed, and, perhaps, unequal. He was a physician of established repute in Paris; a writer of some note; a merry old bachelor, who was welcome in the gay circles for his wit and anecdote, and dear to the philosophers because he loved them. He was full of the "sentiment" of the day; he was one of those republicans of the *salon* so numerous then at Paris, who followed the fortunes of the new Republic with an interest that may, without exaggeration, be called passionate. His enthusiasm carried him away. His letter will enable every reader to understand something of the scene to which Dr. Franklin was himself soon to be transferred, and to make allowance for the errors committed by some who served America in France during the revolutionary period. M. Dubourg, though well informed, was not acquainted with what had transpired in the councils of France respecting America. Few men of that generation were. It is only since Mr. Bancroft, Mr. Sparks, M. de Loménie, and one or two English cotemporaries, have been admitted to peruse and copy the secret records of the French cabinet, that the truth respecting the assistance rendered by France to struggling America has been disclosed. Good old Dr. Dubourg, a man of better heart than head, shall tell the reader all he knew, and to that we may add, by and by, the secrets he would gladly have known. It would be easy to shorten this long epistle, but the passages that most invite the erasive pen are precisely those which elucidate most the future course of the American embassadors, and best excuse the errors of some of them.

Dr. Dubourg to Dr. Franklin:

"PARIS, *June* 10, 1776.

"MY DEAR MASTER:—After being long deprived of it I had at length the pleasure of receiving news on the 4th of May, directly from you, by M. Penet's arriving from Philadelphia. He told me you had intrusted him with a letter and some papers to be delivered to me; but that he had left all his packets at Rotterdam, fearing that they might be intercepted on the journey from Holland to France. This, at first, gave me some inquietude. I hardly dared open myself to him. However, all his answers to my different questions appeared so satisfactory, that I did not longer hesitate to converse with him in the most unreserved manner.

"He astonished me much when he told me that not only the people of the Thirteen United Colonies, but even the Congress, and you yourself, doubted much of the disposition of the Court of France with regard to you, and that you had apprehensions from its connections with the Court of London. When I assured him that all the wishes of our nation in general, and more especially of the Ministry, were in favor of the insurgents, I saw upon his coun-

tenance such a natural diffusion of joy as completely determined me
to confide in him.

"The next day, the 5th of May, I conducted him to Versailles,
that I might convince him, in turn, that I was not under an illusion
myself upon a subject so important. I led him to converse with
our friend Du Pont, who was, as you may have known, the most
confidential intimate of M. Turgot, then Comptroller-general of
Finance, and who told us, among other things, that one of their
most anxious thoughts was, that the Congress might not fail in its
operations through want of money. He even added, that they had
considered together by what means they might, without entering
into the quarrel, procure credit for so unhappy and interesting a
people. That conversation alone quite sufficed to dissipate all the
fears of M. Penet. In consequence, he suddenly took his determination, which was to continue his route as far as Nantes, without
even going back to Paris, if I would undertake the care of American affairs, as well at Paris as at Court, while, in correspondence
with me, he would go to all the ports, and-among the different
manufactures, where the advantage of the same service might call
him.

"He had assured me, from the instant of his arrival, that you had
recommended him to apply to me upon all occasions, and not to
confide in any but such persons as I would answer for, and, as
much as possible, to concert all his operations with me. I was disposed, as you may well think, to second him in every thing within
my power, in a cause in which I have always been so sanguine as
to draw upon me in this country a sort of nickname, at which I do
not hold myself offended. But your envoy demanded of me more
than I thought myself able to promise him, since he wanted to leave
me alone charged with all the business in this city. Moreover, the
conjuncture appeared to me very delicate.

"How should I undertake a long train of weighty affairs and
important negotiations upon the simple word of a stranger, though
calling himself the bearer of letters, which he could not produce?
How should I announce myself to numbers of men, in places known
and unknown, to treat about the affairs of a distant people, without
being furnished with credentials? And, supposing even the necessity of plunging myself into a torrent of circumstances, as essential as they are critical; supposing the possibility of finding every-

where a favorable access, and of being even listened to with confidence by all those with whom I should have to treat, although presenting myself without title and without mission; yet how should I acquit myself, in this work of supererogation, without neglecting the duties which my profession lays upon me, and without exposing myself to lose entirely the position from which I principally gain my living?

"These reflections threw me into a dilemma. But my attachment to you and your respectable friends; my gratitude for the sentiments of kindness with which you have inspired your countrymen towards me; my zeal for the cause of justice, of liberty, and of humanity; in fine, the very necessity of the conjuncture, wherein Providence seemed to have specially intended me, in default of others, for so honorable and indispensable a service, carried my mind above all private considerations, and made me regard it as a sacred duty to devote myself, without reserve, to what was demanded of me in your name. And from that instant I have looked upon myself as the eventual depository of the confidence of the United Colonies of America. I have striven to go through all the functions of a faithful and zealous agent, and I shall thus proceed till their true representatives disavow me. I compare my situation to that of one who, having perceived himself to be the only person at hand to collect precious effects after a shipwreck or a fire, watches more scrupulously over that enforced charge, than over what passes at the same moment in his own house.

"Knowing that United America had pressing need of a certain kind of men, and a certain species of provisions, I have exerted myself to procure both the one and the other for her. I have knocked (if I may so express myself) at every door for that end; I have talked vaguely to some, enigmatically to others; I have half confided to many, and as little as possible have I wholly confided in any one whatever, except the king's ministers and a nephew, of whom I am thoroughly satisfied, and whom I have drawn from his own province on purpose to second me in every thing. I have had the satisfaction of being well received in every quarter, and of seeing that no one demands other assurances than my own word to treat with me upon affairs of the greatest consequence, and concerning which I freely acknowledge to have received neither full power, nor even the least commission or instruction, by word of

mouth any more than by letter.   Ministers to whom I had never
made my court have given me the most flattering marks of confidence from my first interview; have talked to me without winding
or mystery; have discussed with me the weightiest matters; and
have deliberated with me the plans to be pursued, and the means
to accomplish them.   Private individuals, merchants, military men,
and others, have attended without scruple to take from me condi-
tional arrangements, promising to execute them when it shall be
required, though I had declared to them, on my part, that I could
not warrant any thing at all positively.

"On the other hand, I have sometimes been ill directed, and have
been in danger of making a bad choice, or bad purchases, if I had not
kept myself watchfully on my guard, and if I had not drawn information from several quarters upon every affair.   You would hardly
think, for example, that a very friendly minister should point out
and recommend to me for saltpetre and for small-arms, such magazines and salesmen whose saltpetre was too dear, and whose arms
were defective.   Far from taking it ill that I made very different
contracts, he thanked me for the intelligence I gave him.

"I have been six (and three times more in the latter part of
June) different times to Versailles within a month, to see not only
the ministers, but every one who approaches them or continues
near them, and to sound or get sounded the dispositions of every
one; for it must not be thought that they are all equally well-intentioned; however, I wanted to draw some advantage from all.
And, in fact, though I had rather praise some than others, yet
there is not one of whom I could complain without ingratitude.

"I have obtained, among other things, in behalf of M. De la
Tuillerie, the undertaker of a manufactory of arms, that there shall
be delivered to him immediately from the king's arsenals fifteen
thousand muskets for the use of infantry, according to the model of
1763, to be employed in his business on condition that he replaces
them in the course of a year by a like number of new muskets of
his own make, giving good and sufficient security for such return;
and they have taken my security.   The first part of these muskets
are already on the route to Nantes, where M. Penet is looking for
the vessels which your Secret Committee is to send thither.   I hope
your brave soldiers will be pleased with these muskets; but you
must caution them not to trust to the ordinary muskets of com-

merce, called "muskets for exportation," which are almost as dangerous to friends as to enemies.

"I could have obtained brass cannon on the same terms without difficulty, were it not for the circumstance of their bearing the king's arms and cipher, which made them too discoverable. However, if I had been authorized by Congress to insist strongly on it, the L. L. and the fleurs de lis might have been taken off by the file; but all this could not have been executed without expense; and who was to have advanced that? M. Turgot, the only minister from whom I could expect so much favor, had been disgraced the 12th of May, and all the others are so perplexed at this time by the extraordinary cabals of the Court, that each one is too hurried by the care of supporting himself, to take as his proper charge the affairs of the public, which are not absolutely and immediately in his own department. All will kindly listen to a just and honorable cause, but none will espouse it with warmth. It is useless to represent to them the great interest which France has in not losing the opportunity of stripping England of an immense commerce, and of drawing to herself what must certainly increase from year to year; they easily comprehend all this; but France, over head and ears in debt, wants bread, and it is their interest to support her. They would have permitted me to take secretly, from even the Arsenal of Paris, powder and lead, saltpeter, &c., if we had not found as good, and upon better terms, among the merchants, and even in greater quantities than M. Penet has orders to ship.

"I have obtained long furloughs for officers of artillery, and others, and have been promised the like for all such as may be necessary for us, and whom I can make enter into my views. Numbers of good officers are presented to me from every quarter, who ask nothing better than to enter into the service of the colonies, if I was authorized to promise the rank they wish, or such as it is common to give to those who are sent hence to the Indies. But I believe this is what you have the least need of, as it may disgust your valiant countrymen. I have, however, ventured to promise the rank of captain, with some little advances, and his passage, to M. Fareli, an old Lieutenant of Foot, one of those who are called "Soldiers of Fortune;" the same, with the exception of rank, to M. Davin, an old sergeant-major, of great distinction; and his passage only to M. Bois Bertrand, a youth full of honor, courage, and zeal, who was here a brevet lieutenant-colonel, but who insists upon nothing, and whom your generals will place as they shall judge most for the greatest service of your affairs. I regret having nothing to promise to an old officer, under the patronage of M. Turgot, and who has been employed under his brother at Cayenne; but especially to two Irish officers, Messrs. Geoghegan. One of them, whom I have long known, has been, during the last two wars, aidde-camp to a general officer, now Marshal of France, who valued him highly. He is only a brevet lieutenant-colonel of cavalry, but I think him capable of any thing. His cousin has shown himself more advantageously still; when he was only a captain in India, he found himself at the head of a little army, all the superior officers being absent, for good or bad reasons; and he had the fortune, after a well-managed march, to gain a victory over the English. You will readily judge that these two expect to be made general officers.

"With regard to Engineers, there are a number of supernumeraries in France. I have retained two of them upon the single assurance of free passage, and a good recommendation to you. One is M. Potten, of Baldivia, very young, but well-instructed, and a son of a Chevalier of St. Louis, an engineer in the service of the Duke of Orleans, and formerly aid-de-camp to Marshal Saxe; the other is M. Gillet de Lomont, a young man of rare merit, and who wants only an opportunity of practicing in war what he has learned in peace. But engineers who have served in the wars with reputation, are all in places where they are content with their lot. You know that the artillerists and engineers have the greatest affinity with each other. Perhaps you may not know that those two corps have been alternately united and separated here, by different Ministers, so that one may well supply the place of the other. And military men agree in thinking that, in the present situation of the colonies, there is much greater need of officers of artillery than of engineers. This is particularly the opinion of the most capable judge in Europe—the Count de St. Germain. I am well assured of the good disposition of some officers of artillery, active, experienced, and wise. But I have another embarrassment. M. de Gribauval, Lieutenant-General of the King's armies, and Director-General of the Artillery of France, and, consequently, at the head of that corps, and enjoying the highest public esteem, with whom I have had many conferences on this subject, is of opinion that you ought to have three officers of artillery over at a time—one to be chief, and set the whole agoing ; the two others to direct all the operations—one in the Northern Colonies, and one in the Southern. For the chief, he has fixed his eyes, in concert with the minister, upon an officer still in the flower of his age, who is judged equally capable of the whole and of the details, and who has already proved his great talents in Corsica, where every thing was trusted to him, he having been raised over the heads of one hundred and eighty senior officers. I send you herewith a plan, drawn up by the gentleman in question, Monsieur Du Coudray, officer of artillery, which appears to me a very good one ; but I thought, at the same time, to let you know that many persons are less prejudiced in his favor, not only in the corps of artillery, where they are jealous of him, but also out of that corps, as he is engaged in very warm controversies with the military, the chemists, and with Monsieur Buffon.

"Among other officers of artillery who might be persuaded to pass over to America, I particularly distinguish two brothers Messrs. D'Hangest—one a lieutenant-colonel of artillery and Chevalier of St. Louis, the other a captain of artillery, who has also seen action, and is a Chevalier of St. Louis. These Messrs. D'Hangest are brothers-in-law to Monsieur D'Antic, the man in France, perhaps, whom it is most for the interest of America to secure. All agree in thinking him the only one possessed both of the theory and practice of all the arts relative to chemistry, especially glass-making and metallurgy. This learned artist has been cheated by most crafty financiers. Monsieur Turgot proposed to give him the whole direction of all the manufactures of France, if he had continued in place. Monsieur D'Antic is himself in difficulties, being encumbered with a wife and four children, as well as a patrimony loaded with clamorous debts. Gentlemen, whom I believe of your acquaintance, have made him very advantageous offers ; Mr. Hutton, chief of the Moravian Brethren, and Mr. Johnston, to draw him to England ; M. Voltravers to attach him to the Elector Palatine; others form projects to fix him here ; others, in fine, would have him go into Spain ; but I have absolutely fixed him to give you the preference, if you can provide a suitable situation for him. He cannot engage to pass over into the New World, unless you can advance him here twenty thousand crowns of France, making two thousand five hundred pounds' sterling, to clear his goods, and to secure the condition of his family. If he obtains that, he will immediately set off. A crowd of workmen of all sorts will press to follow him ; and you may be certain, in a manner, that this single transmigration would advance all the arts an age in your country. I send you herewith a small memorial, drawn up in concert with him.

"Another person, who would be scarcely less useful to you, is more than half determined to go over to America, to set up there a manufacture of arms, such as is not in Europe, if you can provide the means of transporting him with security. He is rich ; he is extremely expert in his branch ; he is discontented with the court. It is Monsieur De Montieux, formerly undertaker of the Royal Manufacture of Arms, at St. Stephen's in the Forrest, who has been involved in the famous lawsuit with M. Belle-garde, Inspector-General of Artillery, his brother-in-law. This worthy man has ready two small ships of his own, twenty-two finished brass field-pieces, and materials ready for one hundred more. All those who have worked under him would follow him in a crowd. He would take with him all the necessary tools and materials. You have only to speak, and to show how you could secure his safe passage, to what place he should proceed, and what aids could be given to him in his establishments. After our several conversations together, he formed another speculative plan, for forcing a passage through all the cruisers of the English marine, if the Colonies could advance two or three millions of francs for such a decisive expedition. I send you herewith the memorial, which he drew up upon that subject. Also, I have reflected on methods of supporting the vast expenses of your rising Republic.

"The packets which M. Penet mentioned to me have not come to hand in six weeks (this 19th of June), they contain charts of the colonies, plans, pamphlets, a letter from you, and another from Mr. Rush. But I have received, and have several times read, the contract in parchment passed between the Secret Committee of Congress on one part, and Messrs. Plianne, Penet & Co., on the other part, with the instructions of the same committee to the said Commissioners. Upon these authentic proofs M. Penet has given all the explanations which I could desire, and has laid before me his various projects of operation. These appear to me judicious and well concerted. I made him return from Nantes, that I might present him secretly to Monsieur the Count de V., Minister for Foreign Affairs, who wanted to examine him upon the affairs of your colonies. He returned some days after, but, in the interval, we determined together upon further steps to be pursued. In consequence, I have made arrangements with the company of Farmers-General to furnish them directly by commission from the United Colonies with the necessary provision of tobacco for the annual consumption of this kingdom, which they drew heretofore by way of England; thereby saving, on one hand and the other, all that the custom-house and the merchants of Great Britain gained, as well upon the American sales as upon the French purchases. I was extremely satisfied with the frankness with which the Farmers-General, appointed on this occasion, treated with me; opening all their books and showing the original entries. I have proposed to Monsieur de S., Minister of the Marine, to furnish meal and sea-biscuit, timber for ships (and, in course, lumber for cooperage), flax, pitch, tar, &c. He assured me that he should not examine where I procured them for him, provided I did it for him, and for a reasonable price; and that I might take my steps in consequence. But I will not dissemble or conceal from you that I have found this Minister under some mercantile prejudices, which I must combat, and from which I shall find some difficulty to recover him, because they have been suggested to him by such as are reputed to be the most skillful merchants, and who have, or think they have, an interest in maintaining ancient prejudices on such points. I have, however, shaken him a little. He has directed me to throw out, in a small written memoire, my particular ideas upon those articles whereon we differ most; he will give this memoire for the discussion of some skillful merchants, or the Deputies of Commerce; after which he will weigh definitively the reasons on one side and the other. I shall join herewith that memoire, when I shall have shown it to him.

"I have taken the advice of many trading people for a contract of grain, peltries, indigo, whalebone, and spermaceti, and in general all the wares and productions of your climate. And we can flatter ourselves with producing for you a greater advantage than you have ever made. I am still more sure of being able to procure for you in return all the European merchandise which you want, as wine, oil, cloths, linens, drugs, mercury, and hardware, on better terms than you have them from England, because France produces more, and labor is cheaper. I have already an intelligent and vigorous agent, who goes through all the manufactories of needles and pins in Normandy, etc., to put himself soon in a condition of establishing one in Pennsylvania, to which place, upon the encouragement which I have led him to hope for, he intends to proceed, and render himself useful to the Americans, and to build for himself a good house. It appears from the instructions that, next to military stores, your most pressing wants are for needles and pins.

" M. Penet appears a faithful, active, intelligent man, and very much the connoisseur in arms of every kind ; but I have been led to think that your committee, not knowing him sufficiently to trust him with large pecuniary funds, would only engage themselves to repay amply his advances ; and he is not in a condition to do great things in that way, however good his disposition is therefor. This is what retards all the operations, which might have been much accelerated if you had somebody here duly authorized to make bargains, and to pass engagements for their execution in the name of the Thirteen United Colonies, on terms which would be readily acceptable.

" I have learned from our ministers that you have given orders at Liege for having field-pieces cast there. If we had received a commission for them here, we could have had better cast here than at Liege, and could have sent them to you with more ease.

" Further, I have lately had under my eye the state of the cannon in all the arsenals of France, and I have been convinced that there is a superabundance of all bores, and particularly twelve hundred four-pounders. There are scarcely five hundred in actual employ, and about seven hundred pieces without any precise destination. Thus, perhaps, it may not be very difficult for us to' borrow, secretly, two or three hundred, on condition of replacing them ; and these four-pounders are exactly those from which the greatest advantage may be had in the field, where they go at the head of regiments. If you adopt this idea, be so kind as to send us powers in due form ; and to add an assurance of replacing them, either by silver, or merchandise, or bills of exchange, or paper money of the Congress.

" If I could only answer affimatively upon any one of those heads
for a fixed term, you should be left to want nothing.   Stripped of
every means of that kind, we are obliged to reduce ourselves to
send you only a little at a time, by vessels which shall arrive from
your ports ; muskets, powder, lead, flints, saltpeter, and some sub-
altern officers of artillery, chief workmen, founders, armorers, etc.

" June 29th.   M. D'Hangest, the elder, came from La Fere to
this city, on purpose to confer with me upon the means and conditions of his passage to America ; but after having consulted a common friend, in company and separately, we found that better could
be done for him and for us; therefore he returned to his employment.

" It remains for us to choose between two men, and such as I
doubt whether a third like them can be found in Europe of their
profession : one is the M. Du Coudray of whom I have before spoken to you in this letter, and for whom my esteem does but increase ; the other is the famous Chevalier De Tot, who, the day
before yesterday, arrived from Constantinople, where, by the report
of all the Gazettes, he has conducted the artillery of the Turks
much better than could have been hoped; established founderies
for cannon, erected batteries, and constructed fortifications, especially at the straits of the Dardanelles, which he rendered secure
against the invasion of the Russians, very powerful then in the
Mediterranean.   Artists do not think altogether so advantageously
of him; and they regard him as excellent perhaps in Turkey, but
indifferent elsewhere.   However, I should not think I made you a
bad present in sending him.

" In what remains, I shall manage your interests the best way in
my power; but you easily conceive that either of these two men
must be purchased at a very high rate.

" The Chevalier De Tot boasts of having exhibited himself with
the greatest eclat.   M. Du Coudray, by his credit with the minister in the War Department, being in the way of rendering you
greater services than any one else, does not fail to set value upon
that circumstance.   I have seen him often lately to concert how we
may get the loan of some hundreds of field-pieces (cannon or
howitzers), and we are not without hopes of succeeding therein.
I strove to avail myself, for that purpose, of the protection of the
Count D'Aranda, formerly minister of Spain, and now embassa-

dor here.   He showed me much kindness, but important considerations do not permit him to risk a dispute with the French ministry.   Though M. Penet has positively authorized me, by word of
mouth and by writing, to exercise for him and as himself the powers which he has received from your Secret Committee, my mind
is not altogether easy at his not having delivered to me the letter
which you did me the honor to write with your own hand.   In
this perplexity, I have conceived the idea of opening a correspondence with Mr. Arthur Lee, your deputy at London, from whom I
might have frequent intelligence.   Not being known to him, I
have had recourse to the Count de Lamagnais, with whom he is in
connection, to get him to send my first letter.   I have just received one from M. Penet ; he is aiming to procure for the colony
of Virginia twelve pieces of cannon, six-pounders ; that bore is not
common here ; however, we will strive to find them.

"The time is not yet come to speak to you of a musket of new
construction, more simple, and, it is hoped, not less solid; there
will also be a saving in the price.   The inventor (named Reynard)
led me to expect the model, day by day, more than a month ; he
tells me at length that it is finished, and the proof of it will be
made next week, with the most scrupulous exactness, under the
eye of M. De Gribauval, who is pleased to attend it, and who, in
case of success, will be charmed that the first employment of it
should be consecrated to the cause of liberty, of justice, and of
humanity, and that they should not be made use of for the service
of the French armies till after yours shall be abundantly provided
with them.

"July 1st.   I have not yet received the much desired packet
from Rotterdam ; and I must this day close this letter, which I
shall send by M. De Bois Bertrand, who goes post haste to-morrow
to embark at Nantes.   God grant that he may soon deliver it to
you.

"Be assured that I have not trusted it to him till after being
convinced, by good warrants, of his fidelity, his courage, and his
wisdom.   He has given me his word of honor that at least it shall
not fall into the enemy's hands, though such a chance should happen to himself.   He would have given me his oath for it, if I laid
stress upon oaths; but I have never regarded them otherwise than
as the last resource of liars.   Were it not for that, I would swear,

in this within your hands, a full homage and inviolable fidelity to the august Congress of the most respectable Republic which has ever existed. But my attachment to you answers sufficiently for my devotedness to that. May it long enjoy a subject such as you, and produce likenesses of you from generation to generation! And may my services be agreeable to it in an under rank to yours. I would die contented could I see my country and yours intimately united; and could I contribute towards it, I should be at the summit of my wishes.

"I am, with the most perfect esteem, and most tender affection, sir and dear friend, your very humble, and very obedient servant,
"BARBUE DUBOURG.

"As it is very doubtful if these dispatches will reach you, since the sea is porcupined with English cruisers, I have ordered two other copies, which I shall send by two different ships, so that one of the three at least may arrive safely to you.

"July 2d. M. De Bois Bertrand takes at his own charge two subalterns of thorough bravery and irreproachable conduct, of whom may be made very good officers, if they shall be wanted, as is to be presumed. As to him, I have led him to expect the rank of Colonel, from the persuasion I have that he would fill it well, to the satisfaction of your Generals. I have, nevertheless, been upon my guard with him as to giving an absolute promise; but I must observe to you that it is the constant usage here to advance one grade every officer who is sent over to the Indies.

"As to what regards M. Du Coudray and M. De Tot, as I must have taken far too much upon me to make either one or the other to proceed immediately, I thought myself obliged to wait your orders on that head.

"P. S.—I open my letter to tell you that within an hour I have learned some things which make me abate the character which I gave you of M. Montieux. Adieu, fare you well, be prosperous, you and yours, and know that not one in the world is more devoted to you."*

Such was the letter of the worthy Dr. Dubourg; such his overflowing zeal for the country of his friend and "master." The rash engagements into which he had entered, and might enter, were little

---

* "American Archives," Fourth Series, vi., 771.

thought of in the joy excited by the great news he had transmitted which surpassed the hopes of the most sanguine. That the French government should even permit the operations of M. Penet and Dr. Dubourg was a hopeful sign; but the Count de Vergennes had gone the length of seeking an interview with them, and had dismissed them without rebuke. What might not be expected when Mr. Deane, the authorized representative and commissioner of Congress, should exhibit his credentials to the minister? The coming over of so many officers of high rank and higher pretensions would be embarrassing, but there was time to prevent that, and, probably, no one supposed they would venture to cross the ocean unless expressly invited to do so by Congress.

Congress now resolved to send to France an imposing embassy; imposing in the number and the character of its members. It should consist of three persons, to be chosen by ballot. The election occurred on the twenty-sixth of September. Members had already pledged in writing their honor to divulge nothing of what occurred in Congress, except what Congress should order to be made public, and on this occasion they were reminded anew of the infinite and peculiar importance of secrecy. It was difficult enough to elude Lord Howe's cruisers, without stimulating the admiral to greater vigilance by the prospect of capturing commissioners to a foreign court. On the first ballot, as was foreseen, Dr. Franklin was unanimously elected. When the result of the balloting was announced, he is reported to have turned to Dr. Rush, who sat next him, and said : "I am old and good for nothing ; but, as the store-keepers say of their remnants of cloth, 'I am but a fag end, and you may have me for what you please.'" The next balloting elected Thomas Jefferson, then thirty-three years of age, who would be dear to the Salons of Paris as the author of the Declaration of Independence. The third gave a majority to Silas Deane, already in Europe.

Dr. Franklin, regardless of his age, his aversion to voyaging, his longing for repose, and the danger of capture, began forthwith to prepare for his departure. An express was sent to Virginia to notify Mr. Jefferson. Unhappily for Franklin and for Congress, Mr. Jefferson was compelled, by the ill-health of his wife, to decline the mission, and Congress elected in his stead that uneasy spirit, that thorn in Franklin's side, that miracle of ill temper and jealousy, that man formed to stir up strife, enmity, and every evil passion, who spent his whole existence in a broil—Arthur Lee. He, too, had the advantage of being already on the safe side of the Atlantic, and had been for several months in the service of the Secret Committee in London.

Three days after the election of the three commissioners arrived Mr. Thomas Story, with letters from Deane, Dumas, and Arthur Lee, and bearing in his memory intelligence too precious to be intrusted to paper. That this intelligence• may be understood, we must return to France, and enter the council chamber of Versailles, the secret cabinet of the Count de Vergennes, and, perhaps, the boudoir of the young queen, Marie Antoinette.

CHAPTER VII.

HOW FRANCE CAME TO HELP AMERICA.

THERE is in the heart of old Paris an extensive edifice called the Hotel de Hollande, which was built in the reign of Louis XIV. for the residence of the Dutch embassador. In August, 1776, this building, which had been for some time unoccupied, was observed, by the frequenters of the Rue Vieille du Temple, to exhibit the usual signs of again being inhabited. Not that any embassador's carriage rumbled under the sculptured gateway into the ancient court-yard. It soon became evident to the most careless passer-by, that this Hotel, wherein had been represented the majesty of Holland in Holland's palmy days, had been taken by a mercantile firm as a house of business. It was formerly an affectation of great commercial houses in Europe to occupy insignificant edifices, and to dispense with all but the most unobtrusive signs. The firm who had taken the Hotel de Hollande had apparently escaped the domination of a pride so intense, and seemed desirous of even parading the fact, that the new occupants were no other than the great Spanish house of RODERIQUE HORTALEZ AND CO.

Spanish the name was certainly ; but, if any observant Parisian had ventured into the rooms of the Hotel appropriated to business, he would have recognized the clerks as Frenchmen and fellow-citizens ; and if any Spaniard had asked to see the head of the House, he would have been most politely, but most positively, informed that the Señor Hortalez was not then in Paris. The Señor Hortalez never was in Paris. Whoever called, whatever the urgency of business, no Señor Hortalez was ever known to appear in the office of the Hotel de Hollande. It is only with the representative of that great man that we have to do. In an inner office, furnished with heterogeneous elegance, that representative was often to be found ; a tall, slender, fresh-complexioned man of forty-four, who conveyed to strangers the impression that he was in reality a fop and man of pleasure, who, for some reason or other, was *playing* the man of business. This impression would have been confirmed if the visitor had observed that, among the ledgers and other apparatus of the counting-house, there were play-books, billet-doux, riding-whips, music, and musical instruments. The air of the place, the manner of the man, were all that is comprehended in the word, so terrible in the haunts of commerce—" unbusiness-like." It was nevertheless true, that this incongruous person represented the whole dignity, and wielded all the power and resources of the imposing firm of Roderique Hortalez and Co.

To the gay world of Paris no name was more familiar than that of the individual we have described. It was Caron de Beaumarchais, who, last year, had brought out at a Paris theatre one of the most successful of modern comedies, the Barber of Seville, still familiar, through Rossini's music, to all Europe and all America. This was the man who, in August, 1776, in a parlor of the Hotel de Hollande, relieved the monotony of business by trying new airs on the harp, or noting down ideas for scenes in a comedy, and gave audience, by turns, to men of business and men of fashion.

It belongs to our subject to show why M. de Beaumarchais, the dramatist and courtier, had transferred his services to a counting-room, and what was the nature of the business transacted by a firm that had every appearance of being " eminent," but which no merchant in Paris knew any thing about.

Pierre Augustin Caron de Beaumarchais, born in 1732, was the son of a Paris watchmaker of no great note. He was himself brought up to the same vocation, and worked in his father's shop till he was twenty-four years of age, when he washed his hands, changed his clothes, became a frequenter of the court of Louis XV., and, of the king's four daughters, a kind of associate. This start-ling change of condition was effected by Beaumarchais acting upon that *silver* rule of morals, Never to submit to a wrong while there is left one honorable mode of redress. The gallant observance of this maxim brought him all the good fortune he ever enjoyed. At the age of twenty, being, like his father, an enthusiast in his craft, and most eager to excel, he invented an improvement in escape-ments, by which it became possible to make watches of extreme minuteness, as well as of superior accuracy. In the joy of his dis-covery, he communicated the new principle to a neighbor, a watch-maker of great repute, who immediately used the invention in a clock which he was making, and announced it in a newspaper as an idea of his own. The youthful inventor was upon him straight. In a letter to the same newspaper, written with equal spirit and modesty, the youth related the story of his invention and of his imparting the secret. A contest arose between the watchmaker, famous and rich, and this unknown lad, who had only the advan-tage of being in the right, and of being able to say so in an enga-ging manner. Beaumarchais humbly referred the dispute to the Academy of Sciences, apologizing for his audacity in having suc-ceeded in doing what so many older and abler watchmakers had attempted in vain. " Instructed I have been by my father," he said, " from the age of thirteen in the art of watchmaking; and animated by his example and advice to occupy myself seriously in endeavoring to perfect the art, it will not appear surprising that, when only nineteen, I tried to distinguish myself in it, and to enti-tle myself to the esteem of the public. Escapements were the first objects of my attention. To do away with their existing defects, simplify them, and perfect them—such was the aim which excited my ambition. My enterprise was doubtless a rash one : so many great men, whom the application of an entire life will probably not render me capable of equaling, had worked at it without ever arri-ving at the point so much desired, that I ought not to have flattered myself I should ever succeed. But youth is presumptuous ; and shall I not be excusable, gentlemen, if your approbation crowns my work ?"*

* "Beaumarchais and his Times," by M. de Louménie, chap. ii.

The Academy decided in his favor. The contest had attracted attention, and the sympathies of all were on the side of the ingenious youth. One of the results of his victory was, that he was appointed watchmaker to the king.

Now, this Beaumarchais, who knew so well how to assume the air of modest, injured innocence, had, in reality, a most excellent opinion of himself. He was one of those who, from an inch of opportunity, gain an ell or a mile of advantage. He made a watch upon his new principle for the king, which he was allowed to present in person, and the idle monarch was pleased with his new toy. Quick to improve his opportunity, he soon completed the smallest watch in existence, which he affixed to a finger-ring, and presented to the king's mistress, Madame de Pompadour. Her approving smile made it the fashion at court to order a watch of the new construction, and the young "artist," as he styled himself, was perplexed with the multitude of orders. Nor did the favor of Pompadour exclude him from the presence of the king's daughters, for whom he made ingenious clocks and watches, and who were pleased with the vivacity, the wit, the assurance, and the agreeable countenance of the young watchmaker. One of them even took lessons from him in his art ; a fact of some interest in view of Louis Sixteenth's taste for making locks. Watchmaking, we may remark, has always ranked very high among the trades of Paris ; no Parisian could regard with indifference the most elegant and skillful watchmaker of his time.

The retinue of a French king, under the old regime, consisted of several thousand persons, a large number of whom bought their places, and with their places the rank of noble. Montesquieu says : "The king of France has no gold mines like the king of Spain, his neighbor, but he has far greater wealth in the vanity of his subjects, which is more inexhaustible than any mine. He has been known to undertake or continue a war without any resources but the titles of honor which he had to sell, and, owing to a miracle of human conceit, his troops were paid, his towns fortified, and his fleet equipped." It would not, therefore, have been difficult for Beaumarchais to turn courtier—watchmaker that he was. He had but to save a few thousand francs, and buy the place of shoe-buckler-in-ordinary to his most Christian Majesty, to be set up for life in that noble profession. But the entrance of Beaumarchais into the court of

Louis XV. was effected in a manner more romantic.   The beautiful
wife of a controller of the king's kitchen fell in love with him,
brought him a watch to mend, blushed, and caused the susceptible
artist to claim the honor of bringing home the watch as soon as he
had repaired it.   The result was, that in the course of a few months
the aged husband of this amorous lady, in consideration of an annuity guaranteed by the father of Beaumarchais, resigned his office in
favor of the young-man.   He died soon after, and Beaumarchais married the widow, who had some fortune.   The duty of his office was
to march with his sword at his side, "before his majesty's meat,"
and place it on the table.   The salary was three hundred dollars a
year ; but the chances which the post afforded to a man like Beaumarchais were worth a million.   It gave him all he needed—access
to the court.   Audacity, talent, accomplishments, were his already.

His first success was in winning the marked favor of the king's
four daughters, who were glad of any thing that could relieve the
tedium of their hopeless magnificence.   Beaumarchais, from childhood, had been so devoted to music, that his father, fearing he would
never become proficient in the noble art of watchmaking, had often
threatened to deprive him of his musical instruments.   The terrible
threat was not executed, and the youth learned to sing well, to compose tolerably, and to play admirably on the flute, the violin, and
the harp.   The harp, which was then little known in France, becoming at length his favorite instrument, he acquired a certain
celebrity in court and city circles by the force and elegance of his
playing.   The princesses, who studied every thing, and played all
instruments from the jews-harp to the *French horn*, desired to hear
perform the young man, from whom already they had heard exposi-
tions of the mysteries of clockwork.   He played before them.
They asked him to give them lessons.   He conducted the weekly
concert which they were accustomed to give to the king and queen
and a few friends.   He became the indispensable Beaumarchais,
director-general of the pleasures of the princesses, enjoying the
favor and, in a certain sense, the intimacy, of the whole royal family.   And all this, not as the paid servant, but as the fine gentleman,
and gallant, devoted, disinterested courtier.

He bore his new honors not too meekly, it appears.   He had
enemies, but he knew how to meet and baffle them.   A courtier,
who had boasted that he would disconcert the protégé of the

princesses, met him one day as he was leaving their apartment, arrayed in his court suit, and handed him a valuable watch, saying, "Sir, as you understood watch-making, I wish you would have the kindness to examine my watch; it is out of order." A considerable number of courtiers were within hearing. Beaumarchais, with the utmost calmness, replied, "Sir, since I have ceased to practice the art, I have become inexpert." "Oh, sir," continued the gentleman, "do not refuse to look at my watch." "Very well," said Beaumarchais; "but I give you notice that I have become very awkward." He then took the watch, and raising it in the air as if to examine it, let it fall to the floor. Bowing low to the proprietor of the watch, he said, "I warned you, sir, of my extreme awkwardness," and walked away, leaving the discomfited nobleman to pick up the pieces. Another coxcomb of the court put upon him an affront for the avowed and contrived purpose of compelling him to fight. Beaumarchais met him in the field, and ran him through the body, inflicting a fatal wound. The dying man, whom Beaumarchais hastened to succor (for they fought without seconds), confessed his fault, and refused to disclose the name of his antagonist. The favor of the four princesses, in an indirect manner, made the fortune of our gallant adventurer. One of Madame de Pompadour's most assiduous friends was the great banker, Paris Du Verney; and one of their joint projects was the founding of a military college for the education of young officers. Under Du Verney's management, and Pompadour's patronage, the school attained a certain importance; but as the influence of the royal mistress declined, the interest of the king and court in the military school diminished. For *nine* years, we are told, M. du Verney tried in vain all courtly arts and artifices to induce the lazy monarch to bestow upon his school the eclat of a royal visit; until, at length, he took Beaumarchais into his confidence and asked his aid. The young courtier, like a man who understands the heart of man and woman, first prevailed upon the princesses to visit the school; plainly telling them why he desired it, and assuring them that if he could but contrive to gratify the old banker, his fortune was made. With their usual good nature they entered into his scheme, and, upon their return from the school conversed much in the hearing of the king upon what they had seen. The curiosity of the king being aroused, he visited the school of his own accord, merely to enjoy a new pleasure, and thus secured the prosperity of an establishment which is to this day one of the most important in Paris. Such was the ancient *regime!*

M. du Verney, as well to repay this service as to procure others of the same kind, resolved to put his young friend into a way of acquiring wealth. He gave him a share in some of his speculations, lent him money for projects of his own, advanced him eighty-five thousand francs for the purchase of letters of nobility, instructed him in the arts of finance, and gave him a taste for the class of operations which employ capital by the million. We see him, for example, offering to provision the whole Spanish army, and to supply all Spain with white bread. Some years of prosperity he now enjoyed, during which he entertained at his own handsome abode his father and sisters, and granted to each of them an annual allowance. To the public he became, in some degree, known by the production of his two serious dramas, one of which achieved a moderate success, and the other was a failure.

Then followed seven years of calamity, which ended in his becoming one of the poorest, and quite the most popular man in France, and, next to Voltaire and Rousseau, the most famous name in Europe. His patron, Du Verney, died, leaving their account unsettled, which involved Beaumarchais in a series of lawsuits with Du Verney's heir. First, he won his cause. His adversary then appealed to the judicial body, derisively called the Manpeou Parliament, abhorred of all France, as a new device of despotic power. The judge to whom this cause was specially referred was blessed with a wife, whose character may be inferred from a remark which she was once heard to make. " It would be impossible," said this worthy help-meet, " to live decently upon what we get, but we know the art of plucking the fowl without making it cry out." Beaumarchais she had indeed the art to pluck ; only she found it impossible to keep him from crying out. On the contrary, he cried so loud and long that all Europe heard him. A few days before the cause was to be reported upon, Beaumarchais received a hint, that a gift of two hundred louis d'ors to that virtuous lady was the surest way of getting a just judgment. He sent her forthwith money and diamonds to the amount required. She sent back a promise to restore the property, if her husband should decide against Beaumarchais; but she wanted fifteen louis more for her husband's secretary, and this sum would in no case be returned. The money was sent. The judge reported against Beaumarchais, which utterly ruined him in character and estate. The two hundred louis were promptly returned, but not the fifteen. The fowl had been plucked. Unquestionably, *two* fowls had contributed' to feather the nest of this faithful wife; but the plumage of Du Verney's 'heir had afforded better picking than that of Du Verney's protégé.

Beaumarchais learned that the judge's secretary, to whom he had himself given ten louis, had heard nothing of the fifteen. Irritated at once by the loss of his cause and the petty thieving of the woman, he wrote to her demanding the restitution of the fifteen louis. The gods, bent on the destruction of the woman, of her husband, of the Manpeou Parliament and the French monarchy, were pleased to infuse into her mind the madness of the doomed. She denied having received the money; accused Beaumarchais of an attempt to bribe; and induced her husband to denounce him to the parliament as one who had first endeavored to corrupt a judge's wife, and through her a judge, and then to destroy the good name of both. The chances were all against poor Beaumarchais. His property had been seized; he was not in good repute; his princesses had become estranged from him through the evil arts of his adversary; his family was not influential; his friends were few, poor, and powerless. The parliament, moreover, before whom, with closed doors, he was to be tried, could not but regard with extreme aversion a man who had tried to render them more odious by showing that they deserved odium. Death or the galleys threatened the man who had tuned the harps of princesses, and ridden to see his own plays in his own chariot.

But this Beaumarchais happened to be the most irrepressible man in France. In these alarming circumstances, he resorted to the expedient which had served him so well when the villanous watchmaker had stolen his escapement; that is to say, he invoked the power, slumbering in France, but about to be supreme, the power of Public Opinion. No advocate dared plead his cause; he became his own advocate. The tribunal before which he was to be tried was secret; he appealed from its undelivered but inevitable decision, to all reading France. His first "Memorial" called forth replies from the adversary, and he was engaged in a warfare of the pen

which attracted universal attention. The " Memorials" of Beaumarchais are still spoken of by French authors as among the classics
of French literature. "What a man!" wrote Voltaire to one of
his fine friends, " he unites every thing—humor, seriousness, argument, gayety, force, pathos, every kind of eloquence, and he seeks
for none, and he confounds all his adversaries, and he gives lessons
to his judges. His naïveté enchants me." Indeed, nothing more
entertaining or more convincing can be imagined than these unique
productions, which contain narratives the most strange and eventful, and retorts the most telling and happy. But, at the time of
their appearance, they were read with far more than a mere literary
rapture. As the affair proceeded, Beaumarchais, with infinite
prudence but deadly force, assailed the Manpeou Parliament itself,
and thus, from being the defendant in a private cause, became the
spokesman of liberal France—that heaving, eager France, which was
within twenty years of the taking of the Bastile. Add to this the
amiable pleasure we all take in seeing impaled on the nibs of a
brilliant pen, persons whom we are first made to believe deserve
impalement.

Beaumarchais' triumph was glorious, though tardy and incomplete. The judge lost his place, and his wife was compelled to
restore the fifteen louis ; but Beaumarchais was also censured and
deprived of civil rights. If, however, the intense applause of all
France, if social ovations in the most distinguished houses, if the
admiration of literary Europe could console him for the loss of
fortune and the disruption of his career, he was consoled.

One of the readers of his Memorials was the bad old king Louis
XV., who, as a man, enjoyed their perusal, but, as a king, disapproved the audacity of appealing to Public Opinion. He first silenced
Beaumarchais, then suspended the effect of his sentence, and,
finally, determined to employ his talents in secret service. This
potentate, then under the dominion of Madame du Barry, his last
mistress, was in sore tribulation in 1773, through the devices of
a French villain in London, who had written and threatened to
publish a Life of Du Barry, under the title of " Memoirs of a Public
Woman."- For eighteen months, we are told, the King of France
had striven to suppress this man and his work with the strong hand,
desirous to avoid the ignominy of paying black mail. The channel
and the British constitution still baffling the king, the swift Beau-

marchais was dispatched to try his dexterous hand. A few days
sufficed to complete the affair. Regarding the unpublished book
merely as a piece of merchandise to be bargained for and bought,
he procured a copy and brought it to the king, who authorized
him to make the best terms he could. Twenty thousand francs
down, and an annuity for life of four thousand francs a year, well
secured, was the price paid by Beaumarchais for the privilege of
burning the edition of three thousand copies. But, at the same
time, he engaged the author to serve the King of France in the congenial capacity of spy. "He was an audacious poacher," wrote
Beaumarchais to the head of the French police. "I have made him
an excellent game-keeper."

Upon returning to Versailles to receive the reward of his success,
he found the king dying, and Madame du Barry prepared to fly.
May 10th, 1774, Louis XV. died, and Louis XVI., twenty years of
age, and Marie Antoinette, nineteen, ascended the throne. Beaumarchais was not unknown to the young king. The queen, it appears, had read his Memorials, had pitied his misfortunes, had given
him gracious smiles, perhaps had expressed her sympathy in words.
The susceptible Beaumarchais, in common with all susceptible
France, was full of enthusiasm for the youthful sovereigns, who
were expected to usher in the millennium.

A court or a man that pays black mail once, may as well make
an annual appropriation for the same purpose for the rest of his
life. In the first month of the new reign, the king received tidings
of the forthcoming in London of a pamphlet, entitled, "Notice to
the Spanish Branch on its right to the Throne of France in Default
of Heirs." It was a trivial production, but in absolute governments
things the most trivial are frequently invested with supreme importance. This royal pair had been four years married, and there
was yet no heir to the French throne. The subject of the pamphlet
was the very last which the queen could be willing to have publicly discussed, since it kept the public in mind of a circumstance
which diminished her importance in the state, and disappointed the
hopes of two dynasties. Beaumarchais offered his services, and the
king accepted them. He demanded a commission written and
signed with the king's own hand. The minister hesitated to propose such an unprecedented measure. "How can it be feared,"
urged the persistent Beaumarchais, "that I shall compromise the

name of the king? This sacred name will be looked upon by me as the Israelites regarded the supreme name of Jehovah, the syllables of which they dared not pronounce except in cases of supreme necessity. * * The presence of the king, it is said, is worth fifty thousand men to the army : who knows how much his name may spare me in guineas?" The minister still hesitated. "If the work sees the day," Beaumarchais again wrote, "the queen, justly indignant, will soon know that it might have been suppressed, and that you and myself had undertaken to suppress it. I am as yet nothing, and can not fall from very high; but you! Do you know any woman who forgives an insult? 'They could stop,' she would say, 'the work which calumniated the late king and his mistress; by what odious predilection have they allowed this one to circulate?'" *That* was a line of argument which few cabinet ministers could resist. The invincible man obtained the king's autograph, which, with refined ostentation, he wore in a locket of gold, where lovers usually wear the miniature of their beloved. He gave the king this information in these words : "A lover carries round his neck the portrait of his mistress; a miser fastens his keys there; a devotee his reliquary; as for myself, I have had a gold box made, large, oval, and flat, in the form of a lens, in which I have inclosed your majesty's order, suspending it by a little gold chain to my neck, as the thing which is most necessary for my labors and most precious to myself."*

Wonderful adventures now befell him. Two editions of the pamphlet had been printed, one in London, another in Amsterdam ; both the property of a Jew. Fourteen hundred pounds sterling induced the Jew to abandon his speculation, and Beaumarchais had the pleasure of assisting in the destruction of both editions. Well pleased with his success, he permitted himself to live at Amsterdam in the manner of a tourist. Suddenly the news reached him that the speculative son of Abraham had gone to Nuremburg with fourteen hundred pounds in his pocket, and *a copy of the pamphlet*, which he intended to reprint at that city. Beaumarchais instantly prepared to pursue. "I am like a lion," he wrote to the minister, M. de Sartines ; "I have no more money, but I have diamonds and jewels ; I am going to sell every thing, and, with rage in my heart, I must recommence traveling like a postillion. I shall travel day

* Beaumarchais and his Times, by M. de Loménie, chap. xiv.

and night, if I do not drop from fatigue on the road. Woe to the abominable man who forces me to go three or four hundred leagues further, when I thought I was about to repose. If I find him on the road, I shall strip him of his papers and kill him, for the pain and trouble he has caused me."*

He started. Close to Nuremberg, at the beginning of a forest, he descried the Jew, trotting comfortably along on a pony, evidently thinking himself beyond danger. Beaumarchais sprang from his post-chaise, pistol in hand. The Jew, recognizing the man he had betrayed, galloped into the wood. The branches retarding his progress, Beaumarchais soon came up with him, seized him by the boot, twisted him off his horse, and found in his valise the pamphlet and the money, which he seized and bore off. Before he regained his carriage he was attacked by two robbers, with whom he had a fierce combat, and was only saved from death by the timely arrival of assistance. He reached the next inn bleeding from two wounds, and almost beside himself with fatigue and excitement. Still fearing his discomfited Jew, he pushed on to Vienna, made his way to the very presence of the empress, Maria Therese, mother of Marie Antoinette, told his story, and asked the arrest of the Jew. The empress took the zealous agent for an adventurer, and kept him a month in confinement. Satisfied, at length, of the genuineness of his mission, she released him with the gift of a thousand ducats, which the indignant Beaumarchais returned. In October, 1774, he reached Paris, and addressed to the king a narrative of his adventures, written with all the sparkle and vivacity of his famous Memorials. There are many reasons for believing that the queen, from this time, regarded with peculiar favor the man who had shed his blood in her service. Nothing is more certain than that Beaumarchais had some very powerful friends at court, and was himself powerful. Mr. Adams records in his French Diary, that "the confidential friend of M. Beaumarchais at court was the queen's treasurer. I was introduced to him as a personage of great power and respectability, and, with great solemnity, informed that he was the treasurer of the queen, *and* the intimate friend of M. Beaumarchais." We perceive, also, that Beaumarchais wrote to the king with frequency, at great length, and quite in the manner of a minister ; and

---

* Beaumarchais and his Times, by M. de Loménic, chap. xiv.

the ministers wrote to him in the tone of the vizier to the favorite. Neither his celebrity as a writer, nor the favor of the aged Maupertas, is sufficient to account for the great influence which he exerted in the councils of France during the next few years. A score of minute circumstances lead me to the conclusion that the cabinet of France were aware that Queen Marie Antoinette desired M. de Beaumarchais to be honored, employed, and enriched.* For the rest, he was himself the most audacious, indefatigable, and *pushing* man in the world.

During the next twelve months he was much in London, in the secret service of the king—service of a character similar to that in which he had been last employed. Many times he crossed the channel ; voluminous and entertaining were the reports he wrote. In the midst of his career as secret negotiator, he found time to bring out the Barber of Seville, which had a "run" of several weeks, and greatly enhanced his reputation.

One of the houses frequented by Beaumarchais in London was that of John Wilkes, just then doubly triumphant, having been elected Lord Mayor of London, and having secured his seat in the House of Commons, from which he had been four times expelled. The Mansion House of the new Lord Mayor was the special resort of the Americans, and of the politicians who favored their cause. There Beaumarchais met the man who was to embitter his existence for twenty years, Arthur Lee, of Virginia. There he heard the wildest misrepresentations of the state of things in England, and heard them distorted into the French language, for he spoke no English. There he met Americans fresh from the colonies, surcharged with patriotic feeling, and full of confidence in the success of their cause. The impression made on the hasty mind of Beaumarchais was, that England, the ' natural enemy of France,' was in imminent danger of falling to pieces. Convinced of this, he secretly left London in September, 1775, and went to Paris for no other purpose than to impart to his king the startling intelligence, which, he said, was " too important and too delicate to be intrusted to any courier."

" Sire," he wrote, " England is in such a crisis, such a state of disorder within and without, that it would be almost on the point

---

* Thomas Paine, who had the best means of knowing, confirms this opinion. He says: "It is both justice and gratitude to say, that it was the Queen of France who gave the cause of America a fashion at the French Court."—*Rights of Man.*

of ruin if her neighbors and rivals were themselves in a state to occupy themselves seriously about her. I will set forth faithfully the position of the English in America; I received the particulars from an inhabitant of Philadelphia, who had lately arrived from the colonies, and had just been present at a conference with the English ministers, who were thrown into the greatest trouble, and struck with terror by his recital. The Americans, determined to suffer every thing rather than give way, and full of that enthusiasm for liberty which has so often rendered the little nation of Corsica redoubtable to the Genoese, have thirty-eight thousand effective men, armed and resolute, beneath the walls of Boston; they have reduced the English army to the necessity of dying of hunger in this town, or of seeking for winter quarters elsewhere, which it will do forthwith."
* *   "I say, sire, that such a nation must be invincible, above all, when it has at its back as much country as it can possibly require for retreating, even if the English could make themselves masters of all their seaboard, which they are far from having done. All sensible persons, then, are convinced, in England, that the English colonies are lost to the mother-country, and that is also my opinion."

But this was not all: "The open war which is taking place in America is less fatal to England than the intestine war which must yet break out in London; the bitterness between parties has been carried to the greatest excess since the proclamation of the King of England which declares the Americans to be rebels. This absurdity, this masterpiece of madness on the part of the government, has renewed the strength of all the men of the opposition, who have united against it. A resolution has been taken to come to an open collision with the court party during the first sittings of the Parliament. It is thought that these sittings will not pass without seven or eight members of the opposition being sent to the Tower of London, and that is just the appointed time for sounding the tocsin. Lord Rochford, who has been my friend for the last fifteen years, in conversing with me, said these words, with a sigh: '*I am much afraid, sir, that the winter will not pass without some heads being brought down, either among the king's party or the opposition.*' On the other side, the Lord Mayor Wilkes, in a moment of joy and liberty, at the end of a splendid dinner, said to me publicly the following words: 'The king of England has long done me the honor of hating me. For my part, I have always rendered him the justice of despising him. The time has come for deciding which of us has formed the best opinion of the other, and on which side the wind will cause heads to fall.'

" * * * The least check which the royal army receives in America, by increasing the audacity of the people and the opposi- tion, may decide the affair at London at a moment when it is least expected; and if the king finds himself forced to yield, I say it with a shudder, I do not think his crown more secure on his head than the heads of his ministers upon their shoulders. This unhappy English nation, with its frantic liberty, may inspire the man who reflects with true compassion. It has never tasted the sweetness of living peaceably under a good and virtuous king. They despise us, and treat us as slaves because we obey voluntarily; but if the reign of a weak or bad prince has sometimes caused a momentary evil to France, the licentious rage, which the English call liberty, has never left an instant of happiness and true repose to this indomitable nation."*

So wrote Beaumarchais to the King of France, in September, 1775. He merely advised the king, however, to keep out of the broil, and hold the strength of France and Spain in reserve to profit by what might befall.

The winter passed, Beaumarchais still flitting between Paris and London. His acquaintance with Arthur Lee ripened into intimacy; and affairs across the ocean did not stand still. In February, 1776, we find him again addressing a solemn memorial "To THE KING ALONE," on the breach between England and the colonies. He no longer advised the king to observe a neutrality between the belli- gerents. On the contrary, he now endeavored to convince the king that the sole *safety* of France lay in secretly aiding the col- onists. The arguments used by him in maintaining this position were preposterous in the extreme, but we now know that they were the arguments which decided the French government to espouse the cause of the colonists. Those arguments were the following:

" Either England will have the most complete success in America, during the campaign, or the Americans will repel the English with loss.

" Either England will come to the determination, already adopted

* Beaumarchais and his Times, by M. de Loménie, chap. xvii.

by the king, of abandoning the colonies to themselves, or parting from them in a friendly manner; or the opposition, in taking possession of the government, will answer for the submission of the colonies on condition of their being restored to the position they were in in 1763.

" Here are all the possibilities collected together. Is there a single one of them which does not instantly give you the war you wish to avoid? Sire, in the name of God, deign to examine the matter with me.

" First, if England triumphs over America, she can only do so by an enormous expenditure of men and money. Now, the only compensation the English propose to themselves for so many losses is to take possession, on their return, of the French islands, and thus make themselves the exclusive venders of the valuable supply of sugar, which can alone repair all the injuries done to their commerce, and this capture would also render them forever the absolute possessors of the advantages derived from the contraband commerce carried on by the continent with these islands.

" Then, sire, there would remain to you nothing but the option of commencing at a later period an unprofitable war, or of sacrificing to the most shameful of inactive peaces all your American colonies, and of losing 280 millions of capital, and more than thirty millions of revenue.

" 2. If the Americans are victorious, they instantly become free, and the English, in despair at seeing their existence diminished by three quarters, will only be the more anxious, the more eager to seek a compensation, which will have become indispensable, in the easy capture of our American possessions ; and we may be certain that they will not fail to do so.

" 3. If the English consider themselves forced to abandon the colonies to themselves without striking a blow, as it is the secret wish of the king they should do, the loss being the same for their existence, and their commerce being equally ruined, the result for us would be similar to the preceding one, except that the English, less weakened by this amicable surrender than by a bloody and ruinous campaign, would only derive from it more means and facilities for gaining possession of our islands, which they would then be unable to do without, if they wished to preserve their own, and to keep any footing in America.

" 4. If the opposition takes possession of the government, and concludes a treaty of reunion with the colonies, the Americans, indignant with France, whose refusal will alone have caused them to
submit to the mother-country, threaten us from the present moment
to unite all their forces with England in order to take possession of
our islands. They will, indeed, only reunite with the mother-country on this condition, and heaven knows with what joy the ministry,
composed of Lords Chatham, Shelburne, and Rockingham, whose
dispositions toward us are publicly known, would adopt the resentment of the Americans, and carry on against you without cessation
the most obstinate and cruel war.

" What, then, is to be done in this extremity, so as to have peace
and preserve our islands ?

" You will only preserve the peace you desire, sire, by preventing it at all price from being made between England and· America,
and in preventing one from completely triumphing over the other ;
and the only means of attaining this end is by giving assistance to
the Americans, such as will put their forces on an equality with those
of England, but nothing beyond. And believe me, sire, that the
economy of a few millions at present may, before long, cost a great
deal of blood and money to France.

" Believe me, above all, sire, that the necessary preparations for
the first campaign will alone cost you more than all the assistance
you are asked for now ; and that the wretched economy of two or
three millions will certainly make you lose, before two years, more
than three hundred.

" If it be replied that we cannot assist the Americans without
wounding England, and without drawing upon us the storm which
I wish to keep off, I reply in my turn that this danger will not be
incurred if the plan I have so many times proposed be followed,
that of *secretly assisting the Americans without compromising ourselves;* imposing upon them, as a first condition, that they shall
never send any prizes into our ports, and never commit any act
which shall tend to divulge the secret of the assistance, which the
first indiscretion on the part of Congress would cause it instantly to
lose. And if your majesty has not at hand a more clever man to
employ in the matter, I undertake and answer for the execution of
the treaty, without any one being compromised, persuaded that my

zeal will supply my want of talent better than the talent of another could replace my zeal."*

Such reasoning as this, repeated by every courier, urged with the confidence which results from shallowness and conceit, and with the vehemence of a needy man who would provide himself with profitable employment, gradually wore away the scruples of M. de Vergennes, who, at length, laid before the king a memorial of his own, which was little more than a repetition in moderate, official language of Beaumarchais' prognostications, inferences, and advice. The young king, totally unable to grasp the subject, demanded the written opinion of M. Turgot, Minister of Finance ; the last hope of the French monarchy, the greatest and noblest statesman of his day, if not of any day.

If M. Turgot had left no trace of his too brief public life but the paper which he wrote in reply to Beaumarchais' fantastic reasoning, we should be justified in pronouncing him an extraordinary man. He showed, first of all, that the American colonies, whatever the issue of the pending struggle, must, in the nature of things, become independent. If the English succeeded for a few years in holding them in subjection, England would have her hands full, and would not provoke a war with France. If England should fail, she would be exhausted and crippled, and so leave France alone. If the Americans succeeded, as they probably would, it was safe to augur from their prudence and intelligence, that they would give to their government a solid form, and, as a consequence, seek peace with all nations. He then showed (one century in advance of his age) that England would not be essentially injured by the loss of her colonies, and that no nation was benefited by holding colonies in subjection, and compelling them to trade only with their mother-country. "When America is independent," said he, "then the illusion which has lulled our politicians for two centuries will be dispelled ; it will be seen that power, founded on monopoly, is precarious and frail, and that the restrictive system was useless and chimerical at the very time when it dazzled the most." Consider the immensity of the intellect which, in 1776, could have achieved such opinions as these. "Wise and happy," he continued, "will be that nation which shall first know how to bend to the new circumstances, and consent to see in its colonies allies, and not subjects."

* Beaumarchais and his Times, by M. Loménie, chap. xvii.

Finally, M. Turgot pronounced in favor of perfect neutrality; "first of all, for moral reasons," and, then, for reasons of interest. The King of Spain, he said, was not prepared for war, and had not the means of preparing. "As for us," he concluded, and how prophetic the words! "the king knows the situation of his finances; he knows that in spite of economies and ameliorations already made since the beginning of his reign, the expenditure exceeds the receipt by twenty millions. * * For a necessary war, resources could be found; but war ought to be shunned as the greatest of misfortunes, since it would render impossible, perhaps for ever, a reform, absolutely necessary to the prosperity of the state and the solace of the people."

"*Perhaps for ever!*" It proved to be "for ever," if by those words he meant the for ever of the French monarchy.

The king leaned to Turgot's side, for the instincts of this ungifted monarch were sound and noble; it was only capacity that he lacked. But Beaumarchais, De Vergennes, the queen, the court, the philosophers, the salons, and Arthur Lee, exerted an amount of influence which only a great king or an obstinate one could have resisted. The great Turgot was dismissed, and the system of Beaumarchais prevailed. Aid should be sent to the Americans, but with a thousand precautions for keeping it secret.

Beaumarchais hastened to tell the news to Arthur Lee, who immediately dispatched Mr. Story with it to Congress. In communicating the intelligence to Congress, Mr. Lee exaggerated his own influence, and, probably, Beaumarchais' promises. Mr. Story was directed to tell the Committee of Secret Correspondence, that Arthur Lee had had several conferences with the French embassador (a cipher of rank), who had communicated the same to the French court, and, in consequence thereof, the "Duke de Vergennes" had sent a gentleman to Arthur Lee, with the information that the French government could not think of entering into a war with England, but that it would assist America by sending from Holland, that autumn, two hundred thousand pounds' worth of arms and ammunition. The supplies would be sent to one of the French West India islands, the governor of which would be in the secret, and deliver them to any agent of the Congress who should inquire for Monsieur Hortalez.

Beaumarchais, to the end of his life, asserted that he had never delivered a message of this purport to Arthur Lee. Nevertheless, we now know that the first plan meditated by the French government was to send aid to the colonies as a free gift, through a government agent. The probability is, that Beaumarchais, in the exultation of success, said more to Arthur Lee than he afterwards found it convenient to remember, and that Lee announced to Congress as certain, that which Beaumarchais merely hoped was certain. Nowhere, however, do I find any indication that the French government contemplated sending so large a sum as two hundred thousand pounds.

In the French diplomatic correspondence of that year, we find the following letter from M. de Vergennes to the king, dated May 2d : "Sire, I have the honor of laying at the feet of your majesty the writing, authorizing me to furnish a million of livres for the service of the English colonies. I add, also, the draft of an answer I propose to make to the Sieur Beaumarchais. I solicit your approbation to the two propositions. The answer to M. de Beaumarchais will not be written in my hand, nor even in that of either of the clerks or secretaries of my office. I shall employ for that purpose my son, whose handwriting cannot be known. He is only fifteen years old, but I can answer in the most positive manner for his discretion. As it is important that this operation should not be suspected, or, at least, imputed to the government, I entreat your majesty to allow me to direct the return of the Sieur Montaudoin to Paris. The pretext for that proceeding will be, to obtain from him an account of his correspondence with the Americans, though, in reality, it will be for the purpose of employing him to transmit to them such funds as your majesty chooses to appropriate to their benefit, directing him, at the same time, to take all necessary precautions, as if, indeed, the Sieur Montaudoin made the advance on his own account. On this head I take the liberty of requesting the orders of your majesty. Having obtained them, I shall write to the Marquis de Grimaldi,* inform him of our proceedings, and request his co-operation to the same extent."

The king signed the document ordering the royal treasurer to place a million livres at the disposal of the Count de Vergennes.

---

* Prime Minister of the King of Spain.

He also sanctioned the proposed application to the government of Spain. The answer to Beaumarchais, in the handwriting of the son of M. de Vergennes, was probably the letter which furnished the basis of Lee's message to the Secret Committee. Returning to Paris in May, Beaumarchais found the conservative, or, rather, the timorous influence prevailing at court. M. de Vergennes now regarded the direct transmission of aid as too bold a measure; he demanded new precautions against the vigilance of the English embassador. The plan finally adopted was one of the most ingenious pieces of state craft ever devised. The idea of *giving* aid to the colonies was abandoned, and the scheme was formed of founding a great commercial house in Paris, for the sole purpose of *selling* to Congress the warlike stores they needed, on long credit. The capital of this house was to be furnished by the allied kings of France and Spain, each contributing a million francs, which sum, it was expected, would be sunk in doing business on such unbusiness-like principles. In addition to this aid in money, the French government agreed to permit the House to take from the royal arsenals cannon, muskets, and ammunition, to be replaced or paid for at its convenience. This plan, besides being so well calculated to deceive the English embassador, was far better for America than a gift of money and arms. Two millions or ten millions of francs were a trifling boon compared with the privilege of buying unlimited supplies, on terms with which Congress could comply; for not merely was the House to give long credit, but it was to take payment in tobacco, indigo, and rice, a whole crop of which lay spoiling in southern warehouses. To the French government the scheme had the additional advantage of affording an opportunity of rewarding its zealous servant, Beaumarchais, since he was to constitute the new commercial House. It was certainly an odd choice. Nevertheless, it was a good choice; probably, no man in France could, in the very peculiar circumstances, have managed the affair better than he did. A mere merchant could not have done the business at all; it required just such a mixture of courtier, politician, man of genius, man of business, and man of pleasure as Caron de Beaumarchais was.

The delicacy of the task he had undertaken appears from the minister's own explanation of the scheme. "The operation," said M. de Vergennes to the House, "must, in the eyes of the English government, and even in the eyes of the Americans, have the appearance of an individual speculation, to which the French ministers are strangers. That it may be so in appearance, it must also be so, to a certain point, in reality. We will give a million secretly, we will try to induce the court of Spain to unite with us in this affair, and supply you on its side with an equal sum ; with these two millions and the co-operation of individuals who will be willing to take part in your enterprise, you will be able to found a large house of commerce, and at your own risk can supply America with arms, ammunition, articles of equipment, and all other articles necessary for keeping up the war. Our arsenals will give you arms and ammunition, but you shall replace them or shall pay for them. You shall ask for no money from the Americans, as they have none ; but you shall ask them for returns in products of their soil, and we help you to get rid of them in this country, while you shall grant them, on your side, every facility possible. In a word, the operation, after being secretly supported by us at the commencement, must afterward feed and support itself; but, on the other side, as we reserve to ourselves the right of favoring or discouraging it, according to the requirements of our policy, you shall render us an account of your profits and your losses, and we will judge whether we are to accord you fresh assistance, or give you an acquittal for the sums previously granted."*

Such work as this was not to be executed by an ordinary merchant.

On the tenth of June, 1776, Beaumarchais received a million francs from the French treasury, for which he gave the afterwards famous receipt in these words : " I have received from M. Duvergier, conformably to the orders of the Count de Vergennes, dated the 5th instant, which I have remitted to him, the sum, of one million, of which I will render account to the said Count de Vergennes. CARON DE BEAUMARCHAIS."*

Two days after he sent Arthur Lee, with whom he constantly corresponded, a distinct enough intimation of the change of plan : "The difficulties I have met with in my negotiations with the ministry have made me decide to *form a company*, which will send the ammunition and powder to *your friend* as soon as possible, in con-

---

* Beaumarchais and his Times, by M. de Loménie, chap. xvii.

sideration of tobacco being sent in return to the French cape."
They continued to correspond in the most confidential manner for
several weeks more, sometimes in cipher, sometimes over fictitious
signatures. Lee, for example, sent Beaumarchais in this very month
of June, an exact account of Lord Howe's fleet, and urged the
French government to dispatch a fleet to America to destroy it; a
suggestion that may have been creditable to his zeal, but not to his
knowledge of European politics.

CHAPTER VIII.

SILAS DEANE IN PARIS.

Mr. ARTHUR LEE had now done all the useful work he was destined to do for his country in Europe.

Almost on the very day on which Beaumarchais received the
million francs from the French treasury, Silas Deane arrived at
Bordeaux. Disappointment awaited him there; for the cargoes
of fish, rice, and tobacco which the Secret Committee had dispatched after him, and upon the proceeds of which he was to live
and operate, had not arrived. He waited three weeks at Bordeaux, but they did not come. Ship after ship, laden with these
products, was sent to sea by the committee, only to be pounced
upon by British cruisers before the capes were cleared; and, to
add to Mr. Deane's discouragement, ill news had preceded him,
such as the failure of the assault on Quebec, the subsequent loss of
Canada, the mighty armament that had sailed under command of
Lord Howe, and the increase of the war party in England.

He reached Paris about the first of July, and waited immediately
upon Dr. Dubourg. He arrived just as that zealous gentleman was
beginning to doubt the integrity of the merchant, Penet, who had
not yet succeeded in getting his papers from Rotterdam; and who,
like Mr. Deane, depended absolutely upon the expected cargoes.
Upon the credit of tobacco to arrive, Penet, aided by Dr. Dubourg,
had bought, and even got aboard ship, a large quantity of powder,
saltpeter, and muskets. The contagious zeal of the doctor and the

universal enthusiasm for America had brought the affair so far; but there it had stopped. The bad news from Canada, the failure of the ships, doubts of the solvency and authority of M. Penet, all combined to discourage merchants, and the stores remained in port. In the nick of time Mr. Deane appeared upon the scene, with ample credentials, with letters to Dr. Dubourg, with proofs of the genuineness of M. Penet's contracts, with fresh testimonials of the determination of Congress and all America to resist to the death. Arrangements were quickly made, by virtue of which M. Penet succeeded in getting off a quantity of stores.

In a few days, through the good offices of Dr. Dubourg, Mr. Deane and the doctor were closeted with the Count de Vergennes. The Count could not speak English, nor Mr. Deane French; they were obliged to converse through the translations of M. Gerard, chief secretary in the French foreign office. On this occasion, as on all other occasions of intercourse with Americans, M. de Vergennes spoke with perfect frankness and truth. To the English he could lie with the calm assurance of a practical diplomatist of the ancient *regime*. John Adams, who was the most undiplomatic man that ever figured in public life, used to maintain, in his pugnacious, vehement way, that because the French government had deceived England, they were extremely likely to attempt to cheat America also. It did not follow. The Celt, unlike the Saxon, does not object to a lie *per se ;* against an enemy, he can employ falsehoods with as little remorse as cannon-balls; while his sense of honor binds him to act with most scrupulous fidelity to a friend. And, theorizing apart, nothing is now more certainly *known*, than that the French government, from the time of this first interview with Silas Deane, to the close of the war, acted towards America with candor and sincerity. Recent investigation of original papers, in the archives of the three nations concerned, has established this beyond all reasonable, or even unreasonable doubt.

The Count de Vergennes told Mr. Deane, in the course of their two hours' conference, that the "good understanding" which existed between France and England would prevent his openly encouraging the exportation of arms to America, but that no real obstruction would be given to it. A hint should be promptly passed to all the chief officers of the customs, and if any of them should not happen to take the hint, Mr. Deane had only to inform the Count de Vergennes of the circumstance, and he would make it clear to the understanding of the officer. With regard to independency, and the recognition of it by France, that belonged to the future, and would be duly considered at the proper time. Meanwhile, Mr. Deane was requested to consider himself under the immediate protection of the Count de Vergennes, to whom he should always have access on applying to M. Gerard. Not a word was said, during this long interview, nor an allusion made, to M. de Beaumarchais or his million livres.

Mr. Deane and Dr. Dubourg returned from Versailles to Paris well pleased with what had occurred there, and with one another. To Deane the worthy doctor explained the negotiations with Du Coudray, the peerless general of artillery, giving him to understand that scarcely any thing he could do for his country would be so great a boon as the engagement of that officer and his train of subordinates. Mr. Deane, however, was still without resources, and could neither buy his Indian goods, nor advance money to peerless officers of artillery. Credit was pressed upon him ; the mercantile world was eager to supply the illustrious Congress of Republicans ; but, alas ! all the offers of credit were accompanied with the fatal condition, that the notes given by Mr. Deane for stores purchased, should be indorsed by one of the great Paris banking-houses.

While Mr. Deane and Dr. Dubourg were sadly revolving this apparently insurmountable obstacle in their minds, M. de Beaumarchais, the predestined comforter of anxious patriots, appeared to them, bearing in his hand a letter from the Count de Vergennes. The letter introduced Beaumarchais as one " commissioned by the ministry to assist Dr. Dubourg and Mr. Deane by his intelligence, and to undertake the entire and particular direction of all the commerce, exports as well as imports, either of munitions of war or of the usual productions of France, to the united colonies, and of the colonies to France." Dr. Dubourg was grieved and alarmed at this intelligence. Besides having himself expected to take the lead in the American business, he sincerely questioned the commercial ability of Beaumarchais. He at once endeavored to dissuade him from " taking all this immense traffic upon himself," and thus " excluding people who had gone to so much expense, suffered so much fatigue, and run so many risks during the year in the service of Congress." Beaumarchais, with an unsuspected million in his pocket, replied perhaps too warmly, and an altercation arose between them; which ended with the doctor's saying, with unauthorized positiveness : " Mr. Deane, sir, will not and cannot undertake any thing with you." Beaumarchais, conscious of his million and sure of his minister, took his leave and went to Versailles.   Dr. Dubourg immediately sent to Count de Vergennes a letter of remonstrance.   " No one," he wrote, " does more justice than I to M. de Beaumarchais' rectitude, his discretion, and his zeal for all that is good and great.   I believe him to be one of the most fit men in the world for political negotiations, but perhaps, at the same time, one of the least fitted for negotiating in a mercantile sense.   He likes splendor; it is asserted that he maintains young ladies at his expense; in short, he passes for a prodigal; and in France there is no merchant nor manufacturer who is not of this opinion, and who would not hesitate very much to transact the least business with him."

The minister mischievously handed this letter to Beaumarchais, who replied to it with all his wonted humor.   " How does it affect our business," he asked the artless doctor, " if I like pomp and splendor, and maintain young ladies in my house ?   The ladies in my house, who have been there for twenty years, sir, are your very humble servants.   They were five in number, four sisters and a niece.   During the last three years two of these girls have died, to my great sorrow.   I now only keep three, two sisters and my niece, which is, however, display enough for a private individual like myself.   But what would you have thought if, knowing me better, you had been aware that I carried the scandal so far as to keep men too—two nephews, very young and rather good-looking, and even the miserable father who brought such a scandalous person into the world."*

All this was true, for Beaumarchais fulfilled the obligations of kindred with affectionate exactness.   The Count de Vergennes ended the controversy by sending for Dr. Dubourg and Mr. Deane, and informing them that M. de Beaumarchais was indeed the inevitable man, and that he was not less able than willing to supply Congress with all it desired.

Beaumarchais and Deane soon came to a perfect understanding. Dr. Dubourg still served America to the best of his ability, but

* " Beaumarchais and his Times," chap. xviii.

only as a private gentleman. Beaumarchais, deeming Silas Deane the veritable representative of Congress in Europe, dropped Arthur Lee—to that gentleman's extreme and lasting disgust. And now it was, August, 1776, that the Hotel de Hollande cheered the passers-by with the appearance of being inhabited, and informed the neighborhood, in the usual manner, that it had been taken by the firm of RODERIGUE HORTALEZ and Co. Beaumarchais, by residing awhile at Madrid, some years before, had acquired the taste which made him select for his comedies Spanish subjects, and for his House a Spanish name.

These preliminaries settled, the next step of our dramatic merchant was to write the only comic letter which appears in the nineteen volumes of the Diplomatic Correspondence of the Revolution. It was a letter to the Secret Committee, signed Roderigue Hortalez and Co., but written in the first person singular, as though from the Head of that eminent House. "The respectful esteem," began the imaginary Hortalez, "which I bear toward that brave people who so well defend liberty under your conduct, has induced me to form a plan concurring in this great work by establishing an extensive commercial house, solely for the purpose of serving you in Europe, there to supply you with necessaries of every sort. * * Your deputies, gentlemen, will find in me a sure friend, an asylum in my house, money in my coffers, and every means of facilitating their operations, whether of a public or private nature. I will, if possible, remove all obstacles that may oppose your wishes from the politics of Europe."

These brave words would have puzzled the grave Congress, if the name of Hortalez had not been mentioned by Mr. Thomas Story in a manner which prepared them to believe him merely the almoner of the French king. How natural their conclusion, that the writer was merely *playing* merchant; and this impression every succeeding paragraph must have strengthened. "At this very time," continued Señor Hortalez, "and without waiting for any answer from you, I have procured for you about two hundred pieces of brass cannon, four-pounders, which will be sent to you by the nearest way, two hundred thousand pounds of cannon powder, twenty thousand excellent fusils, some brass mortars, bombs, cannon balls, bayonets, platines, clothes and linens for the clothing of your troops, and lead for musket balls. An officer of the greatest merit for artillery and genius, accompanied by lieutenants, officers, artillerists and cannoneers, whom we think necessary for the service, will go for Philadelphia, even before you have received my first dispatches. This, gentlemen, is one of the greatest presents my attachment can offer you. Your deputy, Mr. Deane, agrees with me in the treatment which he thinks suitable to his office." Poor Deane! that sentence helped to ruin him. In truth, he had scarcely any thing to do with the sending of Du Coudray and his troop of followers. Dr. Dubourg began it, at the suggestion of a member of the French Cabinet; Beaumarchais took the affair out of Dr. Dubourg's hands and pressed it upon Deane with his usual resistless ardor. Deane merely did not veto it.

Señor Hortalez continued his epistle to great length, and in a strain of the highest absurdity. Such sentences as these occur: "The secrecy necessary in some part of the operation which I have undertaken for your service requires also, on your part, a formal resolution, that all the vessels and their demands should be constantly directed to our house alone, in order that there may be no idle chaffering or time lost—two things that are the ruin of affairs." * * "I request of you, gentlemen, to send me next spring, if it is possible for you, ten or twelve thousand hogsheads, or more if you can, of tobacco from Virginia, of the best quality." * * "However well-bottomed my house may be, and however I may have appropriated many millions to your trade alone, yet it would be impossible for me to support it, if all the dangers of the sea, of exports and imports, were not entirely at your risk." He concluded with these modest words: "Every thing that passes in your great assemblies, is known, I cannot tell how, at the court of Great Britain. Some indiscreet or perfidious citizen sends an exact account of your proceedings to the palace of St. James. In times of great exigency, Rome had a Dictator; and in a state of danger the more the executive power is brought to a point, the more certain will be its effect, and there will be less to fear from indiscretion. It is to your wisdom, gentlemen, that I make this remark; if it seems to you just and well planned, look upon it as a new mark of my ardor for your rising republic."

Such was the fantastic letter of Beaumarchais to the Secret Committee. So certain were the committee that it was merely part of the game of deceiving the English; so far were they from supposing that there was any reality whatever in the House of Hortalez and Co., that they never thought of answering the letter; a neglect that surprised and wounded the writer thereof.

Beaumarchais now plunged into activity, drawing after him the bewildered and admiring Deane—they two the most noted men of the season. The veil of secrecy which was thrown over their proceedings was of the thinnest. Mr. Deane still gave out that he was a merchant from Bermuda, and Beaumarchais insisted on being regarded as the representative of the great House of Hortalez; but every one in Paris who knew any thing, including the British embassador, knew well enough who they were and what they were doing. As a specimen of Beaumarchais' mode of combining business with pleasure, take this fragment of a report of a chief of police to the minister concerning one of his business journeys to a seaport : " I think that M. de Beaumarchais' journey has done more harm than good : he is known by many people, and he has made himself known to the whole town by having his comedies played, and by hearing the actors repeat their parts, so as to play them better. All this has rendered his caution. of concealing himself under the name of Durand perfectly useless." The man must have felt himself strong at court to dare to act in a manner so ridiculous.

Nevertheless, the work proceeded with creditable expedition. His own account of his exploits this year wears the air of exaggeration, but it is in reality not far from the truth.

" From a Frenchman that I was, I became an American merchant, a politician, and a writer. I imparted my warmth to honest but timid minds, and formed a society under a name unknown. I gathered together merchandise and warlike stores in all our ports, always under fictitious names. Your agent was to have provided vessels to transport them to America, but not one could he find ; and it was still I who, with double zeal and labor, succeeded in procuring them for him at Marseilles, Nantes, and Havre, paying out of my own pocket two-thirds of the freight in advance, and finding security for the remainder.

" The most severe orders everywhere thwarted my operations. What I could not accomplish in the open day, was executed in the night. If government caused my vessels to be unloaded in one port, I sent them secretly to reload at a distance in the roads. Were they stopped under their proper names, I changed them immediately, or made pretended sales, and put them anew under fictitious commissions. Were obligations in writing exacted from my captains to go nowhere but to the West India Islands, powerful gratifications on my part made them yield again to my wishes. Were they sent to prison on their return for disobedience, I then doubled their gratifications to keep their zeal from cooling, and consoled them with gold for the rigor of our government. Voyages, messengers, agents, presents, rewards—no expense was spared. One time, by reason of an unexpected counter order, which stopped the departure of one of my vessels, I hurried by land to Havre twentyone pieces of cannon, which, if they had come from Paris by water, would have retarded us ten days.

" Thus, I scattered money everywhere to surmount the obstacles which constantly came in the way, and, thinking it injurious to the nation which I served to doubt of her gratitude, or of her being fraught with the generous sentiments which actuated myself, I regarded as straw the money I distributed for her, happy in the power at such a price to procure her speedy assistance."*

Which being interpreted signified that, within a period of twelve months, he succeeded in dispatching to America eight ship loads of warlike stores, valued by himself at more than six millions of francs. The capital which enabled him to achieve this great result, was composed, first, of the million received from the French treasury in June, 1776; secondly, the million granted by the Spanish government, which Beaumarchais received in September of the same year; thirdly, another million from the treasury of France in 1777. The stores taken from the royal arsenal were equivalent, perhaps, to a fourth million, and the rest may have been furnished by friends and speculators. Beaumarchais lived, meanwhile, in the style which he supposed became a man who dealt in royal millions. A little later in the war, he mentions in one of his letters that he kept ten horses and three coachmen. Even his head clerk was a man of three horses.

The position of Mr. Silas Deane, during the first six months of his residence in Paris, was immensely difficult, and he was by no means a man of great powers. Such abilities as he had, however, he appears to have faithfully employed in the service of his country.

---

* Diplomatic Correspondence of the United States of America, i., 484.

Left without orders from home, and living amid scenes and circumstances dazzlingly novel to a Connecticut school-master, he committed some errors, but also performed a great deal of real service. All Paris was on the *qui vive* with regard to America and the secret movements of France on her behalf, and the war with England to which those secret movements pointed. Every officer in the French army seemed eager to go and share the campaigns of Washington. "I am well nigh harassed to death with applications of officers to go out to America," he writes in one letter. "Had I ten ships here," he says in another, "I could fill them all with passengers for America." He was even offered troops from Germany and from Switzerland. Merchants of all descriptions tormented him with offers of merchandise on impossible terms. Occasionally, too, a true friend of his country and of mankind, like M. Ray de Chaumont, offered him an admissible credit. M. de Chaumont, without knowing that Congress would ratify the bargain, sold him a million francs' worth of powder and saltpeter on unlimited credit. Chaumont was an army-clothing contractor of great wealth and the highest character, whose whole heart was with America in her struggle for independence.

In all difficulties, Mr. Deane found Beaumarchais a powerful friend. He praises continually, in his letters home, the address, the assiduity, the fertility of resource, the rapidity, the generosity, and the ever hopeful courage of that incredible personage. To Beaumarchais, indeed, he was indebted, at last, for mere subsistence money ; for all his own resources were exhausted long before he obtained any help, or even tidings from America. I attribute to Beaumarchais, also, such hints as this, which occur in the official correspondence of Mr. Deane : " The queen is fond of parade, and, I believe, wishes for war, and is our friend. She loves riding on horseback. Could you send me a fine Narragansett horse or two? The money would be well laid out. Rittenhouse's orrery, or Arnold's collection of insects, a phaeton of American make, and a pair of bay horses, a few barrels of apples, walnuts, cranberries, and butter-nuts, would be great curiosities."* It was Beaumarchais, however, who urged Deane into the great error of sending over so many officers of ex-

---

* Lafayette also, fifty years after these events, told Lady Morgan that the queen favored the American cause, though without understanding any thing about it. See "Lady Morgan's Diary." American edition, p. 112.

travagant pretensions; a measure which both of them considered necessary for the furtherance of their greater objects at court and in the cabinet. But if Du Coudray and his train of forty or fifty artillery officers were a nuisance merely, let us also remember that it was Silas Deane who commissioned Lafayette, De Kalb, and Steuben.

In the course of the autumn Mr. Deane had a taste of Arthur Lee's sweet and confiding disposition. He received a letter from that gentleman desiring him to inform Congress, that Joseph Reed of Philadelphia, military secretary to General Washington, and John Langdon, member of Congress from Connecticut, " were dangerous persons." Mr. Deane being the intimate acquaintance of both the accused, declined doing so unless the charges were explicitly stated and evidence furnished. A few weeks after, Mr. Lee being closeted with Deane in Paris, " I entreated him to inform me on what grounds he had gone in his information respecting Mr. Reed and Mr. Langdon. He told me that as to Mr. Reed, he really knew nothing more than that he formerly corresponded with Lord Dartmouth, and that his brother-in-law, M. de Burdt, was actually intimate with his lordship. But for Mr. Langdon, he said there could be no doubt, as he was the last winter in London, and frequently with the ministry. I replied, that as to the latter, I had spent the last winter with him in Philadelphia; and as to the former, I could not think that such vague and inconclusive circumstances were sufficient to authorize sending general charges to Congress; for, that charges of such a complexion, and coming from such a person as himself, must forever damn the reputation of those accused thereby, and alarm and embarrass the public. To this Mr. Lee said he knew that a person of the name of Langdon had been in London the last winter, and therefore he wrote, supposing him to be Mr. John Langdon of Portsmouth; that he believed that he was too suspicious at times, and was glad that I had not sent forward his letter."*

And so the year wore away; the embarrassments of the American agents not diminishing as events moved onward. With Mr. Deane, the darkest hour was just before the dawn. At the beginning of December, 1776, there were few men in Europe who had a practicable faith in the American cause, and the French government

* "Deane Papers," p. 26.

itself began to depair. Beaumarchais had been to the coast to dispatch two of his vessels, but by consorting with actors and bringing out his plays, as before referred to, had betrayed the secret of his presence, and of his connection with the ships. Lord Stormont, the British embassador, thundered remonstrance with all the force of the British lion. The Count de Vergennes sent orders to stop all the ships loaded and loading for America, and either was or affected to be deeply offended with his dramatic agent. Beaumarchais was understood to be in disgrace, and every thing was in extremity. Deane, oppressed by labors, for he had no secretary, tortured by anxiety, for he was still without news from home, responsible for millions, yet dependent upon a stranger for his subsistence, representing a Power that might have ceased to exist, and inhabiting a country whose policy might at any moment demand his expulsion, his great ally and friend in disgrace, only one ship really off, and half a dozen others eating themselves up in port, England exulting, France giving up—we cannot wonder that he was ready at times to despair. He had written, a month before, asking Congress to send over one of its own members to help him, little supposing that help was near.

In the evening of December the seventh, the overburdened envoy received a note from Nantes, which lifted a mountain load of care from his heart, and sent him to bed a happy man.

PART VI.

RESIDENCE IN FRANCE.

PART VI.

CHAPTER I.

HELP was at hand. The note informed Mr. Deane that Dr. Franklin was at Nantes, two hundred and eight miles southwest of Paris! It was on the twenty-sixth of September, a month after Hortalez and Co. had taken possession of the Hotel de Hollande, that Congress elected the three plenipotentiaries to represent the United States at the friendly court of France. Vain was the attempt to keep the grand embassy a secret. A curious and unique entry in the Records of the Secret Committee acquaints us with the fact that it remained a secret only four days. On the first of October, as we learn from this entry, Mr. Robert Story appeared before Dr. Franklin and Mr. Thomas Morris, the only members of the committee then in Philadelphia, and delivered to them the verbal message with which Arthur Lee had charged him : namely, that the King of France, moved thereto by the powerful intercession of Mr. Lee, had determined to send to America, before the next campaign opened, two hundred thousand pounds worth of arms and ammunition. Intelligence more thrilling has seldom been brought across the ocean than this announcement, as a certainty, of the practical alliance of France with the infant nation. Nevertheless, the two members of the Secret Committee deliberately resolved to conceal it even from Congress, because, as they entered in their records, " we find by fatal experience, that the Congress 'consists of too many members to keep secrets, as none could be more strongly enjoined than the present embassy to France, notwithstanding which, Mr. Morris was this day asked whether Dr. Franklin and others were really going embassadors to France." It was, how-

Chadron State College Library

Chadron, Nebraska

ever, agreed between them, that in case " any unexampled misfortune should befall the States of America, so as to depress the spirits of Congress," then Mr. Morris should cheer them up with this great news; otherwise, he should keep it buried in the archives of the committee, until at least part of the supplies should have escaped the enemy's frigates, and reached an American port.* This was the last official act of any note done by Dr. Franklin before his departure.

One private deed of his, performed during the month of preparation, shines, starlike, in the cloudy records of the time. He collected all the money he could command at such short notice, "between three and four thousand pounds," and lent it to Congress; a practical proof of his faith in the cause, which, we are told, had its effect in replenishing the public coffers. *This* is the man who is regarded by some as the type of penny wisdom!

Two grandsons were to accompany Dr. Franklin on this occasion; William Temple Franklin, his son's son, now a handsome lad of seventeen or eighteen, whom he intended to place at a French or German university, with a view to his adopting the law; and Benjamin Franklin Bache, the eldest son of his daughter, a boy of seven, whom he meant to send to school in Paris. Governor Franklin, then a prisoner in Connecticut, knew nothing of his son's departure for several weeks after he had sailed; as we read in one of his letters to his wife, dated November 27th. "If," wrote the governor, "the old gentleman has taken the boy with him, I hope it is only to put him into some foreign university, which he seemed anxious to do when he spoke to me last about his education."

Franklin's last writing before his departure was a letter to a friend; which, falling into the hands of the enemy, the king and his cabinet had the pleasure of reading a few weeks later. It was written the day before he left home : " Being once more ordered to Europe, and to embark this day, I write this line. * * As to our public affairs, I hope our people will keep up their courage. I have no doubt of their finally succeeding by the blessing of God, nor have I any doubt that so good a cause will fail of that blessing. It is computed that we have already taken a million sterling from the enemy. They must soon be sick of their piratical project. No

---

* Diplomatic Correspondence of the American Revolution, ii., 16.

time should be lost in fortifying three or four posts on our extended coast as strong as art and expense can make them. Nothing will give us greater weight and importance in the eyes of the commercial states, than a conviction that we can annoy, on occasion, their trade, and carry our prizes into safe harbors; and whatever expense we are at in such fortifying, will soon be repaid by the encouragement and success of privateering."*

A swift sloop of war, called the Reprisal, of sixteen guns, Captain Wickes, lay at Marcus Hook, in the Delaware, awaiting the pleasure of Dr. Franklin and his little party. The sloop had three thousand pounds' worth of indigo on board for the first expenses of the plenipotentiaries. There was a fitness in his going by this vessel, since it was he who had originated the policy of reprisals, of which policy this gallant little sloop was one of the prettiest fruits. Readers remember the fiery Preamble which he dashed to paper when the news reached him of the passage of Lord North's Prohibitory bill. On the twenty-sixth of October he and his grandsons left Philadelphia; not attended on this occasion by an escort of three hundred horse; but with precautions to keep their departure secret. That night they lay at Chester, and the next morning rode in a carriage to Marcus Hook, three miles beyond, and embarked on board the sloop, which immediately weighed and stood down the river. Useless precautions! That the British authorities in New York were instantly informed of the event, we learn from a letter of Sir Grey Cooper (an old London friend of Franklin's), written at New York, October 28th, which contains this sentence : " The Arch——Dr. Franklin, has lately eloped under a cloak of plenipotentiary to Versailles ;" i. e., to avoid the inevitable collapse of the revolt.

The voyage was short, rough, and eventful. Several times the vessel was chased by the enemy's cruisers, when Captain Wickes would beat to quarters, and clear for action in a style which Franklin thought could be surpassed in no king's ship. At the same time, the captain made all sail to get away, since his orders were to fight if he must, but avoid fighting if he could. It was one wild November gale nearly all the way over, and the old man was sadly cramped in the contracted cabin; so that of all his eight voyages,

* American Archives.

this was the most distressing.   His grandson assures us, however, that sick or well, sea smooth or sea rough, the ardent experimenter contrived every day to take the temperature of the ocean, in order to verify anew his discovery of the warmth of the Gulf Stream. We may imagine, too, that he spent some hours in furbishing his French, in speaking which he had had but little practice, and that long ago. During his earlier visits to Paris he had depended too much upon his comrade Sir John Pringle; and he told Mr. Adams, a year or two after this voyage, that on reaching France he found it extremely difficult, for a while, to make himself understood, though he read French with perfect ease.   What American embassador has ever crossed the ocean without a furtive phrase-book in his trunk?

William Temple Franklin alone has related with any minuteness, and he too meagerly, the circumstances attending the arrival of his grandfather on the shores of France. "November 27th," he says, "our vessel being near the coast of France, though out of soundings, several sail were seen, and, about noon, the sloop brought to and took a brig from Bordeaux, bound to Cork (being Irish property), loaded with lumber and some wine. She had left Bordeaux the day before. The captain found, by the brig's reckoning, that he was then only sixteen leagues from land. In the afternoon of the same day he came up with, and took another brig, from Rochfort, belonging to Hull, bound to Hamburg, with brandy and flax-seed. Early the next morning land was in sight from the masthead; it proved to be Bellisle; a pilot came on board, and the sloop was brought to an anchor in the evening. On the 29th she ran into Quiberon Bay, where she continued till December 3d; when finding the contrary winds likely to continue, which prevented her entering the Loire, the captain procured a fishing boat to put Dr. Franklin and his grandsons on shore at Auray, about six leagues distant, where they were landed in the evening. The boatmen spoke the Breton language as well as the French; and it appeared to be the common language of the country people in that province. One word only was intelligible, which was Diaul; it signifies Devil, and is the same in the Welsh language. It is said there is a considerable affinity between the two languages, and that the Welsh and Breton fishermen and peasantry can comprehend each other. Auray proved to be a wretched place. No post-chaises to be hired; obliged to send to Vannes for one; which did not arrive till next day; when the party reached that town, late in the evening. Dr. Franklin in the little journal he kept, and from which the above details are taken, adds: 'The carriage was a miserable one, with tired horses, the evening dark, scarce a traveler but ourselves on the road; and to make it more *comfortable*, the driver stopped near a wood we were to pass through, to tell us that a gang of eighteen robbers infested that wood, who but two weeks ago had robbed and murdered some travelers on that very spot.' "

"The same journal contains the following remark: 'December 6th. On the road yesterday,' (traveling to Nantes), 'we met six or seven country women in company, on horseback and astride; they were all of fair white and red complexions, but one among them was the fairest woman I ever beheld. Most of the men have good complexions, not swarthy, like those of the North of France in which I remember that, except about Abbeville, I saw few fair people.'

"Arriving at Nantes on the 7th of December, a grand dinner was prepared on the occasion by some friends of America, at which Dr. Franklin was present, and in the afternoon went to meet a large party at the country seat of Mons. Gruel (senior partner of M. Penet), a short distance from town, where crowds of visitors came to compliment him on his safe arrival, expressing great satisfaction, as they were warm friends to America, and hoped his being in France would be of advantage to the American cause. A magnificent supper closed the evening.

"Being much fatigued and weakened by the voyage and journey, Dr. Franklin was persuaded to remain some time at M. Gruel's country house, where he was elegantly and commodiously lodged: his strength, indeed, was not equal to an immediate journey to Paris." (Franklin himself says, that on landing at Auray, he was so weakened by the voyage, that he could scarcely stand.) "During his stay at M. Gruel's, he was in hopes of living retired, but the house was almost always full of visitors; from whom, however, much useful information was obtained respecting the state of affairs at court, and the character of persons in power."*

At Nantes, a large and important port (now of more than a hun-

---

* William Temple Franklin's Memoirs of Benj. Franklin, vol. i., p. 309.

dred thousand inhabitants, and the fourth seaport of France), America had indeed hosts of friends—interested and disinterested. M. Penet lived there, and had been shipping goods for America; Beaumarchais had been there, collecting and dispatching stores by the shipload to the illustrious Congress. Not a soul in Nantes, not a soul in Europe, knew of Franklin's coming; for the swift Reprisal had outstripped even the rumor of his appointment. The surprise greatly hightened the eclat of his arrival.

The correspondence and diaries of the period, English, French, and German, contain abundant evidence that Dr. Franklin's sudden appearance on the French coast was the "sensation" of that winter. "An account came," wrote Horace Walpole (a stanch friend of America), "that Dr. Franklin, at the age of 72 or 74, and at the risk of his head, had bravely embarked on board an American frigate, and, with two prizes taken on the way, had landed at Nantes in France, and was to be at Paris the 14th, where the highest admiration and expectation of him were raised." Madame du Deffand wrote to Horace Walpole from Paris: "The object of Dr. Franklin's visit is still problematical; and what is the most singular of all is, that no one can tell whether he is actually in Paris or not. For three or four days it has been said in the morning that he had arrived, and in the evening that he had not yet come." The Marquis of Rockingham told Mr. Burke that he considered the presence of Dr. Franklin at the French court "much more than a balance for the few additional acres which the English had gained by the conquest of Manhattan Island." Many similar passages will occur to readers familiar with the letters of that time. Nantes was in a prodigious ferment. He says himself, in his moderate manner: "I find it generally supposed at Nantes, that I am sent to negotiate; and that opinion appears to give great pleasure, if I can judge by the extreme civilities I meet with from numbers of the principal people, who have done me the honor to visit me."

On the 22d of December, Madame du Deffand communicated to Horace Walpole the great event: "Dr. Franklin arrived in town yesterday, at two o'clock in the afternoon; he slept the night before at Versailles. He was accompanied by two of his grandsons, one seven years old the other seventeen, and by his friend, M. Penet. He has taken lodgings in the Rue de l'Université." Even so; at the Hotel de Hamburg, where also lived Silas Deane, now one of the happiest of men. "Here," he wrote exultingly to Mr. Dumas, "is the hero, and philosopher, and patriot, all united in this celebrated American, who, at the age of seventy-four, risks all dangers for his country! I know your heart rejoices with me on this occasion." And more : " He left Philadelphia the last of October, and every thing was favorable in America !" America was *not* endangered, nor even discouraged, by the loss of New York!

Respecting Dr. Franklin's journey from Nantes to Paris, Cobbett has preserved from the old newspapers, an anecdote of some point, and not too improbable for belief. I know not whether there is any truth in it. The story is, that at one of the inns at which he slept on the road, he was informed that Gibbon (the first volume of whose History had been published in the spring of that year) was also stopping. "Franklin sent his compliments, requesting the pleasure of spending the evening with Mr. Gibbon. In answer he received a card, importing that, notwithstanding Mr. Gibbon's regard for the character of Dr. Franklin, as a man and a philosopher, he could not reconcile it with his duty to his king, to have any conversation with a revolted subject ! Franklin in reply wrote a note, declaring, that ' though Mr. Gibbon's principles had compelled him to withhold the pleasure of his conversation, Dr. Franklin had still such a respect for the character of Mr. Gibbon, as a gentleman and a historian, that when, in the course of his writing the history of the *decline and fall* of empires, the *decline and fall* of the British Empire should come to be his subject, as he expects it soon would, Dr. Franklin would be happy to furnish him with ample materials which were in his possession.' "

Cobbett, in the amiable manner usual with him when speaking of Franklin, adds : " Whether this anecdote record a truth or not I shall not pretend to say ; but it must be confessed that the expressions imputed to the two personages were strictly in character. In Gibbon we see the faithful subject, and the man of candor and honor ; in Franklin, the treacherous and malicious ' old Zanga of Boston.' "*

Gibbon, like Hume, was an extreme tory, and supported Lord North unflinchingly in all his American measures ; with the reward, at length, of a sinecure place of eight hundred pounds a

* Cobbett's Works, vol. vii., p. 244.

year. I notice, also, that Mr. Gibbon, in his barren autobiography, mentions having visited France not long after the publication of his first volume ; and he seems to have spent several weeks there, and to have distinguished himself by his opposition to the republican enthusiasm that prevailed in salon, palace, and château. The anecdote, however, stands without support.

In Paris, then, Dr. Franklin was established in the last days of December, 1776. Old friends welcomed him, new ones gathering round, and the public manifesting a strange interest in all that he did. Indeed, his reception in Paris, and his popularity throughout France, during the many years of his residence in that country, were so remarkable, and produced such effects upon public affairs, and upon his own tranquillity, that it seems proper to pause here for a moment on the threshold of his new career, and say a few words respecting the causes of the enthusiasm his presence excited. Generally speaking, popularity is a trivial matter, not worth many words ; but it may be undervalued as well as overvalued. There are times when a popularity, even though evanescent and unmerited, has such results that it cannot be overlooked. Franklin's popularity among the amiable people of France, which was neither evanescent nor unmerited, formed part of the atmosphere in which he lived for so many years. He breathed incense all the time.

A genuine reputation is a growing thing ; and Franklin's European renown was now nearly a quarter of a century old. The electrical discoveries to which he owed his universal celebrity were such as appealed to the uninstructed millions, even more strongly than to the learned few. He had been a printer, editor, and postmaster ; which had brought him into intimate relations with the entire press of one continent, and a part of the press of another. Printers, perhaps, had more *esprit du corps* than any other of the colonial vocations, and the old printers seem to have been never better pleased than when they were giving currency to paragraphs by or concerning Dr. Franklin. Moreover, he was always either saying or doing a good thing ; *i. e.*, shedding the material of paragraphs. Now, as in these modern days, celebrity is simply the having your name often printed in newspapers, Franklin would have been among the most celebrated men of his day from this cause alone. Add to this accident of his former career, his solid and various merits, and we have the material of a very general and vivid celebrity. But this was not all. No people excel the French in the art of living with a certain elegance upon a small revenue. France is full of people who enjoy the *best* results of civilization upon incomes which we should consider synonymous with pinching poverty. Hence, perhaps, the success in France of Poor Richard, whose homely maxims were three times translated into French, and were everywhere known. I may also remark, that Benjamin Franklin, Printer, of Philadelphia, in the Paris of 1776, was the contact of two civilizations that are always pleased with one another when they are properly introduced, and see each other to good advantage. Count Sigur's well-known passage illustrates this point :

" It would be difficult to describe," he says, " the eagerness and delight with which the American Envoys, the agents of a people in a state of insurrection against their monarch, were received in France, in the bosom of an ancient monarchy. Nothing could be more striking, than the contrast between the luxury of our capital, the elegance of our fashions, the magnificence of Versailles, the still brilliant remains of the monarchical pride of Louis XIV., and the polished and superb dignity of our nobility, on the one hand ; and, on the other hand, the almost rustic apparel, the plain but firm demeanor, the free and direct language of the envoys, whose antique simplicity of dress and appearance seemed to have introduced within our walls, in the midst of the effeminate and servile refinement of the 18th century, some sages contemporary with Plato, or republicans of the age of Cato and of Fabius. This unexpected apparition produced upon us a greater effect in consequence of its novelty, and of its occurring precisely at the period when literature and philosophy had circulated amongst us an unusual desire for reforms, a disposition to encourage innovations, and the seeds of an ardent attachment to liberty."*

M. Lacretelle, a French historian, discourses in a similar strain : " Men imagined they saw in Franklin a sage of antiquity, come back to give austere lessons and generous examples to the moderns. They personified in him the republic, of which he was the representative and the legislator. They regarded his virtues as those of his countrymen, and even judged of their physiognomy by the

---

* Memoirs of Count Sigur, vol. i., p. 101.

imposing and serene traits of his own. Happy was he who could gain admittance to see him in the house which he occupied. This venerable old man, it was said, joined to the demeanor of Phocion the spirit of Socrates." And the German, Schlosser, says: "Franklin's appearance in the Paris *salons*, even before he began to negotiate, was an event of great importance to the whole of Europe. Paris, at that time, set the fashion for the civilized world, and the admiration of Franklin, carried to a degree approaching folly, produced a remarkable effect on the fashionable circles of Paris. His dress, the simplicity of his external appearance, the friendly meekness of the old man, and the apparent humility of the Quaker, procured for Freedom a mass of votaries among the court circles, who used to be alarmed at its coarseness and unsophisticated truths." Other chroniclers of the period bear similar testimony.

With regard to the rustic apparel, Count Sigur was in error; neither Silas Deane nor Dr. Franklin was capable of such an affectation. Nevertheless, Franklin did venture upon one bold and wise innovation: he resisted the tyranny of the hair-dressers; he positively would not again submit to the daily nuisance of pigtail and powder. His white hair being now too scanty for the protection of his head, he was accustomed to wear at this time (but soon discarded it) an odd-looking fur cap, which did impart to his appearance something that might pass for rusticity. One of the first letters which he wrote in Paris, contains a humorous description of his appearance: "Figure me, in your mind, as jolly as formerly and as strong and hearty, only a few years older; very plainly dressed, wearing my thin, gray, straight hair, that peeps out under my only *coiffure*, a fine fur cap, which comes down my forehead almost to my spectacles. Think how this must appear among the powdered heads of Paris! I wish every lady and gentleman in France would only be so obliging as to follow my fashion, comb their own heads, as I do mine, dismiss their *friseurs*, and pay me half the money they paid to them. You see, the gentry might well afford this, and I could then enlist these *friseurs*, who are at least one hundred thousand, and with the money I would maintain them, make a visit with them to England, and dress the heads of your ministers and privy counselors; which I conceive at present to be *un peu dérangées*." (A little out of order.)

No one has more forcibly described the estimation in which
Franklin was held in Europe than John Adams; who, unhappily,
was not able to regard his colleague's great fame with equanimity.
"Franklin's reputation," says Mr. Adams, "was more universal
than that of Leibnitz or Newton, Frederick or Voltaire; and his
character more beloved and esteemed than any or all of them. * *
His name was familiar to government and people, to kings, courtiers, nobility, clergy, and philosophers, as well as plebeians, to such
a degree that there was scarcely a peasant or a citizen, a valet de
chambre, coachman or footman, a lady's chambermaid or a scullion
in a kitchen, who was not familiar with it, and who did not consider him a friend to human kind. When they spoke of him they
seemed to think he was to restore the golden age. * * If a collection could be made of all the Gazettes of Europe, for the latter
half of the eighteenth century, a greater number of panegyrical
paragraphs upon *le grand Franklin* would appear, it is believed,
than upon any other man that ever lived. * * The Catholics
thought him almost a Catholic. The Church of England claimed
him as one of them. The Presbyterians thought him half a Presbyterian, and the Quakers believed him a wet Quaker. * * He
was thought to be the magician who had excited the ignorant
Americans to resistance. His mysterious wand had separated the
colonies from Great Britain. He had framed and established all
the American constitutions of government, especially all the best
of them, *i. e.*, the most democratical. His plans and his example
were to abolish monarchy, aristocracy, and hierarchy, throughout
the world."*

Mr. Adams chronicles in his diary a conversation he once had with
M. Marbois, which contains a smothered hint at another cause of the
peculiar affection felt for Franklin in some Parisian circles. "'All
religions,' said M. Marbois, ' are tolerated in America. The embassadors have a right in all courts to a chapel in their own way ; but
Mr. Franklin never had any.' ' No,' said I, laughing, ' because Mr.
Franklin has no———.' I was going to say what I did not say, and
will not say here. I stopped short and laughed. ' No,' said M.
Marbois, ' Mr. Franklin adores only great Nature, which has interested a great many people of both sexes in his favor.' ' Yes,' said

---

* Works of John Adams, i, 660.

I, laughing ; ' all the atheists, deists, and libertines, as well as the philosophers and ladies, are in his train.' "* Mr. Adams could never forgive Franklin's immense importance in Europe. If by the word Religion, he meant any thing which passed in New England by that name, John had little more of it than Benjamin.

Silas Deane, on the contrary, felt an honest pride in the honors bestowed upon his countryman. "Never," he wrote, " did I enjoy greater satisfaction than in being the spectator of the public honors often paid him. A celebrated cause being to be heard before the Parliament of Paris, and the house and street leading to it crowded with people, on the appearance of Dr. Franklin way was made for him in the most respectful manner, and he passed through the crowd to the seat reserved for him amid the acclamations of the people—an honor seldom paid to their first princes of the blood. When he attended the operas and plays, similar honors were paid him, and I confess I felt a joy and pride which was pure and honest, though not disinterested, for I considered it an honor to be known to be an American and his acquaintance."

Such was the number of portraits published of him, that one of his great grandsons in Philadelphia has been able, even at this late day, to collect a hundred and fifty of them, few of which are duplicates. Medallions, medals, busts, in all sizes, styles, and materials, were produced in astonishing numbers. What he says himself on this subject to his daughter, is not a mere humorous exaggeration, but a statement of fact. Writing in 1779 of a certain medallion to which his daughter had alluded, he continued: " A variety of others have been made since of different sizes ; some to be set in the lids of snuff-boxes,† and some so small as to be worn in rings ; and the numbers

* Works of John Adams, iii., 220.

† The following went the round of the press during the Revolution :

"On seeing a small mezzotinto print of Dr. Franklin in the case of a watch, 1778. By an Englishman.

"Had but our nation mov'd like this great man,—
With wisdom's wheel to regulate its plan,—
Not urg'd by rancor, nor disturb'd by rage,—
But guided by the prudence of this sage;
The spring of state had still been strong and tight,
Its *chain* of *friendship* lasting, pure, and *bright*,
Our hand of time had pointed still at noon,
And sable night had not approach'd so soon."

"The author of the above lines immediately after, finding himself in a thoughtful mood, wrote as follows :

"Cheer up, my friend, and view yon western main,
There young day dawns, and Phœbus smiles again,

sold are incredible. These, with the pictures, busts, and prints (of which copies upon copies are spread everywhere), have made your father's face as well known as that of the moon, so that he durst not do any thing that would oblige him to run away, as his phiz would discover him wherever he should venture to show it. It is said by learned etymologists, that the name *doll*, for the images children play with, is derived from the word IDOL. From the number of *dolls* now made of him, he may be truly said, *in that sense*, to be *i-doll-ized* in this country."

In the same humorous manner he always spoke of the extravagant estimation in which he was held. The incense-clouds neither blinded, poisoned, intoxicated, nor inflated him.   In one of his letters to Mrs. Jay occurs this amusing paragraph : " Mrs. Jay does me much honor in desiring to have one of the prints that have been made here of her countryman.   I send what is said to be the best of five or six engraved by different hands, from different paintings.   The verses at the bottom are truly extravagant.   But you must know, that the desire of pleasing, by a perpetual rise of compliments in this polite nation, has so used up all the common expressions of approbation, that they are become flat and insipid, and to use them almost implies censure.   Hence music, that formerly might be sufficiently praised when it was called *bonne*, to go a little further they called it *excellente*, then *superbe*, *magnifique*, *exquise*, *celeste*, all which being in their turns worn out, there only remains *divine ;* and, when that is grown as insignificant as its predecessors, I think they must return to common speech and common sense ; as, from vying with one another in fine and costly paintings on their coaches, since I first knew the country, not being able to go further in that way, they have returned lately to plain carriages, painted without arms or figures, in one uniform color."

On the other side of the channel, the presence of Franklin in the

So 'tis with Liberty—*here* sunk in shade,
While *there* blooms sweetly the celestial maid.
The soil is good, the tree has taken root,
And soon the industrious kind shall reap the fruit.
His persevering toil hath dearly earn'd
Those golden fruits which foolish Britain spurn'd,
While wiser France saw Albion's wretched doom,
Begg'd of it suckers to transplant at home ;
Where her State Husbandmen are now employ'd
To pluck those apples which we once enjoy'd."

French capital excited, as may be imagined, a world of comment, chiefly hostile. "France, my lords," exclaimed the Earl of Chatham in the House of Lords, "has insulted you. She has encouraged and sustained America; and, whether America be wrong of right, the dignity of this country ought to spurn at the officious insult of French interference. The ministers and embassadors of those who are called rebels are in Paris; in Paris they transact the reciprocal business of America and France. Can there be a more mortifying insult? Can even our ministers sustain a more humiliating disgrace? Do they dare to resent it? Do they presume even to hint a vindication of their honor and the dignity of the state, by requiring the dismissal of the plenipotentiaries of America?" Still, it was in this very speech that the aged statesman said, in alluding to the employment of the Hessians: "If I were an American, as I am an Englishman, whilst a foreign troop was landed in my country, I would never lay down my arms—never—*never*—NEVER!"

One penny-a-liner (there were penny-a-liners then) informed the public, that Dr. Franklin had a son, who, though illegitimate, was a "much more honest man than his father;" and as to the mother of that son, nothing was known of her except that her seducer let her "die in the streets." Another writer essayed a satirical piece, in Franklin's own manner, in the form of a "Copy of Dr. Franklin's Proposals from the American Congress to the French Court," a sorry burlesque, much quoted at the time, but not worth copying now. "I have just seen," wrote Franklin in one of his first letters, "seven paragraphs in the (English) papers about me, of which six were lies."

The weakest manifestation of British spleen, however, was an act of the poor, blind king. The Purfleet Powder Magazine, protected by lightning rods of Franklin's own selection, was struck by lightning, and escaped without explosion, or even serious injury. This event having revived the old controversy, whether lightning rods should be blunt or pointed, Dr. Wilson led the assault upon Franklin's opinion, and stoutly contended for blunt. How easy to convince a George III., at such a time, that Franklin's opinions were erroneous! Down came the Franklinian pointed conductors from the Powder Magazine, and from Buckingham Palace, the king's own residence, and in their stead appeared Dr. Wilson's

blunt ones.   The retort of Franklin, when he was informed of this
ridiculous event, has been often quoted : " The king's changing his
pointed conductors for blunt ones is a matter of small importance
to me. If I had a wish about it, it would be, that he had rejected
them altogether as ineffectual. For it is only since he thought
himself and family safe from the thunder of Heaven, that he dared
to use his own thunder in destroying his innocent subjects." The
epigram which the affair evoked in London is also well known :

"While you, great George, for safety hunt,
    And sharp conductors change for blunt,
        The empire 's out of joint.
Franklin a wiser course pursues,
    And all your thunder fearless views,
        By keeping to the *point.*" *

England was strangely divided against herself in this contest.
While the court, the newspapers, the ministry, an increasing ma-

* To show that this story of the blunt conductors was no fiction of the hour, I transcribe Mr.
Weld's account of the controversy, as given in his History of the Royal Society :
    "It was no longer scientific men who were allowed to decide the question, but political parti-
sans, so that the advocates of pointed conductors soon became identified with the insurgent
colonists; and those opposed to blunt points were considered as disaffected subjects. As usual
in such cases, the populace, and even the higher classes of society, took up the quarrel without
inquiring into its merits, or, indeed, knowing any thing about the matter in a scientific point of
view. Wilson thus found protection and support, as he would have done against the theorem
of Pythagoras, had geometry been the subject of dispute.
    "But the most extraordinary part of this dispute is, that George III. is stated to have taken
the side of Wilson, not on scientific grounds, but from political motives; and that he even had
blunt conductors fixed on his palace, and actually endeavored to make the Royal Society rescind
their resolutions in favor of pointed conductors. His majesty, it is declared, had an interview
with Sir John Pringle, during which he earnestly entreated him to use his influence in supporting Mr. Wilson. The reply of the president was highly honorable to himself and the Society
whom he represented. It was to the effect that duty as well as inclination would always induce
him to execute his majesty's wishes to the utmost of his power : but 'Sire,' said he, 'I cannot
reverse the laws and operations of nature.' * * * *
    "Several resolutions and amendments were moved and seconded by the leading fellows, but
not carried. Eventually, it was determined that a reply should be written by the secretary, to
the secretary of the Board of Ordnance. It ran thus :
    "'Sir: In answer to your letter of the 19th May, I am directed to inform you, that the Society
has never since its first institution given an opinion as a body at large, but constantly by committees. And that in the particular instance of the questions lately proposed by the Board of
Ordnance, the Society has no reason to be dissatisfied with the report of its committee.'
    "This letter had the effect of increasing the anger of Wilson and his friends, and, strange as it
now appears, the dispute, which had its origin in a question of Natural Philosophy, was made
one of party politics. This is attributable to the fact, that England was at the hight of her
quarrel with her American colonies, and it was Franklin who invented pointed conductors."—
Weld's History of the Royal Society, ii., 99.

jority of Parliament, and a vast majority of the people (who usually join the war party *en masse* after the first bloodshed) regarded Franklin as a rebel of the deepest dye, nearly every man in England of whom England now is proud, revered him as a patriot and a sage. At the very time of Franklin's arrival in Paris and during the first weeks of his residence there, no one approached him with sincerer homage, no one more prized his society and conversation, than Charles James Fox, the leader of the English opposition. Four years after, in the course of a debate in the House of Commons, a member having spoken of the contest in America as a Holy War, Mr. Fox said: "To others, the application of such an epithet to the actual contest may appear new; but to me it has no novelty. I was in Paris precisely at the time when the present war began, in 1776, and Dr. Franklin honored me with his intimacy. I recollect, that conversing with him on the subject of the impending hostilities, he, while he predicted their ruinous consequences, compared their principle and their consequences to those of the ancient Crusades. He foretold that we should expend our best blood and treasure in attempting an unattainable object; and that like the *holy* war of the dark ages, while we carried desolation and slaughter over America, we should finally depopulate, enfeeble, and impoverish Great Britain."*

Nor was it only such as Fox, Burke, Rockingham, Shelburne, Chatham, Priestley, and Price, who befriended America at this time. All the winter a popular subscription had been going on for the benefit of American prisoners of war in England; prisoners whom the government affected to regard as felons. The subscription in February, 1777, amounted to four thousand six hundred and forty-seven pounds sterling;† and was still proceeding.

For a few weeks Dr. Franklin lived with Mr. Deane at the Hotel de Hamburg amid the whirl and roar of Paris, overwhelmed with the endless rush of visitors. By the time he had discovered that this would not do, the good Genius which in London sent him to Craven Street and Mrs. Stevenson, procured him, near Paris, a most delightful and convenient retreat. At that time Paris, like London, was a great city surrounded by little villages; and the Seine, like the Thames, flowed between verdant

banks, and past gardens and villas almost to the verge of the metropolis.   The villages have long ago been overrun and swallowed
up by the spreading cities, leaving only their names to mark the
districts where once they stood.   Of the villages near Paris one
of the most noted was Passy, situated on a lofty hill overlooking
the river, the city, and a great expanse of gardens, parks, farms,
châteaux, and villages.   It is now included within the fortifica-
tion of Paris, yet retains much of its ancient, leafy, secluded pleasantness, and all its grandeur of situation.   At Passy, in houses of
their own building, live, or have recently lived, Bellini, Rossini,
Lamartine, Erard, Grisi, and other notabilities of Paris and Europe.
Thomas Moore lived and wrote a poem there.   In 1776, one of the
most spacious and sumptuous mansions in the place, called the Hotel
de Valentinois, belonged to that munificent friend of America, M.
Ray de Chaumont, who lived in part of it himself.   M. De Chaumont had been among the first to welcome Dr. Franklin to Paris;
had been with him daily; had conceived for him the warmest affection.   He now pressed Franklin to accept part of his house at
Passy as a place of permanent abode.   It was but two miles from
the center of Paris; far enough to reduce the crowd of idle visitors,
and near enough for easy access.   Dr. Franklin accepted the offer.
M. De Chaumont would accept no rent for his house as long as
the contest of America for independence could be considered
doubtful.   When the war was over and the country happily settled and prosperous, then Congress, if it pleased, might grant him
in compensation a piece of American land.   Early in the year
1777 Dr. Franklin established himself at Passy, in a court of the
Hotel de Valentinois, and there continued to reside during the
whole of his stay in France.   He had his own servants and, in all
respects, an independent establishment.   A chariot and pair was
one of his first and most necessary acquisitions.

The impression prevails that a Spartan simplicity characterized
the household of Dr. Franklin in France.   No such thing.   He
lived liberally, as became his age, his position, and his office.   Spartan simplicity was impossible—as Mrs. Adams discovered, a few
years later.   "It is the policy of France," she observes in one of
her letters home, "to oblige you to keep a certain number of servants, and one will not touch what belongs to the business of another, though he or she has time enough to perform the whole.   In

the first place, there is a coachman who does not an individual thing but attend to the carriages and horses; then the gardener, who has business enough; then comes the cook; then the *maître d'hôtel;* his business is to purchase articles for the family, and oversee that nobody cheats but himself; a *valet de chambre ;* a *femme de chambre ;* a *coiffeuse,*—for this place, I have a French girl about nineteen, whom I have been upon the point of turning away, because Madame will not brush a chamber; 'it is not de fashion, it is not her business.' I would not have kept her a day longer, but found, upon inquiry, that I could not better myself, and hair-dressing here is very expensive, unless you keep such a madam in the house. There is another indispensable servant, who is called a *frotteur ;* his business is to rub the floors. We have a servant who acts as *maître d'hôtel,* whom I like at present, and who is so very gracious as to act as footman too, to save the expense of another servant, upon condition that we give him a gentleman's suit of clothes in lieu of a livery. Thus, with seven servants and hiring a charwoman upon occasion of company, we may possibly make out to keep house; with less, we should be hooted at as ridiculous, and could not entertain any company."

Some such retinue as this, I suppose, Dr. Franklin was compelled to maintain at Passy. He appears to have expended in France an average of about thirteen thousand dollars a year.

CHAPTER II.

DR. FRANKLIN AT WORK.

To cheer the friends, and alarm the enemies of the United States, were among Dr. Franklin's first employments in France. His mere presence was cheering; his countenance, his demeanor, his words, all expressed an honest and perfect confidence in the final triumph of the United States. The circle of Americans and devotees of America at Paris heard with joy his exact and hopeful accounts of affairs at home. Besides putting new heart into the cause in France, he sent witty, warning letters across the channel, full of the unfaltering spirit of America; letters which he knew would be eagerly read in England, and diligently handed about. "We are better armed, better disciplined, better supplied, and more determined than ever," he would write to one friend. "England is undone if she perseveres in so mad a war," he would write to another. To a third, "I sometimes flatter myself that, old as I am, I may possibly live to see my country settled in peace and prosperity, when Britain shall make no more a formidable figure among the powers of Europe." Moral support was what the Cause needed in Europe at that time, and it was moral support that he brought to its aid.

Silas Deane and Beaumarchais, as before intimated, were at their wits' end when Franklin reached Paris. Not only were their laden ships forbidden to depart, but, to complete their misery, the Amphitrite, the only ship they had succeeded in getting off, returned to port after having been at sea three weeks. The precious Du Coudray, peerless General of Artillery, was the ·cause of this mishap; he having ordered the ship back, alleging that the cabin was inconvenient, and the vessel otherwise unsuitable to his dignity. Beaumarchais raved and took to his bed, sick from disgust and anxiety; he ordered Du Coudray out of his ship, bag and baggage, and told him to go about his business.* Deane, too, tried to shake him off, and the French Cabinet interfered, revoked Du Coudray's leave of absence, and ordered him to join his corps. But the impracticable man had friends in the cabinet and at court, whom the American envoys dared not run the risk of disobliging; and so the dispute was arranged, and a passage was found for him and his train in another ship. By exertions that may be literally described as "unheard of," as well as unrecorded, Beaumarchais succeeded in quieting the apprehensions of the ministry, and in procuring permission, expressed or tacit, for the departure of his vessels. The Amphitrite reached Portsmouth in New Hampshire, in April, and two other vessels arrived in time to aid the campaign.

It was agreed between the three envoys, that, as Mr. Deane had alone been concerned with Roderique Hortalez and Co., he should continue to transact business with that mysterious house unassisted. I should not omit, however, to state, that Dr. Franklin

---

* "Beaumarchais and his Times," by M. de Loménie, p. 292.

joined Mr. Deane in recommending General du Coudray to the President of Congress as an officer of "great reputation." Mr. Deane explains how this came to pass : " M. du Coudray came secretly to Paris. I saw him and expostulated with him on what had passed, urging him to give up for the present all thoughts of prosecuting his voyage to America. He was unwilling to agree to it, and chose to go out at any rate. I told him he must not rely on my doing any thing further in his affairs ; he was in danger of being arrested at Paris on account of the order (to join his corps), and left the city privately. After which two gentlemen of high rank, the Duc de Rochefaucault and the Chevalier de Chattelier, waited on Dr. Franklin and myself, Mr. Lee being to the best of my remembrance out of town, and urged that I should not oppose the going out of Monsieur du Coudray. I stated generally my situation, but the character and abilities of this gentleman were so strongly urged by his noble patrons, that Dr. Franklin resolved to write in his favor, and having written the letter, I could no longer refuse joining him in it, which I did, on condition that Monsieur du Coudray should not embark in any of the ships I ordered stores to be sent in, but that he should shift for himself as well as he could."*

So Du Coudray sailed, with his train of hungry officers, carrying in his pocket a letter of introduction signed by Dr. Franklin, and Mr. Deane, and a commission as general-in-chief of artillery in the army of the United States, granted and signed by Silas Deane only. His officers were of all grades, even to sergeants, and were all promised rank in the American army, each one grade higher than he had held in France.

December 28th, five days after Dr. Franklin's arrival in Paris, the three American envoys had their first interview with the Count de Vergennes. The official proceedings against the shipments of Hortalez and Co. were at their hight; i. e., M. de Vergennes was using all his art to soothe Lord Stormont. Nevertheless, he received the envoys with every mark of profound respect. They exhibited their commission, and an outline of such a treaty as Congress desired to conclude with France. They explained the difficulty of making remittances of tobacco and rice from

* Deane Papers, p. 34.

America, the harbors and bays being blockaded by ships of war. America, they said, could cope with English frigates, because she now had frigates of her own, but ships of the line were too much for an infant navy, and, consequently, the resources of the States were locked up. They were instructed to ask the French government to lend Congress eight ships of the line, completely equipped and manned, the whole expense of which Congress would pay, and the possession of which would enable America to carry on with France that renowned commerce which for a hundred years had been enriching England. The minister replied with the vague but cordial politeness of a man who longs to say, Yes, and hopes ere long to be able to say it, but is compelled for the present to await the development of events. The prospects of America to a cool and well-informed minister were dark and darkening. The Count de Vergennes had probably by that time heard something of the great army of eight or ten thousand men with which General Burgoyne was on the point of sailing to America, to co-operate with the twice victorious troops of General Howe. He assured the envoys of the friendly protection of the king during their residence in France; asked them to state in writing the substance of what they had offered, and convey the document to M. Gerard; promised them that its contents should be duly considered; assured them, also (too vaguely for Mr. Deane's anxieties), that whatever commercial privileges France could grant America without violating treaties with Great Britain, should be granted; and, finally, advised them to seek an interview with the embassador of Spain, a power with which France acted in the strictest concert in all affairs that might be supposed to involve the peace of Europe.

The envoys presented their memorial as requested, and received through M. Gerard a polite reply which may be abbreviated thus: "*Not yet, Messieurs!* Meanwhile, we will do all we can for you short of obliging Lord Stormont to demand his passports. For that we are not quite ready. For the present, if a couple of millions of francs, without interest, to be repaid after the war, will be of any use to an illustrious Congress, why, the money is very much at their service. Only, don't say you had it from *us*." To which Arthur Lee penned a reply in his highest style: "We beg to return our most grateful sense of the gracious intentions which his majesty has had the goodness to signify to our states, and to assure his majesty that we shall ever retain the warmest gratitude for the substantial proofs he has given us of his regard," etc., etc. And Dr. Franklin, towards the close of his next letter to the Secret Committee, dated Jan. 17th, observed: "So strong is the inclination of the wealthy here to assist us, that we are offered a loan of two millions of livres, without interest, and to be repaid when the United States are settled in peace and prosperity. No conditions or security are required, not even an engagement from us. We have accepted this generous and noble benefaction; five hundred thousand francs, or one quarter, is to be paid into the hands of our banker this day, and five hundred thousand more every three months. * * P. S., Jan. 22d. We have received the five hundred thousand francs mentioned above, and our banker has orders to advance us the second payment if we desire it." Two months later, a very safe opportunity occurring, the envoys informed the Secret Committee of the truth with regard to this loan.

A week after the date of the cheering postscript just quoted, the envoys received from England their first intelligence of the Burgoyne expedition, which, they were informed, was destined for the invasion of Virginia and Maryland. Arthur Lee, a Virginian, seized with consternation, drew up an earnest appeal to M. de Vergennes, which his colleagues approved and signed, urging France to declare war against England and thus divert this formidable force. If not diverted, argued Lee, "it will be in their power to destroy a great part of those states, as the houses and estates of the principal inhabitants are situated on the navigable waters, and so separated from each other as to be incapable of being defended from armed vessels conveying troops." And "great danger," he added, "is also to be apprehended from the blacks of those states, who, being excited and armed by the British, may greatly strengthen the invaders, at the same time that the fear of their insurrection will prevent the white inhabitants from leaving their places of residence, and assembling in such numbers for their own defense against the English as otherwise they might do." Moreover, "the destruction of these two states probably may make a great impression on the people in the rest, who, seeing no prospect of assistance from any European power, may be more inclined to listen to terms of accommodation." He urged in conclusion, "that notwithstanding the measures taken to convince the court of Britain that France does not countenance the Americans, that court, according to our information, believes firmly the contrary; and it is submitted to the consideration of your excellency, whether, if the English made a conquest of the American states, they will not take the first opportunity of showing their resentment, by beginning themselves the war that would otherwise be avoided." Surely, then, the time for France to strike, is NOW! The answer to this memorial, if any written answer was given, has not come to light. Perhaps the arrival of information that General Burgoyne's field of operations was northern, instead of southern, calmed the apprehensions of Mr. Lee.

But, for the time, the envoys and their friends were penetrated with alarm. Even the faith of Dr. Franklin must have been a little shaken, when, besides the Burgoyne news, the intelligence came (and came through the gazettes of an exulting enemy), that General Washington, with a force of three thousand disheartened militia, was flying across New Jersey before General Howe's victorious troops. Not yet had tidings reached Europe of the battle of Trenton (fought December 26th), which snatched the perishing Revolution from the broken ice of the Delaware, and breathed into it the breath of a new and unquenchable life. The envoys appear to have seriously contemplated the possibility of their being left in Europe without a country. In this midnight of their hopes, they solemnly and formally agreed that, come what might, they would stand by their cause and by one another. They all signed a paper to the effect, that if France and Spain should conclude the desired treaty of amity and commerce with the United States, and should be drawn into a war with Great Britain, through granting aid to the United States, then " it will be right and proper for us " to bind our country to stand by France and Spain to the end, fighting with them and for them until the conclusion of a general peace. To this paper was appended the following mysterious and awful note, signed by the three envoys:

" It is further considered, that in the present peril of the liberties of our country, it is our duty to hazard every thing in their support and defense; therefore resolved unanimously, that if it should be necessary to the attainment of any thing in our best judgment essential to the defense and support of the public cause, that we should pledge our persons, or hazard the censure of the

Congress, by exceeding our instructions, we will for such purpose most cheerfully resign our personal liberty or life."*

It was of just this period, and of the precise series of events which preceded the battle of Trenton, that Thomas Paine wrote that trumpet piece, " *The American Crisis,*" Number One ; beginning, "These are the times that try men's souls ;" a composition of amazing spirit and variety. No wonder the American envoys, to whom the bad news from home came exaggerated and distorted, should have been dismayed and cast down.

It was at this dark period that Lafayette, against the advice of the American envoys, resolved to go to America in a ship of his own. His own artless narrative of this time, contained in the fragment of autobiography which he left, gives us an imperfect, hasty glimpse of the envoys :

" When I first learnt the subject of this (American) quarrel, my heart espoused warmly the cause of liberty, and I thought of nothing but of adding also the aid of my banner. Some circumstances, which it would be needless to relate, had taught me to expect only obstacles in this case from my own family ; I depended, therefore, solely upon myself, and I ventured to adopt for a device on my arms these words, "*Cur non ?*" (Why not ?) that they might equally serve as encouragement to myself, and as a reply to others. Silas Deane was then at Paris ; but the ministers feared to receive him, and his voice was overpowered by the louder accents of Lord Stormont. He dispatched privately to America some old arms which were of little use, and some young officers, who did but little good, the whole directed by M. de Beaumarchais ; and when the English embassador spoke to our court, it denied having sent any cargoes, ordered those that were preparing to be discharged, and dismissed from our ports all American privateers. Whilst wishing to address myself in a direct manner to Mr. Deane, I became the friend of Kalb, a German in our employ, who was applying for service with the *insurgents* (the expression in use at that time), and who became my interpreter. He was the person sent by M. de Choiseul to examine the English colonies ; and on his return he received some money, but never succeeded in obtaining an audience, so little did that minister in reality think of the revolution whose retrograde movements some persons have ascribed to him ! When I presented

* Life of Arthur Lee, 1, 68.

to Mr. Deane my boyish face (for I was scarcely nineteen years of age), I spoke more of my ardor in the cause than of my experience; but I dwelt much upon the effect my departure would excite in France, and he signed our mutual agreement. The secrecy with which this negotiation and my preparations were made appears almost a miracle; family friends, ministers, French spies, and English spies, all were kept completely in the dark as to my intentions. Amongst my discreet confidants, I owe much to M. du Boismartim, secretary of the Count de Broglie, and to the Count de Broglie himself, whose affectionate heart, when all his efforts to turn me from this project had proved vain, entered into my views with even paternal tenderness.

"Preparations were making to send a vessel to America, when very bad tidings arrived from thence. New York, Long Island, White Plains, Fort Washington, and the Jerseys, had seen the American forces successively destroyed by thirty-three thousand Englishmen or Germans. Three thousand Americans alone remained in arms, and these were closely pursued by General Howe. From that moment all the credit of the insurgents vanished; to obtain a vessel for them was impossible; *the envoys themselves thought it right to express to me their own discouragement, and persuade me to abandon my project.* I called upon Mr. Deane, and I thanked him for his frankness. ' Until now, sir,' said I, ' you have only seen my ardor in your cause, and that may not prove at present wholly useless. I shall purchase a ship to carry out your officers; we must feel confidence in the future, and it is especially in the hour of danger that I wish to share your fortune.' My project was received with approbation; but it was necessary afterwards to find money, and to purchase and arm a vessel secretly: all this was accomplished with the greatest dispatch.

"The period was, however, approaching, which had been long fixed, for my taking a journey to England. I could not refuse to go without risking the discovery of my secret, and by consenting to take this journey I knew I could better conceal my preparations for a greater one. This last measure was also thought most expedient by MM. Franklin and Deane, for the doctor himself was then in France; and although I did not venture to go to his home, for fear of being seen, I corresponded with him through M. Carmichael, an American less generally known. I arrived in London with M. de

Poix; and I first paid my respects to Bancroft, the American, and afterwards to his British Majesty. A youth of nineteen may be, perhaps, too fond of playing a trick upon the king he is going to fight with; of dancing at the house of Lord Germain, minister of the English colonies, and at the house of Lord Rawdon, who had just returned from New York; and of seeing at the opera that Clinton whom he was afterwards to meet at Monmouth. But whilst I concealed my intentions, I openly avowed my sentiments; I often defended the Americans; I rejoiced at their success at Trenton; and my spirit of opposition obtained for me an invitation to breakfast with Lord Shelburne."*

He sailed in May, to the delight of all France. "He is exceedingly beloved," wrote Franklin to the Secret Committee, "and everybody's good wishes attend him. * * Those who censure his departure as imprudent in him, do, nevertheless, applaud his spirit; and we are satisfied that the civilities and respect that may be shown him will be serviceable to our affairs here, as pleasing, not only to his powerful relations and to the court, but to the whole French nation. He has left a beautiful young wife, and for her sake particularly, we hope that his bravery and ardent desire to distinguish himself will be a little restrained by the General's prudence, so as not to permit his being hazarded much, but on some important occasion."

Dr. Franklin, during this gloomy winter, presented to the gay world of Paris a serene and smiling face, and amused it with sallies that still form part of the common stock of that immense multitude who are indebted to their memory for their jests. To one who brought to him a story, as from the British embassador, that six battalions of American troops under General Washington had laid down their arms, and asked him if it was "a truth," he replied: "No, monsieur, it is not a truth; it is only a Stormont." The story had great vogue in the saloons, or, to speak in the French manner, "all Paris laughed at it." Franklin was the occasion of another remark which amused the few hundred persons who then constituted "all Paris." The Franklin stove coming into fashion at Paris, one of the French ministers was asked whether he would have one. "By no means," said he, "for if I should, Lord Stormont will never warm himself at my fire." At the time when the ships of Beau-

---

* "Memoirs of Lafayette," vol. i., p. 6.

marchais were struggling vainly to break out to sea through meshes of ministerial orders and counter-orders, Franklin dined in a numerous company, where one of the party informed him that his country at that moment presented a sublime spectacle! " Yes," said Franklin, " but the spectators do not pay."

His letters, too, were unusually merry. January 27th, he added to a letter to Mrs. Hewson in London, this postscript: " They tell me that in writing to a lady from Paris, one should always say something about the fashions. Temple observes them more than I do. He took notice that at the ball in Nantes there were no heads less than five, and a few were seven lengths of the face, above the top of the forehead. You know that those who have practiced drawing, as he has, attend more to proportions than people in common do. Yesterday we dined at the Duke de Rochefoucauld's, where there were three duchesses and a countess, and no head higher than a face and a half. So, it seems, the further from court, the more extravagant the mode." To Dr. Priestley, on the same day: " The hint you gave me jocularly, that you did not quite despair of the *philosopher's stone*, draws from me a request, that, when you have found it, you will take care to lose it again; for I believe in my conscience that mankind are wicked enough to continue slaughtering one another as long as they can find money to pay the butchers." February 8th, he begins a letter to " Mrs. Thompson at Lisle," in these words: " You are too early, *hussy*, as well as too saucy, in calling me *rebel ;* you should wait for the event, which will determine whether it is a *rebellion* or only a *revolution*. Here the ladies are more civil; they call us *les insurgens*, a character that usually pleases them ;" ending the letter with " Adieu, Madcap." Such utterances, we should suppose, were the expression of a light heart and unburdened mind, if we did not know that strong men are often gayest when their load presses heaviest.

It was in February, 1777, that the American envoys had that famous collision with the English embassador. They wrote to Lord Stormont, February 23d: " Captain Wickes, of the *Reprisal* frigate, belonging to the United States of America, has now in his hands near one hundred British seamen, prisoners. He desires to know whether an exchange may be made with him for an equal number of American seamen, now prisoners in England ? We take the liberty of proposing this matter to your lordship, and of requesting your opinion (if there be no impropriety in your giving it), whether such an exchange will probably be agreed to by your court. If your people cannot be soon exchanged here, they will be sent to America."

No answer. The envoys waited one week, and then wrote again: "We did ourselves the honor of writing some time ago to your lordship, on the subject of exchanging prisoners. You did not condescend to give us any answer, and therefore we expect none to this. We, however, take the liberty of sending you copies of certain depositions, which we shall transmit to Congress, whereby it will be known to your court, that the United States are not unacquainted with the barbarous treatment their people receive, when they have the misfortune of being your prisoners here in Europe; and that, if your conduct towards us is not altered, it is not unlikely that severe reprisals may be thought justifiable, from the necessity of putting some check to such abominable practices.

"For the sake of humanity it is to be wished that men would endeavor to alleviate, as much as possible, the unavoidable miseries attending a state of war. It has been said that, among the civilized nations of Europe, the ancient horrors of that state are much diminished; but the compelling men by chains, stripes, and famine, to fight against their friends and relations, is a new mode of barbarity which your nation alone had the honor of inventing; and the sending American prisoners of war to Africa and Asia, remote from all probability of exchange, and where they can scarce hope ever to hear from their families, even if the unwholesomeness of the climate does not put a speedy end to their lives, is a manner of treating captives that you can justify by no other precedent of custom except that of the black savages of Guinea."

In reply, Lord Stormont sent immediately a "paper," undated and unsigned, bearing the well-known words: "The king's embassador receives no applications from rebels, unless they come to implore his majesty's mercy." Which the envoys thus acknowledged: "In answer to a letter which concerns some of the most material interests of humanity, and of the two nations, Great Britain and the United States of America, now at war, we received the inclosed *indecent* paper, as coming from your lordship, which we return, for your lordship's more mature consideration." Lord Stormont's reply extorted from two continents howls of disgust. He acted, however, strictly in character. As the nephew, pupil, and heir of Lord Mansfield, as the embassador of George III., as British tory of that day, what else could he have said? He was a stiff, precise, stingy, honorable man, intent on doing his duty to what he called his " King and country." The American prisoners, therefore, continued to languish in Portsmouth jail, while a large number of the English sea-captives (not less than seven hundred in the year) were set at liberty, from the difficulty and expense of transporting them to America.

As the spring opened, the envoys being assured that no further aid was to be expected of France until the prospect brightened in America, resolved to try other courts; Mr. Lee, that of Spain; Mr. Deane, the Dutch. Mr. Lee started on his mission, but was stopped before reaching Madrid by an official hint, that Spain tenderly loved the United States, but would prefer, just then, not to have an American plenipotentiary at her capital. He did, however, after delay, procure some supplies. Spain, having the fear of British fleets before her eyes, would concede nothing further to Mr. Lee; who returned to Paris, and proceeded thence to Berlin, to learn what Frederick the Great would do to pay off old scores against the tory party of Britain. The wary, wise old king would do nothing. So that the only advantage accruing from these swift, laborious journeys, in the spring and summer of 1777, was that they kept Arthur Lee out of Paris and out of mischief, leaving his colleagues to do their duty unmolested. Mr. Deane made no at-tempt upon the cautious Dutch, having endless work in Paris with his cargoes and the counter-orders.

It is scarcely just to say that the King of Prussia did nothing for America at this critical time. He performed in her favor, to the huge amusement of Europe, a practical joke. We find Franklin writing this spring to a Boston friend: " The conduct of those Princes of Germany who have sold the blood of their people, has subjected them to the contempt and odium of all Europe. The Prince of Anspach, whose recruits mutinied and refused to march, was obliged to disarm and fetter them, and drive them to the sea-side by the help of his guards; himself attending in person. In his return he was publicly hooted by mobs through every town he passed in Holland, with all sorts of reproachful epithets. The King of Prussia's humor of obliging those Princes to pay him the same toll per head for the men they drive through his dominions, as used to be paid him for their *cattle*, because they were sold as such, is generally spoken of with approbation, as containing a just reproof of those tyrants. I send you inclosed one of the many satires that have appeared on this occasion."

Dr. Franklin had been five months from home before he had a line from America, or America a line from him. It was in the very month after his departure that General Howe ravaged across New Jersey and threatened Philadelphia from the banks of the Delaware; his daughter and all her household retiring twenty miles into the country, carrying with them Franklin's library, apparatus, and papers, and all the furniture, except the mahogany. No sooner had the precious little victory at Trenton relieved Philadelphia from apprehension, and raised the spirits of the whole country from the deepest depression, than the Secret Committee resolved to get the good news undiminished across the ocean, if the thing was possible. The swift schooner, Jenifer, Captain Hammond, was expressly designated for this errand. The orders of the committee to Captain Hammond were, to make all speed to Nantes; leave the schooner there in command of the mate; get money from Mr. Thomas Morris or M. Penet; go post-haste to Paris; deliver dispatches to Messrs. Franklin, Deane, and Lee; await their orders and answers; which latter being received, fly over land and sea with them straight to Congress. "The dispatches," added the committee, "will be delivered to you in a box, which you must put into a bag with two shots; so that you can instantly sink them if in danger of capture. And, above all, *secrecy!*" The Jenifer sailed early in tempestuous January; was chased by cruisers; dodged into a Virginia river, where she lay snug for seventeen days, waiting for a chance to slip out to sea. At length, after storms, chasings, and adventures innumerable, Captain Hammond had the satisfaction of delivering his dispatches into the hands of Dr. Franklin at Passy; his news not the less joyful, because it was three months old.

It was agreeable to Dr. Franklin, on reading his dispatches, to find that the orders of the Secret Committee had been anticipated. The committee ordered them to have six men of war built in Europe; men of war were already in progress in Holland. The committee desired them to try for a loan of two millions sterling; they had themselves entertained such a project. The committee sent a commission to Dr. Franklin as plenipotentiary to the court of Spain. Arthur Lee had gone to Spain. The committee wished the envoys to assure the several courts of the unshaken determination of the United States to maintain their independence; they had held no other language. This was pleasant. Captain Hammond bore away dispatches that contained much cheering news for the committee and Congress; but, as ill luck would have it, he was taken by the enemy within sight of the American coast, but succeeded in sinking his dispatch box. It was eleven months, counting from May, 1777, before another letter reached America from the Americans serving Congress on the continent of Europe.

The good news brought by Captain Hammond, the departure of the Marquis de Lafayette, the revived enmity against Great Britain, the presence of Franklin, all contributed to inflame the ardor of Young France for taking part in the American war. Going to America to fight for the noble Insurgents and the illustrious Congress, was so much the rage in Paris, that the applications to Dr. Franklin for recommendatory letters and commissions became the torment of his life. To Dr. Dubourg he wrote, in reply to a letter in behalf of a young officer : " You can have no conception how I am harassed. All my friends are sought out and teazed to teaze me. Great officers of all ranks, in all departments ; ladies, great and small, besides professed solicitors, worry me from morning to night. The noise of every coach now that enters my court terrifies me. I am afraid to accept an invitation to dine abroad, being almost sure of meeting with some officer or officer's friend, who, as soon as I am put in good humor by a glass or two of champagne, begins his attack upon me. Luckily I do not often in my sleep dream of these vexatious situations, or I should be afraid of what are now my only hours of comfort. If, therefore, you have the least remaining kindness for me, if you would not help to drive me out of France, for God's sake, my dear friend, let this your twenty-third application be your last."

For the benefit of young Frenchmen, whose enthusiasm would not permit them " to take No for an answer," he drew up a letter of introduction suited to their case : " The bearer of this, who is going to America, presses me to give him a letter of recommendation, though I know nothing of him, not even his name. This may seem extraordinary, but I assure you it is not uncommon here.

Sometimes, indeed, one unknown person brings another equally unknown, to recommend him; and sometimes they recommend one another! As to this gentleman, I must refer you to himself for his character and merits, with which he is certainly better acquainted than I can possibly be. I recommend him, however, to those civilities, which every stranger, of whom one knows no harm, has a right to; and I request you will do him all the good offices, and show him all the favor, that, on further acquaintance, you shall find him to deserve." His grandson assures us that a form like this was actually employed by him on some occasions.

Franklin's pen was not idle during the first months of his residence in Europe. Of his literary efforts at this time, there was one, the interest and the importance of which readers of the present day cannot be made to conceive. I refer to the translation, executed, I believe, by Dr. Dubourg, but suggested and superintended by Dr. Franklin, of the new Constitutions of the States of the American Confederacy. France, dreaming already of the millenium which she consciously strove for in her own impending Revolution, read those to us so familiar and commonplace productions with the wild interest with which starving mariners on a desert coast might read the Bill of Fare of the last Lord Mayor's banquet. Those Constitutions, says Thomas Paine, in that happy way of his, "were to liberty what grammar is to language: they define its parts of speech, and practically construct them into syntax."* He tells us, also, that "Count de Vergennes resisted for a considerable time the publication in France of the American Constitutions translated into the French language; but even in this he was obliged to give way to public opinion, and a sort of propriety in admitting to appear what he had undertaken to defend."

The effect which this publication had in bringing on, and shaping the early course of the French Revolution, no writer, English, French, or American, appears to have sufficiently noticed. Franklin, who had in view only the honor and prosperity of his own country, had, nevertheless, the idea that the publication might indirectly benefit Europe also. "All Europe," he wrote, in May, 1777, to his old Boston friend, Rev. Samuel Cooper, "is on our side of the question, as far as applause and good wishes can carry

* "Rights of Man."

them. Those who live under arbitrary power do nevertheless approve of liberty, and wish for it; they almost despair of recovering it in Europe; they read the translations of our separate colony constitutions with rapture; and there are such numbers everywhere who talk of removing to America, with their families and fortunes, as soon as peace and our independence shall be established, that it is generally believed we shall have a prodigious addition of strength, wealth, and arts, from the emigrations of Europe; and it is thought that, to lessen or prevent such emigrations, the tyrannies established there must relax, and allow more liberty to their people. Hence it is a common observation here, that our cause is *the cause of all mankind*, and that we are fighting for their liberty in defending our own."

Readers of Horace Walpole's letters and diaries remember how often he repeats the prediction, that if George III. should succeed in subduing America, he would call home his victorious armies only to crush the liberties of England. It could only have been a conviction like this, that induced such patriots as Fox and Burke to rejoice in the dishonor of their country's arms in America, and to count the loss of English armies there a gain to England.

To promote the loan ordered by Congress, Dr. Franklin wrote an ingenious piece, which he caused to be translated into French, Spanish, Dutch, and Italian, and sent to the moneyed capitals of Europe. In borrowing money, said he in this paper, a man's credit depends upon seven particulars, namely : His conduct respecting former loans; his industry; his frugality; the value and condition of his estate; his prospects; his business talent; his honesty. He endeavored to show that in each of these particulars America surpassed England. America at the peace of 1763 was ten millions sterling in debt, and had paid off the whole, principal and interest, in nine years; whereas England, in the same time, had not reduced her debt. With regard to industry and frugality, in America nearly every human being practiced those virtues ; while in England there were large classes of people who were trained to despise both. All America had been governed for seventy thousand pounds a year, while England's king alone consumed a million. As to prudence—good Heavens ! England was always plunging into wars with which she had no concern whatever. " But the most indiscreet of all her wars is the present against America, with whom she might for ages have preserved her profitable connection only by a just and equitable conduct. She is now acting like a mad shop-keeper, who, by beating those that pass his doors, attempts to make them come in and be his customers. America cannot submit to such treatment, without being first ruined, and, being ruined, her custom will be worth nothing. England, to effect this, is increasing her debt, and irretrievably ruining herself." And with regard to downright honesty, as shown in the voluntary payment of debts that might have been avoided, how bright and stainless the record of America! Private debts due to English merchants since the commencement of hostilities, had been paid with remarkable punctuality; though there had not been wanting politicians who had proposed a general stopping of payment until the end of the war.

The money-lending public were doubtless entertained with this production, but they showed not the least inclination to come forward with the two million pounds sterling. Franklin, indeed, had omitted all reference to the money-lender's first consideration—the probability of America maintaining her independence. His seven arguments were excellent; but there were seven on the other side which no capitalist could disregard: the battle of Long Island; the loss of New York; the capture of the upper forts; the affairs about White Plains; the retreat to the Delaware; the sailing of General Burgoyne; Lord Howe's blockading fleet. Penniless patriots and drawing-room enthusiasts see through such shallow reasoning as this, but moneyed men invariably attach to arguments of that description a certain weight.

Another "money article" Dr. Franklin wrote at this time, entitled, "A Catechism relative to the English National Debt;" in which he endeavored to give his readers a vivid conception of its vast amount—one hundred and ninety-five millions. The questions of this catechism elicited the information that it would take a man one hundred and forty-eight years to count the debt in shillings; that the weight of those shillings would be nearly sixty-two millions of pounds, a load for three hundred and fourteen ships, or thirty-one thousand carts. The catechism ended thus: "When will government be able to pay the principal? When there is more money in England's treasury than there is in all Europe. And when will that be? Never." Argument neutralized by the well-known fact that England had never failed to pay the interest of her debt on the day it was due; which is all the capitalist cares for. Where this catechism was published, or whether it was published at all, does not appear.

Another piece of Franklin's fun bears date at this time: " A Dialogue between Britain, France, Spain, Holland, Saxony, and America." To each of these nations in turn Britain applies for help in the business of chastizing rebellious America. Spain replies: " Have you forgotten, then, that when my subjects in the Low Countries rebelled against me, you not only furnished them with military stores, but joined them with an army and a fleet?" France replies: " Did you not assist my rebel Huguenots with a fleet and an army at Rochelle? And have you not lately aided privately and sneakingly my rebel subjects in Corsica? And do you not at this instant keep their chief pensioned, and ready to head a fresh revolt there, whenever you can find or make an opportunity? Dear sister, you must be a little silly!" Holland replies: " 'Tis true you assisted me against Philip, my tyrant of Spain, but have I not assisted you against one of your tyrants, and enabled you to expel him? * * * I shall only go on quietly with my own business. Trade is my profession; 'tis all I have to subsist on. And, let me tell you, I shall make no scruple (on the prospect of a good market for that commodity) even to send my ships to Hell and supply the Devil with brimstone. For you must know, I can insure in London against the burning of my sails." Whereupon, America breaks in: " Why, you old bloodthirsty bully! You, who have been everywhere vaunting your own prowess, and defaming the Americans as poltroons! You, who have boasted of being able to march over all their bellies with a single regiment! You, who by fraud have possessed yourself of their strongest fortress, and all the arms they had stored up in it! You, who have a disciplined army in their country, intrenched to the teeth, and provided with every thing! Do *you* run about begging all Europe not to supply those poor people with a little powder and shot?"

Poor Britain fares no better with Saxony, and cries out at length: " O Lord! where are my friends?" Upon which the nations with one voice inform her that she has no friends, and will have none, until she mends her manners.

The writing of dispatches vastly increased the general labors of the embassy. Not that the dispatches were very numerous, but many copies of each had to be made. Besides the first draft, a corrected copy for preservation and the copy transmitted to Congress, a fresh copy was sent by each of the next three, four, or five opportunities. Few of the more important dispatches were copied less than seven times, which involved, on an average, about a hundred pages of copying. Nor had the Secret Committee made the slightest provision in the way of secretary or clerk. With such prodigious quantities of writing to be executed, Dr. Franklin was compelled to postpone the sending of his grandson to a university, and employ him as a secretary; to whom he was obliged to add a French clerk at "fifty louis per annum." The university scheme was finally abandoned, Dr. Franklin having resolved to train the youth for the diplomatic service of his country, for which his appearance, manners, and tastes appeared to fit him. "Temple," therefore, remained in the household of his grandfather, plying the secretarial pen, during the whole of the revolutionary period.

It was only through this ceaseless multiplying of copies that any dispatches at all reached their destination. In one letter of this year, the envoys mention the loss of four sets of dispatches. "Adams," say they, "by whom we wrote early this summer, was taken on this coast, having sunk his dispatches. We hear that Hammond shared the same fate on your coast. Johnson, by whom we wrote in September, was taken going out of the channel, and poor Captain Wickes (of the Reprisal), who sailed at the same time, and had duplicates, we just now hear foundered near New Foundland, every man perishing but the cook." The affair of General Montgomery's monument gives a lively idea of the extreme difficulty and irregularity of intercourse between the two continents. Congress having ordered the envoys to have the monument made in Paris, the work was executed accordingly, and shipped for America in the summer of 1777. Months passed, and the envoys heard nothing of either the vessel or the marble. At the end of two years vague and casual tidings reached Paris that the ship had arrived at some port in North Carolina. Three years more elapsed, and we still find Franklin earnestly asking his correspondents if they had heard any thing of a very elegant, three-hundred-guinea monument he had sent to sea at the beginning of his residence abroad. Nor does it appear that he ever ascertained what had become of his monument. That it did reach America safely New Yorkers know, since it stands visible to the passing crowd of Broadway, affixed to the front of St. Paul's church. Congress designed it for a wall of the State House, in Philadelphia, Franklin records.

So of the tobacco. "The anxiety of Congress," wrote the committee once to their envoys in Paris, "to get tobacco to you is as great as yours to receive it. We have already lost vast quantities in the attempt, and thereby have furnished our enemies gratis with what was designed for the discharge of your contracts." And Mrs. Bache writes to her father: "The present you sent me this month two years, I received a few weeks ago." As late as 1782 the American plenipotentiaries had to complain that six months passed without their hearing from home.

Such vigilant cruising had the effect of rendering the commerce that did escape most temptingly profitable. Arthur Lee mentions in one of his letters of 1777, that a twenty-two franc French musket sold in America for fifty francs; and for fifty francs two hundred pounds of tobacco could be bought, worth in France one thousand dollars !

Happily, the cruising and the capturing were not all on one side. Dr. Franklin and Mr. Deane were busy enough this summer with the little navy under their direction; whose exploits in the British seas elicited universal applause at the time, and can never be forgotten by Americans who love their country's navy. We belong to a race who have been accustomed, from of old, to fight bunglingly on the land, brilliantly on the sea, successfully on both. Captain Wickes in the sloop-of-war, Reprisal, was the first of our naval officers who fired a hostile gun in European waters. Having admitted his two prizes to ransom, he refitted at Nantes, and boldly cruising in the Bay of Biscay, sent in prize after prize, a Lisbon packet among the rest; and returned to Nantes unharmed. Lord Stormont remonstrated now with such threatening vigor, that the Count de Vergennes was compelled to order both the prizes and the Reprisal to leave the harbor instantly. Whereupon, Captain Wickes invited some Nantes merchants on board of one of his prizes, took all the vessels just outside the port, and there sold them to the merchants, who immediately ordered them in again. As to the Reprisal, he informed the government that she was too leaky to go to sea; and the government was too humane to think of compelling a leaky vessel to encounter the perils of the deep. It was the hundred prisoners captured in these prizes that gave rise to the correspondence between the envoys and Lord Stormont given above. We cannot wonder that his lordship was in ill humor. A still more dashing adventure was in reserve for Captain Wickes and his little sloop. In April, the arrival of the Lexington, sloop-of-war of fourteen guns, Captain Johnson, emboldened the American envoys to plan an expedition to capture the Belfast linen ships, expected to sail in June. About the first of that month the Reprisal, the Lexington, and a cutter of ten guns named the Dolphin (bought from M. de Chaumont to carry dispatches to Congress), the whole under command of Captain Wickes, sailed from Nantes. The little fleet ventured completely round Ireland. It missed the linen ships, but captured or destroyed sixteen prizes less important, and struck terror to the souls of British merchants and underwriters. Near the French coast a line-of-battle ship gave chase to the three vessels, but all escaped into port; the Reprisal having been compelled, however, to let go her guns and cut away her bulwarks. Again, Lord Stormont stormed remonstrance; again, Count de Vergennes issued stringent orders; again, Captain Wickes obediently took his prizes outside the harbor and sold them to French speculators.

Then came that well-contested action between the Lexington and a British cutter called the Alert. It was in September, one day after the Lexington left port, that she fell in with the Alert, a vessel slightly inferior to herself in size and force, but splendidly handled by her commander, Lieutenant Bazely. Both vessels were ludicrously small, and their guns were only four-pounders. The sea being high, these two cock-boats popped away at one another from the foaming summits of Biscay waves, for two hours and a half, without either being able to cripple the other. Then the Lexington, her powder nearly exhausted, ran away before a stiff breeze, thinking to end the affair so, as the Alert had evidently received much damage in her rigging. But no; Lieutenant Bazely, sending all hands to splice and mend, was soon ready to follow, and after a four hours' chase, came up with the Lexington, got abreast of her, and renewed the battle. The American sloop held out for an hour, firing away her last charge of powder, and then struck.

The Reprisal, too, as we have seen, was lost at sea soon after, the gallant Wickes going down in her—to the great sorrow of Franklin, who had himself witnessed and bore witness to his capacity and worth. The impudent doings of Captain Gustavus Conyngham made a great noise in Europe this season, and gave a world of trouble to parties concerned. In the spring our envoys, through a secret agent, bought at an English port a fast-sailing cutter, which they sent to Dunkirk, where she was fitted for her destined work of preying upon British commerce, and named the Surprise. Captain Conyngham was appointed to command her. One of his first exploits was the capture of the Prince of Orange packet, plying and carrying the mail between England and Holland. He did this so neatly, that he himself announced the capture to the captain of the packet as he was sitting in the cabin at breakfast with his passengers. Deeming the mail an important acquisition, he hastened into port with it, and dispatched it to the envoys at Paris. The capture of this vessel following quickly the loss of the Lisbon packet, produced in England the impression of being blockaded. Something like a panic arose. An insurance of ten per cent. was demanded upon the packets plying between Dover and Calais, and forty French ships, it was said, were loading in the Thames, merchants fearing to employ English vessels. Upon this occasion the remonstrances of Lord Stormont were such as compelled the French government to choose between complete restitution or instant war. Captain Conyngham and his crew were seized and imprisoned, the Surprise was confiscated, and the packet set free. The English government, believing from these vigorous measures that the French cabinet really meant peace, went so far as to send two men-of-war to Dunkirk for the purpose of receiving on board Captain Conyngham and his crew, and conveying them to England to be tried as pirates. On arriving, however, the British Captains learned that the "pirates" had *escaped.*

In fact, Messrs. Franklin and Deane had provided another task for the audacious Conyngham, and had "found means," aided by the indomitable Beaumarchais, to procure his release. He and his men, accordingly, exchanged a severe prison regimen of champagne and French cookery for the fare of seamen on active service; the envoys having prepared for them a second cutter, the Revenge, and ordered them to waylay and capture, if possible, some of the transports laden with Hessians. Captain Conyngham sent ashore his guns and crew, took in some freight, and announced his intention of making a commercial voyage to Norway. The French authorities demanding security for his good behavior on the ocean, the American firm of Hodge and Allen, merchants of Dunkirk, were bound for him, and he was permitted to depart. He lay to off the harbor, where late at night came to him a barge bringing his guns and sailors, with which he bore away, and had his usual good luck, though missing the Hessians. The Count de Vergennes was soon notified of these maneuvers by the English embassador, and Mr. Hodge found himself a tenant of the Bastile, where he was confined six weeks, and was supplied with "all the delicacies of the season." At the proper time Dr. Franklin applied for his release, which was granted. Captain Conyngham, however, continued to scour the British seas in the Revenge. On one occasion, it is said, having received much damage in a storm, he stowed his guns below, disguised his vessel, and ran into a British port, where he leisurely repaired damages, and then put to sea again to continue his cruise. On another occasion he entered an Irish port and bought a supply of provisions. And, after all his adventures, he succeeded in getting his cutter safe to America.

Franklin's whole heart was in this business of giving the enemy a taste of the inconveniences of war. How deeply his placid nature had been moved by the atrocities committed on the American coast, we have already seen; he now burned with desire to bring the war to England's own doors. When the English were lulled to security by the apparent determination of the French government to put a stop to such enterprises as those of Captain Wickes and Captain Conyngham, he submitted to Congress a plan for striking a blow that would have most effectually dispelled that security. He advised Congress to send three frigates loaded with tobacco to Nantes or Bordeaux, manned and commanded in the best manner; which, on arriving, should assume all the appearance of common merchantmen; but, on a sudden, dart upon some unprotected British port, seize whole fleets of vessels, levy contributions, burn, plunder, and retire before the alarm could reach the capital. "The burning or plundering of Liverpool or Glasgow," he wrote, " would do us more essential service than a million of treasure and much blood spent on the continent. It would raise our reputation to the highest pitch, and lessen in the same degree that of the enemy. We are confident it is practicable, and with very little danger." Many months passed before the Foreign Committee read these lines, and many more before Franklin had an answer to them. He did not forget the scheme, however. There was one Paul Jones coming to him from over the sea, who would, perhaps, think it feasible. Readers perceive that Franklin was for waging war on warlike principles. His blood was up. He thirsted for vengeance—vengeance for his country's cruel wrongs. Read his heart in the following eloquent letter, addressed, October 14th, 1777, to his English friend, David Hartley, M. P. The letter so belongs to this part of his history, that it would be essentially incomplete without it :

"I have been apprehensive that, if it were known that a correspondence subsisted between us, it might be attended with inconvenience to you. I have therefore been backward in writing, not caring to trust the post, and not well knowing whom else to trust with my letters. But being now assured of a safe conveyance, I venture to write to you, especially as I think the subject such a one as you may receive a letter upon without censure.

"Happy should I have been if the honest warnings I gave, of the fatal separation of interests, as well as of affections, that must attend the measures commenced while I was in England, had been attended to, and the horrid mischief of this abominable war been thereby prevented. I should still be happy in any successful endeavors for restoring peace, consistent with the liberties, the safety, and the honor of America. As to our submitting to the government of Great Britain, it is vain to think of it. She has given us, by her numberless barbarities (by her malice in bribing slaves to murder their masters, and savages to massacre the families of farmers, with her baseness in rewarding the unfaithfulness of servants, and debauching the virtue of honest seamen, intrusted with our property), in the prosecution of the war, and in the treatment of the prisoners, so deep an impression of her depravity, that we never again can trust her in the management of our affairs and interests. It is now impossible to persuade our people, as I long endeavored, that the war was merely ministerial, and that the nation bore still a good will to us. The infinite number of addresses printed in your gazettes, all approving the conduct of your government towards us, and encouraging our destruction by every possible means, the great majority in Parliament constantly manifesting the same sentiments, and the popular public rejoicings on occasion of any news of the slaughter of an innocent and virtuous people, fighting only in defense of their just rights; these, together with the recommendations of the same measures by even your celebrated moralists and divines, in their writings and sermons, that are still approved and applauded in your great national assemblies, all join in convincing us that you are no longer the magnanimous, enlightened nation we once esteemed you, and that you are unfit and unworthy to govern us, as not being able to govern your own passions.

"But, as I have said, should be nevertheless happy in seeing peace restored. For though, if my friends and the friends of liberty and virtue, who still remain in England, could be drawn out of it, a continuance of this war to the ruin of the rest would give me less concern, I cannot, as that removal is impossible, but wish for peace for their sakes, as well as for the sake of humanity, and preventing further carnage.

"This wish of mine, ineffective as it may be, induces me to mention to you, that, between nations long exasperated against each other in war, some act of generosity and kindness towards prisoners on one side has softened resentment, and abated animosity on the other, so as to bring on an accommodation. You in England, if you wish for peace, have at present the opportunity of trying this means, with regard to the prisoners now in your jails. They complain of very severe treatment. They are far from their friends and families, and winter is coming on, in which they must suffer extremely, if continued in their present situation; fed scantily on bad provisions, without warm lodgings, clothes, or fire, and not suffered to invite or receive visits from their friends, or even from the humane and charitable of their enemies.

"I can assure you, from my own certain knowledge, that your people, prisoners in America, have been treated with great kindness; they have been served with the same rations of wholesome provisions with our own troops, comfortable lodgings have been provided for them, and they have been allowed large bounds of villages in the healthy air, to walk and amuse themselves with on their parole. Where you have thought fit to employ contractors to supply your people, these contractors have been protected and aided in their operations. Some considerable act of kindness would take off the reproach of inhumanity in that respect from the nation, and leave it where it ought with more certainty to lay, on the conductors of your war in America. This I hint to you, out of some remaining good will to a nation I once loved sincerely. But, as things are, and in my present temper of mind, not being over fond of receiving obligations, I shall content myself with proposing that your government would allow us to send or employ a commissary to take some care of those unfortunate people. Perhaps on your representation this might speedily be obtained in England, though it was refused most inhumanly at New York.

"If you could have leisure to visit the jails in which they are confined, and should be desirous of knowing the truth relative to the treatment they receive, I wish you would take the trouble of distributing among the most necessitous according to their wants, five or six hundred pounds, for which your drafts on me here shall be punctually honored. You could then be able to speak with some certainty to the point in Parliament, and this might be attended with good effects.

"If you cannot obtain for us permission to send a commissary, possibly you may find a trusty, humane, discreet person at Plymouth, and another at Portsmouth, who would undertake to communicate what relief we may be able to afford those unfortunate men, martyrs to the cause of liberty. Your king will not reward you for taking this trouble, but God will. I shall not mention the gratitude of America; you will have what is better, the applause of your own good conscience. Our captains have set at liberty above two hundred of your people, made prisoners by our armed vessels and brought into France, besides a great number dismissed at sea on your coasts, to whom vessels were given to carry them in. But you have not returned us a man in exchange. If we had sold your people to the Moors at Sallee, as you have many of ours to the African and East India Companies, could you have complained?

"In revising what I have written, I found too much warmth in it, and was about to strike out some parts. Yet I let them go, as they will afford you this one reflection : 'If a man naturally cool, and rendered still cooler by old age, is so warmed by our treatment

of his country, how much must those people in general be exasperated against us ? And why are we making inveterate enemies by
our barbarity, not only of the present inhabitants of a great country, but of their infinitely more numerous posterity ; who will in
future ages detest the name of *Englishman*, as much as the children in Holland now do those of *Alva* and *Spaniard*.' This will
certainly happen, unless your conduct is speedily changed, and the
national resentment falls, where it ought to fall heavily, on your
ministry, or perhaps rather on the king, whose will they only
execute."

A noble, noble letter ; the gush of a compassionate, brave heart,
maddened by the spectacle of meanness and iniquity.

The envoys never ceased their exertions in behalf of their countrymen who languished in British prisons, always finding in Mr.
Hartley a faithful and cordial co-operator. Mr. Hartley, it is extremely probable, showed Dr. Franklin's letter to Lord North, and
Lord North was not a man who could have read it unmoved. For
the moment, however, it produced no perceptible effects.

One unimportant incident of this year casts a gleam of light
upon Franklin's way of life, and, therefore, deserves brief mention.
The emperor, Joseph II., of Austria, brother of the Queen of
France, was in Paris this summer, traveling under the title of
Count Falkenstein : emperor only in name, until the death of his
mother, *King* Maria Theresa. He sought an interview with Dr.
Franklin, but with unusual precautions to make it appear accidental.
Franklin received, one day in May, an invitation to breakfast with
the envoy of the Grand Duke of Tuscany, in terms like these :
" The Abbé Nicoli begs M. Franklin to do him the honor of break-
fasting with him on Wednesday, the 28th instant, at nine o'clock.
The Abbé promises him a good cup of chocolate. He assures Dr.
Franklin of his respect." Upon this invitation, which was found
among Franklin's papers, was written the following explanation :
" The intention of the above was to give the emperor an opportunity of an interview with me, that should appear accidental.
Monsieur Turgot and the Abbé were to be present, and by their
knowledge of what passed, to prevent or contradict false reports.
The emperor did not appear, and the Abbé Nicoli since tells me,
that the number of other persons who visited him (the Abbé) that
morning, of which the emperor was not informed, prevented his com-

ing; that, at 12, understanding they were gone, he came, but I was gone also."* It is said that they afterwards met; which is not improbable, for the two men had much in common. Joseph II., indeed, endeavored to be a kind of crowned Franklin, when, at length, he was really emperor.

So passed the spring and the summer of the year 1777. It can-. not be said, I think, that the prospects of America, as viewed by European observers, had materially brightened as the year wore on. As the two great British armies in America were acting upon a concerted plan, which could not begin to be developed till the spring was far advanced, the accounts of General Burgoyne's movements were late in reaching Europe, and came through England. No man could reasonably doubt that, with such a force as he commanded, he would do great mischief in New York, even if he failed to penetrate to the Hudson, and sever New England from the rest of the States. In June of this year, Dr. Franklin was shown a letter, written by his old friend Dr. Fothergill, and written with a view to its being shown, which contained this passage: "Should thy friend think proper to go to Passy, he may say to Dr. Franklin, that if he has enemies in this country, he has also friends, and must not forget these because the former are ignorant and malicious, yet all powerful. He will, doubtless, inform the Doctor, that there remains not a doubt on this side of the water that American resistance is all at an end—that the shadow of congressional authority scarce exists—that a general defection from that body is apparent—that their troops desert by shoals—that the officers are discontented—that no new levies can be made—that nothing can withstand the British forces, and prevent them from being masters of the whole continent; in short, that the war is *at an end*, and that nothing remains to be done but to divide the country among the conquerors. This is the general language; and that neither France nor Spain will afford them any other than a kind of paralytic aid; enough to enable them to protract a few months longer a miserable existence." †

People did not talk or write in that strain on the continent, but great numbers of them secretly thought so, particularly the better informed. The extreme care taken by the French Government to

† Memoirs of Dr. Franklin, by W. T. Franklin, p. 818.　　　† Ibid., p. 818.

pacify Lord Stormont, the impossibility of borrowing money for Congress, the cautious movements of Spain, the timidity of Holland, the universal dread of giving offense to England, were evidences of a general distrust of the ability of America to maintain her independence.

CHAPTER III.

BEGINNING OF THE ARTHUR LEE MISCHIEF.

BY midsummer, 1777, Congress had as many as twelve agents in Europe, most of whom lived in Paris. On Sundays, when the official Americans and their secretaries dined at Dr. Franklin's, and the American boys came from their schools to join the party, the company must have numbered twenty, or more. Separated as most of these gentlemen were from their country, uncertain, indeed, whether or not they had a country, having similar employments, a common interest and common danger, we should naturally look to see them living in perfect accord—a band of brothers gathered in a foreign land round a venerated father and chief. Alas! the truth is far otherwise. From 1776 to the end of the revolutionary struggle, the persons representing the United States in Europe were generally at open or secret war with one another; envy, jealousy, malice, and all the other passions of a small and morbid brain raged among them. Why was this? Answer: ARTHUR LEE! One such narrow, conceited, fidgety, suspicious, envious, covetous, plantation-bred person as he would be sufficient to introduce discord among a chorus of angels; and the American diplomatists in Paris were not angels.

Perhaps the most convenient way of unfolding the mischief caused by this ridiculous and perfidious man, will be to present here a kind of descriptive catalogue of the servants of Congress in Europe at this time, mentioning them in something like the order of their rank and importance.

DR. BENJAMIN FRANKLIN. As the reader has some acquaintance with this gentleman already, I need but call to mind two cir-

cumstances of his position in France. First : his popularity was
such that, so long as he remained, no other American could be held
in very great or very general estimation. His celebrity was completely overshadowing ; no American could hope to shine in
France, except as his satellite. In this fact, any man, not a fool, or
plantation-bred, would have gladly and proudly coincided, as well
for his own as for his country's sake ; for Dr. Franklin's age,
genius, and services, entitled him to pre-eminence, and the immense esteem in which he was held formed a great part, nay, the
greater part of his country's European capital. Moreover, as we
have seen, he bore his honors better than meekly ; he bore them
airily, gracefully, jocularly ; often amused, never deceived by
them ; something like Gulliver among the Lilliputians. Secondly :
chief as Franklin unquestionably was of the Americans in Europe,
he had no official authority over any of them ; it was only his age,
talents, character, and fame, that gave him the first place.

SILAS DEANE. During the whole of the year 1777 Mr. Deane
continued to co-operate with Beaumarchais, to the great contentment of that gentleman, and with the approval of Dr. Franklin and
the Count de Vergennes. But the contracts with Du Coudray
and his train were giving Congress and General Washington such
a world of trouble, that he was completely out of favor in America.
The artillery service was all arranged before the arrival of Du Coudray ; General Knox, " the father of the American artillery," having been appointed to the chief command. General Knox held the
rank of major-general, and all the other divisions of the army were
commanded by major-generals. " In this state of things," wrote
the Foreign Committee, " arrived General Coudray, with an agreement by which he was to command the artillery and the greatest
part of the major-generals of the army, by being of older commission. A plentiful crop of resignations began presently to sprout up,
and the whole army must have been deranged and thrown into
confusion, just on the opening of a campaign, or this agreement not
acceded to in the whole. But Mons. Du Coudray would have
every thing or nothing. An inflexible ambition that paid no regard to the situation and circumstances of the army, would be gratified. This produced a scene of contention, which was not ended
when the unfortunate General was drowned in the Schuylkill, going
to join the army. Immediately on his death, the rest of his corps

would return to France;" and back to France they went, Congress paying their passage, and continuing their pay until they reached home. General De Coudray, besides the confusion and perplexity he caused, cost Congress a hundred thousand francs; and, I see that, as late as 1785, his heirs were still clamoring at the door of Congress for money which they claimed to be due to his estate.*

The odium of all this fell upon Silas Deane, for whom Congress could not, at that distance, make the requisite allowance. Frank- lin could, and did. Writing to the Foreign Committee on this sub- ject, he observed: "I, who am upon the spot, and know the in- finite difficulty of resisting the powerful solicitations of great men, who, if disobliged, might have it in their power to obstruct the supplies he was then obtaining, do not wonder that, being then a stranger to the people, and unacquainted with the language, he was at first prevailed on to make some such agreements, when all were recommended, as they always are, as *officiers expérimentés, braves comme leurs épées, pleins de courage, de talents, et de zèle pour notre cause,* &c., &c., in short, mere Cesars, each of whom would have been an invaluable acquisition to America. * * * I hope, therefore, that favorable allowance will be made to my worthy col- league on account of his situation at the time, as he has long since corrected that mistake, and daily approves himself to my certain knowledge an able, faithful, active, and extremely useful servant of the public; a testimony I think it my duty to take this occasion of giving to his merit, unasked, as, considering my great age, I may probably not live to give it personally in Congress, and I per- ceive he has enemies."

Long before this letter reached Philadelphia, before it was written even, the fate of Silas Deane was sealed. The question of his re- call was debated in Congress with extreme asperity, since it was originally proposed to accompany the resolution of recall with a preamble of censure. John Jay took the lead in the defense of his absent friend, and succeeded in getting the offensive preamble, which condemned a servant of the public unheard, stricken out. The family seat of the Jays in New York is close to the Connecticut line, and, I presume, Mr. Jay was intimate with Deane before the war. He was warmly his friend and defender, not on this occasion

* Diplomatic Correspondence of the United States, i., 231.

only, but whenever he was attacked in Congress. He even had a
portrait of Deane hanging in his study, which he carried abroad
with him, in later years, when he went embassador to Madrid. It
was not possible, however, at this time, to avert the recall of his
Connecticut friend. December 8th, Congress passed the following
order: " Whereas, it is of the greatest importance that Congress
should at this critical juncture be well informed of the State of
affairs in Europe, and whereas Congress have resolved that the
Hon. Silas Deane be recalled from the Court of France, and have
appointed another Commissioner to supply his place there: ORDERED,
that the Committee of Foreign Affairs write to the Hon. Silas
Deane, and direct him to embrace the first opportunity to return to
America, and, upon his arrival, to repair with all possible dispatch
to Congress." This was the message which, during the exciting,
momentous months of January and February, 1778, was winging its
way across the Atlantic to the envoys at Paris. The reader will
note that it contains not the least intimation of censure: Mr. Deane
was merely notified that Congress desired information respecting
' the state of affairs in Europe."

ARTHUR LEE. This gentleman, never too happy, was miserable
in the extreme on his return to Paris in July, 1777, from the court
of Frederick the Great. He had suffered a long series of galling
disappointments. He had expected to be the medium through
which the French King would convey his liberal subsidies to Congress; but the founding of the great House of Roderique Hortalez
and Co. had deprived him of that honor. With M. de Beaumarchais he had once been in confidential intercourse, writing him mysterious letters signed "Mary Johnson," and receiving epistles from
him in cipher, unfolding the secrets of the French cabinet. The
arrival of Silas Deane had robbed him of this interesting friend;
who much preferred to act with the commissioned envoy of Congress. Then, on reaching Paris in December, 1776, to join his
colleagues, he found all France exulting in the arrival of *le grand
Franklin*; no one much regarding the presence of the **great** Lee.
His unsuccessful missons to Spain, Vienna, and Berlin occupied
most of the spring and summer of 1777, without yielding to his morbid
self-love much consolation. He returned to Paris in July to find
his colleagues immersed in the most important affairs, naval and
commercial, of the details of which he was ignorant, and the whole

history of which it was a work of time to impart to him. He was really a superfluous member of the commission, and conceived that his colleagues both regarded and treated him as a superfluity, which, in the hurry of that stirring time, may have been, in some degree, the case. I presume he had the pleasure of reading in a London newspaper (the *Public Ledger*) of July 12th, a complimentary allusion to himself: " Dr. Lee is certainly joined in the (American) commission, but he understands the business of courts so ill, that not one of the ministers will negotiate with him. He is the straight-laced image of awkward formality. To the preciseness of a Presbyterian he endeavors to add the Jesuitism of a Quaker. The one renders him ridiculous, the other suspected. When he thinks he is imposing on mankind, they are laughing at him." Perhaps, also, he had the comfort of perusing the following lines from the same paper of September 2d: " Two of these commissioners, for the third is a cipher, are protected in their public capacities by the court of Versailles; the court of London hath sent one embassador, the Congress of America have sent two, to France."

It must be owned that these were disagreeable paragraphs, particularly to a man of the disposition of Arthur Lee. But every public man has to submit to such annoyances. He might have read, in other London papers, of the autumn of 1777, paragraphs of which the following is a mild specimen: " They write from Paris that Silas Deane meets with repeated insults every time he goes through the streets of that city, and is pointed at by the populace as one of the wretches who meditated the ruin of his country by the basest strategems. The old fox, Franklin, secures himself from similar treatment by silence and seclusion." How absurd to care for such harmless nonsense !*

---

* An American paper, the New Jersey *Gazette*, of nearly the same date, published the following: "October 2d. A correspondent in Paris says: 'When Doctor Franklin appears abroad, it is more like a public than a private gentleman; and the curiosity of the people to see him is so great, that he may be said to be followed by a genteel mob. A friend of mine paid something for a place at a two-pair-of-stairs window to see him pass by in his coach, but the crowd was so great that he could but barely say he saw him.'

"We are well assured (adds the New Jersey editor) that Dr. Franklin, whose knowledge in philosophical sciences is universally allowed, and who has carried the powers of electricity to a greater length than any of his contemporaries, intends shortly to produce an *electrical machine*, of such wonderful force that instead of giving a slight stroke to the elbows of fifty or a hundred thousand men, who are joined hand in hand, it will give a violent shock even to nature herself, so as to disunite kingdoms, join islands to continents, and render men of the same nation stran-

The result of these various chagrins was, that Mr. Lee fell into direst feud with Beaumarchais and Deane, secretly writhed under the supremacy of Dr. Franklin, held in detestation all their friends, and omitted no opportunity to give them annoyance and disgust. He even conceived, as Mr. Adams relates, an antipathy to France itself, and made no secret of it in the very capital of the country from which his own had received such inestimable benefits. Mr. Deane gives an example of his ill humor with the contractors employed by the envoys. During Lee's absence from France, Dr. Franklin and Mr. Deane had made contracts for many thousands of uniforms, and for a ship in which to convey them and other stores to America.

"Soon after Mr. Lee's return," relates Deane, "he was made acquainted with what had been done in his absence. Mr. Holker, who had the management of the principal contract, waited on Mr. Lee, to inform him of the fashion in which he proposed the coats should be made, and to consult him on an improvement of the lapels by continuing them quite down, so as to join the waistband of the breeches, which would take about one-sixth of an ell of cloth and four buttons more than the usual fashion; but that it would guard the body from the cold in the most tender part of it. Mr. Holker and the gentleman with him met with the most disgusting reception; every thing was by Mr. Lee found fault with. Mr. Holker very patiently heard him, and pertinently answered his several objections : that as to the improvement on the lapels, it was so great, and the expense so very trifling, that sooner than give it up, he would even be content to throw the extra expense out of his account. To which Mr. Lee replied, that if he did, he had still an objection that could not be got over, it was the additional weight of the four buttons and one-sixth of cloth, which must help to fatigue the soldier in his marching. Mr. Holker and the other gentleman at this lost all patience, and refused ever after to have any thing to do with him, as did almost every other person with whom we had formed any connections."*

gers and enemies to each other; and that by a certain chemical preparation from oil, he will bo able to smooth the waves of the sea in one part of the globe, and raise tempests and whirlwinds in another, so as to be universally acknowledged for the greatest physician, politician, mathematician, and philosopher, this day living."

* "Deane Papers," p. 46.

Nor was this the worst of his offenses. He filled his private letters home with the most false and atrocious insinuations against the honor of his colleagues. A *vague* charge is the most injurious of all charges; it is the favorite resort of the calumniating miscreant. Lee would insinuate, in letters to Samuel Adams and Richard Henry Lee, that Deane had involved Congress in debt far beyond its ability to pay ; that Deane was surrounded and aided by men who were traitors to the cause of America; that Dr. Franklin was very old, very idle, and very careless, fit only for some quiet court where there would be nothing to do ; that nothing saved the interest of America in France from total confusion and fatal injury but the presence of such a vigilant, incorruptible, sagacious, and active envoy as Arthur Lee.

Take a few sentences from his correspondence. October 4th, to his brother, Richard Henry Lee : " The journey to Spain I undertook, because Dr. F. would not go through such bad roads in so rigorous a season, and Mr. D. excused himself by a proposition of going to Holland, which he never performed. * * * My idea of adapting characters and places is this : Dr. F. to Vienna, as the first, most respectable, and quiet; Mr. Deane to Holland. * * France remains the center of political activity, and here, therefore, I should choose to be employed." On the same day, to Samuel Adams : " I have within this year been at the several courts of Spain, Vienna, and Berlin, and I find this of France is the great wheel that moves them all. Here, therefore, the most activity is requisite ; and if it should ever be a question in Congress about my destination, I shall be much obliged to you for remembering, that I should prefer being at the court of France." November 4th, to the same correspondent : " Let me whisper to you that I have reason to suspect there is jobbing both with you and with us. The public concerns and the public money are perhaps sacrificed to private purposes. Congress should interfere." January 5th, 1778, to his brother : " If, in the arrangement of things, I could be continued here, and Mr. D. removed to some other place, it would be pleasing to me, and disconcert effectually their wicked measures." To Samuel Adams on the same day : " I have before mentioned to you a Mr. Carmichael" (volunteer secretary to Mr. Deane). " Every day gives me fresh reason for suspecting him. The gentleman who bears this will give you an account of him ; and

the inclosed account will show you in what manner the public
money has been put into his pocket by Mr. Deane, under the pretense of errands, in which the only object was, to tell ignorant
people that he and Mr. Deane were the only persons possessed of
public trust and power. It is impossible to describe to you to
what a degree this kind of intrigue has disgraced, confounded, and
injured our affairs here. The observation of this at head-quarters,
has encouraged and produced through the whole a spirit of neglect, abuse, plunder, and intrigue, in the public business, which it
has been impossible for me to prevent or correct." January 9th,
to his brother: "Things are going on worse and worse every day
among ourselves, and my situation is more painful. I see in every
department, neglect, dissipation, and private schemes. * * There
is but one way of redressing this and remedying the public evil;
that is the plan I before sent you, of appointing the Dr. *honoris
causa*, to Vienna, Mr. Deane to Holland, Mr. Jennings (a friend
of Lee in London) to Madrid, and leaving me here. In that case
I should have it in my power to call those to an account, through
whose hands I know the public money has passed, and which will
either never be accounted for or misaccounted for, by connivance
between those who are to share in the public plunder. If this
scheme can be executed it will disconcert all the plans at one
stroke, without an appearance of intention, and save both the public and me." February 15th, to his brother: "The disputes Mr.
Deane has industriously contrived with me will render my being
his accuser apparently an act of private enmity, not of public justice. And probably this was his object in quarreling with me,
being under great apprehensions from me, as well from my character as from the opportunities my situation would give me of doing
it with effect. Dr. F. has always countenanced his proceedings, I
believe, entirely from a consideration of the business and advantages which he artfully throws into the hands of Mr. Williams"
(nephew of Dr. Franklin at Nantes).

Enough. Such dastardly insinuations (all insinuations are dastardly), repeated occasionally for two years, coming from a man celebrated though unknown in his own country, could not but leave
impressions on many minds that would with difficulty be effaced.
There are those to whom calumny is congenial; who believe Evil
with fatal ease, Good with great difficulty. And this is one of the

reasons why, as Dr. Franklin used to say, " there is no such thing as a little enemy." An offended idiot with a little cunning, such as idiots have, and a box of matches, can burn a city. An Arthur Lee, with his sore vanity and mean ambition, can plant lies in the mind of his generation which shall outlast that generation, besides doing irreparable mischief in it.

I ought to add that, while Arthur Lee was filling the ear of Congress with calumnious insinuations respecting Dr. Franklin and his friends, there was no apparent or avowed ill-will between them. They not only transacted business together, but Lee and his set dined frequently at Franklin's table ; and, occasionally, all the three envoys dined together at the house of Mr. Lee.* Nor could it be said that Lee's isolation or insignificance was the fault of his colleagues ; for we find that several of the memorials addressed by the envoys to the French ministry in the latter part of 1777, as well as one important letter to Lord North, were drawn by Lee, who valued himself upon his rhetorical talent. Doubtless Dr. Franklin strove to conciliate and gratify this uneasy spirit by giving him something to do, and something which he prided himself upon his skill in doing. Nothing delights à gentleman of the Lee caliber more than to be asked to " draw up" a document of form, which affords him a chance to produce a succession of sounding, empty sentences. Pleasures of this nature Mr. Lee abundantly enjoyed in December, 1777, and January, 1778.

WILLIAM LEE. This was an elder brother of Arthur Lee. The beginning of the Revolution found him a merchant and alderman of London, where he had been long settled. Having early espoused the cause of his country, and evinced a willingness to serve it, Congress gave him, in January, 1777, an appointment of joint commercial agent with Thomas Morris, to reside at Nantes. But before the papers relating to this appointment had reached him, came more honorable commissions, naming him envoy to the courts of Berlin and Vienna. These commissions arrived in October ; but as neither Frederick nor Maria Theresa were willing to receive an American envoy, he remained for several months longer in Paris, unemployed, and counting one in the set of his troublesome brother. He had the name in Paris of being avaricious, and of having inherited

---

* " Life of Arthur Lee," i., 848.

a share of the family talent for becoming odious to those with whom they acted. In his diplomatic capacity he accomplished nothing whatever, except draw his salary. In his character of commercial agent we shall have to return to him by and by. RALPH IZARD. A native of South Carolina, of which State his grandfather was one of the founders, and in which he himself had inherited a large estate in land and slaves. He, too, like Arthur Lee, I suppose, was reared among companions whom he could strike without being struck back, whom he could abuse, vilify, and oppress, without receiving a word of remonstrance or reply. No man or woman brought up in that way can have a perfectly sane intellect, or live happily among equals, or co-operate justly in any difficult business. A spoiled child, the reader may have observed, never becomes truly mature; it is so with these unhappy victims of slavery; they either remain children or degenerate into savages; and a savage is merely a selfish, cruel, foolish child. This Ralph Izard was formed by nature to be a good and honorable man, as most men are; but his Carolina education had sadly cramped and perverted him, giving him fantastic notions of "honor," and developing chiefly that false pride for which the people of slave states and countries have always been noted, and upon which they plume themselves. He was, probably, the most passionate man then living; no considerations of prudence or decency could ever restrain the expression of his anger. "Mr. Izard," says John Adams, "was the most passionate, and in his passions the most violent and unbridled in his expressions of any man I ever knew." The breaking out of the revolution found him, also, a resident of London, where he had been living since 1771, much in the confidence of the Americans and their whig friends. It was he who witnessed the outrage upon Franklin in the Cock Pit, and afterwards censured him for not having assaulted Wedderburn on the spot, as he declared he would have done in similar circumstances. He came to Paris early in the war, and the same packet which brought William Lee his twofold commission, conveyed to Ralph Izard an appointment of envoy to the Grand Duke of Tuscany, who was a brother of the queen of France, and a son of the empress of Austria. The same reasons which prevented William Lee from going to Vienna kept Ralph Izard from visiting Florence. He resided in Paris during the whole period of his holding the commission, and, beyond making an unsuccessful attempt to borrow money in Italy, rendered his country no service in Europe. From the first, he was in accord with Arthur Lee. Like Lee, he hated Frenchmen and France. Like Lee, he was at feud with Silas Deane and Beaumarchais. Like Lee, he cooled towards Dr. Franklin, and his coolness grew ever cooler. How entirely he coincided with Lee may be seen from two or three sentences from one of his letters to the President of Congress, dated April 1st, 1778: "I shall avoid entering into any particulars respecting Mr. Deane, and shall only in general give you my opinion of him, which is, that if the whole world had been searched, I think it would have been impossible to have found one on every account more unfit for the office into which he has by the storm and convulsions of the times been shaken. I am under the fullest persuasion that the court of France might long ago have been induced to stand forth in our favor, if America had had proper representatives at that court. I must repeat what I have done in some former letters, that whatever good dispositions were shown by Mr. Lee, they were always opposed and overruled by the two eldest commissioners." This was ignorance and malevolence combined in about equal proportions. Touching Mr. Izard's personal and particular grievance, we shall have to speak further in a future page. He was ripe for collision with Dr. Franklin long before the close of 1777.

THOMAS MORRIS. This was the person originally appointed by the Committee of Secret Correspondence to reside at Nantes, as the commercial agent of the United States, and to him was intrusted the fund of ten thousand pounds designed for the subsistence of the three envoys at Paris. It was an appointment that brought disgrace upon America, infinite trouble upon the envoys, ruin and death upon the agent. Dr. Franklin brought with him from Philadelphia the commission of this miserable man, who came to receive it from London, where he had been living for several months—a man about town. He proceeded immediately to Nantes, where he abandoned himself, at once, to the most sottish debauchery, totally neglecting, for weeks at a time, the duties of his place. "In his paroxysms of intemperance and debauchery," wrote Mr. Deane, "he was unfit for all business, and shut up from all access; these paroxysms usually lasted for several weeks together without a single hour's omission, and there were but very short intervals between the termination of one paroxysm and the commencement of another."

Thomas Morris was a younger brother of Robert Morris, famous as one of the first of colonial merchants, a leading member of Congress, the soul of the Secret Committee, afterwards the self-sacrificing financier who enabled General Washington to transport his army to Yorktown and Lord Cornwallis. It was he who procured the appointment of his brother to the agency; and upon him, of course, would fall a great part of the disgrace of that brother's misconduct. In writing, therefore, to the Secret Committee upon the subject, Mr. Deane did not enter into particulars, but spoke vaguely of the "irregularities" of the agent, and added that he *must* be recalled. Unhappily, Mr. Robert Morris took offense at these words, conceiving that Mr. Deane should have given him *private* information of his brother's misdeeds. He had also received an intimation that Mr. Deane and Dr. Franklin desired the office for a protégé of their own; an intimation which may be found twenty times repeated in the letters of Arthur Lee. Mr. Morris, when at length he was made acquainted with the truth of this sad affair, explained in a letter to the President of Congress, which has recently been disinterred and printed, how he was led into disbelieving Mr. Deane, as well as how he came to recommend the appointment of a person so unworthy of public employment:

"Mr. Thomas Morris and myself," he said, "are descended from a father, whose virtue and whose memory I have ever revered with the most filial piety. Our mothers were not the same, and this youth was born after our father's decease, without any sufficient provision made for his maintenance. The tender regard I bore to the parent, I determined when very young to extend to his offspring, and no sooner had I fixed myself in the world than I took charge of this brother. I gave him the best education that could be obtained in Philadelphia, and took as much care of his morals as my time and capacity enabled. When he was arrived at a proper age, I took him into my counting-house to instruct him in the profession from which he was to draw his future support. In this situation he remained about three years, during which time he discovered on all occasions a good understanding, sound judgment, and clear head, with remarkable facility in dispatching business. His behavior was then modest and innocent, his heart pure, and he possessed a mind strongly actuated by principles of honor; at least these were the opinions I had formed, and such was the character he bore amongst his own acquaintance; from hence I formed the most pleasing expectation, and saw but one source from whence any reverse could spring. This was a fondness he early discovered of being the head of his company, a disposition more dangerous to youth than any other, and which in fact has been his ruin. This it was that first led him to seek improper company, who, readily granting him the pre-eminence he delighted in, soon carried him into the practice of their follies and vices. When I discovered this to be the case, and found that advice had not its proper weight, and thinking frequent exercise of authority might be dangerous, I fell on the expedient of sending him to Spain (in order to break off his connection with worthless companions), and there placed him in an eminent counting-house, where he gained much knowledge and experience, and where he acquired the French and Spanish languages so as to write and speak both with great fluency. At a proper season I recalled him to America, and took him a partner in our house, promising myself assistance and relief from his abilities and *expected* assiduity, and for some time had great satisfaction in him; but unfortunately his former associates found him out and again led him astray.

"At this period the commercial business of America was interrupted by certain resolutions of Congress, and, fearing that idle time and these associates would bring him to ruin, I determined on sending him to Europe well recommended, with money in his pocket, in hopes to open his mind, extend his ideas, and give him a habit of keeping and seeking good company. He traveled through Spain, Italy, and into France, with reputation kept by means of introductions. I procured for him the best company in every place he went to, and I had the pleasure to receive many letters from my friends as well as from himself in the most satisfactory style. These letters, his assurances, and those from some friends on his behalf, regained my confidence, and I judged he had now arrived at the period of proper reflection; for such usually happens to young people who have been too volatile in the first stages of manhood. At this period it happened that a commercial agent became necessary to have a general superintendency of the public business in Europe. My brother was then in France (as I

thought), possessed of my good opinion ; and, reflecting that he
was qualified for that agency by his education in two counting-
houses, where he had seen and executed much business, by his perfect knowledge of the languages, and by his being connected with
some of the best mercantile houses in Europe, and known to many
more, I was prompted to offer his services to the committee, firmly
believing he would be extremely useful, and do honor to himself
and me. Here I must observe that no part of his conduct had ever
given me the least cause to suspect any want of integrity or breach
of honor. Therefore, the only doubts I did or could entertain
were, whether he would bestow that attention that he ought to
this business; and for this I depended on the assurances he had
given in his letters of a faithful execution of any commands I might
lay on him. The committee, of which Dr. Franklin was then a
member, was pleased to accept the offer, and on the doctor's going
to France, he promised me to become a friend and adviser to my
brother if he found it necessary. Mr. Deane had promised this
before his departure, and to make me acquainted with his conduct.
I reposed myself in confidence that he could not do any harm (as
I should soon hear how he managed, and could act accordingly),
and he might do much good. At the same time that I recommended him to the agency, I intrusted him to collect the debts due
to our house in Europe, and pay the balances we might owe there ;
and since then have continued to employ him in the management
of our own business. * * *

"It happened very unfortunately that, about the time Thomas
Morris was appointed in America to this agency, he had gone from
France to London, where, totally unable to withstand the tempting
scenes of pleasure *that sink of iniquity affords*, he gave in to the
pursuit with an eagerness (as I am now informed) that debauched
his mind and laid the foundation for all that has since happened.
He was in London at the time his letters of appointment arrived at
Paris. Mr. Deane sent for him. He came and promised a faithful
attention to business ; he repaired to Nantes, and finding Mr. Penet
had been intrusted with a contract for public business, part of
which had been executed, he readily fell into the proposals made
by that house and became a party in it, but on what terms I do not
know ; consequently he put the public business into their hands
(which was not inconsistent with the instructions under which he

acted). Whilst things were in this train in France, I received a letter from the gentleman in Cadiz with whom my brother had lived, a worthy man, who had great regard for him and wished to promote his welfare. He gave me reason to suppose his conduct in London had been out of character, and this gave the first alarm to my fears.

"In consequence of which, I wrote letters on the 31st January last to Mr. Deane, to Mr. Ross, and to Mr. Thomas Morris, informing them of this intelligence, and pressing their immediate care of, and attention to, the public business, should he neglect it. I requested my friend Ross to visit France on purpose to watch and inform me truly what was his conduct, and insisted to my brother that if he had been guilty of any neglect of duty or misconduct in discharge of his public trust, that he should resign it into the hands of Mr. Deane or Mr. Ross, empowering them *regularly* to act for him until new arrangements were made. This done, I awaited impatiently for the event. * * * By the return of one of our ships came letters from the commissioners, saying, to the best of my remembrance, 'that Mr. Thomas Morris must be immediately displaced from his agency,' and another, quoting the paragraph of Dr. Lee's letter from Bordeaux. Having no private letter *then* from Mr. Deane on this subject, I was astonished at the style of these to Congress; for, supposing my brother guilty of some inattention, which was the most I did suppose, I could not think it right to blast entirely a young man's reputation that was just setting out in the world, merely because he was fond of pleasure; and as the letters he had written respecting the business under his care were full and clear, they were produced to Congress in his justification, and to prevent any hasty measures. I then related to Congress the substance of what I have now written, but not so fully; and many members, as well as myself, were surprised at the affair as it then stood. In consequence of what the commissioners had wrote, I referred myself to Mr. Thomas Morris's private letters more particularly. I found there was no good understanding between Mr. Deane and him (but of Doctor Franklin he wrote respectfully), and he intimated that Mr. Deane was privately his enemy. Not trusting, however, to his letters, I applied to several persons that came from Nantes, who assured me there was nothing amiss in his conduct that they knew or heard of; but more particularly one person who had transacted business with him. This gentleman assured me over and over that he lived two months in the house with my brother; that he saw him assiduous, attentive, and industrious; that if it had not been for him, the business of those ships would not have been done in any reasonable time, and that I might depend my brother would give entire satisfaction; at least he was fully persuaded of this. He said he knew well there were persons in France that envied his appointment, and would leave nothing undone to have him displaced, and particularly mentioned Mr. Williams, who he heard was nephew to one, and concerned in trade with another, of the commissioners, as the person intended to supply his place."*

Acting upon these impressions, Mr. Morris wrote angrily to Mr. Deane; "I think those public letters," he said, "were cruel to my brother and extremely unfriendly to myself. I shall inform him of them, and if he has spirit to resent them, I hope he will also have judgment to do it properly." The letter from which these words are taken, he inclosed open to his brother, asking him to read it before sending it to Mr. Deane. He accompanied it, however, with a few sentences of caution to himself: "As to what I have said about your resenting their letters, I think you had best not think of any thing of that kind, lest your past behavior will not support you in doing it; and the best satisfaction you can have will be by holding your post under such good conduct as will deter them from attacking you again."

Upon receiving this packet, the drunken wretch resolved to convey the letter to Paris himself, and "resent" the conduct of the envoys in their very presence. Mr. Deane related to Mr. Robert Morris what occurred in consequence of this doughty resolution. "Mr. Morris, September 27th, called on me and said he had a letter from you which, though directed to me, respected the commissioners, and therefore he chose to deliver it in the presence of Dr. Franklin. I thereupon conducted him to the doctor's apartments, and he delivered the letter to him. It was open, very much worn and dirty, and the cover in which it was wrapped, without being sealed, was superscribed in the handwriting of Mr. T. Morris. After Dr. Franklin had read the letter, Mr. T. Morris told us we

* "Materials for History," p. 78.

had written to Congress more than was true respecting his conduct; that the Congress were of this opinion, and that he should hereafter despise us, and treat us with the greatest contempt, adding other insulting expressions, not necessary to be repeated; to all which my venerable colleague made this reply: 'It gives me pleasure to be respected by men who are themselves respectable, but I am indifferent to the sentiments of those of a different character, and I only wish that your future conduct may be such as to entitle you to the approbation of your honorable constituents.' On parting, Mr. T. Morris told us he had shown the letter to all whom he thought his friends, and having copied it, he should continue to show it in the same manner. How public it may soon be made by him, or those he communicated it to, I know not, but I am apprehensive that many who are neither friends to him nor to America have already seen it, and that this indiscreet exposure of it may give our enemies an opportunity of using it to strengthen their accounts of our internal divisions and animosities. I must also inform you that Mr. Penet, pretending to have received intelligence from you of what I wrote to Congress concerning him, has had the assurance to send me, open, by Mr. T. Morris, an insulting and menacing letter, which had also been shown in the same manner."*

Here was a coil! And, worse than this, no money could be got from the agent, who began now to draw from the public coffers the means of sustaining his debauchery. Happily his shameful career was short. Early in 1778, after a series of desperate paroxysms of intemperance, he died, leaving Mr. William Lee sole agent. His brother, on learning the truth, handsomely apologized to the envoys for the annoyance he had caused them. "It adds very much," he wrote to Congress, "to the distress and unhappiness this unworthy young man has involved me in, to think I should have passed censures on Dr. Franklin and Mr. Deane (Doctor Lee was not mentioned), which they did not deserve. I did it under a deception that most men of feeling would have fallen into, and I shall as freely own it to them as I do to you, holding it more honorable to acknowledge an error and atone for any injuries produced by it, than with a vindictive spirit to persist, because you

* Deane Papers, p. 121.

happen to have committed it.   My distress is more than I can describe; to think that in the midst of the most ardent exertions I was capable of making to promote the interest and welfare of my country, I should be the means of introducing a worthless wretch to disgrace and discredit it, is too much to bear."* From this time to the end of the war, Mr. Morris remained one of Franklin's stanchest friends.

JONATHAN WILLIAMS. One of Dr. Franklin's Boston nephews, once a clerk in the law office of John Adams. On Dr. Franklin's arrival in France he came from London, where he had been employed as upper or confidential clerk in a sugar house, to visit his uncle; and, while in Paris, offered to serve the envoys for his country's sake, in any capacity in which he could earn a subsistence. Every thing being in confusion at Nantes at the beginning of 1777, Mr. Deane asked him to go to that seaport, and endeavor to extricate from chaos the goods, the cargoes, the prizes, belonging to the United States. He acquitted himself so well, that the true friends of America at Nantes urged the envoys to keep him there. The excesses of Thomas Morris and the absence of William Lee obliged them to employ some one at Nantes, and Mr. Williams was retained. Morris objecting, the envoys, July 4th, 1779, gave him a commission to take charge of *naval* affairs at the port, *i. e.*, the prizes, the refitting of the men-of-war, the purchase of naval stores and provisions, leaving to Morris the business that was merely commercial. Mr. Williams remained at Nantes for more than a year, doing a vast amount of difficult and delicate work, at a rate of compensation exceedingly moderate, to the satisfaction of two of the envoys, and to the great contentment of the gallant captains with whom he had to do; Arthur Lee omitting no opportunity to insinuate that he was a cheating villain, known to be such by Dr. Franklin, who winked at his delinquencies because he was his nephew. It was a pet conviction of Lee, that Jonathan Williams and Silas Deane fitted out privateers with the public money, and, having sold the prizes, shared the proceeds.

WILLIAM CARMICHAEL. This gentleman, a member of the distinguished Maryland family of that name, and a man of fortune, chanced to be at Paris, on his way to America, when Mr. Deane

* Materials for History, p. 85.

arrived there in July, 1776. Becoming intimate with Deane, he perceived his distress from the want of a secretary, and offered to delay his return to America, and devote himself to his assistance. Mr. Deane joyfully accepting the offer, Carmichael remained in the capacity of secretary for more than a year, rendering invaluable service both at Paris and at the seaports. Neither of the envoys, it must be remembered, could personally appear at the ports; since that would have given countenance to Lord Stormont's assertions, that the cargoes of arms were designed for the American Insurgents. Hence the necessity of having young, unknown men of tact and fidelity, like William Carmichael and Jonathan Williams, to aid in getting the ships to sea. Mr. Carmichael, whose letters show him to have been a man of sagacity, of ardent patriotism, and uncommonly fertile in expedients, served his country well in France under the direction of Mr. Deane. It was he who first suggested (many weeks before Dr. Franklin's arrival) the scheme of attacking some British seaport. He also entered *con amore* into the game of deluding Lord Stormont. An item in the bill of expenses of one of his journeys, was this:

" Paid a woman at Dunkirk for complaining to the French admiralty that the English commissary, Frayer, had enticed her husband, a French pilot, into the British service, two guineas."* A mode of saying to the British Government, " You're another," which, Punch informs us, is the " end of all argument." The English ministry, it appears, considered Mr. Carmichael worth buying, and rated him at a high price. In the spring of 1777 an agent of the ministry assured him that " the English Administration saw through the designs of the House of Bourbon, saw that they meant to weaken us both, and by that means command us," and that England was willing to offer peace to America on the basis of 1763, repealing all the obnoxious acts since passed. The agent then offered Mr. Carmichael " an affluent income, to be secured to him in any part of the world he might choose," if he would use his best endeavors to induce his countrymen to accept those terms—" the affluent income" to be his, whether he succeeded or not.† Mr. Carmichael rejected the offer in becoming terms.

---

* Deane Papers, p. 136.
† Diplomatic Correspondence of the American Revolution, ix., 318.

He was of the anti-Lee party. "The age of Dr. Franklin," he wrote in July, 1777, "in some measure hinders him from taking so active a part in the drudgery of business, as his great zeal and abilities would otherwise enable him to execute. He is the Master to whom we children in politics all look up for counsel, and whose name is everywhere a passport to be well received." Mr. Carmichael was also a particular friend of Beaumarchais. Need I add, then, that the "Rogue Lee" (as Beaumarchais styled the amiable Arthur) regarded Mr. Carmichael as Iago regarded Michael Cassio, or Shylock Antonio? Truly the wrath of Arthur Lee burned against this worthy son of Maryland, and he traduced him, in his letters to America, much in the manner of jealous Iago; and this, notwithstanding they had been college companions in bygone years. "I could wish to guard you particularly against Mr. Carmichael, of whose art and enmity I have had sufficient proofs to make me distrust him for the future,"—is a specimen of the mode in which Lee was accustomed to write of his old acquaintance in 1777. There are far worse passages than this in Lee's letters, but I have not patience to copy them. Suffice it to say, that he wrote of Carmichael just as he wrote of Franklin, Deane, Beaumarchais, Chaumont, Williams, Conyngham, Paul Jones, William Franklin, and every other man in France who really helped America in her struggle for independence. All these gentlemen, according to Arthur Lee, had nothing in view, in all that they pretended to do for America, but the dishonest filling of their own pockets. With Carmichael, also, Mr. Lee continued to associate familiarly, and dine, through the whole of the year 1777. This we learn from Lee's own diary.

CARON DE BEAUMARCHAIS. It was upon Beaumarchais that Arthur Lee reeked the fellest and the longest vengeance. During the greater part of 1777, the indefatigable representative of Roderique Hortalez and Co. continued to labor in behalf of Congress, sending off ship after ship laden with arms, ammunition, and clothing. But he received no tobacco, no rice, no indigo, no money, in return; nor even a letter of acknowledgment. The Count de Vergennes sustained the credit of the House by granting another million; which enabled Beaumarchais to wait still longer. But when the year slipped by without his having received from Congress any sign that they knew of his existence, he dissuaded the Firm from sending any more cargoes to America, and devoted him-

self to the business of getting payment for those already dispatched.
The sole cause of this mischief was Arthur Lee, who, in order to
ruin Beaumarchais, did not scruple to write home, not insinuations
merely, but falsehoods pure and simple; conscious, deliberate, and
malicious falsehoods. He *knew* that the French ministry had
changed their original plan of sending money and stores direct to
Congress, and that, in consequence of this change, Beaumarchais
had set up a commercial house in order to accomplish the same end
without risk of premature war with England. Nevertheless, we
find him writing confidentially to Congress such passages as this:
" Mr. de Vergennes, the minister and his secretary, have repeatedly
assured us that no return was expected for the cargoes sent by
Beaumarchais. This gentleman is not a merchant; he is known to
be a political agent, employed by the court of France." And
again : " The ministry *has often given us to understand* that we had
nothing to pay for the cargoes supplied by Beaumarchais; however, the latter, with the perseverance of adventurers of his kind,
persists in his demands." Professor de Loménie, the able and judicious biographer of Beaumarchais, is justified in pronouncing this
assertion " a remarkable falsehood." The invaluable documents
published by him *demonstrate* that the Count de Vergennes and
his Secretary, M. Gerard, uniformly held language of precisely the
opposite tenor, and took almost as much interest in Beaumarchais'
claims upon Congress as *though they were to share in the proceeds
of those claims!* Count de Vergennes could not have made a
statement of this kind to any one without at once betraying and
abandoning the policy of his court ; least of all, could he have made
it to Arthur Lee, whom Beaumarchais had early taught him to
distrust and despise. Lee's assertion, repeated by every opportunity, placed both Deane and Beaumarchais in the most cruel predic-
ament ; Deane, because he supported Beaumarchais' claim, and thus
gave plausibility to Lee's insinuation that there was a corrupt understanding between them : Beaumarchais, because he could get no
return cargoes. Deane could not, and Beaumarchais dared not,
explain the true nature of the House of Hortalez. He dared not
say that it differed from other houses of business *only* in the fact
that the king of France had furnished the capital, and that for the
use of that capital he was *only* accountable to the king of France.
He could merely exhibit his contract with Mr. Deane, send in his

bill, and demand payment; which would have been enough, if Lee
had not continually written, in effect: "Never mind him, gentlemen; he is a dramatist, who is only playing merchant; it is all a
fiction, to disguise the generosity of the king from the prying eyes
of the British ambassador. Don't send him a pound of tobacco."*
Beaumarchais would have been ruined if the French government
had not given other business to the firm of Hortalez and Co., which
enabled him to send to sea whole fleets of ships, and keep his
ten horses and three coachmen.

Attributing the silence and delay of Congress to the artifices of
the "rogue Lee," he sent over to America, at the close of 1777, his
nephew, Francy, to set his affairs right with Congress. Another
nephew was already in America, fighting under General Washington. In his letter of instructions to Francy he wrote "I believe
in the good feeling and equity of the Congress, as in my own and
yours. Its deputies over here are not in easy circumstances, and
want often renders men deficient in delicacy: that is how I explain
the injustice they have endeavored to do me. I do not despair even
of gaining them over by the calmness of my representations, and
the firmness of my conduct. It is very unfortunate, my friend, for
this cause, that its interests in France should have been intrusted to
several persons at once. One alone would have succeeded much
better, and, as far as I am concerned, I owe Mr. Deane the justice
to say, that he is both ashamed and grieved at the conduct of his

---

* The following is an extract from one of Arthur Lee's letters to the Foreign Committee, dated
October 6, 1777.   It is an ingenious and most telling perversion: "Upon the subject of returns, I
think it my duty to state to you some facts relative to the demands of this kind from Hortalez.
The gentleman who uses this name came to me, *about a year and a half ago, in London, as an
agent from this court*, and wishing to communicate something to Congress.   At our first interview he informed me that the court of France wished to send an aid to America of £200,000 sterling in specie, arms, and ammunition, and that all they wanted was to know through which
island it was best to make the remittance, and that Congress should be apprised of it.   We settled the Cape as the place, and he urged me by no means to omit giving the earliest intelligence
of it, with information that it would be remitted in the name of Hortalez.   At our next meeting
he desired me to request that a small quantity of tobacco or some other production might be sent
to the Cape, to give it the air of a mercantile transaction, *repeating over and over again, that it
was for a cover only, and not for payment, as the remittance was gratuitous.*   Of all this I informed Dr. Franklin, by sundry opportunities.   At the same time I stated to Monsieur Hortalez
that if his court would dispatch eight or ten ships of the line to our aid, it would enable us to destroy all the British fleet, and decide the question at one stroke.   I repeated this to him in a
letter after his return to Paris, to which the answer was, that there was not spirit enough in his
court for such an exertion, but that he was hastening the promised succors.   Upon Mr. Deane's
arrival the business went into his hands, and the aids were at length embarked in the Amphitrite, Mercure, and Seine."

colleagues toward me, the fault of which lies altogether with Mr. Lee."

It thus appears that he deemed Franklin also an opponent of his claims. It is certain that Dr. Franklin never understood the nature of the connection between Beaumarchais and the French government. No one ever did, or could, except the parties concerned, until the publication, seven years ago, of M. de Loménie's work, "Beaumarchais and his Times." It appears, also, that Dr. Franklin did not, at this time, know the terms of the contract between Beaumarchais and Deane, or that there was a formal, written contract between them at all. It is probable, too, as M. de Loménie suggests, that he had imbibed a prejudice against the histrionic merchant from his old friend Dr. Dubourg, as well as from the ceaseless and point-blank assertions of Arthur Lee. It does not appear, however, that he took any active part in opposing Beaumarchais' claims upon Congress. Regarding the affair as one of the cabinet mystifications natural to the false and tortuous politics of the time and situation, not intended to be precisely understood by him, he seems to have simply let it alone, having plenty of other business on his hands.

No one can be blamed for not understanding a man who is absolutely unique. M. de Loménie's work upon Beaumarchais presents to our consideration a specimen of human kind so entirely peculiar, that only a master in biography, like himself, could have rendered him credible; nor could he, without the aid of vast stores of the very best material. It is the union in the same character of solid, practical, efficient merit, with the qualities of the consummate charlatan, that renders Beaumarchais so puzzling a personage. If he wrote like Mr. Skimpole in Bleak House, he acted like a small, practical Napoleon, who, also, had a touch of the histrionic in his composition. As another illustration of his various traits, take the plan devised by him of getting his last ship safe to Philadelphia. He had solemnly promised the timid old minister, M. de Maurepas, that the ship should go to St. Domingo, and return to France without having touched at any part of the American continent. This inconvenient promise he communicates to Francy, and then proceeds in the following strain:

"The cargo of this vessel is of much importance to the Congress and myself. It consists of soldiers' coats ready made, of sheets, blankets, etc. It also conveys artillery to the extent of sixty-six bronze cannons, of which four pieces carry thirty-three pounds, twenty-four pieces twenty-four pounds, twenty pieces sixteen pounds, and the rest twelve and eight pounds; besides thirty-three pieces of artillery carrying four pounds, making altogether a hundred bronze cannons, in addition to a great many other things.

"After much thinking, it has occurred to me that you might arrange secretly with the Secret Committee of the Congress to send immediately one or two American privateers up to St. Domingo. One of them will send his shallop to Cape Français, or will make the signal agreed upon long since for all American ships coming to the Cape, that is to say, he will *hoist a white streamer*, display the Dutch flag at the mainmast, and fire three guns; then M. Carabasse (agent of Beaumarchais) will go on board with M. de Montaut, captain of my vessel, 'Le Fier Roderigue.' They will arrange so, that on my vessel going out, the American privateer may seize it, under no matter what pretext, and take it away. My captain will protest violently, and will draw up a written statement threatening to make his complaint to the Congress. The vessel will be taken where you are. The Congress will loudly disavow the action of the brutal privateer, and will set the vessel at liberty, with polite apologies to the French flag; during this time you will land the cargo, fill the ship with tobacco, and send it back to me as quickly as possible, with all you may happen to have ready to accompany it. As M. Carmichael is very rapid, you will have time to arrange this maneuver either with the Congress or with the captain of some privateer who is a friend of yours, and discreet. By this means M. de Maurepas finds himself liberated from his promise to those who have received it, and I from mine towards him, for no one can do any thing against violence, and my operation will meet with success in spite of all the obstacles by which my labors have been so thickly attended."

Such was Caron de Beaumarchais, unique among merchants and men. Whether it was by those or by other maneuvers that this ship was enabled to reach America, no one has informed us. Certain it is that she arrived safely at Yorktown in Virginia, and was loaded with tobacco for her return. I trust M. de Maurepas was satisfied. We leave him, for the present, to struggle with the "obstacles" that so "thickly attended" him.

Dr. Edward Bancroft. A native of Massachusetts, long settled in London as physician, author, and contributor to periodicals. Mr. Adams, who loved him not, tells us that he was a pupil of Silas Deane when that gentleman was a Connecticut schoolmaster, and that, being afterwards apprenticed to a trade, he ran away to sea, as so many Yankee boys did at that day. He held no public or avowed appointment from Congress during the revolution, but he was continually flitting between London and Paris, bringing to the envoys such information as he could gather concerning the plans of the British ministry. He was an old London acquaintance of Franklin, and enjoyed both in London and Paris the particular antipathy of Arthur Lee. It was Mr. Lee's opinion that Dr. Bancroft made immense sums of money by speculating in the stock market on the secrets obtained from the American envoys. In the summer of 1777, being suspected by the British government of a participation in the attempt to burn Portsmouth dockyard, he fled to Passy, and passed several months in Dr. Franklin's house, chiefly employed in assisting Mr. Deane, but occasionally making a rapid journey to London. Dr. Bancroft was highly esteemed at Versailles, and was intrusted with the secrets of the American embassy.

Charles W. F. Dumas. This worthy gentleman, secret agent of Congress at the Hague, continued his services to the end of the war, and for some years after. Though removed from the sphere of Lee's malign activity, he was not exempt from calumny and quarrel; both the Lees having united in misrepresenting him to Congress. Arthur Lee's ground of offense was, that Mr. Dumas, in some of his contributions to the Leyden *Gazette*, had praised Dr. Franklin at his expense. The Lees, however, never quite succeeded in procuring his dismissal, though they contrived to keep his salary insufficient. That he might devote his whole energies to the service of America, Mr. Dumas gave up various employments that yielded him more than the salary paid him by Congress, which was about twelve hundred dollars a year. He was sorely pinched by poverty, for his journeys, his expresses, and postages were exceedingly expensive. He labored, however, with unflagging zeal, proud of the cause and the country he served. The King of France solaced his old age by a pension of fifteen hundred francs, Congress having neglected to provide for him. Imagine him at the Hague,

during these years, corresponding with the envoys at Paris and
with Congress, trying hard to prevail upon Dutch merchants to
lend money to the United States, prying into the movements of the
British embassador, looking after the frigate which the envoys
were building at a Dutch port, writing articles for the newspapers,
and doing all that in him lay to promote the interests of America and
of man. An honest, modest, zealous, learned, indefatigable agent.

WILLIAM TEMPLE FRANKLIN. This young gentleman approved
himself an exact, industrious, and skillful secretary. Of elegant
person and graceful manners, speaking French well, and having inherited much of his grandfather's gayety and humor, young Mr.
Franklin was welcome in the cabinet of M. de Vergennes, and in
the salons of Paris. Congress, neglecting to appoint or provide for
a secretary, Dr. Franklin allowed him, for the first year, six hundred and fifty dollars; the second, eight hundred; the third, nine
hundred; the fourth, twelve hundred; and afterwards, fifteen hundred dollars a year. Few secretaries have earned their salaries by
harder or more various labor; for Dr. Franklin was diplomatist,
banker, commercial agent, naval commissioner, consul, and philosopher, and in each of these capacities required, occasionally, his
grandson's aid. So busy were they both, that there were whole
seasons in which neither of them could snatch a day's holiday. The
faction of the Lees did not spare even this diligent and harmless
youth, who was the solace and stay of Franklin's long exile. So
much prejudice was excited against him in Congress, that his appointment as secretary to the mission was not officially recognized,
and efforts were made, by and by, to insult and wound the grandfather by removing the young man from his place. Such evil could
one perverted mind effect! Such was the spirit of Secession eighty-
five years ago!

MRS. PATIENCE WRIGHT. The mention of young Franklin calls
to mind this venerable lady, who rendered Dr. Franklin some aid
during his residence in France, and of whom his grandson has preserved the memory. Mrs. Patience Wright, reports William Temple Franklin, was a very extraordinary woman. Though born and
reared in Philadelphia, she was a niece of John Wesley, and inherited a share of the indomitable resolution of the family. She
was early distinguished in Philadelphia as a modeler in wax (the
Madame Tussaud of her day), and, a few years before the revolu-

tion, though well advanced in years, brought her famous collection of figures to London, where she gained a good deal of money by exhibiting them. She also modeled in wax the busts of eminent persons in England, which gave her access, sometimes, to important information. A stanch American and whig, and an old Philadelphia acquaintance of Dr. Franklin, she communicated to him every item and rumor which she could gather in the great houses which she frequented. No sooner did she hear of the appointment of a new general, the fitting out of a fleet, the embarking of forces, or the arrival of dispatches, than she busied herself with gleaning details. " The old lady," says Temple, " found means of access to some family where she could get information, and thus, without being at all suspected, she contrived to transmit an account of the number of the troops, and the place of their destination, to her political friends abroad. She, at one time, had frequent access to Buckingham House; and used, it was said, to speak her sentiments very freely to their Majesties, who were amused with her originality. The great Lord Chatham honored her with his visits, and she took his likeness, which appears in Westminister Abbey."

One of Dr. Franklin's letters to this remarkable dame is interesting because it reveals to us the pleasant terms upon which he lived with his merry grandson. The old lady had written to him for advice as to her exhibiting her works at Paris, and then returning to America from a French seaport. He dissuades her from both projects; and, having finished his letter, adds this humorous postscript: " My grandson, whom you may remember when a little saucy boy at school, being my amanuensis in writing the within letter, has been diverting me with his remarks. He conceives that your figures cannot be packed up without damage from any thing you could fill the boxes with to keep them steady. He supposes, therefore, that you must put them into post-chaises, two and two, which will make a long train upon the road, and be a very expensive conveyance; but as they will eat nothing at the inns, you may the better afford it. When they come to Dover, he is sure they are so like life and nature, that the master of the packet will not receive them on board without passes; which you will do well therefore to take out from the secretary's office, before you leave London; where they will cost you *only* the modest price of two guineas and sixpence each, which you will pay without grumbling, because you are sure the money will never be employed against your country. It will require, he says, five or six of the long wicker French stage-coaches to carry them as passengers from Calais to Paris, and a ship with good accommodations to convey them to America; where all the world will wonder at your clemency to Lord North; that, having it in your power to hang, or send him to the lighters, you had generously reprieved him for transportation."

Besides the persons already mentioned, there were other Americans, or friends of America, in Europe, who had more or less to do with Dr. Franklin; such as Simeon Deane, brother of the envoy; J. J. Pringle, secretary to Ralph Izard; Hodge and Allen, merchants; a nephew of Arthur Lee at school; the secretaries of Arthur Lee and William Lee. What employment Izard or William Lee could have found for a private secretary is difficult to conjecture, since they differed from private gentlemen in little more than the peculiarity of drawing from the treasury of Congress two thousand guineas a year each. Neither of them saw the capitals to which they were accredited.

These, then, were the persons composing the American circle of which Dr. Franklin was the center and chief. The two hostile parties were about equal in numbers; but on the side of the Lees were three individuals holding the rank of envoy or commissioner, and having access to the mind of Congress, namely, Arthur Lee, William Lee, and Ralph Izard. During the greater part of the year 1777 Dr. Franklin, who abhorred nothing more than altercation, and who felt deeply the necessity of harmony among the envoys, succeeded in ignoring the controversy, and lived on terms of civility with the men who were traducing him and his friends in every private letter they wrote to America. For his own part, he never mentioned the names of these insidious foes in his letters home, whether public or private, until the quarrel was known to all the world.

CHAPTER IV.

THE DARK HOUR BEFORE THE DAWN.

SEPTEMBER, October, and November, 1777, were anxious months with the servants of Congress in Europe. Not a decisive word of General Burgoyne or General Howe had reached them. Dr. Franklin, I think, must have derived some comfort from reading the exceedingly absurd and pompous Proclamation with which General Burgoyne had begun his southward march into the State of New York. If he had had the privilege of reading as many productions of that kind as the people of the United States have been favored with in recent years, he would, probably, have dismissed all apprehensions of danger from a General capable of opening a difficult campaign with a burst of swelling and boastful words. It was only Napoleon who could both brag and conquer; and Napoleon was then a boy of nine, at school in Corsica. Nevertheless, General Burgoyne's comic opening paragraph was founded on grim fact. "The forces intrusted to my command," said he, " are designed to act in concert, and upon a common principle, with the numerous armies and fleets which already display in every quarter of America the power, the justice, and, when properly sought, the mercy of the king."* So, if General Burgoyne should fight no better than he wrote, there were still General Howe, Sir Henry Clinton, and the fleet.

Nor was the prospect cheering in Europe. No more little naval triumphs; no more prizes; no more privateering; no hope of burning Liverpool and Glasgow; for a strong squadron of British men-of-war cruised off the mouth of the Loire, and shut up the American vessels in Nantes, as though the port were blockaded. Besides, worthy Captain Wickes was drowned; brave Johnson and Nicholson were languishing in British prisons; the bold Conyngham had been obliged at last to fly from British waters; and the alert Hammond had been taken on his way home. In September, too, the envoys had spent all their money; Beaumarchais, all his; Thomas Morris, all the public money under his con-

* For a copy of General Burgoyne's Proclamation, see " Frank Moore's Diary of the Revolution," i., 454.

trol; no cargoes came to their relief; and there were contractors, commissioners, captains, crews, agents, clerks, servants, prisoners escaped from England, a hungry and clamorous host, all looking to the envoys for payment or daily bread. In such dire extremity were they at one time, that Dr. Franklin proposed that they should sell part of the clothing and arms that were waiting for shipment' at Nantes.* They concluded, at length, after many long conferences, to lay the state of their affairs before the King of France; to press him to acknowledge the independence of the United States; and grant them a loan that would really relieve them, say fourteen millions of francs. They also offered to sell the king the frigate they were building in Holland, which, they feared, they would never be able to finish and equip in that cautious, Britain-fearing country. A *mémoire* to this effect was drawn up, which their banker, Mr. Grand, conveyed to the Count de Vergennes on the twenty-fifth of September. The minister engaged to have it immediately translated, and to present it to the king.

September 29th, arrived at Passy a Captain from America with dispatches; but, alas! they proved to be merely duplicates of those last received. Arthur Lee, however, received a private letter, one paragraph of which he read to his colleagues. He made this entry in his diary the next day : " I read a paragraph to the commission-ers, in my brother Richard Henry Lee's letter, stating that without an alliance with France and Spain, with a considerable loan to sup-port their funds, it would be difficult to maintain their independ-ence. Resolved to send Mr. Grand next day to Count Vergennes, for an answer to the mémoire." Mr. Grand went, accordingly. He reported that the count had not yet laid the mémoire before the king, but would do so ere long; that he " seemed to think four-teen millions of francs a great demand ;" and that, as to the pro-posed recognition, it would involve all Europe without materially helping America. The ministers also reproved the envoys for " the unguarded manner in which they did business," saying that " Lord Stormont had apprised Mons. Maurepas that a mémoire was intended before it was presented." " Mr. Grand," continues Arthur Lee, " communicated these things to me in private, and I desired him to do it to all the commissioners together, that it might

* Deane Papers, p. 50.

suggest to them some caution in the conduct of our affairs, which were open to all the world.   He did so ; and it was considered as a pretext for refusing to assist us by one, and as an unjust accusation by the other.   It was said that if Lord Stormont had such information from some one about us, he would not have told it, because that would prevent any further communication, and therefore it seemed improbable that Lord Stormont had told them so.   Mr. Lee said, that in these cases Lord Stormont's object was to excite distrust and destroy all confidence between them, which it appeared he, aided by other things, had but too well effected."

It was on the first of October that Mr. Grand conveyed to the envoys this discouraging report of his interview with the minister. Day after day, week after week passed, and yet no answer to their mémoire came.

We have a specimen of Dr. Franklin's conversation at this dark time, the preservation of which we owe to Arthur Lee; for even Arthur Lee could not, at all times, resist the charms of Dr. Franklin's conversation ; and he records in his diary some interesting particulars of several interviews.   October 25th, the application to the French court for pecuniary aid being still unanswered, Mr. Lee and Dr. Franklin fell into conversation at Passy upon the state of affairs.   Upon reaching home, Mr. Lee made an unusually long entry in his journal, recording chiefly what Franklin had said.

"He seemed to agree with me," wrote Mr. Lee, "in thinking that France and Spain mistook their interest and opportunity in not making an alliance with us now, when they might have better terms than they could expect hereafter.   That it was well for us they left us to work out our own salvation ; which the efforts we had hitherto made, and the resources we had opened, gave us the fairest reason to hope we should be able to do.   He told me the manner in which the whole of this business had been conducted, was such a miracle in human affairs, that if he had not been in the midst of it, and seen all the movements, he could not have comprehended how it was effected.   To comprehend it we must view a whole people for some months without any laws or government at all.   In this state their civil governments were to be formed, an army and navy were to be provided by those who had neither a ship of war, a company of soldiers, nor magazines, arms, artillery, or ammunition.   Alliances were to be formed, for they had none.

All this was to be done, not at leisure nor in a time of tranquillity and communication with other nations, but in the face of a most formidable invasion, by the most powerful nation, fully provided with armies, fleets, and all the instruments of destruction, powerfully allied and aided, the commerce with other nations in a great measure stopped up, and every power from whom they could expect to procure arms, artillery, and ammunition, having by the influence of their enemies forbade their subjects to supply them on any pretense whatever. Nor was this all ; they had internal opposition to encounter, which alone would seem sufficient to have frustrated all their efforts. The Scotch, who in many places were numerous, were secret or open foes, as opportunity offered. The Quakers, a powerful body in Pennsylvania, gave every opposition their art, abilities, and influence could suggest. To these were added all those whom contrariety of opinion, tory principles, personal animosities, fear of so dreadful and dubious an undertaking, joined with the artful promises and threats of the enemy, rendered open or concealed opposers, or timid neutrals, or lukewarm friends to the proposed revolution. It was, however, formed and established in despite of all these obstacles, with an expedition, energy, wisdom, and success, of which most certainly the whole history of human affairs has not, hitherto, given an example. To account for it we must remember that the revolution was not directed by the leaders of faction, but by the opinion and voice of the majority of the people ; that the grounds and principles upon which it was formed were known, weighed, and approved by every individual of that majority. It was not a tumultuous resolution, but a deliberate system. Consequently, the feebleness, irresolution, and inaction which generally, nay, almost invariably attends and frustrates hasty popular proceedings, did not influence this. On the contrary, every man gave his assistance to execute what he had soberly determined, and the sense of the magnitude and danger of the undertaking served only to quicken their activity, rouse their resources, and animate their exertions. Those who acted in council bestowed their whole thoughts upon the public ; those who took the field did so with what weapons, ammunition, and accommodation they could procure. In commerce, such profits were offered as tempted the individuals of almost all nations to break through the prohibition of their governments, and furnish arms and ammunition, for which they received from a people ready to sacrifice every thing to the common cause, a thousand fold. The effects of anarchy were prevented by the influence of public shame, pursuing the man who offered to take a dishonest advantage of the want of law. So little was the effects of this situation felt, that a gentleman, who thought their deliberations on the establishment of a form of government too slow, gave it as his opinion that the people were likely to find out that laws were not necessary, and might therefore be disposed to reject what they proposed, if it were delayed. Dr. Franklin assured me that upon an average he gave twelve hours in the twenty-four to public business. One may conceive what progress must be made from such exertions of such an understanding, aided by the co-operation of a multitude of others upon such business, not of inferior abilities. The consequence was, that in a few months the governments were established; codes of law were formed, which, for wisdom and justice, are the admiration of all the wise and thinking men in Europe. Ships of war were built, a multitude of cruisers were fitted out, which have done more injury to the British commerce than it ever suffered before. Armies of offense and defense were formed, and kept the field, through all the rigors of winter, in the most rigorous climate. Repeated losses, inevitable in a defensive war, as it soon became, served only to renew exertions that quickly repaired them. The enemy was everywhere resisted, repulsed, or besieged. On the ocean, in the channel, in their very ports, their ships were taken, and their commerce obstructed. The greatest revolution the world ever saw is likely to be effected in a few years; and the power that has for centuries made all Europe tremble, assisted by 20,000 German mercenaries, and favored by the universal concurrence of Europe to prohibit the sale of warlike stores, the sale of prizes, or the admission of the armed vessels of America, will be effectually humbled by those whom she insulted and injured, because she conceived they had neither spirit nor power to resist or revenge it."

A valuable passage; which it was a virtuous action in Mr. Arthur Lee to preserve. He had formed the intention of writing a history of the Revolution, and this, I presume, was to be used as "material."

A few days after this conversation, Mr. Grand announced to the envoys that the king would buy their frigate; and, in addition, would make them a furt' er loan of three millions of francs; and endeavor to induce the King of Spain to do the same.   He would, moreover, engage never to leave them unprovided with sufficient means to pay the interest of their debt.

This timely, but inadequate, relief, raised the hopes of the Americans only for a short time ; for, soon came tidings from England, that the city of Philadelphia had fallen (September 20th) into the hands of General Howe.   Franklin turned it off with a joke, but it is evident that the news (though not implicitly believed) dashed the spirits of the whole circle.   " Well, doctor," said an Englishman to Franklin, " Howe has taken Philadelphia."   " I beg your pardon, sir," was the reply, " Philadelphia has taken Howe."*   Which proved true, for he was effectually shut up in Philadelphia for many months.   Dr. Franklin was not yet aware that his daughter, with an infant four days old, had again been removed from the city, and that British Captain André was quartered in his house, playing with his electrical apparatus, his musical glasses, his harps, harpsichords, viols, and books.

November 27th, the three envoys met at Passy to consult upon what they should say to Congress in their next dispatches.   Mr. Deane, who had both to share and console the distress of Beaumarchais (he alone being concerned with that lively, but now disconsolate, personage), was much disheartened.   Mr. Lee has recorded the substance of the conversation :

"Mr. Deane began the discourse; he remarked upon the proceedings of this court with a good deal of ill-humor and discontent; said he thought it was our duty to state the whole to Congress ; that things seem to be going very badly in America; they would be less provided for next campaign, and more pressed than ever. He, therefore, was of opinion we should lay before this court such a statement as would produce a categorical answer to the proposition of an alliance, or satisfy them that without an immediate interposition, we must accommodate with Great Britain.

"Dr. Franklin was of a different opinion ; he could not consent to state that we must give up the contest without their interposition, because the effect of such a declaration upon them was uncertain ; it might be taken as a menace, it might make them abandon

---

* Related by Lafayette to Fanny Wright; by her to Jeremy Bentham.—"*Bowring's Bentham,*" x., 527.

us in despair or in anger. Besides, he did not think it true; he was clearly of opinion that we could maintain the contest, and successfully too, without any European assistance; he was satisfied, as he had said formerly, that the less commerce or dependence we had upon Europe, the better, for that we should do better without any connection with it.

"Mr. Lee was against any such declaration, lest it might deprive them of the assistance they now received, instead of increasing it. He thought this court had acted uniformly and consistently with their declarations; that the violent things done were of necessity, and compelled by the bad conduct of our people;* that we ought to instruct those who were going to America to avoid speaking with bitterness against this country, but rather to soften the resentment of others, arising from considering the injuries and not the benefits we had received from France; he was of opinion that if the credit of their funds was maintained, all would go well; he therefore proposed informing them that the commissioners had funded two millions of livres, to pay the interest of what they borrowed, or bills drawn upon emergent occasions. This, with attention to sending the cannon and clothes, which were ordered, would, it seemed to him, put them on much more firm and respectable ground than ever, and he saw not the least reason to despair of success. Mr. Deane objected to reserving any of the money we received, and to giving Congress any power for money here. He said the court had promised to enable them to pay the interest of what they borrowed, and that was enough; for he knew that if Congress were allowed to draw, they would never rest till they had drawn for every farthing, and that as we were to furnish them with what was necessary there would be no occasion for it. Mr. Lee replied that there was uncertainty in our supplies reaching them, and it might well happen that prevalent as the spirit was of sending adventures to America, they might make offers of these very necessaries upon the spot, which it might not be in their power to pay for in produce, while their ports were blocked up, and which they might purchase by bills on Europe. Dr. Franklin appeared to agree with Mr.

---

* Mr. Lee alludes here to the exploits of Captain Wickes and Captain Conyngham; which exploits he frequently denounces in his letters home, attributing them to the interested machinations of Deane, Beaumarchais, and Williams. He was not aware, perhaps, that there was a party in the French Cabinet and Court which desired such irregularities.

Deane, and it seemed settled that they were to trust to the promise of the minister for paying the interest of their debt; though Mr. Lee observed that promise was vague and verbal," etc., etc.; Mr. Lee continuing, for some time, to multiply objections, and imagine difficulties.

This dismal conversation, it is interesting to know, occurred as late as November 27th, only seven days before the arrival at Passy of Mr. Austin, the messenger sent to convey to the envoys the news of General Burgoyne's surrender, and of General Washington's spirited and all but successful attack upon the British forces at Germantown!

CHAPTER V.

THE ALLIANCE WITH FRANCE.

FEW men have won immortality more agreeably than Mr. Jonathan Loring Austin, the bearer of dispatches who brought to Paris this tremendous intelligence. Let us accompany the young gentleman in his mission ; we shall catch thereby some precious glimpses of that stirring, memorable time.

Massachusetts sent him—spirited, generous, patriotic Massachusetts! No sooner had it become certain that Burgoyne's expedition was frustrated, than the Council of Massachusetts, perceiving the infinite importance of getting the news swiftly to France, completed a fast-sailing vessel, and appointed Mr. Austin (then Secretary to the Massachusetts Board of War) special messenger. The details of the great surrender having arrived, and the dispatches being ready, the vessel sailed on the last day of October, followed by the benedictions of a million patriotic hearts. The Sunday before she sailed, we are told, a note was handed to Dr. Chauncey, minister of the Brick Church in Boston, where Mr. Austin and his family attended, asking the prayers of the congregation for the safety of the messenger and the success of the voyage. The good doctor, it seems, was not a man of perfect tact, and the occasion was one that roused his patriotic feelings to the highest pitch.

"He thanked the Lord," records a writer, "most fervently for the great and glorious event which required the departure of a special messenger. He prayed that it might pull down the haughty spirit of our enemies; that it might warm and inspirit our friends; that it might be the means of procuring peace, so anxiously desired by all good men; and that no delay might retard the arrival in Europe of the packet which contained this great news. He invoked a blessing, as desired, on the person who was about to expose himself to the dangers of the sea to carry this wonderful intelligence across the mighty waters; but," said he, "whatever in thy wise providence thou seest best to do with the young man, we beseech thee most fervently, at all events, to preserve the packet."*

It pleased Heaven to preserve both the packet and the young man. He reached Nantes in thirty-one days, and pushed on rapidly for Paris. Swiftly as he traveled, a rumor preceded him of the arrival of a special messenger, and all the circle of official Americans hurried out to Passy to be present at the opening of the packet. Deane, Lee, William Lee, Izard, Bancroft, Beaumarchais, all appear to have been there. When Mr. Austin's chaise was heard in the court, they went out to meet him, and before he had time to alight, Dr. Franklin cried out:

"Sir, *is* Philadelphia taken?"

"Yes, sir," replied Austin.

Upon hearing this Dr. Franklin clasped his hands, and turned as if to go back into the house.

"But, sir," said Austin, "I have greater news than that. GEN-ERAL BURGOYNE AND HIS WHOLE ARMY ARE PRISONERS OF WAR!"

The effect was thrilling, electric, overwhelming, indescribable. But they did not shout, nor seize each other by the hand, nor rush, French-fashion, into each other's arms. The three envoys and Mr. Austin hastened into the hotel, and spent the rest of the day in reading, copying extracts, and writing dispatches, Austin himself being pressed into the service to assist. "The news," said Mr. Deane afterwards, "was like a sovereign cordial to the dying." Beaumarchais, who had been for several days in an agony of despair, feeling himself to be on the brink of irrecoverable ruin, was almost beside himself with joy. He straightway ordered his carriage, and drove

* Memoirs of Jonathan Loring Austin, in *Boston Monthly Magazine* for July, 1826.

towards Paris at such a furious pace, that the vehicle was overturned, and one of his arms dislocated.* Dr. Bancroft instantly set out for London, for what purpose did not immediately appear, but Mr. Arthur Lee was perfectly sure his errand could be no other than to make a corrupt use of the secret on the stock exchange. No doubt he went, at Dr. Franklin's request, to make known the full details of the intelligence to the heads of the British Opposition, Shelburne, Fox, Burke, and Rockingham; of whom more anon. The envoys busied themselves, first, in preparing a dispatch for Count de Vergennes, containing a summary of the news; which they sent, within a few hours after Mr. Austin's arrival, to Versailles by an express. In a few days all Europe had heard it; and, except the tory party of Great Britain, and the Continental holders of English stock, all Europe rejoiced at it. In Paris the intelligence was received, said Franklin, as if the victory had been won by their own troops over their own enemies; " such is the universal warm and sincere good will and attachment to us and our cause in their nation." Mr. Dumas wrote from the Hague, that the Cafés and the Exchange were all astir with the news, and the colonies were considered lost to the English. England had been haughty and overshadowing since the peace of 1763, and it seemed that all nations and most men exulted in her humiliation; while liberal minds in England† and out of England, rejoiced in the weakening of a power warring against the rights of man.

* Diplomacy of the United States, i., 36.
† A London tory letter of December 9th, 1777, contains this passage : " The account of General Burgoyne's treaty with Mr. Gates, arriving when the two Houses of Parliament were sitting, and in the warmth of high debate, the friends of government were much confounded and staggered by such a shock ; but you cannot imagine how furiously, illiberally, and indecently opposition triumphed on the occasion, opening and roaring like so many bull dogs against administration. The king, God bless him, for we never had a better one, and no other nation had ever so good a one, who feels every calamity and misfortune of his people, was greatly affected ; but, with that magnanimity which distinguishes his character, he soon declared that such a cause could never be given up, that this loss must be retrieved by greater and more vigorous exertions, and that he would even ' sell Hanover and all his private estate, before he would desert the cause of his loyal American subjects, who had suffered so much for him.'
" In two or three days the nation recovered from its surprise, and now is ready to support the king and his ministers in the proper and vigorous use of such means as are adequate to the great end of reducing the revolted colonies to a constitutional subordination. Many in both Houses of Parliament have spoken to this effect with great spirit, and one member of the Commons, Mr. Cambridge, said that he would part with reluctance with one shilling in the pound towards raising another army of ten thousand men for America, yet he would cheerfully pay twelve shillings in the pound towards an additional army of sixty thousand men."—Frank Moore's Diary of the Revolution.

Dr. Franklin, ever after, felt for Mr. Austin a peculiar affection; "as if," remarks the writer quoted above, "he had not
merely been the messenger, but the cause of this glorious information." He took the young gentleman into his own family, and
gave him abundant employment as secretary to the embassy.
Often, in meeting him at breakfast, or when sitting with him in the
office, "Dr. Franklin would break from one of those musings in
which it was his habit to indulge, and, clasping his hands together,
exclaim, 'Oh, Mr. Austin, you brought us glorious news!' He
made it a point to have the young Bostonian accompany him to all
the great houses; wherein, at that period, *Bostonian* was more
distinguishing and honorable than a title of nobility. He taught
him to play chess, and delighted to have him at his bedside during
his fits of the gout. Ere long, he found for him an honorable and
confidential mission, of which we shall have to speak in a
moment.

Events now succeeded one another with great rapidity. It will
be convenient, for a short time, to give our narrative in the form of
a diary.

Dec. 4th. On this, the day of Mr. Austin's arrival, the envoys,
as just related, sent off their dispatch to Versailles; which is ten
miles from Paris, and eight from Passy. Mr. Lee, also, wrote to
the Spanish ambassador (Lee still holding his commission as envoy
to Spain) and to the Prussian prime minister, an outline of the
news.

Dec. 5th. Letter-writing—congratulations—tumultuous joy!

Dec. 6th. M. Gerard, secretary of the king's council and under
secretary for foreign affairs, called upon the envoys at Passy,
charged with messages of the first importance. The Count de
Vergennes, he said, had directed him to convey to the envoys their
congratulations upon the victory, and to assure them that the
tidings had given great pleasure at Versailles. The king, he added,
would be glad to have further particulars of the recent events, and
he assured them that they might depend upon the three millions of
francs from Spain. But the grand object of his visit was to say,
that as there could no longer be a reasonable doubt of the ability
of the States to maintain their independence, it was desired at
Versailles that the envoys should *renew their proposals for an alliance with France;* and the sooner the better, in order that there

might be time to secure the concurrence of Spain, and to prepare for the next campaign. M. Gerard was informed that extracts from American newspapers and dispatches relative to the surrender of Burgoyne and the battle of Germantown were then preparing, and should be sent to the king as soon as they were ready.

December 7th. Dr. Franklin drew up a short memorial to the Count de Vergennes, thanking the king for the three millions of francs last granted by him, and proposing an immediate alliance between France and Spain, and the United States.

December 8th. The memorial was submitted to the other envoys, who approved and signed it; though Mr. Lee snarled a little because the preparation of so short and simple a document had taken two days (one of which was Sunday). "Young Mr. Franklin" conveyed the memorial to Versailles along with the packet of extracts for the king. The Count de Vergennes received him with unusual cordiality and politeness. "In two days," said the minister, "an answer shall be sent to you, and you will then see how much disposed I am to serve the cause of America." Sir George Grand (brother of the banker employed by the envoys), dining with Dr. Franklin to-day, said at the table that the Count de Vergennes, in a note received a few hours before, had spoken of the envoys as "our friends," instead of "your friends," as he had always called them before.

December 10th. Mr. Lee sent a memorial to Count d'Aranda, the Spanish embassador, urging the proposed alliance upon Spain. He asked Sir George Grand to mention to M. de Vergennes that American Commissioners for Prussia, Austria, Tuscany, and Spain, were then in Paris, and would go to their destinations as soon as the French court thought proper. He also requested the banker to say to the minister how extremely convenient it would be if the French government would grant convoy to the fleet of American supply ships that were shut up at Nantes, at a daily expense to Congress. Sir George Grand conveyed these hints to the Count de Vergennes; who replied, that as to the convoy, he would speak of that to the minister of marine; and, as to the commissioners, he saw no objection to their going at once to their courts, but advised him to consult the Spanish embassador on the subject. Grand called upon the Spanish embassador, who made this prudent reply: "I have two ways of thinking, one as the count d'Aranda, and the other as the embassador of my court. As the former, I wish Mr. Lee, in whom I have the greatest confidence, at Madrid ; as the latter, I may give no opinion till I receive orders." The envoys received a note from M. Gerard, informing them that the Count de Vergennes desired to confer with them the day after to-morrow, at ten o'clock in the morning, at Versailles.

December 11th. Letter received from the minister of the King of Prussia, to the effect that Mr. William Lee could not yet be received at Berlin as an envoy of the United States ; but that he might reside there, if he pleased, as a private gentleman. No, thank you, replied Mr. William Lee ; will not give any embarrassment by going to Berlin ; will remain at Paris till the king wants me.

December 12th. To-day occurred the appointed conference with Count de Vergennes. Particular precautions were taken to conceal the fact of the meeting from British spies. On reaching Versailles the envoys repaired to some friendly covert at a distance from the palace, and sent word to M. Gerard that they awaited his pleasure. A hackney coach, conducted by one of M. Gerard's servants, soon drove up, and receiving the Americans, conveyed them to a house half a mile out of town, where they found both the minister and the secretary. Our only knowledge of the important conversation which ensued is derived from the too brief notes of Arthur Lee :

" The minister made us some general compliments upon the present prosperous state of our affairs, and conversed some time upon the situation of the two armies. He said nothing struck him so much as General Washington's attacking and giving battle to General Howe's army. That to bring an army raised within a year to this, promised every thing. He asked Dr. Franklin what he thought of the war. He answered he thought we should succeed, and the English soon be tired of it. Mr. Lee said his excellency might judge what would be the event of the war, from observing that the most signal successes of the enemy were productive of their greatest misfortunes. Howe's advantages on Long Island, New York, and New Jersey, raised a spirit that repelled him with considerable loss. The taking of Ticonderoga, and rapid progress of Burgoyne, had brought upon him a total overthrow. What hopes, therefore, could there be of a war in which the most brilliant success allured them to their ruin ? The fact was, that nothing but a sense of pressing danger and necessity would draw forth the militia, in which the real strength of America consisted, and which, when drawn out, appeared to be irresistible. The minister took our last memorial from his secretary, and read it. He then desired we would give him the information it promised, and any thing we had new to offer. Dr. Franklin said that the entering into the treaty proposed was the object, and if there were any objections to it we were ready to consider them. The count said, that it was the resolution of his court to take no advantage of our situation, to desire no terms of which we might afterwards repent, and endeavor to retract ; but to found whatever they did so much upon the basis of mutual interest, as to make it last as long as human institutions would endure. He said that entering into a treaty with us would be declaring our independency, and necessarily draw on a war. In this, therefore, Spain must be consulted, without whose concurrence nothing could be done."

He showed, however, that he considered that concurrence certain by entering into a long conversation with the envoys upon the details of the proposed treaty. But, not to commit himself irrecoverably, the. wary minister again said, that Independence was an unborn child, whose advent must not be hastened prematurely. He promised to dispatch a courier to Spain immediately, whose return might be expected in three weeks.· Meanwhile, he would do all that he could to facilitate the departure of the supply ships, and would, also, confer with the naval minister upon the subject of the convoy.

December 13th. The envoys renewed their request for convoy— a matter of vital and pressing importance; since the four laden ships at Nantes contained the stores essential for the next campaign. The miseries of Valley Forge were chiefly owing to the detention of this little fleet in the harbor of Nantes.

December 14th. To-day the French government took the significant step of ordering a royal frigate to be prepared for sea, for the purpose of conveying to America the news of the alliance about to be concluded between France and the United States.

December 15th. M. de Sartines, the minister of marine, engaged to furnish one frigate as convoy. This not being deemed adequate, the envoys asked for more ; which, in due time, was granted.

The conduct of Mr. Arthur Lee, during these stirring days, being indescribable, I cannot describe it. Dr. Franklin was of opinion, reports Mr. Deane, that Lee's "head was affected." He found fault with every thing, suspected everybody, and passed his days in terror of not being sufficiently consulted and deferred to. His own diary confirms all that his colleagues charged him with. One day, he complains that his brother had news of the dispatch frigate before he had; the next, he charges his colleagues with rejecting a splendid offer of cheap cannon solely because it was he who had originally called attention to it; again, he records his conviction, that the reason why his colleagues would not buy tent-cloth in Spain was, that it would give no business to Jonathan Williams; on another day, he writhes at the thought of Mr. Carmichael being selected as the bearer of dispatches to Congress; and, when nothing else occurs to him, he chronicles that Mr. Deane failed to keep an appointment, or that Dr. Franklin, instead of talking about business, only "entertained him with some philosophical discourse."

December 17th. A great and joyful day at Passy. M. Gerard came with a message to the envoys from the king and Council, to the effect, that it had been *decided* by the French government to conclude a treaty with the United States, and to maintain their independence, as soon as the courier returned from Spain; which they must wait for as a mark of respect for that court. If war with England should result, the king would ask no stipulation but this, that they should never make peace with Great Britain except as independent States; the object of the king being a just, mutually beneficial and lasting connection with America. For the present, however, the alliance must be kept a most profound secret, because Spain was not yet ready for war, having an immense treasure from her American mines at sea, her fleet in bad condition, and her quarrel with Portugal not adjusted. Mr. Lee not being at Passy during the interview with M. Gerard, he did not hear of this important message till the next day, when he entered in his diary the remark: "It would have been more decent if the other commissioners had sent for Mr. Lee to be present at this transaction;" keeping M. Gerard, who was one of the main-springs of the French government, waiting while Mr. Lee was hunted up in Paris and conveyed to Passy.

The haste of the French government in making this announcement was, probably, due to its knowledge that the English ministry
were in a humor to offer every thing to the envoys except independence. Already, it was said, there were emissaries in Paris
from Downing Street seeking opportunities to sound the Americans.
The time was at hand when, as Gibbon remarked in a letter to
Lord Sheffield (February 23d, 1778): "The two greatest nations
in Europe were fairly running a race for the favor of America;"
England offering 1763; France, 1776.

December 22d. Mr. Arthur Lee visited this evening his friend,
Ralph Izard. Izard asked him whether he had heard any thing,
within the last few days, of a proposal from England to the envoys
respecting terms of peace. "No," said Lee. "Then," continued
Izard, "you are ill-treated, and you ought to call Mr. Deane to a
severe account for his conduct; for that Paul Wentworth had a
meeting with Mr. Deane, to whom he made propositions, which
Mr. Deane gave to the French ministry." Mr. Lee declared that
he had not heard a syllable of this before, and that he would inquire
into it; but as the wrong was of a public or official nature, he could
not take Mr. Izard's advice, and resent it personally.

December 23d. So Mr. Lee, meeting Mr. Deane at Passy,
asked him whether a Mr. Wentworth was in town, and whether he
had seen him. Oh, yes; Mr. Wentworth had sought an-interview,
had expressed a desire for an accommodation, and had asked on
what terms it could be obtained, for, in his (Wentworth's) opinion, the English ministry were disposed to make peace. That
was all.

December 24th. At last, to the great relief of M. de Beaumarchais, one of his ships returned from America, laden with a
hundred and fifty thousand francs' worth of rice and indigo; a mere
drop, as Beaumarchais said, to the ocean of his debts, but still a
drop welcome and refreshing. Conceive his amazement and disgust when he found that this ship, chartered by him, loaded by
him, and dispatched by him, in spite of thundering Stormont, timid
Maurepas, and wary Vergennes, his own Amphitrite, was *not* con-
signed to the house of Hortalez and Co., but to Messrs. Franklin,
Deane, and Lee; who had taken possession and ordered the cargo
to be sold. No mention of Hortalez and Co.; no answer to Beaumarchais' sublime letter to Congress; no recognition whatever of

the existence of the man who had set on foot all this stir in politics and commerce. But Caron de Beaumarchais was not the man to submit to such preposterous injustice. Finding written remonstrance of no avail, he went to Passy; he confronted the "rogue Lee;" he stated his case to the assembled envoys; he showed them the contract between Deane and himself; he exhibited proofs of his having chartered and controlled the vessel; he proved that it was his capital that had loaded her with warlike stores, and that the return cargo of American produce was his stipulated payment. "With tears in his eyes,"* he begged that the cargo might be turned over to him, and the ruin of his house averted. Dr. Franklin could not resist the torrent of evidence; the cargo was unquestionably the property of Hortalez and Co., and to that eminent House it was given with the consent of Messrs. Franklin and Deane; Lee doing his utmost to prevent it.

January 1, 1778. The new year opened with the auspicious sailing from Bordeaux of a vessel bearing dispatches to Congress, announcing that the King of France had determined to conclude a treaty of alliance with the United States.

Jan. 6th. Dr. Franklin was approached by an English baronet. Sir Philip Gibbes, who desired to know what propositions for peace the American envoys were disposed to offer. Dr. Franklin replied that they had no propositions of any kind to make to the English government, those which Congress had offered having been treated with nothing but contempt; and as to the " dependency of the colonies," it " was gone like the clouds of last year." Some intimation of these soundings of the envoys by Wentworth and Gibbes must have reached the French cabinet, as well as certain advices from England, that Lord North desired nothing so much as peace with America, and was disposed to make unprecedented offers. To-day, also, the courier returned from Spain.

Jan. 8th. Another important interview with M. Gerard. It occurred in Paris, in the evening, at the residence of Mr. Deane, to which the other envoys were expressly summoned. Mr. Arthur Lee alone has recorded the particulars of this curious and decisive conversation. While waiting for Dr. Franklin's arrival, M. Gerard told Messrs. Deane and Lee, that a French admiral, M. de la Motte

* Sparks, ix., 390.

Piquet, with three seventy-fours and two frigates, was then clearing the coast of English cruisers; which he could do without collision, since the etiquette of the sea forbade the cruising of a foreign armed vessel " between the French flag and the French coast."
Mr. Lee continues his entry:

"Upon Dr. Franklin's arrival, M. Gerard informed us that he came from the king, and the Counts Maurepas and Vergennes. But before he delivered to us what he had in charge, he desired our parole of honor to observe the most profound secrecy. We each of us promised it; but Dr. Franklin added some insinuation that secrets were not kept on their part, of which M. Girard took no notice, but went into a somewhat tedious harangue, which closed with asking us three questions:

"1st. What would be necessary on the part of this court to satisfy the commissioners of its attachment to the cause of America, and prevent them from listening to the propositions of Great Britain.

"2d. What would be necessary to satisfy the Congress and people of the United States, and prevent them from acceding to the propositions which Great Britain might send to them.

"3d. What assistance would it be necessary for France to give them.

"The commissioners appearing to think it required some consultation before they could give answers, M. Gerard proposed to leave them together, and return in an hour, which he did. Dr. Franklin began to write, and the other two to talk. Mr. Lee said their instructions seemed to furnish them with proper answers. They were sent to negotiate a treaty with France, and the immediate conclusion of that would answer the two first questions; as the granting them eight ships of the line, for which they were instructed to solicit, would be the last. Mr. Deane objected to the latter as dictating to them; to which Mr. Lee replied, it could not possibly be deemed dictation to answer a question, which they to whom they were sent had asked, in the manner in which they who sent them had directed. * * Dr. Franklin said our present business was to consider the answers, which he had written down, and would read to us. This he did as follows:

"Question 1. What is necessary to be done, to give such satisfaction to the American commissioners, as to engage them not to

listen to any propositions from England for a new connection with
your country?

"Answer. The commissioners have long since proposed a treaty
of amity and commerce, which is not yet concluded. The immediate conclusion of that treaty will remove the uncertainty they are
under with regard to it, and give them such a reliance on the
friendship of France, as to reject firmly all propositions made to
them of peace with England which have not for their basis the
entire freedom and independence of America, both in matters of
government and commerce.

"Question 2d. What is necessary to be done, immediately, so to
satisfy the Congress and people of America with the utility and
certainty of the friendship of France in securing their independence,
that they will also reject all propositions from England for peace,
inconsistent with their independence?

"Answer. The supplying them with money to pay the interest
of the bills issued and support their credit, will give them effectual
assurance of the friendship of this court; and the sending them the
aid of eight ships of the line, which they have desired, would enable
them to protect their coast and their commerce, and thereby prevent the inclination or *necessity* of listening to terms of accommodation with England.

"To the first answer the commissioners agreed; and two to the
second, with the addition of the word 'necessity,' proposed by Mr.
Lee. But Mr. Deane began to object to the second, without offering any thing material, when M. Gerard returned. The first
answer was read to him, with which he professed himself satisfied.
As to the second, Dr. Franklin told him we were talking upon it
when he came in. He said it was agreeable to him, if we chose it,
to defer our answer to another time. He then added, that he was
now at liberty to inform us that it was resolved to conclude that
treaty with us immediately, for which he was authorized to give us
his majesty's parole. That farther, it was determined to enter into another treaty offensive and defensive, to guaranty our independency
upon condition of not making a separate peace, or relinquishing our
independency; that he had been ordered to draw up these two treaties, which he expected to lay before the council the next day, and
of which he would send us copies in a few days. He said the king

was not actuated by ambition, or a desire of acquiring new territory, but solely by the desire of establishing the independency of America. That therefore they could not agree to the proposition of assisting us in conquering Canada for us, and the English islands for them. Neither was it their idea of assisting us by land; and they supposed it would not be very agreeable to us to have foreign troops in our country. Their aid therefore would be by sea. Mr. Lee asked him if he thought it proper that Spain should be moved at all. He said that court had not come to a resolution yet, but this would go on alone, reserving to them a right of acceding to the treaties; and they believed they could for some time do without them. That if their object could be secured without a war, it was their wish; but their resolution was to secure it at all events. M. Gerard added, that he was happy now to congratulate us upon the affair being brought to the point he always wished, and he hoped the connection would be as durable, as the terms were mutually beneficial."

Ten days passed before another step was taken.

Jan. 18th. M. Gerard again met the envoys at Mr. Deane's house, in Paris, where he read to them draughts, in French, of two treaties—one of amity and commerce, the other offensive and defensive; the former merely regulating the friendly and commercial intercourse between the two powers; the latter, a compact to make common cause with each other, if England in consequence of the alliance, should declare war against France. M. Gerard left the draughts with the envoys for their revision, assuring them that he would conclude and sign them as soon as they were ready.

During the next eighteen days the envoys were engaged at Passy in translating, copying, discussing, and altering the treaties; meeting nearly every day, and holding long and animated conferences. Mr. Lee complained, querulously, that Dr. Franklin would not make greater haste. One day, when " young Mr. Franklin" humored him so far as to say, that " his grandfather's dining out every day prevented any business from being done," Mr. Lee remarked, in his diary, that it " was a very unpromising state of things, when boys made such observations on the conduct of their grandfathers." But there was really no occasion for extreme haste, now that dispatches were on their way home, containing the promise and substance of the treaties. And, indeed, when we consider that one of the treaties contained thirty-one articles, and the other thirteen, and that, upon every one of these, and every phrase of every one, four men had to agree, and that one of those men was Mr. Arthur Lee, of Virginia; and that each treaty had to be exactly translated into English, and the translation itself debated, and that only one secretary, Temple Franklin, was admitted to the secret; and, when we consider, also, the vast, far-reaching importance of the transaction, we shall not regard eighteen days as a very extravagant expenditure of time.

We may presume, however, that Dr. Franklin, portly and seventy-two, was not the intense and plodding man of business he had been in the early years of Poor Richard. Mr. Lee's diary of these treaty-discussing days contains a parenthesis, which, like a crevice in a wall, lets us peep in upon the envoys during a pause over their work: ("Some philosophical discourse arising, Dr. Franklin said it was his opinion that the matter of light was what entered largely into the nourishment of vegetables. This opinion I mention here for its curiosity, not for its pertinency.") Imagine this in the middle of a large page, treating of the fisheries, the sugar islands, and Mr. Lee's complaints against Mr. Deane and M. de Chaumont. We have, also, a little anecdote of this period. A large cake was sent, one day, to the apartment in which the envoys were assembled, bearing this inscription : " LE DIGNE FRANKLIN :" the worthy Franklin. Upon reading the inscription, Mr. Deane said : " As usual, Doctor, we have to thank you for our accommodation, and to appropriate your present to our joint use." · " Not at all," said Franklin ; " this must be intended for all the commissioners; only, these French people cannot write English. They mean, no doubt, Lee, Deane, Franklin."* " That might answer," remarked the magnanimous Lee, " but we know that whenever they remember us at all, they always put you first." Many pleasant little interruptions like these doubtless occurred, to alleviate the monotony of business, and to give Mr. Lee occasion to complain of Dr. Franklin's waste of time. The biographer of Mr. Austin, to whom we are indebted for this anecdote, and who derived his information from Mr. Austin's own life and letters, excuses Mr. Lee by saying, that the " other commissioners, though the equals of Dr. Franklin

---

* *Digne* is pronounced like Deane.

in political rank, seemed to be forgotten entirely by the French people," and adds, "·that it required considerable address, on the part of the philosopher, to preserve harmony."

In the course of the discussions, there occurred but one serious difference among the envoys, and that arose partly from Mr. Lee's inability to take a joke, and partly from his morbid desire to make himself of consequence. We must explain this matter, for Lee and Izard contrived to make a great deal of what we now call " capital," of it.

It was the article relating to molasses that Mr. Lee could not stomach. Molasses, I should premise, was " the basis on which a great part of the commerce of America rested"—to use the language of Mr. Deane. The West India islands, for example, paid for the flour, fish, beef, pork, butter, staves, boards, cheese, and fruit of New England, in molasses; which the people of New England distilled into rum, and the rum served them in lieu of money ; for, at that day, rum was an article which, it was universally supposed, human nature could not dispense with. " New England rum," in the olden time, was as universal an article, from Maine to Georgia, as Monongahela whisky is now, and far more generally used. Hence Congress ordered the envoys, in case they should succeed in concluding a treaty, to endeavor to get France to engage never to impose a duty upon the molasses exported from the French West Indies to the United States. Congress was desirous to guard against any future disturbance of a branch of commerce upon which the solvency of the merchants so materially depended. Accordingly, in the plan of a treaty, which Congress had matured in 1776, an article was inserted exempting French molasses from export duty, and the envoys, in their secret instructions, were ordered " to press it" upon the French government, but " not to let the fate of the treaty depend upon obtaining it." The article, as finally submitted to M. Gerard, was in these words :

" It is agreed and concluded that there shall never be any duty imposed on the exportation of the molasses that may be taken by the subjects of the United States from the islands of America, which belong, or may hereafter appertain, to his most Christian Majesty."

M. Gerard objected. He said the article was " unequal," inasmuch as the United States obtained a concession or privilege without granting any thing as an equivalent; and, consequently, the article must either be omitted or an equivalent inserted. The envoys concurred in the justice of his objection, but found it impossible to think of any commodity which the French islands took from America which was half as important to them as their molasses was to us. Dr. Franklin mused upon this difficulty for some time, but, at last, the idea came; and a pleasant thing it must have been to see his countenance break into smiles as the conception, in all its comic proportions, became clear to him. He proposed the following:

"In compensation of the exemption stipulated by the preceding article, it is agreed and concluded that there shall never be any duties imposed upon the exportation of any kind of merchandise, which the subjects of his most Christian Majesty may take from the countries and possessions, present or future, of any of the thirteen United States, for the use of the islands which shall furnish molasses."

The reader perceives that it was only an *export duty* which the United States agreed never to impose; a kind of duty which Dr. Franklin well knew, his countrymen never could be so ignorant and foolish as to think of imposing. But France *might;* France, under the ancient *regime;* France, that preferred the folly of Beaumarchais to the wisdom of Turgot. The article, therefore, gave a Nothing for a Something. It was a sane man solemnly promising not to cut off his own nose; and, thereby, binding a flighty neighbor never to close an important thoroughfare that ran across a corner of one of his outlying fields. I wonder the envoys could ever have talked it over without laughing in one another's faces. Besides: taking the thing seriously, the single article of molasses did actually pay for, and was, therefore, the equivalent of the bulk of the numberless articles which Yankee schooners took to the French West Indies.*

---

* Dr. Franklin, I may add, had a peculiar aversion to the principle of export duties, and would gladly have bound his country never to impose them: "To lay duties," he wrote, in July, 1778, to James Lovell, "on a commodity exported, which our neighbors want, is a knavish attempt to get something for nothing. The statesman who first invented it had the genius of a pickpocket, and would have been a pickpocket if fortune had suitably placed him. The nations who have practiced it, have suffered four-fold, as pickpockets ought to suffer. Savoy, by a duty on exported wines, lost the trade of Switzerland, which thenceforth raised its own wine; and (to waive other instances) Britain, by her duty on exported tea, has lost the trade of her colonies. But, as we produce no commodity that is peculiar to our country, and which may not be obtained else-

That profound and sweet-tempered magpie, Arthur Lee, could not or would not see it in this light. "What!" said he, "shall we tie both of our hands for the privilege of binding one of France's fingers? Shall we exempt *every thing* from export duty for the sake of a single article? Monstrous!" M. Gerard, who was content with Franklin's equivalent, said that the king attached slight importance to the two articles, and was equally willing to accept or omit both. Long was the affair debated between the envoys; but, at length, Lee yielded, and they were unanimous for retaining both articles. Mr. Lee even went so far as to draft the joint letter which informed M. Gerard of this unanimous resolve.

So the affair was settled, then, was it? By no means. At the last conference Mr. Lee had urged his colleagues, since they could not agree, to consult the other envoys, Mr. William Lee and Mr. Izard. Dr. Franklin and Mr. Deane refused—of course. Mr. Lee, therefore, *after* having notified the French government of the unanimous acceptance of the two articles, privately consulted his brother and Mr. Izard upon the point in dispute; an act at variance with engagements expressed and implied.

The reader is aware that Ralph Izard and William Lee were brothers in enmity against Dr. Franklin, and I must now make known the particular cause of that enmity. It has been before mentioned that, early in 1777, Congress named William Lee joint commercial agent with Thomas Morris, and that many months elapsed before his commission reached him; so that Morris would have been left at Nantes unchecked in his riotous career, but for the appointment of Jonathan Williams to take charge of the prizes and ships of war. The appointment held by Mr. Williams was naval, not commercial; and it was one which envoys certainly had the right to confer who had been expressly authorized to bestow naval commissions, and had been intrusted with a supply of blank commissions for that purpose. Surely the authority that can make a post-captain, and confer the command of fleets, is competent to appoint a naval agent; especially when the necessity for such an officer is so pressing and so obvious as it was at Nantes in the summer of 1777. Mr.

where, the discouraging the consumption of ours by duties on exportation, and thereby encouraging a rivalship from other nations in the ports we trade to, is absolute folly, which indeed is mixed more or less with all knavery. For my own part, if my protest were of any consequence, I should protest against our ever doing it, even by way of reprisal. It is a meanness with which I would not dirty the conscience or character of my country."

William Lee thought otherwise. The envoys, he knew, had received a notification of his appointment to the joint commercial agency, and he was of opinion that the profits of the business, so ably and economically done by Jonathan Williams, ought to fall into the pocket of a very different style of gentleman. His brother, also, deemed it an indignity that "the clerk of a sugar-baker" should take the place supposed to belong to one who had held the great office of Alderman of London.

Three months before the date of the molasses controversy, Mr. William Lee had made a serious effort to bring over Dr. Franklin and Mr. Deane to this view of the case. Accompanied by the fiery Izard, he went to Passy, in October, 1777, and, after stating the misconduct of Thomas Morris, asked the assembled envoys to furnish him with a letter, addressed to all captains in the naval service of the United States, informing them that he was an agent, duly appointed by Congress, and that they were bound to follow his directions.* Provided with such a letter, he said, he would go to Nantes, and do his utmost to reform all abuses. In other words, "Turn out your nephew, Doctor, who is doing the naval business at Nantes well and cheaply, and put me in his place, who cannot do it better, and am not likely to do it at Mr. Williams's modest two per cent. commission." "This request," says Mr. Izard, in one of his letters to Dr. Franklin, "which appeared to me extremely reasonable, was, to my astonishment, rejected both by you and Mr. Deane." Dr. Franklin, with perfect good nature, and as though Mr. Izard had a right to meddle in the business, proceeded to narrate what he had done with regard to Thomas Morris, and added, that Mr. Robert Morris had "given him a rap over the knuckles," for interfering. "Your reasons," continues Izard, "did not appear satisfactory to me, and I took the liberty of telling you so, which

---

* July 4th, 1777, Dr. Franklin and Mr. Deane had given Mr. Jonathan Williams such a letter as Mr. Lee had now applied for:

PARIS, *July* 4, 1777.

Captain WEEKES, SIR—

We have appointed Mr. Williams to take the direction of such affairs at Nantes as are more particularly within our department, and, accordingly, advise you to address yourself to him for any assistance you stand in want of, in the disposition of your prizes, or your other concerns; you will give directions to Captains Johnson and Nicholson, which renders it unnecessary for us to write to each one separately.

We are yours, &c., &c.

B. FRANKLIN.
SILAS DEANE.

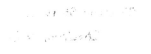

gave you very great offense." Mr. Izard, in fact, had the imperti-nence to say to Dr. Franklin, that it was " unreasonable to allow his resentment against the Secret Committee, for a supposed tacit reproof, and against Mr. Robert Morris for a rap over the knuckles, to operate to the prejudice, perhaps to the destruction, of the com-mercial concerns of his country." Dr. Franklin's reply, says Izard, was direct and positive: "If these consequences should happen, Mr. Robert Morris and the committee must be answerable for them. I am determined not to meddle in the matter."* Mr. Deane concurring in this resolution, the three southern gentlemen, the Messrs. Lee and Izard, took their leave, frustrated and irate; and, from that time, though an appearance of civility was main-tained between them, Mr. Izard was not consulted by Dr. Franklin and Mr. Deane upon public business; an omission which rankled in the breast of the fiery son of South Carolina.

No sooner had Arthur Lee communicated the affair of the mo-lasses to his brother and Ralph Izard, than both those gentlemen declared a determination to protest against the insertion of the ob-noxious article in the treaty. William Lee was dissuaded by his brother from carrying out this resolve, but Izard would not be dis-suaded, and wrote to Dr. Franklin, stating a variety of the most trivial and imaginary objections to the article. One of his points was, that the French were not likely ever to place export duty on molasses. Perhaps not. But was Congress likely to impose an export duty upon any thing?

Jan. 28th. On arriving at Passy, this morning, Arthur Lee found Dr. Franklin and his grandson busy in preparing an exact copy of the translation of the treaty, preparatory to the signing, now daily expected. Izard's letter had been received, and Dr. Franklin remarked that Mr. Izard had evidently heard but one side of the argument, and that the letter had made no change in his opinion. "He seemed much out of humor," reports Lee; said "it would appear an act of levity to renew the discussion of a thing we had agreed to." He reminded Mr. Lee that he had offered, at a former conference, to be of any opinion rather than disagree, for he did not attach to the articles so much importance as Mr. Deane. "Some years before he had left America," he said, "a discovery had

* Diplomatic Correspondence of the American Revolution, ii., 410 to 413.

Chadron State College Library
Chadron, Nebraska

been made that molasses could be procured from cornstalks ; and
who knew that we should not, one day, make our own molasses ?
But now that the articles were settled, translated, copied, and formally communicated to the French government, he was opposed to
the reopening of the subject. Mr. Lee was not satisfied, however,
and continued to argue.

Jan. 30th.   Those cornstalks—Mr. Lee could not get them out
of his head. He went home that evening meditating upon cornstalks, and, probably, called on his friend Izard, and talked cornstalks with him. No; he could not, would not, must not, sign a
treaty containing the molasses article! The result of his cogita-
tions and conferences was, that he sat down, and wrote a long letter to his colleagues, informing them that "fuller lights" upon the
subject had brought him to the firm determination not to consent
to the molasses article, unless his refusal would totally prevent the
alliance. The "fuller lights," he enumerated: 1. M. Gerard had
told them that the French government did not intend to impose any export duty upon molasses; 2. "Dr. Franklin informed
me yesterday that a substitute for molasses had been found in
America, procurable from a substance which is the growth of the
country, and of infinite plenty"; 3. Suppose the treaty *should* bind
the French not to put an export duty upon their molasses, could
they not prohibit its exportation altogether? As though he had
said : You propose to bind them not to cut off their noses, but
leave them perfectly free to amputate their heads ! No such diplomacy for *me*, gentlemen. What is the use of a nose when the
head is off? Mr. Lee, therefore, proposed that "both articles
should be left open to be rejected or admitted by Congress, without
affecting their ratification of the rest of the treaty."

February 1st.   Dr. Franklin and Mr. Deane now resolved, for
the sake of unanimity, to humor their troublesome colleague to the
full. "Although," they replied, "we cannot see the mischievous
consequences of the twelfth article which you apprehended, yet,
conceiving that unanimity on this occasion is of importance, we
have written to M. Gerard this morning that we concur in desiring
that article and the preceding to be omitted, agreeable to his first
proposal." Mr. Lee himself conveyed to M. Gerard at Versailles
the letter of his colleagues asking the omission. M. Gerard informed him that the treaty had been passed upon by the king in

council, and had been engrossed upon parchment; and ministers were of opinion that it would hazard their own credit with the king, and even endanger the treaty, if they should now propose alterations. In any case, an alteration would require to be submitted to the king in council, which would occasion delay. He consented, however, to accept Mr. Lee's proposal, and to leave it to Congress to ratify the treaty either with or without the articles. So Mr. Lee had his way. He had, also, a few weeks later, the triumph of learning that Congress had chosen to ratify the treaty without the disputed articles; a triumph dear to the pride of the Lees for many a year. The reader may imagine that M. Gerard, the Count de Vergennes, and M. de Sartines had their own opinion of Mr. Arthur Lee after this transaction.

February 6th. The treaties were complete, and, to-day, the most glorious except one of Franklin's public life, they were to be signed and sealed. M. Gerard met the envoys in the evening. The treaties were read and compared with the translation, and various preliminaries settled. Mr. Lee then recurred to the vexed subject of the molasses, and did so, as he confesses in his diary, that his colleagues might hear M. Gerard's answer. "Do I understand you aright, M. Gerard, as having said that Congress might reject the eleventh and twelfth articles without affecting the ratification of the rest?" M. Gerard's politeness, it appears, was overtasked by this ill-timed revival of a disgusting subject, and he answered, says Lee, "with an appearance of ill humor which made Mr. Lee believe there had been some private insinuations made to him." M. Gerard said that he had had the honor of telling Mr. Lee at Versailles, "that as the articles were mutual, and it was endeavored to make them all so, and the basis of the treaty was mutual interest, wherever that mutuality was thought not to take place, there could be no objection to omitting them. And he believed upon a representation of it from Congress, there would be no difficulty here relative to the articles in question, which were assented to from an opinion of its being a very desirable thing in America."

The molasses being finally disposed of, the treaties were spread out upon the table, and M. Gerard took up his pen to sign. Again Mr. Lee interposed. There was still a formality wanting, which the veterans present had forgotten, or, else, considered of no importance. Lee, I suppose, had been reading some Diplomatist's

Own Book, and was not going to be balked of a bit of ceremony. "M. Gerard was going to sign," records the punctilious tyro, "when Mr. Lee, having waited till the last moment for Dr. Franklin to propose it, observed that there was a previous ceremony necessary, which was the reading and exchanging their powers. Upon this M. Gerard delivered to them his powers, which were for each treaty, and the commissioners gave him their commission, which was all the powers they had. M. Gerard then sealed and signed, and after him Dr. Franklin. They then went to the fireside and were talking, while Mr. Deane and Mr. Lee were sealing and signing. Mr. Deane inquired of Mr. Lee, with apparent anxiety, how he would sign to distinguish his two characters. Upon which Mr. Lee asked M. Gerard whether he thought it would be necessary for him to sign twice as plenipotentiary for France and for Spain, who said he thought not, but that the characters might be added to the signature. Mr. Deane then asked Mr. Lee how he would word that? to which Mr. Lee answered, Commissioner Plenipotentiary for France and Spain; upon which Mr. Deane observed, that there was no occasion to make this addition to more than the secret and separate article. The treaties were committed to the care of Dr. Franklin. M. Gerard, after some mutual compliments on having happily concluded so important a business, took his leave."

It was remarked by Dr. Bancroft and others, that on this occasion Dr. Franklin wore the same suit of Manchester velvet which he had worn on the day when Wedderburn, with the applause of a great concourse of lords, had insulted him in the Privy Council. "It had been intended," says Dr. Bancroft, "that these treaties should be signed on the evening of Thursday, the fifth of February; and when Dr. Franklin had dressed himself for the day, I observed that he wore the suit in question; which I thought the more extraordinary, as it had been laid aside for many months. This I noticed to Mr. Deane; and soon after, when a messenger came from Versailles with a letter from M. Gerard, the French plenipotentiary, stating that he was so unwell from a cold that he wished to defer coming to Paris to sign the treaties until the next evening, I said to Mr. Deane, 'Let us see whether the Doctor will wear the same suit of clothes to-morrow; if he does, I shall suspect that he is influenced by a recollection of the treatment which he received at the Cockpit.' The morrow came, and the same clothes were again worn, and the treaties signed. After which these clothes were laid aside, and, so far as my knowledge extends, never worn afterwards. I once intimated to Dr. Franklin the suspicion, which his wearing these clothes on that occasion had excited in my mind, when he smiled, without telling me whether it was well or ill founded. I have heard him sometimes say that he was not insensible to injuries, but that he never put himself to any trouble or inconvenience to retaliate."

The envoys, on this memorable occasion, affixed their signatures to three documents : 1. The Treaty of Amity and Commerce; whose thirty-one articles were only thirty-one variations upon the twin themes suggested by its title. It bound both nations to be good friends, and trade fairly, and grant no superior privilege to any other nation. It aimed to provide against all probable, and many improbable, causes of misunderstanding, descending even to mention what should be done in case a ship of one of the parties should "stick upon the sands" of the other. 2. The Treaty of Alliance; to be operative only in case France, by recognizing and aiding America, should be drawn into a war with Great Britain. It declared that "the essential and direct end of the present defensive alliance is to maintain effectually the liberty, sovereignty, and independence, absolute and unlimited, of the United States, as well in matters of government as of commerce;" and ordained, that "neither of the two parties shall conclude either truce or peace with Great Britain without the formal consent of the other first obtained," nor lay down arms until the independence of the United States was secured. If Canada should be conquered, it should belong to the United States : if any West India islands, they should belong to France. 3. A Secret Article, providing for the admission of Spain to the alliance, as soon as that tardy power should desire it ; which would be, it was hoped, as soon as the silver ships had arrived and the Spanish navy had been put in order.*

---

* As a curious specimen of the kind of lie that passes by the name of Historical Anecdote, I insert the following from a French work, entitled "Historical Anecdotes of the Reign of Louis XVI.:"

"Mr. Deane, tired out by the delays, and even excuses of M. de Sartines, then minister of the marine, wrote to him, that unless within forty-eight hours he made up his mind to get the treaty of alliance signed, he would negotiate with England for a reconciliation. He adopted this hasty and irregular course without the participation of his colleagues. The moment Dr. Franklin heard of it, he thought all was lost. 'You have offended the court of France and ruined Amc.:-

The deed was done; but it was not avowed. M. Gerard solemnly bound the envoys to keep all that had passed between them relative to the alliance in the strictest secresy, until they had received notification that Congress had ratified the treaties; of which, strange to say, the French government had some doubts, thinking it possible Congress might be shaken by the offers of England. He, nevertheless, assured them that France and the United States had now a common cause, and that M. le Motte Piquet, the admiral who was to command the convoying fleet, had received strict orders not to give way one inch to the English, nor suffer any of his convoy to be touched; and if upon that ground the English chose to commence hostilities, "France was determined."*

I have remarked before, that Dr. Franklin habitually made use of his acquaintance with the leaders of the English Opposition to convey to England correct information of the state of things in America. The interests of America and the interests of that Opposition were identical; a victory in the United States over the king's troops presaged and hastened the decisive victory in the House of Commons over the king's hired majority. During the progress of the late negotiations, Dr. Franklin resolved upon sending to England Mr. Austin, for the sole purpose of giving Lord Shelburne, Mr. Fox, Mr. Burke, Lord Rockingham, and the liberal members of Parliament, such a complete insight into American affairs as would enable them to demonstrate the impossibility of reducing the States to submission. The strange spectacle was then afforded of the most eminent British statesmen associating with, and entertain-

---

ca,' exclaimed the philosopher. ' Be easy until we get an answer,' replied the negotiator. 'An answer! we shall be thrown into the Bastile.' 'That remains to be seen.'

"After the lapse of a few hours, M. de Sartines, chief secretary, made his appearance. 'You are requested, gentlemen, to hold yourselves in readiness for an interview at midnight; you will be called for.'

"'At midnight!' cries Dr. Franklin, the moment the Secretary had gone; 'my prediction is verified; Mr. Deane, you have ruined all.'

"They were, of course, called upon at the appointed hour. The American envoys got into a carriage and reached a country house, where M. de Sartines chose to receive them, the better to hide this step under the veil of mystery. They were introduced to the minister, and the declaration so imperiously demanded by Mr. Deane was instantly signed.

"The American deputies returned to Paris in triumph; and Franklin confessed, that in politics patience was not always the only thing to be relied on."

The most remarkable thing about this narrative is, that it contains one grain of truth. Mr. Deane did *propose* demanding a categorical answer from the French government, and the decisive interview with the Count de Vergennes *did* take place in a cottage five miles from Versailles. Who manufactures these "anecdotes," of which the libraries of the world contain tons?

* "Life of Arthur Lee," i., 398.

ing in their houses, a commissioned emissary of their king's revolted subjects; the king's own son and heir not disdaining his society. The secret was well kept, however, and few persons, even at this late day, are aware that such an audacious mission was ever undertaken. At the death of Mr. Austin, in 1826, his family gave the public a brief account of this singular adventure, to the following effect:

"As a preparatory measure, Dr. Franklin required Mr. Austin to burn, in his presence, every letter which he had brought from his friends in America; in exchange for which he gave him two letters, which he assured him would open an easy communication to whatever was an object of interest or curiosity. * * * Trusting to his prudence, and enjoining on him the most scrupulous attention to preserve from all but the proper persons the secret of his connection with the commissioners, Dr. Franklin furnished him with the means of a conveyance to England. * * *

"The letters of Dr. Franklin, and the desire that was felt by the leaders of opposition to see and converse with an intelligent American, who possessed the confidence of that distinguished man, and was recently from the country of their all-engrossing interest, brought Mr. Austin into personal and familiar intercourse with the master-spirits of the age.

"In reporting the progress of his mission, Mr. Austin writes: 'My time passes with so little of the appearance of business, that if I was not assured it was otherwise, I should think myself without useful employment. The mornings I devote to seeing such objects of curiosity or interest as I am advised to, and wholly according to my own inclination. I attend constantly the debates of Parliament, to which I have ready admission, and have been particularly enjoined to attend, that I may not miss any question on our affairs. Dinner, or, as it ought to be called, supper, which follows, is the time allotted to conversation on the affairs of our country. I am invariably detained to parties of this kind, sometimes consisting of seven or eight, and sometimes of the number of twenty. The company is always composed of members of Parliament, with very few others; and no question which you can conceive is omitted, to all which I give such answers as my knowledge permits. I am sadly puzzled with the various titles which different ranks require. My small knowledge of French prevented this trouble in Paris; but here I frequently find myself at fault, which subjects me to embarrassment that is yet forgiven to a stranger.'

" Mr. Austin was domesticated in the family of the Earl of Shelburne; placed under the particular protection of his chaplain, the celebrated Dr. Priestley—introduced to the present king (George IV.), then a lad, in company with Mr. Fox—was present at all the coteries of the Opposition—and was called upon to explain and defend the cause and character of his countrymen in the freedom of colloquial discussion, before the greatest geniuses of the age, amid the doubts of some, the ridicule of others, the censure of many, and the inquiries of all. * * *

" The object of his visit to England was accomplished to the perfect satisfaction of Dr. Franklin, in whose family he continued for some time after his return to Paris. Being charged with the dispatches of the commissioners to Congress, he left France and arrived at Philadelphia in May, 1779. A very liberal compensation was made him by Congress for his services in Europe, and Mr. Austin. returned to his business at Boston."*

Going again to Europe, later in the war, on public business, he was taken prisoner and conveyed to England ; but his old friends of the Opposition procured his liberation, and he proceeded to the performance of his errand in Spain and Holland, as though he had merely visited England. on his way. Such conduct as this, on the part of the Opposition, had been treason to the king, if the king himself had not been a traitor to the British Constitution.

CHAPTER VI.

THE TREATIES AVOWED AND CELEBRATED.

In connection with this great fact of the alliance between the ancient kingdom and the young republic, and quickly following it, were several striking and memorable historic scenes; which serve to show us the importance attached to the event by the men of that generation.

One of these occurred in the British House of Commons, Feb-

* *Boston Monthly Magazine*, for July, 1826.

ruary 17th, eleven days after the signing of the treaties at Paris. It had been known, for a day or two, to the very selectest circle of the Opposition in London, that France had concluded an alliance with the United States ; a secret too momentous to be kept by the sixteen persons—six Americans and ten Frenchmen—who had been intrusted with it. The House, on the night of the 17th, was crowded with members and peers, not one of whom, to his dying day, forgot the impressive and startling events of the sitting. No corps of reporters then sat assiduous, in a gallery replete with every convenience, to reproduce and improve the debates. If Mr. Horace Walpole had not taken the trouble to make, in his diary, a brief chronicle of what occurred, nearly all knowledge of the details must have perished with the generation that witnessed them. Amid breathless silence, Lord North rose to introduce his Conciliation Bill, which gave the colonies just what Dr. Franklin had demanded for them the last winter he was in England. The premier now owned that he and his party had been all in the wrong with regard to America, and he expressed a most earnest desire to make peace with the colonies on almost any terms. The astonishment, says Walpole, of a great majority of the House at the prime minister's confessions and proposals, was totally indescribable. The Opposition, led by Fox and Burke, promptly seconded Lord North's plan, not omitting to remind him that he then proposed only what they had advocated two years before ; and every day since. The tories, though for some time dumb with mere amazement, could not but follow their leader ; and so Lord North seemed likely to have an evening of triumph.

"But," continues Horace Walpole, " Charles Fox threw a bomb, that much disconcerted the minister. My cousin, Thomas Walpole, had acquainted me that the treaty with France was signed. We agreed to inform Charles Fox ; but, as we both distrusted Burke (i. e., his prudence), and feared the childish fluctuations of Lord Rockingham, we determined that Fox should know nothing of the secret till an hour or two before the House met. Accordingly, Thomas Walpole communicated the notice of the treaty to the Duke of Grafton on the 16th, and engaged him to acquaint Charles Fox but just before the House should meet next day. This was done most exactly, and Burke knew nothing of the matter until he came into the House. As soon as Lord North had opened his two bills, Charles Fox rose, and after pluming himself on having sat there till he had brought the noble Lord to concur in sentiment with him and his friends, he astonished Lord North by asking him whether a commercial treaty with France had not been signed by the American agents at Paris, within the last ten days? 'If so,' said he, 'the Administration is beaten by ten days, a situation so threatening, that in such a time of danger the House must concur with the propositions, though probably now they would have no effect.' Lord North was thunderstruck, and would not rise.

"Burke called on him to answer to the fact of the treaty. Still the Minister was silent, till Sir G. Savile rose, and told him that it would be criminal, and a matter of impeachment, to withhold an answer, and ended with crying, 'An answer! an answer! an answer!' Lord North, thus forced up, owned he had heard a report of the treaty, but desired to give no answer to the House at that moment; he had no official intelligence on that subject. The report might be vague. Some time ago the Ministers of France had denied it. Such evasive answers convinced everybody of the truth of the report."

Another spectacle, which occurred in Versailles, a few weeks later, our grandfathers were deeply interested in. The American envoys, after the signing, pressed upon the French ministry the importance of publicly acknowledging the alliance, without waiting for the ratification of the treaties; and all France seemed impatient for the hour. But, for nearly six weeks, the government hesitated; during which the alliance was a secret, just as the authorship of Waverly was once a secret; twenty persons knew it, and, in all Europe, twenty persons may have doubted it. M. Gerard's argument against immediate avowal, was this: If we should publish the treaties in Europe, and they should then be rejected in America, how deeply humiliating it would be to France, and how exasperating to Frenchmen! "There cannot be a doubt," said Mr. Lee, one day, at the end of a long harangue on the subject, "that Congress will ratify the treaties." "Do you think so, sir?" asked M. Gerard. Mr. Lee's comment upon this innocent inquiry, is an amusing instance of his morbid and mad suspiciousness: "M. Gerard's manner struck me with some surprise, but I now suppose it arose from the very friendly suspicions my colleagues had been endeavoring to infuse." At length, however, the envoys were notified that the fact of the alliance would be formally announced, and that they would be presented to the king on the twentieth of March.

Vain were the attempt to convey to American readers of 1864 an adequate sense of the importance attached to this ceremonial by Europeans of 1778. I can only relate the few incidents of the august occasion which chance has preserved.

Dr. Franklin, we are informed, began his preparations by ordering a wig; since no man had yet dared to contemplate the possibility of exhibiting uncovered locks to a monarch of France. Mr. Austin used to say, that, not only was the court costume exactly prescribed, but each season had its own costume, and if any one presented himself in lace ruffles, when the time of year demanded cambric, the chamberlain of the palace would refuse him admission. Readers of Madame Campan remember her lively pictures of the intense etiquette which worried the soul of Marie Antoinette in these very years. So Dr. Franklin ordered a wig. On the appointed day, says tradition, the peruquier himself brought home the work of his hands, and tried it on; but the utmost efforts of the great artist could not get it upon the head it was designed to disfigure. After patiently submitting for a long time to the manipulations of the peruquier, Dr. Franklin ventured to hint that, perhaps, the wig was a little too small. "Monsieur, it is impossible." After many more fruitless trials, the peruquier dashed the wig to the floor, in a furious passion, exclaiming, "No, Monsieur; it is not the wig which is too small; it is your head which is too large." It was too late, continues the anonymous chronicler who recorded this anecdote, to procure another, and, therefore, the audacious philosopher resolved to approach the presence of majesty "without a bag." "The size and appearance of Franklin's head," he concludes, "became a subject of common conversation. 'Yes, sir,' was the usual remark: 'Il a une grosse tête, et une grande tête. He has a big head, and a great head.' "

Having abandoned the wig, he ventured to discard the still more indispensable sword, as well as the universal chapeau that was carried under the arm. On the morning of the great day he dressed as he would have dressed if he were going out to dine with the president of Congress—in a suit of plain, black velvet, with the usual snowy ruffles at wrist and bosom, white silk stockings and silver buckles. And a more superb costume than that has never been worn by an old gentleman in any age or country. So General Washington was attired on occasions of state, with the addition of yellow gloves, a cocked hat and plume, and sword with steel hilt and white leather scabbard. Dr. Franklin's costume, I need not say, was a most brilliant success. Mr. Austin intimates that the chamberlain hesitated a moment about admitting him, but it was only for a moment; and all the court were captivated at the noble, well-timed effrontery of his conduct. Better for the whole tribe of chamberlains if that chamberlain had done his duty, and sent the American home for his wig. The recoil from the French Revolution (in which we are now living) has given the chamberlain class another century of life, but Franklin really announced their departure when he went to court without a court dress, amid the ecstatic applause of Europe. Mr. Deane and Mr. Lee, as was proper, conformed to the custom, and wore both wig and sword.

On the morning of the twentieth of March the three envoys, each in his own carriage, and attended by the usual train of servants, drove into Versailles, and alighted at the residence (in a wing of the palace) of M. de Vergennes, the appointed rendezvous. Mr. Izard, Mr. William Lee, and a great crowd of Americans assembled at the apartments of the minister, to whom the more important individuals were presented. A concourse of Parisians filled the court-yard of the palace. At the proper moment, Count de Vergennes conducted the envoys, who were followed by all the Americans, to the king's ante-chamber; and, a few minutes after, the doors were thrown open, and the whole crowd admitted to the king's dressing-room. The five envoys, Franklin, Deane, Lee, William Lee, and Ralph Izard, were then presented to the king, by the Count de Vergennes, the rest of the Americans looking on from behind. The king is reported to have addressed them thus : " Gentlemen, I wish the Congress to be assured of my friendship ; I beg leave also to observe that I am exceedingly satisfied, in particular, with your own conduct during your residence in my kingdom." He then left the apartment. Arthur Lee records, that the king, on this great occasion, " had his hair undressed, hanging down on his shoulders; no appearance of preparation to receive us, nor any ceremony in doing it. The king appeared to speak with manly sincerity."*

Leaving the king's dressing-room, the envoys, still followed by the crowd of Americans, were conducted across the spacious court-yard of the palace to be presented to the other members of the cabinet. As soon as they appeared, the crowd, regardless of the etiquette of the place, clapped and cheered with great enthusiasm. The introductions over, the five envoys returned to the residence of Count de Vergennes, where a magnificent company of the nobility were invited to meet them at dinner. The other Americans repaired to a hotel, where a dinner had been ordered for them by Dr. Franklin and his colleagues. In the evening, Madame Campan records, "the envoys went by particular invitation to the ' Jeu de la Reine,' where they found the royal family seated at play round a large table; a considerable heap of louis d'ors lay before each of the players, and from the number of these, which, from time to time, were shoveled by the losers to the winners, the gaming appeared to be high. On this occasion Dr. Franklin was honored by the particular notice of the queen, who courteously desired him to stand near to her, and as often as the game did not require her immediate attention, she took occasion to speak to him in very obliging terms."

The next morning Lord Stormont left Paris on his way to England without having taken leave of the king.· Ominous event! But Paris took it lightly. When his household goods were advertised for sale, one of the items in the catalogue was, " a quantity of table furniture that has never been used." " No wonder," said some one, " he never gave us any thing to eat;" at which all Paris laughed.

The day after this significant departure, the envoys went again to Versailles to attend a levee of the queen. Mr. Lee gives a sorry account of this adventure. " It was with great difficulty the commissioners could pass through an unordered crowd, all pressing to

---

* One of the New York tory newspapers of the time gave this account of the presentation : " When Dr. Franklin and Silas Deane were introduced to the French King in the quality of embassadors from North America, they went in elegant coaches, attended by domestics in superb French liveries, with a *suite*. On their entrance into the court-yard, martial music struck up, the soldiers were under arms, and the French flag was lowered as a solemn salute, which all the officers accompanied. In the inner part of the palace they were received by *les cent Suisses*, the major of which announced ' *Les ambassadeurs des trieze provinces unies*,' i. e., The ambassadors from the ' Thirteen United Provinces.' When they were ushered into the royal presence, the college of Paris, the bishops, the nobility, ministers, foreign and domestic, and ladies arose and saluted them. Old Franklin was observed to weep, but the Count de Vergennes relieved the confusion of the philosopher, by waiving certain forms, and immediately presenting him to the king, who, *à l'Anglaise*, took the embassador by the hand, and viewing his credentials, entered directly into conversation."—*New York Journal.* July 6,1778.

get into the room where the queen was. When they got in, they stood a moment in view of the queen, and then crowded out again. They were neither presented nor spoken to, and every thing seemed in confusion. They went next to Monsieur and Madame, the king's eldest brother and his wife : then to Madame, the king's maiden sister. The youngest brother, Count d'Artois, was at this time under a temporary banishment from court for having fought a duel with Duke Bourbon, a prince of the blood. They then visited the chancellor, whose office is for life, and he is obliged always to wear the robe of it. After this they dined with the Americans in their suite at Monsieur Gerard's."

That was the last dinner party given by M. Gerard in France for many a day ; for he had been secretly appointed plenipotentiary to the Congress, and was to sail in the French fleet destined to cruise in American waters, and about to depart. Mr. Deane, too (March 4th), had received his letters of recall, and was going in the same ship. Four American captains had been engaged by Mr. Deane to go out in the fleet as pilots, and had been presented to the Count de Vergennes. Mr. Deane received from the king the usual gift of a diamond snuff box, from M. de Vergennes a cordial and complimentary letter of farewell, and from Dr. Franklin a particularly emphatic declaration of the ability and zeal with which he had served his country in circumstances of extreme novelty and difficulty. All these movements, the destination of the fleet, the appointment of M. Gerard, the intended departure of Mr. Deane, the diamond snuff box, and the four pilots,—were, by the express injunction of the Count de Vergennes, concealed from Arthur Lee ; because the private secretary of that gentleman was suspected to be the channel of communication with the English ministry, and it was deemed a matter of the first importance to keep secret as long as possible the sailing of the fleet. The night of March 31st Mr. Deane, M. Gerard, the four captains and their attendants, secretly left Paris, each by a different route. Near Toulon, M. Gerard and Mr. Deane met, and traveled together to that port, "happy," writes Deane, "in the great prospects before us." He had no doubt that, after giving Congress the information they said they were in want of, he should return to Europe to continue his labors. On the very day of his departure from Paris, Mr. John Adams arrived at Bordeaux to take his place, bringing in a prize worth seventy thousand pounds.

The mention of Mr. Adams calls to mind a curious circumstance preserved in the letters of his wife. During these weeks of joy and glory, when the compliments of the king and the smiles of the queen had made Dr. Franklin ten times more the fashion in Paris than ever, his friends in America supposed him dead, the victim of an assassin. Mrs. Adams heard the story a week after her husband's departure for France, and evidently believed it. In her first letter to Mr. Adams she wrote: "'Tis a little more than three weeks since the dearest of friends and tenderest of husbands left his solitary partner, and quitted all the fond endearments of domestic felicity for the dangers of the sea, exposed, perhaps, to the attack of a hostile foe, and, O good Heaven! can I add, to the dark assassin, to the secret murderer, and the bloody emissary of as cruel a tyrant as God, in his righteous judgments, ever suffered to disgrace the throne of Britain. I have traveled with you over the wide Atlantic, and could have landed you safe, with humble confidence, at your desired haven, and then have set myself down to enjoy a negative kind of happiness, in the painful part which it has pleased Heaven to allot me; but the intelligence with regard to that great philosopher, able statesman, and unshaken friend of his country, has planted a dagger in my breast, and I feel, with a double edge, the weapon that pierced the bosom of a Franklin." She says, in another letter, that "the horrid story of Dr. Franklin's assassination was received from France, and sent by Mr. Purveyance, of Baltimore, to Congress and to Boston. Near two months before that was contradicted."

It was in this spring of 1778 that Voltaire, at the age of eighty-four, came to Paris, after an exile of twenty-seven years, to be overwhelmed and destroyed by the enthusiasm of his countrymen. What crowds followed his carriage; what cheers welcomed him to the theatre; how nobles disguised themselves as tavern-waiters to get sight of him, and how he finally sank under the weight of his own glory, all the world knows, and will not soon forget, for the pathetic story has been greatly told. The American envoys (so Arthur Lee used to relate) sent to ask permission to wait upon the patriarch of literature. They found him lying upon a couch, feeble, attenuated, sick, his countenance all withered into wrinkles; only his eyes, "glittering like two carbuncles," showing the quality of the man. Seeing them enter, he feebly raised himself from his pil-

low, and repeated several lines from Thomson's Ode to Liberty; a
poet that had sprung into celebrity during Voltaire's residence in
England fifty years before:

> " Lo ! swarming southward on rejoicing suns,
> Gay Colonies extend, the calm retreat
> Of undeserv'd Distress, the better home
> Of those whom bigots chase from foreign lands :
> Not built on rapine, servitude, and woe,
> And in their turn some petty tyrant's prey;
> But, bound by social Freedom, firm they rise.' '

He then began to converse with Dr. Franklin in English ; when
his niece, Madame Denis, begged them to speak in French, in order
that she and others present might understand what was said.   " I
beg your pardon," said the polite and spirited old man; " I have,
for a moment, yielded to the vanity of showing that I can speak in
the language of a Franklin."   Dr. Franklin presenting his grandson, Voltaire lifted his arms over the head of the young man, and
said to him : " My child, God and Liberty!   Recollect those two
words."   After a short interview, for the old man could not bear a
long one, the envoys withdrew, deeply impressed with the language
and demeanor of the dying genius.

Voltaire himself wrote, a few days after: " When I gave my
benediction to the grandson of the sage and illustrious Franklin,
the most respectable man of America, I uttered only these words,
God and Liberty !   All who were present shed tears."

But this was not the only scene between Franklin and Voltaire.
Another occurred, April 29th, in the presence of a concourse of
"philosophers" at a session of the Academy of Sciences.   The meeting was attended by Voltaire and Franklin, who sat near each other
on the platform in full view of the audience.   At a pause in the
proceedings, a confused cry arose, in which could be distinguished
the names of the two favorites, and which was interpreted to mean
that they should be introduced.   This was done.   They rose,
bowed, and spoke to one another.   But the clamor did not sub-
side ; the people were evidently dissatisfied; something more must
be done.   They shook hands.   Even this was not enough.   At
length, the words of the clamor were distinguished : " Il faut s'em-
brasser, à la Françoise ;" "you must embrace, French fashion."

Then, says John Adams, who witnessed the spectacle, "the two aged actors upon this great theatre of philosophy and frivolity, embraced each other by hugging one another in their arms, and kissing each other's cheeks, and then the tumult subsided. And the cry immediately spread through the whole kingdom, and, I suppose, over all Europe, 'How charming it was to see Solon and Sophocles embrace?'"*

Another month, and Voltaire lay dead, his brilliant eyes quenched at last, and his friends seeking surreptitious burial for him in consecrated ground. It was at this time that Beaumarchais, a true disciple of Voltaire, conceived the idea of publishing a complete edition of his master's works, upon which he squandered many millions of francs; for the edition was in eighty-one volumes, and he only sold two thousand sets out of fifteen thousand printed. Truly our friend must have been in a good way of business to indulge in such luxuries as this, and yet build a great mansion, keep three coachmen, and give away the profits of Figaro, the most successful comedy of the time.

Another Scene.—General Washington's camp at Valley Forge, May 6th. The long winter is over; the thrilling news of the alliance has come to greet the opening May; and this is the day named by the General-in-chief for the celebration of the great event in camp. At nine in the morning, the whole army was drawn up without arms in brigades, each brigade on its own parade ground. The brigade chaplains, according to the programme issued the day before by the General, then mounted their rostrums, and read to the troops the outline of the news and the leading articles of the treaty of alliance, as published by order of Congress in the Pennsylvania *Gazette*.† Prayers and thanksgivings followed; after which

* "Life and Works of John Adams," iii., 147.

† The tories affected to disbelieve the alliance. Rivington, in his New York *Gazette*, said: "This may be looked upon as the masterpiece, or keystone of the arch that supports that system of lies with which the good people of America have been gulled and deceived; but the foundation is rotten, and the whole fabric must soon fall to the ground. Franklin knew this, and makes use of the last effort to support his own consequence. But the deception is too gross, too palpable almost for the Congress itself. They have only ventured to publish in an indirect manner, three of the most conspicuous articles, by which, supposing them to be really genuine, France engages to do nothing."

The Pennsylvania *Ledger* commented thus: "Of this extraordinary publication, we doubt not but our readers will think as we do—that we have good reason to suspect it is, what many former publications from the same quarter certainly have been, a *seasonable* piece of *misrepresentation*. There is an art, well known to these adepts, of *mixing* truth and falsehood, or of conveying falsehood in the vehicle of truth."

each chaplain delivered a patriotic discourse, with such eloquence as nature had bestowed upon him, and the men were then dismissed. At half-past ten a cannon summoned the troops again, armed, and in their best uniforms, to their several parade grounds, where they were inspected, and drawn up in marching order. At half-past eleven, at the sound of the second cannon, the brigades began their march to the review ground, and, in an instant, the scene became animated and picturesque in the highest degree—the whole plain covered with moving coils and lines of troops, their arms glittering in the bright May sun, colors flying, mounted officers in gay if not splendid uniforms, prancing at the head of each column. "I can convey," wrote an eye-witness, "no adequate idea of their movements to their several posts—of the appearance of His Excellency during his circuit round the lines—of the air of our soldiers—the cleanliness of their dress—the brilliancy and good order of their arms, and the remarkable animation with which they performed the necessary salute as the General passed along. Indeed, during the whole of the review, the utmost military decorum was preserved, while at the same time one might observe the hearts of the soldiery struggling to express their feelings in a way more agreeable to nature."

The review over, General Washington, the Marquis de Lafayette, Lord Stirling, General Greene, and the officers of their staffs, retired to the center of the field to witness the feu de joie, which was conducted with strictest decorum. First, there was a salute of thirteen cannon; then a running fire of musketry, that flashed and rolled from right to left, and then back again from left to right. Then, one cannon as a signal; upon hearing which, the whole army, in unison, cried "HUZZA! LONG LIVE THE KING OF FRANCE!" Again thirteen cannon; again the running fire of musketry, from right to left, and from left to right. Then, at the sound of the signal gun, a second shout, "HUZZA! LONG LIVE THE FRIENDLY EUROPEAN POWERS!" A third salute of thirteen guns, another fire of musketry, another signal gun, and the troops cry "HUZZA FOR THE AMERICAN STATES!" The men then marched back to their camps, and the officers advanced to the entertainment provided for them by the General-in-chief, of which our eye-witness gives a pleasing account:

"Some of the ancients," he remarks, "were not more attached

to their mystical figures than many of the moderns. We of America have our number THIRTEEN. The officers approached the place of entertainment in different columns, thirteen abreast, and closely linked together in each other's arms. The appearance was pretty enough. The number of officers composing each line signified the Thirteen American States; and the interweaving of arms a complete union and most perfect confederation. The amphitheater looked elegant. The outer seats for the officers were covered with tent canvas stretched out upon poles ; and the tables in the center shaded by elegant markees, raised high, and arranged in a very striking and agreeable style. An excellent band of music attended during the entertainment ; but the feast was still more animating by the discourse and behavior of His Excellency to the officers, and the gentlemen in the country (many of them our old Philadelphia acquaintances) who were present on this occasion. Mrs. Washington, the Countess of Stirling, Lady Kitty, her daughter, Mrs. Greene, and a number of other ladies, favored the feast with their company, amongst whom good humor and the graces were contending for the pre-eminence. The wine circulated in the most genial manner—to the King of France—the friendly European powers— the American States—the Honorable Congress, and other toasts of a similar nature, descriptive of the spirit of freemen. About six o'clock in the evening the company broke up, and His Excellency returned to head-quarters. The French gentlemen of rank and distinction seemed peculiarly pleased with this public approbation of our alliance with their nation. The General himself wore a countenance of uncommon delight and complacence."*

And yet another scene.—August 6th.   In Congress.   This was the day named for the reception by Congress of M. Gerard, who had arrived some weeks before. The reception was conducted with the same rigorous, exact, and yet affecting decorum, which marked the military celebration just described. Divine Decorum ! how pleasant to read these old narratives in these days of slang and expectoration. In the well-known chamber of the State House at Philadelphia, Congress was arranged in a large semicircle within the bar. At one extremity of the semicircle was a platform, raised two steps, for the President, and at the other extremity a chair for the Embassador on the floor. The space below the bar

* New York Journal, May, 1778.

was filled by two hundred of the principal gentlemen of the State, among whom were the chief officers of the State Government, a number of French gentlemen, and several officers of the army. At the appointed hour, we are told—

"In pursuance of the ceremonial established by Congress, the Hon. Richard Henry Lee, Esq., and the Hon. Samuel Adams, Esq., in a coach and six provided by Congress, waited upon the minister at his house. In a few minutes the minister and the two delegates entered the coach, Mr. Lee placing himself at the minister's left hand on the back seat, Mr. Adams occupying the front seat; the minister's chariot, being behind, received his secretary. The carriages being arrived at the state-house, the two members of Congress, placing themselves at the minister's left hand, a little before one o'clock, introduced him to his chair in the Congress chamber, the President and Congress sitting. The minister being seated, he gave his credentials into the hands of his secretary, who advanced and delivered them to the President. The secretary of Congress then read and translated them; which being done, Mr. Lee announced the minister to the President and Congress. At this time the President, the Congress, and the minister rose together; he bowed to the President and the Congress—they bowed to him; whereupon, the whole seated themselves. In a moment the minister rose and made a speech to Congress, they sitting. The speech being finished, the minister sat down, and giving a copy of his speech to his secretary, he presented it to the President. The President and the Congress then rose, and the President announced their answer to the speech, the minister standing. The answer being ended, the whole were again seated, and the President, giving a copy of the answer to the secretary of Congress, he presented it to the minister. The President, the Congress, and the minister then again rose together: the minister bowed to the President, who returned the salute, and then to the Congress, who also bowed in return; and the minister having bowed to the President, and received his bow, he withdrew, and was attended home in the same manner in which he had been conducted to the audience."

After the audience, the members and the minister met at a banquet provided by Congress for his entertainment, which was "conducted with a decorum suited to the occasion, and gave perfect satisfaction to the whole company." We may justly boast, I

think, that the Congress of rustic America received the first plenipotentiary ever accredited to them in a style not *less* becoming than
that in which their own envoys were received at the court which
was supposed to be the politest in Europe.

CHAPTER VII.

ENGLISH EMISSARIES IN PARIS.

OUR envoys soon learned the altered mood of the British ministry.
A few days after the arrival of the Burgoyne news, Arthur Lee
drafted a letter, in the Junius Americanus vein, to Lord North,
calling attention anew to the harsh treatment of American prisoners
in England, proposing an exchange, and asking that an agent appointed by the envoys might be permitted to visit the prisoners,
and minister to their necessities. This letter, signed by all the
envoys, was carried to England by a special messenger, Major
Thornton, afterwards private secretary to Mr. Lee. Far different
was the reception of this communication from that bestowed, only
a few months before, upon a similar one by Lord Stormont. Lord
North gave Major Thornton civil and explicit answers, to this
effect :

" His majesty's servants do not approve of the appointment of
inspectors. They understand the establishment of the prisoners to
be what has been usual and proper in such cases. If there has been
any neglect they have given strict orders to have it rectified ; and
they will be always ready to redress any complaints that shall be
made. The prisoners shall be permitted to receive, under proper
regulations, any charitable donations in their favor. Besides, this
government is disposed and have it in their intentions, as opportunities shall offer, to exchange them in America against British
prisoners there. If any complaints are made through the hands of
Mr. Hartley, or through any other proper channel, they will be
taken into consideration according to the case, and redressed."*

Thus, the requests of the envoys were all complied with except

* Life of Arthur Lee, i., 104.

the one relating to the appointment of a prison agent, and even that
was practically granted.*

At Portsmouth, where the prisoners were confined, lived a dissenting clergyman, named Thomas Wren, whose name should be
mentioned with honor in every American account of these transactions. Moved by his sympathy with the cause of America, not less
than by pity for the distressed Americans, he devoted a great part
of his time for several years to the relief of the prisoners in Forton
jail, near Portsmouth; access to which was expressly granted him
by the government. The biographer of this forgotten benefactor
says: "When American prisoners were continually carried into
Portsmouth during the late war, and many of them were in the
most wretched condition, he was struck with compassion, and flew
to their relief. He contributed most liberally to their necessities
out of his own small fortune, and sought the assistance of his friends.
One of his first objects was to procure, from his acquaintances in
the metropolis and other places, a large supply of clothes, these
being particularly wanted. After this, he set on foot that subscription for the relief of the prisoners, which extended so liberally
through the kingdom. As he was the cause, so he was the distrib-
utor, of the bounties that were raised; and this work employed
his constant attention for several years. The management of the
affair not only required his daily visits to the captives, but engaged
him in a very large correspondence, both at home and abroad."†

Dr. Franklin, who was in constant correspondence with him during the whole period of the Revolution, for it was through Mr.
Wren that the allowance of eighteen pence a week each, granted
by the envoys, was paid to the prisoners, had the liveliest sense of
his worth. It was in consequence of Franklin's suggestion, that

---

* George III. in a note to Lord North, comments upon Lee's letter thus:

21 *Decr.* 1777.

"A letter written by Franklin or by his instructions; singular. The writer adds, 'Offensive,
and calculated to increase animosity;' but Franklin is too deep to draw it up solely from Malevolence; it occurs to me, therefore, that if he could obtain any answer, it would be tacitly acknowledging him and his Colleagues in the capacity they assume, and consequently admitting the right
of the rebel Colonists to make such appointments and to be united States; and perhaps if he does
not succeed in that object, of publishing something in Europe that may carry the air of our having acted with cruelty, which I am certain no officer, either military or civil in my service, could
be guilty of. They certainly could not make much *distinction among rebels;* but if they have
erred, I rather think it has rather been from too much civility towards them."—*Brougham's Statesmen of George III.*, i., 100.

† Gentlemen's Magazine for November, 1787.

Congress, in 1783, sent him a vote of thanks, and that Princeton College conferred upon him the degree of Doctor of Divinity.

Hard, indeed, was it for England to believe, that America could really prefer an alliance with Catholic France, a power with which she had waged three bloody, bitter wars, to a connection with Protestant England on the basis of having every thing she wanted except Independence. During the whole of 1778 and part of 1779, secret emissaries, more or less in the confidence of ministers, kept coming over to Paris to sound Dr. Franklin on the subject, all bearing essentially the same message: " Take all you ever asked for, take several things you never asked for, only don't forsake your mother country, and throw yourselves into the arms of our and your natural enemy, perfidious France."

Three such gentlemen we hear of even in December, 1777, but know nothing of them, except that they were extremely solicitous to learn on what terms, short of independence, the envoys were authorized to treat for peace. Then, early in 1778, James Hutton, an old London friend of Franklin, crossed the channel in search of similar information. Mr. Hutton, a patriarch of the Moravians, was one of those benevolent persons who, in their character of " good old soul," have access to everybody, everywhere ; equally at home and equally welcome in cottage and palace. Without his ear-trumpet Mr. Hutton was as deaf as a post, and, though a man of fortune, wore a thread-bare coat, in order that he might have more coats to give to men who had none ; and in his countenance shone that bland and heavenly light which beams from the faces of men, women, and angels, all whose actions, for a long period of time, have been just, and all their emotions friendly and affectionate. Mr. Hutton, it seems, was a frequenter of Buckingham palace, where he had an occasional chat with the king and queen. Horace Walpole, in his Journal, says he was told, " on good authority," that the king approved Hutton's mission to Paris. Hutton himself, however, says, " I was a loving volunteer, loving both people with no common ardor, a friend of peace, a hater of discord, with horror at all bloodshed, wishing you secure in your liberties, and guarded for ever against all apprehensions."

This good man left Paris no wiser than he came. Upon reaching home, he wrote to Franklin : " I got to my own house in seventy-three hours from Paris. I shall never forget your kindness to me, and your kind intentions to serve my brethren. The sensation I had of the certain miseries of war, that would attend all parties embarked in it, caused my heart almost to break. I always thought it a sad misfortune that there was such a thing as war upon earth. When I left England, I fancied that you and Mr. Deane could treat about peace. I wished it ardently; but, having no commission, nor any thing to offer, I was sorry to hear nothing on your side that I could mention, as a ground to treat upon, to such as I fancied could give it weight."

Franklin's reply to this letter must have been edifying to his Majesty, George III. It amounted to this : Dismiss and disgrace the bad ministers who advised the oppression of America; acknowledge our independence; and, by way of conciliation and remuneration, throw in Canada, Nova Scotia, and Florida. In one particular, Dr. Franklin was able to gratify his good old friend; it was in exempting from seizure the annual supply-ship which the Moravians sent to their Labrador Mission.

A few weeks after Mr. Hutton's departure, Mr. William Pultney, M. P., arrived at Paris, and, under the name of Williams, sought interviews with Franklin. Mr. Pultney was a veritable agent of the ministry, and as he asked the same information for which the benevolent Moravian had applied, he obtained from Dr. Franklin answers of a similar purport : " Acknowledge the independence of the United States, and then enter at once into a treaty with us for a suspension of arms, with the usual provisions relating to distances; and another for establishing peace, friendship, and commerce, such as France has made. This might prevent a war between you and that kingdom, which, in the present circumstances and temper of the two nations, an accident may bring on every day." This was written March 30th, ten days after the American envoys had been presented to the king.

Mr. Pultney, on one occasion, submitted to Dr. Franklin a series of propositions, such as, he said, the British government could be induced to make to the colonies ; but as they were based on the dependence of America, Franklin told him, with emphasis, that he did not approve them, and they would not be approved in America. " But," continued Franklin, " there are two other commissioners here ; I will, if you please, show your propositions to them, and you will hear their opinions. I will also show them to the ministry here, without whose knowledge and concurrence we can take no step in such affairs." " No," said Pultney, " as you do not approve of them, it can answer no purpose to show them to anybody else ; the reasons that weigh with you will also weigh with them; therefore, I now pray, that no mention may be made of my having been here, or my business."

About the same time another member of Parliament, Mr. Chapman, had a conversation on the same subject with Dr. Franklin, and received a similar answer. But the ministry appeared still unsatisfied. In April, two more English gentlemen of rank presented themselves at Passy: David Hartley, M. P., the old friend of Franklin and of America, and Mr. George Hammond, father of that George Hammond who, years after, was minister plenipotentiary from England to the United States. All the spring Mr. Hartley had been writing to Dr. Franklin, imploring him to "arrest the conclusion of any fatal treaty with the House of Bourbon." Franklin replied : " In return for your repeated advice to us, not to conclude any treaty with the House of Bourbon, permit me to give (through you) a little advice to the Whigs in England. Let nothing induce them to join with the Tories in supporting and continuing this wicked war against the Whigs of America, whose assistance they may hereafter want to secure their own liberties, or whose country they may be glad to retire to for the enjoyment of them." So, in April, Mr. Hartley and his friend Hammond crossed the channel to see if they could effect any thing by personal interviews with this contumacious rebel. Hartley, I should add, though belonging to the Opposition, was a friend of Lord North, and came to Paris on this occasion with the knowledge and consent of that minister. Wraxall and others describe him as a well-intentioned, dull, long-winded gentleman, whose rising in the House of Commons had the effect upon members of a dinner-bell.

He found upon his arrival, that the " fatal treaty with the House of Bourbon" was already concluded, and soon learned, besides, that one of the provisions of that treaty bound the United States to make common cause with France in case England should declare war against her. His mission, of course, was fruitless, and he returned home in despair. On the day of his departure from Paris, having occasion to write a note to Dr. Franklin, he added this postscript : " If tempestuous times should come, take care of your

own safety; events are uncertain, and men may be capricious."
Franklin made light of his apprehensions, and wrote in reply, that,
perhaps, the best use such an old fellow as himself could be put to
was to make a martyr of him. Hartley appears to have derived
the impression that Franklin was surrounded with French spies.
This being told to Dr. Franklin, he replied, that "he did not care
how many spies were placed about him by the court of France,
having nothing to conceal from them." I observe from his correspondence at this time, that he promptly transmitted to Count de
Vergennes full accounts of his interviews with these various emissaries.

The great soul of Arthur Lee was deeply moved by the too evident fact that these gentlemen from England cared for nothing but
to learn the opinion of Dr. Franklin. The innocent and soft-hearted
Hartley, whose sole motive in coming over was his yearning for
peace, excited such animosity in Lee's mind that he had to relieve
himself by writing about him to the Count de Vergennes. He informed the minister that "Mr. Hartley, in conversing with French
people whose opinions he thinks may have weight, insinuates to
them, that engaging in a war in our favor is very impolitic, since
you can expect nothing from us but the ingratitude and ill faith
with which we have repaid Great Britain. To us, he says, the
French have done nothing for you, they can never be trusted; no
cordial connection can be formed with them, therefore you had better return back to your former connection, which may be upon your
own terms if you will renounce France." The minister, on the
same day, received Dr. Franklin's official account of Mr. Hartley's
visit, and marked his sense of Lee's tattle by replying to Franklin
at length, and with cordiality, while bestowing upon Lee four
short sentences of cold, diplomatic civility, apologizing for his
brevity by saying that he was "obliged to go immediately to
Council." John Adams, too, a man worth a thousand Arthur Lees,
yet sharing Lee's foibles of vanity and suspicion, conceived a violent distrust of poor Hartley. "This mysterious visit," he says, " I
did not at all admire. I soon saw that Hartley was a person of
consummate vanity, as Hammond was a plain, honest man; but I
considered both as spies, and endeavored to be as reserved and as
much on my guard as my nature would admit." So that Mr.
Hartley, on his return to London, remarked to a friend, "Your

Mr. Adams, that you represent as a man of such good sense—he may have that, but he is the most ungracious man I ever saw ;" a remark which Mr. Adams attributed to his not having sufficiently extolled Mr. Hartley's inventions of fire plates and Archimedes mirrors.

During all the remaining years of the revolutionary struggle, Mr. Hartley never long intermitted his exertions for restoring peace ; sometimes suggesting a truce for five or seven years, sometimes advising the " relinquishment" of the French alliance with the consent of France—the alliance, as he said, being the great stumbling-block in the way to peace. I am tempted to insert Dr. Franklin's warm and witty reply to the latter proposition :—

" The long, steady, and kind regard you have shown for the welfare of America, by the whole tenor of your conduct in Parliament, satisfies me, that this proposition never took its rise with you, but has been suggested from some other quarter; and that your excess of humanity, your love of peace, and your fear for us, that the destruction we are threatened with will certainly be effected, have thrown a mist before your eyes, which hindered you from seeing the malignity and mischief of it. We know that your king hates Whigs and Presbyterians ; that he thirsts for our blood, of which he has already drunk large draughts; that weak and unprincipled ministers are ready to execute the wickedest of his orders, and his venal Parliament equally ready to vote them just. Not the smallest appearance of a reason can be imagined, capable of inducing us to think of relinquishing a solid alliance with one of the most amiable, as well as most powerful princes of Europe, for the expectation of unknown terms of peace, to be afterwards offered to us by *such a government ;* a government that has already shamefully broken all the compacts it ever made with us. This is worse than advising us to drop the substance for the shadow. The dog, after he found his mistake, might possibly have recovered his mutton ; but we could never hope to be trusted again by France, or indeed by any other nation under heaven. Had Lord North been the author of such a proposition, all the world would have said it was insidious, and meant only to deceive and divide us from our friends, and then to ruin us ; supposing our fears might be so strong as to procure an acceptance of it. But, thanks to God, that is not the case. We have long since settled all the account in our own minds. We know the worst you can do to us, if you have your wish, is, to confiscate our estates and take our lives, to rob and murder us; and this you have seen we are ready to hazard, rather than come again under your detested government.

"You must observe, my dear friend, that I am a little warm. Excuse me. It is over. Only let me counsel you not to think of being sent hither on so fruitless an errand as that of making such a proposition.

"It puts me in mind of the comic farce entitled, *Godsend, or The Wreckers.* You may have forgotten it; but I will endeavor to amuse you by recollecting a little of it.

SCENE. *Mount's Bay.*

[*A ship riding at anchor in a great storm. A lee shore full of rocks, and lined with people, furnished with axes and carriages to cut up wrecks, knock the sailors on the head, and carry off the plunder ; according to custom. The boat goes off, and comes under the ship's stern.*]

Spokesman. So ho, the ship, ahoa!

Captain. Hulloa.

Sp. Would you have a pilot?

Capt. No, no!

Sp. It blows hard, and you are in danger.

Capt. I know it.

Sp. Will you buy a better cable? We have one in the boat here.

Capt. What do you ask for it?

Sp. Cut that you have, and then we'll talk about the price of this.

Capt. I shall do no such foolish thing. I have lived in your parish formerly, and know the heads of ye too well to trust ye; keep off from my cable there; I see you have a mind to cut it yourselves. If you go any nearer to it, I'll fire into you and sink you.

Sp. It is a damned rotten French cable, and will part of itself in half an hour. Where will you be then, Captain? You had better take our offer.

Capt. You offer nothing, you rogues, but treachery and mischief.

My cable is good and strong, and will hold long enough to balk all your projects.

Sp. You talk unkindly, Captain, to people who came here only for your good.

Capt. I know you came for all our *goods*, but, by God's help, you shall have none of them ; you shall not serve us as you did the Indiamen.

Sp. Come, my lads, let's be gone. This fellow is not so great a fool as we took him to be.———"

Mr. Hartley's failure appears to have only provoked the British king to make an attempt of another description upon the American envoys. Former emissaries had assailed their discretion ; an attack was now made upon their fidelity. On a morning in June, a packet was thrown into a window at Passy, which proved to be a long letter, addressed to Dr. Franklin, written in the English language, but dated, "Brussels, June 16th," and signed, Charles de Weissenstein. The English, moreover, was not the English of a foreigner ; the letter was evidently a home product, and, as Franklin thought, a message from the king himself—certainly written with the king's knowledge and consent. It began by conjuring Dr. Franklin, in the name of the Just and Omniscient God, before whom we must soon appear, and by his hopes of future fame, to consider if some expedient could not be found for putting a stop to the desolation of America, and for preventing the impending war in Europe. The writer proceeded to vilify the French, asserting that they would certainly betray America at last, and to lay down a plan of union with Great Britain. His plan provided, that "the judges of the American courts shall be named by the king, and hold their offices for life, and shall either bear titles as peers of America, or otherwise, as shall be decided by His Majesty ; that a Congress shall assemble once in seven years, or oftener, if His Majesty thinks fit to summon it, but all its proceedings are to be transmitted to the British Parliament, without whose consent no money shall ever be granted by Congress or any separate state to the crown ; that the great offices of state shall be named in the compact, and that America shall provide for them ; that the whole naval and military force shall be directed by His Majesty ; that the British Parliament shall fix the naval and military force, and vote the sums necessary for its maintenance, etc., etc." The letter con-

tained, also, the following passage : " And as the conspicuous part
which some American gentlemen have taken, may expose them to
the personal enmity of some of the chief persons in Great Britain,
and as it is unreasonable that their services to their country should
deprive them of those advantages which their talents would otherwise have gained them, the following persons shall have *offices*, or
pensions for life, at their option, namely, Franklin, Washington,
Adams, Hancock, etc., etc. In case His Majesty, or his successors,
should ever create American peers, then these persons or their descendants shall be among the first created, if they choose it ; Mr.
Washington to have immediately a brevet of lieutenant-general, and
all the honors and precedence incident thereto, but not to assume
or bear any command without a special warrant, or letter of service, for that purpose, from the king."

The writer requested a personal interview with Dr. Franklin for
the purpose of discussing the details of the project ; or, if that were
inadmissible, then he would be at a certain part of the church of
Notre Dame on a certain day, at noon precisely, with a rose in his
hat, to receive a written answer from Dr. Franklin, which he would
transmit to the king without the intervention of ministers.

Dr. Franklin consulted with his colleagues, and they agreed that
he should answer the letter, and that both letter and answer should
be laid before the Count de Vergennes, and the answer sent or
withheld, as he should recommend. Franklin's reply, written for
the very eye of the king, the author, as Franklin well knew, of all
the calamities his country had suffered, was all fire, point, and sar-
casm. Alluding to the solemn conjurations with which Charles de
Weissentein had begun his epistle, he said it should have been addressed, not to one who had striven for years to prevent the war,
but " to your sovereign and his venal parliament," who " wickedly
began and madly continue a war for the desolation of America."
" You think," Franklin continued, " that we flatter ourselves, and
are deceived into an opinion that England *must* acknowledge our independence. We, on the other hand, think you flatter yourselves
in imagining such an acknowledgment a vast boon, which we strongly desire, and which you may gain some great advantage by granting or withholding. We have never asked it of you ; we only tell
you, that you can have no treaty with us but as an independent
State ; and you may please yourselves and your children with the

rattle of your right to govern us, as long as you have done with
that of your King's being King of France, without giving us the
least concern, if you do not attempt to exercise it."

Weissentein had intimated that the title of Great Britain to the
colonies being indisputable, it would never be relinquished, even
though the fortune of war should compel the Government, for a
time to relinquish possession of the country. Franklin's reply to
this point was aimed full at the King: "I thank you for letting me
know a little of your mind, that, even if the Parliament should acknowledge our independency, the act would not be binding to posterity, and that your nation would resume and prosecute the claim
as soon as they found it convenient. * * * I now indeed recollect my being informed, long since, when in England, that a certain very great personage (George III.), then young, studied much
a certain book, called *Arcana Imperii*. I had the curiosity to procure the book and read it. There are sensible and good things in
it, but some bad ones; for, if I remember rightly, a particular king
is applauded for his politically exciting a rebellion among his subjects, at a time when they had not strength to support it, that he
might, in subduing them, take away their privileges, which were
troublesome to him; and a question is formally stated and discussed, *Whether a prince, who, to appease a revolt, makes promises of
indemnity to the revolters, is obliged to fulfil those promises.* Honest and good men would say, Ay; but this politician says, as you
say, No. And he gives this pretty reason, that, though it was
right to make the promises, because otherwise the revolt would
not be suppressed, yet it would be wrong to keep them, because
revolters ought to be punished to deter from future revolts."

He ridiculed, very happily, the secresy with which this correspondence was proposed to be carried on, and observed that, if the
government of England desired peace, they should propose it
openly to Congress, not send mysterious agents to corrupt and betray their servants. He concluded his letter with a paragraph,
which, really, the king *ought* to have been permitted to read:

"This proposition of delivering ourselves, bound and gagged,
ready for hanging, without even a right to complain, and without
a friend to be found afterwards among all mankind, you would
have us embrace upon the faith of an act of Parliament! Good
God! an act of your Parliament! This demonstrates that you do

not yet know us, and that you fancy we do not know you; but it
is not merely this flimsy faith that we are to act upon; you offer
us *hope*, the hope of PLACES, PENSIONS, and PEERAGES. These,
judging from yourselves, you think are motives irresistible. This
offer to corrupt us, sir, is with me your credential, and convinces me
that you are not a private volunteer in your application. It bears
the stamp of British court character. It is even the signature of
your king. But think, for a moment, in what light it must be
viewed in America. By PLACES, you mean places among us, for
you take care, by a special article, to secure your own to yourselves. We must then pay the salaries, in order to enrich ourselves
with these places. But you will give us PENSIONS, probably to be
paid, too, out of your expected American revenue, and which none of
us can accept without deserving, and perhaps obtaining, a SUS-*pension*. PEERAGES! alas! sir, our long observation of the vast servile majority of your peers, voting constantly for every measure
proposed by a minister, however weak or wicked, leaves us small
respect for that title. We consider it as a sort of *tar-and-feather*
honor, or a mixture of foulness and folly, which every man
among us, who should accept it from your king, would be obliged
to renounce, or exchange for that conferred by the mobs of their
own country, or wear it with everlasting infamy."*

The French government decided that the answer should not be
sent. On the day named for the rendezvous at Notre Dame, an
agent of the French police was on the watch, who reported, that
at noon, a gentleman appeared at the place appointed, and, finding
no one, wandered about the church, looking at the altars and pictures, but never losing sight of the spot, and often returning to it,
gazing anxiously about, as if he expected some one. After waiting for two hours he left the church, and went to his hotel, where
his name was ascertained to be " Colonel Fitz–something," says
John Adams, " an Irish name, that I have forgotten."†

Mr. Adams mentions in his diary, that the reasons for believing
the letter of Weissenstein to have been written with the consent
of the king, were such as completely convinced Dr. Franklin,
" who affirmed to me that he *knew* it came from the king, and that

---

* This letter was copied from the original, in the Office of Foreign Affairs, at Paris, by Dr.
Jared Sparks.—See *Sparks's Franklin*, viii., 278.
† Life and Works of John Adams, iii., 179.

it could not have come from any other without the king's knowledge." Mr. Adams was puzzled to account for Franklin's extreme
aversion to his majesty. "He often, and, indeed, always, appeared
to me to have a personal animosity and very severe resentment
against the king. In all his conversations, * * he mentioned the
king with great asperity, and even upon the margin of a book he
introduced his habitual acrimony against his majesty." Puzzling,
indeed, to a man constitutionally disposed to venerate a monarch,
and who was not acquainted with the secret of the British court!
Franklin himself was long in finding out George III.; but, at this
time, he knew him well, and spoke of him according to his
knowledge.

George III., as his letters show, reciprocated Franklin's antipathy. "That insidious man," the king calls him, in a note to Lord
North of March, 1778. And again : "The many instances of the
inimical conduct of Franklin makes me aware that hatred to this
country is the constant object of his mind."*

A few months after the abortive mission of Colonel Fitz–something, there came to Paris an amiable young barrister, who was
afterwards an eminent judge and renowned Indian scholar, Sir
William Jones. Dr. Franklin had frequently met this gentleman
at the house of his friend, the Bishop of St. Asaphs, to whose
daughter the still briefless barrister was already engaged. It was
the lot of Mr. William Jones to make another, and the last attempt, to ascertain from Dr. Franklin whether England could prevail upon America to accept any thing less than complete and final
independence. He acted, however, not as the agent of king or
ministry, but as the representative of that noble few of Englishmen who had championed the cause of America, from the days of
the Repeal of the Stamp Act, of whom the good Bishop of St.
Asaphs was among the worthiest. Modestly clothing his ideas in
the garb of antiquity, he presented to Dr. Franklin, in May, 1779,
a paper, entitled, " A Fragment of Polybius," in which the political situation was depicted under ancient names ; England figuring
as Athens, France as Caria, the United States as the Islands,
Franklin as Eleutherion, and himself as an Athenian lawyer sojourning at the capital of Caria. The proposals of the Athenian

* Lord Brougham's Statesmen of George III., i., 112.

Jones were founded upon the conviction that England could *never*
be brought to give up America. "This I *know*," he observed,
" and positively pronounce, that, while Athens is Athens, her proud
but brave citizens will never *expressly* recognize the independence
of the Islands; their resources are, no doubt, exhaustible, but will
not be exhausted in the lives of us and of our children. In this
resolution all parties agree."

The leading suggestions of this worthy peace-maker were these :
That there should be " a perfect co-ordination between Athens and
the Thirteen United Islands, they considering her not as a parent,
whom they must obey, but as an elder sister, whom they cannot help
loving, and to whom they shall give pre-eminence of honor and co-
equality of power;" that the new Constitutions of the Islands
should remain; that " on every occasion requiring acts for the
general good, there shall be an assembly of deputies from the Senate of Athens, and the Congress of the Islands, who shall fairly
adjust the whole business, and settle the ratio of the contributions on
both sides ; and this committee shall consist of fifty Islanders and
fifty Athenians, or of a smaller number chosen by them ;" and that
" if it be thought necessary, and found convenient, a proportionable number of Athenian citizens shall have seats, and power of
debating and voting on questions of common concern, in the great
assembly of the Islands, and a proportionable number of Islanders shall sit with the like power in the Assembly at Athens."

This amiable dream of an impossible re-union had as much effect
upon the course of events as a school-girl's composition on the
Horrors of War may be supposed to have in hastening the return
of peace. Nevertheless, the mission of Mr. Jones does credit to
his heart. It had, also, the effect of giving him sundry opportunities of conveying letters, messages, and gifts, from Dr. Franklin to
the beloved family of his betrothed, and from them to Dr. Franklin ; reward enough for the lover of Georgiana Shipley.

CHAPTER VIII.

PAUL JONES.

IT was in the spring of 1778 that the name of John Paul Jones became so terrible along the western coasts of Britain—his native coasts, as familiar to him as to a Solway fisherman. This man was so intimately connected and associated with Dr. Franklin, and held him in such affectionate veneration, that I cannot but give a slight sketch of his brilliant career in the service of Congress.

And what a tough, valiant, indomitable, audacious hero·he was, with his foppish ways and costume, his romantic, fantastic courtesy and enthusiasm! He had been a Nelson, if he had had Nelson's opportunities; for he was just such another soft-hearted, lady-loving, impetuous, imaginative Knight of the Quarter Deck. He was a little man, too, like Nelson, though compactly knit, and his voice was "soft and still, and small, and his eye had keenness, and wildness, and softness in it;"* and full as he was of the spirit of mastery, he was all gentleness, consideration, generosity to men who obeyed him. Mr. Adams mentions, also, that he was a sea-dandy, who would have his full share of gold lace and epaulette, and liked to see his officers, marines, men, boat, and ship all handsomely attired. Like all the greatest fighters, he performed his immortal exploits while he was young; he was but thirty-two when he did his greatest day's work.

On the southwestern coast of Scotland he was born; a natural son of a Mr. Craig, but brought up in the family of Mr. Craig's gardener, from whom he was named John Paul.† Nothing could keep him from the sea. At twelve, therefore, he was apprenticed to a merchant in the American trade, in whose ships he served seven years, as cabin boy, boy, and sailor before the mast. At the age of twenty-four we find him settled at Tobago, engaged in commerce, and possessing considerable property. In 1774, for a reason unknown, but which he himself styles an "accident," and "a very great misfortune," he was obliged suddenly to leave Tobago, and abandon all his property there, except fifty pounds. He came to

---

* John Adams, iii., 202.
† Encyclopedia Britannica, xiii., 2.

the colonies, where he lived twenty months in great poverty, through the neglect or dishonesty of his agent at Tobago. The revolution breaking out, and his fifty pounds being exhausted, he made known his situation and his qualifications to persons of influence, through whom he obtained a lieutenant's commission in the forming navy of the United States. He acquired sudden and very great distinction. In one short cruise he took sixteen prizes, of which he burnt eight, and sent in eight. He had some sharp actions with king's ships, and captured one which had on board a company of British troops, and ten thousand suits of clothes—a most precious acquisition in 1776. In a few months he made a fortune .in prize money, and swept the northern seas of America clear of unconvoyed British vessels.

It was Paul Jones who first hoisted the Stars and Stripes upon a national vessel. On the very day (June 14th, 1777) on which Congress resolved " that the flag of the thirteen United States be thirteen stripes, alternate red and white, and that the Union be thirteen stars, white in a blue field, representing a new constellation," they also resolved "that Captain John Paul Jones be appointed to command the ship Ranger." In the Ranger he was to go to France, and there take command of that fine frigate which the envoys had been building in Holland. As he had been the first to hoist the flag of the United States on a ship-of-war, so, on entering the harbor of Brest in February, 1778, seven days after the signing of the treaty of alliance, he was the first naval officer who had the pleasure of acowledging a salute to that flag from a foreign power.*

Disappointment! The envoys had been obliged, as we have seen, to sell the fine Dutch frigate ; it was then the property of the French Government. Dr. Franklin explained and consoled, as best he could. After two months of delay, caused by the discontent of his first lieutenant, who had expected to command the Ranger in Europe, Captain Jones sailed in the Ranger for the Scottish coast, on his first cruise in British waters.

With ports closed, and all other signs of armament carefully removed, the Ranger could have sent in a daily prize, but Captain Jones had other designs which obliged him to husband his men, and keep his ship clear of prisoners. One brigantine and one ship,

* Sherburne's Life and Character of John Paul Jones, p. 43.

however, he condescended to take on his way; sunk the brigantine, and sent the ship to Brest. On the seventh day he was between the Island of Man and Whitehaven; waters which he knew as familiarly as New Yorkers do the Narrows. Whitehaven was the town at which he had been apprenticed, and from which he had sailed for ten years. It was a town then of several thousands of inhabitants, and its harbor contained three or four hundred vessels, moored close together in large masses. Jones had formed the daring scheme of running in near the port, landing two parties, burning all these ships, and retiring before an armed force could be raised to repel him. At ten o'clock in the evening of April 18th he was off the harbor, with parties of volunteers ready for landing, when, suddenly, the wind veered so as to make the landing impossible, and even his own retreat difficult.

Cruising northward, he was near the harbor of Carrickfergus on the 21st. An unsuspecting fisherman coming alongside, Jones learned from the crew, that in the roads lay at anchor the British ship-of-war, Drake, of twenty guns. He sent the fishermen below as prisoners, their boat towing astern. He had determined to grapple with the Drake that very night, as she lay at anchor, and take her out from the harbor, a prize. His plan was to run in close to the very bow of the ship, cast anchor, rake her fore and aft with great guns and musketry, and force her quickly to surrender. Before a stiff breeze, the Ranger swept in upon her prey in the darkness of the evening, having all the appearance of a common merchant ship returning from a voyage. Unluckily, the anchor of the Ranger, upon which the success of the dashing maneuver depended, was let go a few seconds too late, which brought her to at half a cable's length from the Drake. Then it was that Captain Jones displayed his genius for command. Perceiving that his chance was lost, he instantly ordered his cable to be cut. The Drake's men supposing the cable had parted from the strain caused by the gale, saw nothing extraordinary in the circumstance, and the Ranger soon tacked out of sight and range, without having excited the slightest alarm.

The next afternoon he was again nearing Whitehaven—England, Ireland, and Scotland all in sight at once, and all white with snow. At midnight, with two boats and thirty-one men, provided with combustibles and dark lanterns, he left his ship and made for Whitehaven pier. Day was dawning when he reached it, for the

light wind had made him hours too late in starting. He would
not abandon the enterprise, however, unpromising as it seemed.
Sending one boat to the north side of the harbor to fire the vessels
collected there, he went himself to do the same office to the
stranded fleet on the south side. Familiar with every foot of the
ground he had to traverse, he boldly landed under the guns of the
two forts that protected the harbor, and he himself climbed the
wall of one of them, and spiked every gun without giving alarm.
All the sentinels, he found, had gone to the guard-house; and there
he secured and disarmed every one of them without giving or receiving a scratch. Then, accompanied by one man, he scaled the
other fort and spiked its guns. Returning to the pier to begin the
conflagration, he found there the other boat, which had come back
for a light, the candles in the lanterns having burnt out. Jones now
discovered that all his own candles were consumed, and there was not
in either boat a spark of fire, or the means of kindling one. The day,
too, had dawned, and every second was precious. Nevertheless, he
sent one of his men to a house near by for a light, who soon
returned successful, and the boats again separated for the work of
destruction.

Ten minutes later a barrel of tar, ignited in the steerage of a ship
that lay surrounded by a hundred and fifty others, all left high and
dry by the receded tide, shot a bolt of roaring flame through the
hatchway. The people of the town, in hundreds, were soon running to the pier. Captain Jones stood by the side of the burning
vessel, pistol in hand, and ordered the crowd to keep their distance,
which they did. Not till the flames had caught the rigging and
wreathed about the mainmast—not till the sun was an hour high—
not till the whole town was rushing amazed to the scene—did Jones
give the order to embark. His men entered the boats without
opposition, the captain releasing, at the last moment, all his prisoners but three, who were all he had room for. He stood on the pier
till his men were seated in the boats, and for some little time
after, then stepping gracefully into his place, he gave the word, the
oars splashed into the water, and they moved towards the ship;
while from every eminence in the vicinity hundreds and thousands
of silent, astounded spectators gazed upon the incredible scene.

To the forts! was the cry on shore, as soon as the spell of the
enemy's presence was removed. "Their disappointment," says

Jones, "may easily be imagined, when they found at least thirty heavy cannon, the instruments of their vengeance, rendered useless. At length, however, they began to fire; having, as I apprehend, either brought down ship guns, or used one or two cannon which lay on the beach at the foot of the walls dismounted, and which had not been spiked. They fired with no direction; and the shot falling short of the boats, instead of doing us any damage, afforded some diversion, which my people could not help showing, by discharging their pistols, in return of the salute."* He had the mortification, however, to perceive that the people of the town succeeded in confining the ravages of the fire to two or three ships. Had it been possible, he remarks, to have landed a few hours sooner, he could have burnt three hundred vessels.

On regaining his ship he stood over to the Scottish coast. At noon, with a single boat and a small crew, he landed near the place of his birth, where stood the seat of the Earl of Selkirk, the great man of the neighborhood. . He meant to take the earl prisoner, convey him to France, and hold him as a hostage for the better treatment and fair exchange of the American prisoners in England and America. "I wished," wrote Jones to the Countess of Selkirk, some time after, "to make him the happy instrument of alleviating the horrors of hopeless captivity, when the brave are overpowered and made prisoners of war." The earl was absent from home. On learning this, near the landing-place, the chivalric captain gave the order to return to the boat. The crew grumbled at this, alleging that when English parties landed on the coasts of America they never left them empty-handed, but plundered, destroyed, and burnt, without let or hindrance. "That party," as Jones explained to the countess, "had been with me the same morning, at Whitehaven; some complaisance therefore was their due. I had but a moment to think how I might gratify them, and at the same time do your ladyship the least injury. I charged the two officers to permit none of the seamen to enter the house, or to hurt any thing about it,—to treat you, Madam, with the utmost respect,—to accept of the plate which was offered,—and to come away without making a search, or demanding any thing else. I am induced to believe that I was punctually obeyed; since I am in-

---

* Sherburne's Paul Jones, p. 48.

formed that the plate which they brought away is far short of the quantity expressed in the inventory which accompanied it. I have gratified my men; and when the plate is sold I shall become the purchaser, and will gratify my own feelings by restoring it to you by such conveyance as you shall please to direct."

He kept his word, and, though the earl at first haughtily refused to receive the plate, Jones persisted in his resolve to return it, and did return it, after *eleven years* of effort and negotiation. The Earl then handsomely acknowledged the courtesy of Captain Jones, and paid a just tribute to the excellent behavior of his officers and boat's crew. "Your officers and men," wrote the Earl, "did exactly as ordered, and not one man offered to stir from his post on the outside of the house, nor entered the doors, nor said an uncivil word; the two officers staid not a quarter of an hour in the parlor and butler's pantry, while the butler got the plate together, behaved politely, and asked for nothing but the plate, and instantly marched their men off in regular order, and both officers and men behaved in all respects so well that it would have done credit to the best disciplined troops."*

Now for the Drake again! The audacious captain was determined to have that ship if he was obliged to enter the harbor of Carrickfergus and fight her in broad daylight, in full view of the town and garrison. He was off the harbor the next morning, and was about to enter, when he perceived the Drake coming out. At the same moment the Drake saw *him*, and, the wind being extremely light, sent a boat ahead to reconnoiter, and ascertain whether the stranger knew any thing of the terrible vessel that had been ravaging sea and land the last ten days. Jones, guessing the object of the boat, kept the Ranger's unrecognizable stern towards it, and the boat hailed and came alongside. The officer coming on deck was astounded to find himself sent below, a prisoner. Jones learned from him that the Drake was coming out in search of the Ranger, of whose exploits at Whitehaven an account had arrived the night before. Five small vessels filled with people were following in the wake of the British ship, to witness the expected engagement; " but," remarks Captain Jones, " when they saw the Drake's boat at the Ranger's stern they wisely put back. Alarm-smokes,"

* Sherburne's Paul Jones, p. 58.

he adds, " now appeared in great abundance on both sides of the Channel." The country was thoroughly roused.

All day the Drake was working out of the harbor before the light breeze, and against the tide; the Ranger tacking up and down, waiting for her. On approaching the Ranger, at length, she hoisted British colors, and her antagonist flung out the stars and stripes, unseen till then in the waters of Britain. The Drake hailed :

" What ship is that ?"

Jones ordered his master to reply : " The American Continental ship Ranger. We are waiting for you. Come on. The sun will set in an hour, and it is time to begin."

The Drake, being at the moment astern of the Ranger, Jones put up his helm, and gave him the first broadside, which was gallantly returned. " The action," reported our captain, " was warm, close, and obstinate. It lasted an hour and four minutes, when the enemy called for quarters ; her fore and main-topsail yards being both cut away, and down on the cap; the topgallant yard and mizzen-gaff both hanging up and down along the mast; the second ensign which they had hoisted shot away, and hanging on the quarter-gallery in the water ; the jib shot away, and hanging in the water; her sails and rigging entirely cut to pieces ; her masts and yards all wounded, and her hull also very much galled." A minute before the Drake struck her colors, her commander fell mortally wounded, her first lieutenant having, just before, received his mortal wound. The Drake's loss, in killed and wounded, was forty-two ; the Ranger's, nine.

In his letter to the Countess of Selkirk, Captain Jones discourses of this victory in his lofty, fantastic style. " Had the Earl," he comically observes, " been on board the Ranger, he would have seen the awful pomp and dreadful carnage of a sea engagement ; both affording ample subject for the pencil, as well as melancholy reflection to the contemplative mind. Humanity starts back from such scenes of horror, and cannot sufficiently execrate the vile promoters of this detestable war.

> " 'For *they*, 'twas *they* unsheathed the ruthless blade,
> And Heaven shall ask the havoc it has made.'

* * * " The ships met, and the advantage was disputed with great fortitude on each side for an hour and four minutes, when the gallant commander of the Drake fell, and victory declared in favor of the Ranger. The amiable lieutenant lay mortally wounded, besides near forty of the inferior officers and crew killed and wounded. A melancholy demonstration of the uncertainty of human prospects, and of the sad reverse of fortune which an hour can produce. I buried them in a spacious grave, with the honors due to the memory of the brave. * * * As the feelings of your gentle bosom cannot but be congenial with mine, let me entreat you, Madam, to use your persuasive art with your husband's to endeavor to stop this cruel and destructive war, in which Britain never can succeed."

The battle over, Captain Jones thought it time to release the poor fishermen, through whom he had learned the whereabouts of the Drake, a few days before. "As the poor fellows," he says, " had lost their boat, she having sunk in the late stormy weather, I was happy in having it in my power to give them the necessary sum to purchase every thing new which they had lost. I gave them also a good boat to transport themselves ashore; and sent with them two infirm men, on whom I bestowed the last guinea in my possession, to defray their traveling expenses to their proper home in Dublin. The grateful fishermen were in raptures; and expressed their joy in three huzzas as they passed the Ranger's quarter."

And so the Ranger and her glorious prize sailed away without molestation for Brest, leaving terror in every town, in every mansion, in every cottage, on the coasts of the Three Kingdoms.*

---

* "Paul Jones," says Henderson, " was the dread of all, old and young (and pamphlets of his depredations were as common in every house as almanacs). He was looked upon as a sea-monster, that swallowed up all that came in his power. The people all flocked to the shore to watch his movements, expecting the worst consequences. There was an old Presbyterian minister in the place, a very pious and good old man, but of a most singular and eccentric turn, especially in addressing the Deity, to whom he would speak with as much familiarity as he would to an old farmer, and seemingly without respect, as will appear from the following. He was soon seen making his way through the people with an old black oak arm-chair, which he lugged down to low-water mark (the tide flowing), and sat down in it. Almost out of breath, and rather in a passion, he then began to address the Deity in the following singular way:—

" 'Now *deed* Lord, *dinna* ye think it's a shame for *ye* to send this vile *pireet* to *rub* our *folk* o' *Kirkaldy;* for ye *ken* they're *a' puir* enough already, and *hae naething to spare.* They are *a' gaily guid,* and it *wad* be a *peety* to serve them in *sic in a wa.* The *wa* the *wun blaws,* he'll be here in a *jiffie,* and *wha kens* what he may do. He's *nane* too *guid* for *ony* thing. *Meickle's* the mischief he has *dune* already. *Ony pecket gear* they *hae* gathered *thegither* he will *gang wi' the heal o't;* may burn their *hooses, tak* their *vary claes,* and *tirl* them to the *sark;* and *waes me,! wha kens* but the *bluidy* villain might *tak* their lives. The *puir weemen ere maist freightened* out o' their *wuts,* and the *bairns skirling* after them. I *canna' tho'lt ! I canna tho'lt ! I hae* been *lang* a *faithfu'* servant to *ye, Laird;* but *gin ye dinna* turn the *wun* about, and *blaw* the scoundrel out of our *gate,* I'll *na stur a fit,* but will *juist* sit here, until the tide comes and *drouns* me. *Sae tak yere wull o't.* ' "

The victory electrified France; France whose fondest dream was to see the naval power of Britain humbled. Nothing else was talked of in the drawing-rooms of Paris. The name of the victorious captain was extolled to the skies; and Franklin was overwhelmed with congratulations. It was, indeed, a most timely and splendid inauguration of the alliance.

It was only Arthur Lee and his faction who gave a cold welcome to the young hero. Through Lee's machinations, a bill drawn by Captain Jones on the envoys for five thousand dollars, for the support and solace of his crew, his wounded, and his two hundred prisoners, was refused payment, and a letter was written him on the subject, in which he was damned with faintest praise, and severely snubbed for petty or imaginary omissions. The caitiff Lee had taken it into his preposterous head that Captain Jones had not treated him with the profound respect due to his high mightiness, and being now joined by an ally, John Adams, did all that was possible to hinder and annoy the gallant man who had done such signal honor to his country's flag. Captain Jones, fiery and audacious as he was in the presence of a foe, had all a sailor's respect for lawful superiors, and properly constituted authorities. He defended himself against Lee's charges of disrespect and irregularity with patience, dignity, and completeness, proving that the money for which he had drawn was necessary for the maintenance of his men, as well as authorized by Act of Congress. But Lee remained his enemy to the last, and tormented his susceptible soul to the last.

In Franklin, however, he had a hearty and a powerful friend. A few weeks after his return to Brest, he had the delight of receiving from Dr. Franklin a notification, that the king had asked the *loan of him* to the French navy for a while, and offered him that very frigate which Congress had sent him to Europe to command. "She is at present," wrote Franklin, "the property of the king; but, as there is no war yet declared, you will have the commission and flag of the United States, and act under their orders and laws. * * * The other Commissioners are not acquainted with this proposition as yet, and you see, by the nature of it, that it is necessary to be kept a secret till we have got the vessel here, for fear of difficulties in Holland, and interruption. You will therefore direct your answer to me alone, it being desired that, at present, the affair rest between you and me. Perhaps it may be best for you to take a trip up here to concert matters, if in general you approve the idea."

He did approve the idea. He came to Paris, to Passy, to Versailles; conferred with ministers, dined with princes, supped familiarly with the most distinguished ladies, and played, for some weeks, the *role* of first lion. Between Franklin and himself a warm friendship sprang up, which never grew cold. He returned to Brest to await the coming of his ship, in which he hoped to surpass all his previous exploits; for he was as covetous of honor as the men generally are who know that they are able to win it.

But there's many a slip 'twixt a man and his ship, as naval officers well know. The Holland ship was not half ready. Then, cabals arose among the French naval officers against the interloper who was going to retard their promotion. Month after month passed away, and still this ardent spirit was unemployed. Plans were formed, changed, postponed, abandoned. Chafing under this miserable inactivity, his soul in arms and eager for the fray, Captain Jones besought, implored, complained; wrote to the minister, wrote to Franklin, wrote to members of the Royal Family, and, at last, wrote to the King himself. Franklin did all that he could to assuage his irritation and promote his interests; obtained for him an abundance of most positive promises, and duly transmitted them by post.

One day the wretched Jones chanced to light on a copy of one of Poor Richard's Almanacs, in which he read this sentence: "If you would have your business done, go; if not, send." He took the hint, went to Versailles, and soon obtained an order for the purchase of that famous ship, which, in honor of the source of his inspiration, he named *Bon Homme Richard*. She was a large but very old vessel, and was furnished with forty guns, and a most miscellaneous crew of three hundred and eighty men—Americans, Irish, English, Scotch, French, Portuguese, Maltese, and Malays. To her were added the Congress ship Alliance, thirty-six, Captain Landais; the Pallas, thirty-two; the Cerf, eighteen; and the Vengeance, twelve; the whole under the command of Commodore John Paul Jones, and bound on a cruise in the waters of Great Britain. He sailed under the orders of Dr. Franklin, who directed him *not* to imitate the barbarism of the British in America, who burned defenseless towns without giving the old, the sick, the women and children, time enough to escape. He ordered him not to burn a town at all unless its inhabitants should refuse to pay a proper ransom. August 14th, 1779, at daybreak, this little fleet weighed anchor and stood out to sea.

The weak point of the expedition was the incompetency and bad temper of Captain Landais, the second in command; who was a kind of French Arthur Lee, suspicious, jealous, conceited, insubordinate, sentimental.

I pass over the first five weeks of this immortal cruise. Suffice it to say, that the fleet took a prodigious number of prizes, and that the grand object of Captain Jones, which was to lay the town of Leith (the port of Edinburgh) under a contribution of two hundred thousand pounds, failed through Captain Landais' want of sense and spirit. It is merely the events of a single day of the cruise which I wish briefly to relate.

It was the 23d of September, and the fortieth day of the voyage; the Bon Homme Richard having then four hundred and fifty prisoners on board. At one in the afternoon, when the Commodore was about to close with a large ship, which he had been chasing off the coast of Yorkshire, a fleet of forty-one merchantmen hove in sight, convoyed by two men-of-war. The signal for a general chase was displayed from the Bon Homme Richard, and the merchantmen were soon observed to crowd all sail for the coast, like a flock of frightened geese; while the two men-of-war stood out from the shore, and having got between their convoy and the enemy, awaited his approach. They proved to be the Serapis, forty-four, and the Countess of Scarborough, twenty; the Serapis being a new ship of the best model and construction then known, and manned by a picked crew of three hundred and seventy-five men. As the breeze was light, it was seven o'clock in the evening before the Bon Homme Richard came within hail of the Serapis, and even then the Alliance was several miles astern. The sun was near setting, but the moon was rising, and the evening promised to be clear. The ships were within two or three miles of the Yorkshire coast, and the two headlands of Scarborough and Flamborough were crowded with spectators.

A short conversation took place between the two vessels:

SERAPIS. "What ship is that?"

BON HOMME RICHARD. (*not quite ready*, *perhaps*). "The Princess Royal."

SERAPIS. "Where from?"

BON HOMME RICHARD. "Can't hear you."

SERAPIS. "Answer immediately, or I shall fire into you."

The Bon Homme Richard obeyed this order by firing a broadside into the Serapis, which the Serapis instantly returned, and so the battle was begun. About the same time the Pallas engaged the Countess of Scarborough; Captain Landais and the Alliance being still far from the scene of strife. It was a battle, therefore, of a forty-gun old ship against a forty-four-gun new ship, and of the Pallas, thirty-two, against the Countess of Scarborough, twenty. The smaller vessels of the American fleet, the Cerf and the Vengeance, had parted company, and took no part in either fight.

FIRST HOUR. Commodore Jones, finding that he had an enemy of superior force on his hands, used all his art to gain an advantage over the Serapis in point of position, so as to rake her. But Captain Pearson of the Serapis being as good a sailor as himself, and having a better ship and a better-trained crew, not only balked this design, but gave the Bon Homme Richard some raking fires. Jones soon saw that his only chance for an equal fight was to close with his adversary, and fight it out, muzzle to muzzle, and hand to hand. His first attempt to close failed, from the defective training of his crew—his Malays understanding neither English nor navigation. He ran his bowsprit on board the Serapis, but in such a manner that he could not bring a gun to bear.

"Have you struck?" shouted an officer on board the English ship.

"I have not begun to fight," replied Commodore Jones.

He backed off; but the Serapis, wearing round "upon her heel," ran her jibboom into the mizzen rigging of the Bon Homme Richard. Jones instantly lashed the bowsprit of the enemy to his own mizzen-mast; and, in another minute or two, the two vessels swung round alongside of each other, the stern of one to the bow of the other, the yards and rigging all entangled, the muzzles of the one touching the side of the other, the end of the main-yard of the American ship being directly over the main hatchway of the Serapis.

Not a moment too soon had Commodore Jones closed with his

powerful adversary. It was eight o'clock when the ships came together, and the action had lasted just an hour. By that time, though the Serapis had suffered no very serious damage, the Bon Homme Richard had received eighteen shots below the water; had four feet of water in her hold; was leaking as fast as her pumps could clear her; had had four guns burst; had every gun on the side next the enemy silenced, except two nine-pounders on the quarter-deck; and had lost a hundred men in killed and wounded. Some officers had abandoned their posts, many more were disabled, and all fighting on the decks seemed at an end. The *ship*, in fact, was beaten; it was the indomitable heart of John Paul Jones, supported by a few gallant spirits below and aloft, that was not conquered. In the tops he received efficient aid, particularly in the main-top, where Lieutenant Stack commanded a most expert, vigilant, and daring body of sailors and marines.

The Pallas, meanwhile, was gaining on the Countess of Scarborough; but the Alliance was still an hour and a half distant, unless the breeze should freshen.

SECOND HOUR. Brilliant moonlight. The commodore being now the only officer left on the quarter-deck, rallied the men that still had fight in them, and shifted over one of the nine-pounders on the other side of the deck, to the side next the Serapis. The rest of the action was fought with the three nine-pounders and the musketry in the tops; not a gun below, nor a gun forward of the quarter-deck was fired after the ships closed. Jones himself handled the nine-pounders. One of them he charged with round shot, and pointed it continually at the main-mast of the Serapis; the others, filled with grape and canister, swept the enemy's decks with most destructive effect; while from the tops rained a murderous fire of musketry. The commander of the Serapis relied chiefly upon his lower-deck guns, and poured broadside after broadside into the battered old hulk of the Bon Homme Richard, hoping to sink her. Both ships repeatedly caught fire; and "the scene," as Captain Jones observes, "was dreadful, beyond the reach of language." But the terror on board the Bon Homme Richard was water, not fire; for it soon began to be doubtful if she could be kept afloat long enough to fight the action fairly out. Towards nine, one of her pumps being shot away, and the carpenter crying out the ship must go down, a panic arose among the group near the pumps, and the gunner ran aft to strike the flag. "Fortunately for me," says Jones, "a cannon-ball had done that before;" which the gunner perceiving, he shouted, "Quarters! Quarters!" in the tone of a man who thinks his ship is sinking. "Do you call for quarters?" shouted Captain Pearson. "No!" replied Jones, with savage emphasis. The answer was unheard in the noise of the battle, and Captain Pearson ordered a party to board. On mounting the bulwarks of the Bon Homme Richard, the boarders were met by a vigorous charge of pikemen, who had been stationed along the deck for the purpose, under cover of the bulwarks. The boarders returned to their guns, and the battle was renewed with redoubled fury. At the moment of the panic on board the American ship, a petty officer had set at liberty the four hundred and fifty prisoners confined below, meaning to give them a chance for their lives; and, before they could be again secured, one of them, the captain of a twenty-gun ship taken a day or two before, leaped into a port-hole of the Serapis, and told Captain Pearson, that if he could but hold out a few minutes longer, the enemy's ship must sink. This news, equal to a re-enforcement of two hundred men, gave new heart to the brave commander of the Serapis.

And so the battle raged another hour, Jones being well seconded by the best of his crew, and efficiently aided by some of the volunteers. Even his purser, Mr. Matthew Mease, most nobly fought on the quarter-deck; and when, at last, he was wounded in the head so seriously that it was afterwards trepanned in six places, he only remained below long enough to have it bound with a handkerchief, and then returned to his gun. A young Parisian, named Baptiste Travallier, a friend of the Chaumonts, amused the band of fighting men on the quarter-deck. One of the sailors calling for wadding, young Travallier took off his coat and thrust it into the muzzle of the gun. Soon after, the ship catching fire, he took off his shirt, and dipping it into water, used it "with great dexterity" to extinguish the flames; and fought the rest of the action in a cool undress of trowsers and shoes.

THIRD HOUR. The sharpshooters in the tops of the Bon Homme Richard, aided by the commodore's grape and canister, had, by the end of the second hour of the battle, killed, wounded, or driven below, most of the men on the deck of the Serapis, and every man

above the deck. Emboldened by this, the sailors in the main-top
of the American formed a line along the main-yard, the end of
which hung directly over the enemy's main hatchway. A cool and
daring sailor, seated at the end of the yard, dropped hand-grenades
into the hatchway. One of these exploding in a heap of cartridges,
they blew up with appalling effect. Twenty men were instantly
blown to pieces; forty more were disabled, and, as some report,
forty more were slightly wounded. The ship was set on fire in
half a dozen places at once, nor was the fire extinguished until the
next day. Thus, while one ship was threatened with one element,
the other had to contend with another; and the question was,
which was likely to gain the faster, the water in the hold of the
Richard, or the fire between the decks of the Serapis. At this
crisis of the fight, to the boundless relief and joy of Commodore
Jones, the tardy Alliance hove in sight.

"I now," says Jones, "thought the battle at an end; but to my
utter astonishment, Captain Landais discharged a broadside full
into the stern of the Bon Homme Richard. We called to him for
God's sake to forbear firing into the Bon Homme Richard; yet
he passed along the off side of the ship, and continued firing.
There was no possibility of his mistaking the enemy's ship for the
Bon Homme Richard, there being the most essential difference in
their appearance and construction; besides, it was then full moonlight, and the sides of the Bon Homme Richard were all black,
while the sides of the prizes were yellow; yet, for the greater security, I showed the signal of our reconnoissance. Every tongue
cried that he was firing into the wrong ship, but nothing availed,
he passed round, firing into the Bon Homme Richard's head, stern,
and broadside, and by one of his volleys killed several of my best
men, and mortally wounded a good officer on the forecastle. My
situation was really deplorable. The Bon Homme Richard received various shots under water from the Alliance; the leak gained
on the pumps; and the fire increased much on board both ships.
Some officers persuaded me to strike, of whose courage and good
sense I entertain a high opinion."

But, no! "I would not," he adds, "give up the point. The enemy's
main-mast began to shake, their firing decreased, ours rather increased." So the battle still went on. The Alliance, at last, discovered her almost fatal mistake (for a mistake it doubtless was) and

gave the Serapis a few ineffective shots ; ineffective but discouraging. By this time (ten o'clock) the Countess of Scarborough had struck to the Pallas, but the victor was unable to come to the assistance of the Bon Homme Richard. THE END OF IT. Scottish grit carried the day on this occasion, against English pluck. At half-past ten, when the combat had lasted three hours and a half, Captain Pearson ordered his flag to be struck. As not a man offered to obey a command which involved so much peril, he went himself into the rigging, and with his own hand hauled down his flag. At the same moment his main-mast fell. Mr. Richard Dale, the first lieutenant of the Bon Homme Richard, immediately informed his captain, and asked permission to board, which was granted. He swung himself over to the quarter deck of the Serapis. " I found Captain Pearson," he wrote long after, " standing on the leeward side of the quarter-deck, and, addressing myself to him, said—' Sir, I have orders to send you on board the ship alongside.' The first lieutenant of the Serapis coming up at this moment, inquired of Captain Pearson whether the ship alongside had struck to him ? To which I replied, ' No, sir, the contrary ; he has struck to us.' The lieutenant renewing his inquiry, have you struck, sir ? was answered, ' Yes, I have.' The lieutenant replied, ' I have nothing more to say ; ' and was about to return below, when I informed him he must accompany Captain Pearson on board the ship alongside. He said, ' If you will permit me to go below, I will silence the firing of the lower-deck guns.' This request was refused, and with Captain Pearson was passed over to the deck of the Bon Homme Richard. Orders being sent below to cease firing, the engagement terminated."* The excitement of the action over, Mr. Dale discovered, to his great astonishment, that he was badly wounded.

All night the fire raged on board the Serapis and the water gained in the hold of her antagonist. It was ten the next morning before the fire was subdued ; but no exertions availed to keep afloat the Bon Homme Richard's battered hulk. Her rigging and spars were cut to pieces, her rudder was shot away, and " her timbers," as Captain Jones reports, " from the main-mast to the stern, being greatly decayed with age, were mangled beyond my power of de-

* Sherburne's Paul Jones, p. 128.

scription; and a person must have been an eye-witness to form a just idea of the tremendous scene of carnage, wreck, and ruin that everywhere appeared. Humanity cannot but recoil from the prospect of such finished horror, and lament that war should produce such fatal consequences." He adds, "I was determined to keep the Bon Homme Richard afloat, and, if possible, to bring her into port. For that purpose the first lieutenant of the Pallas continued on board with a party of men to attend the pumps, with boats in waiting, ready to take them on board, in case the water should gain on them too fast. The wind augmented in the night and the next day, so that it was impossible to prevent the good old ship from sinking. They did not abandon her till after 9 o'clock; the water was then up to the lower deck, and a little after ten I saw with inexpressible grief the last glimpse of the Bon Homme Richard."

The American fleet, with its prizes and more than a thousand prisoners, made the best of its way to Holland, where the Commodore, after great difficulty, found a temporary shelter for his four hundred wounded men. Half his own crew and half the crew of the Serapis had fallen in the battle, either killed or hurt.

The effect of this wonderful cruise, crowned by a victory so brilliant, can scarcely be conceived. Every town on the coast of England had its association for defense, its system of signals, its lookouts by night and day. Twenty men-of-war were kept cruising in the British waters, in search of this terrible rover of the seas. Continental Europe and all America were filled with the just renown of these splendid exploits, which reflected glory, also, upon the cause and name of America. Franklin, Lafayette, De Chaumont, Dumas, De Sartines, and many fair ladies of the court, sent letters of congratulation to the victors. The King of France gave Lieutenant Stack, who commanded in the main-top, a captain's commission in the French navy, and a pension of four hundred francs a year. It was the king of England who paid Commodore Jones the most striking compliment, when he conferred upon Captain Pearson the honor of Knighthood, and appointed him to the command of a new forty-four gun frigate. Jones gayly remarked, when this was told him: "He deserved it; and should I have the good fortune to fall in with him again, I will make a Lord of him."

Splendid as his success was deemed, the Commodore himself was extremely dissatisfied with it, being persuaded that if he had been well seconded by Captain Landais, he could have brought into port the greater part of the fleet of merchantmen that were convoyed by the Serapis and Scarborough. Determined to have no more to do with mixed expeditions, of which he could not be the sole and absolute commander, he prepared to return to America, and seek future employment from Congress alone.

Both Dr. Franklin and the French ministry shared the resentment of Captain Jones against the insubordinate and bungling Landais. At the request of M. de Sartines, Franklin ordered Landais to come to Paris and explain his conduct. Upon receiving this order he threw up his command, and said to officers on board the Alliance, and to Franklin at Paris, that he should return no more to that ship. After investigating his conduct and receiving the written testimony of all the leading officers of the Bon Homme Richard, Franklin transmitted the whole of the evidence to Congress; himself pronouncing no judgment, not conceiving that he was authorized to cashier or otherwise punish an officer holding a commission from Congress itself. Landais was dissatisfied with his silence, and desiring to be restored to the command of the Alliance, asked Franklin his opinion of him, and made known his wish for a command. Dr. Franklin gave him a most candid and forcible reply : " I think you," he wrote, " so imprudent, so litigious, and quarrelsome a man, even with your best friends, that peace and good order, and consequently the quiet and regular subordination so necessary to success, are, where you preside, impossible; these are within my observation and apprehension; your military operations I leave to more capable judges. If, therefore, I had twenty ships of war in my disposition, I should not give one of them to Captain Landais."

In Arthur Lee, who took naturally to every man who did his country harm, and who inevitably quarreled with all who had served his country well, Captain Landais found a patron and a friend—as shall be shown in a moment.

Besides the exploits of Commodore Jones, some privateers commissioned by the American envoys did great execution upon British commerce. In the summer of 1779, for example, a little schooner called the Black Prince, with a motley crew of all nations, and a sprinkling of Americans among them, sailed round the British Islands, and, in the course of a three months' cruise, took thirty-seven prizes.

CHAPTER IX.

THE FATE OF SILAS DEANE.

UNHAPPY Deane! Upon arriving at Philadelphia he discovered, to his sorrow, that Arthur Lee, insignificant as he might be in Europe, was far from being powerless in America. Virginia ruled the country then, and in Virginia the Lee families were ancient, numerous, wealthy, and influential. As for poor Deane, he had, it is true, the portrait of the king set in diamonds, and other proofs that he stood very high in the esteem of the French ministry and of Dr. Franklin, but he had no family influence, little wealth, small tact, and no great general ability. Besides the black and constantly repeated insinuations of Lee and Izard, he had to contend with the odium excited by Du Coudray and his followers, as well as the inexplicable mystery of Beaumarchais and Hortalez, whose agent, De Francy, was then at Philadelphia asking Congress to pay him sundry millions for goods which Arthur Lee kept telling them were the free gifts of a gracious monarch.

A circumstance occurred between the recall of Deane and his arrival in America, which served to increase the growing distrust in the mind of Congress respecting their servants in Europe. In January, 1778, when nine months had elapsed since a letter had been received from the envoys at Paris, arrived Captain John Folger, with a large packet of dispatches from them. With his own hands, as he had promised, the captain conveyed the precious packet to the door of Congress, which was then sitting at York. How this packet had been longed for, how eagerly it was opened, every one can imagine. But who can portray the astonishment and mortification of the Foreign Committee when they discovered that the dispatches had been stolen, and blank paper put in their stead? Externally, the packet was regular and perfect, directed in Franklin's own hand, and sealed with the seal of Arthur Lee; within, it was mere sheets of white paper folded in the proper form. Honest Captain Folger was instantly arraigned, and subjected to the severest cross-questioning, but he told a straightforward story, which only showed that he knew nothing whatever of the matter. His reputation was high, both as a citizen and as a sailor.

He was thrown into prison, however, and held for several weeks. His passengers were examined without result; and, in short, the affair was investigated on both sides of the ocean without eliciting any single fact implicating an individual. In this total absence of evidence, every one interested in the affair indulged in conjectures that accorded with his disposition. Dr. Franklin, Mr. Adams, and all other rational beings who had attended to the case, concluded that the theft had been accomplished, before the ship left France, by some light-fingered agent of the British ministry. But Arthur Lee's evil mind led him to the conviction that the thief was an emissary of Silas Deane, who, he thought, wished to destroy the letters of the Lee party, because they contained accusations against him. No charge more destitute of evidence or probability was ever made: nevertheless, the insinuation, doubtless, had its effect upon some minds, and the loss of the dispatches gave ground for the general feeling, that there was villany *somewhere* among the agents of Congress in Europe. In private letters, Lee did not scruple to hint a belief that Dr. Franklin himself, whose superscription the packet bore, was privy to the abstraction of the dispatches.

All unconscious of impending evil, Silas Deane, after a three months' voyage, arrived in Delaware Bay, passenger on board the ship of Admiral D'Estaing, accompanied by M. Gerard. How natural that he should expect a distinguished welcome—he, who had stolen across the sea, two years before, in a hired sloop, the secret emissary of revolted colonies, and now returned, the acknowledged minister of a victorious nation, the honored guest of a French admiral, bringing back a powerful fleet (twelve line-of-battle ships and four frigates), to aid his country, and accompanied by an embassador of the King of France! Accordingly, when the fleet dropped anchor in Delaware Bay, on the tenth of July, Mr. Deane wrote an exulting letter to the president of Congress, which he sent express to Philadelphia, by the hands of Captain Nicholson. " I shall embark this afternoon," he concluded, " in company with his excellency, Monsieur Gerard, for Philadelphia, and hope soon to have the honor of paying my respects to your excellency and the honorable Congress in person, and to congratulate you on the late glorious events." And then, in the style of a victorious general, recommending his favorite aid-de-camp for promotion, he besought for his messenger, Captain Nicholson, the favorable consideration of Congress.

He reached Philadelphia. He was not received as a conquering hero of diplomacy. Congress did not hasten to throw open its doors for his reception, and showed no desire to receive from him the "information," which in their resolution of recall they said they were in want of. Seven weeks passed away without his having been summoned. He had brought with him from France only a hundred pounds, not expecting to be detained in America many weeks: his private estate in Connecticut was not large; and, thus it happened, that the man whom Arthur Lee charged with having gained a fortune of three hundred thousand dollars by trading in France with the public money, was beginning to be embarrassed for the means of subsistence. He ventured, at length, to remind Congress of his presence, and to solicit an "early audience." An audience was then granted him, and he told his story. But he told it not to admiring and grateful countrymen, but to distrustful and estranged employers. All the friends and relations of Arthur Lee, all of Franklin's ancient foes, and a large proportion of the faction who desired to put Horatio Gates into the place filled by George Washington, were disposed to believe the foul calumnies sent over by every ship from Paris. Arthur Lee had redoubled his malign activity after Deane's departure; averring, even in his public letters, that Deane had assumed to himself the entire management of business, and had refused to explain any thing to his virtuous colleague; that he had left his accounts in Paris in "studied confusion," and spent nearly twice as much money on his private account as either of the other envoys. "All that we can find," wrote Lee, "is, that millions have been expended, and that almost every thing remains to be paid for." Millions of francs *had* been expended, and almost every thing *did* remain to be paid for; but what had that to do with the charges against Silas Deane? Deane had drawn more money on his private account than either Lee or Franklin; because upon him had fallen the chief burden of business, the minor expenses of the embassy, and the charges of an establishment in Paris.

Against these vague, vile, groundless insinuations, the luckless Deane could do little more than reply, that he had left all his papers and accounts in Paris; that those accounts were regular and correct; and that Arthur Lee was a suspicious, quarrelsome, false-hearted knave, whose word was totally unworthy of consideration.* Congress evidently did not believe him. Nor can we wonder that they did not; for, even if the Lee insinuations were set aside, there remained the Beaumarchais mystery, which no man ever penetrated or could penetrate, until M. de Loménie brought to light the masses of Beaumarchais' papers, which he found, only seven years ago, in a Paris garret. Take out of Deane's case the Beaumarchais papers, and poor Deane cannot be cleared of conniving at fraud; since, without the testimony of those papers, Beaumarchais' entire claim wears the appearance of being an impudent attempt to cheat Congress of six millions of francs. This claim Deane constantly supported. It was his name which the Hortalez contracts bore, and which gave them authority and importance. I presume that no one ever looked into this complicated affair, previous to the publication of M. de Loménie's work, without deriving an impression, that there must have been a corrupt understanding be-

* Mr. Deane afterwards defended himself very happily against the assertions and insinuations of Lee's public letters of the summer of 1778. Take one brief passage, which sums up a long and thorough examination of one of Lee's letters:

"Mr. Lee asserts:

"1. That he cannot find any satisfaction as to the expenditures of public money, and says, all we can find is, that millions have been expended, and almost every thing remains to be paid for.

"It has been proved that Mr. Lee had, when he wrote this letter, an account in his hands of all the expenditures of public money until I left Paris, of the sums paid, and to whom.

"2. That one hundred thousand livres had been advanced to Mr. Hodge for the purchase of a vessel which cost but three thousand pounds sterling, or seventy-two thousand livres, &c.

"The truth is, Mr. Hodge did not in the whole receive that sum, and he purchased and fitted out two vessels instead of one.

"3. Speaking of the contracts, he says: 'You will see that my name is not to the contracts.'

"The fact is, he was not in France when the principal part of them were made.

"4. He says there was the greatest profusion and dissipation in the purchases.

"The clothes are now in use in the army, and a suit complete delivered on board cost but thirty-two or thirty-three shillings sterling, and better clothes no army was ever furnished with.

"5. He says that Mr. Williams had received near a million of livres without accounting.

"The truth is, Mr. Lee was privy to the contracts made with Mr. Williams, and signed the orders for the principal part of the money put into his hands by the Commissioners; and when he wrote this letter, he could not be ignorant that Mr. Williams was then adjusting his accounts for a settlement, which was actually made, to the satisfaction of Dr. Franklin and Mr. Adams, but a few weeks after.

"6. Mr. Lee says, 'that the contracts were industriously concealed from him.'

"His dispute with Mr. Holker, the principal contractor, now the honorable agent of France in America, about the lapels and buttons, and his assisting personally to settle those accounts and afterwards his signing the bills for the payment thereof himself (for the truth of which I freely appeal to Mr. Holker and to M. Grand's account delivered), is a sufficient answer."— Deane Papers, p. 68.

tween Deane and Beaumarchais. I do not wonder, therefore, that
Congress was puzzled and distrustful, and knew not either what
to believe, or what to do. In censuring Congress for their hesitation and delay, M. de Loménie is unjust. I can declare, that until
I had had the pleasure (and a great pleasure it was) of reading his
elegantly executed work, I supposed that both Deane and Beaumarchais were dishonest—the one a villain of genius, like Robert
Macaire, the other a bungler and tool, like Jacques Strop.

So Mr. Deane had his audience of the honorable Congress, after
waiting nearly seven weeks. Then he waited five weeks more,
without receiving any intimation of the will of Congress. He
wrote to the president, praying him to remind Congress that he
awaited their orders. Civil reply, that he, the president, had done
so. And still the hapless embassador waited. He waited all that
summer. He waited all the succeeding autumn. He wrote to the
president of Congress letter after letter; short letters, long letters,
exculpatory letters, argumentative letters, imploring letters, beseeching letters. At last, he was directed to prepare a written
statement of his conduct in France. He did so, and sent it to
Congress. Then more waiting. At length, in an evil hour, forgetting that he had not the wit of Beaumarchais, and that America
was not France, he resolved to try Beaumarchais's favorite expedient, and appeal to Public Opinion. Doubtless, Beaumarchais
had related to him the singular story of his life—how, when the
rich watchmaker or the corrupt magistrate had striven to rob him
of his rights, he had transferred his cause to another tribunal, and
frustrated nefarious schemes by giving them publicity.

In December, 1778, in a Philadelphia newspaper, Mr. Deane
published the fatal narrative, which revealed to all the world,
which only a few officials had known before, that the American
embassy at Paris was a scene of the bitterest contentions. That Mr.
Deane's story was substantially true, that Arthur Lee really *was*
the cause of those contentions, availed him nothing ; the educated
public saw in his publication a *betrayal* of an official trust, and the
public in general regarded it as the effusion of an angry and detected man. In France, no less than in America, the act was universally condemned ; and, particularly, in the official circles, which
hitherto had sustained Mr. Deane against his malign and odious
adversary. Before adopting the tactics of Beaumarchais, Mr.

Deane should have borrowed his pen.   It is a true old saying, that
he who leaps the hedge of custom for a short cut to his object,
should be well mounted.   Beaumarchais bestrode a winged and
flashing Pegasus ; the horse of Silas Deane was only a common
nag.

Strange to relate, Deane's publication, which completed the ruin
of its author, caused Congress immediately to pay two or three
millions of francs to Beaumarchais.   Thomas Paine, who, as Secretary to the Foreign Committee, had charge of its papers, replied
to Mr. Deane, in the *Pennsylvania Packet,* and betrayed the authorship of the reply, by entitling it, " Common Sense to the Public on Mr. Deane's Affair."   In the course of his article Paine said :
" If Mr. Deane, or any other gentleman, will procure an order
from Congress to inspect an account in my office, or any of Mr.
Deane's friends in Congress will take the trouble of coming themselves, I will give him or them my attendance, and show them, in
a hand-writing, which Mr. Deane is well acquainted with, that the
supplies he so pompously plumes himself upon, were promised and
engaged, and that *as a present,* before he even arrived in France,
and that the part which fell to Mr. Deane, was only to see it done ;
and how he has performed that service, the public are now acquainted with."   Mr. Paine here referred to the message of Arthur
Lee, recorded in the summer of 1776, and brought over by Mr.
Thomas Story.

Paine's article, which, in effect, charged the King of France
with a deliberate violation of a treaty with England, aroused M.
Gerard, who well knew how keenly the amiable Louis XVI. would
feel such an imputation, and how mischievous the disclosure might
prove in future complications.   He explained the affair to Mr.
Paine in person, assuring him, as he had already assured Congress,
that " all the supplies furnished by M. de Beaumarchais to the
States, whether merchandise or cannons and military goods, were
furnished *in the way of commerce,* and that the articles which came
from the king's magazines and arsenals, were *sold* to M. de Beaumarchais by the Department of Artillery, and that he has furnished his obligations for the price of those articles."   Paine refusing
to retract, M. Gerard complained to Congress.   That puzzled and
distracted body, though they all secretly surmised that M. Gerard
spoke only in a diplomatic or Pickwickian sense, resolved unani-

mously, that " Congress do fully, in the clearest and most explicit manner, disavow" Mr. Paine's publication ; and " as they are convinced by indisputable* evidence, that the supplies shipped in the Amphitrite, Seine, and Mercury, were not a present, and that his most Christian Majesty, the great and generous ally of these United States, did not preface his alliance with any supplies whatever, sent to America, so they have not authorized the writer of said publication to make any such assertions as are contained therein, but, on the contrary, do highly disapprove of the same."† And more. After having neglected Beaumarchais for two years and a half, Congress now formally thanked him for his services,‡ and paid him a large part of his claim in long bills. Thomas Paine resigned his office. M. de Francy went home rejoicing.

But all this did not help Silas Deane, who still languished and memorialized in Philadelphia. He waited all the spring and summer of 1779. In August, Congress granted him ten thousand five hundred of their paper dollars, in compensation for the fourteen months' delay. He returned the paper, as being absurdly inadequate. Late in the year, Congress having appointed an American accountant, residing in Paris, to audit the accounts of their envoys in Europe, Mr. Deane crossed the ocean to meet the accountant, and vindicate his claims and his character. On reaching Paris he learned, to his unspeakable dismay, that the gentleman had declined the appointment. Dr. Franklin then proposed appointing, in his stead, Mr. James Searle, who had recently arrived from Philadelphia, commissioned to negotiate a loan in Europe for the State of Pennsylvania; but to him Mr. Deane objected, on the ground that Mr. Searle was his personal enemy. Twelve tedious

---

* The reader will note this word, "indisputable." It was, doubtless, used with a full sense of its exact meaning. The solemn asseveration of the French Embassador, was certainly *indisputable*, but it was far from being convincing.

† Diplomatic Correspondence of the American Revolution. x., 263.

‡ " By express Order of the Congress, sitting at Philadelphia, to M. de Beaumarchais.

"SIR:—The Congress of the United States of America, grateful for the great efforts you have made in their favor, presents you its thanks, and the assurance of its esteem. It grieves for the misfortunes you have suffered in support of its States. Unfortunate circumstances have prevented the accomplishment of its desires ; but it will take the promptest measures for acquitting itself of the debts it has contracted with you.

"The generous sentiments, and the exalted views, which alone could dictate a conduct such as yours, are your greatest eulogium, and are an honor to your character. While, by your great talents, you have rendered yourself useful to your prince, you have gained the esteem of this rising republic, and merited the applause of the New World. JOHN JAY, President."
—*Beaumarchais and his Times*, p. 318.

and miserable months he waited in Paris, imploring Congress, by every opportunity, to appoint another accountant. No answer came to his most just and reasonable petition. At length, however (in March, 1782), an accountant, Mr. Barclay, arrived from America, who proceeded to examine his papers. This gentleman was authorized merely to examine, not to order payment, nor even to pronounce a binding judgment. In his last letter to the President of Congress, dated Ghent, March 17th, 1782, Mr. Deane wrote: "Mr. Barclay, after viewing my accounts, proposed that auditors or arbitrators should be named at Paris, to audit and settle the accounts. I have not the least objection to this, nor shall I have against any person or persons named by Congress, provided they are such as have a competent knowledge of accounts, and are impartial. I am willing either to nominate one part of them, or leave the whole nomination to Dr. Franklin, as Congress shall prefer, or to submit my accounts to the examination of Mr. Barclay alone, provided that he be empowered to take the opinion of disinterested persons on the spot, as to any dubious or uncertain articles, and to make a final close of the affair."*

This letter, together with Mr. Barclay's favorable judgment, and Franklin's influence, might have prevailed against the malign activity of the Lees; but, before it came to hand, other letters of Deane were intercepted on the ocean, which showed only too plainly, that his cruel wrongs had, at length, estranged his weak heart, not merely from Congress, but from his country's sacred cause. Upon reading these letters in European papers, Mr. Robert R. Livingston, the head of the Foreign Department, wrote to Dr. Franklin asking whether these letters could be genuine. Franklin replied: "There is no doubt of their being all genuine. His conversation, since his return from America, has, as I have been informed, gone gradually more and more into that style, and at length come to an open vindication of Arnold's conduct; and, within these few days, he has sent me a letter of twenty full pages, recapitulating those letters, and threatening to write and publish an account of the treatment he has received from Congress. He resides at Ghent, is distressed both in mind and circumstances, raves and writes abundance, and I imagine it will end in his going

* Diplomatic Correspondence of the American Revolution, i., 219.

over to join his friend Arnold in England. I had an exceeding good opinion of him when he acted with me, and I believe he was then sincere and hearty in our cause. But he is changed, and his character ruined in his own country and in this, so that I see no other country but England to which he can now retire. He says that we owe him about twelve thousand pounds sterling; and his great complaint is, that we do not settle his accounts and pay him."

"His *friend*, Arnold." Arnold was a Connecticut man, and he and Deane were early friends. Deane did, at last, join Arnold in England, where he renewed his acquaintance with the traitor, and associated with the traitor's friends. Upon hearing this shocking intelligence, John Jay, who, like Franklin, had stood by Deane in all his misfortunes, took down his portrait from the wall of his study, tore it into pieces, and threw it into the fire. Some time after, when Deane presumed to call upon Mr. Jay, in London, the indignant patriot wrote to reject his proffered civilities, saying, " Every American who gives his hand to Benedict Arnold, in my opinion, pollutes it."*

Even after Deane's removal to England, Dr. Franklin did not refuse publicly to testify to the correctness of his conduct while he was in the service of the United States. In justice to the memory of both, I insert the following explicit statement by Dr. Franklin, dated December 18, 1782 :

" Certain paragraphs having lately appeared in the English newspapers, importing that Silas Deane, Esq., formerly Agent and Commissioner Plenipotentiary of the United States of America, had some time after his first 'arrival in France, purchased in that kingdom, for the use of his countrymen, thirty thousand muskets ; that he gave three livres for each of them, being old condemned arms: that he had them cleaned and vamped up, which cost near three livres more, and that for each of these, he charged and received a louis d'or.' And that he also committed similar frauds, in the purchase of other articles for the use of his country ; and Mr. Deane having represented that the said paragraphs are likely to injure him in the opinions of many persons unacquainted with his conduct whilst in public service ; I think it my duty, in

---

* "Life of John Jay," ii., 144.

compliance with his request, to certify and declare, that the paragraphs in question, according to my best knowledge and belief, are entirely false, and that I have never known or suspected any cause to charge the said Silas Deane with any want of probity, in any purchase or bargain whatever made by him for the use or account of the United States."

This was published by Mr. Deane in the pamphlet which he issued in London in 1784, entitled "An Address to the United States of North America."

For a few months the ill-starred Deane basked in the smiles of tory, and, it is said, of *royal* favor; which is not unlikely, for George III. had Arnold continually at his side, and bestowed upon him the most conspicuous marks of favor. But after the peace Deane was totally neglected. He died at a small country town, a few years later, in extreme poverty.

Such was the unhappy fate of Silas Deane, the first diplomatic agent of the United States. It was not the malignity of Arthur Lee which ruined him, although that was the cause of heavy sorrows and bitter mortifications. Patience, fortitude and tact would have enabled him, at length, to overcome the Lees, and restore both his fortune and his good name. It was Arnold's example, acting upon a mind, not originally strong, exasperated by ill-usage, and weakened by long anxiety, which led him fatally astray.

The reader may be interested to know that, in 1835, forty-five years after the death of Silas Deane, Congress paid his heirs a considerable part of the sum due to them. Mr. Alfred Smith, of the Connecticut Historical Society, having fallen upon a mass of Mr. Deane's papers at Hartford, among which was a complete statement of his case by Deane himself, fortified by convincing testimony, was so struck with the injustice done him, that he advised the family, even at that late day, to apply to Congress for redress. His advice was taken, and Mr. Smith spent a winter in Washington "engineering" the claim. The sum awarded the heirs was thirty-eight thousand dollars. Dr. Franklin's emphatic testimony had much to do with convincing members of Mr. Deane's integrity, and of the justice of the claim.

CHAPTER X.

ARTHUR LEE SUPPRESSED.

WE shall now have the pleasure of settling accounts with Mr. Arthur Lee and his two chief adherents. They died hard, but the reader may comfort himself with the assurance that Europe, Franklin, and the French ministry were rid of them at last. In order to render the story of their discomfiture complete, it is necessary for us to return to the time of Mr. Deane's secret departure from Paris in the spring of 1778.

That event, though it was a triumph for the Lee party, did not have the effect of improving their temper ; since the circumstances attending it were such as to grate severely upon the susceptible jealousy of their chief. So rancorous was the animosity of the Lees at that time, that they would not, if they could avoid it, send dispatches in the ships employed by Dr. Franklin and his friends, but cherished captains of their own selection for the purpose. And after the departure of Mr. Deane, both the malignant Lee and the irascible Izard redoubled their exertions, in public and private letters, to place his conduct in the most odious light, and to involve Dr. Franklin in the ignominy of his alleged peculations.

We have seen, in previous pages, how seriously the mind of Mr. Ralph Izard was perturbed by the molasses articles of the commercial treaty, and, still more, by the omission of Dr. Franklin to consult him during the negotiations. He had now another grievance. Dr. Franklin had not vouchsafed to answer the impertinent and foolish letter which he had written him upon the molasses articles. After writing many letters upon this alleged neglect, he summed up all his complaints in a short and angry note, which he sent to Dr. Franklin by the hands of Mr. John Julius Pringle, his " private secretary." Mr. Pringle delivered the note, conversed with Dr. Franklin upon Izard's complaints, and drew up a report of the interview for the solace of his irritable employer. This document, ridiculous as it may seem, will serve to show on what puerile grounds these shallow progenitors of rebels based their long catalogue of accusations against the ornament of their country and their kind.

"Dr. Franklin," reported Mr. Pringle, "had scarcely read your note, when he said: 'Mr. Izard has written me a very angry letter; please to tell him that he has only made use of general assertions of my having done wrong, which I cannot otherwise answer than by denying. If I have given him any causes of offense, he should let me know what they are.' To this I replied, ' that you had been kind enough to form so good an opinion of me, as to admit me into a share of your confidence; therefore I could take upon me to say, that you were persuaded you had clearly stated, in the several letters he had received from you, circumstances affording sufficient grounds of offense.' He said, ' he should be glad to know what these circumstances were.' I answered, in the first place, 'that, conceiving it your duty as a member of the States, having a considerable fortune there, and intrusted with a commission from Congress, to communicate as occasion offered all the intelligence you could, you found this communication greatly obstructed by a concealment on the part of Dr. Franklin of proper opportunities, when it was quite unnecessary, or when the end of secrecy might be answered, though you had been intrusted with the knowledge of them.' Upon which Dr. Franklin told me, 'that you had only complained of this in the present letter, and as to the particular opportunity you mentioned by M. Gerard, or Mr. Deane, he had not himself looked upon it as a good or proper one, and had not himself made use of it to write.'

"As another ground of complaint I observed, ' that, while the commercial treaty was on the carpet, you considered one article as highly unreasonable and inexpedient, and therefore expressly objected to it; you had in a letter fully specified the reasons upon which your disapprobation was founded, and had sent this letter to Dr. Franklin, in hopes of his removing your scruples, and setting you right if you were wrong, or letting your reasons and objections, if they were just, produce some good effect before the conclusion of the treaty, but you had never been favored with any answer on the subject, though you had repeatedly requested it.' Dr. Franklin alleged, ' that he would have given a full and satisfactory answer, but he had been prevented by business and various avocations; that he was still willing to give one, but could not conceive why you should be so impatient. Suppose he could not give it for a month hence, what great inconvenience would it oc-

casion?' I observed, 'that the sooner you had it, you might be
the better prepared to guard against any misrepresentation.' Dr.
Franklin assured me that he had not been, nor would he ever be,
guilty of any misrepresentation; so far from it, that he had not even
written any thing concerning the matter. I told him, perhaps you
might choose to lay it before Congress, and his answer might enable
you to do it more fully and satisfactorily. Dr. Franklin said you
should have an answer, but you must be patient; for he really was
very much engaged by other business, and interrupted by people
continually coming in upon him, though upon some frivolous errands, as was the case with the two Frenchmen, just gone away,
who came only to ask him to buy cloth.

"I suggested as a third ground of complaint, that you had been
directed by the Congress to propose to the court of Tuscany a
commercial treaty similar to the one concluded with this court,
which you therefore required as necessary for your regulation, in
pursuance of the instructions of Congress, who directed you should
have, not only the original treaty, but also the alterations which
might be proposed; both were nevertheless withheld from you by
Dr. Franklin without the least regard to your applications. Dr.
Franklin replied, 'Did he go into Tuscany? Has not the treaty
been sent to him?' I said, you had good reasons for staying; that
the treaty was kept from you till the other day, when perhaps it
was necessary for you to have had it as early as possible, even
previous to your departure, to give it the maturer consideration,
and because there might be explanations you would like to have
made here; or observations might occur to you, which you might
think it advisable to communicate to Congress, to have their further instructions as soon as you could.

"I do not recollect that Dr. Franklin made any direct reply to
this. He observed, that he was clear he had not given you any
just cause of offense, or reasonable grounds of complaint, that he
was studious to avoid contention; he acknowledged that he owed
you an answer, but, though he was in your debt, he hoped you
would be a merciful creditor; he would say, as the debtor in the
Scripture, 'have patience, and I will pay thee all;' that you certainly ought to give him time, as you had urged so much matter as
would require a pamphlet in answer. I told him that I was sure
it was far from your disposition to court quarrels; that if the

reasons he gave in his answer to you were just and satisfactory, you would undoubtedly allow them their full weight; that satisfaction you were desirous of having, and were anxious to have the affair ended. He said he should endeavor to do it as soon as possible; in the mean time, he hoped to have no more such angry letters from you; his answer he promised should be a cool one, and that people who wrote such angry letters should keep them till they sufficiently reflected on the contents, before they sent them."

With regard to the ceaseless interruptions from visitors and parcels to which Dr. Franklin was subjected at Passy, he has left us a striking illustration in the memoranda of a single day, December 18, 1778. This is the record:

"A man came to tell me he had invented a machine which would go of itself, without the help of a spring, weight, air, water, or any of the elements, or the labor of man or beast, and with force sufficient to work four machines for cutting tobacco; that he had experienced it; would show it me if I would come to his house, and would sell the secret of it for two hundred louis. I doubted it, but promised to go to him in order to see it.

"A Monsieur Coder came with a proposition in writing to levy six hundred men, to be employed in landing on the coast of England and Scotland, to burn and ransom towns and villages, in order to put a stop to the English proceedings in that way in America. I thanked him, and told him I could not approve it, nor had I any money at command for such purposes; moreover, that it would not be permitted by the government here.

"A man came with a request that I would patronize and recommend to government an invention he had, whereby a hussar might so conceal his arms and habiliments, with provision for twenty-four hours, as to appear a common traveler; by which means a considerable body might be admitted into a town, one at a time, unsuspected, and, afterwards assembling, surprise it. I told him I was not a military man, of course no judge of such matters, and advised him to apply to the *Bureau de la Guerre*. He said he had no friends, and so could procure no attention. The number of wild schemes proposed to me is so great, and they have heretofore taken so much of my time, that I begin to reject all, though possibly *some* of them may be worthy notice.

"Received a parcel from an unknown philosopher, who submits

to my consideration a memoir on the subject of *elementary fire,*
containing experiments in a dark chamber.   It seems to be well
written, and is in English, with a little tincture of French idiom.
I wish to see the experiments, without which I cannot well judge
of it."

This " unknown philosopher," upon inquiry, proved to be Jean
Paul Marat, who was destined to play so memorable a part in the
French Revolution, and to receive his death at the hands of Char-
lotte Corday.   Marat had recently returned from England, where
he had earned a scanty living by teaching French ; and was then
trying to live in Paris by his pen and by his experiments.   Failing
in this, he sold medicines in the streets.   The Revolution found
him in the employment of a veterinary surgeon.

Dr. Franklin's explanations, given both to Arthur Lee and
Ralph Izard, were not satisfactory to the Carolinian.   He laid his
silly complaints before Congress, in a long and minute dispatch, in
which he accused Dr. Franklin of " effrontery," of " chicanery,"
and of sacrificing the interests of the country to the interests of one
section of it.   " His abilities," wrote Izard, " are great, and his reputation high.   Removed as he is at so considerable a distance
from the observation of his constituents, if he is not guided by principles of virtue and honor, those abilities and that reputation may
produce the most mischievous effects.   In my conscience, I declare
to you, that I believe him under no such restraint, and God knows
that I speak the real, unprejudiced sentiments of my heart."

In May, 1778, another character appeared upon the scene, Mr.
John Adams ; the most undiplomatic of men, and of all honest
men, the least able to endure a superior.   Mr. Bancroft has sketched his character with truth, charity, and elegance ; and his own
diary portrays him to the life, as an honest, valiant, patriotic, fussy,
vain, blundering Yankee John Bull.   " He was humane," says Mr.
Bancroft, " and frank, generous, and element ; yet he wanted that
spirit of love which reconciles to being out-done.   He could not
look with complacency on those who excelled him, and regarded
another's bearing away the palm as a wrong to himself ; he never
sat placidly under the shade of a greater reputation than his own."*
The marble bust of Mr. Adams, which now stands over the plat-

---

* Bancroft's " History of the United States," viii., 309.

form, in Faneuil Hall, reveals plainly the same traits. The head is of a great size, but curiously short and low, like a line-of-battle ship razeed into a stocky gunboat ; having still the strength of the original ship, though not its grace and swiftness. You say to yourself, as you look at this most interesting and truth-telling of all the revolutionary relics in Boston, " What a man had this been, if he could have been raised a story higher !" It is as though that vast, bald, polished crown of his pressed down upon the great volume of brain, and kept it from having free play. A great tuft of hair, on each side of the head, increases the effect of breadth and shortness. He only lacks a uniform to look the very picture of a bluff, hearty, irascible, brave old British Admiral, all of the olden time. A great sailor, indeed, he might have been ; but never has there figured in courts a man with less of the diplomatist in him than John Adams. Yet such is the force of absolute, downright, incorruptible honesty, that his court life, though it often excites our mirth, never provokes contempt.

We are, also, to bear in mind, that Mr. Adams, in crossing the ocean at this time, left a country in which he was a great man, perhaps the foremost civilian of all the nation, and came to a country in which he was very nearly unknown, and where he must be, till he could acquire the language and manners of the people, completely insignificant. He felt the change, and had the weakness to attribute it to the machinations of a faction. He records in his diary, that, on his arrival at Bordeaux, the question arose among the friends of America, whether or not he was the *famous* Adams : " Le fameux Adams ! Ah, le fameux Adams !" Portions of Paine's " Common Sense," it appears, had been published in France, and attributed to the " celebrated Adams." All that he could say would not convince the people of Bordeaux that he was not this distinguished person. " ' C'est un homme celebre ! Votre nom est bien connu ici !' My answer was, it is another gentleman whose name of Adams you have heard ; it is Mr. Samuel Adams, who was exempted from pardon by General Gage's proclamation. ' Oh non, Monsieur, c'est votre modestie.' But when I arrived at Paris, I found a very different style. I found great pains taken, much more than the question was worth, to settle the point that I was not the famous Adams. * * I soon found, too, that it was effectually settled in the English newspapers that I was not the famous Adams. * * I behaved with as much prudence and civility and industry as I could; but still it was a settled point at Paris, and in the English newspapers, that I was not the famous Adams; and, therefore, the consequence was settled, absolutely and unalterably, that I was a man of whom nobody had ever heard before—a perfect cipher, a man who did not understand one word of French, awkward in his figure, awkward in his dress; no abilities; a perfect bigot and fanatic."* What a wild exaggerater is human vanity! I have found the very paragraph of the *London Morning Post*, which evidently gave rise to all this misconception. It occurs in the course of a long tory letter from Paris, in which *all* the American envoys, in due order, are severely satirized and execrated—Dr. Franklin most severely of all. Here is the passage relating to the new comer: " John Adams, the now third Commissioner at Paris, was appointed to succeed the recalled Mr. D——e. His proscribed relation and namesake, who is still the political ruler of Congress, obtained for him this appointment, to which trust he had neither property nor abilities enough to recommend him; but his being the most flaming, violent *patriot* of all his Bostonian friends, made up for all other deficiencies. He is a mere cipher at Paris as yet; does not understand a word of French, is disgusted with the volatile spirits of the Parisians, extremely awkward in his manners, warm in his passions, uncouth in his dress and figure, and a truly fanatic bigot He was bred to the law, and has no other character at home than that of a cunning, hard-headed attorney."†

Upon such a trifling basis as this, a man of susceptible vanity will erect a formidable superstructure of vague accusation and complaint. In this trait of his character, John Adams was but another Arthur Lee. In the whole world there could not another honest man have been found so fitted by nature, so prepared by circumstances, to sympathize with Lee in his mean jealousies and mad suspicion.

At remote Bordeaux, hundreds of miles from Paris, he already began to hear of the enmities that raged in the American embassy at Paris. He was informed that " the animosity was very rancorous, and had divided all the Americans and all the French people connected with Americans or American affairs, into parties

---

* Works of John Adams, iii., 189.
† "Morning Post," Jan. 12, 1779, in Upcott Collection. v., 178. N. Y. Hist. Society.

very bitter against each other." Lee, Izard, and Bancroft, he had never seen, though he had sat with two brothers of Arthur Lee in Congress. With Dr. Franklin he was well acquainted, and Jonathan Williams had studied law under him at Boston. " I determined," he says, " to be cautious and impartial ; knowing, however, very well the difficulty and the danger of acting an honest and upright part in all such situations."

A week later he met Dr. Franklin at Passy, who greeted the stranger with an invitation to dinner from the greatest man in France, M. Turgot ; and, after dinner, Mr. Adams went home with Dr. Franklin, and supped with him " on cheese and beer." It was soon arranged between them, that Mr. Adams should occupy the apartments at Passy vacated by Mr. Deane.

" The first moment," says Mr. Adams, " Dr. Franklin and I happened to be alone, he began to complain to me of the coolness, as he very coolly called it, between the American ministers. He said there had been disputes between Mr. Deane and Lee ; that Mr. Lee was a man of an anxious, uneasy temper, which made it disagreeable to do business with him ; that he seemed to be one of those men, of whom he had known many in his day, who went on through life quarreling with one person or another, till they commonly ended with the loss of their reason. He said Mr. Izard was there too, and joined in close friendship with Mr. Lee ; that Mr. Izard was a man of violent and ungoverned passions ; that each of these had a number of Americans about him, who were always exciting disputes, and propagating stories that made the service very disagreeable ; that Mr. Izard, instead of going to Italy, and having nothing else to do, spent his time in consultations with Mr. Lee, and in interfering with the business of the commission to this court."

This exactly true and very charitable statement of the case, Mr. Adams heard, as he tells us, " with inward grief and external patience and composure ;" and assured Dr. Franklin that he deplored the " misunderstanding," and should think only of harmonizing and composing it.

From the first hour of his arrival in Paris, he had been constantly associating with Arthur Lee ; but Mr. Lee was politic enough to be extremely " reserved " upon the subject of the quarrel. Mr. Adams, however, was not left to wonder at his silence. " I was

informed by others," he tells us, " that Mr. Lee had said he would
be silent on this subject, and leave me to learn by experience the
state and course of the public business, and judge for myself whether it had been or was likely to be done right or wrong." Mr.
Izard, however, had no reserve. His hatred of Dr. Franklin had become a fanaticism, and he gave Mr. Adams such a tale as " shocked
him beyond measure;" a tale compounded of Lee's malign imagin-
ings and his own savage resentments. It is but too evident that
John Adams believed the substance of Izard's story. He speaks of
Izard as a man of violent passions, but as one who had " a fund of
honor, integrity, candor and benevolence in his character, which
must render him eternally estimable in the sight of all moral and
social beings." I do not think that Mr. Adams, after this conversation with Ralph Izard, ever heartily believed in Franklin. He
endeavored to act fairly towards him as towards all men ; he could
not but be amused by his wit, and moved by his benevolence; he
could never quite resist the genial magic of his presence; he had
some pride in his discoveries and his celebrity ; but this horrible
tale coined in Lee's evil heart, and thundered from Izard's infuriate
tongue, poisoned his mind against the man with whom he ought, at
once, to have made common cause against those shallow maligners.
And though, at first, he was gratified by the attentions shown him
at Paris, soon, as we have already seen, he began to imagine that
some one, or some party, was interested in keeping Europe advised
that, after all, he was *not* the famous Adams.

The first important official act done by Mr. Adams in France
was to join Arthur Lee in expelling Jonathan Williams from the
naval agency at Nantes, to which Franklin and Deane had appointed him. William Lee had, at length, offered to give the commercial agency to Mr. Williams on condition of receiving one-half its
profits. Dr. Franklin advised his nephew not to accept the post,
and himself notified William Lee (March 6th, 1778) that he would
have no hand either in appointing his nephew to the commercial
agency, or in approving it, " not being desirous of his being in any
way concerned in that business."* Consequently, Mr. Lee gave the
appointment to Mr. Schweighauser, a respectable merchant of Nantes.
There was immediate collision between the commercial agent and

* Diplomatic Correspondence of the American Revolution, ii., 104.

the naval agent. Arthur Lee demanded that the drafts of Mr. Williams should be dishonored, he having no authority to draw upon the funds of the envoys. He also thought it monstrous that Mr. Williams should ever have been permitted to draw directly upon the banker of the embassy. Franklin replied : " The reason of permitting him to draw on our banker instead of ourselves, was, as I understand it, to mask more effectually our building and equipping vessels of force. If, in a single instance, he is known or suspected to have abused this confidence placed in him, I am ready to join with you in putting a stop to his proceedings by ordering his bills to be protested. If not, I think the public service requires that he should complete his orders, which, as far as I have ever heard, he has hitherto executed with great care, fidelity, and ability."

Thus the affair stood on the day of Mr. Adams's arrival in Paris. Within four days after, Mr. Adams concurred in ordering Mr. Williams to close his accounts as soon as possible and to enter into no new ones; in short, dismissed him from the naval agency. Dr. Franklin finding them resolved, disappointed Arthur Lee and astonished Mr. Adams by quietly signing the order. I have not space to dwell upon this transaction, but, if it were necessary, I think it could be demonstrated, that the preference of Mr. Schweighauser to Mr. Williams was neither just nor wise, nor required either by the letter or the spirit of the orders of Congress. Mr. Adams, moreover, agreed to draft and sign the dismissal of Mr. Williams before it was possible for him to have been fully informed upon the points in dispute. He seemed to throw himself into the arms of Arthur Lee at the very first opportunity. Mr. Schweighauser acknowledged the substantial compliment paid him by receiving into his counting-room a nephew of the Lees, whom they had attempted to get into the military school at Paris, but could not, because the young gentleman was not a Catholic.*

---

* I see by Franklin's later letters, that the change of agents proved to be a very costly one to Congress. Mr. Williams, on all the public business done by him, charged a uniform commission of two per cent. ; but several of the agents appointed by William Lee were far less reasonable. " For instance," wrote Dr. Franklin in May, 1779, " Mr. Schweighauser, in a late account, charges five per cent. on the simple delivery of the tobaccos to the officer of the farmers-general in the port, and by that means makes the commission on the delivery of the two last cargoes amount to about six hundred and thirty pounds sterling. As there was no sale in the case, he has, in order to calculate the commission, valued the tobacco at ninety livres the hundred weight ; whereas, it was, by our contract with the farmers, to be delivered at about forty livres. I

Mr. Adams, with all his impetuosity, was a man of method; and, like the genuine Yankee that he was, was seldom happy or satisfied unless hard at work. Franklin, a somewhat disorderly man of genius, old, fond of society, very willing to serve his country by dining out six days in the week, and able to see that that *was* serving his country, did not keep the papers and books of the embassy in the perfect order to which the Boston lawyer was accustomed. We have seen in an early chapter, that when Franklin was striving after moral perfection, he found no part of his scheme so difficult as that which related to Order. There is not a more exquisite page in his Autobiography than that in which he relates his failure to acquire orderly habits.

" I made so little progress in amendment, and had such frequent relapses, that I was almost ready to give up the attempt, and content myself with a faulty character in that respect. Like the man, who, in buying an axe of a smith, my neighbor, desired to have the whole of its surface as bright as the edge. The smith consented to grind it bright for him, if he would turn the wheel; he turned, while the smith pressed the broad face of the axe hard and heavily on the stone, which made the turning of it very fatiguing. The man came every now and then from the wheel to see how the work went on; and at length would take his axe as it was, without further grinding. ' No,' said the smith, ' turn on, turn on, we shall have it bright by and by; as yet it is only speckled.' ' Yes,' said the man, ' but *I think I like a speckled axe best.*'   And I believe this may have been the case with many, who, having for want of some such means as I employed, found the difficulty of obtaining good and breaking bad habits in other points of vice and virtue, have given up the struggle, and concluded that ' *a speckled axe is best.*' For something, that pretended to be reason, was every now and then suggesting to me, that such extreme nicety as I exacted of myself might be a kind of foppery in morals, which, if it were known, would make me ridiculous; that a perfect character might be attended with the inconvenience of being

got a friend, who was going upon change, to inquire among the merchants what was the custom in such cases of delivery. I send inclosed the result he has given me of his inquiries. In consequence, I have refused to pay the commission of five per cent. on this article, and I know not why it was, as is said, agreed with him at the time of his appointment, that he should have five per cent. on his transactions, if the custom is only two per cent., as by my information."

envied and hated; and that a benevolent man should allow a few
faults in himself, to keep his friends in countenance. In truth, I
found myself incorrigible with respect to *Order ;* and now I am
grown old, and my memory bad, I feel very sensibly the want
of it."

Red tape has been much spoken against in late years; it is in
bad odor everywhere. It is, nevertheless, one of the minor essen-
tials of public business, and a perfect minister must have a few
yards of it in his composition.

Mr. Adams objected to the disarrangement of the papers, and
very properly addressed himself to the task of putting the embassy in order. He procured letter books and pigeon-holes, and
performed a great deal of useful, and, perhaps, some superfluous
labor, in arranging and rectifying the affairs of the office. In a
word, he put the office into red tape. I suppose he attempted at
the embassy what he did on board the frigate crossing the ocean.
In his sea Diary he wrote: "I am constantly giving the captain
hints concerning order, economy, and regularity, and he seems to
be sensible of the necessity of them, and exerts himself to introduce them. He has cleared out the 'tween decks, ordered up the
hammocks to be aired, and ordered up the sick, such as could bear
it, upon deck for sweet air. * * This was in pursuance of the
advice I gave him in the morning: 'If you intend to have any
reputation for economy, discipline, or any thing that is good, look
to your cockpit.'" An amusingly characteristic passage. He had
never been out of sight of land before in his life.

Accustomed to the plain, frugal ways of New England, he appears to have been a little uncomfortable amid the grandeurs and
elegancies of the Hotel de Valentinois; and his discomfort was
only increased when he learned, that M. de Chaumont had only
lent a part of the house to Dr. Franklin, merely stipulating that
when the war was over, Congress might, if it pleased, grant him
a tract of land in America; not as rent or compensation, but only
as an honorary souvenir—that he might be able to boast of owning
a portion of the soil which he had assisted to deliver. Mr. Adams
did not like such an arrangement; it was not business-like. Accordingly, he wrote a very polite letter on the subject to M. de
Chaumont, requesting him to name the rent of that part of the
hotel occupied by Dr. Franklin and himself. He thanked him for

his constant politeness and generosity to the Americans in Paris; "yet," he added, "it is not reasonable that the United States should be under so great an obligation to a private gentleman as that two of their representatives should occupy, for so long a time, so elegant a seat, with so much furniture and so fine accommodations, without any compensation; and in order to 'avoid the danger of the disapprobation of our constituents, on the one hand, for living at too great or too uncertain an expense, and, on the other, the censure of the world for not making sufficient compensation to a gentleman who has done so much for our convenience, it seems necessary that we should come to an eclàircissement upon this head."

Now, M. de Chaumont was a most ardent Franklinite, and he evidently regarded this letter as a measure of the Lee party, and replied accordingly. "When," said he, "I consecrated my house to Dr. Franklin and his associates who might live with him, I made it fully understood that I should expect no compensation, because I perceived that you had need of all your means to send to the succor of your country, or to relieve the distresses of your countrymen escaping from the chains of their enemies. I pray you, sir, to permit this arrangement to remain, which I made when the fate of your country was doubtful. When she shall enjoy all her splendor, such sacrifices on my part will be superfluous or unworthy of her, but, at present, they may be useful, and I am most happy in offering them to you. There is no occasion for strangers to be informed of my proceeding in this respect. It is so much the worse for those who would not do the same if they had the opportunity, and so much the better for me to have immortalized my house by receiving into it Dr. Franklin and his associates."*

"Dr. Franklin and his associates!" Always Dr. Franklin! How tired certain persons must have been of hearing Aristides called the Just!

It is curious to observe that, with all this contention and jealousy, the envoys long contrived to remain on terms of outward civility. As late as the third of May, 1778, Dr. Franklin still occasionally invited Mr. Izard, Mrs. Izard, and Arthur Lee to his Sunday dinners, which were usually attended by a large circle of Americans and the

* Diplomatic Correspondence of the American Revolution, iv., 269.

young gentlemen at school, as well as by such stanch friends of America as Dr. Dubourg and M. de Chaumont. At Dr. Dubourg's residence, too, they all met, now and then; much to the satisfaction of Mr. Adams, who thought Dr. Dubourg's house one of the most agreeable in Paris, and his pictures chosen with true taste. During this summer, however, Dr. Franklin, placable as he was, ceased to invite Mr. Izard. The fourth of July approached, and the two envoys who lived at Passy resolved to celebrate the day by a grand banquet, to which should be invited the leading Americans and friends of America. Mr. Adams tells us that, knowing Dr. Franklin would not invite Mr. Izard and his adherents, he sent the invitation in his own name; an expedient to which Franklin consented. He was resolved, he says, to " bring them all together, and compel them, if possible, to forget their animosities." The day, he adds, " passed joyously enough, and no ill humor appeared from any quarter." " Afterwards Mr. Izard said to me, that he thought we should have had some of the *gentlemen* of France; he would not allow those we had" (*i. e.*, the wits, the philosophers, the republicans) " to be the gentlemen of the country. They were not ministers of State, nor embassadors, nor princes, nor dukes, nor peers, nor marquises, nor cardinals, nor bishops. But neither our furniture nor our finances would have borne us out in such an ostentation. We should have made a most ridiculous figure in the eyes of such company."

Mr. Adams's diary affords us three glimpses of Franklin in his social moments; when, during the hours of business, he paused to interject an anecdote or a remark. This is one: " Franklin told us one of his characteristic stories. A Spanish writer of certain visions of hell relates, that a certain devil, who was civil and wellbred, showed him all the apartments of the place, among others, that of deceased kings. The Spaniard was much pleased at so illustrious a sight, and, after viewing them for some time, said he should be glad to see the rest of them. ' The rest !' said the demon ; ' here are all the kings that ever reigned upon earth, from the creation of it to this day. What the devil would the man have ?' Another : A certain tailor once stole a horse, and was found out, and committed to prison, where he met another person who had long followed the trade of horse-stealing. The tailor told the other his story. The other inquired why he had not taken such a road, and assumed such a disguise, and why he had not disguised the horse. ' I did not

think of it.' ' Who are you, and what has been your employment ?'
' A tailor.' ' You never stole a horse before, I suppose, in your life ?'
' Never.' ' G—d—you! what business had you with horse-stealing ?
Why did you not content yourself with your cabbage ?' " Another
and a better—one of the best things ever said by man :
" ORTHODOXY IS MY DOXY, AND HETERODOXY IS YOUR DOXY."
Mr. Adams's benevolent efforts on the fourth of July were not rewarded with the success he had hoped for; Arthur Lee and his
fiery friend from South Carolina were not mollified in the least.
Lee, indeed, now laid aside all moderation and decency in his de-
nunciations of Dr. Franklin. Nevertheless, when Mr. Deane's appeal to the public reached France, Mr. Adams made haste to write
to the Count de Vergennes, defending Lee and denouncing Deane,
ludicrously exaggerating the importance of the affair. He told Dr.
Franklin that Deane's publication was " one of the most wicked and
abominable productions that ever sprang from a human heart." In
fact, it was nothing more than a moderate and ill-timed exposure
of Arthur Lee, who was one of the most impracticable and incompetent men that ever, in any age or country, held a public station.

But relief was at hand. On one point, and only on one, the five
envoys were agreed; and that was in recommending Congress to
appoint a single plenipotentiary to each court. Franklin, Adams,
Izard, and both Lees, all wrote letters to this effect, each, perhaps,
cherishing some expectation of being the happy man whom Congress would appoint sole plenipotentiary to the court of France.
Congress acted upon their unanimous recommendation, revoked the
joint commission of Franklin, Lee, and Adams, and elected Dr.
Franklin sole plenipotentiary. In February, 1779, General Lafayette returning to France on leave of absence, brought the new commission and the new instructions. This measure threw Mr. Adams
out of employment, while Arthur Lee still retained his place as envoy to Spain. Mr. Adams submitted with excellent grace, and prepared forthwith to return to America. " This masterly measure
of Congress," he wrote to the Count de Vergennes in his letter of
leave, " which has my most hearty approbation, and of the necessity of which I was fully convinced before I had been two months
in Europe, has taken away the possibility of those dissensions
which I so much apprehended." Not so. Dr. Franklin wrote a
note to Mr. Arthur Lee, a day or two after that sentence was

written, asking him to send to Passy " the public papers in your
hands belonging to this department." Mr. Lee replied that he had
" no papers belonging to the department of minister plenipotentiary
to the court of Versailles." All the public papers in his possession,
he said, belonged to the late joint commission, which no single
commissioner had a right to demand or hold, and he would not
give them up. Mr. Adams returned the papers in his possession
without being asked.

Every true friend to America in Paris rejoiced in this triumph
of Franklin over his mean, insidious foes. The French court and
ministry were especially gratified. M. Gerard was ordered to say
to Congress that " the King and ministry were -extremely pleased
with the exclusive appointment of so steady and honest a man, and
so firm and solid a patriot as Dr. Franklin." M. Gerard observed, in explanation of this order, that " the personal character of
Dr. Franklin will enable the Court to act with a frankness becoming the alliance, and they will have no occasion to withhold any
more the secrets which may interest the United States and the alliance." A fit of the gout prevented Dr. Franklin from immediately
appearing at court ; but, in April, as soon as he could hobble, he
went to Versailles, and was presented to the King with all the
forms, and with unusual eclat. Art has portrayed or imagined the
scene—as our picture-shop windows daily attest. The leading incident of the picture, a lady of the Court placing a wreath upon
Franklin's head, has, at least, the authority of Madame Campan.

The appointment of Dr. Franklin as plenipotentiary caused a
flutter in the circle of diplomatists at Paris. Shall we return his
official visit—we whose courts have not acknowledged the independence of the United States ? The agreement was general not
to do so. Dr. Franklin, " by good luck," as he says, heard of this resolution, and " disappointed their project by visiting none of them."

General Lafayette, besides Dr. Franklin's new commission and
instructions, brought over a curious resolution of Congress, enjoining their servants in Europe to live together in harmony. Dr.
Franklin sent a copy of this resolution to each of the gentlemen
concerned, and assured them that he concurred most heartily with
the desire of Congress, and should do all in his power to comply
with it. They all replied in a similar strain ; each protesting himself the most peaceful of all possible men. Nevertheless, Dr. Frank-

lin, before he could be rid of them, was destined to have a quarrel
with each of the three, so intense and bitter as almost to obliterate.
the recollection of the disputes which had preceded it.

And, first, with Ralph Izard. This individual, as we have before
mentioned, was a man of large fortune. He had now held the appointment of envoy to Tuscany for fifteen months, during which
period he had lived in Paris in the style supposed to be becoming
a plenipotentiary, and had not performed one act calculated to be
of the slightest benefit to his country. The Grand Duke of Tuscany had not acknowledged the independence of the United States,
would not receive their embassador, and could have done nothing
for them if he had. The appointment held by Mr. Izard, necessarily useless, became absurd when the politics of Europe were better
understood. He clung to it, however, and even charged Congress
with the education of his children at Paris schools. Already, Dr.
Franklin and his colleagues had advanced to him and William Lee
two thousand pounds each. This he did soon after the arrival of
their commissions in 1777, and for reasons which he himself explains : " These gentlemen having represented to us that no provision had arrived for their subsistence, and that they were nearly
ready to set out for their respective destinations, but wanted money
to defray the expense of their journeys ; for which they therefore
requested us to furnish them with a credit on our banker ;—the
commissions, fearing that the public interests might possibly suffer if those journeys were delayed till the necessary provision or
orders should arrive from America, thought they might be justified
in giving such a credit, for the expense of those journeys ; and Mr.
Lee, being asked what sum he imagined would be necessary, said,
justly, that the expense of his journey could not be exactly ascertained beforehand ; but, if he were empowered to draw on our
banker, he should certainly only take, from time to time, what was
absolutely necessary, and therefore it was of little importance for
what sum the credit should be ordered ; it would, however, look
handsome and confidential, if the sum were two thousand louis.
We thereupon, confiding that no more of this money would be
taken out of our disposition than the expenses of the journeys as
they should accrue, did frankly but unwarily give the orders. Mr.
Deane and myself were, however, soon surprised with the intelligence, that the gentlemen had gone directly to the banker, and by

virtue of these orders had taken out of our account the whole sum
mentioned, and carried it to their own; leaving the money indeed
in his hands, but requiring his receipt for it as their money, for
which he was to be accountable to them only."

Ten months after, Mr. Izard applied to Messrs. Franklin, Lee,
and Adams for five hundred guineas more. Dr. Franklin drafted
a reply, revealing the financial condition of the United States,
showing him that the credit of Congress in Europe was in imminent, daily peril, through the enormous and unexpected drafts from
America. "It is not a year," wrote Franklin, "since you received
from us the sum of two thousand guineas, which you thought necessary on account of your being to set out immediately for Florence.
You have not incurred the expense of that journey. You are a
gentleman of fortune. You did not come to France with any dependence on being maintained here with your family at the expense
of the United States, in the time of their distress, and without rendering them the equivalent service they expected. On all these
considerations we should rather hope, that you would be willing to
reimburse us the sum we have advanced to you, if it may be done
with any possible convenience to your affairs. Such a supply
would at least enable us to relieve more liberally our unfortunate
countrymen, who have long been prisoners, stripped of every thing,
of whom we daily expect to have near three hundred upon our
hands by the exchange."

This letter, Mr. Adams and Mr. Arthur Lee declined to sign,
and it was not sent. Upon Izard's drawing for the money, Dr.
Franklin refused to accept his bill. It was accepted, however, by
Messrs. Adams and Lee, and Izard obtained the five hundred
guineas. This occurred in January, 1779. In May, Dr. Franklin
being sole plenipotentiary, and the financial peril not less threatening than before, Izard and William Lee both applied for more
money for their subsistence. Dr. Franklin positively declined to
furnish it. "They produced to me," wrote Franklin, "a resolve
of Congress empowering them to draw on the Commissioners in
France for their expenses at foreign courts; and doubtless Congress, when that resolve was made, intended to enable us to pay
those drafts; but, as that has not been done, and the gentlemen
(except Mr. Lee for a few weeks) have not incurred any expense
at foreign courts, and, if they had, the five thousand five hundred

guineas, received by them in about nine months, seemed an ample provision for it, and as both of them might command money from England, I do not conceive that I disobeyed an order of Congress, and that, if I did, the circumstances will excuse it; and I could have no intention to distress them, because I must know it is out of my power, as their private fortunes and credit will enable them at all times to pay their own expenses."

Dr. Franklin had, also, the pleasure, in the course of the year, of refusing to supply Arthur Lee with money for a journey to Spain; which journey he *knew* would be useless. And, again, when William Lee desired the aid of Dr. Franklin in procuring official interviews with the Count de Vergennes for purposes of transparent inutility, Dr. Franklin refused either to accompany him to Versailles on those idle errands, or to write to M. de Vergennes recommending Mr. Lee's proposals to the consideration of the government.

The wrath of the three worthies at these rebuffs, their letters, public and private, still attest. Arthur Lee went so far as to say, in a letter to a member of Congress, that Paul Jones's glorious expedition of this year, was "a cruising job of Chaumont and Dr. Franklin." Here is the passage: "There is nothing of which I am more persuaded than that Duane" (the well known, patriotic member of Congress from the State of New York) "is a secret, treacherous, and dangerous enemy to the United States. If Congress are satisfied, that, while from the feebleness of our marine the enemy's vessels of every description are plundering our commerce and our coast, one of our best frigates, the *Alliance*, should be kept upon a cruising job of Chaumont and Dr. Franklin, I shall be much surprised. I am sure that the latter would never have ventured to do so criminal an act, were he not resolved never to return to his country to give an account of his conduct, which, without some extraordinary conjuncture, or a total violation of justice, could not escape the severest condemnation." A paragraph from another Lee letter of this year: "So effectually have the seeds, sown by the father of corruption here, prospered both in Europe and America, that every thing yields to it. Dumas has been at Passy some weeks, but is not permitted to come near me. Sayre tells me, his object is to get the agency for a loan into the hands of a French house. If he offers good· *private* reasons, it will embarrass the good Doctor exceedingly, because the house of Grand, in whose hands it is at present, is in partnership with Deane (in which probably the Doctor may share), and therefore it will wound those honorable and friendly feelings which bind them together. As to the public, that is out of the question." With equal malice, but less insanity, wrote William Lee and Ralph Izard.

It is worth noticing, before we finally dispose of Mr. Arthur Lee, that while he was so fierce a critic of other men, he himself was signally faulty and incompetent. It was he who was cheated in buying fusils at Berlin—as he himself confesses. It was *his* secretary who betrayed the secrets of the legation. It was he who had his papers stolen. It was he who caused repeated delays in the shipping of stores. He made himself abhorred by the government and people whom it was his first duty to conciliate. He sanctioned the indecent drafts of Izard and his brother upon the public treasury. He alone asked a personal favor of the French ministry. It was he who caused the long misery arising from the transactions of Beaumarchais, which lasted from 1777 until 1835. It was he who lent his influence to the expulsion from the naval agency of that efficient, prompt, economical Bostonian, Jonathan Williams, and the appointment of the highly respectable but very expensive Herr Schweighauser. He it was who recommended to public employment in London the Maryland merchant, Digges, who cheated the American prisoners in England of more than four hundred pounds of the money intrusted to him by the envoys for the prisoners' weekly allowance. Franklin has damned this wretch to eternal infamy in a familiar passage : " He that robs the rich even of a single guinea is a villain ; but what is he who can break his sacred trust, by robbing a poor man and a prisoner of eighteen pence given in charity for his relief, and repeat that crime as often as there are weeks in a winter, and multiply it by robbing as many poor men every week as make up the number of near six hundred ? We have no name in our language for such atrocious wickedness. If such a fellow is not damned, it is not worth while to keep a devil." This was a protégé of Arthur Lee. All men are liable to be deceived; but none are *so* liable as those who habitually and savagely denounce the conduct of others.

Congress soon discovered that the appointment of Franklin as sole plenipotentiary had not allayed the dissensions among their envoys in Europe ; and again those dissensions were the theme of warm discussion. A committee of thirteen was appointed to consider the matter and report. Many propositions were considered by this committee. Some members were in favor of recalling all the envoys and sending out a new set. A powerful faction aimed at the recall of Dr. Franklin, and the election of Arthur Lee in his stead. There are reasons for believing that this project would actually have prevailed, but for the direct and energetic influence of the French Embassador. All accounts agree that the majority in the committee for sustaining Dr. Franklin was very small, probably it was for a time a majority of one. M. Gerard distinctly claims the honor of having defeated the Lees on this occasion. One of his letters to M. de Vergennes contains these sentences : " The stories of Mr. Arthur Lee are but an absurd tissue of falsehoods and sarcasms, which can only compromise those who have the misfortune of being obliged to have any correspondence with him. Permit me, Monseigneur, to congratulate myself at least on having relieved you of this burden." Another letter has the following : " I explained myself gradually, and not until the very instant when it was indispensable, to prevent this dangerous and bad man (Arthur Lee) from replacing Franklin, and being, at the same time, charged with the negotiations with Spain. I cannot conceal from you, Monseigneur, that I rejoice every day more and more in having been able to assist in preventing this misfortune."*

The struggle was long and severe ; it lasted all the spring and part of the summer of 1779, until the country clamored for an end of the strife, that Congress might turn to the support of its failing credit. Truth, justice, and good policy prevailed at length ; Dr. Franklin was confirmed in his post. Arthur Lee, William Lee, and Ralph Izard were recalled.

It is humiliating to think that such a creature as Arthur Lee could, for a single instant, have stood to Franklin in the light of a competitor. We are to consider, however, that Lee was personally unknown to Congress ; that many of his letters, though transparently false to the well-informed, read plausibly enough to persons not familiar with the events and characters involved ; that he and his two confederates possessed great family influence in the

* " Beaumarchais and his Times," p. 320.

two leading States of the South ; that for two years they had been assiduously employed in poisoning the mind of Congress against Franklin; that he had never deigned, until after the question was decided, to so much as *allude* to their efforts to undermine him ; and that Congress, owing to the irregularity of the packets, had only such knowledge of their affairs in Europe as they could gather and infer from the few letters of their correspondents which escaped capture. In a letter of this very year Dr. Franklin mentions, that of four copies of his new commission, sent to him by as many different ships, he received only the one brought by the Marquis de Lafayette. Every man, moreover, of any force or individuality has enemies. Franklin, during the long contests in Pennsylvania, in which he had been the head and champion of the popular party against the wealth and rank of the province, had inflicted some wounds which time had not healed. Nay, time *has* not healed them; for there is to this hour a certain narrow, dismally respectable circle in Philadelphia, who cherish, besides sundry silver teapots, cracked punch-bowls, family pictures, ancient furniture, and other trumpery of the Past, an hereditary antipathy to Dr. Franklin, of which they are very proud.

His grandson, William Temple Franklin, did not escape the malevolence of the factions. Mrs. Bache informed her father that a cabal was plotting his removal. He assured her that he would resign if the youth were taken from him; and to Mr. Bache he wrote : " I am surprised to hear that my grandson, Temple Franklin, being with me, should be an objection against me, and that there is a cabal for removing him. Methinks, it is rather some merit that I have rescued a valuable young man from the danger of being a Tory, and fixed him in honest, republican Whig principles ; as I think, from the integrity of his disposition, his industry, his early sagacity, and uncommon abilities for business, he may in time become of great service to his country. It is enough that I have lost my *son;* would they add my *grandson?* An old man of seventy, I undertook a winter voyage at the command of the Congress, and for the public service, with no other attendant to take care of me. I am continued here in a foreign country, where, if I am sick, his filial attention comforts me, and, if I die, I have a child to close my eyes and take care of my remains. His dutiful behavior towards me, and his diligence and fidelity in business, are both pleasing and

useful to me. His conduct, as my private secretary, has been un-
exceptionable, and I am confident the Congress will never think of
separating us."

It is well for us to know that Franklin suffered such things as
these. Perhaps, every estimable man who has lived forty years in
the world, has had his Arthur Lee. It is comforting to know that
such disordered beings can only sting and perplex, not permanently
injure, and that the greatest and wisest men are not exempt from
their attacks. Franklin's own comments upon the enmity of Lee
and Izard are amusing : " As to friends and enemies, I have hitherto,
thanks to God, had plenty of the former kind ; they have been my
treasure ; and it has perhaps been of no disadvantage to me, that I
have had a few of the latter. They serve to put us upon correcting the faults we have, and avoiding those we are in danger of
having. They counteract the mischief flattery might do us, and
their malicious attacks make our friends more zealous in serving us
and promoting our interest. At present, I do not know of more
than two such enemies that I enjoy, viz., Arthur Lee and Ralph
Izard. I deserved the enmity of the latter, because I might have
avoided it by paying him a compliment, which I neglected.* That
of the former I owe to the people of France, who happened to respect me too much and him too little ; which I could bear, and he
could not. They are unhappy that they cannot make everybody hate
me as much as they do ; and I should be so, if my friends did not love
me much more than those gentlemen can possibly love one another."

To the last hour of their stay in Europe, these two individuals
were a plague and a shame to all honest men concerned with them.
Paul Jones, covered with the glory of his late expedition, and desirous to return to America, Dr. Franklin had appointed to the
command of the frigate Alliance, which had been so shockingly
misgoverned, and then abandoned by Captain Landais. In this
ship Franklin had, also, obtained passage for Lee and Izard. The
crew of the Alliance refused to sail until large disputed arrears of
pay and prize money were paid them. Lee and Izard openly supported them in this mutinous resolution. Many weeks were consumed in this dispute, though the Alliance was to convey stores to
America, of which the army was in pressing need. Commodore

---

* i. e., he might have paid Izard the compliment of consulting him during the negotiations
of 1778, vol. ii., 17.

Jones went to Paris, at length, to seek the advice and authority of Dr. Franklin; and, in his absence, Captain Landais reappeared, and assumed command of the ship. On the return of Jones, the ship being upon the point of sailing, the contest for the command was referred to Arthur Lee. Landais exhibited merely his original commission from Congress, appointing him to the command of the Alliance. Against his claim to the present control of the ship were the following considerations: 1. His conduct in the late expedition, which was attested by every officer of the Bon Homme Richard, in writing, and which misconduct was capital; 2. His public abandonment of the ship, and the removal therefrom of all his effects; 3. His written request to Dr. Franklin for money and a passage to America, to take his trial there before a court-martial; 4. Dr. Franklin's written and very emphatic refusal to restore him; 5. Franklin's order to Captain Jones, assigning him to the command; 6. Captain Jones's actual command of the ship for eight months; 7. The evident, notorious, undeniable unfitness of Landais for any post of trust and difficulty; 8. The pre-eminent ability and reputation of Captain Jones, and the gratitude due to him from every citizen of America. Need I say that Arthur Lee disregarded these considerations, and assigned the command of the Alliance to Captain Landais? Jones left the frigate, rather than sail under such a commander. News of these proceedings reaching Paris, Franklin annulled his order assigning a passage in the vessel to Arthur Lee; and the French government dispatched an order for the arrest of Captain Landais; but before the documents reached the coast, the Alliance had sailed.

The vessel had not been many days at sea before Landais gave such alarming evidences of flightiness and incompetency, that the passengers deposed him from the command, and the ship was taken into port by the first lieutenant. Beyond all question, Jones was right when he wrote to Mr. Robert Morris, that "Mr. Lee has acted in this manner merely because I would not become the enemy of the venerable, the wise, and good Franklin, whose heart and head does, and always will do, honor to human nature." The honest sailor added: "I know the great and good in this kingdom better, perhaps, than any other American who has appeared in Europe since the treaty of alliance; and if my testimony would add any thing to Franklin's reputation, I could witness the universal veneration and esteem with which his name inspires all ranks, not only at Versailles, and all over this kingdom, but also in Spain and in Holland ; and I can add, from the testimony of the first characters of other nations, that envy itself is dumb when the name of Franklin is but mentioned."

On his arrival in America, Arthur Lee assured Gen. Wayne, on his honor as a gentleman, that Dr. Franklin was alone responsible for the delay of the supplies, which, he said, were wantonly and causelessly held back by Franklin for the space of four months. The plausible, lying villain, added : "Dr. Franklin and his agents have given no explanation of their conduct. Perhaps they may, and it is fit they should be heard. But while there is a tory party here strong enough to prevent Dr. Franklin from being called to answer for what is charged against him, I do not see how it can be expected but that the impunity of the past will encourage new and greater crimes against the public."

Izard, too, railed against Franklin on every occasion, and in all companies, "filling the country with jealousies." All the agents which Congress had in Europe, he would say, were corrupt, excepting only the Lees and himself; and the reason why Franklin procured their recall was, simply, because he found it inconvenient to have near him such honest and clear-sighted witnesses of his faithless conduct. Graydon records, that when this irascible Carolinian visited Carlisle (Pennsylvania), in 1783, his abhorrence of Franklin was still an active principle within him. "Izard's manner," reports Graydon, "though blunt, announced the style of the best company ; and, though one of those who deliver their opinions with freedom and decision, he seemed untinctured with asperity upon every subject but one ; but this never failed to produce some excitement, and his tone ever derived some animation from the name of Dr. Franklin. When, therefore, the Doctor's daughter, Mrs. Bache, in speaking of the Carolinians, said that she hated them all, from B. to Izard, the saying, I presume, must be taken inclusively ; since, though I know nothing of the sentiments of Mr. Bee, I am enabled to pronounce those of Mr. Izard to have been anti-Franklinian in the extreme."

And now, I trust, we may leave these angry gentlemen to vent their fury at their leisure. It may fall to the lot of others to trace the effects of this quarrel upon the politics of the country, and to

show whether or not John Adams ever could have been President
of the United States, if in France he had not sided with the Lees
against Franklin. But, for our part, we are now at liberty to turn
to topics more congenial.

CHAPTER XI.

FRANKLIN SOLE PLENIPOTENTIARY.

DR. FRANKLIN was now, to use a well-worn phrase, "master of
the situation"—in Europe the supreme American—director and
controller of his country's affairs on that continent, naval, commercial, financial, political. He and his grandson, aided by their
single clerk, now transacted business in their own rational and
successful way, with as much or as little of red tape as they chose
to employ, and with no restless, malign, or impracticable spirits to
criticize or interfere. But if his life flowed on more tranquilly
than before, it was not because his labors were less arduous, but
because his hands were freer to perform them. Labor and care
are the basis of all noble lives led on this earth ; nor does nature
produce a great, energetic brain without meaning to get from it
all that it was made capable of furnishing. In a universe conducted with such exact economy, it would be surprising, indeed,
if the rarest and most precious of all things, a superior human
mind, were allowed to waste any portion of its intelligent power.
We find, accordingly, that men of real ability are, generally,
heroic workers to the last. They cannot extricate themselves
from the coil of affairs. The majority of us are so prodigiously
stupid and ignorant, that a man of a little true insight cannot be
spared while there is yet remaining a gleam of his original sense.
During the whole of his long and busy career, Franklin never
worked harder, never suffered more anxiety, than in the next three
years after becoming sole plenipotentiary.

The burden of his thoughts was—money. Upon his broad
shoulders rested the credit of the infant republic. As the congressional paper depreciated, and the resources of the country
were exhausted, Congress acquired a fearful facility in drawing

bills upon Dr. Franklin.   When all other resources failed, recourse
was invariably had to him; and it was he, also, who had to find
means to pay the interest on the always growing debt of Congress
in Europe.   He always *had* been able to honor the drafts of Congress, and, therefore, Congress appeared to think he always would.
And besides the interest of the debt and the drafts from America, he
had to pay the salary of every agent employed by Congress in
Europe, and to defray the endless expenses attending the ships engaged in transporting stores.   To meet all these demands, he
received an occasional cargo of tobacco or rice from America ;
but his great resource was the treasury of the King of France.
When the drafts came rushing in upon him, and terror possessed
his soul lest the credit and the cause of his country should be overwhelmed, and all other means had failed, then would he conquer
his all but unconquerable repugnance to asking further aid from so
generous an ally, and apply to the Count de Vergennes.   Never
did he apply in vain.   Never was he obliged to defer the payment
of a draft for an hour.

The very means employed by Congress to relieve him of his
embarrassment only served to increase it.   Early in 1780, Mr. Jay
arrived at Madrid to solicit the alliance and aid of Spain.   So confident was Congress of his obtaining money, that they began forthwith to draw upon him; but as no money could be wrung from
the Spanish court, all these drafts came upon Dr. Franklin for payment.   " The storm of bills," he wrote to Mr. Jay, " which I found
coming upon us both, has terrified and vexed me to such a degree,
that I have been deprived of sleep, and so much indisposed by continual anxiety, as to be rendered almost incapable of writing."   The
Count de Vergennes, as usual, came to his rescue.

In this letter to Mr. Jay, occurs the once famous passage respecting the value to the United States of the Mississippi River:
" Poor as we are, yet, as I know we shall be rich, I would rather
agree with them to buy at a great price the whole of their right
on the Mississippi, than sell a drop of its waters.   A neighbor
might as well ask me to sell my street door."

The last two years of the revolutionary war were little more than
one long agonizing struggle for money.   The very facility with
which aid had been obtained from France, and the evident zeal of
France in the common cause, tended to make the States languid in

enforcing the requisite taxation. For the campaign of 1781, there seemed absolutely no resource but the French treasury. "We must have one of two things," wrote General Washington to Franklin, "peace or money from France;" and to similar purport, wrote Robert Morris and members of Congress. Franklin was at length ordered to lay the state of affairs before the French ministry, and ask for a loan of *twenty-five millions of francs*, as well as for stores requisite for the campaign. Mr. Morris, then at the head of the department of finance, was of opinion that, with the assistance of that amount of capital, he could put the finances of the country upon a sound basis, and maintain the credit of Congress in all probable contingencies. Without such aid, he knew not how to take the first step towards solvency. Franklin obeyed the orders of Congress, and wrote an eloquent memorial to the Count de Vergennes, asking for the loan. As usual with him when he had a great point to carry, he appealed not to one motive only, but to *all* the motives which were likely to come into play in the minds of the persons whom he sought to influence. Thus, in this memorial, after stating the case in all its leading points, he concluded with a kind of personal appeal, and yet mingled with that some weighty sentences addressed to the fears of the French people.

"I am grown old," he wrote; "I feel myself much enfeebled by my late long illness, and it is probable I shall not long have any more concern in these affairs. I therefore take this occasion to express my opinion to your Excellency, that the present conjuncture is critical; that there is some danger lest the Congress should lose its influence over the people, if it is found unable to procure the aids that are wanted; and that the whole system of the new government in America may thereby be shaken; that, if the English are suffered once to recover that country, such an opportunity of effectual separation as the present may not occur again in the course of ages; and that the possession of those fertile and extensive regions, and that vast seacoast, will afford them so broad a basis for future greatness, by the rapid growth of their commerce, and the breed of seamen and soldiers, as will enable them to become the *terror of Europe*, and to exercise with impunity that insolence which is so natural to their nation, and which will increase enormously with the increase of their power."

He had to wait three anxious weeks for an answer, during which arrived Colonel John Laurens, the minister sent expressly by Congress to promote the loan. The arrival of Colonel Laurens gave Dr. Franklin an excuse for pressing his request anew upon the Count de Vergennes; who sent for him, at length. "He assured me," Franklin wrote, " of the king's good will to the United States; remarking, however, that, being on the spot, I must be sensible of the great expense France was actually engaged in, and the difficulty of providing for it, which rendered the lending us twenty-five millions at present impracticable. But that to give the States a signal proof of his friendship, his Majesty had resolved to grant them the sum of six millions, not as a loan, but as a free gift. This sum, the minister informed me, was exclusive of the three millions which he had before obtained for me, to pay the Congress drafts for interest, expected in the current year. He added, that, as it was understood the clothing, with which our army had been heretofore supplied from France, was often of bad quality, and dear, the ministers would themselves take care of the purchase of such articles as should be immediately wanted, and send them over; and it was desired of me to look over the great invoice that had been sent hither last year, and mark out those articles."

It was a timely and a priceless gift. It enabled Dr. Franklin to sustain the credit of America in Europe, and it contributed essentially to the success of the campaign which ended in the surrender of Lord Cornwallis at Yorktown. The sum total of the money obtained from France at the solicitation of Franklin was twenty-six millions of francs; in 1777, two millions; in 1778, three millions; in 1779, one million; in 1780, four millions; in 1781, ten millions; in 1782, six millions. These aids were given at a time when France herself was at war, and while the minister of finance, M. Necker, constantly opposed the grants. Franklin, without knowing it, helped bleed the French monarchy to death.*

---

* In relation to the loans and gifts procured by Dr. Franklin from France, the following passages from the letters of the Count de Vergennes to the French Minister in America, are important and interesting:

December 4th, 1780: "I have too good an opinion of the intelligence and wisdom of the members of Congress, and of all true patriots, to suppose that they will allow themselves to be led astray by the representations of a man [Arthur Lee] whose character they ought to know, or that they will judge of us from any other facts, than the generous proceedings of his Majesty. As to Dr. Franklin, his conduct leaves nothing for Congress to desire. It is as zealous and patriotic, as it is wise and circumspect; and you may affirm with assurance, on all occasions where you think proper, that the method he pursues is much more efficacious than it would be if he

Dismissing this topic of money, we may pass lightly and rapidly over these three busy, honorable years (1779, 1780, 1781), gleaning only the few anecdotes, events, and utterances which ought not to be omitted.

In 1779, with a felicity all his own, Franklin obeyed the resolve of Congress which ordered him to have made in Paris and to present to the Marquis de Lafayette a sword in the name of the United States. The sword, which cost two hundred guineas, being. completed, he sent his grandson with it to Havre, where the young general then was. " Congress directed it," wrote Franklin to Lafayette, " to be ornamented with suitable devices. Some of the principal actions of the war, in which you distinguished yourself by your bravery and conduct, are therefore represented upon it. These, with a few emblematic figures, all admirably well executed, make its principal value. By the help of the exquisite artists France affords, I find it easy to express every thing but the sense we have of your worth and our obligations to you. For this, figures and even words are found insufficient."

were to assume a tone of importunity in multiplying his demands, and above all in supporting them by menaces, to which we should neither give credence nor value, and which would only tend to render him personally disagreeable.

" Furthermore, that Congress may be enabled to judge that they ought to rely much more on our good will than the importunity of Dr. Franklin, you may inform them that, upon the first request of their minister, we have promised to give him a million of livres to put him in a condition to meet the demands made on him from this time to the end of the year ; that we are occupied in providing for him new resources for the year coming; and that, in short, we shall in no case lose sight of the interests of the American cause. I flatter myself that these marks of regard will be understood by the patriots, and will destroy any prepossessions which the ill-advised language of Mr. Izard and Mr. Arthur Lee may have produced."

February 15th, 1781. " Congress rely too much on France for subsidies to maintain their army. They must absolutely refrain from such exorbitant demands. The great expenses of the war render it impossible for France to meet these demands if persisted in. You must speak in a peremptory manner on this subject; and, to give more weight, you must observe, that the last campaign has cost us more than one hundred and fifty millions extraordinary, and what we are now about to furnish will surpass that sum. You may add, that our desire to aid Congress to the full extent of our power has engaged us to grant Dr. Franklin (besides the one million, of which he had need to meet the demands for the last year) four millions more, to enable him to take up the drafts which Congress have drawn on him for the present year. I dare believe that this procedure will be duly estimated in America, and convince Congress that they have no occasion to employ the false policy of Mr. Izard and Mr. Lee to procure succors. If you are questioned respecting our opinion of Dr. Franklin, you may without hesitation say, that we esteem him as much on account of the patriotism as the wisdom of his conduct; and it has been owing in a great part to this cause, and to the confidence we put in the veracity of Dr. Franklin, that we have determined to relieve the pecuniary embarrassments in which he has been placed by Congress. It may be judged from this fact, which is of a personal nature, if that minister's conduct has been injurious to the interests of his country, or if any other would have had the same advantages."— *Writings of Washington*—Sparks, vii., 379.

Lafayette and France were keenly gratified by this well-timed gift; for the reader must know that in 1779 presentation swords were not an article of ordinary manufacture, and "kept constantly on hand." The compliment derived value from its rarity. In his letter of acknowledgment, the marquis spoke warmly of the manner in which Dr. Franklin had performed the duty assigned him, and omitted not to commend the politeness "with which Mr. Temple Franklin was pleased to deliver that inestimable sword."

Franklin united his influence with that of Lafayette in inducing the ministry to adopt the measure, long discussed, of sending French troops to America to co-operate with those under General Washington; and when the troops sailed, he wrote many letters to his friends in Massachusetts and Pennsylvania, introducing the officers, and commending the troops to their friendly attentions. The French soldiers were received with boundless and universal welcome—as Franklin had maintained they would be. Let me also record, that in all their long and wearisome marches through the country, they scrupulously respected the rights and property of the people. Not a barn, not a henroost, not an orchard was robbed by them. The "hereditary enemies," from whom so much was feared, proved to be most generous and considerate allies. The biographer of James Otis mentions that Franklin's old clerical friend, Dr. Cooper, of Boston, to whom he had specially written on behalf of the French officers, was exceedingly delighted with the new comers, "papists as they were," and they not less with him—the courtly, grand old Puritan, versed in languages, sciences, and mankind.

A less agreeable duty devolved upon Dr. Franklin in the summer of 1780. In February of that year, Mr. John Adams reappeared in Paris, having returned from America as commissioner to treat for peace, whenever England should be disposed to end the contest. Having explained the object of his appointment to the Count de Vergennes, he was cordially welcomed by that minister, who presented him to the king, and invited him to communicate news from America, from time to time, as he should gather it from newspapers and correspondence. Unwary minister! to make such a request of a man greedy of work, and with nothing particular to do. Mr. Adams bored the Count with interminable letters, which led, at length, to something worse than boring. First, there arose a mild controversy between them as to whether or not Mr. Adams should announce his mission to the British ministry. By no means, said the French Secretary for Foreign Affairs; the time has not come for it; it would look as if you were too anxious for peace. Mr. Adams assented, though he was evidently not convinced. From time to time he renewed the subject, arguing the case at various lengths, to the scarcely concealed weariness of the Count de Vergennes. In June, Mr. Adams chanced to mention, in one of his news letters to the minister, that Congress had resolved to redeem their depreciated currency at the rate of forty paper dollars for one silver one; a *liberal* rate, considerably above the current value of the notes, and a rate which had the immediate effect of raising their value at least ten per cent.! The minister took alarm at this piece of intelligence, not perceiving that the act was beneficial to every holder of the notes, whether native or foreign; and he besought Mr. Adams to exert his influence to induce Congress to redeem their paper held by Frenchmen at par! In vain did Mr. Adams demonstrate, not the injustice merely, but the impossibility of making such an exception. Mr. Adams talked for hours, and wrote a letter long enough for a pamphlet, on the subject; but such was the universal ignorance at that day of the simplest laws of finance, that this accomplished minister, so well skilled in the routine of his office, could not be made to understand the matter, and took deep offense at Mr. Adams's refusal to recommend the exception desired. He finally sent a copy of his correspondence with Mr. Adams to Dr. Franklin, and desired him, in the king's name, to lay the whole before Congress.

Now, Mr. Adams's long letter, though it was as unanswerable as the forty-seventh proposition of Euclid, was not the letter of a diplomatist. It contained none of the usual expressions of gratitude for the goodness of the king in concluding an equal treaty with an infant state; and in the passages which placed the French merchant upon an equality with all others, there seemed to be a kind of intentional, if not defiant ignoring of such transactions as those of Roderique Hortalez and Co. The argument of the letter was perfect; but in dealing with such persons as Louis XVI. and his ministers, something more is requisite than incontrovertible argument, particularly when it is upon them you depend for sustaining the

credit and cause of your country. In truth, it is only a very wise
man who should be trusted to deal with fools, and, happily, there
was a wise man at hand to rectify the mischief which Mr. Adams
had done.

Franklin had a difficult task before him. He did not desire to
offend or injure Mr. Adams, little claim as that gentleman had upon
his forbearance. Nor could he presume to advise Congress, at
the distance of three thousand miles from the scene of their labors,
upon a point which he could not be supposed to understand better
than they. Least of all could he think of offending the French
court, assailed as he was by a "storm of bills," raining in upon
him from every quarter, and with no sure shelter but the French
treasury. It was evident, moreover, from the language of Count
de Vergennes' letter to him, that he relied upon Dr. Franklin for
aid in soothing the self-complacency of the soft-hearted king,
ruffled by Mr. Adams's robust and uncompromising argument.
"The king," he wrote, "is so firmly persuaded, sir, that your
private opinion respecting the effects of that resolution of Congress,
as far as it concerns strangers, and especially Frenchmen, differs
from that of Mr. Adams, that he is not apprehensive of laying you
under any embarrassment by requesting you to support the representations which his minister is ordered to make to Congress.
* * The king expects that you will lay the whole before Congress; and his Majesty flatters himself that that assembly, inspired
with principles different from those which Mr. Adams has discovered, will convince his Majesty that they know how to prize those
marks of favor which the king has constantly shown to the United
States."

How admirably adroit was Franklin's reply! "I have taken
some pains to understand the subject, and obtain information of
facts from persons recently arrived, having received no letters myself that explain it. I cannot say that I yet perfectly understand
it; but in this I am clear, that if the operation directed by Congress
in their resolution of March the 18th occasions, from the necessity
of the case, some inequality of justice, that inconvenience ought to
fall wholly on the inhabitants of the States, who reap with it the
advantages obtained by the measure; and that the greatest care
should be taken, that foreign merchants, particularly the French,
who are our creditors, do not suffer by it. This I am so confident

the Congress will do, that I do not think any representations of mine
necessary to persuade them to it. I shall not fail, however, to lay
the whole before them; and I beg that the king may be assured,
that their sentiments, and those of the Americans in general, with
regard to the alliance, as far as I have been able to learn them, not
only from private letters, but from authentic public facts, differ
widely from those that seem to be expressed by Mr. Adams in his
letter to your Excellency, and are filled with the strongest impressions of the friendship of France, of the generous manner in which
his Majesty was pleased to enter into an equal treaty with us, and
of the great obligations our country is under for the important aids
he has since afforded us."

The packet of correspondence between the Count and Mr. Adams
was, accordingly, directed to the Foreign Committee, and placed
on board a ship bound for America. The ship, as was not uncommon in those days, was detained in port two or three months longer
than was expected; which gave time for Mr. Adams to offend the
French court still more seriously.

It happened thus : Mr. Adams wrote to the Count, reminding
him of the vast importance of gaining a naval superiority in American waters. The minister replied by communicating to Mr.
Adams, what was still a secret, that a powerful fleet, under the
Count de Rochambeau, had actually sailed for that purpose. Mr.
Adams replied, that " scarcely any news he ever heard gave him
more satisfaction," and he felt sure the result would prove the wisdom of the scheme. But, a few days after, Mr. Adams wrote to
the minister another letter on the same subject, curiously at variance with these joyful sentiments. He said that he had been thinking over an expression in the Count de Vergennes' last letter, and
had come to the conclusion that he ought not to let it pass without
comment. That expression was, that the king had sent out this
fleet " without having been solicited by the Congress." Mr.
Adams (for what purpose I cannot imagine) proceeded to refute
this statement by recounting the several occasions in which Congress, through their envoys, had solicited naval assistance. Having disposed of this subject, he proceeded to show that the fleet of
the Count de Rochambeau was insufficient, and, unless greatly
strengthened, would fail to secure important objects. " I may be
mistaken," said Mr. Malaprop, " but it would answer no good pur-

pose to deceive myself, and I certainly will not disguise my sentiments from your Excellency."

The minister was so violently disgusted with this ill-timed and
unnecessary letter, that he refused to hold further correspondence
with Mr. Adams. "When," wrote M. de Vergennes, "I took upon
myself to give you a mark of confidence by informing you of the
destination of Messrs. de Ternay and Rochambeau, I did not expect
the animadversion which you have thought it your duty to make on
a passage of my letter. To avoid any further discussion of that
sort, I think it my duty to inform you, that Mr. Franklin being the
sole person who has letters of credence to the king from the United
States, it is with him only that I ought and can treat of matters
which concern them, and particularly of that which is the subject
of your observations. Besides, sir, I ought to observe to you that
the passage of my letter, which you have thought it your duty to
consider more particularly, * * * had nothing further in view
than to convince you, that the king did not stand in need of your
solicitations to induce him to interest himself in the affairs of the
United States."

This correspondence, also, the offended minister sent to Dr.
Franklin, and requested him to transmit it to Congress; "that
they may judge whether Mr. Adams is endowed with that concili-
ating spirit which is necessary for the important and delicate business with which he is entrusted."

Dr. Franklin complied with this request, and, in his next letter
to the President of Congress, treated the affair in the terms following:

"Mr. Adams has given offense to the court here, by some sentiments and expressions contained in several of his letters written to
the Count de Vergennes. I mention this with reluctance, though
perhaps it would have been my duty to acquaint you with such a
circumstance, even were it not required of me by the minister
himself. He has sent me copies of the correspondence, desiring I would communicate them to Congress; and I send them
herewith. Mr. Adams did not show me his letters before he sent
them. I have, in a former letter to Mr. Lovell, mentioned some
of the inconveniences that attend the having more than one minister at the same court; one of which inconveniences is, that they do
not always hold the same language, and that the impressions made

by one, and intended for the service of his constituents, may be effaced by the discourse of the other. It is true that Mr. Adams's proper business is elsewhere; but, the time not being come for that business, and having nothing else here wherewith to employ himself, he seems to have endeavored to supply what he may suppose my negotiations defective in. He thinks, as he tells me himself, that America has been too free in expressions of gratitude to France; for that she is more obliged to us than we to her; and that we should show spirit in our applications. I apprehend that he mistakes his ground, and that this court is to be treated with decency and delicacy. The king, a young and virtuous prince, has, I am persuaded, a pleasure in reflecting on the generous benevolence of the action in assisting an oppressed people, and proposes it as a part of the glory of his reign. I think it right to increase this pleasure by our thankful acknowledgments, and that such an expression of gratitude is not only our duty, but our interest. A different conduct seems to me what is not only improper and unbecoming, but what may be hurtful to us. Mr. Adams, on the other hand, who, at the same time, means our welfare and interest as much as I, or any man, can do, seems to think a little apparent stoutness, and a greater air of independence and boldness in our demands, will procure us more ample assistance. It is for Congress to judge and regulate their affairs accordingly.

"M. de Vergennes, who appears much offended, told me, yesterday, that he would enter into no further discussions with Mr. Adams, nor answer any more of his letters. He is gone to Holland to try, as he told me, whether something might not be done to render us less dependent on France. He says, the ideas of this court and those of the people in America are so totally different, that it is impossible for any minister to please both. He ought to know America better than I do, having been there lately, and he may choose to do what he thinks will best please the people of America. But, when I consider the expressions of Congress in many of their public acts, and particularly in their letter to the Chevalier de la Luzerne, of the 24th of May last, I cannot but imagine that he mistakes the sentiments of a few for a general opinion. It is my intention, while I stay here, to procure what advantages I can for our country, by endeavoring to please this court; and I wish I could prevent any thing being said by any of our countrymen here, that may have a contrary effect, and increase an opinion lately showing itself in Paris, that we seek a difference, and with a view of reconciling ourselves to England. Some of them have of late been very indiscreet in their conversations."

Before the ship sailed which conveyed this dispatch and the offensive letters, Dr. Franklin wrote to Mr. Adams, informing him of what had occurred, and suggesting that he should do something to remove the ill impression created. " I was myself sorry to see those passages," wrote Franklin. "If they were the effects of inadvertence, and you do not, on reflection, approve of them, perhaps you may think it proper to write something to efface the impressions made by them. I do not presume to advise you, but mention it only for your consideration." Mr. Adams merely replied that he had himself transmitted the correspondence to Congress, leaving Franklin to infer that he had taken his course deliberately, and meant to abide by it.

When the letters reached America they created considerable apprehension, and a motion was made in Congress to censure Mr. Adams for offending the French court. The motion was lost, and resolutions were passed which justly extolled the patriotism of Mr. Adams, and yet conveyed to him a gentle intimation that the advice of the Count de Vergennes must not be lightly disregarded. His able defense of the action of the Government in redeeming their paper at the rate of forty for one was rewarded with the thanks of Congress.

So no harm befell Mr. Adams, in consequence of his indiscretion. And what, I would ask the candid reader, could have been more scrupulously right and proper than the conduct of Dr. Franklin in this affair? Could he have done less? Could he have done what he had to do with a more delicate regard for *all* the interests intrusted to his care? Mr. Adams, however, when he read the letter of Franklin, quoted above, was offended by it past forgiveness. Thirty-one years after these events, we find him still denouncing it in the Boston newspapers, at great length and with much plausibility. I regret, also, to see that the grandson of Mr. Adams revives the ancient feud, and founds upon Dr. Franklin's conduct in this matter the most offensive charge that one human being can bring against another:—namely, that Franklin, though wanting in the courage to utter a falsehood, had the meanness to profit by one which it was his duty to expose. The comments of Mr. Charles Francis Adams may be profitably studied by one who is investigating the law of hereditary transmission. " The errors of Franklin's theory of life," remarks this gentleman, " may be detected almost anywhere in his familiar compositions. They sprang from a defective early education, which made his morality superficial even to laxness, and undermined his religious faith. His system resolves itself into the ancient and specious dogma of *Honesty the best policy.* That nice sense which revolts at wrong for its own sake, and that generosity of spirit which shrinks from participation in the advantages of indirection, however naturally obtained, were not his. If they had been, he would scarcely have consented to become the instrument to transmit the stolen letters of Hutchinson and others to Massachusetts, neither could he have been tempted to write the confession of Polly Baker, still less to betray the levity of such a reason as he gave for disseminating its unworthy sophistry in print."* This is highly absurd. John Adams's own grandson speaks in these words; though I hardly think the indomitable old patriot could have been so insensible to a joke as to talk in that priggish way of Polly Baker.

In these differences at Paris we discern the origin of the two American parties, which contended for the mastery from 1780 to the general peace of 1815 : the French or democratic party, and the English or federal party. John Adams was a leader of the one ; Benjamin Franklin was the founder of the other. Yes ; of that great party, right upon almost every leading issue that ever divided the country, until it struck upon the rock of slavery and went to pieces, Franklin was most assuredly the father.

In these years, Dr. Franklin exerted his influence frequently in favor of the principle, then new, that free ships should make free goods. In connection with this subject, he took every opportunity of calling attention to a favorite opinion of his own, that privateering was not legitimate warfare, and ought to be abolished. " I wish," he wrote to Robert Morris, " the powers would ordain, that unarmed trading ships, as well as fishermen and farmers, should be respected, as working for the common benefit of mankind, and never be interrupted in their operations, even by national enemies ; but let those only fight with one another whose trade it is, and who are

* Life and Works of John Adams, i., 319.

armed and paid for the purpose." I fear that this amiable idea has too much of the spirit of "rose water" in it to be wise or practicable. Privateering seems to be the natural and just resource of a nation of small naval resources when warring against a great naval power. At this moment, England's commerce is a kind of bond for the good behavior of her fleet. Abolish privateering, give England a great minister, and all commercial nations except one exist only because she permits them to exist.

Mr. Adams has a word to say upon Dr. Franklin's proposal to exempt farmers and mariners from molestation in time of war. In an explosion of disgust at the writings of Plato, he declares that he learned from that philosopher just two things. One was, that this idea for which his colleague obtained so much credit, was Plato's, not Franklin's. The other was, that sneezing is a cure for hiccough. "Accordingly," he adds, "I have cured myself and all my friends of that provoking disorder, for thirty years, with a pinch of snuff."*

A strange commission was given to Franklin in 1780. Congress, moved by the barbarities committed by British troops in America, and desiring to instill into the minds of the young a salutary horror of the perpetrators, requested Franklin to "make a school book of them." He was to have, as he wrote to his English friend, Hart-ley, "thirty-five prints designed here by good artists, and engraved, each expressing one or more of the different horrid facts, to be in-serted in the book, in order to impress the minds of children and posterity with a deep sense of your bloody and insatiable malice and wickedness." The work was never executed. "Every kind-ness," he wrote to the same friend, "done by an Englishman to an American prisoner, makes me resolve not to proceed in the work, hoping a reconciliation may yet take place. But every fresh instance of your devilism weakens that resolution, and makes me abominate the thought of a reunion with such a people;" i. e., a reunion of hearts, not of political ties.

Franklin's curious suggestion with regard to the copper coin of the United States, belongs to these years: "Instead of repeating continually, upon every half-penny the dull story that everybody knows (and what it would have been no loss to mankind if nobody had ever known), that George the Third is King of Great Britain,

* Works of John Adams, x., 103.

Chadron State College Library

Chadron, Nebraska

France, and Ireland, &c., &c., to put on one side some important proverb of Solomon, some pious moral, prudential or economical precept, the frequent inculcation of which, by seeing it every time one receives a piece of money, might make an impression upon the mind, especially of young persons, and tend to regulate the con-duct; such as, on some, *The fear of the Lord is the beginning of wisdom ;* on others, *Honesty is the best policy ;* on others, *He that by the plow would thrive, himself must either hold or drive.*" The other side of the coin, he says, it was once proposed to fill " with good designs, drawn and engraved by the best artists in France, of all the different species of barbarity with which the English have carried on the war in America, expressing every abominable circumstance of their cruelty and inhumanity that figures can express, to make an impression on the minds of posterity as strong and durable as that on the copper." For the sake of our zealous friends, the coin-collectors, it is to be regretted that a few of these coppers were not struck.

A beautiful and noble letter was that which Dr. Franklin wrote to General Washington in the spring of 1780; it was a tribute of veneration worthy of both. The acquaintance of these two con-trolling men of the revolution, which dated back to the days of General Braddock, had been, of late, exalted into that grand kind of friendship which one great monarch may be supposed to en-tertain for another. It found fitting expression in this fine compo-sition :

" I have received but lately the letter your Excellency did me the honor of writing to me, in recommendation of the Marquis de Lafayette. His modesty detained it long in his own hands. We became acquainted, however, from the time of his arrival at Paris ; and his zeal for the honor of our country, his activity in our affairs here, and his firm attachment to our cause, and to you, impressed me with the same regard and esteem for him that your Excellen-cy's letter would have done, had it been immediately delivered to me.

" Should peace arrive after another campaign or two, and afford us a little leisure, I should be happy to see your Excellency in Eu-rope, and to accompany you, if my age and strength would permit, in visiting some of its ancient and most famous kingdoms. You would, on this side of the sea, enjoy the great reputation you have acquired, pure and free from those little shades that the jealousy and envy of a man's countrymen and contemporaries are ever endeavoring to cast over living merit. Here you would know, and enjoy, what posterity will say of Washington. For a thousand leagues have nearly the same effect with a thousand years. The feeble voice of those groveling passions cannot extend so far either in time or distance. At present I enjoy that pleasure for you; as I frequently hear the old generals of this martial country, who study the maps of America, and mark upon them all your operations, speak with sincere approbation and great applause of your conduct; and join in giving you the character of one of the greatest captains of the age.

"I must soon quit this scene, but you may live to see our country flourish, as it will amazingly and rapidly after the war is over; like a field of young Indian corn, which long fair weather and sunshine had enfeebled and discolored, and which in that weak state, by a thunder gust of violent wind, hail, and rain, seemed to be threatened with absolute destruction; yet the storm being past, it recovers fresh verdure, shoots up with double vigor, and delights the eye, not of its owner only, but of every observing traveler."

I question if General Washington ever received a letter which gave him more delight than this; for, it was not merely eloquent, and touching as a composition, but was well adapted to the character of the person to whom it was addressed. It appears plainly in Washington's letters, that he cared much to know what others thought of him.

Few events of these times made so much noise in Europe as the capture, at sea, of Mr. Henry Laurens, formerly President of Congress, now sent abroad to negotiate a treaty with Holland. The capture occurred in September, 1780, off Newfoundland, a few days after Mr. Laurens had sailed. When, after a chase of five hours, it became certain that the ship could not escape, his papers, loaded with shot, were thrown into the sea. Unfortunately, the trunk which contained them did not immediately sink, and a dexterous British sailor caught it in the nick of time, and it was taken on board the man-of-war. What a batch of treason then fell into British hands! Proof positive that Holland was almost, if not altogether, persuaded to become the ally of the United States. Holland, wherein British influence, wielded by the arrogant and domineering Sir Joseph Yorke, had been for so many years predominant! The principal papers were: a copy of the proposed treaty, drawn up "agreeably to the orders and instructions of the Counselor and Pensionary of the city of Amsterdam;" and a mass of letters to, from, and concerning various magnates of Holland, proving that they abhorred the domination of Britain, and desired nothing so much as to join the powers at war with her. The consequences of the capture were, that England declared war against Holland, and placed Mr. Laurens in the Tower of London, where he remained for fifteen months.

A great number of Dr. Franklin's letters of this period relate to Mr. Laurens's imprisonment. Hearing that his health suffered from confinement, Franklin wrote to an old friend, Sir Grey Cooper, asking him to use his influence to obtain the release of the prisoner on parole. "The fortune of war," wrote Franklin, "which is daily changing, may possibly put it in my power to do the like good office for some friend of yours, which I shall perform with much pleasure, not only for the sake of humanity, but in respect to the ashes of our former friendship." In reply, Sir Grey Cooper enclosed a letter from the lieutenant-governor of the Tower, stating that Mr. Laurens was extremely well and comfortable, and felt it an honor to be lodged in so illustrious a prison. Mr. Laurens, however, used very different language, when, a year later, he wrote his famous pencil note to Mr. Burke. In that note he said, that he had "in many respects, particularly by being deprived (with very little exception) of the visits and consolations of his children, and other relations and friends, suffered under a degree of rigor, almost, if not altogether, unexampled in modern British history. That, from long confinement and the want of proper exercise, and other obvious causes, his bodily health is greatly impaired, and that he is now in a languishing state." Dr. Franklin continued his good offices to the prisoner, kept his daughters in America advised of his condition, and placed money at his disposal in London.

Mr. Burke exerted himself to effect the exchange, offered by Congress, of General Burgoyne for Mr. Laurens. In August, 1781, on hearing that Congress was about to demand the return of Burgoyne, he had the boldness to write to Dr. Franklin, entreating his good offices to prevent a measure so inconvenient to his friend. General Burgoyne, who, after his return from America, had openly joined the Opposition, and proclaimed his belief that America

could not be subdued, was punished for his audacity by the refusal
of the proffered exchange, and had, in consequence, resigned all
his valuable military appointments. If, in addition to this indignity, and the loss of his emoluments, he was to suffer captivity in
America, his case, Mr. Burke thought, would be hard beyond precedent ; and hence his application to Dr. Franklin.

"I feel," began Mr. Burke, "as an honest man and as a good citizen ought to feel, the calamities of the present unhappy war. The
only part, however, of those calamities which personally affects
myself is, that I have been obliged to discontinue my intercourse
with you; but that one misfortune I must consider equivalent to
many. I may, indeed, with great truth, assure you that your
friendship has always been an object of my ambition; and that, if
a high and very sincere esteem for your talents and virtues could
give me a title to it, I am not wholly unworthy of that honor. I
flatter myself that your belief in the reality of these sentiments,
will excuse the liberty I take, of laying before you a matter in
which I have no small concern." He then stated the case of
General Burgoyne, and besought the aid of Franklin in procuring
for him the indulgence of Congress. "If," concluded Mr.
Burke, "I were not fully persuaded of your liberal and manly way
of thinking, I should not presume, in the hostile situation in which
I stand, to make an application to you. But in this piece of experimental philosophy, I run no risk of offending you. I apply
not to the embassador of America, but to Dr. Franklin, the philosopher—the friend, and the lover, of his species."

Franklin replied: "Since the foolish part of mankind will make
wars from time to time with each other, not having sense enough
otherwise to settle their differences, it certainly becomes the wiser
part, who cannot prevent those wars, to alleviate as much as possible the calamities attending them. Mr. Burke always stood high
in my esteem; but his affectionate concern for his friend renders
him still more amiable, and makes the honor he does me of admitting me of the number still more precious. I do not think the
Congress have any wish to persecute General Burgoyne. I never
heard, till I received your letter, that they had recalled him; if
they have made such a resolution, it must be, I suppose, a con-
ditional one, to take place in case their offer of exchanging him
for Mr. Laurens should not be accepted; a resolution intended

merely to enforce that offer.   I have just received an authentic
copy of the resolve containing that offer, and authorizing me to
make it.   As I have no communication with your ministers, I send
it inclosed to you.   If you can find any means of negotiating this
business, I am sure the restoring another worthy man to his family
and friends will be an addition to your pleasure."

Mr. Burke did not succeed in the negotiation.   To his impru-
dence in corresponding with Dr. Franklin, he added the defiance
of reading Franklin's letter to the House of Commons; an act
which brought upon him a storm of execration from the ministerial benches.   It was as though Fernando Wood should read in
the House of Representatives a friendly letter which he had received from Mr. Slidell.   " Good God !" exclaimed Lord Newhaven, " do not my senses deceive me !   can a member of this assembly, not only avow his correspondence with a rebel, but dare to
read it to us !"   Lord North said: " Far from feeling either the
contrition or the repentance for the acts of his past administration,
which gentlemen opposite asserted would become him, he experienced, on the contrary, the most perfect calm, arising from the
consciousness of not having done any wrong.   If, indeed," continued he, " in any of my speeches in this house, or in any which I
have made out of doors, or in any part of my conduct, I had held
out hopes to the Americans that they possessed friends in this
country, professing to be their advocates, and who embraced every
occasion to advance their interests, in preference to those of their
native country—then, I confess, I should think I had acted in a
manner that called for deep contrition and sincere repentance :
nay, even for humiliation, for self-abasement, and for shame."*

It is a strange condition of affairs when a government contents
itself with an indirect, verbal rebuke of such an act as that of Mr.
Burke.   The Speaker of the House of Commons even called to
order Lord Newhaven for the vehemence of his denunciation.   The
truth was, that Mr. Burke expressed the real sense of every uncor-
rupt man in England who could be said to have any sense.   The
state of England was such, that even Horace Walpole's letters, usually so placid and so trivial, became earnest and eloquent.   At his
superb retreat upon Strawberry Hill, thus wrote the elegant Eng-

* " Wraxall's Memoirs."

lish Horace, in the spring of one of these distracting years: "I have been here ever since Tuesday, enjoying my tranquillity, as much as an honest man can do who sees his country ruined. It is just such a period as makes philosophy wisdom. There are great moments when every man is called on to exert himself—but when folly, infatuation, delusion, incapacity, and profligacy fling a nation away, and it concurs itself, and applauds its destroyers, a man who has lent no hand to the mischief, and can neither prevent nor remedy the mass of evils, is fully justified in sitting aloof, and beholding the tempest rage, with silent scorn and indignant compassion. Nay, I have, I own, some comfortable reflections. I rejoice that there is still a great continent of Englishmen who will remain free and independent, and who laugh at the impotent majorities of a prostitute parliament."

In such a strain as this must every sane inhabitant of the Southern States have written, during these years of mad rebellion, if he had had the temerity to trust his thoughts to paper. Mr. Burke would not have dared, would not have wished, to correspond, on friendly terms, with an "enemy of his country," if that enemy had not been more truly his country's friend than the king and the ministers who were misleading it. England was, in truth, at war with that which made England England; as our slave rebels conspired to destroy that which makes America America. George III. was the true rebel.

Mr. Laurens was not released from the Tower until General Washington and his French associates had provided Congress with another British General for exchange—Lord Cornwallis.

I believe I need not dwell further upon this part of the public life of Dr. Franklin. It was, indeed, his desire that his public life should end with the year 1781; but Congress decreed otherwise. Early in the spring of that year he asked to be relieved of his office, in terms so full of dignity and pathos that, perhaps, his biography may justly lay claim to the passage:

"I must now," said he, after disposing of public topics, " beg leave to say something relating to myself; a subject with which I have not often troubled the Congress. I have passed my seventy-fifth year, and I find that the long and severe fit of the gout which I had the last winter, has shaken me exceedingly, and I am yet far from having recovered the bodily strength I before enjoyed. I do not know that my mental faculties are impaired ; perhaps I shall be the last to discover that ; but I am sensible of great diminution in my activity, a quality I think particularly necessary in your minister for this court. I am afraid, therefore, that your affairs may some time or other suffer by my deficiency. I find, also, that the business is too heavy for me, and too confining. The constant attendance at home, which is necessary for receiving and accepting your bills of exchange (a matter foreign to my ministerial functions), to answer letters, and perform other parts of my employment, prevents my taking the air and exercise which my annual journeys formerly used to afford me, and which contributed much to the preservation of my health. There are many other little personal attentions which the infirmities of age render necessary to an old man's comfort, even in some degree to the continuance of his existence, and with which business often interferes.

" I have been engaged in public affairs, and enjoyed public confidence, in some shape or other, during the long term of fifty years, and honor sufficient to satisfy any reasonable ambition ; and I have no other left but that of repose, which I hope the Congress will grant me, by sending some person to supply my place. At the same time, I beg they may be assured, that it is not any the least doubt of their success in the glorious cause, nor any disgust received in their service, that induces me to decline it, but purely and simply the reasons above mentioned. And, as I cannot at present undergo the fatigues of a sea voyage (the last having been almost too much for me), and would not again expose myself to the hazard of capture and imprisonment in this time of war, I purpose to remain here at least till the peace ; perhaps it may be for the remainder of my life ; and, if any knowledge or experience I have acquired here may be thought of use to my successor, I shall freely communicate it, and assist him with any influence I may be supposed to have, or counsel that may be desired of me.

" I have one request more to make, which, if I have served the Congress to their satisfaction, I hope they will not refuse me ; it is, that they will be pleased to take under their protection my grandson, William Temple Franklin. I have educated him from his infancy, and I brought him over with an intention of placing him where he might be qualified for the profession of the law ;

but the constant occasion I had for his services as a private secretary during the time of the Commissioners, and more extensively since their departure, has induced me to keep him always with me; and indeed, being continually disappointed of the secretary Congress had at different times intended me, it would have been impossible for me, without this young gentleman's assistance, to have gone through the business incumbent on me. He has therefore lost so much of the time necessary for law studies, that I think it rather advisable for him to continue, if it may be, in the line of public foreign affairs; for which he seems qualified by a sagacity and judgment above his years, and great diligence and activity, exact probity, a genteel address, a facility in speaking well the French tongue, and all the knowledge of business to be obtained by a four years' constant employment in the secretary's office, where he may be said to have served a kind of apprenticeship.

" After all the allowance I am capable of making for the partiality of a parent to his offspring, I cannot but think he may in time make a very able foreign minister for Congress, in whose service his fidelity may be relied on. But I do not at present propose him as such, for though he is now of age, a few years more of experience will not be amiss. In the mean time, if they should think fit to employ him as a secretary to their minister at any European court, I am persuaded they will have reason to be satisfied with his conduct, and I shall be thankful for his appointment, as a favor to me."

Such was Franklin's letter of resignation, in the seventy-fifth year of his age. Mr. Jay and Col. John Laurens were aware of his intention to resign, and both of them besought Congress not to dispense with the services of a man whose mere presence in Europe was a tower of strength to the American cause. " I confess," wrote Mr. Jay, " it would mortify my pride as an American, if his constituents should be the only people to whom his character is known, that should deny his merit and services the testimony given them by other nations. Justice demands of me to assure you, that his reputation and respectability are acknowledged and have weight here, and that I have received from him all that uniform attention and aid, which was due to the importance of the affairs committed to me." Col. Laurens, too, urged the appointment of a competent secretary of legation upon whom the burden of business might devolve, and used his influence to secure the appointment of Franklin's grandson. He advised Dr. Franklin to send the young gentleman to America with the last remittance of money from the French treasury, in order to remove, by a personal introduction to Congress, the prejudices which calumny and his father's defection had excited against him. No, replied Franklin; "I have too much occasion for his assistance, and cannot spare him to make the voyage. He must take his chance, and I hope he will in time obtain, as well as merit, the consideration of our government."

Congress did more than decline to accept Dr. Franklin's resignation; they conferred upon him a new appointment, that of joint commissioner with Mr. Adams and Mr. Jay, to negotiate for peace. "I must therefore buckle again to business," he wrote to Mr. Carmichael, "and thank God that my health and spirits are of late improved. I fancy it may have been a double mortification to those enemies you have mentioned to me, that I should ask as a favor what they hoped to vex me by taking from me; and that I should nevertheless be continued. But this sort of considerations should never influence our conduct. We ought always to do what appears best to be done, without much regarding what others may think of it. I call this continuance an honor, and I really esteem it to be a greater than my first appointment, when I consider that all the interest of my enemies, united with my own request, were not sufficient to prevent it."

To another friend, who had congratulated him upon these new honors, and styled him the keystone of the American arch, he wrote in a more amusing strain. The compliment, he said, was very pretty, and tended to make him content with his situation. "But," he humorously added, "I suppose you have heard our story of the *harrow ;* if not, here it is. A farmer, in our country, sent two of his servants to borrow one of a neighbor, ordering them to bring it between them on their shoulders. When they came to look at it, one of them, who had much wit and cunning, said : 'What could our master mean by sending only two men to bring this harrow ? No two men upon earth are strong enough to carry it.' 'Poh !' said the other, who was vain of his strength, 'what do you talk of two men ? One man may carry it. Help it upon my shoulders, and see.' As he proceeded with it, the wag kept exclaiming, 'Zounds, how strong you are ! I could not have thought it. Why, you are a Samson! There is not such another man in America. What amazing strength God has given you! But you will kill yourself! Pray, put it down and rest a little, or let me bear a part of the weight.' 'No, no,' said he, being more encouraged by the compliments, than oppressed by the burden ; 'you shall see I can carry it quite home.' And so he did. In this particular I am afraid my part of the imitation will fall short of the original."

<hr>

CHAPTER XII.

HIS PRIVATE LIFE IN FRANCE.

BENJAMIN FRANKLIN was the American who discovered France. It has only been since his day, that "all good Americans when they die, go to Paris."* To that British contempt for Frenchmen, which appears in Hudibras, Hogarth, Smollett, and, indeed, in all the popular English literature and art of that age, the colonists of New England added an aversion to them as Catholics, and a hatred of them as enemies in three bloody wars. Franklin learned to like the French, and taught his countrymen to like them. He imbibed, also, an esteem for the French character, and a respect for the French intellect. He admired their universal politeness, and found them "a most amiable people to live with." "They have some frivolities," he once wrote to Josiah Quincy, "but they are harmless. To dress their heads so that a hat cannot be put on them, and then wear their hats under their arms, and to fill their noses with tobacco, may be called follies, perhaps, but they are not vices. They are only the effects of the tyranny of custom. In short, there is nothing wanting in the character of a Frenchman, that belongs to that of an agreeable and worthy man. There are only some trifles surplus, or which might be spared.'

For the intellectual women of Paris, he had a particular esteem. In new and in poor countries, women are necessarily immersed in household cares; and, consequently, that most enchanting of all be-

* "Autocrat of the Breakfast Table." By Oliver Wendell Holmes.

ings, a woman of sense, spirit, and culture, capable of associating on equal terms with intellectual men, is seldom produced. In England, moreover, where Franklin had lived so many years, society is dislocated and vulgarized by that ponderous incubus of an aristocracy, which debauches the minds of women, and infects them with a mean ambition for what is called "social distinction." In Paris, for the first time, Franklin found a circle of ladies who could well discharge the duties of their sphere, and yet have an abundant reserve of vivacity and leisure for society, and who paid to his genius that homage which English ladies are said to bestow, with *perfect* sincerity, upon rank alone. He is reported to have said, that the purest and most useful friend a man could have was a Frenchwoman of a certain age, who had no designs upon his person : "they are so ready," he would add, "to do you service, and from their knowledge of the world, know so well how to serve you wisely."*

In Paris, what men he found! what an interest in social problems! what a stir in the domain of the intellect! In his list of friends he could number nearly every person of literary or scientific distinction in Paris : the brothers Turgot, Raynal, Morellet, Rochefoucault, Buffon, D'Alembert, Condorcet, Cabanis, Le Roy, Mabley, Mirabeau, D'Holback, Marmontel, Necker, Malesherbes, Watelet, Madame de Genlis, Madame Denis, Madame Helvetius, Madame Brillon, and La Veillard, were all his friends or acquaintances.

We must observe, however, that he saw little of France except the best of her—her most enlightened men, her most pleasing women, her most pleasant places. Confined at home by his duties, he did not, like his successor, Mr. Jefferson, wander forth into the provinces, and stroll into the peasant's hovels, and furtively peep into the boiling pot, and feel the hardness of the crust and the bed, his heart swelling with mingled rage and pity at the hideous spectacle of hopeless want in the midst of wasted plenty. Consequently, in all Franklin's writings, there is not a passage from which we can infer that he understood the condition of France, or the peril of the monarchy; which to less sagacious observers had for many years been apparent. He may, nevertheless, have comprehended the danger in all its imminence, and not recorded the fact; for it

* Seward's Anecdotes, iv., 223.

was not his cue to descant upon any thing he may have seen amiss in France, and his talent for silence was as remarkable as his felicity of utterance. We are, also, to consider, that during the first few years of the reign of Louis XVI., affairs in France wore a deceptive show of improvement and prosperity, which had vanished utterly when Mr. Jefferson saw the country in 1784. Wars are not paid for in war time ; when the war is done, then the bill comes in. Franklin, then, felt at home in France. He lived a full, a joyous life there, apart from the round of his official duties. It is of that private life that we are now to speak, before entering upon the events which led to the general peace, and Franklin's triumphant return to his native land. The material here is as abundant as it is interesting ; I know not how to reduce the chaotic mass to order, or to present it in reasonable compass.

Let us first take note that Dr. Franklin was still a natural philosopher. He continued to exchange scientific information and conjecture with his old friends of the Royal Society, and with the searchers after truth in America and on the continent of Europe. He appears to have been the first to observe that the atmosphere of Europe is damper than that of America ; which he was led to discover from the uniform shrinking in America of the wooden instrument-cases made in Europe. It was chiefly, however, as an encourager of other men's experiments and observations that his writings of this period reveal him. He regretted the shortness of life, for the limitations it imposed upon the advance of science. He would often say how much he should like to revisit the earth a hundred years after his death, in order to see what improvements and discoveries had been made in his absence. To Priestley he wrote in 1780 : " The rapid progress *true* science now makes, occasions my regretting sometimes that I was born so soon : it is impossible to imagine the hight to which may be carried, in a thousand years, the power of man over matter ; we may perhaps learn to deprive large masses of their gravity, and give them absolute levity for the sake of easy transport. Agriculture may diminish its labor and double its produce; all diseases may by sure means be prevented or cured (not excepting even that of old age), and our lives lengthened at pleasure, even beyond the antediluvian standard. Oh ! that moral science were in as fair a way of improvement ; that men would cease to be wolves

to one another; and that human beings would at length learn what
they now improperly call humanity!"

This was a favorite train of thought with him. He enlarges upon
the theme, in his most delightful manner, in another letter to Dr.
Priestley : "I should rejoice much if I could once more recover the
leisure to search with you into the works of nature ; I mean the *in-
animate*, not the *animate* or moral part of them; the more I discovered of the former, the more I admired them; the more I know
of the latter, the more I am disgusted with them. Men I find to be
a sort of beings very badly constructed, as they are generally more
easily provoked than reconciled, more disposed to do mischief to
each other than to make reparation, much more easily deceived than
undeceived, and having more pride and even pleasure in killing
than in begetting one another; for without a blush they assemble
in great armies at noonday to destroy, and when they have killed
as many as they can, they exaggerate the number to augment the
fancied glory; but they creep into corners, or cover themselves
with the darkness of night, when they mean to beget, as being
ashamed of a virtuous action. A virtuous action it would be, and
a vicious one the killing of them, if the species were really worth
producing or preserving; but of this I begin to doubt.

"I know you have no such doubts, because, in your zeal for their
welfare, you are taking a great deal of pains to save their souls.
Perhaps as you grow older, you may look upon this as a hopeless
project, or an idle amusement, repent of having murdered in me-
phitic air so many honest, harmless mice, and wish, that to prevent
mischief, you had used boys and girls instead of them. In what
light we are viewed by superior beings, may be gathered from a
piece of late West India news, which possibly has not yet reached
you. A young angel of distinction being sent down to this world
on some business, for the first time, had an old courier-spirit assigned him as a guide. They arrived over the seas of Martinico,
in the middle of the long day of obstinate fight between the fleets
of Rodney and De Grasse. When, through the clouds of smoke,
he saw the fire of the guns, the decks covered with mangled limbs,
and bodies dead or dying; the ships sinking, burning, or blown
into the air; and the quantity of pain, misery, and destruction, the
crews yet alive were thus with so much eagerness dealing round to
one another; he turned angrily to his guide, and said, 'You blun-

dering blockhead, you are ignorant of your business; you undertook to conduct me to the earth, and you have brought me into hell!' 'No, sir,' said the guide, 'I have made no mistake; this is really the earth, and these are men. Devils never treat one another in this cruel manner; they have more sense, and more of what men (vainly) call humanity.'

"But to be serious, my dear old friend, I love you as much as ever, and I love all the honest souls that meet at the London Coffee-house. I only wonder how it happened that they and my other friends in England came to be such good creatures in the midst of so perverse a generation. I long to see them and you once more, and I labor for peace with more earnestness, that I may again be happy in your sweet society."

What gayety and spirit in a man of seventy-six!

Once in Paris he figured as a philosopher in public; it was when, in the Spring of 1779, he read, or caused to be read, before the Royal Academy of Sciences, a paper upon the Aurora Borealis. The popularity of the envoy, and of the American, gave eclat to this occasion, and the paper gained extraordinary applause, not in the learned circles merely, but at court, and in the world of the drawing-room.

To electricity, Dr. Franklin referred the splendid phenomena of the Aurora Borealis. His theory (or conjecture) may be summed up in these five sentences of his essay :

1. "Water, though naturally a good conductor, will not conduct well when frozen into ice by a common degree of cold; not at all where the cold is extreme. 2. Snow falling upon frozen ground has been found to retain its electricity; and to communicate it to an isolated body, when, after falling, it has been driven about by the wind. 3. The humidity contained in all the equatorial clouds that reach the polar regions, must there be condensed and fall in snow. 4. The great cake of ice that eternally covers those regions may be too hard frozen to permit the electricity, descending with that snow, to enter the earth. 5. It will therefore be *accumulated upon that ice*." These words give but the essence of the paper; they are both preceded and followed by plausible conjectures and ingenious reasoning. For simplicity and clearness of style, as well as for novelty of suggestion, this essay, I think, is one of the best of his scientific papers. Mr. Sparks does

well to quote, in connection with it, Sir Humphrey Davy's remarks upon Franklin's electrical writings, for the essay is exactly described by them. "A singular felicity of induction," says Sir Humphrey, "guided all Franklin's researches, and by very small means he established very grand truths. The style and manner of his publication on electricity are almost as worthy of admiration, as the doctrine it contains. He has endeavored to remove all mystery and obscurity from the subject. He has written equally for the uninitiated and for the philosopher; and he has rendered his details amusing as well as perspicuous, elegant as well as simple. Science appears in his language in a dress wonderfully decorous, the best adapted to display her native loveliness. He has in no instance exhibited that false dignity, by which philosophy is kept aloof from common applications; and he has sought rather to make her a useful inmate and servant in the common habitations of man, than to preserve her merely as an object of admiration in temples and palaces."

Thus, in the essay upon the Aurora Borealis, though it was read before a learned society, he prepares the way for his grand conception by showing what goes on continually in the atmosphere of an ordinary room. The drawing-rooms of Paris praised the essay for several reasons, but one of them was, that they could understand it.

His very spectacles were the spectacles of a philosopher. In England he had usually carried two pairs of spectacles, one for reading, the other for surveying distant objects. In France he had the two combined into a single pair, the glasses of which were in two parts, the upper half for distant objects, the lower for reading. As the invention has not come into general use, I presume it has not proved very serviceable. He, however, found it extremely useful, and wore no others for several years; "the glasses," as he remarked, "that serve me best at table to see what I eat, not being the best to see the faces of those on the other side of the table who speak to me; and when one's ears are not well accustomed to the sounds of a language, a sight of the movements in the features of him that speaks helps to explain; so that I understand French better by the help of my spectacles."

Watson, the annalist of Philadelphia, preserves a curious philosophic anecdote of Franklin, which he derived from the son of the gentleman to whom Franklin himself related it. While living in France, he sometimes extemporized an Æolian harp by stretching a silken string across some crevice that admitted a current of air. On revisiting a village, after the lapse of several years, he found the house in which he had formerly lodged deserted, from its having gained the ill repute of being haunted. Strange melodious sounds, he was told, could be heard in its empty rooms. On entering the house he found some shreds of the silk still remaining which had caused all the mischief.*

John Adams records in his Diary, that, on his saying one day to Dr. Franklin that he thought he did not take as much exercise as formerly, Franklin replied : " Yes ; I walk a league every day in my chamber ; I walk quick, and for an hour, so that I go a league ; I make a point of religion of it."

To Mr. Jefferson we owe two or three of the most amusing anecdotes of Franklin's life in France that have been preserved. One of these brings the learned Abbé Raynal and the naughty Polly Baker into unexpected conjunction. " The Doctor," says Mr. Jefferson, " and Silas Deane were in conversation one day at Passy, on the numerous errors in the Abbé's *Histoire des deux Indes*," when the author happened to step in. After the usual salutations, Silas Deane said to him : ' The Doctor and myself, Abbé, were just speaking of the errors of fact into which you have been led in your history.' ' Oh, no, sir,' said the Abbé, ' that is impossible. I took the greatest care not to insert a single fact for which I had not the most unquestionable authority.' ' Why,' says Deane, ' there is the story of Polly Baker, and the eloquent apology you have put into her mouth when brought before a court in Massachusetts to to suffer punishment under a law which you cite, for having had a bastard. I know there was never such a law in Massachusetts." ' Be assured,' said the Abbé, ' you are mistaken, and that it is a true story. I do not immediately recollect indeed the particular information on which I quote it ; but 1 am certain that I had for it unquestionable authority.' Doctor Franklin, who had been for some time shaking with unrestrained laughter at the Abbé's confidence in his authority for that tale, said, ' I will tell you, Abbé, the origin of that story. When I was a printer and editor of a newspaper, we were sometimes slack of news, and, to amuse our customers, I used to fill up our vacant columns with anecdotes and

* Annals of Philadelphia, i., 533.

fables, and fancies of my own, and this of Polly Baker is a story of my making on one of these occasions." The Abbé, without the least disconcert, exclaimed with a laugh: "Oh, very well, Doctor, I had rather relate your stories than other men's truths."[*]

Another of Mr. Jefferson's stories: "Dr. Franklin had a party to dine with him one day at Passy, of whom one-half were Americans, the other half French, and among the last was the Abbé Raynal. During the dinner he got on his favorite theory of the degeneracy of animals, and even of man in America, and urged it with his usual eloquence. The Doctor, at length, noticing the accidental stature and position of his guests at table, 'Come,' says he, 'M. l'Abbé, let us try this question by the fact before us. We are here one-half Americans and one-half French, and it happens that the Americans have placed themselves on one side of the table, and our French friends are on the other. Let both parties rise, and we will see on which side nature has degenerated.' It happened that his American guests were Carmichael, Harmer, Humphreys, and others of the finest stature and form; while those on the other side were remarkably diminutive, and the Abbé himself particularly, was a mere shrimp. He parried the appeal by a complimentary admission of exceptions, among which the Doctor himself was a conspicuous one."

Mr. Jefferson relates, also, the following: "He was invited to all court parties. At these he sometimes met the old Duchess of Bourbon, who, being a chess player of about his force, they very generally played together. Happening to put her king into prize, the Doctor took it. 'Ah,' says she, 'we do not take kings so.' 'We do in America,' said the Doctor."

William Temple Franklin has something surprising to tell us of his grandfather's chess-playing. "Dr. Franklin," he says, "was so immoderately fond of chess, that one evening at Passy, he sat at that amusement from six in the afternoon till sunrise. On the point of losing one of his games, his *king* being attacked by what is called a check, but an opportunity offering at the same time of giving a fatal blow to his adversary, provided he might neglect the defense of his king, he chose to do so, though contrary to the rules, and made his move. 'Sir,' said the French gentleman, his antag-

---

[*] Works of Jefferson, vol. viii., p. 501.

onist, ' you cannot do that, and leave your king *in check*.' ' I see he is in check,' said the Doctor, ' but I shall not defend him. If he was a good king like yours, he would deserve the protection of his subjects; but he is a tyrant, and has cost them already more than he is worth. Take him, if you please, I can do without him, and will fight out the rest of the battle, *en Républicain*.' "*

There is yet another version of this chess story, which some future inquirer into the natural history of anecdotes may value. I find it in Jeremy Bentham, who heard it related by Fanny Wright as from General Lafayette : " When Franklin was negotiating in Paris, he sometimes went into a café to play at chess. A crowd usually assembled, of course to see the man rather than the play. Upon one occasion Franklin lost in the middle of the game; when, composedly taking the king from the board, he put him into his pocket and continued to move. The antagonist looked up. The face of Franklin was so grave, and his gesture so much in earnest, that he began with an expostulatory, 'Sir!' ' Yes, sir; continue,' said Franklin, ' and we shall soon see that the party without a king will win the game.' "†

With the young and lovely queen of France, tradition reports him to have been a favorite. The paragraph to this effect, which had had such a run in the American newspapers during the revolution, may have had a foundation of truth. It originated in the New Hampshire Gazette : " A gentleman just returned from Paris informs us that Dr. Franklin has shaken off entirely the mechanical rust, and commenced the complete courtier. Being lately in the gardens of Versailles, showing the queen some electrical experiment, she asked him, in a fit of raillery, if he did not dread the fate of Prometheus, who was so severely served for stealing fire from Heaven ? ' Yes, please your Majesty' (replied old Franklin, with infinite gallantry), ' if I did not behold a pair of eyes this moment, which have stolen infinitely more fire from Jove than ever I did, pass unpunished, though they do more mischief in a week than I have done in all my experiments.' "‡ Of course, Franklin was never capable of uttering such an elephantine compliment; yet he may have shown the queen electrical experiments at Versailles, and said pretty things to her while he was doing so.

* William Temple Franklin's Memoir of Franklin, vol. i., pp. 448–9.
† Bowring's Bentham, x., 527.
‡ Frank Moore's Diary of the Revolution, ii., 82.

He was, indeed, a very gallant old gentleman. Mr. Adams tells us that at seventy-two Dr. Franklin had lost neither his love of beauty nor his taste in judging it. The most beautiful girl in the French circle frequented by the Americans, was Mademoiselle de Passy, a daughter of M. Boulainvilliers, the author. "He called her his favorite, and his flame, and his love," says Mr. Adams, "which flattered the family, and did not displease the young lady." Why should it? Mr. Adams adds that when the Marquis de Tonnerre had wooed and won the lady, Madame de Chaumont, who was a wit, cried out, on seeing Franklin approach, "Alas! all the conductors of Monsieur Franklin have not kept the thunder-bolt (*le tonnerre*) from falling upon Mademoiselle de Passy."

Madame Brillon, the wife of a wealthy gentleman of a neighboring village, was another of Franklin's friends. He describes her as "a lady of most respectable character and pleasing conversation; mistress of an amiable family in this neighborhood, with which I spend an evening twice in every week. She has, among other elegant accomplishments, that of an excellent musician; and, with her daughters, who sing prettily, and some friends who play, she kindly entertains me and my grandson with little concerts, a cup of tea, and a game of chess. I call this *my Opera*, for I rarely go to the Opera at Paris." It is in a letter to this lady that his story of paying too dear for the whistle occurs; and for her entertainment he wrote his amusing piece upon the ephemera, which was copied and recopied so often in Paris, that it became as well known as though it had been published. The "Petition of the Left Hand," the "Handsome and Deformed Leg," "Morals of Chess," the "Dialogue between Franklin and the Gout," and other witty effusions of this period, were written for the amusement of the circle which assembled twice a week at Madame Brillon's. These pieces were, probably, composed by Franklin in English, and translated into French by some member of the company.

The Gout dialogue contains a passage which, though purposely exaggerated, has doubtless a good deal of biographic truth in it. It gives us a view of Franklin's pleasant surroundings on the lofty, umbrageous banks of the Seine.

"Let us," says Gout, "examine your course of life. While the mornings are long, and you have leisure to go abroad, what do you do? Why, instead of gaining an appetite for breakfast by salutary exercise, you amuse yourself with books, pamphlets, or newspapers, which commonly are not worth the reading. Yet you eat an inordinate breakfast, four dishes of tea, with cream, and one or two buttered toasts, with slices of hung beef, which I fancy are not things the most easily digested. Immediately afterward you sit down to write at your desk, or converse with persons who apply to you on business. Thus the time passes till one, without any kind of bodily exercise. But all this I could pardon, in regard, as you say, to your sedentary condition. But what is your practice after dinner? Walking in the beautiful gardens of those friends, with whom you have dined, would be the choice of men of sense; yours is to be fixed down to chess, where you are found engaged for two or three hours! This is your perpetual recreation, which is the least eligible of any for a sedentary man, because, instead of accelerating the motion of the fluids, the rigid attention it requires helps to retard the circulation and obstruct internal secretions. Wrapt in the speculations of this wretched game, you destroy your constitution. What can be expected from such a course of living, but a body replete with stagnant humors, ready to fall a prey to all kinds of dangerous maladies, if I, the Gout, did not occasionally bring you relief by agitating those humors, and so purifying or dissipating them? If it was in some nook or alley in Paris, deprived of walks, that you played awhile at chess after dinner, this might be excusable; but the same taste prevails with you in Passy, Auteuil, Montmartre, or Sanoy, places where there are the finest gardens and walks, a pure air, beautiful women, and most agreeable and instructive conversation; all which you might enjoy by frequenting the walks. But these are rejected for this abominable game of chess. Fie, then, Mr. Franklin! But amidst my instructions, I had almost forgot to administer my wholesome corrections; so take that twinge,—and that.

"FRANKLIN. Oh! Eh! Oh! Ohhh! As much instruction as you please, Madame Gout, and as many reproaches; but pray, Madame, a truce with your corrections!"

Of all the ladies composing this amiable and brilliant circle, Franklin loved best Madame Helvetius, widow of the celebrated author. A great part of the immense fortune which M. Helvetius gained in his office of farmer-general, he left to his wife, who, at an age when ladies usually prefer the repose of domestic life, enter-

tained with noble hospitality, the savans and literary men of Paris.
Fortunately, we have the means of exhibiting the friendship that
existed between Madame Helvetius and Franklin in the most agreeable manner; one of the frequenters of the lady's house, the Abbé
Morellet, having left, in his memoirs, a whole chapter of his recollections of the time when Franklin was Madame Helvetius' neighbor. This chapter was translated, some years ago, for a Philadelphia periodical (Bizarre) by Mr. William Duane, a great grandson
of Dr. Franklin, and an inheritor of his humor and benevolence.
I shall use, with his permission, the greater part of this entertaining piece.

" Franklin resided," says the Abbé," at Passy, and the intercourse
between Passy and Auteuil, where Madame Helvetius lived, was
easy. We went to dine at his house once a week—Madame Helvetius, Cabanis, and the Abbé de la Roche, her two guests and myself, who often accompanied them. He also came very frequently
to dine at Auteuil, and our meetings were very gay.

" It was for one of these dinners, for the anniversary of his birthday or of American liberty, I cannot say which, that I made the
following song :

> " Let hist'ry our Franklin's name
> Grave on brass with pen of fame;
> 'Tis to me the task belongs,
> Him to sing in drinking songs ;
>   Come begin
> Drink and sing our Benjamin.

> " Great in politics is he,
> At the table gay and free;
> Founding empires, see him quaff
> Flowing cups, and hear him laugh,
>   Gay and grave as a capuchin,
> Such is our Benjamin.

> " Like an eagle, see him rise,
> Nobly daring, to the skies;
> And carry off, as plunder,
> The earth-alarming thunder ;
>   Happy sin
> Of the clever Benjamin.

" The American regains
  Liberty, and breaks his chains ;
And this great work of our age,
A fresh exploit of our sage,
    Has finished been
By Louis and Benjamin.

" Never did mankind engage
  In a war with views more sage ;
They seek freedom with design
To drink plenty of French wine ;
    Such has been
The intent of Benjamin.

" If you see our heroes brave
  Both the English and the wave,
'Tis that our Cath'lic wine
May, America, be thine,
    Clear and fine,
Such as loveth Benjamin.
   *   *   *   *   *
" May we on the sea surpass
  That so proud and jealous race ;
But when we our vict'ry win,
Let us teach them to begin
    To fill their skin,
In healths to Benjamin.

" Franklin was very fond of Scotch songs; he recollected, he said, the strong and agreeable impressions which they had made him experience. He related to us, that, while traveling in America, he found himself beyond the Alleghany mountains, in the house of a Scotchman, living remote from society, after the loss of his fortune, with his wife, who had been handsome, and their daughter, fifteen or sixteen years of age ; and that on a beautiful evening, sitting before their door, the wife had sung the Scotch air, ' So merry as we have been,' in so sweet and touching a way, that he burst into tears, and that the recollection of this impression was still quite vivid, after more than thirty years.

" This was more than was wanting to make me try to translate, or imitate in French, the song which had given him so much pleasure. It may be found, with five others of the same kind, and the romance of Mary Stuart, in a collection of music copied by my hand. He sometimes accompanied me in these airs upon the harmonics, an instrument of his invention, as is well known.

"His conversation was exquisite—a perfect good nature, a simplicity of manners, an uprightness of mind that made itself felt in the smallest things, an extreme gentleness, and, above all, a sweet serenity that easily became gayety; such was the society of this great man, who has placed his country among the number of independent States, and made one of the most important discoveries of the age.

"He seldom spoke long, except in composing tales—a talent in which he excelled, and which he greatly liked in others. His tales always had a philosophical aim; many had the form of apologues, which he himself invented, and he applied those which he had not made with infinite justice.*

"But I cannot give a juster idea of the amiable disposition of this man, otherwise so distinguished by his genius and the strength of his reason, than by introducing a letter which Madame Helvetius received from him one morning, after he had spent the previous day in uttering many pieces of amusing nonsense with her. This letter is perhaps found elsewhere, but no one will be sorry to read it again.

"'PASSY.

"'Chagrined at your resolution, pronounced so decidedly last evening, to remain single for life, in honor of your dear husband, I went home, fell upon my bed, thought myself dead, and found myself in the Elysian Fields.

---

* The following is a specimen of the tales to which the Abbé Morellet refers: "An officer named Montrèsor, a worthy man, was very ill. The curate of his parish, thinking him likely to die, advised him to make his peace with God, that he might be received into Paradise. 'I have not much uneasiness on the subject,' said Montrèsor, 'for I had a vision last night which has perfectly tranquilized my mind.' 'What vision have you had?' said the good priest. 'I was, replied Montrèsor, 'at the gate of Paradise, with a crowd of people who wished to enter, and St. Peter inquired of every one what religion he was of. One answered, 'I am a Roman Catholic. 'Well,' said St. Peter, 'enter, and take your place there among the Catholics.' Another said he was of the Church of England. 'Well,' said the Saint, 'enter and place yourself there among the Anglicans.' A third said he was a Quaker. 'Enter,' said St. Peter, 'and take your place among the Quakers.' At length my turn being come, he asked me of what religion I was. 'Alas!' said I, ' poor Jacques Montrèsor has none.' ''Tis pity,' said the Saint; 'I know not where to place you; but enter nevertheless and place yourself where you can.'"

" 'They asked me if I had any desire to see any persons in parti-
ular. 'Lead me to the philosophers.' 'There are two that reside
here in this garden. They are very good neighbors, and very
friendly to each other.' 'Who are they?' 'Socrates and Helvetius.'
'I esteem them both prodigiously; but let me see Helvetius first,
because I understand a little French, and not a word of Greek.'
He viewed me with much courtesy, having known me, he said, by
reputation for some time. He asked me a thousand things about
the war, and the present state of religion, liberty, and Government
in France. 'You ask me nothing, then, respecting your friend,
Madame Helvetius, and yet she loves you still excessively; it is
but an hour since I was at her house.' 'Ah!' said he, 'you make
me recollect my former felicity; but I ought to forget it to be
happy here. For many years I thought of nothing but her. At
last I am consoled. I have taken another wife, the most like her
that I could find. She is not, it is true, quite so handsome; but
she has as much good sense and wit, and loves me infinitely. Her
continued study is to please me; she is at present gone to look for
the best nectar and ambrosia to regale me this evening; stay with
me, and you will see her.'

" 'I perceive,' said I, 'that your old friend is more faithful than
you; for many good matches have been offered her, all which she
has refused. I confess to you that I loved her myself to excess;
but she was severe to me, and has absolutely refused me, for love
of you.' 'I commiserate you,' said he, 'for your misfortune; for
indeed she is a good woman, and very amiable. But the Abbé de
la Roche and the Abbé Morellet, are they not still sometimes at her
house?' 'Yes, indeed, for she has not lost a single one of your
friends.' 'If you had gained over the Abbé Morellet with coffee
and cream to speak for you, perhaps you would have succeeded : for
he is as subtle a reasoner as Scotus or St. Thomas, and puts his
arguments in such good order, that they become almost irresistible;
or if you had secured the Abbé de la Roche, by giving him some
fine edition of an old classic to speak against you, that would have
been better; for I have always observed that when he advises any
thing, she has a very strong inclination to do the reverse.' At
these words, the new Madame Helvetius entered with the nectar;
I instantly recognized her as Mrs. Franklin, my old American
friend. I reclaimed her, but she said to me coldly, 'I have been

your good wife forty-nine years and four months, almost half a century; be content with that.' Dissatisfied with this refusal of my Eurydice, I immediately resolved to quit those ungrateful shades, and to return to this good world to see again the sun and you. Here I am. *Let us avenge ourselves.*'

"I shall be pardoned, I believe, for publishing another pleasantry of Franklin's, which will confirm what I have said of his frank gayety, and the happy sociability of his character.

"As he loved drinking songs almost as much as Scotch songs, and as I had made some of them for him, he bethought himself, in one of his moments of pleasantry, of addressing me the following letter:

"'You have often enlivened me, my very dear friend, with your excellent drinking songs; in return, I desire to edify you by some Christian, moral and philosophical reflections upon the same subject.

"'In vino veritas,' says the wise man; truth is in wine.

"'Before Noah, men having only water to drink could not find the truth. So they went astray; they became abominably wicked and were justly exterminated by the water which they loved to drink. This good man Noah, having seen that all his contemporaries had perished by this bad drink, took an aversion to it; and God, to quench his thirst, created the vine and revealed to him the art of making wine of it. With the aid of this liquor he discovered more truth; and since his time the word, *to divine*, has been in use, commonly signifying to discover by means of wine. Thus the patriarch Joseph pretended to discover by means of a cup or glass of wine, a liquor which has received its name to show that it was not owing to a human invention, but divine; another proof of the antiquity of the French language against M. Gébelin. Therefore, since this time, all excellent things, even the deities, have been called divine or divinities.

"'We speak of the conversion of water into wine, at the marriage of Cana, as a miracle. But this conversion is performed every day by the goodness of God before our eyes. Behold the water which falls from the skies upon our vineyards; there it enters into the roots of the vines to be changed into wine; a constant proof that God loves us, and that he loves to see us happy. The particular miracle was performed only to hasten the operation, upon an occasion of sudden need which required it.

" 'It is true that God has also taught men to bring back wine into water. But what kind of water? Brandy (eau de vie); in order that they might thereby themselves perform the miracle of Cana in case of need, and convert the common water into that excellent species of wine called punch. My Christian brother, be benevolent and beneficent like him, and do not spoil his good beverage. He has made wine to rejoice us. When you see your neighbor at table pouring wine into his glass, do not hasten to pour water into it. Why do you wish to mix the truth? It is likely that your neighbor knows better than you what suits him. Perhaps he does not like water: perhaps he only wishes to put in some drops of it out of regard to the fashion: perhaps he does not wish another to observe how little of it he puts into his glass. Therefore, offer water only to children. It is a false complaisance and very inconvenient. I say this to you as a man of the world. But I will finish, as I began, like a good Christian, by making a religious remark to you very important, and drawn from Holy Writ, namely, that the Apostle Paul very seriously advised Timothy to put some wine into his water for his health's sake; but not one of the apostles nor any of the holy fathers have ever recommended putting water into wine.

" 'P. S.—To confirm you still more in your piety and gratitude to Divine Providence, reflect upon the situation which he has given to the elbow. You see in figures 1 and 2, that the animals which ought to drink the water that flows upon the earth, if they have long legs have also long necks, in order that they may reach their drink without the trouble of falling on their knees. But man, who was destined to drink wine, ought to be able to carry the glass to his mouth. Look at the figures below: if the elbow had been placed near the hand, as in figure 3, the part A, would be too short to bring the glass to the mouth; if it had been placed nearer the shoulder, as in figure 4, the part B, would have been so long, that it would have carried the glass quite beyond the mouth: thus would we have been tantalized. But owing to the present situation, represented in figure 5, we are in a condition to drink at our ease, the glass coming exactly to the mouth. Let us adore then, glass in hand, this benevolent wisdom; let us adore and drink.'

"To this fine dissertation were annexed the following drawings from the hand of his grandson, under the direction of this excel-

Fig. 1.

Fig. 2.

Fig. 3.

Fig. 4.

Fig. 5.

lent man, in whom I contemplated Socrates, mounted on a stick, playing with his children."

So far the Abbé Morellet. If space permits, we may converse again with this merry ecclesiastic, further on.

I must append to the Abbé's delineation of " Our Lady of Anteuil," a portrait of her by another hand, which is not flattering. Mrs. Adams, who joined her husband in Paris before Franklin left the country, dined with Madame Helvetius at Passy one day, and did not like her in the least. The orderly and decorous matron of New England, but lately arrived in France, was astonished at the lady's free ways.

"She entered the room," Mrs. Adams relates, " with a careless, jaunty air ; upon seeing ladies who were strangers. to her, she bawled out, ' Ah! mon Dieu, where is Franklin ? Why did you not tell me there were ladies here ?' You must suppose her speaking all this in French. 'How I look!' said she, taking hold of a chemise made of tiffany, which she had on over a blue lute-string, and which looked as much upon the decay as her beauty, for she was once a handsome woman ; her hair was frizzled ; over it she had a small straw hat, with a dirty gauze half-handkerchief round it, and a bit of dirtier gauze than ever my maids wore was bowed on behind. She had a black gauze scarf thrown over her shoulders. She ran out of the room ; when she returned, the Doctor entered at one door, she at the other; upon which she ran forward to him, caught him by the hand, ' Helas ! Franklin ; then gave him a double kiss, one upon each cheek, and another upon his forehead. When we went into the room to dine, she was placed between the Doctor and Mr. Adams. She carried on the chief of the conversation at dinner, frequently locking her hand into the Doctor's, and sometimes spreading her arms upon the backs of both the gentlemen's chairs, then throwing her arm carelessly upon the Doctor's neck.

" I should have been greatly astonished at this conduct, if the good Doctor had not told me that in this lady I should see a genuine Frenchwoman, wholly free from affectation or stiffness of behavior, and one of the best women in the world. For this I must take the Doctor's word ; but I should have set her down for a very bad one, although sixty years of age, and a widow. I own I was highly disgusted, and never wish for an acquaintance with any ladies of this cast. After dinner she threw herself upon a settee, where she showed more than her feet. She had a little lap-dog, who was, next to the Doctor, her favorite. This she kissed, and when he wet the floor she wiped it up with her chemise. This is one of the Doctor's most intimate friends, with whom he dines once every week, and she with him. She is rich, and is my near neighbor; but I have not yet visited her. Thus you see, my dear, that manners differ exceedingly in different countries. I hope, however, to find amongst the French ladies manners more consistent with my ideas of decency, or I shall be a mere recluse."*

We may presume that a longer acquaintance with Madame Helvetius lessened Mrs. Adams's disgust. These two amiable and richly endowed women approached each other from the extremes of two most diverse civilizations. Fancy Madame Helvetius transported to a New England village, and descanting upon a New England Sunday in a letter to the Abbé Morellet!

In the spring of 1781, Sophia, Countess d'Houdetot, in the gardens of her château at Sanoy, near Paris, entertained Dr. Franklin at a superb and peculiar fête champêtre, which was much celebrated at the time. Although no guests were present except the members of the d'Houdetot family and its connections, the company was numerous and distinguished. The occasion must have been a trying one to the modesty of Franklin, for he was deluged with versified eulogium. As soon as it was known that his carriage was approaching, the whole company set off on foot to meet him. At the distance of half a mile from the château they gathered round the doors of the carriage, and walked with it, as an escort, to the entrance of the grounds, where the countess herself handed him out. "The venerable sage," says the French chronicler of the fête, "with his gray hairs flowing down upon his shoulders, his staff in his hand, the spectacles of wisdom on his nose, was the perfect picture of true philosophy and virtue." As soon as he had alighted, the company formed a group around him, and the countess pronounced some lines, which may be roughly translated thus:

"Life of the valiant and the wise,
    Oh, Liberty! first gift of the gods!

* "Letters of Mrs. Adams," ii., 55.

Alas ! it is but from afar that we pay thee our vows :
And with longing hearts we offer homage
To the man who rendered his fellow citizens happy."

They then wound slowly through the gardens to the château
Dinner was soon announced, and the company sat down to a ban
quet which displayed all the resources both of the kitchen and the
cellar of the mansion. At the first glass of wine, a few soft instruments played an air, when the company rose, and sang a
stanza which served as the standing chorus of the occasion :

" Of Benjamin let us celebrate the memory ;
Let us sing the good he has done to mortals.
In America he will have altars ;
Then in Sanoy let us drink to his glory."

When the second glass of wine was about to be drunk, the
Countess d'Houdetot sang the following stanza :

" To human nature he restores its rights ;
To make men free he would enlighten them ;
And Virtue's self, in order to be adored,
Assumes the form of Benjamin."

At the third glass, the Viscount d'Houdetot sang these lines :

" William Tell was brave but barbarous ;
I love far more our dear Benjamin.
While fixing the destiny of America,
At table he laughs—just the way with your true sage."

As prelude to the fourth glass, the Viscountess d'Houdetot sang
this stanza :

" I say, live Philadelphia, too !
Independence—how it allures me !
I would gladly dwell in that country,
Though there is neither ball nor play there.

When the next glass was called, Madame de Pernan sang :

> " All our children shall learn of their mothers
> To love, to believe, and to bless you.
> You teach that which could reunite
> All the race of men as in the arms of one Father."

At the sixth glass, the aged Count de Tressau took up the strain :

> " Live Sanoy, say I ! It is my Philadelphia.
> When I see here our dear Legislator
> I grow young again in this home of delight,
> Where I laugh, where I drink, and list to Sophia."

The next glass was preceded by a bold stanza from the Count d'Apeché :

> " To obtain the sacred charter
> Which Edward yielded to the English,
> I think there is no French Knight
> Who would not desire to draw his sword."

It was certainly time for the company to leave the table when such a revolutionary sentiment as that had been offered. It savored of the coming revolution. The substitution of Edward for John was, perhaps, owing to the stanza being the herald of the *seventh* glass of wine.

When every individual present had complimented the guest in a similar manner, the company left the table, and the Countess d'Houdetot conducted Franklin, followed by the whole family, to an arbor in the gardens. The gardener there presented to him a Virginia locust, which the family desired he should plant with his own hands. When he had complied with their request, the Countess pronounced some verses, which were afterward engraved on a marble pillar, placed near the tree :

> " Sacred tree ! the lasting monument
> Of the visit to these scenes, a Wise Man deigned to pay ;
> Of these gardens henceforth the pride ;
> Receive, receive the just homage
> Of our vows and of our incense !

> And may'st thou, all down the ages,
> Touched gently by the hand of Time,
> Last as long as his name, his laws, and his writings."

The band of music then approached, and accompanied the family in the following song:

> "May this tree, planted by his beneficent hand,
> Raise in future years its verdant top
> Far above the unthrifty elm,
> And by its fragrant blossoms
> Perfume the air of this sequestered vale!
> The thunderbolt will not strike it;
> It will respect its summit and its branches.
> 'Twas Franklin who, by his happy toils,
> Taught us to direct, at once, and quench the lightning;
> And this, while restraining the enemies of man
> From ravaging the earth."

The ceremonial over, the company returned to the château, where they passed some agreeable hours in conversation. Late in the afternoon, all the family conducted Dr. Franklin to his carriage. When he was seated, they gathered round the open door of the vehicle, and the amiable countess exclaimed:

> "Legislator of one world, and benefactor of two!
> To the latest time men will owe honors to thy name.
> To-day I do but pay part of the debt
> Due to thee from all the ages."

The carriage door was then closed, and the guest was allowed to depart. A programme of the proceedings on this unique occasion, with the verses sung and pronounced, was handed about at Paris, and reprinted in America. From the American edition* I have drawn up this account. Very seldom in the history of mankind has a person of *real* merit been called upon to endure such a long sustained torrent of adulation. The hardest heart must com-

---

* Obligingly lent me from the Zenger Club's Collection of Materials for History by its worthy custodian, Mr. Frank Moore.

miserate the wretched philosopher who, for so many hours, had to smile responsive to quickly succeeding explosions of compliment. To suffer is the lot of man, but not many of us are required to suffer, and look as if we liked it. Poor Franklin might as well, for that day, have been a king.

The reader perceives that it was not possible to convince the French people that Franklin was not the whole of the American revolution. M. Turgot's happily composed verse,

" Eripuit Cœlo fulmen, sceptrumque tyrannis,"*

appeared to be taken in its literal acceptation, and the burden of most of the French songs made in his honor, was that he had despoiled heaven of its avenging bolt, and snatched the emblem of sovereignty from George the Third's thirteen tyrannical governors. It was in vain that he waved aside the prodigious compliment, protesting that the revolution was the work of many brave men, among whom to have a humble place was honor enough for him.† In more jocular moments he would say, that, as to the thunder, he left

---

* For very full and interesting information respecting the origin and effects of this celebrated verse, see an article in the Atlantic Monthly for November, 1863, by the Hon. Charles Sumner.

† As a specimen of the newspaper adulation of Franklin in France, take the following from the *Gazette of Amiens*, of April, 1780: "M. Fragouard, the King's painter at Paris, has lately displayed the utmost efforts of his genius in an elegant picture dedicated to the genius of. Franklin, Mr. Franklin is represented in it, opposing with one hand the ægis of Minerva to the thunderbolt, which he first knew how to fix by his conductors, and with the other commanding the god of war to fight against avarice and tyranny; whilst America, nobly reclining upon him, and holding in her hand the fasces, a true emblem of the union of the American States, looks down with tranquillity on her defeated enemies. The painter, in this picture, most beautifully expressed the idea of the Latin verse, which has been so justly applied to Mr. Franklin:

"'Eripuit Cœlo fulmen, sceptrumque Tyrannis.'

"'He snatched the thunderbolt from Heaven,
And the scepter from the hands of Tyrants.'

"The name of Franklin is sufficiently celebrated that one may glory in bearing it; and a nation prides herself in having given birth to the ancestors of a man who has rendered that name so famous. We think ourselves entitled to dispute with the English nation an honor of which they have rendered themselves so unworthy. Franklin appears rather to be of a French than of an English origin. It is certain that the name of Franklin, or Franquelin, is very common in Picardy, especially in the districts of Vimeu and Ponthieu. It is very probable that one of the Doctor's ancestors has been an inhabitant of this country, and has gone over to England with the fleet of Jean de Biencourt, or that which was fitted out by the nobility of this province. In genealogical matters there are bolder conjectures than this. There was at Abbeville, in the fifteenth and sixteenth centuries, a family of the name of Franklin. We see in the public records of the town, one John and Thomas Franquelin, woolen drapers, in 1521. This family remained at Abbeville till the year 1600; they have since been dispersed through the country, and there are still some of their descendants so far as Auz le Château. These observations are a new homage which we offer to the genius of Franklin."—*Frank Moore's Diary of the Revolution.*

it where he found it, and that more than a million of his country-men co-operated with him in snatching the scepter.

We must not omit to notice that, amid the gayeties and glories of his life in France, he still cherished his ancient tastes, and loved his old and distant friends. In his house at Passy, he had a small print-ing press and fonts of type, with which he printed copies of the "Bagatelles," those amusing essays of which we have spoken, for distribution among his friends. Among his fine acquaintances in Paris, he would speak of his business career in Philadelphia with the most unaffected nonchalance. At dinner, one day, when a dis-tinguished company was present, he thus addressed one of his guests, a young gentleman just arrived from Philadelphia: "I have been under obligation to your family; when I set up business in Philadelphia, being in debt for my printing materials and wanting employment, the first job* I had was a pamphlet written by your grandfather; it gave me encouragement and was the beginning of my success." He continued to show the young stranger particular attention during his stay in Paris.

His printing press he put to a curious use on one occasion.

We have seen how deeply he was moved, during the whole of the revolutionary struggle, by the barbarous manner in which some of the English officers had conducted the war, and, particularly, their employing the Indians, whose only notion of war is indiscriminate slaughter. In writing on this subject to his old friend, James Dutton, in 1782, he used remarkable language. "The dispensa-tions of Providence," said he, " puzzle my weak reason.   *   *
Why has a single man in England, who happens to love blood and to hate Americans, been permitted to gratify that bad temper by hiring German murderers, and, joining them with his own, to destroy in a continued course of bloody years near one hundred thousand human creatures, many of them possessed of useful talents, virtues, and abilities, to which he has no pretension? It is he who has furnished the savages with hatchets and scalping knives, and engages them to fall upon our defenseless farmers, and murder them with their wives and children, paying for their scalps, of which the account kept in America already amounts, as I have heard, to near *two thousand.*
*   *   * And yet this man lives, enjoys all the good things this

---

* Dr. Franklin must have meant the first job of any importance, for he says, in his Antobiog-raphy, that his *first* job was one from a chance countryman, which only came to five shillings.

world can afford, and is surrounded by flatterers; who keep even his conscience quiet by telling him he is the best of Princes! I wonder at this, but I cannot therefore part with the comfortable belief of a Divine Providence."

To bring the horrors of Indian warfare home to the minds of the rulers of England, he printed a leaf of an imaginary American newspaper, which he styled, "Supplement to the *Boston Independent Chronicle.*" For this supplement he wrote an "Extract of a letter from Captain Gerrish, of the New England Militia;" imitating, with great enactness, the usual style of such performances in the newspapers of New England. Captain Gerrish said: "The peltry taken in the expedition [see the account of the expedition to Oswegatchie, on the River St. Lawrence, in our paper of the 1st instant] will, as you see, amount to a good deal of money. The possession of this booty at first gave us pleasure; but we were struck with horror to find among the packages eight large ones, containing SCALPS of our unhappy country folks, taken in the three last years by the Seneca Indians from the inhabitants of the frontiers of New York, New Jersey, Pennsylvania, and Virginia, and sent by them as a present to Colonel Haldimand, governor of Canada, in order to be by him transmitted to England."

The captain added, that the packages of scalps were accompanied by an explanatory letter from one James Crauford, a trader, to the governor of Canada, which he inclosed. In the composition of this letter Franklin displayed great ingenuity. The opening paragraphs will serve to show the leading idea:

"May it please your Excellency : At the request of the Seneca chiefs, I send herewith to your Excellency, under the care of James Boyd, eight packs of scalps, cured, dried, hooped, and painted, with all the Indian triumphal marks, of which the following is invoice and explanation :

"No. 1. Containing forty-three scalps of Congress soldiers, killed in different skirmishes; these are stretched on black hoops, four inches diameter; the inside of the skin painted red, with a small black spot to note their being killed with bullets. Also sixty-two of farmers killed in their houses; the hoops red; the skin painted brown, and marked with a hoe; a black circle all round, to denote their being surprised in the night; and a black hatchet in the middle, signifying their being killed with that weapon.

"No. 2. Containing ninety-eight of farmers killed in their houses; hoops red; figure of a hoe, to mark their profession; great white circle and sun, to show they were surprised in the daytime; a little red foot, to show they stood upon their defense, and died fighting for their lives and families."

The other packages were described in similar style. No. 3 contained ninety-seven scalps of farmers, and No. 4 one hundred and two; of which eighteen were "marked with a little yellow flame, to denote their being of prisoners burnt alive, after being scalped, their nails pulled out by the roots, and other torments; one of these latter supposed to be a rebel clergyman, his band being fixed to the hoop of his scalp. Most of the farmers appear by the hair to have been young or middle-aged men; there being but sixty-seven very gray heads among them all; which makes the service more essential." No. 5 contained eighty-eight scalps of women, and Nos. 6, 7, 8, some hundreds of boys and girls. In No. 8 was found "a box of birch bark, containing twenty-nine little infants' scalps of various sizes; small white hoops; white ground; no tears; and only a little black knife in the middle, to show they were ripped out of their mothers' bellies."

These packages, according to James Crauford, the governor of Canada was requested by the chiefs to send to the King of England, that he might know and reward their zeal in his service.

The imaginary editor of the paper appended to the whole a postscript of his own, in which he stated that the scalps had just reached Boston, and that thousands of people were flocking to see them, their mouths full of execrations. "Fixing them to the trees is not approved," added the editor. "It is now proposed to make them up in decent little packets, seal and direct them; one to the king, containing a sample of every sort for his museum; one to the queen, with some of women and little children; the rest to be distributed among both Houses of Parliament; a double quantity to the bishops."

To fill out the supplement, Franklin inserted a fictitious letter from Commodore Paul Jones to Sir Joseph Yorke, in which the Commodore defended himself with spirit from the charge of piracy, which the embassador had brought against him. He showed Sir Joseph that the real pirate, the common enemy of men and nations, was George III. "It afflicts me, therefore," he concluded, "to see a gentleman of Sir J. Y——'s education and talents, for the sake of a red ribbon and a paltry stipend, mean enough to style such a —— *his master*, wear his livery, and hold himself ready at his command even to cut the throats of fellow-subjects. This makes it impossible for me to end my letter with the civility of a compliment, and obliges me to subscribe myself simply, JOHN PAUL JONES, whom you are pleased to style a '*pirate.*' "

To what extent this ingenious " hoax" was distributed, and what effects it produced, no one has recorded. I have an indistinct re-collection of seeing part of the scalp letter quoted in a work relating to the revolutionary war, as though it were a genuine production.

In English periodicals of these years, weekly, monthly, and annual, I notice articles and letters by Dr. Franklin, not unfrequently published with editorial commendation. And, what is more strange, a new volume of his works, edited by his old friend Benjamin Vaughan, appeared in London in 1779 ; the proof-sheets of which, in spite of the war, he read himself in his study at Passy. The good bishop of St. Asaphs suggested the motto from Horace that appeared under the portrait of the author : *Non sordidus auctor naturæ verique.* It was entitled " Political, Miscellaneous, and Philosophical Pieces," the greater number of which were then first collected. With all his old English friends he occasionally corresponded, particularly with the members of the good bishop's family, whose portraits adorned his study, and who cherished the recollection of his visits to their abode as among the happiest days of their lives. " You can scarcely imagine," Dr. Price once wrote to him, " with what respect and affection you are talked of there."

It is pleasant to notice that Franklin's cordial praise cheered the heart of poor Cowper, then just coming into notice as a poet. An English friend having sent Franklin, in the spring of 1782, a copy of the poet's first venture (which did not contain the Task), he sent back a few words of hearty commendations,* and desired that his respects might be presented to the author. Cowper wrote to Mr.

---

* " The relish for reading poetry had long since left me ; but there is something so new in the manner, so easy, and yet so correct in the language, so clear in the expression, yet concise, and so just in the sentiments, that I have read the whole with great pleasure, and some of the pieces more than once. I beg you to accept my thankful acknowledgments, and to present my respects to the author."—*Franklin to a friend*, March, 1782.

Unwin in great enthusiasm: "A friend of ours sent my poems to one of the first philosophers, one of the most eminent literary characters, as well as one of the most important in the literary world, that the present age can boast of. Now perhaps your conjecturing faculties are puzzled, and you begin to ask, 'who, where, and what is he? Speak out, for I am all impatience.' I will not say a word more; the letter in which he returned his thanks shall speak for me. We may now treat the critics as the Archbishop of Toledo treated Gil Blas, when he found fault with one of his sermons. His Grace gave him a kick, and said, 'Begone for a jackanapes, and furnish yourself with a better taste, if you know where to find it.'"

The reader perceives that Franklin was still a name of honor in England among men of honor. Perhaps, if I should insert here a vituperative article upon him from the scurrilous tory press of London, the space were not unprofitably bestowed. Such things, alas! still appear in the newspapers both of London and New York; and, perhaps, it may console some good men, not yet newspaper-hardened, to know what a fine insight into character, motives, and events, party hacks were wont to exhibit eighty years ago.

"Dr. Franklin," observed the writer of this veracious piece, "may be looked upon as the most ripened republican politician in the new world. In this business of independence, however, he seems to have overshot his mark; for he has nearly ruined his own country, and brought France into a war with her *new* and *great* *allies*, that he will scarcely extricate her from for some years. The old veteran in mischief was in England, was an agent for New England and Pennsylvania at the breaking out of the war in America, and after sowing the seeds of commotion in this country, went out to reap the benefits of them with his friends in Congress; and on his arrival was chosen delegate to Congress for Philadelphia, one of the secret council, and president of the Assembly of the State of Pennsylvania.

"He is said to be the father and promoter of the thirteen Articles of Confederation and *perpetual* union; and after establishing this (I hope) rope of sand, he assisted in forming plans for foreign negotiations, and had the art to get himself appointed with very extensive powers, and a salary of a thousand pounds a year, to the court of France. He formed this plan with his old friend Monsieur Maurepas, before he took shipping last from London, and was consequently received with open arms by that subtle and cunning minister, on his arrival at Paris in the winter of 1776. It was much lamented in England that he was permitted to return again to America, and more so, when his arrival at Paris was announced to all Europe. He arrived rather unexpectedly in France; and from his grotesque habit of a Canada fur-cap covering his straight silver locks, and a bear skin pelisse, he was at first talked of and stared at as a meteor. Whatever Mr. D——e might have done prior to this old snake's arrival, the Doctor, nevertheless, has the credit in his country of forming the regulations in trade, procuring loans both in France and Holland, framing the treaties of amity and partition, &c., &c., and the event only can show whether they will be beneficial to the *new* and mighty *states*.

"Exclusive of the literati, the Doctor's principal guide and friend at Paris, is old Maurepas ; and there is not, perhaps, two geniuses existing so similar in vindictive subtlety, watchfulness, and political trick. The Doctor is now about eighty-five years of age, was born of very mean parents, in Boston, and there served an early and short apprenticeship to a printer. Supposing, as most of his countrymen did at that early period, that Philadelphia was the seat of arts, learning, and commerce, he quitted his master and friends, and begged his way to that once flourishing capital. He worked as a printer's devil long enough to earn as much money as brought him to London, where he, for some years, labored as a journeyman, and was very soon obliged to write and print half-penny songs, for the common ballad singers, in order to procure himself a dinner. His poverty and friends prevailed on him to return again to Philadelphia, where he became the editor and proprietor of a newspaper, which, together with his profits as a writer and vender of almanacs, soon placed him above want. His rage, however, for the purchase of mathematic and electric machines, always kept him low and needy : and, I believe, at this period, he inherits very little, if any thing in America.

"Although his education was very narrow and contracted, he certainly ranks among the foremost of philosophers, and some of his literary productions are well spoken of ; he is, however, thought by some to be rather more triflingly amusing, than substantially

convincing. He has a good political head, his conversation is
fluent and pleasing, without being argumentative; and his address
remarkably stiff and awkward. In the line of his former politics,
he ever had as many enemies as friends, and his rectitude and honesty (before very much doubted) received a severe stroke on the
affair of purloining the papers of Governor H——n, from Mr.
W———ly, and which was so ably argued, and the transaction
so severely condemned to the Doctor's face, before the Privy
Council, as to need no comment."*

Thus, the *Morning Post*. Thus, do we still often misinterpret
the men who serve us best.

The correspondence of Dr. Franklin with his family, during his
residence in France, affords us many pleasing touches. He was
relieved to learn that no great harm had come to his daughter's
family, or to his own property, from the nine months' occupation
of Philadelphia by the British army. Captain André, who was
the chief tenant of his house, seems to have preserved the greater
part of its contents from injury. Nevertheless, Mr. Bache wrote:
"They stole and carried off with them some of your musical instruments, viz., a Welsh harp, ball harp, the set of tuned bells,
which were in a box, viol-de-gambs, all the spare armonica glasses,
and one or two spare cases; your armonica is safe. They took
likewise the few books that were left behind, the chief of which
were Temple's school-books, and the history of the Arts and Sciences in French, which is a great loss to the public; some of your
electric apparatus is missing also. Captain André also took with
him the picture of you, which hung in the dining-room. The rest
of the pictures are safe."

In one of his letters to his daughter, there was a passage which
did her injustice, and gave her great pain. The reader is aware
that all the drafts sent from America to Europe passed through
his hands; and he, consequently, knew how much money his countrymen spent abroad, and what they spent it for. Now, the United States, during the Revolutionary War, enjoyed just that kind
of inflated paper prosperity, which has so much surprised us during
the great rebellion of 1861 and 1862, and which England enjoyed
during her stupendous wars with Napoleon, and which is usually

---

* *Morning Post*, Jan. 12, 1779.

the lot of nations in war time.   Hence, as the struggle went on, the drafts upon France increased ; and while every ship brought private orders for tea, ribbons, silks, velvet, feathers, and trinkets, the doleful theme of half the public letters that arrived was the emptiness of the Congressional treasury. The ladies and the dandies, thought Franklin, are loaded with French finery, while the soldiers, who fight for them, are naked in their huts. At length came a request from Mrs. Bache for some decorative article. He thus replied to her application :

"When I began to read your account of the high prices of goods, ' a pair of gloves seven dollars, a yard of common gauze twenty-four dollars, and that it now required a fortune to maintain a family in a very plain way,' I expected you would conclude by telling me that everybody, as well as yourself, was grown frugal and industrious ; and I could scarce believe my eyes in reading forward, that ' there never was so much pleasure and dressing going on ;' and that you yourself wanted black pins and feathers from France, to appear, I suppose, in the mode ! This leads me to imagine, that, perhaps, it is not so much that the goods are grown dear, as that the money has grown cheap, as every thing else will do when excessively plenty ; and that people are still as easy, nearly, in their circumstances, as when a pair of gloves might be had for half a crown. The war, indeed, may in some degree raise the prices of goods, and the high taxes, which are necessary to support the war, may make our frugality necessary ; and, as I am always preaching that doctrine, I cannot in conscience or in decency encourage the contrary, by my example, in furnishing my children with foolish modes and luxuries. I therefore send all the articles you desire, that are useful and necessary, and omit the rest ; for, as you say you should ' have great pride in wearing any thing I send, and showing it as your father's taste,' I must avoid giving you an opportunity of doing that with either lace or feathers. If you wear your cambric ruffles as I do, and take care not to mend the holes, they will come in time to be lace; and feathers, my dear girl, may be had in America from every cock's tail."

In the same letter he said : "I was charmed with the account you gave me of your industry, the tablecloths of your own spinning, &c. ; but the latter part of the paragraph, that you had sent for linen from France because weaving and flax were grown dear, alas! that dissolved the charm; and your sending for long black pins, and lace, and *feathers!* disgusted me as much as if you had put salt into my strawberries. The spinning, I see, is laid aside, and you are to be dressed for the ball! You seem not to know, my dear daughter, that, of all the dear things in this world, idleness is the dearest, except mischief."

The lady did not submit in silence to this reproof. She replied: "How could my dear papa give me so severe a reprimand for wishing a little finery. He would not, I am sure, if he knew how much I have felt it. Last winter (in consequence of the surrender of General Burgoyne) was a season of triumph to the whigs, and they spent it gayly; you would not have had me, I am sure, stay away from the Embassadors' or Gerard's entertainments, nor when I was invited to spend a day with General Washington and his lady; and you would have been the last person, I am sure, to have wished to see me dressed with singularity. Though I never loved dress so much as to wish to be particularly fine, yet I never will go out when I cannot appear so as to do credit to my family and husband. The Assembly we went to, as Mr. Bache was particularly chosen to regulate them; the subscription was fifteen pounds; but to a subscription ball, of which there were numbers, we never went to one, though always asked. I can assure my dear papa that industry in this house is by no means laid aside; but as to spinning linen, we cannot think of that till we have got that wove which we spun three years ago. Mr. Duffield has bribed a weaver that lives on his farm to weave me eighteen yards, by making him three or four shuttles for nothing, and keeping it a secret from the country people, who will not suffer them to weave for those in town. This is the third weaver's it has been at, and many fair promises I have had about it. 'Tis now done and whitening, but forty yards of the best remains at Litiz yet, that I was to have had home a twelve-month last month. Mrs. Keppele, who is gone to Lancaster, is to try to get it done there for me, but not a thread will they weave but for hard money. My maid is now spinning wool for winter stockings for the whole family, which will be no difficulty in the manufacturing, as I knit them myself. I only mention these things that you may see that the balls are not the only reason that the wheel is laid aside."*

* "Letters to Franklin," p. 106.

Let us hope that she was consoled in her father's next letter. He had the pleasure, in 1781, of hearing that she was at the head of the band of Philadelphia ladies who were employed in making shirts for the soldiers of General Washington's army. The French embassador wrote to him, that in raising money for this purpose, " she showed the most indefatigable zeal, and the most unwearied perseverance, and a courage in asking, which surpassed even the obstinate reluctance of the Quakers in refusing. Rivington tried to turn her zeal into ridicule. Her patriotism, he called superstition and foolish fanaticism ; he pretended, that her officiousness went beyond all bounds. In a word, she could not have been praised more skillfully."

The first boy borne by Mrs. Bache after ,the conclusion of the French alliance, she named Louis. Before its birth she had asked her father which of the queen's numerous names she should bestow upon the coming girl. But the coming girl proved.to be a boy.

Franklin was far from forgetting his good old sister, Jane Mecom, the being who, of all the friends he ever had from youth to hoary age, loved him most. I cannot help giving a few sentences from her letters to him during his long residence abroad, there is something so sweet and touching in her admiring fondness. July, 1779, she acknowledges the receipt of a letter from him : " wherein you, like yourself, do all for me that the most affectionate brother can be desired or expected to do ; and though I feel myself full of gratitude for your generosity, the conclusion of your letter affects me more, where you say you wish we may spend our last days together. O my dear brother, if this could be accomplished, it would give me more joy than any thing on this side of Heaven could possibly do. I feel the want of a suitable conversation—I have but little here. I think I could assume more freedom with you now, and convince you of my affection for you. I have had time to reflect and see my error in that respect. I suffered my diffidence and the awe of your superiority to prevent the familiarity I might have taken with you, and ought, and [which] your kindness to me might have convinced me would be acceptable ; but it is hard overcoming a natural propensity, and diffidence is mine. * * * Friends flock around me when I receive a letter, and are much disappointed that they contain no politics. I tell them you dare not trust a woman with politics, and perhaps that is the truth ; but if there is any thing we could not possibly misconstrue or do mischief by knowing from you, it will gratify us mightily if you add a little to your future kind letters."

Again, in September of the same year :. " Your very affectionate and tender care of me all along in life excites my warmest gratitude, which I cannot even think on without tears. What manifold blessings I enjoy beyond many of my worthy acquaintance, who have been driven from their home, lost their interest, and some have the addition of lost health, and one the grievous torment of a cancer, and no kind brother to support her, while I am kindly treated by all about me, and ample provision made for me when I have occasion. * * * When shall I have any foundation for the hope that we shall again meet and spend our last days together ? America knows your consequence too well to permit your return, if they can possibly prevent it; and your care for the public good will not suffer you to desert them till peace is established, and the dismal sound of fifteen years from the commencement of the war dwells on my mind, which I once heard you say it might last. If it does, it is not likely I shall last so long."

And in 1783 : " Believe me, my dear brother, your writing to me gives me so much pleasure that the great, the very great presents you have sent me are but a secondary joy. I have been very sick this winter at my daughter's; kept my chamber six weeks, but had a sufficiency for my supply of every thing that could be a comfort to me of my own, before I received any intimation of the great bounty from your hand, which your letter has conveyed to me, for I have not been lavish of what I before possessed, knowing sickness and misfortunes might happen, and certainly old age; but I shall now be so rich that I may indulge in a small degree a propensity to help some poor creatures who have not the blessing I enjoy. My good fortune came to me all together to comfort me in my weak state; for as I had been so unlucky as not to receive the letter you sent me through your son Bache's hands, though he informs me he forwarded it immediately. His letter with a draft for twenty-five guineas came to my hand just before yours, which I have received, and cannot find expression suitable to acknowledge my gratitude how I am by my dear brother enabled to live at ease in my old age (after a life of care, labor, and anxiety), without which I must have been miserable."

It is when we read such passages as these, that we know what Dr. Samuel Cooper meant when he wrote to Dr. Franklin in one of these years: "Your friendship has united two things in my bosom that seldom meet, pride and consolation: it has been the honor and the balm of my life."

CHAPTER XIII.

DAWN OF PEACE.

AUGUST 30th, 1781. A high day in Philadelphia. The City Light-Horse and the uniformed militia were out, and the whole city was astir. General Washington was coming, and he was to be accompanied by the Count de Rochambeau, by the Chevalier Chastellux, by General Knox, by General Moultrie, and a great troop of cavaliers, French and American, the retinue of those generals. From the banks of the Hudson they had swiftly marched, the whole army following swiftly, and they were going southward to join General Lafayette near Yorktown, where they hoped, with the assistance of Admiral de Grasse, if he should arrive in time, to hem in, and, perhaps, capture Lord Cornwallis. At one o'clock, the Generals reached the suburbs. The city soldiery and a great number of gentlemen on horseback received them there, and gave them honorable escort through the streets to the City Tavern, where the General-in-chief gave audience to the principal citizens. Thence, to the residence of Mr. Robert Morris, the Superintendent of Finance, who entertained all the generals and a large party of civilians at dinner; and while they were drinking, in full bumpers and with sedate enthusiasm, the United States, the King of France, the King of Spain, the United Provinces, and the Speedy Arrival of Count de Grasse, the ships that lay at anchor in the river thundered to the Jersey shore "the triumph of their pledge." In the evening the city was illuminated, and General Washington walked forth to view the spectacle, followed by a concourse of people "eagerly pressing to see their beloved General."

Justly fell to Robert Morris the honor of entertaining General Washington on this occasion; for it was to him the General owed the possibility of this sudden transfer of the army to Virginia. All his own money, all the money he could borrow upon his personal credit, and twenty thousand silver dollars borrowed by him, at the last moment, from the money chest of the French army, just paid the hire of the boats, and an indispensable half month's pay of the troops. Next to Washington, the country owes the triumph at Yorktown to Robert Morris.

October 16th, ten o'clock in the evening, at Yorktown. Sixteen large barges were drawn up along the shore of the York River. Cornwallis had determined upon a last effort to escape; for, defend Yorktown he now knew he could not. Silently the troops file in, till nearly all his force is embarked. At the critical moment, when already some of the barges were in the stream, a violent storm of wind and rain broke upon them, drove the boats down the river, and frustrated the scheme. With extreme difficulty, and some loss, the men were got back to the town. The next day, the very anniversary of the surrender of General Burgoyne, four years before, while in every camp, at every post, and in numberless places of festivity all over the country, that glorious event was commemorated, Lord Cornwallis signified to the American General that he, too, had given up.

November 3d. Another high day in Philadelphia—perhaps the most profoundly joyful one that city has known since William Penn first viewed its tangled and woody site. The City Light-Horse were out again, and again they went out of town to meet something which all the city was eagerly expecting. To-day they rode southward a few miles, and met, not a splendid calvacade of Generals and staff officers, but only two of General Washington's aids, Colonel Humphrey and Colonel Tilghman, bearing the colors captured at Yorktown, twenty-four in number. These were given to the light-horsemen, and were borne by them to the city, each flag in the hand of one of the privates. Down all the length of Market Street, to the Delaware River, then along the river to Chestnut Street, and so to the State House, the colors were carried, crowds of people looking on, not exultant merely, but amazed and awe-struck. The colors were then presented to Congress. "And many of the members," wrote Robert Morris in his diary that night, "tell me, that in-

stead of viewing this transaction as a mere matter of joyful ceremony, which they expected to do, they instantly felt themselves impressed with ideas of the most solemn nature. It brought to their
minds the distress our country has been exposed to, the calamities
we have repeatedly suffered, the perilous situations which our affairs
have almost always been in ; and they could not but recollect the
threats of Lord North that he would bring America to his feet in
unconditional submission."*

November 25th, Sunday, in London. At noon a messenger from
the coast reached Pall Mall, bearing the news of the surrender of
Cornwallis. He rode to the house of Lord George Germain, the
minister having special charge of American affairs. An under Secretary of State chanced to be there at the time, Lord Walsingham,
who was to second the address on the following Tuesday in the
House of Lords, and who was therefore particularly concerned to
know the state of affairs. To him Lord George Germain read the
stunning dispatch, and then both of them, to save time, took a hackney coach and drove to Lord Stormont's, then a cabinet minister,
the individual who " would hold no intercourse with rebels unless
they came to implore his majesty's mercy." Lord Stormont having
joined them in the coach, the three proceeded to the house of Lord
North, who had as yet heard nothing of the news. The prime
minister received the intelligence (so Lord George Germain afterwards said) " as he would have taken a ball in his breast." He
threw his arms apart. He paced wildly up and down the room, exclaiming from time to time, " Oh God ! it is all over !" When the
first agony had subsided, the four ministers sat down to consult,
and they conversed together for several hours.

Wraxall has an interesting reminiscence of that memorable Sunday. " I dined on that day," he tells us, " at Lord George Germain's; and Lord Walsingham, who likewise dined there, was the
only guest that had become acquainted with the fact. The party,
nine in number, sat down to table. Lord George appeared serious,
though he manifested no discomposure. Before the dinner was
finished, one of his servants delivered him a letter, brought back by
the messenger who had been dispatched to the king. Lord George
opened and perused it : then looking at Lord Walsingham, to whom
he exclusively directed his observation, " The king writes," said he,

* Diplomatic Correspondence of the American Revolution, xii., 7.

" just as he always does, except that I observe he has omitted to
mark the hour and the minute of his writing, with his usual precision.'
This remark, though calculated to awaken some interest, excited no
comment; and while the ladies, Lord George's three daughters,
remained in the room, we repressed our curiosity. But they had
no sooner withdrawn, than Lord George having acquainted us, that
from Paris information had just arrived of the old Count de Maurepas, first minister, lying at the point of death; 'It would grieve
me,' said I, 'to finish my career, however far advanced in years,
were I first minister of France, before I had witnessed the termination of this great contest between England and America.' 'He
has survived to see that event,' replied Lord George, with some
agitation. Utterly unsuspicious of the fact which had happened
beyond the Atlantic, I conceived him to allude to the indecisive
naval action, fought at the mouth of the Chesapeake, early in the
preceding month of September, between Admiral Graves and Count
de Grasse; an engagement which in its results might prove most
injurious to Lord Cornwallis. Under this impression, 'My meaning,' said I, 'is, that if I were the Count de Maurepas, I should
wish to live long enough to behold the final issue of the war in
Virginia.' 'He has survived to witness it completely,' answered
Lord George: 'The army has surrendered, and you may peruse the
particulars of the capitulation, in that paper;' taking at the same
time one from his pocket, which he delivered into my hand, not
without visible emotion. By his permission I read it aloud, while
the company listened in profound silence. We then discussed its
contents, as affecting the ministry, the country, and the war. It
must be confessed that they were calculated to diffuse a gloom over
the most convivial society, and that they opened a wide field for
political speculation.

" After perusing the account of Lord Cornwallis's surrender at
Yorktown, it was impossible for all present not to feel a lively curiosity to know how the king had received the intelligence; as well
as how he had expressed himself in his note to Lord George Germain, on the first communication of so painful an event. He gratified our wish by reading it to us; observing at the same time, that it
did the highest honor to his majesty's fortitude, firmness, and consist-
ency of character. The words made an impression on my memory,
which the lapse of more than thirty years has not erased; and I

shall here commemorate its tenor, as serving to show how that prince felt and wrote, under one of the most afflicting, as well as humiliating occurrences of his reign. The billet ran nearly to this effect : 'I have received with sentiments of the deepest concern, the communication which Lord George Germain has made me, of the unfortunate result of the operations in Virginia. I particularly lament it, on account of the consequences connected with it, and the difficulties which it may produce in carrying on the public business, or in repairing such a misfortune. But, I trust that neither Lord George Germain, nor any member of the cabinet, will suppose that it makes the smallest alteration in those principles of my conduct, which have directed me in past time, and which will always continue to animate me under every event, in the prosecution of the present contest.' Not a sentiment of despondency or of despair was to be found in the letter ; the very hand-writing of which, indicated composure of mind."*

November 27th. Parliament met. Fox, Burke, Sheridan, Thomas Pitt, the youthful William Pitt, and all the usual speakers on the liberal side, assailed the ministry and the war, as no ministry has ever since, or had ever before, been assailed. The result was merely to diminish Lord North's majority to fifty-four. But, out-of-doors, the clamor against the war increased ; and though the hirelings of the ministry stood firm, the independent members were changing their opinions and beginning to think of changing their votes. The ministry was felt to be shaky. It lost strength daily during the rest of the year.

January, 1782. A kind of informal, second-hand negotiation for peace was going on during this month, between Lord North and Dr. Franklin ; and another, more secret and direct, between Lord North and the French Ministry. In writing to Mr. David Hartley, December 15th, to acknowledge the receipt of a plan for securing play-goers against fire, Dr. Franklin chanced to remark : "But what are the lives of a few idle haunters of play-houses compared with the many thousands of worthy men, and honest industrious families, butchered and destroyed by this devilish war? Oh that we could find some happy invention to stop the spreading of the flames, and put an end to so horrid a conflagration !" Now, the bearer of this letter was a certain ill-informed, indiscreet American,

* " Wraxall's Memoirs."

named Alexander: and in converging with Hartley, Mr. Alexander expressed the opinion that America desired peace so much,
that she would willingly waive a formal recognition of her independence, and would not object to enter into a *separate* peace. Mr. Hartley, who lived but to promote the longed-for peace, jumped at the
wild conclusion that Mr. Alexander, in these admissions, expressed
the sense of Dr. Franklin and of America. Full of this thought, he
hastened to report them to Lord North. The minister caught eagerly at the straw, and asked Mr. Hartley which of the American ministers in Europe was authorized to treat. Was it Dr. Franklin?
Was it Mr. Adams? or was it both? He inquired, also, whether
the *"propositions"* mentioned by Mr. Alexander *"* would be
acknowledged as general grounds of negotiation towards peace,
by the person or persons authorized to treat; because it was necessary, before he could lay a matter of so great importance before the
Cabinet Council, that he should be entitled to say, these propositions and general outlines come to me from responsible and authorized persons."

Mr. Hartley, now one of the happiest of men, instantly wrote a
letter of vast length to Dr. Franklin, making the requisite inquiries,
and urging Franklin to come into the plan of a separate peace. " I
believe," wrote Hartley, " that it has been the unfortunate union
or common cause between America and France, which has for the
last three years turned aside the wish of the people of England for
peace. I verily believe (so deep is the jealousy between England
and France), that this country would fight for a straw to the last
man, and the last shilling, rather than be dictated to by France. I
therefore consider this as the greatest rub out of the way." He
added: " I have the strongest opinion, that if it were publicly
known to the people of England, that a negotiation might be
opened with America, upon the terms above specified, that all the
ministry together, if they were ill-disposed to a man, would not
venture to thwart such a measure."

Franklin, indignant, gave a prompt and most emphatic denial to
the intimations of Mr. Alexander. He told Mr. Hartley that his
previous urgings of a separate treaty had given him more disgust
than his friendship had permitted him to express. " But," added
Franklin, " since you have gone so far as to carry such a proposition to Lord North, as arising from us, it is necessary that I should be

explicit with you, and tell you plainly, that I never had such an idea; and I believe there is not a man in America, a few *English Tories* excepted, that would not spurn at the thought of deserting a noble and generous friend, for the sake of a truce with an unjust and cruel enemy. * * * Believe me, my dear friend, America has too much understanding, and is too sensible of the value of the world's good opinion, to forfeit it all by such perfidy. The Congress will never instruct their commissioners to obtain a peace on such ignominious terms; and though there can be but few things in which I should venture to disobey their orders, yet, if it were possible for them to give me such an order as this, I should certainly refuse to act; I should instantly renounce their commission, and banish myself forever from so infamous a country. We are a little ambitious, too, of your esteem; and, as I think we have acquired some share of it by our manner of making war with you, I trust we shall not hazard the loss of it by consenting meanly to a dishonorable peace."

In conclusion, he apologized for his warmth, and said : "Whatever may be the fate of our poor countries, let you and me die as we have lived, in peace with each other."

Not less stanch were the French ministry in adhering to the compact of 1778. Dr. Franklin, having sent a copy of his correspondence with Hartley to the Count de Vergennes, was informed by him, that while that correspondence was in progress, Lord North had sent over a secret emissary to sound France respecting peace, and to offer advantageous propositions in case she should be disposed to treat separately. The emissary was charged to say to the English minister, " that the King of France is as desirous of peace as the King of England; and that he would accede to it as soon as he could with dignity and safety ; but it is a matter of the last importance for his most Christian Majesty to know, whether the court of London is disposed to treat on equal terms with the allies of France."

So this attempt to separate the allies failed.

February 28th, one o'clock in the morning, in the House of Commons. For many hours the House had been in session, and all the great orators had spoken. The debate was upon the motion of General Conway—the same General Conway whom we saw moving the repeal of the stamp act seventeen years before—to the effect that the reduction of the colonies by force of arms was impracticable. Lord North's majority had been falling away from him daily, until, a few days before, he had been left in a majority of a single vote. To-night the hearts of the opposition beat high with expectation of triumph. Soon after one, the cry of question became general and vehement, and, on the house dividing, General Conway carried his motion by a majority of nineteen, and so ended the American war. No sooner was the result known, says Wraxall, than " the acclamations pierced the roof, and might have been heard in Westminster Hall. Information of the event was instantly transmitted, notwithstanding the advanced hour, to his majesty, at the queen's house. Conway following up the blow, carried without any division, before the assembly adjourned, an address to the throne, soliciting the sovereign to 'stop the prosecution of any further hostilities against the revolted colonies, for the purpose of reducing them to obedience by force.' It was ordered to be presented by the whole house."

The same morning, Burke wrote to Franklin announcing the result, and hailing it as the almost certain harbinger of peace. The motion, he said, was the *declaration* of two hundred and thirty-four members, but it was the *opinion*, he thought, of the whole house.

The ministry, still supported by the most obstinate and unteachable of kings, indecently held out twenty days longer; the king threatening, as usual, to relinquish the crown of England, and retire to his hereditary Hanover. George IV. used to amuse his companions with the story of his father's scheme of retirement; " describing," says Lord Holland, " with more humor than filial reverence, his arrangement of the details, and, especially, of the liveries and dresses, about which he was so earnest that it amounted almost to insanity." But the poor blind king was compelled to yield, at length, and the whigs came into power towards the end of March: Fox and Lord Shelburne, secretaries of state; Conway, commander-in-chief; the Marquis of Rockingham, premier; Burke, paymaster-general; Colonel Barré, treasurer of the navy; Dunning (Franklin's old friend and counsel), a peer and chancellor of the Duchy of Lancaster; and Lord Howe, raised a step in the peerage. All of these were old friends of America and of Franklin.

The prospect was fair for an immediate peace, because all parties most earnestly desired it, and to some of them it was necessary.

Holland was, constitutionally, of Franklin's opinion, that there never was a good war, nor a bad peace. Spain had long ago ceased to be a warlike nation. France began the war embarrassed, and was now approaching exhaustion. And as to America, it was a question whether or not her army could be fed another month. Robert Morris, alarmed at the backwardness of the States in imposing taxes, had just engaged Thomas Paine, at a secret salary of eight hundred dollars a year, to rouse them to a sense of their duty by the exercise of his pen.* With a liberal ministry in England and reasonable commissioners at Paris, what was to hinder the prompt conclusion of a tolerable peace?

---

* Mr. Morris left a record of this curious transaction, as follows, dated February, 1782.

"Having lately had several meetings with Mr. Thomas Paine, the writer of a pamphlet, styled *Common Sense*, and of many other well-known political pieces, which, in the opinion of many respectable characters, have been of service to the cause of America, I thought this gentleman might become far more serviceable to the United States by being engaged to write in the public newspapers in support of the measures of Congress and their ministers. My assistant, Mr. Gouverneur Morris, is clearly of the same opinion, and in all our conferences with him we have pointedly declared, that we sought the aid of his pen only in support of upright measures and a faithful administration in the service of our country. We disclaim private or partial views, selfish schemes or plans of any and every kind. We wish to draw the resources and powers of the country into action. We wish to bring into the field an army equal to the object for which we are at war. We wish to feed, clothe, move, and pay that army as they ought to be done, but we wish also to effect these on such terms as may be least burdensome to the people, at the same time that the operations shall be every way effective.

"Having these for our objects, we want the aid of an able pen to urge the Legislatures of the several States to grant sufficient taxes; to grant those taxes separate and distinct from those levied for State purposes; to put such taxes, or rather the money arising from them, in the power of Congress, from the moment of collection;

"To grant permanent revenues for discharging the interest on debts already contracted, or that may be contracted;

"To extend by a new confederation the powers of Congress, so that they may be competent to the Government of the United States, and the management of their affairs;

"To prepare the minds of the people for such restraints, and such taxes and imposts, as are absolutely necessary for their own welfare;

"To comment from time to time on military transactions, so as to place in a proper point of view the bravery, good conduct, and soldiership of our officers and troops, when they deserve applause, and do the same on such conduct of such civil officers or citizens, as act conspicuously for the service of their country.

"Finding Mr. Paine well disposed for the undertaking, and observing that General Washington had twice in my company expressed his wishes that some provision could be made for that gentleman, I took an opportunity to explain my design to the General, who agreed entirely in the plan. I then communicated the same to Mr. Robert R. Livingston, Secretary for Foreign Affairs, and proposed that he should join me in this business, by furnishing from his department such intelligence as might be necessary from time to time to answer the useful purposes for which Mr. Paine is to write; and in order to reward this gentleman for his labors, and enable him to devote his time to the service of the United States, it was agreed to allow him eight hundred dollars a year, to be paid quarterly. But it was also agreed, that this allowance should not be known to any other persons than those already mentioned, lest the publications might lose their force if it were known that the author is paid for them by government."—*Diplomatic Correspondence of the American Revolution*, xii., p. 95.

CHAPTER XIV.

AN ATTEMPT TO NEGOTIATE.

MADAME BRILLON and her daughters—those amiable neighbors of Dr. Franklin who entertained him twice a week with tea, talk, chess, and music—spent the winter following the surrender of Cornwallis, at Nice; which was an Italian city then, but only four miles from the French frontier. Among the crowd of foreigners there, in quest of health or pleasure, was an English set, with whom Madame Brillon, who was familiar with their language, fell into a watering-place intimacy. In her letters to Franklin she wrote of her new friends, and mentioned, particularly, Lord Cholmondely, who, she said, had promised, on his return homeward, to stop at Passy, and join the circle of tea-drinkers and chess-players accustomed to assemble at her house. To Lord Cholmondely she could not but speak of Franklin and his unequaled talent for making happy those with whom he lived.

Lord Cholmondely, as it chanced, preceded Madame Brillon to Paris. Nevertheless, he introduced himself to Dr. Franklin, talked with him upon the political situation, and offered to convey a letter to his old friend, Lord Shelburne, who was about as every one supposed, to come into power. Dr. Franklin, accordingly, wrote a note to Lord Shelburne (March 22d), congratulating him upon the late triumph of the whigs in the House of Commons, and expressed the hope that it would produce a " *general peace.*"* To give an unofficial air to this note, Franklin mentioned that Madame Helvetius had been made very happy by receiving in excellent order the gooseberry bushes which his lordship had lately sent her.

When Lord Shelburne received this letter he had become a Secretary of State. At that time, the foreign business of the British court was divided between two secretaries, one having charge of the southern department, and the other of the northern. The southern department, which included France, belonged to Mr. Fox, and the northern department, which included America, to Lord Shelburne. Lord Shelburne, therefore, could treat with Dr. Franklin, but not with the Count de Vergennes, and Mr. Fox could treat

* Franklin's own italics.

with the Count de Vergennes, but not with Dr. Franklin. If the two secretaries had been on cordial terms, and had agreed in their system of foreign politics, no great inconvenience would have arisen from this most awkward distribution of duties. Unhappily, this was not the case; they were the leaders of two "wings" of the whig party, which could unite to win a victory, but were likely to quarrel over the distribution of the spoils. Mr. Fox had, also, a personal antipathy to Lord Shelburne, and thought him insincere.

Three weeks after the departure of Lord Cholmondely from Paris, an old London friend of Dr. Franklin called upon him at Passy, and presented a stranger, Mr. Richard Oswald, who, he said, had a great desire to see Dr. Franklin. After the usual compliments and some general conversation, Mr. Oswald produced a letter from Lord Shelburne and one from Mr. Henry Laurens, both of which introduced Oswald as the confidential messenger of the British ministry. "He is fully apprised of my mind," wrote Lord Shelburne, "and you may give full credit to every thing he assures you of." Mr. Oswald was a retired London merchant of very large fortune, who had had extensive dealings with America for many years, and had friends and connections there. Mr. Laurens wrote of him to Franklin: "He is a gentleman of the strictest candor and integrity. I dare give such assurances from an experience little short of thirty years, and to add, you will be perfectly safe in conversing freely with him on the business he will introduce, a business which Mr. Oswald has disinterestedly engaged in, from motives of benevolence; and from the choice of the man a persuasion follows that the electors mean to be in earnest."

Dr. Franklin entered, at once, into political conversation with this gentleman, with a view to learn Lord Shelburne's "mind." All he could gather was, that the new ministry really meant peace, and that they were prepared to concede the independence of the United States. Mr. Oswald said that they considered the object of the war, so far as regarded France and America, as obtained; since America had won independence, and France had severed the colonies from England. What, then, he asked, was there to hinder a pacification? He intimated, however, that if France should demand concessions too humiliating to England, England could still fight, as she was yet far from having exhausted her resources. Franklin merely said, in reply, that the United States would never treat but in concert with France, and that as he could do nothing of importance in the absence of all his colleagues, he would, if Mr Oswald wished it, present him to the Count de Vergennes. Oswald consenting, Dr. Franklin wrote to the minister a narrative of what had occurred, inclosing copies of all the letters that had passed, and proposing to bring Mr. Oswald to Versailles.

Two days after (April 18th), Dr. Franklin, Mr. Oswald, and M. de Vergennes, were closeted in the minister's cabinet, and conversed nearly an hour. The minister, who received Mr. Oswald with particular cordiality, assured him that the French court reciprocated, to the full, the good dispositions towards peace which were entertained by the government of England; but that France, positively, could not treat without the concurrence of her allies. They must, therefore, treat for a general peace, or not treat at all. He advised the selection of Paris as the place of negotiation, but would not object to Vienna; and, indeed, the king was so desirous of ending the war, that he would consent to any place the King of England might prefer. He told Mr. Oswald, frankly, that in case the treaty was entered upon, France had certain demands for reparation to make of England; meaning, probably, compensation for the French ships taken by surprise at sea before war had been declared. Mr. Oswald wished to obtain some propositions to convey to London. "No," said the minister; "there are four nations engaged in the war against you, who cannot, till they have consulted and know each other's minds, be ready to make propositions. Your court being without allies and alone, knowing its own mind, can express it immediately. It is therefore more natural to expect the first proposition from you."

In the carriage, on their return from Versailles to Passy, Mr. Oswald again warned Dr. Franklin of the consequences which would certainly follow if France should attempt to impose on England conditions too humiliating. There is no lack of money in England, said he; the only difficulty is to invent new modes of taxation : and even if taxation should fail, there is always the resource of stopping the payment of the interest upon the public debt, which alone would afford five millions sterling a year! " I made no reply to this," records Franklin in his diary of the negotiation : " for I did not desire to discourage their stopping payment, which I considered as cutting the throat of the public credit, and a means

of adding fresh exasperation against them with the neighboring nations. Such menaces were besides an encouragement with me, remembering the adage, that *they who threaten are afraid.*"
The next morning, Mr. Oswald being about to set out for England, Dr. Franklin waited upon him with the letter he had written in reply to Lord Shelburne ; in which he applauded the wisdom which had chosen so honest and capable a negotiator as Mr. Oswald. Further conversation ensued. Dr. Franklin observed, that as England seemed to desire, not peace merely, but reconciliation, perhaps she might think it best not to wait for America to *demand* reparation for the burning of towns and the ravages of the Indians, but *offer* something which might serve as partial compensation, and, at the same time, conciliate the people whom she had so cruelly wronged. Say *Canada*, for example. Mr. Oswald had admitted that it was politic in France to give up Canada at the peace of 1763 ; why, asked Franklin, would it not be just as politic for England to surrender it now, and thus remove one most probable cause of future quarrel ? In discoursing upon this topic, Dr. Franklin often glanced at a paper of memoranda which he held in his hand. Mr. Oswald at length asked to be allowed to read it, and Franklin, after some delay, handed it to him. It was entitled " Notes for Conversation," and read as follows :

" To make a peace durable, what may give occasion for future wars should if practicable be removed.

" The territory of the United States and that of Canada, by long extended frontiers, touch each other.

" The settlers on the frontiers of the American provinces are generally the most disorderly of the people, who, being far removed from the eye and control of their respective governments, are more bold in committing offenses against neighbors, and are forever occasioning complaints and furnishing matter for fresh differences between their States.

" By the late debates in Parliament, and public writings, it appears, that Britain desires a *reconciliation* with the Americans. It is a sweet word. It means much more than a mere peace, and what is heartily to be wished for. Nations make a peace whenever they are both weary of making war. But, if one of them has made war upon the other unjustly, and has wantonly and unnecessarily done it great injuries, and refuses reparation, though there may, for the present, be peace, the resentment of those injuries will remain, and will break out again in vengeance when occasions offer. These occasions will be watched for by one side, feared by the other, and the peace will never be secure; nor can any cordiality subsist between them.

"Many houses and villages have been burnt in America by the English and their Allies, the Indians. I do not know that the Americans will insist on reparation; perhaps they may. But would it not be better for England to offer it? Nothing would have a greater tendency to conciliate, and much of the future commerce and returning intercourse between the two countries may depend on the reconciliation. Would not the advantage of reconciliation by such means be greater than the expense?

"If then a way can be proposed, which may tend to efface the memory of injuries, at the same time that it takes away the occasions of fresh quarrels and mischief, will it not be worth considering, especially if it can be done, not only without expense, but be a means of saving?

"Britain possesses Canada. Her chief advantage from that possession consists in the trade for peltry. Her expenses in governing and defending that settlement must be considered. It might be humiliating to her to give it up on the demand of America. Perhaps America will not demand it; some of her political rulers may consider the fear of such a neighbor as a means of keeping the thirteen States more united among themselves, and more attentive to military discipline. But on the mind of the people in general would it not have an excellent effect, if Britain should voluntarily offer to give up this province; though on these conditions, that she shall in all times coming have and enjoy the right of free trade thither, unencumbered with any duties whatsoever; that so much of the vacant lands there shall be sold, as will raise a sum sufficient to pay for the houses burnt by the British troops and their Indians; and also to indemnify the royalists for the confiscation of their estates?

"This is mere conversation matter between Mr. Oswald and Dr. Franklin, as the former is not empowered to make propositions, and the latter cannot make any without the concurrence of his colleagues."

Mr. Oswald, with most undiplomatic readiness, declared that, in his opinion, nothing could be clearer or more satisfactory and convincing, than the reasonings in that paper. He said he would do his utmost to bring over Lord Shelburne to the same views, and, to that end, begged to be permitted to take the paper with him to England, promising to return it safely to Dr. Franklin's own hands. After much hesitation, Franklin consented. " We parted exceeding good friends," says Franklin, " and he set out for London."

It is usual to represent this attempt to procure the cession of Canada, merely as a piece of sly diplomacy—an endeavor to get the start of the other side in demanding, and to gain an advantage through the susceptible heart of Richard Oswald. Earl Russell, in his Memoirs of Mr. Fox, betrays an opinion of this kind.

" The truth is," says Lord Russell, " Dr. Franklin very quickly discovered that Mr. Oswald was a simple-minded, well-meaning man, on whom he could make the impression he chose, and desired nothing better than to have such a negotiator to deal with. Such confidence had he in Mr. Oswald that, at the moment of parting, he trusted him confidentially with a paper to Lord Shelburne, in which, *on pretense* of bringing about a thorough reconciliation between England and America, and of preventing future quarrels, he suggested the cession of Canada to the United States."

It is true that Franklin's suggestion of the voluntary surrender of Canada was a masterly stroke, viewed as mere diplomacy. But the reader of these pages is aware that the opinions expressed in the paper of memoranda had long been entertained by Franklin. He regarded the war in its true light, as a wanton outrage upon a loyal and unoffending people, for every single act of which reparation was justly due ; and he could himself remember three of the wars into which his country had been drawn, because Canada had belonged to a power different from that to which the thirteen colonies were subject. Mr. Oswald simply yielded to arguments that were irresistible, and paid homage to a mind that was just, as well as superior. Dr. Franklin, in fact, was ashamed of having been so little of a diplomatist as to let the paper go. He says, in his diary, that he gave Mr. Adams a narrative of what had transpired, but omitted all reference to this paper ; and " the reason," he added, " of my omitting it was, that, on reflection, I was not pleased with my having hinted a reparation to tories for their forfeited estates, and

I was a little ashamed of my weakness in permitting the paper to go out of my hands."

I think it probable, that if Dr. Franklin had been alone in the negotiation, on the American side, he would have procured the cession of Canada ; and that, too, without surrendering any thing essential, or even important, which the final treaty contained. Unfortunately, of his four colleagues, the only one who could have really understood and co-operated with him, namely, Mr. Jefferson, did not reach Europe till the treaty was concluded. Mr. Laurens was an aged invalid, and took little part in the negotiations. Mr. Adams was—Mr. Adams. Mr. Jay, one of the purest of men, was not skilled in diplomacy, nor acquainted with the scene in which he was so suddenly called upon to act. Jefferson alone would have taken the correct view of affairs, and been willing to make the trivial concessions that were needful, in order to secure so vast and lasting an advantage. The possession of Canada by the United States, would have changed the course of events. Years ago, it would have given an ascendency to freedom and civilization which the slaves of slavery would not have thought of calling in question ; and, perhaps, it would have given the free States, in 1787, the courage to reject the fatal compromises of the Constitution, the cause of all our woe. In these later days, Canada wisely holds aloof from a nation which must be distracted and debilitated, as long as any part of it, or any party in it, cherishes the blight of slavery. So the opportunity, which escaped in 1782, escaped, perhaps, never to return.

Mr. Oswald returned to Paris on the fourth of May, having been absent sixteen days ; during which Dr. Franklin informed each of his colleagues of what had occurred—Mr. Jay, at Madrid, Mr. Adams, in Holland—Mr. Laurens, on parole, in London.

The letter from Lord Shelburne, which Mr. Oswald brought with him, showed that the British ministry had taken Dr. Franklin's hint touching "sweet" reconciliation. Dr. Franklin had suggested that Mr. Laurens should be released from his parole, and that the American prisoners of war in England should be sent home in circumstances somewhat more comfortable than was usual. Both these suggestions were adopted. "Transports," said Lord Shelburne, "are actually preparing, for the purpose of conveying your prisoners to America, to be there exchanged ; and we trust, that you will learn, that due attention has not been wanting to their accommodation and good treatment." Lord Shelburne, also, announced, that as the negotiations with France belonged to the department of the other Secretary of State, Mr. Fox was about to dispatch a proper person to confer with the Count de Vergennes. Meanwhile Mr. Oswald was instructed to communicate to Dr. Franklin the sentiments of Lord Shelburne.

Mr. Oswald proceeded to do so. He again said, that the whole ministry were sincerely disposed to peace; that they were all agreed in conceding independence to the Thirteen Colonies; that " a good deal of confidence was placed in Dr. Franklin's character for open, honest dealing;" and that it was generally believed there was still remaining in his mind some part of his ancient love for Old England. He said he had shown the paper of memoranda to Lord Shelburne, and even left it with him for a night, upon his lordship's solemn promise of returning it. It had made an impression, Mr. Oswald thought, and he " had reason to believe that matters might be settled to our satisfaction towards the end of the treaty; but, in his own mind, he wished it might not be mentioned at the beginning." Nevertheless, said Oswald, Lord Shelburne had not imagined reparation would be demanded. Mr. Oswald formally announced, that his court was willing to treat for a general peace, and at Paris; and that the agent about to arrive from Mr. Fox was the Honorable Thomas Grenville, son of that Mr. George Grenville under whose fatal ministry the Stamp Act was passed, and who had questioned Dr. Franklin, during his administration, before the House of Commons. All these things Mr. Oswald repeated to the Count de Vergennes; " who seemed to think it odd," says Franklin, " that he had brought nothing more explicit " On their return from Versailles, Mr. Oswald again expressed the opinion to Dr. Franklin, that the affair of Canada " would be settled to our satisfaction;" only it had better not be mentioned just then. It was as though he had said: We, too, have some demands to make, which may be hard for you to grant; and we must keep Canada in reserve to throw in at the pinch of the negotiation.

On the 8th of May, Mr. Grenville arrived at Passy, and presented a letter of introduction from Mr. Fox. " Mr. Grenville," wrote that minister, " is fully acquainted with my sentiments and with the sanguine hopes which I have conceived, that those with whom we are contending are too reasonable to continue a contest, which has no longer any object, either real or even imaginary. I know your liberality of mind too well to be afraid, lest any prejudices against Mr. Grenville's *name* may prevent you from esteeming those excellent qualities of heart and head which belong to him, or from giving the fullest credit to the sincerity of his wishes for peace, in which no man in either country goes beyond him." Upon conversing with Mr. Grenville, Dr. Franklin was surprised to find that he had not yet seen nor sent to the Count de Vergennes, but expected Dr. Franklin to introduce him. An express was immediately dispatched to Versailles to announce his arrival and to solicit an appointment for an interview. Mr. Grenville waited at Passy all day for the return of the express, dined with Franklin, conversed with him for several hours, but communicated nothing in addition to what he had previously learned from Mr. Oswald. Dr. Franklin tells us that he found him a " sensible, intelligent, judicious, good tempered, and well instructed young man, answering the character which Mr. Fox had given him."

At Versailles, the next morning, Dr. Franklin, Mr. Grenville, and M. de Vergennes had a long and earnest conference, of which we find an interesting report in Franklin's diary :

" Mr. Grenville intimated, that, in case England gave America independence, France, it was expected, would restore the conquests she had made of British islands, receiving back those of Miquelon and St. Pierre. And, the original object of the war being obtained, it was supposed that France would be contented with that. The minister seemed to smile at the proposed exchange, and remarked, the offer of giving independence to America amounted to little. 'America,' said he, 'does not ask it of you; there is Mr. Franklin, he will answer you as to that point.' 'To be sure,' I said, ' we do not consider ourselves as under any necessity of bargaining for a thing that is our own, which we have bought at the expense of much blood and treasure, and which we are in possession of.' ' As to our being satisfied with the original object of the war,' continued the Count, 'look back to the conduct of your nation in former wars. In the last war, for example, what was the object ? It was the disputed right of some waste lands on the Ohio and the frontiers of Nova Scotia. Did you content yourselves with the recovery of those lands ? No, you retained, at the peace, all Canada, all Louisiana, all Florida, Grenada, and other West India islands, the greatest part of the northern fisheries, with all your conquests in Africa and the East Indies.' Something being mentioned of its not being reasonable that a nation, after making an unprovoked and unsuccessful war upon its neighbors, should expect to sit down whole, and have every thing restored which she had lost in such a war, I think Mr. Grenville remarked, the war had been provoked by the encouragement given by France to the Americans to revolt. On which the Count de Vergennes grew a little warm, and declared firmly, that the breach was made, and our independence declared, long before we received the least encouragement from France ; and he defied the world to give the smallest proof of the contrary: 'There sits,' said he, ' Mr. Franklin, who knows the fact, and can contradict me if I do not speak the truth.'

"He repeated to Mr. Grenville what he had before said to Mr. Oswald respecting the king's intention of treating fairly, and keeping faithfully the conventions he should enter into, of which disposition he should give at the treaty convincing proofs by the fidelity and exactitude with which he should observe his engagements with his present allies, and added, that the points which the king had chiefly in view were *justice* and *dignity ;* these he could not depart from. He acquainted Mr. Grenville that he should immediately write to Spain and Holland, communicate to those courts what had passed, and request their answers ; that, in the mean time, he hoped Mr. Grenville would find means of amusing himself agreeably, to which he should be glad to contribute ; that he would communicate what had passed to the king, and he invited him to come again the next day.

" On our return, Mr. Grenville expressed himself as not quite satisfied with some part of the Count de Vergennes' discourse, and was thoughtful. He told me that he had brought two State messengers with him, and perhaps, after he had had another interview with the minister, he might dispatch one of them to London. He did not ask me to go with him the next day to Versailles, and I did not offer it.

" The coming and going of these gentlemen were observed, and made much talk at Paris; and the Marquis de Lafayette, having learned something of their business from the minister, discoursed with me about it. Agreeably to the resolutions of Con-

gress, directing me to confer with him, and take his assistance in
our affairs, I communicated to him what had passed. He told me
that, during the treaty at Paris for the last peace, the Duke de
Nivernais had been sent to reside in London, that this court might,
through him, state what was from time to time transacted in the
light they thought best, to prevent misrepresentations and misunderstandings. That such an employ would be extremely agreeable
to him on many accounts; that as he was now an American citizen, spoke both languages, and was well acquainted with our interests, he believed he might be useful in it; and that, as peace
was likely from appearances to take place, his return to America
was perhaps not so immediately necessary. I liked the idea, and
encouraged his proposing it to the ministry. He then wished I
would make him acquainted with Messrs. Oswald and Grenville,
and for that end proposed meeting them at breakfast with me,
which I promised to contrive if I could, and endeavor to engage
them for Saturday."

Mr. Grenville, according to appointment, had a second interview
with the French minister on the day following, unaccompanied by
Dr. Franklin. M. D'Aranda, the Spanish embassador, was present; a fact of which Dr. Franklin does not appear to have been
aware. Mr Grenville retired, not too well pleased. He sat in his
hotel that night till three o'clock, writing dispatches to Mr. Fox,
and private elucidations for "dear Charles;" while his courier,
booted and spurred, waited in an ante-chamber, impatient to mount.
He told "dear Charles," that "the language of Monsieur de Vergennes, his manner, and those little expressions which it is easier
to feel the force of than to put into a dispatch, seem, as far as one
can judge in two pretty long conversations, to promise a most un-
governable extent to the sense of the two terms he repeats so often, justice and dignity; that he wishes for peace, I do believe, but
that the expectation of our being obliged to make peace as a country, and most particularly of your being obliged to make peace to
support your new Administration, is what makes great part of his
desire for peace, I cannot but believe likewise. Every expression
that M. D'Aranda and he used to-day were those of a very close
pruning."* So, added Grenville, you may as well begin to think,

* "Memoirs of C. J. Fox," by Earl Russell, i., 275.

already, of your ultimatum. At four o'clock in the morning, the
tired envoy, his arm aching, sent off his dispatches, and, at ten,
was at Passy, sitting down to breakfast with Dr. Franklin, Mr.
Oswald, and the Marquis de Lafayette.

A day or two after, Mr. Oswald announced his intention to set
out immediately for England, and to travel with the utmost expedition. Dr. Franklin was surprised and puzzled, but asked no
questions. He wrote, however, to the Earl of Shelburne, that he
hoped Mr. Oswald would return: "As I esteem him more, the
more I am acquainted with him, and believe his moderation, prudent counsels, and sound judgment may contribute much, not only
to the speedy conclusion of a peace, but to the framing such a peace
as may be firm and lasting."

Mr. Grenville had another interesting conversation with Dr.
Franklin after Mr. Oswald's departure. He says, in his letters to
Mr. Fox, that he had not the slightest expectation of peace, and
that, therefore, the only good likely to result from his mission, was
his "learning Franklin's ideas;" which, though not then practicable, might come to be so. "To that," he says, "I now chiefly direct my attention." And again: "I shall lose no opportunity with
Franklin that I can lay hold of; one must watch one's time with
him, for he is not a man that can be pressed." Hence the conversation just referred to, of which Dr. Franklin gives us some amusing details. Grenville began in the Hartley vein : "Suppose France
should insist on points totally different from the original and avowed
objects of the alliance, would America feel herself bound to continue the war merely in order to enable her to carry those points ?"

"I thought," relates Dr. Franklin, "I could not give him a better answer to this kind of discourse, than what I had given in two
letters to Mr. Hartley, and, therefore, calling for those letters, I
read them to him. He smiled, and would have turned the conversation ; but I gave a little more of my sentiments on the general
subject of benefits, obligation, and gratitude. I said, I thought
people had often imperfect notions of their duty on those points,
and that a state of obligation was to many so uneasy a state, that
they became ingenious in finding out reasons and arguments to
prove that they had been laid under no obligation at all, or that
they had discharged it, and they too easily satisfied themselves with
such arguments.

" To explain clearly my ideas on the subject, I stated a case. A, a stranger to B, sees him about to be imprisoned for a debt by a merciless creditor ; he lends him the sum necessary to preserve his liberty. B then becomes the debtor of A, and, after some time, repays the money. Has he then discharged the obligation ? No. He has discharged the money debt, but the obligation remains, and he is a debtor for the kindness of A, in lending him the sum so seasonably. If B should afterwards find A in the same circumstances that he, B, had been in when A lent him the money, he may then discharge this obligation or debt of kindness *in part*, by lending him an equal sum. *In part*, I said, and not *wholly*, because, when A lent B the money, there had been no prior benefit received to induce him to it. And, therefore, if A should a second time need the same assistance, I thought B, if in his power, was in duty bound to afford it to him.

" Mr. Grenville conceived that it was carrying gratitude very far, to apply this doctrine to our situation in respect to France, who was really the party served and obliged by our separation from England, as it lessened the power of her rival and relatively increased her own.

" I told him, I was so strongly impressed with the kind assistance afforded us by France in our distress, and the generous and noble manner in which it was granted, without exacting or stipulating for a single privilege, or particular advantage to herself in our commerce, or otherwise, that I could never suffer myself to think of such reasonings for lessening the obligation ; and I hoped, and, indeed, did not doubt, but my countrymen were all of the same sentiments.

" Thus he gained nothing of the point he came to push; we parted, however, in good humor. His conversation is always polite, and his manner pleasing. As he expressed a strong desire to discourse with me on the means of a reconciliation with America, I promised to consider the subject, and appointed Saturday the first day of June, for our conversation, when he proposed to call on me."

Affairs were at a stand still during the absence of Mr. Oswald, no one having yet received from England the requisite formal powers to treat. During this lull in the negotiation, came news of Admiral Rodney's great victory over the French fleet of Count de Grasse in the West Indies, which elated the English people to an extraordinary degree. Fears were entertained of its restoring the war party to a majority in the House of Commons, and of its raising the demands even of the liberal ministry, to a point which would necessitate another campaign. Dr. Franklin chanced to dine on the day the news reached Paris at the Count d'Estaing's, with a large party of naval officers. " We were all a little dejected with the news," he records. " I mentioned, by way of encouragement, the observation of the Turkish bashaw, who was taken with his fleet at Lepanto by the Venetians. 'Ships,' says he, ' are like my master's beard ; you may cut it, but it will grow again. He has cut off from your government all the Morea, which is like a limb, which you will never recover." A very apt quotation.

A ludicrous incident occurred during this interval. " The Count du Nord," says Franklin, " who is son of the Empress of Russia, arriving at Paris, ordered, it seems, cards of visit to be sent to all the foreign ministers. One of them, on which was written, ' *Le Comte du Nord et el Prince Bariatinski*,' was brought to me. Being at court the next day, I inquired of an old minister, my friend, what was the etiquette, and whether the Count received visits. The answer was, ' No ; you leave your name; that's all.' This is done by passing the door, and ordering your name to be written on the porter's book. Accordingly, on Wednesday I passed the house of Prince Bariatinski, embassador of Russia, where the Count lodged, and left my name on the list of each. I thought no more of the matter ; but this day, May the 24th, comes the servant who brought the card, in great affliction, saying he was like to be ruined by his mistake in bringing the card here, and wishing to obtain from me some paper, of I know not what kind, for I did not see him.

" In the afternoon came my friend, M. Le Roy, who is also a friend of the Prince's, telling me how much he, the Prince, was concerned at the accident, that both himself and the Count had great personal regard for me and my character, but that, our independence not yet being acknowledged by the court of Russia, it was impossible for him to permit himself to make me a visit as minister. I told M. Le Roy it was not my custom to seek such honors, though I was very sensible of them when conferred upon me ; that I should not have voluntarily intruded a visit, and that, in this case, I had only done what I was informed the etiquette required of me ; but if it would be attended with any inconvenience to Prince Bariatinski, whom I much esteemed and respected, I thought the remedy was easy ; he had only to erase my name out of his book of visits received, and I would burn their card."

Mr. Laurens wrote, at this time, to decline serving on the commission for negotiating a peace ; but, to encourage Franklin in the arduous work, he discoursed of the *blessings* which, he said, would be showered upon his head if he should succeed in terminating the war. Not so, replied Franklin. " I have never yet known of a peace made, that did not occasion a great deal of popular discontent, clamor, and censure on both sides. * * * So that the blessing promised to peacemakers, I fancy, relates to the next world, for in this they seem to have a greater chance of being cursed. And as another text observes, that in ' *the multitude of counselors there is safety,*' which I think may mean safety to the counselors as well as to the counseled, because, if they commit a fault in counseling, the blame does not fall upon one or a few, but is divided among many, and the share of each is so much the lighter, or because when a number of honest men are concerned, the suspicion of their being biased is weaker, as being more improbable; or because *defendit numerus ;* for all these reasons, but especially for the support your established character of integrity would afford me against the attacks of enemies, if this treaty take place, and I am to act in it, I wish for your presence, and the presence of as many of the Commissioners as possible, and I hope you will reconsider and change your resolution." Late in the negotiations, therefore, Mr. Laurens took part in the business. For some time longer, however, Dr. Franklin was alone. Would that he could have remained alone to the end !

The pause in the negotiations was broken by an incident which had consequences important and lasting. Mr. Grenville, on the twenty-sixth of May, announced to Dr. Franklin that a courier had arrived from London bringing him full powers, in form, to treat with *France and her allies.* But, a day or two after, the Count de Vergennes sent the Marquis de Lafayette to Dr. Franklin to inform him, that the document produced by Mr. Grenville empowered him to treat with France only, and contained not a word respecting the allies. Suspicion seized upon the French court. They hurried to the conclusion, that Rodney's victory had given England fresh courage and new designs, and that this defective power was an expedient for gaining time. The omission, in truth, arose from the unfortunate distribution of duties between Lord Shelburne and Mr. Fox, and the want of a good understanding between those ministers. It was due, in part, also, to the strong preference which Dr. Franklin had expressed for treating with Mr. Oswald. Lord Shelburne had imparted scarcely any thing of Oswald's preliminary negotiations to Mr. Fox; had said nothing to him even of the paper respecting Canada; and had, apparently, taken it for granted that Mr. Fox's envoy would negotiate with the Count de Vergennes, and leave to Mr. Oswald the negotiation with the Americans. Mr. Grenville's powers were worded in accordance with this scheme, and Mr. Oswald was to follow him to Paris, and continue to treat with Dr. Franklin. Mr. Grenville soon discovered that Franklin, as well as the French minister, was more reserved in his communications.

On the Saturday appointed, Mr. Grenville had a long conference with Dr. Franklin. He could not explain the defect in his powers. Unfortunately, he attributed the consequent reserve of Dr. Franklin to the wrong cause, and the error took such violent hold of his mind, that he was on the point of instantly starting for London to communicate it to Mr. Fox. On second thoughts, he adopted the more prudent resolution of sending a courier with a long, confidential letter.

"You will easily see," wrote Grenville on this occasion, "from the tenor of the correspondence we have hitherto had, that what little use I could be of to you here, appeared to me to be in the communication that I had with Franklin. I considered the rest of the negotiation as dependent upon that, and the only possible immediate advantages which were to be expected seemed to me to rest in the jealousy which the French court would entertain of not being thoroughly supported in every thing by America. The degree of confidence which Franklin seemed inclined to place in me, and which he expressed to me, more than once, in the strongest terms, very much favored this idea, and encouraged me in wishing to learn from him what might be, in future, ground for a partial connection between England and America; I say in future, because I have never hitherto much believed in any treaty of the year 1782, and my expectation, even from the strongest of Franklin's expressions, was not of an immediate turn in our favor, or any positive advantage from the Commissioners in Europe, till the people of America should cry out to them, from seeing that England was meeting their wishes. It was in this light, too, that I saw room to hope for some good effects from a voluntary offer of unconditional independence to America; a chance which looked the more tempting, as I own I considered the sacrifice as but a small one, and such as, had I been an American, I had thought myself little obliged to Great Britain in this moment for granting, except from an idea that, if it was an article of treaty, it would have been as much given by France as by England.

"I repeat this only to remind you that, from these considerations, the whole of my attention has been given to Franklin, and that I should have considered myself as losing my time here, if it had not been directed to that subject. I believe I told you in my last that I had very sanguine expectations of Franklin's being inclined to speak out, when I should see him next; indeed, he expressly told me that he would think over all the points likely to establish a solid reconciliation between England and America, and that he would write his mind upon them, in order that we might examine them together more in order, confiding, as he said, in me, that I would not state them as propositions from him, but as being my own ideas of what would be useful to both countries. (I interrupt myself here, to remind you of the obligation I must put you under not to mention this.) For this very interesting communication, which I had long labored to get, he fixed the fourth day, which was last Saturday; but on Friday morning Mr. Oswald came, and having given me your letters, he went immediately to Franklin, to carry some to him.

"I kept my appointment at Passy the next morning, and in order to give Franklin the greatest confidence, at the same time, too, not knowing how much Mr. Oswald might have told him, I began with saying, that though under the difficulty which M. de Vergennes and he himself had made to my full power, it was not the moment as a politician, perhaps, to make further explanations till that difficulty should be relieved; yet to show him the confidence I put in him, I would begin by telling him that I was authorized to offer the independence in the first instance, instead of making it an article of general treaty. He expressed great satisfaction at this, especially he said, because, by having done otherwise, we should have seemed to have considered America as in the same degree of connection with France which she had been under with us, whereas America wished to be considered as a power free and clear to all the world; but when I came to lead the discourse to the subject which he had promised four days before, I was a good deal mortified to find him put it off altogether till he should be more ready, and notwithstanding my reminding him of his promise, he only answered that it should be in some days.

" What passed between Mr. Oswald and me will explain to you the reason of this disappointment. Mr. Oswald told me that Lord Shelburne had proposed to him, when last in England, to take a commission to treat with the American ministers; that upon his mentioning it to Franklin now, it seemed perfectly agreeable to him, and even to be what he had very much wished, Mr. Oswald adding that he wished only to assist the business, and had no other view; he mixed with this a few regrets that there should be any difference between the two offices, and when I asked upon what subject, he said owing to the Rockingham party being too ready to give up every thing. You will observe though—for it is on that account that I give you this narrative—that this intended appointment has effectually stopped Franklin's mouth to me, and that when he is told that Mr. Oswald is to be the Commissioner to treat with him, it is but natural that he should reserve his confidence for the quarter so pointed out to him; nor does this secret seem only known to Franklin, as Lafayette said laughingly yesterday, that he had *just left Lord Shelburne's embassador at Passy*. Indeed, this is not the first moment of a separate negotiation, for Mr. Oswald, suspecting by something that I dropped, that Franklin had talked to me about Canada (though, by the by, he never had), told me this circumstance, as follows: When he went to England the last time but one, he carried with him a paper intrusted to him by Franklin under condition that it should be shown only to Lord Shelburne and returned into his own hands at Passy. This paper, under the title of ' Notes of a Conversation,' contained an idea of Canada being spontaneously ceded by England to the thirteen provinces, in order that Congress might sell the unappropriated lands and make a fund thereby, in order to compensate the damages done by the English army, and even those too sustained by the Royalists; this paper, given with many precautions for fear of its being known to the French Court, to whom it was supposed not to be agreeable, Mr. Oswald showed to Lord Shelburne, who, after keeping it a day, as Mr. Oswald supposes, to show to the king, returned it to him, and it was by him brought back to Franklin. I say nothing to the proposition itself, to the impolicy of bringing a *strange* neighborhood to the New-foundland fishery, or to the little reason that England would naturally see, in having lost thirteen provinces, to give away a fourteenth; but I mention it to show you an early trace of separate negotiation which perhaps you did not before know."

He concluded by saying that he could not fight a daily battle with Mr. Oswald and *his* Secretary of State; and advised Mr. Fox to have both Oswald and himself recalled, and to send over, in their stead, a man of rank charged with the entire negotiation, who would be necessarily under the exclusive control of Mr. Fox. Thus, Lord Shelburne would be frustrated, Mr. Fox reinstated, and the treaty advanced.

This letter broke up the British cabinet. Mr. Fox was in favor of an immediate explosion, but he was overruled, and the two factions held office together for a few weeks longer. The Marquis of Rockingham, never a robust man, sunk under the unwonted fatigues and excitement of office; Lord Shelburne became premier in his stead; Mr. Fox and his more intimate connections threw up their places; Mr. Grenville was recalled from Paris, and Mr. Oswald remained. Although these events did not immediately occur, we may now rule out Mr. Grenville and Mr. Fox from the negotiation, and confine our attention to Lord Shelburne and Mr. Oswald. Perhaps I should state, however, that Dr. Franklin was not long in discovering the want of harmony between Lord Shelburne and his colleagues. He says in his diary for June 17th (eleven days after the date of Mr. Grenville's letter quoted above) : "I find myself in some perplexity with regard to these two negotiators. Mr. Os-wald appears to have been the choice of Lord Shelburne, Mr. Gren-ville that of Mr. Secretary Fox. Lord Shelburne is said to have lately acquired much of the king's confidence. Mr. Fox calls himself the minister of the people, and it is certain that his popularity is lately much increased. Lord Shelburne seems to wish to have the management of the treaty; Mr. Fox seems to think it in his department. I hear that the understanding between these ministers is not quite perfect. Mr. Grenville is clever, and seems to feel reason as readily as Mr. Oswald, though not so ready to own it. Mr. Oswald appears quite plain and sincere; I sometimes a little doubt Mr. Grenville. Mr. Oswald, an old man, seems now to have no desire but that of being useful in doing good. Mr. Grenville, a young man, naturally desirous of acquiring reputation, seems to aim at that of being an able negotiator." All true, except the last. Mr. Grenville, as we see in his private letters, desired only to wash his hands of the whole business, and get back to his pleasures in England.

Dr. Franklin continued to converse in a desultory way with Mr. Oswald, who appears to have been the most frank negotiator of whom we have any account. In his first interview after his return from England, he told Dr. Franklin that the ministry desired peace as much as ever, notwithstanding Rodney's victory. One of them, he said, observing his coolness when the victory was spoken of, asked him if he did not think it a good thing. " Yes," replied Oswald, " if you do not rate it too high." Franklin relates, that " he. went on with the utmost frankness to tell me, that the peace was absolutely necessary for them. That the nation had been foolishly involved in four wars, and could no longer raise money to carry them on, so that if they continued, it would be absolutely necessary for them to stop payment of the interest money on the funds, which would ruin their future credit. He spoke of stopping on all sums above one thousand pounds, and continuing to pay on those below, because the great sums belonged to the rich, who could better bear the delay of their interest, and the smaller sums to poorer persons, who would be more hurt, and make more clamor, and that the rich might be quieted by promising them interest upon their interest. All this looked as if the matter had been seriously thought on. Mr. Oswald has an air of great simplicity and honesty, yet I could hardly take this to be merely a weak confession of their deplorable state, and thought it might be rather intended as a kind of intimidation, by showing us that they had still that resource in their power. But, he added, our enemies may now do what they please with us ; *they have the ball at their foot*, was his expression, and we hope they will show their moderation and magnanimity."

At their next interview Mr. Oswald produced a paper of memoranda written by Lord Shelburne, as follows :

" 1. That I am ready to correspond more particularly with Dr. Franklin, if wished.

" 2. That the *Enabling Act* (an Act to enable the king to make peace with America) is passing, with the insertion of commissioners recommended by Mr. Oswald; and, on our part, commissioners will be named, or any character given to Mr. Oswald which Dr. Franklin and he may judge conducive to a final settlement of things between Great Britain and America; which Dr. Franklin very properly says, requires to be treated in a very different manner from the peace between Great Britain and France, who have always been at enmity with each other.

" 3. That *an establishment for the loyalists must always be on Mr. Oswald's mind, as it is uppermost in Lord Shelburne's,* besides other steps in their favor to influence the several States to agree to a fair restoration or compensation for whatever confiscations have taken place."

With regard to the loyalists, Dr. Franklin explained, that " their estates had been confiscated by the laws made in particular States where the delinquents had resided, and not by any law of Congress, who, indeed, had no power either to make such laws or to repeal them, or to dispense with them, and, therefore, could give no power to their commissioners to treat of a restoration for those people; that it was an affair appertaining to each State. That if there were justice in compensating them, it must be due from England rather than America; but, in my opinion, England was not under any very great obligations to them, since it was by their misrepresentations and bad counsels she had been drawn into this miserable war. And that if an account was to be brought against us for their losses, we should more than balance it by an account of the ravages they had committed all along the coasts of America." To all of which Mr. Oswald assented, and again said, voluntarily, that Canada ought to be given up to the United States. He assured Dr. Franklin that he had said so to the ministry, and that neither Lord Rockingham nor Lord Shelburne were " very averse to it," though " Mr. Fox appeared to be startled at the proposition."

We cannot wonder, therefore, that when they came to talk over the " character to be given to Mr. Oswald," Dr. Franklin should have again expressed a very decided preference for Oswald as a negotiator, and urged his appointment upon Lord Shelburne.

The Enabling Act lingered in Parliament; the cabinet was torn by dissensions within; and, so, several weeks passed during which nothing material was done. Towards the end of June, Dr. Franklin was seized with an influenza, which brought on other maladies, that gradually rendered him almost incapable of business. It was, indeed, three months before he regained his usual health. A few days before his seizure, Mr. John Jay, one of his colleagues in the peace commission, reached Paris, after a laborious journey, overland, from Madrid. Mr. Adams was still detained in Holland. Here, then, the first stage of the negotiation, that which was conducted by Franklin alone, terminates, and another begins, during which Mr. Jay was the chief actor on the part of the United States.

It will not be denied, I think, that Dr. Franklin left the negotiation in a prosperous way. That gentle, preliminary suggestion respecting Canada was a masterly move, however it may be interpreted; and he hinted, too, at the only mode in which a British ministry could ever have faced Parliament upon the cession of Canada, namely, a provision in it for the American tories. Nor could Congress have been induced to consent to a provision for the tories on any other terms than the cession of a province for the purpose. At the very start, he struck the right trail, and he had made good progress in it when the influenza laid him aside. Then, again, he had procured from the king and cabinet of England a distinct, written, reiterated, public, irrevocable acknowledgment of the Independence of the United States. That Dr. Franklin was the procuring cause of this important preliminary concession, we know from the words in which it was communicated by the British ministry to General Sir Guy Carlton, commanding the king's forces in America. June 25th, Sir Guy was thus instructed : " It has been said that great effects might be obtained by something being done *spontaneously* from England. Upon this and other considerations, his majesty * * has commanded his ministers to direct Mr. Grenville, that the independence of America should be proposed by him in the first instance, instead of making it the condition of general peace." And this Sir Guy Carlton was directed to communicate to Congress. Franklin had secured, moreover, the appointment of Richard Oswald as the negotiator on the part of England, and assisted to shelve, not merely the far less manageable Grenville, but that portion of the British ministry least disposed to make concessions; for Mr. Fox and his friends not only did not believe peace probable, but were of opinion that peace *ought not* to be made on any terms which the allies seemed likely to agree to.

I may add, that a few days after Mr. Jay's arrival, but before he had begun to negotiate, Dr. Franklin read to Mr. Oswald a paper of hints for the treaty, which, really, contained nearly all which the treaty finally gave us. "He took out a minute," Oswald wrote to Lord Shelburne, July 10th, " and read from it a few hints or articles; some, he said, as *necessary* for them to insist on; others, which he could not say he had any orders about, or were not absolutely demanded, and yet such as it would be *advisable* for England to offer for the sake of reconciliation and her future interest, viz. :

" 1st. Of the first class, *necessary* to be granted; independence, full and complete in every sense, to the thirteen States; and all troops to be withdrawn from thence.

" 2dly. A settlement of the boundaries of *their* colonies and the loyal colonies.

" 3dly. A confinement of the boundaries of Canada; at least to what they were before the last Act of Parliament, I think in 1774, if not to a still more contracted state, on an ancient footing.

" 4thly. A freedom of fishing on the Bank of Newfoundland and elsewhere, as well for fish as whales. I own I wondered he should have thought it necessary to ask for this privilege.

" He did not mention the leave of drying fish on shore in Newfoundland, and I said nothing of it. I do not remember any more articles which he said they would insist on, or what he called necessary to them, to be granted.

" Then, as to the *advisable* articles, or such as he would, as a friend, recommend to be offered by England, viz. :

" 1st. To indemnify many people, who had been ruined by towns burnt and destroyed. The whole might not exceed five or six hundred thousand pounds. I was struck at this. However, the Doctor said, though it was a large sum, it would not be ill-bestowed, as it would conciliate the resentment of a multitude of poor sufferers, who could have no other remedy, and who, without some relief, would keep up a spirit of secret revenge and animosity for a long time to come against Great Britain; whereas a voluntary offer of such reparation would diffuse a universal calm and conciliation over the whole country.

2dly. Some sort of acknowledgment, in some public act of Parliament or otherwise, of our error in distressing those countries so much as we had done. A few words of that kind, the Doctor said, would do more good than people could imagine.

" 3dly. Colony ships and trade to be received, and have the same privileges in Britain and Ireland, as British ships and trade. I did not ask any explanation on that head for the present. British and Irish ships in the colonies to be in like manner on the same footing with their own ships.

" 4thly. Giving up every part of Canada.

" If there were any other articles of either kind, I cannot now recollect them; but I do not think there were any of material consequence, and I perhaps was the less attentive in the enumeration, as it had been agreed to give me the whole in writing. But, after some reflection, the Doctor said he did not like to give such writing out of his hands, and, hesitating a good deal about it, asked me if I had seen Mr. Jay, the other commissioner, lately come from Madrid. I said I had not. He then told me it would be proper I should see him, and he would fix a time for our meeting, and seemed to think he should want to confer with him himself before he gave a final answer. * * *

" From this conversation, I have some hopes, my lord, that it is possible to put an end to the American quarrel in a short time; and when that is done, I have a notion that the treaty with the other powers will go more smoothly on."

To promote his views respecting the treaty, he wrote, and printed upon his private press, an imaginary piece, as from a peasant philosopher, who had trudged on foot from the mountains of Provence to recommend justice and good will to the great men at Paris. His rustic and poor appearance, said Franklin, prevented his access to them; so he had himself taken him by the hand and struck off a few copies of his production. The piece, unfortunately, has not been preserved. I mention it to show that in this, the most important transaction of his life, he fell upon expedients similar to those by which he had promoted affairs of less consequence; the great feature of his policy as a public man being *to enlighten public opinion, and to bring an enlightened public opinion to bear upon the counsels of public men.* He wanted this treaty negotiated, not as jockeys with jockeys, each assuming that the other has no thought but to cheat; but as statesmen with statesmen, strenuous solely to know and do what justice and the interests of man required.

CHAPTER XV.

SECOND ATTEMPT TO NEGOTIATE.

"Mr. Jay likes Frenchmen as little as Mr. Lee and Mr. Izard did. He says they are not a moral people; they know not what it is; he don't like any Frenchman; the Marquis de Lafayette is clever, but he is a Frenchman." So wrote John Adams in his Diary, one day in November, 1782, of a man whose great grandfather was a French protestant refugee.

But in John Jay the vivacious blood of his French ancestors was tempered by that of the Dutch Van Cortlandts, a fair daughter of whom his father married. How could John Jay like the French of 1782?—he, the pure, devout Episcopalian, nurtured in that clean, plain, paternal mansion in rural Westchester, by parents who knew no standard of human worth except that which is expressed with such severe simplicity in their prayer-book. Obey the commandments of God, and you go to Heaven when you die: disobey them, and you go to hell, unless you repent. This was the simple creed of the excellent Jay, and he. held it in the literal sense of moral and pious Westchester county, in the State of New York, in the year of our Lord, one thousand seven hundred and eighty-two. Franklin, and all the good men that have ever lived, held precisely the same opinion; only, Franklin would have given to the words a larger, a wiser interpretation. It was as natural and as *right* for John Jay to abhor the French, as it was for Benjamin Franklin to like them, and to be happy in their society. It was unfortunate, though, that a gentleman who detested Frenchmen should have been selected to negotiate a difficult treaty in conjunction with Frenchmen. He tried hard to escape the task, but Congress would not let him off.

He was, moreover, a young man, only thirty-seven, and without experience in diplomacy; and being most sensitively conscientious, and having a painful sense of the responsibility of his position, he fell into a state of miserable distrust. He suspected the English, he suspected the Spanish, and he more than suspected the French.

When Franklin's sickness, later in the year, left him practically alone, he was like an Alpine traveler out on the mountains after dark, who dreads a precipice at every step, and dares not stir till he has felt the ground before him. Franklin knew the road, and, sick as he was, could have guided the timid adventurer safely through; but Mr. Jay, though he was never capable of distrusting the integrity of Dr. Franklin, became thoroughly distrustful of the soundness of his judgment.

Mr. Jay reached Paris at noon on the 23d of June, and as soon as he had placed his family at a hotel, went out to Passy, and spent the rest of the day in learning from Dr. Franklin the state of the negotiation. A few days after, they called together upon the Count d'Aranda, the Spanish Embassador, with whom Mr. Jay was to negotiate. This call was a notable event, for it was the first time that the plenipotentiaries of the United States had had official intercourse with any of the diplomatic corps in Paris. D'Aranda gave them a reception of unusual cordiality. As one of the grandest of the grandees of Spain, and one of the richest men in Europe, he lived at Paris in great splendor. He had such a profusion of plate that he maintained a silversmith in his house to keep it burnished as bright as new; and instead of buying his wine of wine merchants, he employed agents to go from vineyard to vineyard, selecting the choicest varieties.* "On our going out," says Dr. Franklin, "he took pains himself to open the folding doors for us, which is a high compliment here; and told us he would return our visit (*rendre son devoir*), and then fix a day with us for dining with him." He said, also, that he should be ready to begin business as soon as Mr. Jay found it convenient.

Mr. Jay was taken sick a few days after this visit, and was laid aside for a month. No time was lost, however; for, during the interval, the British cabinet was recast, Mr. Grenville recalled, a new agent, Mr. Alleyne Fitzherbert, sent over in his stead, and Mr. Oswald formally commissioned to treat with the Americans. By the middle of August, when Oswald's commission arrived, Mr. Jay, though still debilitated, was able to attend to business.

Upon reading over Mr. Oswald's commission, Mr. Jay observed that he was empowered to treat with the thirteen "Colonies or

* "Life of John Jay," i., 40.

Plantations." The document was long and minute, but wherever there was occasion to speak of the United States, they were called by the same name, "Colonies or Plantations." Mr. Jay was surprised at this appellation, and the more he thought of it, the less he liked it. The wildest suspicions tormented him. The English ministry, he thought, had changed their system, and meant to withhold the acknowledgment of independence. It chanced that two Englishmen, Franklin's old acquaintance, William Jones, and a Mr. Paradise, passed through Paris on their way to America. Paradise, who had inherited an estate in Virginia, was going out to take possession, and Jones was accompanying him as his friend and legal adviser. But, on arriving at the coast, Paradise was seized with such a terror of the sea, that he could not be persuaded to embark. Jones returned to England, and Paradise to Paris ; where Mr. Jay again met him, and found him "very reserved" upon the cause of his return—as well he might be. Mr. Jay was so sure that this mysterious affair contained some lurking peril for America, that he gave a dozen pages of details respecting it, in one of his public letters to the Foreign Secretary. Colonies and Plantations ! NEVER !

Mr. Jay carried the document to the Count de Vergennes, pointed out the offensive words, and said to him that it would be " descending from the ground of independence," to treat under the denomination of Colonies and Plantations. The minister thought not. Names, said he, signify little ; the King of England styles himself King of France, yet the King of France treats with him. Besides, an acknowledgment of independence would naturally occur in the treaty, not precede it ; for that would be to place the effect before the cause. In various ways, too, the King of England _had_ acknowledged the independence of the United States. The minister turned to Dr. Franklin, and asked him what he thought of the matter. "I think the commission will do," he replied ; " what do you think, Mr. Jay ?" Mr. Jay said he did not like it, and that it was best to proceed cautiously.

In the carriage, on their return to Passy, Mr. Jay expressed to Dr. Franklin a total distrust of all the courts. It was evident he said, that M. de Vergennes did not want to see our independence acknowledged by Britain until "they had made all their uses of us." It was easy for France to foresee, he added, that Spain would, with great difficulty, be brought to conclude a reasonable treaty, and " if we once found ourselves standing on our own legs, our independence acknowledged, and all our other terms ready to be granted, we might not think it our duty to continue the war for the attainment of Spanish objects. But, on the contrary, as we were bound by treaty to continue the war until our independence should be attained, it was the interest of France to postpone that event until their own views, and those of Spain, could be gratified." Only in that way, Mr. Jay said, could he account for the minister's advising us to act in a manner inconsistent with our dignity, and for reasons which he himself had too much understanding not to see the fallacy of.

In vain, did Dr. Franklin essay to remove these groundless impressions from the mind of Mr. Jay. In vain, he dwelt upon the past generosity, the tried honor, the proved sincerity, of the French court during the whole of the war. In vain, he produced the instructions of Congress, which ordered the commissioners to defer to the advice of the French government. In vain, he pointed out the true reasons of M. de Vergennes' conduct—his moderation, and his desire to remove every obstacle to peace. In vain, did Mr. Oswald offer to write to the American Commissioners a letter, in which he would expressly state, that he treated with them as the representatives of an independent power. In vain, did he exhibit an article of his instructions, which empowered him to concede " the complete independence of the Thirteen Colonies." Mr. Jay remained unconvinced, and, at length, refused, point blank, to go on with the negotiation, until a commission was shown in which the power he represented was styled the United States.

This is not the road to Canada, Franklin must often have groaned, during the month that was wasted upon this nonsense. He lay on his bed much of the time, tormented with the pains of the gravel ; and Mr. Jay had every thing his own way.

Mr. Oswald, finding him inflexible, communicated the difficulty to the Secretary of State, who replied that it was the king's " determination to exercise, in the fullest extent, the powers with which the act of Parliament had invested him, by granting to America full, complete, and unconditional independence, in the most explicit manner, as an article of treaty."

But even this did not satisfy Mr. Jay. On the contrary, it did but convert strong suspicion into absolute certainty. He had no longer the slightest doubt that there was a conspiracy among those scurvy politicians to pick his pocket of his country's independence. One trifling incident will serve to show how completely he was the prey of Distrust, and, at the same time, how groundless that distrust was.

I have mentioned before that the chief secretary to the Count de Vergennes and the secretary to the king's council (offices formerly filled by M. Gerard), was M. de Rayneval: who was as active in negotiating a peace as Mr. Gerard had formerly been in negotiating the treaty of alliance. While Mr. Oswald's courier was bearing to England Mr. Jay's positive refusal to treat under the old commission, word was brought to Mr. Jay that M. de Rayneval had suddenly set out for London. It was given out that he had gone into the country, and particular precautions had been taken to keep his real destination a secret. On the same day, Mr. Jay learned that the Spanish Embassador, contrary to his usual practice, had gone with *post horses* (Mr. Jay's own italics) to Versailles, and had been in consultation for two or three hours with the Count de Vergennes and M. de Rayneval; immediately after which, de Rayneval had taken his departure. On the day following, Mr. Jay obtained, by an unknown hand, from the French foreign office, a copy of a letter from M. de Marbois, the French minister in Philadelphia, to the Count de Vergennes, in which de Marbois expressed *surprise* that the Americans should claim the right of fishing on the banks of Newfoundland, and advised the Count to let them know at once that he would not support them in it. These facts taken together, Mr. Jay says, led him to conjecture, that M. de Rayneval had been sent to England to dissuade Lord Shelburne from acknowledging independence, and urge him to keep the Americans out of the fisheries, and limit their western boundary.

Penetrated with alarm, nothing would serve Mr. Jay but to dispatch a secret messenger of his own to Lord Shelburne, to counteract the baleful influence of the French emissary. Mr. Benjamin Vaughan, Franklin's old friend and the editor of his works, was the messenger employed by Mr. Jay on this occasion; and away he sped to England, charged to the brim with arguments calculated to neutralize the reasonings which M. de Rayneval was expected to bring forward. All this was kept secret from Dr. Franklin, who still afflicted the soul of Mr. Jay by maintaining that the French court was acting towards them in good faith. "It would have relieved me from much anxiety and uneasiness," wrote Mr. Jay, "to have concerted all these steps with Dr. Franklin; but on conversing with him about M. de Rayneval's journey, he did not concur with me in sentiment respecting the objects of it, but appeared to me to have a great degree of confidence in this court." Time, he adds, will show which of us is right.

Time *has* shown. Hear the explicit testimony of Dr. Jared Sparks on this point: "I have read in the office of Foreign Affairs in London the confidential correspondence of the British ministers with their commissioners for negotiating peace in Paris. I have also read in the French office of Foreign Affairs the entire correspondence of the Count de Vergennes, during the whole war, with the French ministers in this country, developing the policy and designs of the French court in regard to the war, and the objects to be obtained by the peace. I have, moreover, read the instructions of the Count de Vergennes when de Rayneval went to London, and the correspondence which passed between them while he remained there, containing notes of conversations with Lord Shelburne on one part, and Count de Vergennes' opinions on the other. After examining the subject with all the care and accuracy which these means of informations have enabled me to give to it, I am prepared to express my belief most fully that Mr. Jay was mistaken both in regard to the aims of the French court, and the plans pursued by them to gain their supposed ends."*

M. de Rayneval, in fact, went to London to ascertain, from personal interviews with Lord Shelburne, whether the British Government was sincerely desirous of concluding a peace, and he was ordered not to converse at all upon American topics except to insist upon the independence of the United States as a *sine qua non.*

Good Mr. Jay was soon relieved of his anxiety. Mr. Vaughan returned in about fifteen days, and with him came a courier who brought a new commission for Mr. Oswald, in which Mr. Jay's country was called by its proper name, "the United States;" "and very happy," he says, "were we to see it." Then, and not before, the negotiation could really begin. It was on the 27th

* Diplomatic Correspondence of the American Revolution, viii., 209.

of September when the new commission arrived, nine months after the first overture had reached Dr. Franklin from Lord North's ministry. The importance which this affair of the commission had assumed in the mind of Mr. Jay may be inferred from the fact, that his principal memoir on the subject to the Count de Vergennes was a manuscript of fifty or sixty pages. He ransacked all modern history for precedents and illustrations, and made a very learned argument. Nevertheless, that was not the way to Canada, which should have been *the* object of the negotiation, and to the acquisition of which nearly every thing else might have been postponed. Well, said Talleyrand to the clerks in his office: "Above all, gentlemen, *no zeal!*"

Congress having authorized the commissioners, "or a majority of such of them as should assemble," to appoint a secretary, at a thousand pounds a year, Mr. Jay and Dr. Franklin gave the office to William Temple Franklin. His commission was signed by them on the first of October.

During the month of October, Mr. Jay and Mr. Oswald, Mr. Jay and the Spanish embassador, Mr. Jay, Dr. Franklin and Mr. Oswald, discussed the details of the treaty, without making any great progress towards agreement on the troublesome points. Mr. Jay was still the slave of distrust. One evening, while he was in conference with Oswald, at the hotel of the latter, Mr. Oswald, wishing to refer to his instructions, opened his desk to get them; when, to his alarm, he found the paper missing ; *i. e.,* he could not find it. Oh, never mind, said Jay, you will find it in its place as soon as the minister has done with it. "In a few days," adds Mr. Jay's biographer, "the prediction was verified;" *i. e.,* Mr. Oswald found the paper. So convinced was Mr. Jay that the French ministry had spies in their employ who hovered about the lodgings of the diplomatic corps, picking locks and abstracting papers, that he "made it a rule to carry his confidential papers about his person."* He lent a credulous ear, too, to a tale told him by Mr. Oswald, that the Count de Vergennes, in the course of a conversation with "an Englishman of distinction here," had proposed to make a partition of America, France to possess one half, and England the other.

* "Life of Jay," i., 156.

October 26th, a gentleman, long expected, arrived in Paris, who was prepared to sympathize with Mr. Jay in his worst suspicions, and to sustain him in any measures growing out of the same; a gentleman who, to a general dislike of Frenchmen, added a particular recollection of a disagreeable collision with the Count de Vergennes. It was Mr. John Adams, flushed with his double success in Holland, in having concluded a treaty of commerce and started a loan.

CHAPTER XVI.

PEACE CONCLUDED.

Mr. ADAMS begins his Paris diary by saying, that the first thing to be done after arriving at the French capital, is to send for a tailor, peruke-maker, and shoe-maker; for France had established such a domination over the fashion that neither clothes, wigs, nor shoes, made in any other place, would do in Paris. So he did not see Mr. Jay the first day; still less, Dr. Franklin. On the next, which was Sunday, he called on his younger colleague, but did not find him at home. In the course of the day, however, he found out his old friend Ridley, who told him the news as learned from the friends of Mr. Jay. "Ridley says, Franklin has broke up the practice of inviting everybody to dine with him on Sunday at Passy; that he is getting better; the gout left him weak, but he begins to sit at table; * * Jay refused to treat with Oswald until he had a commission to treat with the commissioners of the United States of America; Franklin was afraid to insist upon'it; was afraid we should be obliged to treat without; differed with Jay. * * * Ridley is full of Jay's firmness and independence; has taken upon himself to act without asking advice, or even communicating with the Count de Vergennes, and this even in opposition to an instruction;" (ultimately to be governed by the advice and opinion of the French ministry).

Mr. Adams added a few lines of comment upon Mr. Ridley's version of the state of things: "Between two as subtle spirits as any in the world, the one malicious, the other, I think, honest, I shall have a delicate, a nice, a critical part to act. Franklin's cunning will be to divide us ; to this end, he will provoke, he will insinuate, he will intrigue, he will maneuver. My curiosity will at least be employed in observing his invention and his artifice." Horace correctly described inordinate self-love as *blind*.

He was closeted with Mr. Jay on the day following. I suppose that, corporeally speaking, they merely shook hands, after the Anglo-Saxon manner ; but, in a spiritual sense, they rushed into each other's arms, and hugged one another with the violence of true love. " Nothing," wrote Mr. Adams, " that has happened since the beginning of the controversy in 1761, has ever struck me more forcibly, or affected me more intimately, than that entire coincidence of principles and opinions between him and me." He thought Mr. Jay's compelling Oswald to get the phraseology of his commission changed, " a noble triumph," and regarded Franklin's conciliatory policy as base subserviency. Mr. Jay said, " we must be honest and grateful to our allies, but think for ourselves."

On the *fourth* day, in the evening, Mr. Adams went out to Passy, and paid his respects to Dr. Franklin. " I told him," says Adams, " without reserve, my opinion of the policy of this court, and of the principles, wisdom and firmness with which Mr. Jay had conducted the negotiation in his sickness and my absence, and that I was determined to support Mr. Jay to the utmost of my power in the pursuit of the same system. The Doctor heard me patiently, but said nothing." Wise doctor ! Franklin, indeed, never displayed more wisdom and self-control than in not quarreling with these two rare diplomatists, and letting them go on in their sage way without hinderance. They were a majority, and John Adams was at the head of the commission. A serious opposition on Franklin's part might have retarded the peace, might have broken up the commission ; but it could not have gained any solid advantages for his country. *That* game had been spoiled months ago. So, the first time the commissioners met, Dr. Franklin gave in to Mr. Jay's proposal, which was supported by Mr. Adams, to go on negotiating without consulting the French court at all. This he consented to the more readily, because Mr. Fitzherbert's negotiation with the Count de Vergennes was kept secret from them, and because nothing final or binding could be concluded without the formal consent of the French government first obtained. In truth, Mr. Jay's determination was such, that there was no choice left to Franklin but to withdraw from the commission, or let him have his way. " Would you break your instructions?" Franklin asked him, one day. " Yes," replied Jay, taking his pipe from his mouth, " as I break this pipe," and, so saying, threw the fragments into the fire.*

Now they set to work in earnest. Two long conferences every day; sometimes three. Couriers went and came continually. " The eyes of the universe" were upon Paris, and the press of all lands teemed with rumors and surmises respecting the negotiations. It was already November; Parliament would meet in a month; could Lord Shelburne sustain himself, if, when Parliament met, he could not announce the signing of acceptable preliminaries, at least, by Mr. Oswald and the Americans? Oswald thought not. All the adherents of the ministry feared not.

There were but three troublesome points, namely, the boundaries, the fisheries, and the tories. England claimed the province of Maine; said it was part of Canada; clung to it tenaciously. Spain as stoutly resisted the demand of the Americans for the Mississippi River as their western boundary. Some Frenchmen were disposed to keep American fishermen from the banks of Newfoundland, and England objected to their curing their fish on the Newfoundland shores. With one voice, the people of England demanded that, whatever else might be omitted from the treaty, a provision for the American tories must not be; their confiscated estates must be restored, their offenses forgiven, their losses made good. They had stood by England; England must stand by them. Lord Shelburne's office was daily besieged by American refugees, applicants for redress and compensation (Governor Franklin, perhaps, among them). He said that no part of his duty was so painful as to give them audience, and listen to the tale of their distresses; and well did he know that no ministry could stand who should make a peace without providing for them.

To demonstrate the justice of their claim to the province of Maine, who should the ministry send over but that Mr. Strachey, whom Mr. Adams and Dr. Franklin had met on Staten Island at the beginning of the revolution, when they conferred with Lord Howe? It was reserved for Mr. Adams to refute this gentleman. In the

---

* Diplomacy of United States, i., 121.

olden time, long before the revolution, Mr. Adams had been employed to investigate the boundaries of Massachusetts, of which Maine was then a part, and had even drawn up an elaborate report for the legislature upon the subject.   He was, therefore, at home upon the boundary question, and had, with wise foresight, brought with him a mass of documents and papers relating to it.   Mr. Adams, in his entertaining, vain-glorious manner, tells us how he discomfited the venerable Strachey.

"Messengers and couriers," he says, "were continually passing and repassing between Paris and London, from the British embassadors to the British ministry.   One gentleman, I have been informed, crossed the Channel eight or ten times upon these errands during the negotiation.   And whenever a new courier arrived, we were sure to hear some new proposition concerning the province of Maine.   Sometimes the English gentlemen appeared to soften down a little, and to be willing to compromise with us, and to condescend to agree upon Kennebec River as the boundary, and at last they seemed to insinuate that for the sake of peace they might retreat as far as Penobscot.   But Penobscot must at all events be theirs.   We concluded from all these appearances, that they had instructions to insist upon this point; but we insisted upon the river St. Croix, which I construed to mean the river St. John's, for St. John's had as many holy crosses upon it as any other river in that region, and had as often been called St. Croix River.

"One morning, I am not able to say of what day in November, but certainly many days after the commencement of conferences, the British minister introduced to us a special messenger from London, as the oldest clerk in the board of trade and plantations, and a very respectable character.   He was sent over by the British cabinet with huge volumes of the original records of the board of trade and plantations, which they would not trust to any other messenger, in order to support their incontestable claim to the province of Maine.   We all treated the gentleman and his records with respect.   After the usual ceremonies and salutations were over, the gentleman produced his manuscripts and pointed to the passages he relied on, and read them.

"I said nothing at first; but I thought the British cabinet believed that Doctor Franklin was too much of a philosopher to have been very attentive to these ancient transactions, and that Mr.

Adams and Mr. Jay were too young to know any thing about them ; and, therefore, that they might, by the venerable figure and imposing title of the most ancient clerk in the board of trade and plantations, and by the pompous appearance of enormous volumes of ancient records, be able to chicane us out of the province of Maine, or at least to intimidate us into compromise for the river Kennebec, or, at the worst, for Penobscot. When the aged stranger had read some time in his aged volumes, I observed that I had, at my apartments, documents which I flattered myself would sufficiently explain and refute whatever might be contained in those records which should be construed or alleged against our right to the province of Maine, and requested that the deliberation might be postponed till I could produce my books and papers. This was agreed. Accordingly, at the next meeting, I produced my documents."*

And those documents were convincing. " Before I had gone half way," says Mr. Adams, " I saw that all the gentlemen, not excluding the clerk himself, were fully convinced that they had taken possession of ground they could not maintain or defend. Although they did not expressly acknowledge their error, the subject subsided, and we heard little more concerning it."

A day or two after (November 5th), Mr. Strachey set out for London to report progress to the ministry, and to procure final instruction on the points in dispute. He had tried hard to induce the commissioners to concede something on the tory question ; and, shortly before stepping into his carriage, he wrote a note entreating them to reconsider the subject, and, if they could change their mind upon it, to send a messenger in pursuit of him with the intelligence. "How far," wrote the old man, " you will be justified in risking every favorite object of America is for you to determine. Independence, and more than a reasonable possession of territory, seems to be within your reach. Will you suffer them to be outweighed by the gratification of resentment against individuals ?" The American commissioners stood their ground, however, and Mr. Strachey took no new proposals to London.

Mr. Adams informs us, too, that he "silenced all the praters at Versailles," on the Maine topic. He let two whole weeks pass without paying even a visit of ceremony to the Count de Vergennes,

* " Works of John Adams," i., 665.

and would not then have gone if the minister had not caused both the Marquis de Lafayette and Dr. Franklin to remind him of the omission. M. de Vergennes said that he knew of Mr. Adams's arrival in Paris only from the reports of the police. So, early on Sunday morning, November 10th, Mr. Adams rode out to Versailles, and waited on the minister for foreign affairs. His reception was all that he could desire. The Count asked how he and his colleagues got on with the English commissioner. Mr. Adams replied that they were divided on two points, Maine and the tories, but, for his own part, he did not believe that Lord Shelburne or England cared for either, and they were only insisted upon for reasons unavowed. Mr. Adams proceeded to exhibit his Maine documents, which, as he has told us, "silenced all the praters of Versailles;" though there were only two praters present, the Count de Vergennes and M. de Rayneval. After a long conversation, the minister invited Mr. Adams to dinner, and Mr. Adams accepted the invitation. The company, it seems, fooled him to the top of his bent.

"I went up to dinner," he says, "with the Comte alone. He showed me into the room where were the ladies and the company. I singled out the Countess, and went up to her to make her my compliments. The Countess and all the ladies rose up; I made my respects to them all, and turned round and bowed to the rest of the company. The Count, who came in after me, made his bows to the ladies, and to the Countess last. When he came to her, he turned round and called out, 'Monsieur Adams, come here; here is the Comtesse de Vergennes.' A nobleman in company said, 'Mr. Adams has already made his court to Madame la Comtesse.' I went up again, however, and spoke again to the Countess, and she to me. When dinner was served, the Comte led Madame de Montmorin, and left me to conduct the Countess, who gave me her hand with extraordinary condescension, and I conducted her to table. She made me sit next her on her right hand, and was remarkably attentive to me the whole time. The Comte, who sat opposite, was constantly calling out to me to know what I would eat, and to offer me tid bits, claret, and madeira. In short, I was never before treated with half the respect at Versailles in my life.

"In the ante-chamber, before dinner, some French gentlemen came to me and said they had seen me two years ago; said that I had shown in Holland that the Americans understood negotiation

as well as war. The compliments that have been made since my
arrival in France, upon my success in Holland, would be considered
as a curiosity if committed to writing. 'I congratulate you upon
your success,' is common to all. One adds, 'Sir, by my faith, you
have succeeded marvelously well. You have established your independence; you have made a treaty; and you have negotiated a
loan. You afford us the spectacle of a perfect success.' Another
says: 'You have done wonders in Holland; you have floored the
Stadtholder and the English party; you have maneuvered admirably,
and made a prodigious stir in the world.' Another said: 'Sir, you
are the Washington of the negotiation.' This is the finishing stroke.
It is impossible to exceed this. Compliments are the study of this
people, and there is no other so ingenious at them."*

This last compliment appears to have given Mr. Adams particular delight, as he qotes it several times in his diary. A day or
two after this Versailles Sunday, he dined out again, and he recorded the pleasing fact, that more than one person told him he
was the Washington of the negotiation. " I answered," he says,
'Sir, you do me the greatest honor, and the compliment is the sublimest possible.' ' Oh, sir, in truth, it is no more than your due.'
A few more of these compliments would kill Franklin, if they
should come to his ears."

Mr. Adams records a curious conversation with Mr. Oswald:
" 'You are afraid,' says Mr. Oswald to-day, ' of being made the
tools of the powers of Europe.' 'Indeed I am,' says I. 'What
powers?' said he. 'All of them,' said I. 'It is obvious that
all the powers of Europe will be continually maneuvering with us,
to work us into their real or imaginary balances of power. They
will all wish to make of us a make-weight candle, when they are
weighing out their pounds. Indeed, it is not surprising; for we
shall very often, if not always, be able to turn the scale. But I
think it ought to be our rule not to meddle; and that of all the
powers of Europe, not to desire us, or, perhaps, even to permit us
to interfere, if they can help it.' 'I beg of you,' says he, 'to get
out of your head the idea that we shall disturb you.' ' What!'
said I, 'do you yourself believe that your ministers, governors,
and even nation, will not wish to get us on your side in any future
war?' 'Damn the governors!' said he. 'No! we will take

* Works of John Adams, iii., 305.

off their heads if they do an improper thing towards you.'
'Thank you for your good will,' said I, 'which I feel to be sincere. But nations don't feel as you and I do ; and your nation,
when it gets a little refreshed from the fatigues of the war, when
men and money are become plenty, and allies at hand, will not feel
as it does now.' 'We never can be such sots,' says he, 'as to
think of differing again with you.' 'Why,' says I, 'in truth, I
have never been able to comprehend the reason why you ever
thought of differing with us thus far.' "*

During these critical days of the negotiation, Mr. Adams perfectly realized Dr. Franklin's well-known description of him : "Always an honest man, often a wise one, but sometimes, and in some
things, absolutely out of his senses." Mr. Adams, let us own,
thought no better of Franklin. During this final month of the negotiation, he wrote to a friend at home : "Luckily, Mr. Deane out
of the question, every American minister in Europe, except Dr.
Franklin, has discovered a judgment, a conscience, and a resolution
of his own, and, of consequence, every minister that has come
over, has been frowned upon. On the contrary, Dr. Franklin, who
has been pliant and submissive in every thing, has been constantly
cried up to the stars, without doing any thing to deserve it." He
wrote in a similar strain thirty years afterward ; for John Adams
belonged to the class of mortals who learn nothing and forget
nothing.

During the negotiations, Dr. Franklin failed not to bring forward
his favorite scheme for the suppression of privateering. He drew
up an article for insertion in the treaty, prohibiting the practice,
and exempting farmers, fishermen, artisans, manufacturers, and unfortified towns, from attack and molestation.† The article was not

---

* "Works of John Adams," iii., 316.

† The following is a copy of the proposed article : "If war should hereafter arise between
Great Britain and the United States, which God forbid, the merchants of either country, then residing in the other, shall be allowed to remain nine months, to collect their debts, and settle
their affairs, and may depart freely, carrying off all their effects without molestation or hindrance. And all fishermen, all cultivators of the earth, and all artisans or manufacturers unarmed
and inhabiting unfortified towns, villages, or places, who labor for the common subsistence and
benefit of mankind, and peaceably follow their respective employments, shall be allowed to continue the same, and shall not be molested by the armed force of the enemy, in whose power, by
the events of the war, they may happen to fall ; but, if any thing is necessary to be taken from
them, for the use of such armed force, the same shall be paid for at a reasonable price. And all
merchants or traders, with their unarmed vessels, employed in commerce, exchanging the products of different places, and thereby rendering the necessaries, conveniences, and comforts of

inserted, and does not appear to have been seriously discussed. His argument on this subject, which he read to Mr. Oswald, Mr. Jay, and Mr. Adams, is ingenious, and does infinite honor to his noble old heart. But ingenious arguments are lost upon the human mind when passion sways it; else, there had never been a war.

The month of November wore rapidly away in endless discussions of the three vexed topics : the fisheries, the boundaries, and the tories. Mr. Strachey's return with the ultimatum of the ministry could alone bring the affair to a conclusion. After an absence of twenty days, that ancient clerk arrived, and was again in conference with the commissioners. With regard to the boundaries claimed by the Americans, he said the ministry thought them far too extended, but would not make a difficulty about them; in short, they conceded the boundaries. As to the fisheries, the Americans could not be allowed to dry their fish on the Nova Scotia shores, nor fish within three leagues of the coast, nor within fifteen leagues of Cape Breton. With regard to the tories, Mr. Strachey said, that he had called upon every member of the cabinet, and that they were all strenuous in demanding the restitution of the confiscated estates. A long and most earnest conference ensued. Mr. Adams, who, in the course of his law-practice among the fishermen of Cape Cod, had acquired a perfect familiarity with the business of fishing and the habits of fish, luminously expounded those subjects to Mr. Strachey and Mr. Oswald. The tory question was deferred for further consultation. Toward the close of the interview, Mr. Jay inquired if the propositions brought by Strachey were the ultimatum of the ministry. With much reluctance Mr. Strachey answered, No; upon which, hope revived in the minds of the American commissioners. Mr. Jay also asked whether Mr. Oswald had authority to conclude and sign. " Absolutely," replied Mr. Strachey. " We agreed," records Mr. Adams, " that these were good signs of sincerity."

That evening, Dr. Franklin drew up a long letter to Mr. Oswald, in which the tory question was exhaustively discussed. He

human life more easy to obtain, and more general, shall be allowed to pass freely, unmolested. And neither of the powers, parties to this treaty, shall grant or issue any commission to any private armed vessels, empowering them to take or destroy such trading ships, or interrupt such commerce."

showed, first, that the confiscation of the estates was the act of the legislatures of the States in which they were situated, and that, therefore, the Congress of the United States could not restore them; and, secondly, that the losses entailed on the tories by those confiscations were as nothing compared with the stupendous sum of damage inflicted on loyal citizens through the lawless conduct of the king's troops. He treated the latter point with singular ingenuity and force. He recounted the burning of Charlestown, Falmouth, Norfolk, New London, Fairfield, Esopus; the desolation of vast tracts of country; and the slaughter of hundreds of unoffending farmers. Restitution! "The British troops," said he, "can never excuse their barbarities. They were unprovoked. The loyalists may say in excuse of theirs, that they were exasperated by the loss of their estates, and it was revenge. They have then had their revenge. *Is it right they should have both?* Some of those people may have merit in their regard for Britain, and who espoused her cause from affection; these it may become *you* to reward. But there are many of them who were waverers, and were only determined to engage in it by some occasional circumstance or appearances; these have not much of either merit or demerit; and there are others, who have abundance of demerit respecting your country, having by their falsehoods and misrepresentations brought on and encouraged the continuance of the war; these, instead of being recompensed, should be punished. * * *

"Your ministers require, that we should receive again into our bosom those who have been our bitterest enemies, and restore their properties who have destroyed ours, and this, while the wounds they have given us are still bleeding! It is many years since your nation expelled the Stuarts and their adherents, and confiscated their estates. Much of your resentment against them may by this time be abated; yet, if we should propose it, and insist on it as an article of our treaty with you, that that family should be recalled and the forfeited estates of its friends restored, would you think us serious in our professions of earnestly desiring peace?

"I must repeat my opinion, that it is best for you to drop all mention of the refugees. We have proposed, indeed, nothing but what we think best for you as well as ourselves. But, if you will have them mentioned, let it be in an article, in which you may provide, that they shall exhibit accounts of their losses to the commissioners, hereafter to be appointed, who should examine the same, together with the accounts now preparing in America of the damages done by them, and state the account; and that, if a balance appears in their favor, it shall be said by us to you, and by you divided among them as you shall think proper; and if the balance is found due to us, it shall be paid by you. Give me leave, however, to advise you to prevent the necessity of so dreadful a discussion by dropping the article."

The American commissioners breakfasted together, the next morning, at Mr. Jay's hotel, when Dr. Franklin produced his letter, and it was agreed that he should read it to Mr. Oswald as his private opinion merely. On this day, for the first time, Mr. Fitzherbert joined the conference. The whole day was spent in discussing the two disputed points, but without producing on either party the slightest discernible effect.

"Dr. Franklin," says Mr. Adams, "is very stanch against the tories; more decided a great deal on this point than Mr. Jay or myself." Perhaps, he thought of his son, however, when he suggested in his letter to Oswald, that it would become England to reward some of the tory refugees. William Temple Franklin, it seems, went so far as to ask Mr. Vaughan to use his influence with Lord Shelburne to procure compensation for his father; and Mr. Vaughan repeatedly urged it upon the premier for the sake of the effect it might have upon the negotiation. Whether Governor Franklin owed his eight hundred a year, or any part of it, to this recommendation, I do not know. It was, certainly, very pardonable in the young secretary to say a word for his father, when a word might so materially benefit him. Dr. Franklin, however, was "stanch" in the opinion, that all compensation to tories must come from the treasury of England, not from the coffers of Congress. I doubt, too, if he reckoned his son in the class of tories who deserved compensation.

November 27th. Mr. Benjamin Vaughan returned from London, where he had conversed with Lord Shelburne on all the topics of the treaty. He brought no comfort with him. He could only say that the ministry were exceedingly anxious to procure something for the tories, since their honor and their places seemed to depend upon their doing so. Mr. Vaughan entreated Franklin to yield this point. It was now or never with the peace, he urged.

"We have liberal American commissioners at Paris, a liberal English commissioner, and a liberal first minister for England. All these circumstances may vanish to-morrow, if this treaty blows over." "I know," said he, "you have justice on your side; I know you may talk of precedents; but there is such a thing as forgiveness, as generosity, and as a manly policy, that can share a small *loss*, rather than miss a greater *good*."

The next day, November 28th, was spent in another long and fruitless conference. Mr. Laurens arrived, mourning the loss of his son, killed in battle a few weeks before, in South Carolina, yet "proud that he had had a son willing to die for his country." He joined the conference the next morning; "his judgment as sound," says Mr. Adams, "and his heart as firm as ever."

Friday, November 29th, was the great day of the negotiation; it was also the last. Present, Mr. Oswald, Mr. Fitzherbert, Mr. Strachey, Mr. Adams, Dr. Franklin, Mr. Jay, Mr. Laurens, William Temple Franklin, and Mr. Caleb Whitefoord, the secretary of Mr. Oswald. The conference was held at the rooms of Mr. Jay, in the Hotel d'Orleans, Rue des Petits Augustins. The fisheries were the first topic discussed. Mr. Adams presented an article on the subject, newly drawn, which he said expressed the claims of America. Mr. Strachey proposed to change the "right" of fishing into the "liberty" of fishing; and Mr. Fitzherbert said that the word *right* was an obnoxious expression. Then rose up Mr. Adams, and gave one of those bursts of eloquence, which, in 1776, had so much to do in bringing Congress to the point of declaring the colonies independent.

"Gentlemen," said he, "is there or can there be a clearer right? In former treaties,—that of Utrecht and that of Paris,—France and England have claimed the right, and used the word. When God Almighty made the banks of Newfoundland, at three hundred leagues' distance from the people of America, and at six hundred* leagues' distance from those of France and England, did he not give as good a right to the former as to the latter? If Heaven in the creation gave a right, it is ours at least as much as yours. If occupation, use, and possession, give a right, we have it as clearly as you. If war, and blood, and treasure, give a right, ours is as good as yours. We have been constantly fighting in Canada, Cape Breton, and Nova Scotia, for the defense of this fishery, and have expended beyònd all proportion more than you. If, then, the right cannot be denied, why should it not be acknowledged, and put out of dispute? Why should we leave room for illiterate fishermen to wrangle and chicane?"

Mr. Fitzherbert replied : " The argument is in your favor. I must confess your reasons appear to be good ; but Mr. Oswald's instructions are such, that I do not see how he can agree with you. And, for my part, I have not the honor and felicity to be a man of that weight and authority in my country that you, gentlemen, are in yours." (Mr. Adams interjects here, "This was very genteelly said.") " I have the accidental advantage of a little favor with the present minister; but I cannot depend upon the influence of my own opinion, to reconcile a measure to my countrymen. We can consider ourselves as little more than pens in the hands of government at home; and Mr. Oswald's instructions are *so* particular."*

Mr. Adams said : " The time is not so pressing with us but that we can wait till a courier goes to London, with your representations on this subject." To which Mr. Fitzherbert replied, that " to send again to London, and have all laid loose before Parliament, was so uncertain a measure—it was going to sea again. Suppose," he added, " we were to sign the other articles, and leave this matter of the fishery to be settled at the definitive treaty?" Adams, Jay, and Laurens, at once declared that they could sign no articles which did not expressly concede the right to the fishery. Without that, said Mr. Jay, it could not be a peace—it would only be an insidious truce.

" If another messenger is to be sent to London," said Dr. Franklin, " he ought to carry something more respecting a compensation to the sufferers in America." He then drew from his pocket a paper, which he said was an article that he proposed for insertion in the treaty. He read it, as follows :

" It is agreed, that his Britannic Majesty will earnestly recommend it to his Parliament, to provide for and make a compensation to the merchants and shopkeepers of Boston, whose goods and merchandize were seized and taken out of their stores, warehouses, and shops, by order of General Gage, and others of his commanders and officers there ; and also to the inhabitants of Philadelphia,

---

* " Works of John Adams," iii., 333.

for the goods taken away by his army there ; and to make compensation, also, for the tobacco, rice, indigo, and negroes, &c., seized and carried off by his armies, under Generals Arnold, Cornwallis, and others, from the States of Virginia, North and South Carolina, and Georgia, and also for all vessels and cargoes belonging to the inhabitants of the said United States, which were stopped, seized, or taken, either in the ports, or on the seas, by his governors, or by his ships-of-war, before the declaration of war against the said States. And it is further agreed, that his Britannic Majesty will also earnestly recommend it to his Parliament, to make compensation for all the towns, villages, and farms, burnt and destroyed by his troops, or adherents, in the said United States."

To this he had appended a brief statement of " Facts," in support of the article.*

This inimitable stroke finished the business. There was nothing more said of compensating the tories, or annulling confiscations. The three English commissioners withdrew to another apartment, for consultation. Upon their return, Mr. Fitzherbert said that Mr. Strachey and himself had agreed to advise Mr. Oswald to accept the terms proposed on behalf of America, and Mr. Oswald had consented to do so. The articles were then read over and corrected, and the next day appointed for the signing of the preliminary treaty.

The articles, nine in number, were in substance these : I. Inde-

---

* " FACTS.

" There existed a free commerce, upon mutual faith, between Great Britain and America. The merchants of the former credited the merchants and planters of the latter with great quantities of goods, on the common expectation, that the merchants, having sold the goods, would make the accustomed remittances; that the planters would do the same by the labor of their negroes, and the produce of that labor, tobacco, rice, indigo, &c.

" England, before the goods were sold in America, sends an armed force, seizes those goods in the stores, some even in the ships that brought them, and carries them off; seizes, also, and carries off the tobacco, rice, and indigo, provided by the planters to make returns, and even the negroes, from whose labor they might hope to raise other produce for that purpose.

" Britain now demands that the debts shall, nevertheless, be paid.

" Will she, can she, justly refuse making compensation for such seizures ?

" If a draper, who had sold a piece of linen to a neighbor on credit, should follow him, and take the linen from him by force, and then send a bailiff to arrest him for the debt, would any court of law or equity award the payment of the debt, without ordering a restitution of the cloth ?

" Will not the debtors in America cry out, that, if this compensation be not made, they were betrayed by the pretended credit, and are now doubly ruined ; first, by the enemy, and then by the negotiators at Paris, the goods and negroes sold them being taken from them, with all they had besides, and they are now to be obliged to pay for what they have been robbed of ?"

pendence. II. Boundaries. III. People of the United States to have the right of fishing on the Banks of Newfoundland and in the Gulf of St. Lawrence, and cure their fish on the unsettled shores of Nova Scotia and Labrador. IV. Private debts to be paid on both sides. V. Congress to recommend the State legislatures to restore confiscated estates of real British subjects, and to permit American tories to remain unmolested for twelve months, in their endeavors to obtain the restoration of their rights and property. VI. No more confiscations or prosecutions for acts done during the war. VII. British troops to be withdrawn, and no American property taken away with them. VIII. The navigation of the Mississippi, from its source to the ocean, shall forever remain free and open to the subjects of Great Britain and the citizens of the United States. IX. Any place taken before the arrival of these articles in America, to be at once restored.

There was, also, a separate and secret article defining the boundaries of West Florida, in case that province should fall to Great Britain at the conclusion of the general peace. The whole was prefaced by a declaration that the "treaty is not to be concluded until terms of peace shall be agreed upon between Great Britain and France."

The conference over, Dr. Franklin, for the first time, reported progress to the Count de Vergennes, in these words: "I have the honor to acquaint your Excellency, that the commissioners of the United States have agreed with Mr. Oswald on the preliminary articles of the peace between those States and Great Britain. To-morrow I hope we shall be able to communicate to your Excellency a copy of them."

The next morning, November 30th, the commissioners met at the rooms of Mr. Oswald, when the preliminaries were duly signed, sealed, and delivered; after which, says Mr. Adams, "we all went out to Passy to dine with Dr. Franklin." In the course of the day, Dr. Franklin sent a copy of the articles to the Count de Vergennes, with the announcement that they had been that morning signed. Doubtless, the commissioners were very merry over their wine at Passy. Times had changed since Mr. Adams and Dr. Franklin had slept together and discussed the philosophy of colds, on their way to Perth Amboy to meet Lord Howe, in 1776.

No congratulatory letter, no answer or acknowledgment of any kind, came from the French minister. When some days of this ominous silence had elapsed, Dr. Franklin went to Versailles and called upon the Count, who did not receive him with the usual cordiality. " I allowed myself," the minister afterward wrote, " to make him perceive that his proceeding in this abrupt signature of the articles had little in it which could be agreeable to the king. He appeared sensible of it, and excused in the best manner he could, himself and his colleagues. Our conversation was amicable." I know not what excuses Dr. Franklin advanced to soften the minister's resentment on this occasion. Mr. Adams made this defense of the " abrupt" signing in one of his public letters : " We must have signed (then) or lost the peace. The peace depended on a day. Parliament had been waiting long, and once prorogued. The minister was so pressed he could not have met Parliament and held his place without an agreement upon terms, at least, with America.   If we had not signed, the ministry would have changed, and the coalition (of Fox and Lord North) come in ; and the whole world knows the coalition would not have made peace upon the present terms, and, consequently, not at all this year (1783).   The iron was struck in the few critical moments when it was of a proper heat. If it had been suffered to cool, it would have flown in pieces like glass."*   A good excuse ; and offered, doubtless, in perfect sincerity.   The ministry was, indeed, in a tottering condition, and being censured by Parliament for making peace without securing a provision for the tories, resigned in February, 1783. Nevertheless, the true reason for the abrupt signing was, that John Adams and John Jay believed that the French government wished to limit the power, the growth, and the boundaries, of the United States ; and they meant, simply, to steal a march upon the Count de Vergennes and M. de Rayneval.

The Count was by no means satisfied with Dr. Franklin's apology.   A week or two later, when Franklin proposed sending the preliminaries to America by a ship for which a passport was sent him by the English commissioners, the Count sharply remonstrated.   "I am at a loss, sir," he wrote, "to explain your conduct, and that of your colleagues on this occasion.   You have concluded your preliminary articles without any communication between us,

* " Works of John Adams," viii., 88.

Chadron State College Library

Chadron, Nebraska

although the instructions from Congress prescribe, that nothing shall be done without the participation of the king. You are about to hold out a certain hope of peace to America, without even informing yourself on the state of the negotiation on our part. You are wise and discreet, sir; you perfectly understand what is due to propriety; you have all your life performed your duties. I pray you to consider how you propose to fulfill those, which are due to the king! I am not desirous of enlarging these reflections; I commit them to your own integrity. When you shall be pleased to relieve my uncertainty, I will entreat the king to enable me to answer your demands (for money)."

Franklin hastened to mollify the minister; for Congress was still in the utmost extremity of need. " Nothing," he urged, " has been agreed in the preliminaries contrary to the interests of France; and no peace is to take place between us and England, till you have concluded yours. Your observation is, however, apparently just, that, in not consulting you before they were signed, we have been guilty of neglecting a point of *bienséance*. But, as this was not from want of respect for the king, whom we all love and honor, we hope it will be excused, and that the great work, which has hitherto been so happily conducted, is so nearly brought to perfection, and is so glorious to his reign, will not be ruined by a single indiscretion of ours. And certainly the whole edifice sinks to the ground immediately, if you refuse on that account to give us any further assistance. * * * It is not possible for any one to be more sensible than I am, of what I and every American owe to the king, for the many and great benefits and favors he has bestowed upon us. All my letters to America are proofs of this; all tending to make the same impressions on the minds of my countrymen, that I felt in my own. And I believe that no prince was ever more beloved and respected by his own subjects, than the king is by the people of the United States. *The English, I just now learn, flatter themselves they have already divided us.* I hope this little misunderstanding will therefore be kept a secret, and that they will find themselves totally mistaken."

The money was granted. Congress had asked a loan of twenty millions of francs; but this was beyond the resources of the French treasury at the close of a long war, and only six millions could be spared.

M. de Vergennes gave the French minister at Philadelphia a narrative of the abrupt signing, and of Mr. Adams's neglecting to call upon him. " I think it proper," wrote the Count, " that the most influential members of Congress should be informed of the very irregular conduct of their commissioners in regard to us. You may speak of it not in the tone of complaint. I accuse no person; I blame no one, not even Dr. Franklin. He has yielded too easily to the bias of his colleagues, who do not pretend to recognize the rules of courtesy in regard to us. All their attentions have been taken up by the English whom they have met in Paris. If we may judge of the future from what has passed here under our eyes, we shall be but poorly paid for all that we have done for the United States, and for securing to them a national existence." The conduct of the commissioners, as Mr. Madison reports, was most sharply criticised in Congress, and there was talk even of their recall. Probably some decisive act of censure would have followed, if the news of the general peace, so quickly succeeding, had not banished the recollection of every thing that was not in harmony with the universal joy. Mr. Livingston, however, in his next letter to the commissioners, gave strong expression to his disapprobation of the conduct complained of by the Count de Vergennes. Each of the gentlemen returned a defense of that conduct, which reads plausibly enough. Franklin succeeded, at length, in removing the ill impression from the mind of the French minister, and no bad consequences resulted from the affair.

I do not think Dr. Franklin was to blame for the act of discourtesy to the French minister; for, linked with two such colleagues, it was, perhaps, the best of all the evils in his choice. He must have seen how *essential* it was to keep Mr. Adams and Mr. Jay apart from the French minister and his secretary—men formed by nature and by education to misunderstand and undervalue one another. It was only a Franklin who could have extricated the peace from such a conjunction of antagonisms.

Mr. Fitzherbert and the Count de Vergennes agreed upon terms on the eighteenth of January, 1783. Two days after, in the Count's office, at Versailles, in the presence of Dr. Franklin and Mr. Adams, the representatives of England, France, and Spain, signed the preliminaries of the general peace. Documents were immediately signed, declaring hostilities suspended. The war was at an end.

The United States, with the assistance of France, had achieved their independence. There was no ceremony observed or emotion expressed on this interesting occasion; the commissioners merely showing their powers, and signing the various documents, in a composed, business-like manner. "Thus," says Mr. Adams, "was this mighty system terminated with as little ceremony, and in as short a time, as a marriage settlement." The Americans went to dine at the Duc de la Rochefoucault's. In that hospitable abode, the spell of official etiquette dissolved, and Franklin exclaimed, as he embraced the Duke, "My friend! could I have hoped, at my age, to enjoy such a happiness!"*

In the United States, the articles gave universal satisfaction, and every heart swelled with gratitude and exultation. Contrary to Franklin's prediction, blessings without number were bestowed upon the peace-makers.

The negotiation of the definitive treaty was conducted on the part of England by Mr. David Hartley; Mr. Oswald having retired from public life on the retirement of his patron, Lord Shelburne. From May to September, the commissioners were busy enough. New articles were proposed, discussed, rejected; or, if agreed upon in Paris, rejected in London. Mr. Adams became more suspicious and unmanageable than ever, almost to the point of being "absolutely out of his senses." "One of my colleagues," wrote Franklin, July, 1783, "thinks the French minister one of the greatest enemies of our country; that he would have straitened our boundaries, to prevent the growth of our people; contracted our fishery, to obstruct the increase of our seamen; and retained the royalists among us, to keep us divided; that he privately opposes all our negotiations with foreign courts, and afforded us, during the war, the assistance we received, only to keep it alive, that we might be so much the more weakened by it; that to think of gratitude to France is the greatest of follies, and that to be influenced by it would ruin us. He makes no secret of his having these opinions, expresses them publicly sometimes in presence of the English ministers, and speaks of hundreds of instances which he could produce in proof of them." His jealousy of Dr. Franklin sometimes amounted to a mania.† He accused him of arrogating to himself the

---

* Rochefoucault's Eulogium of Franklin, Paris, June 13, 1790.
† Such passages as the following occur in Mr. Adams's private letters of 1783: To Elbridge Gerry,

power and consequence which belonged to the whole commission, and thought that the Count de Vergennes and Franklin were plotting his ruin, and employing the newspapers of Europe to depreciate his character. He was sorely affronted, too, by the appointment of Franklin's grandson to the secretaryship, and, at first, refused to sign his commission ; but, after holding out many months, he was induced to append his signature. He had the grace, also, to bear voluntary testimony, in two of his public letters, to Dr. Franklin's ability and firmness, as displayed at the crisis of the negotiation in November, 1782.

In a word, nothing could be agreed upon between the American commissioners and the English ministry, save only the preliminary articles signed in 1782. After eight or nine months of fruitless negotiation, those preliminaries were accepted as the definitive treaty, with only the requisite alterations of form. On Wednesday, September 3d, 1783, at Mr. Hartley's apartments at the *Hotel de York*, in Paris, the definitive treaty between Great Britain and the United States was signed. The treaty between England and France was signed on the same day, at Versailles ; the Count de Vergennes making it a point to delay the ceremony until a messenger from Paris brought him the news that the signing of the American treaty had taken place. The treaty was unanimously ratified by Congress, January 14th, 1784 ; and ratified by the king of England, on the 9th of April ; so that, from the beginning of the negotiation to the final ratification, was a period of two years and three months.

Liberal Europe rejoiced. Young Europe began to realize its dream of emigrating to free America. The great movement westward, that has since known but two brief intervals of pause, began. Men of family and fortune, widows seeking chances for their children, young adventurers with small "ventures" of goods or capital, and hosts of poor men who sold their all, or mortgaged

April 15th : "John Jay, in his present circumstances, wants, as well as all your faithful ministers, all the support which Congress can give them. You will never have another honest minister trumpeted by the court where he is. Dr. Franklin alone is, and will be, trumpeted by the *commis* at Versailles, and their tools." To the same, Sept. 3d : "The moment an American minister gives a loose to his passion for women, that moment he is undone ; he is instantly at the mercy of the spies of the court, and the tool of the most profligate of the human race. * * If you make it a principle that your ministers should be agreeable at the court and have the good word of the courtiers, you are undone. No man will ever be pleasing at a court in general, who is not depraved in his morals or warped from your interest."

their labor, to pay their passage, hastened to embark for the land of promise. Among those who did so, I observe, just after the conclusion of the definitive treaty, was a young German from Baden, son of a small farmer, who took out with him to sell on commission a few hundred dollars' worth of musical instruments— John Jacob Astor, founder of the Astor Library in the city of New York.

CHAPTER XVII.

AFTER THE PEACE.

THE definitive treaty signed, Mr. Jay went to England to try the Bath waters, and Mr. Adams soon followed him on a tour of pleasure. Dr. Franklin himself had thoughts of crossing the Channel once more, and dropping in, some Thursday evening, at his old Whig Club at the London Coffee-House, and taking up his quarters, for a while, in Craven street. But the autumn was too far advanced, he thought; and his old friend, the Gout, gave him warning not to venture too far; to say nothing of the severer admonitions of a new acquaintance, the Stone. The completion of the treaty, however, gave him more leisure than he had enjoyed before in France, and his grandson, Ben Bache, a fine lad then of fifteen, came home from his Swiss boarding-school to enliven his heart and home. The boy, he found, had learned something of many languages, but had half forgotten his English.

Twice Dr. Franklin had asked his recall: first, in 1781; the second time, soon after the signing of the preliminaries, in 1782. His first resignation was answered by his being appointed a member of the commission to treat for peace, and by an assurance that when peace was made he should be allowed to retire, if he should then wish to do so. To his second request for recall he had received no answer, though a year had elapsed since he had sent it. Some weeks after the signing of the definitive treaty, he wrote a third resignation, more decided than those previously forwarded. In each of these three letters he called the attention of Congress to the merits and services of William Temple Franklin, and asked for him a suitable diplomatic appointment in Europe. "He has been seven years in the service," he wrote in December, 1783, "and is much esteemed by all that know him, particularly by the minister here, who, since my new disorder (the stone) makes my going to Versailles inconvenient to me, transacts our business with him in the most obliging and friendly manner. It is natural for me, who love him, to wish to see him settled before I die in some employ that may probably be permanent; and I hope you will be so good to me as to get that affair likewise moved and carrie l through in his favor. He has, I think, this additional merit to plead, that he has served in my office as secretary several years, for the small salary of three hundred louis a year, while the Congress gave one thousand a year to the secretaries of other ministers, who had not half the employ for a secretary that I had."

No answer at all ever came to *this* part of his letters. He wished Congress to make his grandson their minister at one of the secondary courts; and, perhaps, if his desires had been gratified, he would never have summoned courage to cross the ocean again, for he loved him, as Lafayette says, "better than any thing in the world"—certainly better than any one else in the old world. There was some justice in Dr. Franklin's claim upon Congress for the adoption of the young man; for he had spent those years in the service of Congress which would otherwise have been employed in acquiring a profession. Perhaps, too, his grandfather perceived that the seven years passed about the French court had unfitted him to excel in any career open to him in the United States; where, indeed, the young gentleman had only lived a year or two of his life.

It was long before Dr. Franklin received the desired permission to retire. Meanwhile, he was agreeably enough employed in negotiating treaties with other powers of Europe, and making vain attempts to induce Great Britain to enter into just commercial relations with the young nation over the sea.

After a French war, crowds of English hasten to enjoy once more the delights of a "trip to Paris." This year, and the next, therefore, the gay city was overflowing with English visitors, and most of them who were worth knowing, and many who were not, found their way to Passy; Franklin being, at this time, incomparably the most distinguished person in Europe. Among his new acquaintances, just after the peace, were William Pitt and his friend William Wilberforce; both in Parliament, both opponents of the American war, both very young. We have no record, I believe, of William Pitt's impressions, and Wilberforce merely mentions that he was pleased to see how cordially Dr. Franklin greeted the young orator, whose first triumphs had been won in defending America. Mr. Wilberforce, it appears, was particularly struck with the strange, and even portentous position of the Marquis de Lafayette, whom he styles "a pleasing, enthusiastical man." "He seemed to be the representative of the democracy in the very presence of the monarch, the tribune intruding with his veto within the chamber of the patrician order. His own establishment was formed upon the English model, and amidst the gayety and ease of Fontainbleau he assumed an air of republican austerity. When the fine ladies of the court would attempt to drag him to the card-table, he shrugged his shoulders, with an affected contempt for the customs and amusements of the old régime. Meanwhile, the deference which this champion of the new state of things received, above all from the ladies of the court, intimated clearly the disturbance of the social atmosphere, and presaged the coming tempest."*

In Mr. Wilberforce's diary, I discover the origin of the tradition so long current, that Dr. Franklin signed the treaty of peace, also, in the coat which he had worn when Wedderburn insulted him in the Privy Council, ten years before. The entry to which I refer is this: "Friday, Lord St. Helens" (formerly, Mr. Alleyne Fitzherbert) "dined with me tête-à-tête—pleasant day—free conversation—much politics and information. Franklin signed the peace of Paris in his old spotted velvet coat (it being the time of a court-mourning, which rendered it more particular). 'What,' said Lord St. Helens, 'is the meaning of that harlequin coat?' 'It is that in which he was abused by Wedderburn.' He showed much rancor and personal enmity to this country—would not grant the common passports for trade, which however were easily got from Jay or Adams." Dr. Bancroft has told us that the same suit was worn at the signing of the treaty of alliance in 1778. It must have been a poor soul that could conceive of no other reason for such a significant reminder than "rancor and personal enmity."

* "Life of Wilberforce," by his sons.

Two other young Englishmen were often at Passy this autumn; and, fortunately, they were more profuse in recording what passed there than the two rising members of Parliament. One of them was Mr. Samuel Romilly, afterward Sir Samuel Romilly; the other, his friend, Mr. Baynes; barristers both, and both young men of liberal opinions, and a noble cast of character. Mr. Romilly, who was the descendant of French refugees, speaks of Franklin, in his autobiography, with French enthusiasm. "Of all the celebrated persons," he says, " whom in my life I have chanced to see, Dr. Franklin, both from his appearance and his conversation, seemed to me the most remarkable. His venerable, patriarchal appearance, the simplicity of his manner and language, and the novelty of his observations, at least the novelty of them at that time to me, impressed me as of one of the most extraordinary men that ever existed."

Mr. Baynes, who kept a diary during his travels on the continent, recorded much of the conversation which passed at these interviews.* The young gentlemen bore a letter of introduction from Dr. Jebb. "Dr. Franklin's house," wrote Mr. Baynes, "is delightfully situated, and seems very spacious; and he seemed to have a great number of domestics. We sent up the letter, and were then shown up into his bedchamber, where he sat in his nightgown, his feet wrapped up in flannels, and resting on a pillow, he having, for three or four days, been much afflicted with the gout and the gravel." Parliamentary reform, then agitated in England, became a topic of conversation, and Mr. Baynes said, that Dr. Jebb was for having every man vote. "Dr. Jebb is right," said Franklin, "for the all of one man is as dear to him as the all of another." But he afterward appeared to qualify this remark, by " expressing his approbation of the American system, which excludes minors, servants, and others, who are liable to undue influence."† The retirement of General Washington from the army, had been spoken of in a French paper as a dissolution of the compact between the States. Dr. Franklin said his retirement had no more political significancy or effect than the resignation of a constable. Mr. Baynes mentioned the absurd comments of the Eng-

* Life of Sir Samuel Romilly, i.. 447.

† IMPERTINENT NOTE BY THE AUTHOR. All illiterate persons are "liable to undue influence." In affairs political, people who cannot read are absolutely at the mercy of those who can. Hence the justice of the proposed law to exclude from voting all who cannot read.

lish press upon the same event, and added that, for his own part, he always believed a man to act from good motives, until he saw cause to think otherwise. "Yes," said Franklin; "so would every honest man." He reprobated the maxim that all men are equally corrupt; upon which Mr. Romilly remarked, that that had been the favorite maxim of Lord North's administration. Such men, rejoined Franklin, had reason to think so, as they judged mankind from themselves, and those whom they knew. "A man," he added, "who has seen nothing but hospitals, must naturally have a poor opinion of the health of mankind." The subject of religious toleration having been introduced, Dr. Franklin said he had once had a conversation upon the rights of Dissenters with Lord Bristol, the Bishop of Derry, who had in contemplation a scheme of exempting Catholics from the payment of tithes. "And pray, my lord," said Franklin to the bishop, "while your hand is in, do extend your plan to Dissenters, who are clearly within all the reasons of the rule." "His lordship was astonished—no—he saw some distinction or other, which he could not easily explain." In fact, added Franklin, the bishop's revenues would have suffered, if Dissenters had been allowed to pay their tithes to their own pastors.

In concluding his entry of this visit, Mr. Baynes wrote: "I never enjoyed so much pleasure in my life, as in the present conversation with this great and good character. He looked very well, notwithstanding his illness, and, as usual, wore his spectacles. He desired us, on taking leave, to come and visit him again, which we resolved to do."

Three weeks after, Mr. Baynes visited Passy a second time. "On entering Dr. Franklin's house," he wrote in his diary, "a confounded Swiss servant told me to go up stairs, and I should meet with domestics. I went up, but not a domestic was there; I returned, and told him there was nobody. He then walked up with me, and told me I might enter, and I should find his master alone. I desired him to announce me. 'Oh, sir, it is unnecessary; go in, go in;' on which I proceeded, and, rapping at the door, I perceived that I had disturbed the old man from a sleep he had been taking, on a sofa. My confusion was inexpressible. However, he soon relieved me from it, saying that he had risen early that morning, and that the heat of the weather had made a little rest not unacceptable; and desiring me to sit down." Religious toleration again became the subject of conversation, in the course of which Dr. Franklin commended some features of the Quaker system. "I rather incline to doubt," he said, "the necessity of having teachers or ministers for the express purpose of instructing people in their religious duties." He also expressed a doubt of the necessity of salaried judges. "The Quakers," he said, "have no judges, except such as are determined at their own meetings; there is an appeal from the monthly to the annual meeting. All is done without expense, and nobody grumbles at the trouble of deciding. In fact, the honor of being listened to as a preacher, or of presiding to decide lawsuits, is in itself sufficient. A salary only tends to diminish the honor of the office. Persons will play at chess by the hour without being paid for it; this you may see in every coffee-house in Paris. Deciding causes is, in fact, only a source of amusement to sensible men. Here, in France, a *bourgeois* gives a sum of money for his seat in parliament. The fees of his office do not bring him in more than three per cent. Therefore, for the *noblesse*, or honor which his seat gives him, he pays two-fifths of the price of his office, and at the same time gives up his labor without any recompense."

Mr. Baynes asked if imprisonment for debt was still practiced in America? Dr. Franklin replied that it was, and expressed strong disapprobation of the system. He said he could not compare any sum of money with imprisonment—they were not commensurable quantities. He inclined to think that all methods to compel payment were very impolitic; nor did he regard the diminution of credit as an evil, for the commerce which arose from credit was in a great measure detrimental to a state. He said, that in the interval between the declaration of independence and the formation of the code of laws, there was no method of compelling payment of debts in America; yet, debts were paid as regularly as ever; and if any man had refused to pay a just debt because he was not legally compellable, he durst not have shown his face in the street.

Upon making his third visit to Passy, Mr. Baynes took care to be properly announced. "I found Dr. Franklin," he wrote, "with some American gentlemen and ladies, who were conversing upon American commerce, in which the ladies joined. On their departure, I was much pleased to see the old man attend them down stairs, and hand the ladies to their carriage. On his return I expressed my pleasure in hearing the Americans, and even the ladies, converse entirely upon commerce. He said that it was so throughout the country; not an idle man, and, consequently, not a poor man, to be found." They talked upon the plan for preventing wars by referring national disputes to a congress. He thought the plan impracticable, but added: "Two or three sovereigns might agree upon an alliance against all aggressors, and agree to refer all disputes between each other to some third person, or set of men, or power. Other nations, seeing the advantage of this, would gradually accede; and, perhaps, in a hundred and fifty or two hundred years, all Europe would be included."

A few days after, when Mr. Baynes again sought the pleasant shades of Passy, he had much interesting conversation with Dr. Franklin. The young Englishman asked him if he thought the scheme of parliamentary reform would be successful. "I fear," he replied, "you are too corrupt a nation to carry the point. I have not patience to read even your newspapers; they are full of nothing but robberies, murders, and executions; and when a nation comes to that, nothing short of absolute government will keep it in order." Mr. Baynes expressed a doubt whether the United States would be able to maintain themselves without a more efficient armed force. "America," replied Dr. Franklin, "is not, like any European power, surrounded by others, every one of which keeps an immense standing army; therefore she is not liable to attacks from her neighbors; at least, if attacked, she is on an equal footing with the aggressor; and if attacked by any distant power, she will always have time to form an army. Could she possibly be in a worse condition than at the beginning of the late war, and could we have had better success?" The standing armies of Europe became a subject of conversation. Mr. Baynes asked Franklin if he could think of any plan for their reduction. At present, said Mr. Baynes, a compact among the powers of Europe seemed to be the only plan, but that was not likely to be entertained, because a large standing army was necessary to support an absolute government. "That is very true," said Franklin; "I admit that if one power singly were to reduce their standing army, it would be instantly overrun by other nations; but yet, I think, there is one effect of a standing army which must in time be felt in such a manner as to bring about the total abolition of the system.

A standing army not only diminishes the population of a country, but even the size and breed of the human species; for an army is the flower of the nation; all the most vigorous, stout, and well-made men in a kingdom are to be found in the army, and these men in general never marry."

Mr. Baynes said, that in England the army was not large enough to cause a degeneration of the race, but suggested that the prevalence of luxury and the law of primogeniture had that tendency. "Yes," said Franklin, "I have observed that myself in England. I remember dining at a nobleman's house where they were speaking of a distant relation of his who was prevented from marrying a lady whom he loved by the smallness of their fortunes. Everybody was lamenting their hard situation, when I took the liberty to ask the amount of their fortunes. 'Why,' said a gentleman near me, 'all they can raise between them will scarce be forty thousand pounds.' I was astonished. However, on recollecting myself, I suggested that forty thousand pounds was a pretty handsome fortune; that it would, by being vested in the three per cents., bring in twelve hundred pounds a year. 'And pray, sir,' said the gentleman, 'consider what is twelve hundred a year? There is my lord's carriage and my lady's carriage,' etc., etc. So he ran up twelve hundred a year in a moment. I did not attempt to confute him; but only added, that notwithstanding all he had said, I would endow four hundred American girls with it, every one of whom should be esteemed a fortune in her own country. As to the custom of giving the eldest son more than the others, we have not been able to get entirely rid of it in America. The eldest son in Massachusetts has, without rhyme or reason, a share more than any of the rest. I remember before I was a member of the Assembly (of Pennsylvania), when I was clerk to it, the question was fully agitated. Some were for having the eldest son to have the extraordinary share; others were for giving it to the youngest son, which seemed, indeed, the most reasonable, as he was the most likely to want his education, which the others might probably have already had from their father. After three days' debate, it was left as it stood before, namely, that the eldest son should have a share more."

Talking upon leases, Dr. Franklin said he was convinced that no man should cultivate any land but his own, and that the policy was erroneous which tended to the accumulation of great landed estates.

In another conversation he reverted to his favorite theory, that offices should not be a source of revenue to the incumbents, and need not be. He said that he had sat in the Assembly twelve years, and had never solicited a single vote, and that this was not peculiar to himself—hundreds had done the same. The office of Assemblyman was looked upon as an office of trouble, and you perpetually saw the papers filled with advertisements requesting to decline the honor. "Anciently, when the office of sheriff was instituted in America, the fees were fixed at rather too small a rate to make a sufficient salary, there being then very few writs; the fees were therefore increased; but since that time, the number of lawsuits having increased, the salary is increased so much as to make the office an object of desire." The sheriff's place was then sought by many candidates; but if he lived to return to America he should endeavor to diminish the emoluments of the office. In England, seats in Parliament were sought as an indirect means of obtaining places; make the places unprofitable, and one source of corruption would be stopped.

Dr. Franklin mentioned in the course of this conversation, that he had subscribed to "another balloon," and that one of the conditions of the subscription was, that "a man should be sent up along with it." He showed his young friend several books as specimens of printing, particularly a Spanish edition of Don Quixote, one of the most superbly executed works then existing.

The reader will remember that this was the period of the first balloon ascensions. From 1782, when one of the brothers Montgolfier sent up his first paper bag, inflated with smoke, until the end of 1784, ballooning was the rage in Paris, in France, in Europe. Besides subscribing to various balloons, and watching the progress of the daring experiments, Dr. Franklin wrote a paper on the subject for the Royal Society, which Sir Joseph Banks commends for its concise completeness. Since Franklin's sublime invasion of the clouds with his electrical kite, nothing had so startled and excited scientific circles as these balloon ascensions; which, like the kite experiment, interested the multitude not less than the learned.

"What is the use of this new invention?" some one asked

Franklin.   "What is the use of a new-born child?" was his reply.*

Another of Dr. Franklin's visitors was young Lord Fitzmaurice, son of Lord Shelburne, who arrived in July, 1784. We have a fragment of a diary, in which Franklin chronicles some interesting particulars of the visit. "July 22d.—Lord Fitzmaurice arrives; brought me sundry letters and papers. He thinks Mr. Pitt in danger of losing his majority in the House of Commons, though great at present; for he will not have wherewithal to pay them. I said, that governing by a Parliament which must be bribed, was employing a very expensive machine, and that the people of England would in time find out, though they had not yet, that, since the Parliament must always do the will of the minister, and be paid for doing it, and the people must find the money to pay them, it would be the same thing in effect, but much cheaper, to be governed by the minister at first hand, without a Parliament. Those present seemed to think the reasoning clear. Lord Fitzmaurice appears a sensible, amiable young man.

"Tuesday, 27th.—Lord Fitzmaurice called to see me. His father having requested that I would give him such instructive hints as might be useful to him, I occasionally mentioned the old story of Demosthenes' answer to one who demanded what was the first point of oratory. *Action.* The second? *Action.* The third? *Action.* Which, I said, had been generally understood to mean the action of an orator with his hands in speaking; but that I thought another kind of action of more importance to an orator who would persuade people to follow his advice, viz., such a course of action in the conduct of life, as would impress them with an opinion of his integrity as well as of his understanding; that, this opinion once established, all the difficulties, delays, and oppositions, usually occasioned by doubts and suspicions, were prevented; and such a man, though a very imperfect speaker, would almost always carry his points against the most flourishing orator, who had not the character of sincerity. To express my sense of the importance of a good private character in public affairs more strongly, I said the advantage of having it, and the disadvantage of not having it, were so great, that I even believed, if George the Third had had a

* Memoirs of Baron de Grimm.

bad private character, and John Wilkes a good one, the latter might have turned the former out of his kingdom. Lord Shelburne, the father of Lord Fitzmaurice, has, unfortunately, the character of being *insincere ;* and it has much hurt his usefulness, though, in all my concerns with him, I never saw any instance of that kind."

To this period belongs the rise of "Mesmerism." We must by no means omit to notice Dr. Franklin's curious labors in exposing the pretensions of the charlatan who gave his name to that delusion. Whatever may be thought of Mesmerism, there can be no doubt that Mesmer himself was a villain in grain, and Dr. Franklin had a share of the honor of demonstrating the fact.

Baffled and disgraced in Germany, his native land, Mesmer, in 1778, took up his abode in Paris, where he soon became the lion of the day. In the spacious salon of his hotel, magnificently furnished, and provided with mysterious and half concealed apparatus, he received vast crowds of patients daily, upon whom, with magic wand, he appeared to operate with miraculous effect. Mesmerism became the rage in the world of fashion, and made some converts among men of repute in scientific circles. Besides gaining large sums from his practice, Mesmer received from his admirers a gift of three hundred and forty thousand francs. One of his pupils, Deslon, was believed to have cleared two millions. Such was the assurance of Mesmer, that he asked of the French government, as a reward for his discoveries, a château and an estate, which being refused, he had the still more sublime assurance to threaten to leave France! The government, at one time, actually offered him a pension of twenty thousand francs a year for his secret. Mesmer himself contrived always to elude investigation, but his most renowned and successful pupil, Deslon, consented, in 1784, to submit the whole subject to the investigation of commissioners appointed by the king.

The celebrity of these commissioners shows what importance was attached to this investigation. The king first appointed four eminent physicians of Paris—Borie, Sallin, D'Arcet, and Guillotin ; but, at the request of these, added afterward five members of the Royal Academy, Franklin, Le Roy, Bailly, De Bory, and Lavoisier. M. Bory having died early in the affair, M. Majault was appointed to succeed him. Bailly was the French astronomer, and Guillotin was he who gave a new name, his own, to an ancient instrument. The commissioners were appointed in March, 1784, and reported in August of the same year. The report, which was a model of perspicuity and completeness,* drawn up by M. Bailly, contains many traces of Franklin, whose name, at the request of the polite commissioners, headed the list of signatures.

First, the commissioners visited the operating room of M. Deslon, where they saw strange things. To quote the report: "They saw in the center of a large apartment a circular box, made of oak, about a foot and a half deep, which is called the bucket. The lid of this box is pierced with a number of holes, in which are inserted branches of iron, elbowed and movable. The patients are arranged in ranks about this bucket, and each has his branch of iron, which by means of the elbow may be applied immediately to the part affected; a cord passed round their bodies connects them one with the other; sometimes a second means of communication is introduced, by the insertion of the thumb of each patient between the fore-finger and thumb of the patient next him; the thumb thus inserted is pressed by the person holding it; the impression received by the left hand of the patient, communicates through his right, and thus passes through the whole circle. A piano-forte is placed in one corner of the apartment, and different airs are played with various degrees of rapidity; vocal music is sometimes added to the instrumental. The persons who superintend the process, have each of them an iron rod in his hand, from ten to twelve inches in length."

Such was the apparatus. M. Deslon, before proceeding to operate upon patients, explained some parts of it. He said that the rod or wand which he held in his hand was a conductor of the magnetism, had the power of concentrating it at its point, and of rendering its emanations more considerable; that sound, according to the theory of M. Mesmer, was also a conductor of the magnetism, and that to communicate the fluid to the piano-forte, noth-

---

* Copy in Philadelphia City Library, entitled: "Report of Dr. Benjamin Franklin, and other Commissioners, charged by the king of France with the examination of the Animal Magnetism as now practiced at Paris. Translated from the French, with an Historical Introduction. London, 1785." Pamphlet of 108 pp. Report dated Aug. 11, 1784. Signed

B. FRANKLIN,	SALLIN,	DE BORY,
MAJAULT,	BAILLY,	GUILLOTIN,
LE ROY,	D'ARCET,	LAVOISIER.

ing more was necessary than to approach to it the iron rod; that the person who played upon the instrument furnished also a portion of the fluid, and that the magnetism was transmitted by the sounds to the surrounding patients; that the cord which was passed round the bodies of the patients was designed, as well as the union of their fingers, to augment the effects by communication; that the interior part of the bucket was so constructed as to concentrate the magnetism, and was a grand reservoir, from which the fluid was diffused through the branches of iron that were inserted in its lid.

After quoting, with the utmost gravity, this nonsense, the author of the report quietly remarks: "The commissioners in the progress of their examination discovered, by means of an electrometer and a needle of iron not touched with the loadstone, that the bucket contained no substance either electric or magnetical; and from the detail that M. Deslon made to them respecting the interior construction of the bucket, they cannot infer any physical agent capable of contributing to the imputed effects of the magnetism."

The explanation over, M. Deslon gave the commissioners an exhibition of his powers as a mesmeriser. The patients, ranged round the mysterious bucket in circles, each holding his bar of iron, sat motionless, while the piano was played, and M. Deslon waved his wand, and applied his hands to various parts of the patients' bodies. This curious scene the commissioners had the patience to witness for a considerable time without observing any effects of the magnetism. But, at last, the spell began to work. "The patients," when they are affected, "offer a spectacle extremely varied, according to their different habits of body. Some of them are calm, tranquil, and unconscious of any sensation; others cough, are affected with a slight degree of pain, a partial or a universal burning, and perspiration; a third class are agitated and tormented with convulsions. These convulsions are extraordinary from their frequency, their violence, and their duration, and as soon as one person is convulsed, others presently are affected by that sympton."

It needed not a body of learned commissioners to discover in all this the trick of a man who was trading upon the ignorance and credulity of his followers. The difficulty was to so prove it a trick as to convince the ignorant and credulous; and it was in doing this that the commissioners were particularly aided by the sagacity and ingenuity of Dr. Franklin. As he was at that time scarcely able to leave his house, several of the more élaborate experiments were performed at Passy. On one occasion, as we learn from the report, Dr. Franklin and all his family were magnetized by M. Deslon. " The assembly was numerous ; every person who was present underwent the operation. Some sick persons, who had come to Passy with M. Deslon, were subjected to the effects of the magnetism in the same manner as at the public process; but Madame de B——, Dr. Franklin, his two relations, his secretary, and an American officer, felt no sensation, though one of Dr. Franklin's relations was convalescent, and the American officer had at that time a regular fever."

To prove that the marvelous effects of the mesmeric process were due to the imagination of the patients, two classes of experiments were tried. In one class, the patients were made to believe that the operation had been performed, when it had not been ; in the other, the operation was performed, and the fact concealed from the patients. In both cases, the effects were precisely the same. A ridiculous scene occurred in Dr. Franklin's garden one day, when the commissioners were endeavoring to ascertain whether the imagination alone was sufficient to cause the magnetic convulsions. It was one of the mesmeric fancies, that a tree could be so magnetized, that a very susceptible person who should go under it would be sensibly affected. The commissioners selected this experiment as one favorable for their purpose: " M. Deslon, therefore, brought with him a boy of about twelve years of age ; an apricot tree was fixed upon in the orchard of Dr. Franklin's garden, considerably distant from any other tree, and calculated for the preservation of the magnetic power which might be impressed upon it. M. Deslon was led thither alone to perform the operation, the boy in the mean time remaining in the house, and another person along with him. We could have wished that M. Deslon had not been present at the subsequent part of the experiment, but he declared that he could not answer for its success, if he did not direct his cane and his countenance toward the tree, in order to augment the action of the magnetism. It was therefore resolved, that M. Deslon should be placed at the greatest possible distance, and that some of the commissioners should stand between him and the boy, in order to ascertain the impracticability of any signals being made by M. Deslon, or any intelligence being maintained between them. These precautions in an experiment the essence of which must be authenticity, are indispensable, without giving the person with respect to whom they are employed a right to think himself offended. The boy was then brought into the orchard, his eyes covered with a bandage, presented successively to four trees upon which the operation had *not* been performed, and caused to embrace each of them for the space of two minutes, the mode of communication which had been prescribed by M. Deslon himself. M. Deslon, present, and at a considerable distance, directed his cane toward the tree which had been the object of his operations. At the first tree, the boy being interrogated at the end of a minute, declared that he prespired in large drops; he coughed, expectorated, and complained of a slight pain in his head. The distance of the tree which had been magnetized was about twenty-seven feet. At the second tree he felt the sensations of stupefaction and pain in his head; the distance was thirty-six feet. At the third tree the stupefaction and headache increased considerably; he said that he believed he was approaching to the tree which had been magnetized; the distance was then about thirty-eight feet. In fine, at the fourth tree which had not been rendered the object of the operation, and at the distance of about twenty-four feet from the tree which had, the boy fell into a crisis; he fainted away, his limbs stiffened, and he was carried to a neighboring grass-plot, where M. Deslon hastened to his assistance and recovered him."

This was pretty decisive, and other experiments of a similar nature were not less so Again: "One day, the commissioners were all together at Passy at the house of Dr. Franklin, and M. Deslon was with them; they having previously entreated the latter to bring some of his patients with him, selecting those of the lower class, who were most susceptible to the magnetism. M. Deslon brought two women; and while he was employed in performing the operation upon Dr. Franklin and several persons in another apartment, the two women were separated, and placed in different rooms. One of them, Dame P——, had films over her eyes; but as she could always see a little, the bandage already described was employed. *She was persuaded that M. Deslon had been brought into the room to perform the magnetical operation;* silence was recommended; three commissioners were present, one to interrogate, another to take minutes of the transaction, and the third to personate M. Deslon.

The conversation was pretended to be addressed to M. Deslon; he was desired to begin the operation ; the three commissioners in the mean time remained perfectly quiet and solely occupied in observing her symptoms. At the end of three minutes the patient began to feel a nervous shuddering ; she had then successively a pain in the back of her head, in her arms, a creeping in her hands (that was her expression) ; she grew stiff, struck her hands violently together, rose from her seat, stamped with her feet. The crisis had all the regular symptoms. Two other commissioners who were in the adjoining room with the door shut, heard the stamping of the feet and the clapping of the hands, and without seeing any thing were witnesses to this noisy experiment. The two commissioners we have mentioned were with the other patient, Mademoiselle B——, who was subject to nervous distempers. No bandage was employed upon her, but her eyes were at liberty ; she was seated with her face toward a door which was shut, and persuaded that M. Deslon was on the other side, employed in performing upon her the magnetical operation. This had scarcely taken place a minute, before she began to feel the symptom of shuddering ; in another minute she had a chattering of the teeth and a universal heat ; in fine, in the third minute she fell into a regular crisis. Her respiration was quick, she stretched out both her arms behind her back, twisting them extremely, and bending her body forward : her whole body trembled ; the chattering of her teeth became so loud that it might be heard in the open air ; she bit her hand, and that with so much force, that the marks of the teeth remained perfectly visible."

The report of the commissioners, which, of course, pronounced Mesmerism baseless and pernicious, was immediately printed by order of the Government. The disciples of Mesmer attempted, in various ways, to break the force of the blow, but Mesmer himself soon saw that the game was up. He fled to England with a prodigious booty, and passed the rest of his life in obscurity. Indeed, the report was annihilating, as the passages quoted above indicate. It is possible there may be more in Mesmerism than the commissioners discovered, but it is impossible to doubt, after reading their report, that Mesmerism as then practiced in Paris for the purpose of gaining money, was a scandalous cheat.

Franklin seemed to renew his youth after the peace, at least the youth of his mind. He was seventy-eight years old. He had outlived, not merely his early friends, but many of those whom he had not known till he had passed the midday of his life; among them, Sir John Pringle, Dr. Fothergill, Lord le Despencer, Lord Kames, Mrs. Stevenson, and Dr. Dubourgh. He could scarcely hobble about his garden, at times; and he was occasionally laid up for many days with the stone. But his intellect was never clearer, more acute, more active, or more fruitful. The essays which he wrote in 1784, are among the very best of his writings. Who ever wrote better things of their kind than his " Information to those who would remove to America," his new treatise on Privateering, his essay on the raising of Wages in Europe by the American Revolution, his piece on the Savages of North America, or his letter to Vaughan upon Luxury? And what father of seventy-eight ever wrote to his daughter a letter more ingenious and witty than his elaborate epistle to Mrs. Bache satirizing the hereditary principle, as proposed to be incorporated in the Society of the Cincinnati. There is point, wit, fun, originality, and good sense in every paragraph of it. He abhorred and derided the hereditary principle. "What is your opinion, sir, of the establishment of the Cincinnati?" asked Lafayette, who was an eager champion of the project. " Why, truly, Marquis," replied Franklin, " I have no opinion of it at all."

It is in one of his letters of this year that the familiar passage occurs in ridicule of dueling: " A man says something which another tells him is a lie. They fight; but, whichever is killed, the point at dispute remains unsettled. To this purpose they have a pleasant little story here. A gentleman in a coffee-house desired another to sit further from him. ' Why so?' ' Because, sir, you stink.' ' That is an affront, and you must fight me.' ' I will fight you, if you insist upon it; but I do not see how that will mend the matter. For if you kill me, I shall stink too; and if I kill you, you will stink, if possible, worse than you do at present.' How can such miserable sinners as we are entertain so much pride, as to conceit that every offense against our imagined honor merits *death?*"

Another anecdote, almost equally well-known, is in place here. One Benjamin Webb, being in distress for money, applied to Dr. Franklin for aid. He replied: " I send you herewith a bill for ten louis d'ors. I do not pretend to *give* such a sum; I only *lend* it to you. When you shall return to your country with a good character, you cannot fail of getting into some business that will in time enable you to pay all your debts. In that case, when you meet with another honest man in similar distress, you must pay me by lending this sum to him; enjoining him to discharge the debt by a like operation, when he shall be able, and shall meet with such another opportunity. I hope it may thus go through many hands, before it meets with a knave that will stop its progress. This is a trick of mine for doing a deal of good with a little money. I am not rich enough to afford *much* in good works, and so am obliged to be cunning and make the most of a *little*."

The Percy Anecdotes contain an incredible tale, to this effect: "Dr. Franklin, dining with the English and French embassadors' the following toasts were drunk. By the British embassador: 'England—the sun, whose bright beams enlighten and fructify the remotest corners of the earth.' The French embassador, glowing with national pride, but too polite to dispute the previous toast, drank, 'France—the moon, whose mild, steady, and cheering rays are the delight of all nations: consoling them in darkness.' Doctor Franklin then arose, and said, 'George Washington—the Joshua, who commanded the sun and moon to stand still, and they obeyed him.'" This is related as by one of the guests. All may believe it who can. If such toasts were given, it must have been late in the third bottle, or at the opening of the fourth.

In July, 1784, Governor William Franklin broke the silence of years, and wrote a sorrowful letter to his father, asking a renewal of their former affectionate intercourse, and proposing to visit Passy to converse upon family affairs that required their joint attention. Dr. Franklin wrote a forgiving, conciliatory reply. He said the renewal of their intercourse would be "very agreeable" to him, though nothing had ever hurt him so much as to find himself deserted in his old age by his only son, and to see him taking up arms against a cause upon which he had staked life, fortune, and honor.

"I send your son over," he continued, "to pay his duty to you. You will find him much improved. He is greatly esteemed and beloved in this country, and will make his way anywhere. * * * I am here among a people that love and respect me, a most amiable nation to live with; and perhaps I may conclude to die among them; for my friends in America are dying off, one after another,

and I have been so long abroad, that I should now be almost a
stranger in my own country. I shall be glad to see you when convenient, but would not have you come here at present. You may
confide to your son the family affairs you wished to confer upon
with me, for he is discreet; and I trust that you will prudently
avoid introducing him to company that it may be improper for him
to be seen with." So the young gentleman went to London, and
intercourse was re-established between fathers and sons. Nevertheless, Dr. Franklin could never quite forgive, still less forget, his
son's defection; for he thought it was something more than an error
of the head.

Readers have not forgotten the Rev. John Carroll, of Maryland,
the companion of Franklin's toilsome journey to Canada in 1776.
Dr. Franklin had an opportunity, in 1784, of giving an important
professional lift to that worthy gentleman, by making known his
merits, and those of his family, to the papal nuncio, who was busied
in adjusting the affairs of the Catholic Church in the United States
to the new order of things. It was in consequence of this recommendation, as the nuncio himself relates, that Mr. Carroll became
the first Catholic bishop of North America, and died an archbishop.

Franklin had some concern, too, in arranging similar difficulties
in the Protestant Episcopal Church of the United States, severed
by the revolution from the parent Church in England. Two young
gentlemen from America having been churlishly refused Episcopal
ordination by the Archbishop of Canterbury, applied to Dr. Franklin for advice. He asked the Pope's nuncio to ordain them; but
the nuncio said, "The thing is impossible unless the gentlemen become Catholics." He then advised them to try the Irish bishops,
and, if they refused, the Danish or Swedish. If, however, as was
most probable, all of these should refuse to perform the rite, then
he recommended them to follow the example of the first Scottish
clergy in a similar dilemma. "When their king," said Franklin,
"had built the cathedral of St. Andrew's, and requested the King
of Northumberland to lend his bishops to ordain one for them,
that their clergy might not as heretofore be obliged to go to
Northumberland for orders, and their request was refused; they
assembled in the cathedral; and, the miter, crosier, and robes of
a bishop being laid upon the altar, they, after earnest prayers for
direction in their choice, elected one of their own number; when

the king said to him, '*Arise, go to the altar, and receive your office at the hand of God.*' His brethren led him to the altar, robed him, put the crosier in his hand, and the miter on his head, and he became the first Bishop of Scotland.

"If the British Islands," he continued, "were sunk in the sea (and the surface of this globe has suffered greater changes), you would probably take some such method as this; and, if they persist in denying you ordination, it is the same thing. A hundred years hence, when people are more enlightened, it will be wondered at, that men in America, qualified by their learning and piety to pray for and instruct their neighbors, should not be permitted to do it till they had made a voyage of six thousand miles out and home, to ask leave of a cross old gentleman at Canterbury; who seems, by your account, to have as little regard for the souls of the people of Maryland, as King William's attorney-general, Seymour, had for those of Virginia. The Reverend Commissary Blair, who projected the college of that province, and was in England to solicit benefactions and a charter, relates, that, the queen, in the king's absence, having ordered Seymour to draw up the charter, which was to be given, with two thousand pounds in money, he opposed the grant; saying that the nation was engaged in an expensive war, that the money was wanted for better purposes, and he did not see the least occasion for a college in Virginia. Blair represented to him, that its intention was to educate and qualify young men to be ministers of the Gospel, much wanted there; and begged Mr. Attorney would consider, that the people of Virginia had souls to be saved, as well as the people of England. '*Souls !*' said he, '*damn your souls! Make tobacco.*'"

The point was conceded by the Church of England in 1787, when the Archbishop of Canterbury consecrated two American bishops, Samuel Provost, of New York, and William White, of Pennsylvania. But this was not done until the difficulty had been otherwise solved; for Samuel Seabury, of Connecticut, in 1784, acting upon Franklin's hint, went to Scotland and there received consecration at the hands of three nonjuring bishops. If the king had not meanly frustrated Mr. Fox's intention, Dr. Franklin's "good bishop" of St. Asaph's would have been, at this time, Archbishop of Canterbury; and very happy would he have been to ordain American priests, and consecrate American bishops.

A new town of Norfolk county in Massachusetts, organized in 1778, the year of the alliance with France, gave itself the name of Franklin; a bustling place now, containing, says the *Gazetteer*, ten mills, thirteen schools, and two thousand inhabitants. It was a rare compliment, then, and Franklin was touched by it. The town, it seems, sent him word of the honor they had done him, and said they would build a steeple to their church if he would give them a bell for it. He replied, advising them to spare the expense of a steeple at present, and asking them to accept from him a present of books instead of a bell, "sense being preferable to sound." Books of the value of twenty-five pounds were sent accordingly; which being received, the pastor of the church, Rev. Nathaniel Emmons, celebrated the event by preaching a sermon upon it. This production, when published in 1787, was entitled: "The Dignity of Man; a Discourse addressed to the Congregation in Franklin, upon the Occasion of their receiving from Dr. Franklin the Mark of his Respect in a rich Donation of Books, appropriated to the Use of a Parish Library." The sermon was thus dedicated: "To his Excellency Benjamin Franklin, President of the State of Pennsylvania; the Ornament of Genius, the Patron of Science, and the Boast of Man; this Discourse is inscribed, with the greatest Deference, Humility, and Gratitude, by his obliged and most humble Servant, the Author." The text of the discourse was "Show thyself a man"; in enlarging upon which, the preacher adduced the example of Franklin. I should mention that the selection of the books devolved upon Dr. Price, Franklin requesting him to choose "such as are most proper to inculcate principles of sound religion and just government. Besides your own works, I would only mention, on the recommendation of my sister, 'Stennet's *Discourse on Personal Religion*,' which may be one book of the number, if you know and approve it."*

---

* The following is a list of the books selected by Dr. Price, his own works being presented by him to the town. I copy from the printed catalogue of about the year 1800, sent me by Mr. S. Fishe, postmaster of Franklin in 1863:

"Clarke's Works; Hoadley's Works; Barrow's Works; Ridgeley's Works; Locke's Works; Sydney's Works; Montesquieu's Spirit of Laws; Blackstone's Commentaries; Watson's Tracts; Newton on the Prophecies; Law on Religion; Priestley's Institutes; Priestley's Corruptions; Price and Priestley; Lyndsey's Apology; Lyndsey's Sequel; Abernethy's Sermons; Duchal's Sermons; Price's Morals; Price on Providence; Price on Liberty; Price's Sermons; Price on the Christian Scheme; Needham's free State; West and Lyttleton on the Resurrection; Stennet's Sermons; Addison's Evidences; Gordon's Tacitus; Backus's History; Lardner on the Logas; Watts's Orthodoxy and Charity; Brainerd's Life; Bellamy's true Religion; Doddridge's Life;

At present, there is no State in the Union which has not, at least, one town named Franklin. Ohio has nineteen. Twenty States have a Franklin county. The name occurs on the map of the United States one hundred and thirty-six times; Washington and Jackson being the only names that are more frequently repeated.

A year had elapsed since the peace, and still no recall. Mr. Jefferson arrived in August, 1784, to co-operate with Franklin and Adams, in the negotiation of commercial treaties; but he had nothing to report touching the release of Dr. Franklin. Perhaps this neglect was owing to the repeated insinuations contained in Mr. Adams's letters, that his resignation was not meant to be accepted. Mr. Adams would write thus to his friend, Elbridge Gerry : " Dr. Franklin showed me yesterday a letter from Mr. Jay, in which he says, ' that the Doctor's letter requesting leave to return to America, was committed, and not reported on.' You can judge best from his letters whether he is sincere in his request ; if he is, you will make a new arrangement. He may be sincere, for a voyage seems the only chance he has for his life. He can now neither walk nor ride, unless in a litter; but he is strong, and eats freely, so that he will soon have other complaints besides the stone, if he continues to live as entirely without exercise as he does at present."*

At length Congress accepted his resignation. March 7th, 1785, a resolution was passed, permitting " the Honorable Benjamin Franklin, Esquire, to return to America as soon as convenient;" and, March 10th, " the Honorable Thomas Jefferson, Esquire," was appointed Plenipotentiary at the Court of Versailles, in his stead. Franklin had been busy all the winter in preparing for his departure ; so that when the news of his recall reached him, on the second of May, he had but to arrange the mode of his return.

" You replace Dr. Franklin, I hear," said the Count de Ver-

Bellamy's Permission of Sin; Fordyce's Sermons; Hemmenway against Hopkins; Hopkins on Holiness; Life of Cromwell; Fulfilling of the Scriptures; Watts on the Passions; Watts's Logic; Edwards on Religion; Dickinson on the Five Points; Christian History; Prideaux's Connections; Cooper on Predestination; Cambridge Platform; Stoddard's Safety of Appearing; Burkett on Personal Reformation; Barnard's Sermons; Shepard's Sound Believer; History of the Rebellion; Janeway's Life; Hopkins's System; American Preacher; Emmons's Sermons; Thomas's Laws of Massachusetts; American Constitutions; Young's Night Thoughts; Pilgrim's Progress; Ames's Orations; Spectators; Life of Baron Trenk; Cheap Repository; Moral Repository; Fitch's Poem; Erskine's Sermons."

* Written in January, 1785.

gennes to Mr. Jefferson. "I *succeed;* no one can *replace* him," replied the new plenipotentiary.*

Mr. Jefferson bore honorable testimony, at a later day, to Dr. Franklin's merits, as his country's representative at the French court: "Particulars of great dignity," he wrote in 1791, "happened not to occur during his stay of nine months, after my arrival in France. A little before that, Argand had invented his celebrated lamp, in which the flame is spread into a hollow cylinder, and thus brought into contact with the air within as well as without. Doctor Franklin had been on the point of the same discovery. The idea had occurred to him; but he had tried a bullrush for a wick, which did not succeed. His occupations did not permit him to repeat and extend his trials to the introduction of a larger column of air than could pass through the stem of a bullrush.

"The animal magnetism, too, of the maniac, Mesmer, had just received its death-wound from his hand, in conjunction with the brethren of the learned committee appointed to unvail that compound of fraud and folly. But after this, nothing very interesting was before the public, either in philosophy or politics, during his stay; and he was principally occupied in winding up his affairs there.

"I can only, therefore, testify in general, that there appeared to me more respect and veneration attached to the character of Dr. Franklin in France, than to that of any other person in the same country, foreign or native. I had opportunities of knowing particularly how far these sentiments were felt by the foreign embassadors and ministers at the court of Versailles. The fable of his capture by the Algerines, propagated by the English newspapers, excited no uneasiness; as it was seen at once to be a dish cooked up to the palate of their readers. But nothing could exceed the anxiety of his diplomatic brethren on a subsequent report of his death, which, though premature, bore some marks of authenticity.

"I found the ministers of France equally impressed· with the talents and integrity of Dr. Franklin. The Count de Vergennes particularly gave me repeated and unequivocal demonstrations of his entire confidence in him. * * *

"The succession to Dr. Franklin, at the court of France, was an

* Randall's Life of Jefferson, i., 415.

excellent school of humility.   On being presented to any one as the minister of America, the common-place question used in such cases was, " *c'est vous, Monsieur, qui remplace le Docteur Franklin ?*" " It is you, sir, who replace Dr. Franklin ?"   I generally answered, " No one can replace him, sir ; I am only his successor."*

Again, in 1818, Mr. Jefferson wrote : " As to the charge of subservience to France, besides the evidence of his friendly colleagues, nine months of my own service with him at Paris, daily visits, and the most friendly and confidential conversation, convince me it had not a shadow of foundation.   He possessed the confidence of that government in the highest degree, insomuch, that it may be truly said, that they were more under his influence than he was under theirs.   The fact is, that his temper was so amiable and conciliatory, his conduct so rational, never urging impossibilities, or even things unreasonably inconvenient to them, in short, so moderate and attentive to *their* difficulties as well as our own, that what his enemies called subserviency, I saw was only that reasonable disposition, which, sensible that advantages are not all to be on one side, yielding what is just and liberal, is the more certain of obtaining liberality and justice.   Mutual confidence produces, of course, mutual influence, and this was all which subsisted between Dr. Franklin and the government of France."†

CHAPTER XVIII.

RETURN TO PHILADELPHIA.

BEAUTIFUL and becoming was the return of Dr. Franklin to his native land, after nine years' absence spent in her service.   No circumstance was wanting to it which his dignity or his comfort, or the honor of either nation required.   France dismissed him nobly ; nobly his countrymen welcomed him home.

As he could not bear the motion of a carriage, he was unable to

* Works of Jefferson, iii., 212.   † Works of Jefferson, vii., 108.

go to Versailles for an audience of leave. He therefore wrote his farewell in a letter to the minister of Foreign Affairs. "May I beg the favor of you, sir," he wrote, "to express respectfully for me to his majesty, the deep sense I have of all the inestimable benefits his goodness has conferred on my country; a sentiment that it will be the business of the little remainder of life now left me, to impress equally on the minds of all my countrymen. My sincere prayers are, that God may shower down his blessings on the king, the queen, their children, and all the royal family to the latest generations! Permit me, at the same time, to offer you my thankful acknowledgments for the protection and countenance you afforded me at my arrival, and your many favors during my residence here, of which I shall always retain the most grateful remembrance."

The minister replied: "I can assure you, sir, that the esteem the king entertains for you does not leave you any thing to wish, and that his majesty will learn with real satisfaction, that your fellow-citizens have rewarded, in a manner worthy of you, the important services that you have rendered them."

The portrait of the king, usually given to departing ministers, was not forgotten òn this occasion. The one bestowed upon Franklin was decorated with the extraordinary number of four hundred and eight diamonds, arranged in two circles round the picture, which was literally framed with brilliants. The bauble was worth about ten thousand dollars.

It had been his intention to float down the Seine to Havre, and there take passage for America. But as he could not leave till the summer heats had lowered the river so much as to render the navigation slow and difficult, one of the queen's litters was placed at his disposal, designed to be borne between two large mules. The last official act done by him in Europe was the signing, a day or two before his departure, of the treaty with Prussia; which left only Portugal and Denmark, among all the Christian powers, unconnected by treaty with the United States. The treaty with Prussia was one after Franklin's own heart, since it contained an article against privateering, and others, securing private property against seizure on the sea and destruction on the land, in time of war. This was the treaty which General Washington commended, as marking "a new era in negotiation," and which he styled the most original and the most liberal treaty ever negotiated between independent powers.

July 12th, 1785, accompanied by M. de Chaumont, and one of his daughters, and by his affectionate neighbor, M. Le Veillard, Dr. Franklin and his two grandsons began their journey to the coast. " When he left Passy," says Mr. Jefferson, " it seemed as if the village had lost its patriarch." The street in which he had · lived for so many years bears to this day the name of Franklin. It was at four o'clock in the afternoon when they set out ; the Chaumonts in their carriage, M. Le Veillard and the two grandsons in another, and Dr. Franklin in his litter. The motion of the litter did not seriously incommode him. At St. Germain they stopped for the night ; and, the next morning, M. de Chaumont and his daughter, after breakfasting with the party, returned to Passy. M. Le Veillard, who loved Franklin with a peculiar devotion, and was resolved to see the last of him, still accompanied the travelers. And so they jogged on ; their average day's work being eighteen miles. We may note a few incidents from Franklin's diary :

July 13th, the second day of the journey. " A messenger from the Cardinal de la Rochefoucauld meets us, with an invitation to us to stop at his house at Gaillon the next day, acquainting us, at the same time, that he would take no excuse ; for, being all-powerful in his archbishopric, he would stop us *nolens volens* at his habitation, and not permit us to lodge anywhere else. We consented. Lodged at Mantes. Found myself very little fatigued with the day's journey, the mules going only foot pace.

" July 14th. Proceed early, and breakfast at Vernon. Received a visit there from Vicomte de Tilly and his Comtesse. Arrive at the Cardinal's without dining, about six in the afternoon. It is a superb ancient château, built about three hundred and fifty years since, but in fine preservation, on an elevated situation, with an extensive and beautiful view over a well-cultivated country. The Cardinal is archbishop of Rouen. ˙ A long gallery contains the pictures of all his predecessors. The chapel is elegant in the old style, with well-painted glass windows. The terrace magnificent. We supped early. The entertainment was kind and cheerful. .We were allowed to go early to bed, on account of our intention to depart early in the morning. The Cardinal pressed us to pass another day with him, offering to amuse us with hunting in his park ;

but the necessity we are under of being in time at Havre, would not permit. So we took leave, and retired to rest. The Cardinal is much respected and beloved by the people of this country, bearing in all respects an excellent character.

"July 15th. Set out about five in the morning, traveled till ten, then stopped to breakfast, and remained in the inn during the heat of the day. We got to Rouen about five; were most affectionately received by Mr. and Mrs. Holker. A great company of genteel people at supper, which was our dinner. The chief President of the Parliament, and his lady, invite us to dine the next day; but, being pre-engaged with Mr. Holker, we compounded for drinking tea. We lodge all at Mr. Holker's.

"July 16th. A deputation from the Academy of Rouen came with their compliments, which were delivered in form, and a present for me by one of the directors, being a magical square, which I think he said expressed my name. I have perused it since, but do not comprehend it. The Duke de Chabot's son, lately married to a Montmorency, and colonel of a regiment now at Rouen, was present at the ceremony, being just come in to visit me. I forgot to mention that I saw, with pleasure, in the Cardinal's cabinet, a portrait of this young man's grandmother, Madame la Duchesse d'Enville, who had always been our friend, and treated us with great civilities at Paris; a lady of uncommon intelligence and merit.

"I received here, also, a present of books, 3 vols. 4to, from Dr. ———, with a very polite letter, which I answered.

"We had a great company at dinner; and at six went in a chair to the President's, where were assembled some gentlemen of the robe. We drank tea there, awkwardly made, for want of practice, very little being drunk in France. I went to bed early; but my company supped with a large invited party, and were entertained with excellent singing.

"July 17th. Set out early. Mr. Holker accompanied us some miles, when we took an affectionate leave of each other. Dine at Yvetot, a large town, and arrive at Bolbec, being the longest day's journey we have yet made. It is a market-town, of considerable bigness, and seems thriving; the people well-clad, and appear better fed than those of the wine countries. A linen-printer here offered to remove to America, but I did not encourage him.

" July 18th. Left Bolbec about ten o'clock, and arrive at Havre at five P. M., having stopped on the road at a miserable inn to bait. We were very kindly received by M. and Mde. Ruellan. The governor makes us a visit, and some other gentlemen."

Three days they passed at Havre, receiving honorable attentions from the inhabitants. As the ship which had been engaged to convey them to America, was to call for them at Portsmouth, they crossed the channel to Southampton to await her arrival. Thither hastened, from all quarters, Franklin's old friends, to see him for the last time. The British government sent down an order, exempting the effects of the party from custom-house examination. Governor Franklin came, and embraced his father for the first time in ten years. The seat of the good Bishop of St. Asaphs was only a few miles distant, and Franklin instantly notified him of his arrival. The Bishop replied : " The first emotion of my heart is, to thank Heaven that you are onc e more so near me, and that I shall have the happiness of seeing you in a few hours. Some of our good friends are come most untimely to dine with us. As soon as we are rid of them, my wife and I, and the only daughter that is now with us, will hasten to welcome you, and to enjoy till the last moment of your departure as much of the blessing of your conversation as we can without being tiresome. Adieu, till seven or eight in the evening."

They came. " The Bishop and family," diarizes Franklin, " lodging in the same inn, the Star, we all breakfast and dine together. I went at noon to bathe in Martin's salt-water hot-bath, and, floating on my back, fell asleep, and slept near an hour by my watch, without sinking or turning ! a thing I never did before, and should hardly have thought possible. Water is the easiest bed that can be. Read over the writings of conveyance, &c., of my son's lands in New Jersey and New York to my grandson."

The next day the deeds were signed between Governor Franklin and Temple Franklin, and on the next, Dr. Franklin gave his son a power of attorney to collect the unpaid balance of his claim against the British government for supplies furnished the army of General Braddock, in the old French war. The Bishop and his family dined with the departing voyagers for the last time ; and, after dinner, they all embarked in a shallop, to go on board the ship. The Bishop resolved to spare both families the pain of taking leave; so, after supping in the cabin, and accepting Captain Truxton's invitation to remain on board all night, they quietly withdrew, and returned to Southampton. When Dr. Franklin awoke the next morning (July 28th) he found his friends gone, and the ship at sea, under full sail. "We all left the ship," wrote the Bishop's daughter, "with a heavy heart; but the taking leave was a scene we wished to save you as well as ourselves. God grant you may have a good voyage; it is our constant *toast* every day at dinner. * * * We are forever talking of our good friend; something is perpetually occurring to remind us of the time spent with you. We never walk in the garden, without seeing *Dr. Franklin's room*, and thinking of the work that was begun in it. * * * Indeed, my dear sir, from my father and mother, down to their *youngest child*, we all respect and love you."

To the latest moment of their lives, the good Bishop's family cherished the memory of Franklin with a warmth of affection indescribable. Thirty-seven years after this sad parting, Washington Irving met in Paris one of the last survivors, whom he calls "old Lady Jones, widow of Sir William Jones." She was still lively and cheerful, he says, and told stories of Dr. Franklin, and felt for America all the old love.[*]

The Bishop's family and M. Le Veillard had urged him to spend the leisure of the voyage in continuing his Autobiography, begun long ago in the Bishop's garden-house at Troyford; and he appears to have promised to do so. But the wonderful old man, his health being renewed by traveling, and by the enforced exercise on board the ship, devoted his time to severer labors. It was during this voyage of seven weeks, that he wrote three of his most extensive and useful essays, one on navigation, another on chimneys, the third a description of his smoke-consuming stove. In the paper upon navigation he embodied the whole of his reflections, observations and discoveries relating to the construction, rigging, sailing, loading, provisioning and saving of ships, and the winds, currents, and temperature of the ocean; illustrated by twenty-five drawings and a chart of the Atlantic, and accompanied by six tables of thermometrical observations. Eight times he had crossed the Atlantic, his active mind always on the alert to study the wondrous phenom-

---

[*] Life and Letters of Washington Irving, by Pierre M. Irving, ii., 87.

ena of the sea, and the sublime art of navigation.   In this essay he recorded the results of so much observation and thought.   Several of his suggestions have proved to be of vast utility, particularly this one: " While on the topic of sinking, one cannot help recollecting the well-known practice of the Chinese, to divide the hold of a great ship into a number of separate chambers by partitions tight caulked, so that, if a leak should spring in one of them, the others are not affected by it; and, though that chamber should fill to a level with the sea, it would not be sufficient to sink the vessel." This, also, might be of use : " If the crew of a ship happen, in any circumstance, such as after shipwreck, taking to their boat, or the like, to want a compass, a fine sewing needle laid on clear water in a cup, will generally point to the north, most of them being a little magnetical, or may be made so by being strongly rubbed or hammered, lying in a north and south direction.   If their needle is too heavy to float by itself, it may be supported by little pieces of cork or wood."   This also : " The accidents I have seen at sea with large dishes of soup upon a table, from the motion of the ship, have made me wish that our potters or pewterers would make soup dishes in divisions, like a set of small bowls united together, each containing about sufficient for one person ; for then, when the ship should make a sudden heel, the soup would not in a body flow over one side, and fall into people's laps and scald them, as is sometimes the case, but would be retained in the separate divisions."

In the preparation of this essay, he was aided by the intelligence of Captain Thomas Truxton, who commanded the ship, a man destined to illustrate, by his valor and conduct, the naval service of his country.   Temple Franklin, I presume, executed the drawings. Truxton tried some of Franklin's suggestions, and was always fond of talking of the time when he and Dr. Franklin sailed and " chopped logic" together.

The essay on the Cause and Cure of Smoky Chimneys, was very sprightly and entertaining, as well as valuable.   At that time, we may boldly say, all chimneys smoked sometimes ; and it was a trade in large cities to cure them.   By revealing the correct principle of chimney construction, as Franklin did in this paper, he rid all Christendom of a most afflicting nuisance.   The discourse was enlivened by good stories, as usual.   " A puzzling case," he says, " I met with at a friend's country-house near London.   His best

room had a chimney, in which, he told me, he never could have a
fire, for all the smoke came out into the room.   I flattered myself,
I could easily find the cause, and prescribe the cure.   I had a fire
made there, and found it as he said.   I opened the door, and perceived it was not want of air.   I made a temporary contraction of
the opening of the chimney, and found that it was not its being too
large, that caused the smoke to issue.   I went out and looked up
at the top of the chimney ; its funnel was joined in the same stack
with others, some of them shorter, that drew very well, and I saw
nothing to prevent its doing the same.   In fine, after every other
examination I could think of I was obliged to own the insufficiency
of my skill.   But my friend, who made no pretension to such kind
of knowledge, afterward discovered the cause himself.   He got to
the top of the funnel by a ladder, and looking down, found it filled
with twigs and straw cemented by earth, and lined with feathers.
It seems the house, after being built, had stood empty some years
before he occupied it ; and he concluded, that some large birds had
taken the advantage of its retired situation to make their nest
there.   The rubbish, considerable in quantity, being removed, and
the funnel cleared, the chimney drew well, and gave satisfaction."

The paper upon the smoke-burning stove is remarkably full and exact.   It abounds in striking observations, and is profusely illustrated by drawings.

These three essays, written in despite of the languor of ship-
board and the infirmities of fourscore, would fill about one hundred of these pages.   Nor did he neglect to verify again his discovery respecting the warmth of the Gulf Stream.   The Autobiography was wholly neglected.

On the morning of September 13th, Dr. Franklin awoke to hear
the joyful news that the ship was in Delaware Bay, abreast of the
lighthouse, and between Cape May and Cape Henlopen.   A fine
breeze wafted them so swiftly up the river, that they passed New-
castle at sunset, and anchored, when the wind failed and the tide
turned, near Red Bank, a short distance below Philadelphia.
" With the flood in the morning," wrote Franklin in his diary,
" came a light breeze, which brought us above Gloucester Point,
in full view of dear Philadelphia ! when we again cast anchor to
wait for the health officer ; who, having made his visit, and finding
no sickness, gave us leave to land.   My son-in-law came with a

boat for us; we landed at Market Street wharf, where we were received by a crowd of people with huzzas, and accompanied with acclamations quite to my door. Found my family well. God be praised and thanked for all his mercies!"

The next day, the Assembly of Pennsylvania voted him a congratulatory address, in which they said: "We are confident, Sir, that we speak the sentiments of the whole country, when we say, that your services, in the public councils and negotiations, have not only merited the thanks of the present generation, but will be recorded in the pages of history, to your immortal honor." The faculty of the University, the Philosophical Society, and many other public bodies also, addressed him; and to all these addresses he gave suitable replies. General Washington wrote to him: "Amid the public gratulations on your safe return to America, after a long absence and the many eminent services you have rendered it, for which as a benefited person I feel the obligation, permit an individual to join the public voice in expressing a sense of them; and to assure you, that, as no one entertains more respect for your character, so no one can salute you with more sincerity or with greater pleasure, than I do on the occasion."

Among the many who were made happy by his arrival, no one was so deeply moved as his sister, Jane Mecom; for no one loved him as she loved him. She had felt all the anguish of his malady when the ocean rolled between them. Before he left France, she had written: "Oh! that after you have spent your whole life in the service of the public, and have attained so glorious a conclusion, as I thought, as would now permit you to come home and spend (as you used to say) the evening with your friends in ease and quiet, that now such a dreadful malady should attack you! My heart is ready to burst with grief at the thought. How many hours have I lain awake on nights, thinking what excruciating pains you might then be encountering, while I, poor, useless, and worthless worm, was permitted to be at ease. O that it was in my power to mitigate or alleviate the anguish I know you must endure!" And when she heard of his arrival, she wrote: "I long so much to see you that I should immediately seek for some one that would accompany me, and take a little care of me, but my daughter is in a poor state of health, and gone into the country to try to get a little better, and I am in a strait between two; but the comfortable reflection that you are at home among all your dear children, and no more seas to cross, will be constantly pleasing to me till I am permitted to enjoy the happiness of seeing and conversing with you." She told him, too, that his old friend, Mrs. Catherine Greene, wife of the Governor of Rhode Island, was so overjoyed at the news of his arrival that her children thought she was seized with hysterics.

His letters to his sister continued to be unspeakably considerate and tender. One of them has been particularly admired, not for its humor merely, but for the thoughtful, ingenious benevolence of it. "You need not," said he, "be concerned, in writing to me, about your bad spelling; for, in my opinion, as our alphabet now stands, the bad spelling, or what is called so, is generally the best, as conforming to the sound of the letters and of the words. To give you an instance. A gentleman received a letter, in which were these words—*Not finding Brown at hom, I delivered your meseg to his yf.* The gentleman finding it bad spelling, and therefore not very intelligible, called his lady to help him read it. Between them they picked out the meaning of all but the *yf*, which they could not understand. The lady proposed calling her chambermaid, because Betty, says she, has the best knack at reading bad spelling of any one I know. Betty came, and was surprised, that neither Sir nor Madam could tell what *yf* wa.. 'Why,' says she '*y f* spells *wife;* what else can it spell?' And, indeed, it is a much better, as well as shorter method of spelling *wife*, than *doubleyou, i, ef, e*, which in reality spell *doubleyifey.*"

"I think," replied she, in her simple way, "Sir and Madam were very deficient in sagacity that they could not find out *yf* as well as Betty, but sometimes the Betties have the brightest understandings."

PART VII.

LAST YEARS AND LABORS.

PART VII.

CHAPTER I.

PRESIDENT OF PENNSYLVANIA.

THE long sea voyage gave Dr. Franklin a new hold upon life. He could walk the streets of "dear Philadelphia," and could endure the motion of an easy carriage. He told Mr. Jay that he hoped to visit him in New York ere long, as he thought he could bear riding along the sandy, level roads of New Jersey, from Burlington to Amboy, and "the rest was water." Nor did he despair of seeing once more his native Boston, well beloved. His cheeks were ruddy, his eye was bright, his voice was firm, his spirits were high, and his conversation was as merry and vigorous as ever. He said that he sometimes forgot that he was an old man. His townsmen, too, were not disposed to consider him past doing them service.

Pennsylvania was in a stress of politics in the summer of 1785. The election of a president and vice-president of the State was to occur in October; and between the two parties, the Constitutionalists and the Republicans, the struggle for triumph was waxing warm. The chief point in dispute was whether the legislature of the State should consist of one house, as the Constitution then ordained, or of two houses, as the Republicans desired. People then were not so accustomed to political strife as we are now, and, consequently, many timid individuals feared that the Commonwealth itself was in danger of being torn to pieces by the contending factions. In August came the announcement that Dr. Franklin was, in very truth, coming home; nay, had actually left Paris in one of the royal litters, and would, in all probability, reach Philadelphia before the election. Dr. Franklin, as we know, was a Constitutionalist—a one-house man—the great champion of that system.

But for ten years he had been absent from the State, and he was coming home covered with the glory of a vast success, and illustrious with the esteem of civilized man. If, on the one hand, the Constitutionalists saw their opportunity, the Republicans, on the other, willingly bowed to the necessity of the situation.

"The expected arrival," said one of the newspapers of Philadelphia, "of that great philosopher, that great politician, and, to add a wreath of glory of a more immortal texture, that truly benevolent citizen of the world, Dr. Franklin, in this State, cannot fail to produce a most sensible effect on the public weal. To doubt of his being chosen President on the vacation of that office, should he fortunately arrive prior thereto, would be to call in question not only the honor and gratitude, but even the common sense of Pennsylvania. With his profound penetration, which will instantaneously see through the complicated system of government, and develop the most minute incoherence or irregularity capable of impeding the progress of society toward perfection—with his benevolence, his magnanimity, and his unbounded patriotism, with his capacious understanding and enlarged views, which will teach him to despise equally those members of both parties, who, under the false mask of patriotism, have no other views than their own aggrandizement, and to select from both parties those whose only object is the safety and well-being of the state, and whose only difference is in the *mode* of promoting that object—he will authoritatively command the effectual support of all the real friends of Pennsylvania. Confided in and obeyed by all persons of this description, he will, doubtless, induce our contending parties to bury the war-hatchet, to send the belt of peace, and to embrace each other as brethren. Party disputes to a certain degree are inevitable in, and perhaps essential to a free government. But when they arrive at such a hight, that the public welfare is esteemed but a secondary consideration, and is liable to be sacrificed to private piques and resentments (as is too much the case on both sides at present), they threaten a dissolution of government, and the introduction of disorder, anarchy, and all the horrors of civil commotion!"

This article, which appeared two or three weeks before his arrival, evidently expressed the feeling of the State. As soon as he reached the city he was put in nomination for the office of Councilor for Philadelphia, to which he was elected early in October with remarkable unanimity; and when he took his seat in the Council he was unanimously elected chairman. Such events as these soon made it apparent to him that his long cherished dream of escaping from politics, and spending the evening of his life in tranquil study, with his family and friends around him, could be realized only by disappointing the vehement wishes of the entire commonwealth. Friends in other States joined their entreaties. Mr. Jay wrote to him that if Dr. Franklin did not restore harmony in Pennsylvania he did not know who could; "and if you accomplish it, much honor and many blessings will result from it." To the solicitations of his countrymen he gave a not very reluctant consent. Gratified as he had been by the warmth of his welcome home, he was still more keenly touched by this signal proof, given in the view of the whole world, that his diligent maligners had not been able to despoil him of the confidence of those who had known him longest and trusted him most. He was a modest man, moreover; and a modest man values the esteem of his countrymen.

"I had not firmness enough," he wrote to an old friend, "to resist the unanimous desire of my country folks; and I find myself harnessed again in their service for another year. They engrossed the prime of my life. They have eaten my flesh, and seem resolved now to pick my bones."

The election lay with the Executive Council and the Assembly, seventy-seven votes in all; of which seventy-six were cast for Dr. Franklin. Charles Biddle (father of Nicholas and Commodore James Biddle), was elected Vice-President.

The day of the election was also the day of the inauguration. Modern Philadelphians may be amused with the original record of these events in the archives of their State: "Council and Assembly having met, and their votes collectively being taken, it appeared that his Excellency Benjamin Franklin, Esq., was duly elected President, and the Honorable Charles Biddle, Esquire, Vice-President, of the Supreme Executive Council of this Commonwealth.

"Proclamation was then made of the said President and Vice-President, and the following order of procession observed:

"Constables with their staves; Sub-Sheriffs with their wands; High Sheriff and Coroner with their wands: Judges of the Supreme Court and Judges of the High Court of Errors and Appeals; Attorney-General and Prothonotary of the Supreme Court; Marshall of the Admirality; Judge and Register of the Admirality; Wardens of the Port of Philadelphia; Naval Officer, Collector of the Customs, and Tonnage Officer; Treasurer and Comptroller-General of the State; Secretary of the Land Office; Receiver and Surveyor-General; Justices of the Peace; Prothonotary of the Court of Common Pleas and Clerk of the Court of General Quarter Sessions; Clerk of the City Court; Master of the Rolls and Register of Wills; Secretary of the Council; His Excellency the President, and Honorable the Vice-President; Members of the Council, two and two; Doorkeeper of the Council; Sarjeant-at-arms with the mace; Honorable the Speaker of the General Assembly; Clerk of the General Assembly; Members of the General Assembly, two and two; Doorkeeper of the General Assembly; Provost and Faculty of the University; Officers of the Militia; Citizens."*

Thus escorted, the newly elected magistrates entered the state-house, where, with the ancient solemnity, they were sworn in. Among the great crowd who on that day saw, with delight and veneration, Dr. Franklin as he went into the building, was a young journeyman printer from Ireland, Matthew Carey by name, afterward the head of the leading publishing house of Philadelphia. He essayed to express his feelings on the occasion in blank verse—not with striking success:

> "Each wistful gazer, wond'ring, seemed to say,
> And is that Franklin? the great, the good,
> The sage whose pains incessant, and mature advice
> Conflicting storms for us have weather'd,
> And safely steer'd our bark into the port
> Of independence—where ease, and happiness,
> And plenty, inviting, tempt acceptance—
> And where, unless by party broils
> We mar our fortune, we bliss may taste
> Beyond the ancient fictions of poetic fancy.
> Almighty power! whose eye benignly doth regard
> Fair virtue's sons with love paternal,
> Preserve his precious life from harm," etc., etc.

The noise of party contention died away for the time, and Dr.

* Colonial Records of Pennsylvania, xiv., 565.

Franklin ruled over a peaceful, happy, and prosperous State. The day after his election he wrote to his old friend David Hartley: "Your newspapers are filled with accounts of distresses and miseries that these States are plunged into since their separation from Britain. You may believe me when I tell you, that there is no truth in those accounts. I find all property in lands and houses augmented vastly in value; that of houses in towns at least fourfold. The crops have been plentiful, and yet the produce sells high, to the great profit of the farmer. At the same time, all imported goods sell at low rates, some cheaper than the first cost. Working people have plenty of employ and high pay for their labor."

In this general prosperity the President of Pennsylvania, whose property consisted chiefly of houses in Philadelphia, abundantly shared. He accepted the government with the determination to appropriate the whole of his salary to public objects; for it had now become a fixed article of his political faith, that offices of honor, in a Democratic State, ought never to be offices of emolument. He gave large sums toward the founding and support of colleges and other institutions, and bequeathed the remainder for a benevolent scheme to be described in due time. His official labors, except during the sessions of the legislature, were not arduous; it was the conspicuousness of the situation, crowding his house with visitors, and his letter-box with correspondence, that alone made him ever regret his election.

He was now permanently domiciled in the house in Market Street, of which his wife had superintended the building twenty years before; both expecting to pass therein the residue of their lives. He was at home at last, with his daughter and her seven beautiful children, and a very happy household it was. "The companions of my youth," he wrote, in the spring of 1786, "are indeed, almost all departed, but I find an agreeable society among their children and grandchildren. I have public business enough to preserve me from *ennui*, and private amusement besides in conversation, books, my garden, and *cribbage*. Considering our well-furnished, plentiful market as the best of gardens, I am turning mine, in the midst of which my house stands, into grass plots and gravel walks, with trees and flowering shrubs. Cards we sometimes play here, in long winter evenings; but it is as they play at chess, not for money, but for honor, or the pleasure of beating one another."

This will not be quite a novelty to you, as you may remember we played together in that manner during the winter at Passy. I have indeed now and then a little compunction in reflecting that I spend time so idly; but another reflection comes to relieve me, whispering, '*You know that the soul is immortal; why then should you be such a niggard of a little time, when you have a whole eternity before you?*' So, being easily convinced, and, like other reasonable creatures, satisfied with a small reason when it is in favor of doing what I have a mind to, I shuffle the cards again, and begin another game.

"As to public amusements, we have neither plays nor operas, but we had yesterday a kind of oratorio, and we have assemblies, balls, and concerts, besides little parties at one another's houses, in which there is sometimes dancing, and frequently good music; so that we jog on in life as pleasantly as you do in England; anywhere but in London, for there you have plays performed by good actors. That, however, is, I think, the only advantage London has over Philadelphia.

"Temple has turned his thoughts to agriculture, which he pursues ardently, being in possession of a fine farm, that his father lately conveyed to him. Ben is finishing his studies at college, and continues to behave as well as when you knew him."

He was much occupied in these years with building a new wing to his house. It was of three stories, of which the first was a large apartment for the meetings of the Philosophical Society, the second was his library, and the third was composed of lodging rooms. The new wing presented some novelties of construction: "None of the wooden work of one room communicates with the wooden work of any other room; and all the floors, and even the steps of the stairs, are plastered close to the boards, besides the plastering on the laths under the joists. There are also trap-doors to go out upon the roofs, that one may go out and wet the shingles in case of a neighboring fire. But, indeed, I think the staircases should be stone, and the floors tiled as in Paris, and the roofs either tiled or slated." It was for this new library that he contrived his "long arm," an instrument for taking down books from high shelves, which he took particular pleasure in showing to visitors. Against a recurrence of his malady, he had a sedan chair made, a vehicle not known then in America.

A pleasing incident appears in Franklin's correspondence of the spring of 1786. Dr. Benjamin Rush, discoursing to the Philosophical Society upon the "Influence of Physical Causes on the Moral Faculty," broke into an eulogium of Dr. Franklin, who was presiding. Franklin addressed to the orator the following note:

"During our long acquaintance, you have shown many instances of your regard for me; yet I must now desire you to add one more to the number, which is, that, if you publish your ingenious discourse on the *Moral Sense*, you will totally omit and suppress that most extravagant encomium on your friend Franklin, which hurt me exceedingly in the unexpected hearing, and will mortify me beyond conception if it should appear from the press." Dr. Rush replied: "Agreeably to your request, I have suppressed the conclusion of my oration, but I cannot bear to think of sending it out of our State or to Europe without connecting it with your name. I have therefore taken the liberty of inscribing it to you by a simple dedication, of which the inclosed is a copy. And, as you have never in the course of our long acquaintance refused *me* a single favor, I must earnestly insist upon your adding to my great and numerous obligations to you the permission, which I now solicit, to send my *last* as I did my *first* publication into the world under the patronage of your name."

Dr. Rush had one intention with regard to Dr. Franklin which it is a thousand pities he did not fulfill. He meant to write out and publish a volume of Franklin's conversation. What a book it might have been!

In general politics, this year, the exciting topic was the delay of the English in evacuating the frontier posts, on the pretext that American merchants did not pay their old debts. Franklin wrote a remarkably witty and spirited piece on this subject, entitled the Retort Courteous: in which he showed that England, in destroying American commerce in 1775, without notice or provocation, had herself rendered the payment of many of those debts impossible. I observe in this tract, that Franklin held in just contempt the claims of Dr. Samuel Johnson to the character of "moralist." The Johnson, however, whom Franklin disliked was not the leading character in an entertaining work by James Boswell, but quite another person, the unworthy author of "Taxation no Tyranny."

In another article of this year, Dr. Franklin humorously suggested

the transportation of American felons to England, as English felons
were formerly transported to America. " No due returns," said he,
" have yet been made for these valuable consignments. We are
therefore much in her debt on that account ; and, as she is of late
clamorous for the payment of all we owe her, and some of our debts
are of a kind not so easily discharged, I am for doing, however, what
is in our power. It will show our good-will as to the rest. The
felons she planted among us have produced such an amazing in
crease, that we are now enabled to make ample remittance in the
same commodity. * * * * * I am of opinion that, besides
employing our own vessels, every English ship arriving in our ports
with goods for sale, should be obliged to give bond, before she is
permitted to trade, engaging that she will carry back to Britain at
least one felon for every fifty tons of her burden. Thus we shall
not only discharge sooner our debts, but furnish our old friends
with the means of ' *better peopling*,' and with more expedition,
their promising new colony of Botany Bay." This amusing article
appeared in the Pennsylvania *Gazette*, the paper founded by himself, wherein other pieces from the same pen, or inspired by the
same mind, were not unfrequently published during his presidency.

One glory in his old age Franklin missed. When he returned
from France in September, 1785, that most unfortunate of men of
genius, JOHN FITCH, clock-cleaner and brass-smith, was six months
gone with his conception of a steamboat, and was assailing all ears,
willing and unwilling, with descriptions of his plan, and prognostications of the day when all rivers and all oceans should be navigated by steam-propelled vessels. He was a poor, ungainly,
illiterate man, without the smallest faculty to win or persuade, and
of a zeal so intense, a conviction so absolute, a disinterestedness so
pure, that people sometimes said, after hearing him talk, " Poor fellow
what a pity he is crazy !" With as tender a heart as ever beat, a
mind quick to comprehend, and a hand as diligent as it was expert,
he had seldom prospered, and had always been misunderstood and
undervalued. He was the son of a singularly mean Connecticut
farmer, whose merciless exactions stunted his growth and placed
such obstacles in the way of his acquiring knowledge as only the
John Fitches of the world can surmount. In spite of the niggard-
liness of this paternal churl, he managed to pick up a little geog-
raphy, a little arithmetic, a little geometry, a little skill in brass

and clock work. After a forty years' battle with the world, there he was in Philadelphia, with not a guinea in his pocket, and not a second coat to his back; but with as clear a conception of a steamboat, and as entire a certainty of the practicability of his idea, as we now have who see steamboats daily passing before our eyes. And, what is more surprising, he knew nothing of the steam-engine, had never seen one, had never heard of one, until after he had conceived the idea of using the mighty force of steam in the propulsion of boats. Nothing was then known in America of the new English firm of Watt and Bolton (formed in 1774) and their improved steam-engines, which were soon to change the face of the globe and the condition of every creature on it. In all America there were only three or four steam engines, and those of the old construction, used to pump water from mines. " Although it was not to my credit," says poor John Fitch, in his unpublished Autobiography,* " I did not know that there was a steam-engine on earth when I proposed to gain a force by steam ;" and when he was shown a drawing of one, he confesses that he " was very much chagrined."

The glory which Dr. Franklin missed was that of giving effectual aid to this forlorn, uncouth man of genius in his costly experiments. At the first meeting of the Philosophical Society which occurred after Franklin's arrival, John Fitch was present, with his drawings and his models, his rustic manner and his choking zeal. He expounded his plan, and the knot of philosophers commented upon it. But, he says, no new ideas were advanced, and some of the most material were not hinted at. A few days after, the inventor called upon Dr. Franklin, who, he says, spoke so flatteringly of the scheme, that he had hopes of securing his patronage. Again, before leaving the city, he wrote a letter to Franklin beseeching his attention to the darling, daring project. " The subscriber," says John Fitch, " is full in the belief, that it will answer for sea voyages as well as for inland navigation, in particular for packets, where there may be a great number of passengers. He is also of opinion, that fuel for a short voyage would not exceed the weight of water for a long one, and it would produce a constant supply of fresh water. He also believes, that the boat would make head against the most violent tempests, and thereby escape the danger of a lee-

* Quoted in Thompson Westcott's excellent Life of John Fitch, p. 122. Will not Mr. Westcott give us the Autobiography entire?

shore; and that the same force may be applied to a pump to free a leaky ship of her water." All true; but it made only a very slight impression upon the minds of contemporaries. Dr. Franklin thought so little of Fitch's dream, that in his paper upon Navigation, written on board Captain Truxton's ship, and read before the Philosophical Society, six or seven weeks after the date of Fitch's letter, he does not even mention the project of propelling vessels by steam. Still worse: upon the return of Fitch from his journey, Franklin unwittingly wounded his sensitive feelings most acutely. The poor inventor called upon Dr. Franklin again to solicit his patronage, asking particularly for a written certificate of the value of the invention, to aid him in procuring subscriptions for building a steamboat. Franklin declined to give any written opinion upon the subject, though he again spoke highly of the ingenuity of Fitch's plans. At length, he asked him to come into another room, where he opened a desk, took out five or six dollars, and offered them to the evidently needy inventor. Poor Fitch, stung with the indignity, refused to accept the money unless he could take it as Dr. Franklin's subscription to the steamboat. Franklin refused to give it as a subscription, and John Fitch withdrew, respectful in manner, but most deeply incensed. "I esteem it," he says, "one of the most imprudent acts of my life, that I had not treated the insult with the indignity which he merited, and stomped the paltry Ore under my feet."

He persevered in his project, however, and, with the aid of a few subscribers, won for himself the immortal distinction of being the first man who constructed a steamboat that answered the purpose of a steamboat. In 1788 he had one running upon the Delaware, and in the summer of 1790 his boat made thirty-one successful trips, carrying passengers for money, as many advertisements in the newspapers attest.* A well-known Philadelphian describes its last trip: "I often witnessed the performance of the boat in 1788, '89, and '90. It was propelled by paddles in the stern, and constantly

---

* Mr. Westcott, the worthy biographer of John Fitch, publishes twenty-three such advertisements as the following from Philadelphia Newspapers, of 1790:

"The Steam-boat will set out this morning, at 11 oclk, for Messrs. Gray's Garden, at a quarter of a dollar for each passenger thither. It will afterward ply between Gray's and middle ferry, at 11d each passenger. To morrow morning, Sunday, it will set off for Burlington at eight oclock, to return in the afternoon.

"Sept. 4, 1790."   *Pennsylvania Packet.*

getting out of order. I saw it when it was returning from a trip
to Burlington, from whence it was said, to have arrived in little
more than two hours. When coming to off Kensington, some part
of the machinery broke, and I never saw it in motion afterward.
I believe it was his last effort. He had, up to that period, been
patronized by a few stout-hearted individuals, who had subscribed
a small capital, in shares, I think, of £6 Pennsylvania currency;
but this last disaster so staggered their faith and unstrung their
nerves, that they never again had the hardihood to make other contributions. Indeed, they already rendered themselves the subjects
of ridicule and derision, for their temerity and presumption in giving
countenance to this wild projector and visionary madman. The
company thereupon gave up the ghost, the boat went to pieces, and
Fitch became bankrupt and broken-hearted. *Often have I seen
him stalking about like a troubled spectre*, with downcast eye and
lowering countenance, his coarse, soiled linen, peeping through the
elbows of a tattered garment.*

He removed to Kentucky, where he died by his own hand, firm
to the last in the conviction that the Ohio, on whose banks he lived,
would, ere many years had elapsed, be navigated by steamboats.
" The day will come," he would say, " when some more powerful
man will get fame and riches from my invention; but nobody will
believe that poor John Fitch can do any thing worthy of attention."

In the Philadelphia directory for 1785, we read: " Robert Fulton,
miniature painter, corner of Second and Walnut Street."

It were highly absurd to hold Dr. Franklin censurable for not
having bestowed upon this noble and ingenious patriot the powerful
sanction of his name and influence. Such schemes as that of John
Fitch are not for old men. Youth does the greatest things. It
must have been apparent to Franklin, not yet acquainted with
Watt's improved engine, that the construction of a really useful
steamboat was work for a long lifetime, if, indeed, it were possible
at all; and he properly hesitated to countenance a scheme which,
being countenanced by him, would have probably involved many of
his friends in loss. If John Fitch had met Benjamin Franklin in
the old leathern-apron days, or even when he received from Peter
Collinson the first electrical tube, the two men would have under-

* Thomas P. Cope in Hazard's Register, vii., 91.

stood one another. Still, we cannot help coveting even for the aged Franklin the honor of having seen through the rags, the igno- rance and the ungainliness of John Fitch, and discovered that he, too, was a genius and a peer.*

After all, the steamboat, like gunpowder, the printing-press, America, the steam-engine, the locomotive, the telegraph, and the mowing machine, came as soon as it was wanted. The great in- ventions and discoveries have all been exquisitely timed.

There is a famous, undated letter among the writings of Franklin that appears to belong to this period of his life, which is too impor- tant to be passed by without notice. The letter is in reply to a friend who had sent him, for his opinion, a manuscript treatise con- troverting the doctrine of a "particular Providence," and inveighing generally against religion. The treatise has been generally supposed to be the "Age of Reason" by Thomas Paine; a work which Paine explicitly states was not begun until Dr. Franklin had been dead three years. Besides, upon looking over the "Age of Reason," I do not find any thing in it about a particular Providence, nor any thing against religion. It is merely a strong statement of the fact, that Thomas Paine was no believer in miracles, and that he found especially and utterly incredible the miraculous production of any of the works composing the Bible.† It is, in fact, a leaf of the con-

---

* "His bones," says Mr. Westcott, "still rest near the Ohio, unhonored by any fitting memorial. * * * On some fair promontory near the Ohio, a monument to the inventor of the steamboat should be raised, having inscribed upon it the beautiful paraphrase of the expression of his hopes written by John F. Watson:

> "'His darling wish [he said] was to be buried
> On the margin of the Ohio ;
> Where the song of the boatman might penetrate
> The stillness of his resting-place,
> And where the sound of the steam-engine
> Might send its echoes abroad.'"

† Paine sums up his argument in these words:

"First—That the idea or belief of a word of God existing in print, or in writing, or in speech, is inconsistent in itself for reasons already assigned. These reasons, among many others, are the want of an universal language; the mutability of language; the errors to which translations are subject; the possibility of totally suppressing such a word ; the probability of altering it, or of fabricating the whole, and imposing it upon the world.

"Secondly—That the Creation we behold is the real and ever existing word of God, in which we cannot be deceived. It proclaims his power, it demonstrates his wisdom, it manifests his good- ness and beneficence.

"Thirdly—That the moral duty of man consists in imitating the moral goodness and beneficence of God manifested in the creation toward all his creatures. That seeing as we daily do the good- ness of God to all men, it is an example calling upon all men to practice the same toward each other ; and, consequently, that every thing of persecution and revenge between man and man, and every thing of cruelty to animals, is a violation of moral duty."

troversy which has raged in the world from the days of Boling-
broke and Voltaire, to those of Theodore Parker, Renan, and
Bishop Colenso, and which is likely to continue for some time to
come. Paine, moreover, was a resident of Philadelphia, a frequenter
of Franklin's house, and was as well aware as we are of Dr. Franklin's religious opinions. Nor is there much in the "Age of Reason"
to which Franklin would have refused his assent. The person replied to in the letter which I am about to quote was, perhaps, Dr.
Edward Bancroft.

No man then living had a stronger conviction than Dr. Franklin
of the necessity, not only of religion, but of *a* religion. The events,
too, of the recent revolution had given him, as they had General
•Washington, a revival of belief in particular Providence. Hence
the warmth and decision of the following letter :

"I have read your manuscript with some attention. By the
argument it contains against a particular Providence, though you
allow a general Providence, you strike at the foundations of all
religion. For without the belief of a Providence, that takes cogni-
zance of, guards, and guides, and may favor particular persons,
there is no motive to worship a Deity, to fear his displeasure, or to
pray for his protection. I will not enter into any discussion of
your principles, though you seem to desire it. At present I shall
only give you my opinion, that, though your reasonings are subtle,
and may prevail with some readers, you will not succeed so as to
change the general sentiments of mankind on that subject, and the
consequence of printing this piece will be a great deal of odium
drawn upon yourself, mischief to you, and no benefit to others.
He that spits against the wind spits in his own face.

"But, were you to succeed, do you imagine any good would be
done by it ? You yourself may find it easy to live a virtuous life,
without the assistance afforded by religion ; you having a clear
perception of the advantages of virtue, and the disadvantages of
vice, and possessing â strength of resolution sufficient to enable you
to resist common temptations. But think how great a portion of
mankind consists of weak and ignorant men and women, and of in-
experienced, inconsiderate youth of both sexes, who have need of
the motives of religion to restrain them from vice, to support their
virtue, and retain them in the practice of it till it becomes *habitual*,
which is the great point for its security. And perhaps you are in-

debted to her originally, that is, to your religious education, for the
habits of virtue upon which you now justly value yourself. You
might easily display your excellent talents of reasoning upon a less
hazardous subject, and thereby obtain a rank with our most distinguished authors. For among us it is not necessary, as among the
Hottentots, that a youth, to be raised into the company of men,
should prove his manhood by beating his mother.

"I would advise you, therefore, not to attempt unchaining the
tiger, but to burn this piece before it is seen by any other person ;
whereby you will save yourself a great deal of mortification by the
enemies it may raise against you, and perhaps a good deal of regret
and repentance. If men are so wicked *with religion*, what would
they be *if without it* ?"

It has been objected to this letter that the same reasoning would
have closed the mouth of St. Paul, Luther, Channing, Carlyle,
Parker, Buckle, Colenso, Maurice, all of whom had to do a good deal
of spitting against the wind ; nay, would have deprived the world
of the benign utterances of Jesus Christ himself. The letter *does*
seem incomplete. I feel the want in it of a sentence like this:
"These are my candid opinions, Dr. Heretic ; weigh them ; but, if
upon full and calm consideration, you still feel it to be your duty
to publish your treatise, then PUBLISH IT, though the heavens fall."
Franklin, however, knew his man, and, probably, gave his objections
a general form from politeness. It is not always proper to say :
"Your work, sir, is trivial—far beneath the mighty theme upon
which you have essayed to enlighten mankind. Burn it, sir, burn it !"

The year of his presidency rolled round ; but Pennsylvania was
not yet inclined to spare him. In the fall of 1786, he was unanimously re-elected ; an event which he owns was "agreeable" to him,
since it was a proof that "the esteem of his country with regard to
him was undiminished." And still the country prospered. "Our
husbandmen," wrote Franklin, in November, 1786, "who are the
bulk of the nation, have had plentiful crops, their produce sells at
high prices, and for ready, hard money ; wheat, for instance, at
eight shillings, and eight shillings and sixpence, a bushel. Our
working people are all employed and get high wages, are well fed
and well clad. Our estates in houses are trebled in value by the
rising of rents since the revolution. Buildings in Philadelphia increase amazingly, besides small towns rising in every quarter of the

country. The laws govern, justice is well administered, and property as secure as in any country on the globe. Our wilderness
lands are daily buying up by new settlers, and our settlements extend rapidly to the westward. European goods were never so
cheaply afforded us, as since Britain has no longer the monopoly of
supplying us. In short, all among us may be happy, who have happy
dispositions ; such being necessary to happiness even in Paradise."
His own health, too, was still tolerable, and his estate throve.

During the second year of his presidency he was active in the
promotion of a long-cherished scheme, the founding of a college for
the education of young Germans. Lancaster, sixty miles from
Philadelphia, was the site chosen for the institution ; and when the
corner-stone was ready to be laid, the generous old man underwent
the fatigue and pain of a journey thither, to give eclat to the occasion by performing the ceremony. It was a great day for Lancaster.
All the country seemed present. There was a grand procession,
and, what was especially pleasing to Franklin, a religious service
on the ground, in which Episcopalians, Presbyterians, Lutherans,
Catholics, Moravians, and Quakers, all harmoniously joined.

We have a pleasing relic of this journey, in a conversation with
President Franklin, reported by Hector St. John, author of " Letters
from an American Farmer." St. John was a Frenchman, who saw
every thing in America in an Arcadian light, and whose report of
this conversation has evidently something of the character of the
speeches in Thucydides. His report, however, is highly interesting.

" In the year, 1787," he begins, " I accompanied the venerable
Franklin, on a journey to Lancaster, where he had been invited to
lay the corner-stone of a college, which he had founded there for
the Germans. In the evening of the day of the ceremony, we were
talking of the different nations which inhabit the continent, of their
aversion to agriculture, &c., when one of the principal inhabitants
of the city said to him :

" ' Governor, where do you think these nations came from ? Do you
consider them aborigines ? Have you heard of the ancient fortifications and tombs which have been recently discovered in the west ?'

" ' Those who inhabit the two Floridas,' he replied, ' and lower
Louisiana, say, that they came from the mountains of Mexico. I
should be inclined to believe it. If we may judge of the Esqui-
maux of the coasts of Labrador (the most savage men known) by

the fairness of their complexion, the color of their eyes, and their enormous beards, they are originally from the north of Europe, whence they came at a very remote period. As to the other nations of this continent, it seems difficult to imagine from what stock they can be descended. To assign them an Asiatic and Tartar origin, to assert that they crossed Behring's Straits, and spread themselves over this continent, shocks all our notions of probability. How, indeed, can we conceive that men almost naked, armed with bows and arrows, could have undertaken a journey of a thousand leagues, through thick forests, or impenetrable marshes, accompanied by their wives and children, with no means of subsistence, save what they derived from hunting? What could have been the motives of such an emigration? If it were the severe cold of their own country, why should they have advanced to Hudson's Bay and Lower Canada? Why have they not stopped on their way at the beautiful plains on the banks of the Missouri, the Minnesota, the Mississippi, or the Illinois? But it will be said, they *did* settle there, and those with whom we are acquainted are but the surplus population of these ancient emigrations. If it were so, we should discover some analogy between their languages; and it is ascertained, beyond a doubt, that the languages of the Nadouassees and Padoukas no more resemble the Chippewa, the Mohawk, or the Abenaki, than they do the jargon of Kamschatka.

" ' On the other hand,' he continued, ' how can we suppose them to be the aborigines of a region like this, which produces scarcely any fruits or plants on which the primitive man could have subsisted until he had learned to make a bow and arrow, harpoon a fish, and kindle a fire? How could these first families have resisted the inclemency of the seasons, the stings of insects, the attacks of carnivorous animals? The warm climates, therefore, and those that abound in natural fruits, must have been the cradle of the human race; it was from the bosom of these favored regions that the exuberant portion of the early communities gradually spread over the rest of the world. Whence came the nations which inhabit this continent, those we meet with in New Zealand, New Holland, and the islands of the Pacific? Why have the people of the old world been civilized for thousands of ages, while those of the new still remain plunged in ignorance and barbarism?

Has this hemisphere more recently emerged from the bosom of the waters? These questions, and a thousand others we might ask, will ever be to us, frail beings, like a vast desert where the wandering eye sees not the smallest bush on which it may repose.

" 'This planet is very old,' he continued. 'Like the works of Homer and Hesiod, who can say through how many editions it has passed in the immensity of ages? The rent continents, the straits, the gulfs, the islands, the shallows of the ocean, are but vast fragments on which, as on the planks of some wrecked vessel, the men of former generations who escaped these commotions, have produced new populations. Time, so precious to us, the creatures of a moment, is nothing to nature. Who can tell us when the earth will again experience these fatal catastrophes, to which, it appears to me, to be as much exposed in its annual revolutions, as are the vessels which cross the seas to be dashed in pieces on a sunken rock? The near approach or contact of one of those globes whose elliptical and mysterious courses are perhaps the agents of our destinies, some variation in its annual or diurnal rotation, in the inclination of its axis or the equilibrium of the seas, might change its climate, and render it long uninhabitable.

" 'As to your third question,' continued the governor, 'I will give you some reflections which occurred to me on reading the papers lately presented to our philosophical society by Generals Varnum and Parsons, and Captains John Hart and Sarjeant, in relation to the intrenched camps and other indications of an ancient population, of whom tradition has transmitted no account to our indigenous population. In traveling through parts of this State beyond the Alleghanies, we often find on the high ground near the rivers remains of parapets and ditches covered with lofty trees. Almost the whole of the peninsula of Muskingum is occupied by a vast fortified camp. It is composed of three square inclosures; the central one, which is the largest, has a communication with the former bed of the river, whose waters appear to have retreated nearly three hundred feet. These inclosures are formed by ditches and parapets of earth, in which no cut stones or brick have been found. The center is occupied by conical elevations of different diameters and hights. Each of these inclosures appears to have had a cemetery. As a proof of the high antiquity of these works, we are assured as an undisputed fact, that the bones are converted into calcareous matter, and that the vegetable soil with which these fortifications are covered, and which has been formed merely by the falling off of the leaves and of the fragments of trees, is almost as thick as in the places around about them. Two other camps have been likewise discovered in the neighborhood of Lexington. The area of the first is six acres; that of the second, three. The fragments of earthenware which have been found in digging, are of a composition unknown to our Indians. * * * *

" ' At what period, by what people, were these works constructed? What degree of civilization had this people reached? What has become of them? Can we conceive that nations sufficiently powerful to have raised such considerable fortifications, and who buried their dead with such religious care, can have been destroyed and replaced by the ignorant and barbarous' hordes we see about us at the present day? Could the calamities occasioned by a long state of war have effaced the last traces of their civilization and brought them back to the primitive condition of hunters? Are our Indians the descendants of that ancient people?

" ' Such are the doubts and conjectures which arise in our minds on contemplating the traces of the passage and existence of the nations which inhabited the regions of the west; traces which are not sufficient to guide us in the vagueness of the past. Although neither arms nor instruments of iron have yet been discovered, how can we conceive that they could dig such deep ditches, or raise such large masses of earth, without the aid of that metal? This ancient people must have had chiefs, and been subject to laws; for without the bonds of subordination, how could they have collected and kept together so great a number of workmen? They must have been acquainted with agriculture, since the products of the chase would never have sufficed to support them. The extent of these camps also proves that the number of the troops destined to defend these works, and that of the families to which, in moments of danger, they afforded an asylum, was immense. The cemeteries prove that they sojourned there a long time. This people must therefore have been much further advanced in civilization than our Indians.

" ' When the population of the United States shall have spread over every part of that vast and beautiful region, our posterity, aided by new discoveries, may then perhaps form more satisfactory conjectures. What a field for reflection! A new continent, which, at some unknown period, appears to have been inhabited by agricultural and warlike nations! Were it not for my advanced age, I would myself cross the mountains to examine those old military works. Perhaps a careful and minute inspection would give rise to conjectures which now elade all the combinations of the mind.' "*

Such a vigorous, sweeping intelligence as this at "fourscore and upward"—what an argument for the soul's immortality!

Dr. Franklin's happiness at home, the honors bestowed upon him by his countrymen, and the prosperity of the young republic, gave great joy to the circle of his friends in France, particularly to those who revolved round Our Lady of Auteuil, Madame Helvetius. They not only wrote to him by every opportunity, but sent him copies of the humorous pieces which they were still accustomed to compose for the entertainment of the "Wednesday diners" at Madame Helvetius' house. The Abbé Morellet was his most frequent and most affectionate correspondent.

"Thrice welcome to your own country, which you have enlightened and liberated!" wrote the vivacious Abbé, on hearing of his safe arrival at Philadelphia. "Enjoy there glory and repose, a thing more substantial than the glory which you have so well deserved. May your days be prolonged and be free from pain; may your friends long taste the sweetness and the charm of your society, and may those whom the seas have separated from you be still happy in the thought that the end of your career will be, as our good La Fontaine says, 'the evening of a fine day.' You know how true and sincere these wishes are, which I repeat daily. I cannot express to you the pleasure, the transport which I felt at the news of your arrival at Philadelphia, which a friend of Mr. Jefferson has brought me. I sent immediately to tell it to our friends at Auteuil.

"I left them five or six days ago, after having passed three weeks with *our lady*, during which the Abbé de la Roche had been to make a journey into Normandy. I return thither in a few days, and we are about to speak much of you and of our joy at seeing that you were better during the passage than on shore. You must have learned that it was said in all the public papers that you had

---

* "Duyckinck's Cyclopædia of American Literature," i., 175. Translated from St. John's "Voyage Dans la Haute Pennsylvania."

been taken by an Algerine corsair. I never believed it at all; but perhaps there were some people in England who, for the beauty of the contrast, would have been well pleased to see the founder of the liberty of America, a slave among the people of Barbary. That would have been a fine subject for a tragedy twenty or thirty years hence; you would have had a very fine part. And have you not some regret at having missed so fine an opportunity of being a tragic personage? You must, however, dispense with this glory.

"We have been told that you were very well received, and had the huzzas of the people. These are very good and very just dispositions; but for the welfare of your country they should be durable, they should be extended, and all enlightened and virtuous citizens should second them, that your wise counsels and large views for the happiness and liberty of America may influence the measures that remain to be taken, and consolidate the edifice whose foundations you have laid in company with other good citizens. It is a wish that I express from the bottom of my heart, not as your friend and for your glory, but as a citizen of the world, and desiring that there should be on the face of the earth one country in which the government should be really occupied with the happiness of men; where property, liberty, safety, and toleration, should be possessions as natural, so to speak, as those that the sun and climate furnish; whither European governments, when they wish to return from their errors, may go to seek models. The Greek colonies were obliged to relight their sacred fires at the altar of their mother country. This will be the reverse, and the mother countries of Europe will go to seek in America that which will reanimate among them all the principles of national happiness which they have allowed to become extinct. *   *   *

"After having soared to these great objects, I must come down again to earth, and speak to you a little of your friends. *Our Lady of Auteuil* is very well, although she takes coffee too often, contrary to the decrees of D'r Cabanis, and always robs me of my share of cream, contrary to all justice. The bull-dog that your grandson brought us from England is become insupportable, and even vicious; he has again bitten the Abbé de la Roche, and affords us a glimpse of a ferocity truly disquieting. We have not yet made his mistress decide to send him to the bull-fight, or to have him drowned; but we are laboring at it. We have also domestic enemies less ferocious, but very offensive; a great number of cats, that have multiplied in her wood-house and barn-yard, owing to the care that she has taken to feed them very abundantly; for, as you have so well explained in your essay ' On Peopling Countries,' population being always in proportion to the means of subsistence, they are now eighteen, and will soon be thirty, eating all they can get, doing nothing but keeping their paws in their furred gowns, and warming themselves in the sun, and leaving the house infested with mice. It had been proposed to catch them in a snare and drown them; a cunning sophist, one of those people who know how to render every thing problematical, and who, as Aristophanes says of Socrates, know how *to make the worst cause appear the best*, has undertaken the defense of the cats, and has composed a *Petition* for them, that may serve as a companion-piece to the *Thanks* that you made for the flies of your rooms, after the destruction of the spiders ordered by *Our Lady*. We have sent you this piece, begging you to aid us in replying to the cats. We might also propose a pleasanter course for them, which might turn to the advantage of your America. I remember having heard you say, that you had many squirrels in the fields and many rats in the cities, that cause great havoc, and that you have not yet been able to arrange between the country people and the cits the imposition of a tax intended to rid you of these two kinds of enemies. But, for that, our cats will be of great assistance to you. We could send you a cargo of them from Auteuil; and though we have ever so little time, we shall have enough to load a small vessel with them. In truth, there is nothing so suitable. These cats will but return into their real country: friends of liberty, they are entirely out of place under the governments of Europe. They might also set you some good examples; for, in the first place, according to your charming apologue, they know how to turn against the eagle that carries them off, and, by striking their claws into his belly, to compel him to descend again to the earth to get rid of them. We ought also to do them this justice, that we have never seen among them the least dispute over the wooden platter that is regularly carried to them twice a day. Each takes his share, and eats it in peace in a corner. In short, after being saved from the mouth of the bulldog, as you Americans from that of John Bull, they never endanger themselves by intestine dissensions: they have some good in them.

" Here are some absurdities, my dear and respectable friend ; I indulge myself in them, because you love them, and are yourself very much inclined to say them, and, what is worse, to write them. But, if you are afraid to lose your consideration among your countrymen, by letting them perceive this taste, you will shut yourself up to read me, and will say nothing to Congress about the project that I open to you of sending cats from Europe. Besides, one obstacle is in the way at present : our treaty of commerce with you is no more advanced than at the peace ; and, whilst waiting for the conclusion of this treaty, I know not what duties they would make my cats pay on arriving at Philadelphia ; and then, if my vessel should find nothing to load with among you but grain, it could not touch at our islands to take in sugar, or to bring me back good rum either, which I love much, and which would pay in France some little duty of seventy-five per cent. on the value. All that embarrasses my cat-trade, and I must think of some other speculation.

" I finish my letter at Auteuil. *The lady* is about to write to you, and to answer your little note. The Abbé de la Roche and M. de Cabanis will also write to you."*

Franklin's reply was cordial and humorous. " Your project," he wrote, " of exporting the eighteen cats of *Our Lady of Auteuil,* rather than drown them, is very humane ; but the good treatment which they receive from their present mistress may make them averse to change their situation. However, if they are of the race of Angoras, and if you could apprise them how the two cats of their tribe, brought over by my grandson, are caressed here and almost adored, you might perhaps dispose them to emigrate of their own accord, rather than remain a mark for the hatred of the abbés, who will finish, sooner or later, by obtaining their condemnation. Their petition is perfectly well drawn up ; but if they continue to multiply as they do, they will make their cause so bad, that it will be impossible to defend it any longer ; wherefore their friends would do well to advise them to submit to transportation, or to—castration.

" The pains that you have taken to translate the congratulatory addresses that I received on my arrival, are a fresh proof of the continuance of your friendship towards me, which has given me as

* "Memoirs of the Abbé Morellet."

much satisfaction as the addresses themselves, and you may well believe that is saying not a little; for this welcome of my fellow-citizens has much exceeded my expectations. Popular favor, which is not the most constant thing in the world, is maintained towards me. My election to the Presidency for the second year has been unanimous. Will there be the same inclination for the third? Nothing is more doubtful. A man who occupies a high post is so often in danger of disobliging some one, whilst discharging his duty, that those whom he thus disobliges, having more resentment than those whom he has served have gratitude, it almost always happens that, whilst he is vigorously attacked, he is feebly defended; you will not, therefore, be surprised if you learn that I have not finished my political career with the same eclat as I have begun it."

He concludes with the usual friendly messages to " all the Wednesday diners, to the Stars, and to your family." The Abbé explains, in a note to this letter, that the Stars were the two daughters of Madame Helvetius, so named by Franklin, in allusion to the story of a mother who, on being asked by her little daughter what became of the old moons, replied, that they were broken into five or six pieces to make stars of.

In the spring of 1787, Dr. Franklin introduced to France, as he had formerly introduced to America, Thomas Paine; who now crossed the ocean to dispose of his newly invented bridge. He had made some noise in America; he was not to remain undistinguished in France. The letters which he bore from Franklin gave him immediate and most welcome access to the great party who were about to witness, as they supposed, the fulfillment of their dearest hopes in the coming together of the Assembly of the Notables. How little Franklin foresaw the consequences of that convocation, fraught with ruin to so many of his friends ! " The newspapers tell us," he wrote in one of the letters which Paine carried, " that you are about to have an Assembly of Notables, to consult on improvements of your government. It is somewhat singular that we should be engaged in the same project here at the same time; but so it is, and a convention for the purpose of revising and amending our Federal constitution, is to meet at this place next month. I hope both assemblies will be blessed with success, and that their deliberations and counsels may promote the happiness of both nations."

Our Lady of Auteuil gave Mr. Paine the welcome due to him as the friend of Franklin and of Washington.   "It must have been," wrote Paine to Franklin, "a very strong attachment to America, that drew you from this country, for your friends are very numerous and very affectionate." The Abbé Morellet, too, bestirred himself in behalf of the inventor of the improved bridge, and procured the remission of duties upon the model.   "The custom-house officers," he wrote to Franklin, "had not foreseen, that it might one day happen that a bridge should be constructed in Philadelphia or New York, to be thrown over the Seine at Paris. They are now aware of the fact, and will not forget this article in the new tariff. They must also enter houses on the list, if you acquire the habit of making them for Europeans." The Abbé was one of the stanchest of free-traders.

He concluded this letter with a touching outburst of affection : " I shall never forget the happiness I have enjoyed in knowing you, and seeing you intimately.   I write to you from Auteuil, seated in your arm-chair, on which I have engraved, *Benjamin Franklin hic sedebat*,* and having by my side the little bureau, which you bequeathed to me at parting, with a drawer full of nails to gratify the love of nailing and hammering, which I possess in common with you.   But, believe me, I have no need of all these helps to cherish your endeared *remembrance*, and to love you,

'Dum memor ipse mei, dum spiritus hos reget artus.' "†

CHAPTER II.

FRANKLIN IN THE CONVENTION OF 1787.

THE people of the United States had been, for some time past, resolving themselves into a Committee of the Whole upon the state of the Union.   The country was bewilderingly prosperous, yet the work of the revolution was felt to be incomplete while the government remained unsettled.   The simple expedient of a general Congress which, with the help of France, had carried

---

* Benjamin Franklin used to sit here.
† While memory holds her seat ; while life itself remains.

the country through the war, was deemed inadequate for its government in time of peace and prosperity. That something must be done to effect a more perfect union and a more stable government, most were agreed ; but no two States or men were in·perfect accord as to what. Hence, a universal discussion of the principles of government; hence, a general study of the ancient republics ; hence, essays, pamphlets, clubs, debating societies, fireside conferences, and wayside chats ; all to elucidate the nature and tendency of republican institutions, and the just terms of the proposed federal union. Dr. Franklin himself was president of a Society for Political Inquiries, which met in the large room of his new wing, and listened to weekly "Papers" upon the topics uppermost in the public mind.

The project of a convention to frame a new government, originally suggested by Alexander Hamilton in 1780, ripened slowly, and was only adopted after six years' delay and discussion. Finally, however, a convention was appointed ; delegates were elected ; Philadelphia was named as the place of meeting, and a day fixed for the assembling,—the second Monday in May, 1787. President Franklin, who was not at first elected a member of the Pennsylvania delegation, was added to it, in order that there might be in the Convention one man whom all could concur in calling to the chair, in case General Washington should still decline to attend. The insurrection in Massachusetts overcame the General's scruples, and the Convention therefore had the countenance of the two men whose names had most weight in the country. The aid of both appeared to be essential to its success. The opponents of the Convention were so numerous, and the opposition to the constitution framed by it was so warm and general, that the absence of Washington and Franklin would have probably rendered the scheme abortive. General Washington's awful dignity in the chair, Dr. Franklin's contagious good temper on the floor, and the influence of both out-of-doors, if these had been wanting, I think the Convention would either have made no constitution at all, or made one which the States would have rejected.

The delegates came in slowly, and there was no quorum on the day appointed for the sessions to begin. General Washington, always a punctual man, was among the first to arrive ; and, with his usual punctilious observance of etiquette, his first visit was to the venerable president of Pennsylvania. On one of the days of waiting, Dr. Franklin had the delegates at his house to dinner, when a cask of porter just received from London was broached, and its contents, says Franklin, " met with a most cordial reception and universal approbation." On another evening, a newspaper tells us, " notwithstanding the tempestuous weather, the equally amiable and illustrious General Washington, accompanied by a brilliant crowd of his friends of both sexes, proceeded to the University to hear a Lady deliver a Lecture on the Power of Eloquence. This," adds the editor, " a superficial observer, accustomed to undervalue all female talents, might denominate condescension, so it certainly was ; but the man of judgment and penetration would conclude, that a soul, like Cyrus or Scipio, only could be capable of such attention and patronage."

May 25th, delegates from seven States having arrived, and others being hourly expected, the Convention met in the State-house. Dr. Franklin was to have proposed General Washington as the president of the body. A heavy rain and some admonitory symptoms of his malady prevented his attendance, and the motion was made by another member of the Pennsylvania delegation, Mr. Robert Morris. It was deemed becoming and graceful in Pennsylvania, says Mr. Madison, to pass by her own distinguished citizen as president, and take the lead in giving that pre-eminence to the late Commander-in-chief, which the country felt to be his due. The Convention had an opportunity gracefully to reciprocate ; but it did not improve that opportunity. As soon as General Washington had taken the chair, Alexander Hamilton moved that Major Jackson be appointed Secretary of the Convention. Mr. James Wilson, of Pennsylvania, proposed the name of William Temple Franklin. The Convention, voting by States, elected Major Jackson, five States to two. Other preliminary business being concluded, the Convention adjourned from Friday to Monday.

On Monday morning Dr. Franklin was in his place, and he attended the Convention thenceforward regularly, five hours a day, for more than four months. His friends thought his health improved by the daily exercise of going and returning, though the distance from his house to the State-house was considerably less than half a mile.

The Convention sat with closed doors, bound itself to secrecy, and published no record of its proceedings. The little we now know of the daily debates and transactions is chiefly derived from the papers of Mr. Madison, who has preserved entire several of Dr. Franklin's speeches, because they were written out in full by Franklin himself. The malady under which Dr. Franklin labored made it painful for him to remain standing long at a time. When, therefore, he had any thing of importance to say to the Convention, he was accustomed to write a speech, and hand it to one of his colleagues (usually the learned lawyer, James Wilson), to read for him. Mr. Madison copied the speeches from Franklin's own manuscript, and hence their preservation entire, while all others delivered in the Convention have been lost or abridged. Upon many points of the first importance, however, it is impossible to discover the course of individual members, owing to the fact that on leading questions the vote was taken by States; and only the votes of States were recorded; and doubtless, many an amusing anecdote and happy repartee fell from the lips of Dr. Franklin during the sessions, which a reporter less intent on the main business of the occasion than James Madison would have contrived to interpolate among the more grave and matter-of-fact details.

Such bodies as this Convention naturally divide into two parties, one favoring a powerful and imposing government, the other a government of very limited powers and resources. All his life, Dr. Franklin had been called to contemplate the abuses of arbitrary power. For many years he had battled in Pennsylvania with the stupid tyranny and meanness of the Penns. Then, for many years more, he had been painfully conversant with the working of the English government under George III. Finally, he had resided near the court of Versailles, where he had had an opportunity of observing the ill results of arbitrary government, even when the monarch is benevolent and patriotic. We find Dr. Franklin, therefore, opposing every measure that tended to endow the new government with powers likely to be abused, and favoring the class of measures that tend to keep governments in due subordination and subjection to the people. In common with the vast majority of his fellow-citizens, he *abhorred* the institution of monarchy; and most solicitous was he to guard against the possibility of a future lapse into that barbarism.

A leader of the opposite party in the convention was that spirited young Englishman, Alexander Hamilton, whose birth and early education in the West Indies had given him that *distant* view of .

the British Constitution which made it appear so enchanting in his
eyes. That constitution he loved, as Charles Lamb loved his
friends, "faults and all." Young Hamilton* leading the reactionists,
and old Franklin the democrats, was a curious reversal of the usual
distribution of *roles*. Hamilton, however, during his short public
life had had his attention continually called, and in the most forcible
manner, to the difficulties which arise from a lack of power in the
central authority. The aged democrat and the young conservative
were on excellent terms personally, for Hamilton with all his foibles
was a gentleman; and knowing what was due to age and long
service, forbore to assail the opinions of Dr. Franklin as he did the
similar ones of Mr. Jefferson a year or two later, when he and Jefferson were daily "pitted against each other like two fighting cocks"
in the cabinet of President Washington.

The history of the Convention has been elaborately written.† I
need, therefore, only glean from the scenes in which Dr. Franklin
prominently figured, the characteristic things said and done by him.

The first topic upon which he formally addressed the Convention
was the compensation to be settled upon the head of the nation.
He thought the chief magistrate should have *no* pecuniary compensation, and he supported his opinion in a remarkable speech. The
casual reader, accustomed to see governments occupying themselves
in a thousand illegitimate ways, and the chief executive officer surrounded with preposterous grandeur, may smile at Dr. Franklin's
scheme of disinterested service, as Utopian. But *he* had in view
a government unimposing, inexpensive; a simple contrivance for
executing the will of the people respecting a very few objects of
general concern—such a government, in short, as that which he
himself administered with so much ease and dignity in Pennsylvania.
We must take his ideas on this subject as a part of *his* scheme of
government, not of ours.

"Sir," said he, "there are two passions which have a powerful
influence in the affairs of men. These are *ambition* and *avarice;*
the love of power and the love of money. Separately, each of these
has great force in prompting men to action; but, when united in
view of the same object, they have in many minds the most violent

---

* Aged 30 years.

† "History of the Origin, Formation, and Adoption of the Constitution of the United States. By
George Ticknor Curtis." 2 vols. 8vo.

effects.   Place before the eyes of such men a post of *honor*, that shall at the same time be a place of *profit*, and they will move heaven and earth to obtain it.   The vast number of such places it is, that renders the British government so tempestuous.   The struggles for them are the true source of all those factions which are perpetually dividing the nation, distracting its councils, hurrying it sometimes into fruitless and mischievous wars, and often compelling a submission to dishonorable terms of peace.

"And of what kind are the men that will strive for this profitable pre-eminence, through all the bustle of cabal, the heat of contention, the infinite mutual abuse of parties, tearing to pieces the best of characters?   It will not be the wise and moderate, the lovers of peace and good order, the men fittest for the trust.   It will be the bold and the violent, the men of strong passions and indefatigable activity in their selfish pursuits.   These will thrust themselves into your government, and be your rulers.   And these, too, will be mistaken in the expected happiness of their situation; for their vanquished competitors, of the same spirit, and from the same motives, will perpetually be endeavoring to distress their administration, thwart their measures, and render them odious to the people.

" Besides these evils, sir, though we may set out in the beginning with moderate salaries, we shall find, that such will not be of long continuance.   Reasons will never be wanting for proposed augmentations; and there will always be a party for giving more to the rulers, that the rulers may be able in return to give more to them. Hence, as all history informs us, there has been in every state and kingdom a constant kind of warfare between the governing and the governed ; the one striving to obtain more for its support, and the other to pay less.   And this has alone occasioned great convulsions, actual civil wars, ending either in dethroning of the princes or enslaving of the people.   Generally, indeed, the ruling power carries its point, and we see the revenues of princes constantly increasing, and we see that they are never satisfied, but always in want of more.   The more the people are discontented with the oppression of taxes, the greater need the prince has of money to distribute among his partisans, and pay the troops that are to suppress all resistance, and enable him to plunder at pleasure.   There is scarce a king in a hundred, who would not, if he could, follow the example of Pharaoh,—get first all the people's money, then all their lands, and then make them and their children servants forever. It will be said, that we do not propose to establish kings. I know it. But there is a natural inclination in mankind to kingly government. It sometimes relieves them from aristocratic domination. They had rather have one tyrant than five hundred. It gives more of the appearance of equality among citizens; and that they like. I am apprehensive, therefore,—perhaps too apprehensive,— that the government of these States may in future times end in a monarchy. But this catastrophe, I think, may be long delayed, if in our proposed system we do not sow the seeds of contention, faction, and tumult, by making our posts of honor places of profit. If we do, I fear, that, though we employ at first a number and not a single person, the number will in time be set aside; it will only nourish the foetus of a king (as the honorable gentleman from Virginia very aptly expressed it), and a king will the sooner be set over us.

"It may be imagined by some, that this is an Utopian idea, and that we can never find men to serve us in the executive department, without paying them well for their services. I conceive this to be a mistake. Some existing facts present themselves to me, which incline me to a contrary opinion. The high sheriff of a county in England is an honorable office, but it is not a profitable one. It is rather expensive, and therefore not sought for. But yet it is executed, and well executed, and usually by some of the principal gentlemen of the county. In France, the office of counselor, or member of their judiciary parliaments, is more honorable. It is therefore purchased at a high price; there are indeed fees on the law proceedings, which are divided among them, but these fees do not amount to more than three per cent. on the sum paid for the place. Therefore, as legal interest is there at five per cent., they in fact pay two per cent. for being allowed to do the judiciary business of the nation, which is at the same time entirely exempt from the burden of paying them any salaries for their services. I do not, however, mean to recommend this as an eligible mode for our judiciary department. I only bring the instance to show, that the pleasure of doing good and serving their country, and the respect such conduct entitles them to, are sufficient motives with some minds, to give up a great portion of their time to the public, without the mean inducement of pecuniary satisfaction.

" Another instance is that of a respectable society, who have made the experiment, and practiced it with success, now more than a hundred years. I mean the Quakers. It is an established rule with them that they are not to go to law, but in their controversies they must apply to their monthly, quarterly, and yearly meetings. Committees of these sit with patience to hear the parties, and spend much time in composing their differences. In doing this, they are supported by a sense of duty, and the respect paid to usefulness. It is honorable to be so employed, but it was never made profitable by salaries, fees, or perquisites. And indeed, in all cases of public service, the less the profit the greater the honor.

" To bring the matter nearer home, have we not seen the greatest and most important of our offices, that of general of our armies, executed for eight years together, without the smallest salary, by a patriot whom I will not now offend by any other praise; and this, through fatigues and distresses, in common with the other brave men, his military friends and companions, and the constant anxieties peculiar to his station ? And shall we doubt finding three or four men in all the United States, with public spirit enough to bear sitting in peaceful council, for perhaps an equal term, merely to preside over our civil concerns, and see that our laws are duly executed ? Sir, I have a better opinion of our country. I think we shall never be without a sufficient number of wise and good men to undertake, and execute well and faithfully, the office in question.

" Sir, the saving of the salaries, that may at first be proposed, is not an object with me. The subsequent mischiefs of proposing them are what I apprehend; and therefore it is that I move the amendment. If it is not seconded or accepted, I must be contented with the satisfaction of having delivered my opinion frankly, and done my duty."

It is mentioned as an instance of Mr. Hamilton's complaisance to a venerable patriot, that he seconded Dr. Franklin's motion, although there was no man in the house more opposed than himself to the substantial meaning of the speech. Dr. Franklin's plan was *in effect* adopted; for the salaries affixed to the offices of president, vice-president, foreign embassador, and cabinet minister, were not equal to the expenditures of those who have usually held them. President Washington spent more than his salary, and Hamilton was compelled to retire from the cabinet in order to support an increasing family. The inconveniences which have arisen from the low, salary system appear to be owing to the fact, that one part of the Franklinean scheme was adopted without the rest. Franklin fixed the salaries, and Hamilton arranged the scale of expenditure. Hamilton, too, it was who afterwards bought a few southern votes by agreeing to build the capital of the republic in the woods on the Potomac, when there was clean, cheap, and comfortable Philadelphia ready made to his hand. Economical government was, is, and long will be impossible in the city of Washington. As well expect to raise cheap pine-apples in a hot-house.*

The first two months of the convention were chiefly spent in debating the terms upon which States so small as Delaware and Rhode Island could safely and justly enter a confederacy with such powerful sovereignties as Pennsylvania and Virginia. The small States were unwilling to be overshadowed, and feared to be oppressed by the large. The large States could not consent to forego the weight and influence due to their superior wealth and population. The small States demanded an equal representation in the national legislature; a claim which the large States could not but regard as fatally unreasonable and unjust even to absurdity. Dr. Franklin, who had traversed the ground of this debate in the Pennsylvania Convention of 1776, was the man of all others most opposed to the demand of the smaller States, because he both felt its injustice and believed that an unjust compact contains the seeds of its own dissolution. No such confederation, he thought, could be consented to by the people of New York, Pennsylvania, and Virginia; nor, if formed, could it endure.

* The following appeared in the New York Historical Magazine for September, 1862:

"In looking over the early history of the United States, it is surprising to see with what reluctance persons accepted and held offices of the highest consideration. Take, for instance, the U. S. Senate, in the first thirty years from the adoption of the Federal Constitution, there were no less than 110 resignations; the Senators generally holding the position only a couple of years. (There were 17 deaths in the same period.) The longest term held by any one, was that of Mr. Benton, from October 2, 1820, to March 3, 1851, the shortest that of Pierre Soulé, from Feb. 3, 1847, to March 3, 1847, 28 days; David J. Baker, of Illinois, was appointed by the governor, Nov. 12th, 1830, but was superseded by the Legislature, Dec. 11, 1830, Mr. B. nominally enjoying the honor 29 days; though in that period of slow traveling in the West, it was said in the newspapers that he actually sat but one day in the Senate before his successor was elected. W. R. King held the office from Oct. 28, 1819, to April 22, 1844; and John Gaillard, from Dec. 6, 1804, to February 26, 1826.   *   *   *   *

"One can see by Washington's letters, how much difficulty he had in organizing the Supreme Court of the United States, absolutely begging distinguished men to accept the judgeships; Cushing declined the office of Chief-justice, and both Jay and Ellsworth resigned that distinguished position after a short enjoyment of its honors. Of the associate-justices, ten resigned the office, or declined the appointment, during the first thirty years of our Government."

The debates were long and earnest; they became at length, hot and acrimonious. The wise men of the Convention began to fear that it would dissolve, without accomplishing its purpose. Dr. Franklin now proposed a measure which, he hoped, would have the effect of allaying the excitement, and restoring the Convention to that calm temper which was needful for the proper discussion of subjects so important. June 28th, he moved,

" That, henceforth prayers, imploring the assistance of Heaven and its blessing on our deliberations, be held in this Assembly every morning before we proceed to business; and that one or more of the clergy of this city be requested to officiate in that service."

His short speech in support of this motion belongs to his biography, familiar as it is to many readers :

" Mr. President : The small progress we have made, after four or five weeks' close attendance and continual reasonings with each other, our different sentiments on almost every question, several of the last producing as many *Noes* as *Ayes*, is, methinks, a melancholy proof of the imperfection of the human understanding. We, indeed, seem to *feel* our own want of political wisdom, since we have been running all about in search of it. We have gone back to ancient history for models of government, and examined the different forms of those republics which, having been originally formed with the seeds of their own dissolution, now no longer exist ; and we have viewed modern states all round Europe, but find none of their constitutions suitable to our circumstances.

" In this situation of this Assembly, groping, as it were, in the dark, to find political truth, and scarce able to distinguish it when presented to us, how has it happened, sir, that we have not hitherto once thought of humbly applying to the Father of Lights to illuminate our understandings ? In the beginning of the contest with Britain, when we were sensible of danger, we had daily prayers in this room for the Divine protection ! Our prayers, sir, were heard ; and they were graciously answered. All of us who were engaged in the struggle, must have observed frequent instances of a superintending Providence in our favor. To that kind Providence we owe this happy opportunity of consulting in peace, on the means of establishing our future national felicity. And have we now forgotten that powerful friend ? or do we imagine we no longer need its assistance ? I have lived, sir, a long time ; and the longer I live, the more convincing proofs I see of this truth : *That* GOD *governs in the affairs of men!* And if a sparrow cannot fall to the ground without his notice, is it probable that an empire can rise without his aid ? We have been assured, sir, in the Sacred Writings, that ' except the Lord build the house, they labor in vain that build it.' I firmly believe this; and I also believe, that without his concurring aid, we shall succeed in this political building no better than the building of Babel; we shall be divided by our little partial local interests, our projects will be confounded, and we ourselves shall become a reproach and a by-word down to future ages. And, what is worse, mankind may, hereafter, from this unfortunate instance, despair of establishing government by human wisdom, and leave it to chance, war, and conquest."

Strange to relate, the motion met with immediate and invincible opposition. Mr. Hamilton, and " several others,"* expressed apprehensions that prayers begun at that late day, would expose the Convention to " some disagreeable animadversions." It might have been well, added Hamilton, to have had prayers at first, but if the practice were then commenced, people out-of-doors would be greatly alarmed, as they would naturally conclude the Convention to be in some dire extremity of disagreement. Dr. Franklin replied, that past delinquency could not excuse present and continued neglect ; and, as to the alarm out-of-doors, that might do as much good as harm. Another gentleman bluntly said, that the true cause of the opposition could not be mistaken : the Convention had no money to pay the clergyman. Edmund Randolph proposed that a clergyman be invited to preach a sermon to the Convention on the approaching fourth of July, and that, thenceforth, prayers be said every morning at the opening of the session. Dr. Franklin seconded this motion. But, says Mr. Madison, " after several unsuccessful attempts for silently postponing this matter by adjourning, the adjournment was at length carried without any vote on the motion." We cannot help wishing that Mr. Madison had vouchsafed a little light on the true cause of the opposition to prayers. Dr. Franklin appended this note to his speech : " The Convention, except three or four persons, thought prayers unnecessary."

I think it not improbable, that the cause of this opposition to a proposal so seldom negatived in the United States, was the preva-

* " Madison Papers," p. 986.

lence in the Convention of the French tone of feeling with regard to religious observances. If so, it was the more remarkable to see the aged Franklin, who was a Deist at fifteen, and had just returned from France, coming back to the sentiments of his ancestors.

The debates on the vexed topic continued. They grew even more excited and bitter than before. Mr. Dickenson, always an unmanageable man, who now represented the State of Delaware, went so far as to say, that rather than be deprived of an equality of representation in the legislature of the nation, he would prefer to become the subject of a foreign power. Another member said, and truly, " We are now come to a full stop."

In this extremity, Dr. Franklin suggested a compromise. " The diversity of opinion," said he, in his homely, familiar manner, " turns on two points. If a proportional representation takes place, the small States contend that their liberties will be in danger. If an equality of votes is to be put into its place, the large States say, their money will be in danger. When a broad table is to be made, and the edges of the planks do not fit, the artist takes a little from both, and makes a good joint." He proceeded to propose : 1, that all the States should send an equal number of delegates ; 2, that on all questions affecting the authority or sovereignty of a State, every State should have an equal vote ; 3, that in acting upon appointments and confirmations, every State should have an equal vote ; but, 4, on all bills to raise or expend money, every State should have a vote proportioned to its population.

This ingenious plan was amply debated. The small States, however, led by Mr. Dickenson, still contended, and with a vehemence worthy of a wrong cause, for an equality absolute and entire. Virginia and Pennsylvania were equally resolute against their preposterous demand, and the Convention seemed again on the point of breaking up. A committee was at length appointed to consider the subject apart from the excitements of the main body, and to report a compromise. As a member of that committee, Dr. Franklin proposed the simple, the admirable expedient, which was adopted, and which has ever since satisfied the largest and the smallest States. He proposed, that in the Senate, every State should have an equal representation ; but in the other House, every State should have a representation proportioned to its population ; and in that House all bills to raise or to expend money should originate. This suggestion, it is said by men conversant with the state of feeling in the Convention, saved the Constitution ; and to it we owe the wonderful fact, that no ill feeling has ever existed in a State growing out of its superiority or inferiority in population and importance. Rhode Island and Delaware, New York and Pennsylvania, were thus made equal members of the same confederacy, without peril to the smaller, and without injustice to the larger. Of political expedients this was, perhaps, the happiest ever devised. Its success in gaining the objects aimed at has been simply perfect—so perfect that scarcely any one has remarked it. We have all been as unconscious of the working of this system as a healthy man is of the process of digestion.

It was not adopted, however, until the heated disputants had exhausted every artifice of debate and intimidation, and had discovered that the representatives of the great States would abandon the attempt to form a constitution rather than yield. It needed all the benign and fertile genius of Franklin, and all the commanding influence of Washington, to save the republic from making early shipwreck upon this great rock of difficulty.

The proposed article fixing the presidential term at seven years, and declaring a president ineligible for a second term, was supported by Franklin. " It seems to have been imagined," said he, " that returning to the mass of the people was degrading to the magistrate." This, he thought, was contrary to republican principles. In free governments, the rulers are the servants, and the people their superiors and sovereigns. For the former, therefore, to return among the latter was not to degrade but to promote them. And it would be imposing an unreasonable burden on them to keep them always in a state of servitude, and not allow them to become again one of the masters.

He opposed most earnestly the proposal to limit the suffrage to freeholders. " It is of great consequence," said he, in the debate on this vital topic, " that we should not depress the virtue and public spirit of our common people, of which they displayed a great deal during the war, and which contributed principally to the favorable issue of it." He related the honorable refusal of the American seamen, who were carried in great numbers into the British prisons during the war, to redeem themselves from misery, or to seek their fortunes, by entering on board the ships of the enemies to their country, contrasting their patriotism with a contemporary instance, in which the British seamen made prisoners by the Americans readily entered the ships of the latter on being promised a share of the prizes that might be made out of their own country. This proceeded from the different manner in which the common people were treated in America and Great Britain. He did not think that the elected had any right, in any case, to narrow the privileges of the electors. He quoted, as arbitrary, the British statute setting forth the danger of tumultuous meetings, and, under that pretext, narrowing the right of suffrage to persons having freeholds of a certain value; observing that this statute was soon followed by another, under the succeeding parliament, subjecting the people who had no votes to peculiar labors and hardships. He was persuaded, also, that such a restriction as was proposed would give great uneasiness in the populous States. The sons of a substantial farmer, not being themselves freeholders, would not be pleased at being disfranchised, and there were a great many persons of that description."*

Again, some days after, " Dr. Franklin expressed his dislike to every thing that tended to debase the spirit of the common people. If honesty was often the companion of wealth, and if poverty was exposed to peculiar temptation, it was not less true that the possession of property increased the desire of more property. Some of the greatest rogues he was ever acquainted with were the richest rogues. We should remember the character which the Scripture requires in rulers, that they should be men hating covetousness. This Constitution will be much read and attended to in Europe; and if it should betray a great partiality to the rich, will not only hurt us in the esteem of the most liberal and enlightened men there, but discourage the common people from removing to this country."†

The clause giving Congress the power to impeach the President was much opposed by the strong government party. Franklin favored it; arguing that where the head of the government cannot be lawfully called to account for his conduct, the people have no resource against oppression but revolution and assassination. He strongly opposed investing the President with an absolute veto, citing the conduct of the Penn governors of Pennsylvania, whose

* Madison Papers, p. 1254.   † Madison Papers, p. 1284.

assent to the most unobjectionable bills had to be bought. He opposed the requirement of a fourteen years' residence before admitting foreigners to citizenship. He thought four years sufficient. The article upon treason, defining it to be an " overt act," and requiring the evidence of two witnesses to the overt act, had his emphatic approval. He took a leading and laborious part in the long debates upon the powers of the two houses of Congress ; and his ideas on this difficult subject were substantially embodied in the Constitution.

Precisely what part he took in arranging the fatal " compromises of the constitution" does not appear in the outline report from which we derive nearly all our knowledge of what transpired in the Convention. We know, however, that in common with the civilized portion of his countrymen, North and South, his abhorrence of slavery had been deepened and intensified by the revolution. In his old age, he added to his other titles of honor the only name known to political parties in the United States which confers on him who bears it nothing *but* honor—that of ABOLITIONIST. Whig, tory, democrat, republican—all these are associated with self-seeking and ignoble subserviency. It is the abolitionist alone who has always sought noble ends by worthy means. Benjamin Franklin was an abolitionist ; but he felt it to be his duty to assent to the compromises of the Constitution, rather than see the Confederation broken up, and the malign predictions of European ill-wishers so speedily fulfilled. And thus the inevitable collision was postponed to the year 1861.

We have a pleasing view of the aged Franklin at home, during the sittings of the Convention, surrounded by his books, his apparatus, and his friends. A noted clergyman and botanist of Massachusetts, Dr. Manasseh Cutler (afterward a member of Congress), visited Philadelphia in July, 1787, and called upon the President of Pennsylvania at his house in Market Street. To Dr. Jared Sparks we owe the publication of the delightful pages of Dr. Cutler's diary which describe the visit.

" Dr. Franklin's house," wrote the clerical botanist, " stands up a court, at some distance from the street. We found him in his garden, sitting upon a grass-plot, under a very large mulberry tree, with several other gentlemen and two or three ladies. When Mr. Gerry introduced me, he rose from his chair, took me by the hand,

expressed his joy at seeing me, welcomed me to the city, and begged me to seat myself close to him. His voice was low, but his
countenance open, frank, and pleasing. I delivered to him my letters. After he had read them, he took me again by the hand, and,
with the usual compliments, introduced me to the other gentlemen,
who are most of them members of the Convention.

"Here we entered into a free conversation, and spent our time
most agreeably, until it was quite dark. The tea table was spread
under the tree, and Mrs. Bache, who is the only daughter of the
Doctor, and lives with him, served it out to the company. She
had three of her children about her. They seemed to be excessively fond of their grandpapa. The Doctor showed me a curiosity
he had just received, and with which he was much pleased. It
was a snake with two heads, preserved in a large phial. It was
taken near the confluence of the Schuylkill with the Delaware,
about four miles from this city. It was about ten inches long, well
proportioned, the heads perfect, and united to the body about one-
fourth of an inch below the extremities of the jaws. The snake
was of a dark brown, approaching to black, and the back beautifully speckled with white. The belly was rather checkered with
a reddish color and white. The Doctor supposed it to be full
grown, which I think is probable; and he thinks it must be a *sui
generis* of that class of animals. He grounds his opinion of its
not being an extraordinary production, but a distinct genus, on the
perfect form of the snake, the probability of its being of some
age, and there having been found a snake entirely similar (of which
the Doctor has a drawing, which he has showed us) near Lake
Champlain, in the time of the late war. He mentioned the situation of this snake, if it was traveling among bushes, and one head
should choose to go on one side of the stem of a bush, and the
other head should prefer the other side, and neither of the heads
would consent to come back, or give way to the other. He was
then going to mention a humorous matter, that had that day occurred in the Convention, in consequence of his comparing the
snake to America; for he seemed to forget that every thing in the
Convention was to be kept a profound secret. But this secrecy of
Convention matters was suggested to him, which stopped him, and
deprived me of the story he was going to tell.

"After it was dark we went into the house, and he invited me into his library, which is likewise his study. It is a very large chamber, and high-studded. The walls are covered with book-shelves, filled with books ; besides there are four large alcoves, extending two-thirds the length of the chamber, filled in the same manner. I presume this is the largest and by far the best private library in America. He showed us a glass machine for exhibiting the circulation of the blood in the arteries and veins of the human body. The circulation is exhibited by the passing of a red fluid from a reservoir into numerous capillary tubes of glass, ramified in every direction, and then returning in similar tubes to the reservoir, which was done with great velocity, without any power to act visibly upon the fluid, and had the appearance of perpetual motion. Another great curiosity was a rolling press, for taking the copies of letters or any other writing. A sheet of paper is completely copied in less than two minutes ; the copy as fair as the original, and without defacing it in the smallest degree. It is an invention of his own, extremely useful in many situations of life. He also showed us his long, artificial *arm and hand*, for taking down and putting up books on high shelves, which are out of reach ; and his great arm-chair, with rockers, and a large fan placed over it, with which he fans himself, keeps off the flies, &c., while he sits reading, with only a small motion of the foot; and many other curiosities and inventions, all his own, but of lesser note. Over his mantel he has a prodigious number of medals, busts, and casts in wax, or plaster of Paris, which are the effigies of the most noted characters in Europe.

" But what the Doctor wished principally to show me was a huge volume on botany, which indeed afforded me the greatest pleasure of any one thing in his library. It was a single volume, but so large, that it was with great difficulty that he was able to raise it from a low shelf, and lift it on the table. But, with that senile ambition, which is common to old people, he insisted on doing it himself, and would permit no person to assist him, merely to show us how much strength he had remaining. It contained the whole of Linnæus's *Systema Vegetabilium*, with large cuts of every plant, colored from nature. It was a feast to me, and the Doctor seemed to enjoy it as well as myself. We spent a couple of hours in examining this volume, while the other gentlemen amused themselves with other matters. The Doctor is not a botanist, but lamented he did not in early life attend to this science. He delights in Natural History, and expressed an earnest wish, that I should pursue the plan that I had begun, and hoped this science, so much neglected in America, would be pursued with as much ardor here as it is now in every part of Europe. I wanted, for three months at least, to have devoted myself entirely to this one volume; but, fearing lest I should be tedious to him, I shut up the volume, though he urged me to examine it longer.

"He seemed extremely fond, through the course of the visit, of dwelling on philosophical subjects, and particularly that of Natural History; while the other gentlemen were swallowed up with politics. This was a favorable circumstance for me; for almost the whole of his conversation was addressed to me, and I was highly delighted with the extensive knowledge he appeared to have of every subject, the brightness of his memory, and clearness and vivacity of all his mental faculties, notwithstanding his age. His manners are perfectly easy, and every thing about him seems to diffuse an unrestrained freedom and happiness. He has an incessant vein of humor, accompanied with an uncommon vivacity, which seems as natural and involuntary as his breathing. He urged me to call on him again, but my short stay would not admit. We took our leave at ten, and I retired to my lodgings."[*]

A beautiful picture of a noble old man! It reminds us of some of the glimpses we catch, in contemporary letters, of the aged Goethe, a man who had much in common with Franklin.

The labors of the Convention drew toward a conclusion early in September. When the Constitution had been completed, Dr. Franklin, in a speech of much humor and good feeling, urged the members who were dissatisfied with it, to sacrifice their opinions to the general good, and send the Constitution forth stamped with the seal of unanimity. The speech had its effect, and all the members signed. Mr. Madison records, that while "the last members were signing, Dr. Franklin, looking toward the president's chair, at the back of which a rising sun happened to be painted, observed to a few members near him, that painters had found it difficult to distinguish in their art, a rising, from a setting sun. 'I have,' said he, 'often and often, in the course of the session, and the vicissitudes of my hopes and fears as to its issue, looked at that behind

* "Life and Works of Franklin," by Jared Sparks, i., 519

the president, without being able to tell whether it was rising or
setting : but now, at length, I have the happiness to know, that it
is a rising and not a setting sun.' "*

The Convention adjourned on the 17th of September. Perhaps,
I may mention, as a striking illustration of the *uneven front* with
which civilization marches, that while these wise men were settling the details of the most liberal and advanced government ever
devised by mortals, a poor harmless old woman was thrice assaulted in the streets of Philadelphia, because she was accused of being
a witch.† So, in 1862, when all the nobler forces of the nation
were arrayed against the slave power, a few unhappy men were
found petitioning the legislature of a Northern State to re-establish
slavery, and many more poor creatures took delight in all the thousand modes of " spelling negro with two g's." Nay, a person calling
himself Bishop of a Christian church essayed to prove American
slavery an institution ordained of God; and another person, supposed to be a man of science, declared it to be as holy, wise, and
necessary as matrimony, or the relation between parent and child.
Such men, if they had lived in 1787, would have headed the mob
that stoned this poor woman, and justified their act from the Old
Testament.

After the adjournment of the Convention, Dr. Franklin exerted
all his influence to promote the adoption of the Constitution by
the States. When ten States had signified their acceptance, the
event was celebrated in Philadelphia with great splendor and enthusiasm. There was a grand procession of the trades, a banquet,
and an oration by James Wilson, in the open air, to twenty thousand people. The printers were represented in the procession by
a car, upon which a printing-press was placed ; and, as it moved

---

* " Madison Papers," p. 1624.

† The following is the newspaper account of one of these scenes: " We are sorry to hear that the
poor woman who suffered so much, some time ago, under the imputation of being *a witch*, has
again been attacked by an ignorant and inhuman mob. On Tuesday last she was carted through
several of the streets, and was hooted and pelted as she passed along. A gentleman who interfered in her favor was greatly insulted, while those who recited the innumerable instances of her
art, were listened to with curiosity and attention. The repetition of this outrage calls for the
serious interposition of the officers of government, not merely for the sake of the wretched
object herself (though surely she has a peculiar claim to the protection of the laws), but for the
sake of the illiterate and youthful part of society, who will naturally imagine that the charge of
sorcery must be just, when such persecution is publicly practiced with impunity. It is with
pleasure we add, that several respectable citizens, who were present, have determined to bear
testimony against these violators of tranquillity and common sense, and that a gentleman of the
law has voluntarily undertaken the prosecution."—*Independent Journal, July* 18, 1787.

along, a song, in honor of the trades, was struck off, and scattered
among the people. The author of this homely ditty was no other
than the President of Pennsylvania. It contained such stanzas as
these:

> " Ye TAILORS ! of ancient and noble renown,
> Who clothe all the people in country and town,
> Remember that Adam, your father and head,
> Though lord of the world, was a tailor by trade.

> " Ye SHOEMAKERS ! noble from ages long past,
> Have defended your rights with your *awl* to the *last ;*
> And cobblers so merry, not only stop holes,
> But work night and day for the good of our *soles.*

> " Ye HATTERS ! who oft with hands not very fair,
> Fix hats on a block for a blockhead to wear,
> Though charity covers a sin now and then,
> You cover the heads and the sins of all men.

> " And CARDERS, and SPINNERS, and WEAVERS attend,
> And take the advice of Poor Richard, your friend,
> Stick close to your looms, your wheels, and your card,
> And you never need fear of the times being hard.

> " Ye COOPERS ! who rattle with drivers and adz,
> A lecture each day upon hoops and on heads,
> The famous old ballad of Love in a Tub,
> You may sing to the tune of your rub-a-dub-dub.

> " Each tradesman turn out with his tools in his hand,
> To cherish the arts and keep peace in the land ;
> Each 'prentice and journeyman join in my song,
> And let the brisk chorus go bounding along."

The late Major Noah, who began his literary life as a writer of
patriotic dramas, used to say, that his mind received its bent in
that direction from his frequent gazing at the sign of a tavern in
Philadelphia, called " The Federal Convention." " It was an excellent piece of painting of its kind." he once wrote. " representing

a group of venerable personages, engaged in public discussion, with the following distich:

"'These thirty-eight great men have signed a powerful deed,
That better times to us shall very soon succeed.'

"The sign," he adds, "must have been painted very soon after the adoption of the Federal Constitution, and I remember to have stood, 'many a time and oft,' gazing when a boy, at the assembled patriots, particularly the venerable head and spectacles of Dr. Franklin, always in conspicuous relief."*

CHAPTER III.

SETTING HIS HOUSE IN ORDER.

THE second year of Dr. Franklin's presidency of Pennsylvania expired in the autumn of 1787. He had hoped to be allowed to retire. It was his wish to revisit once more, before he died, his native city, to embrace his aged sister, and converse with the few surviving friends of other days. He desired, also, to spend the last years of his life at the farm of his grandson, away from the ceaseless interruptions of Philadelphia, and there work at his leisure upon the Autobiography, which his friends were so anxious he should complete. But, it appears, his grandson did not find an agricultural life so pleasant as he had hoped. He hankered after the society of Paris, and sought every opportunity to relieve the tedium of his existence by visiting Philadelphia. Probably he did not urge his grandfather to carry out his scheme of retirement to the country. At the expiration of the second term, Dr. Franklin was unanimously re-elected, and he consented to forego his anticipations of literary leisure. "I must own," he wrote to Mrs. Mecom, "that it is no small pleasure to me, and I suppose it will give my sister pleasure, that, after such a long trial of me, I should be elected a third time by my fellow-citizens, without a dissenting vote but my own, to fill the most honorable post in their power to

* "Cyclopedia of American Literature," ii., 74.

bestow. This universal and unbounded confidence of a whole people, flatters my vanity much more than a peerage could do.

" ' Hung o'er with ribbons, and stuck round with strings.' "

There is a fine thought in one of his letters of this year with regard to his advanced age. " I am grown so old," he wrote, " as to have buried most of the friends of my youth, and I now often hear persons whom I knew when children, called *old* Mr. such-a-one, to distinguish them from their sons now men grown and in business ; so that, by living twelve years beyond David's period, *I seem to have intruded myself into the company of posterity,* when I ought to have been abed and asleep."

He was still fond of life. He told one of his friends that when he dwelt upon the rapid progress mankind was making in philosophy, politics, morals, and the arts of living, and when he considered that, as one improvement begets another, the future progress of the race was likely to be more rapid than it ever had been, he almost wished it had been his destiny to be born two or three centuries later. He sometimes amused his friends with humorous predictions of inventions yet to be, and expressed a wish to revisit the earth at the end of a century to see how man was getting on. Would that he could ! How pleasant to show the Shade of Franklin about the modern world ! What would he say of the Great Eastern, the Erie Canal, the locomotive, the telegraph, the Hoe printing-press, the steam type-setter, chloroform, the sewing machine, the Continental Hotel, the Fairmount Water-Works, the improved strawberry, an omnibus, gas-light, the Sanitary Commission, Chicago, Buckle's History, Mills's Political Economy, Herbert Spencer's " First Principles," Adam Bede, David Copperfield, the Newcomes, the Philadelphia High School, Henry Ward Beecher's church, the Heart of the Andes ? Surely, he would admit that we have done pretty well in the seventy-five years that have passed since he left us. Perhaps he knows more of these things than we suppose. If his youthful theory of the minor gods is true, he may be serving now as the secondary Providence of that portion of North America which lies between Mason and Dixon's Line and British America—where, certainly, the Spirit of Franklin is universally manifest. Over the territory south of that Line, the busy, verbose, malign, and distrustful Soul of

Arthur Lee appears to have borne sway.   Hence the rebellion of 1861 !

If Franklin was fond of life, *this* life, he had only pleasing expectations of the life to come, and he founded his hope of future happiness on the justice of God. He felt that at the hands of a just and good Father he deserved little but happiness. " You tell me," he wrote in 1788, " that our poor friend Ben Kent is gone ; I hope to the regions of the blessed ; or at least to some place where souls are prepared for those regions. I found my hope on this, that, though not so orthodox as you and I, he was an honest man, and had his virtues. If he had any hypocrisy, it was of that inverted kind, with which a man is not so bad as he seems to be. And, with regard to future bliss, I cannot help imagining, that multitudes of the zealously orthodox of different sects, who at the last day may flock together in hopes of seeing each other damned, will be disappointed, and obliged to rest content with their own salvation."

He had, indeed, a peculiar tenderness for honest men who had been so unfortunate as to incur obloquy for opinion's sake, and particularly for those who had been unable to conform to established creeds and prevalent religious usages, a class of men to whom mankind are deeply indebted. In writing to one of his English friends, about this time, he desired to be remembered affectionately to " good Dr. Price, and to the honest heretic, Dr. Priestley." He added : " I do not call him *honest* by way of distinction ; for I think all the heretics I have known have been virtuous men. They have the virtue of fortitude, or they would not venture to own their heresy ; and they cannot afford to be deficient in any of the other virtues, as that would give advantage to their many enemies ; and they have not, like orthodox sinners, such a number of friends to excuse or justify them. Do not, however, mistake me. It is not to my good friend's heresy that I impute his honesty. On the contrary, it is his honesty that has brought upon him the character of heretic."

In December, 1787, his aged frame was severely shaken by a fall down the stone steps that led to his garden. He was much bruised, his right wrist was sprained, and the shock brought on a bad fit of the stone. He rallied, however, in the following spring, and pursued his usual avocations. The topic of the new year was the election of a President of the United States. " General Washington," he wrote, "is the man that all our eyes are fixed on for President, and what little influence I may have, is devoted to him." The accident in his garden, perhaps, led him to think that it was time to put his house in order against his final departure. He inquired out all his relations, endeavored to collect his debts, many of which were of fifty years' standing, tried to get his accounts with the United States settled, catalogued his books, and put his affairs, important and unimportant, in perfect order, so far as he could control them. He made his will with the most thoughtful consideration for all who had claims upon his remembrance. His will, indeed, is one of the most carefully drawn productions of the kind which have been published.

His estate, in 1788, was worth, at a liberal estimate, one hundred and fifty thousand dollars, of which about two-thirds was productive. Besides his residence in Market Street, with its valuable accumulations of books, apparatus, furniture, and plate, he possessed in the same street two new and large houses, two others of less value, and the printing-house recently built for his grandson. He had also a small house in Sixth Street, two houses in Pewter Platter Alley, a lot in Arch Street, some lots near the center of the city, and a pasture ground in Hickory Lane. He owned a tract of land in Nova Scotia, three thousand acres in Georgia, some lands on the Ohio, and a house and lot in Unity Street, Boston. Bonds he held of the value of seven or eight thousand pounds. He had twelve shares in the Bank of North America, about five thousand pounds in money, and the portrait of the King of France adorned with four hundred and eight diamonds. A balance of unknown amount was due to him from the United States, besides numberless small debts dating back to the time when he was a printer and stationer.

The will opens with this sentence :—" I, Benjamin Franklin, of Philadelphia, printer, late Minister Plenipotentiary from the United States of America to the Court of France, now President of the State of Pennsylvania, do make and declare my last will and testament as follows "

To his son, William Franklin, he left his lands in Nova Scotia, and forgave the debts due to him from his son. "The part he acted against me," the will continued, "in the late war, which is of public notoriety, will account for my leaving him no more of an estate he endeavored to deprive me of." The bulk of his Philadelphia property he left to his daughter and her husband, and to their children after them. To his son-in-law, Mr. Bache, he forgave a bond he held against him for more than two thousand pounds, " requesting that, in consideration thereof, he would immediately after my decease manumit and set free his negro man, Bob." He gave him also, the lands on the Ohio and sundry debts and bonds remaining to be collected. The picture of the King of France with its diamonds he bequeathed to his daughter ; " requesting, however, that she would not form any of those diamonds into ornaments, either for herself or daughters, and thereby introduce or countenance the expensive, vain, and useless fashion of wearing jewels in this country ; and that those immediately connected with the picture may be preserved with the same."

He left to his sister, Jane Mecom, his house and lot in Boston, and an annuity of sixty pounds. To William Temple Franklin, he gave the three thousand acres in Georgia. " I also," said the will, " give to my grandson, *William Temple Franklin*, the bond and judgment I have against him of four thousand pounds sterling, my right to the same to cease upon the day of his marriage ; and, if he dies unmarried, my will is, that the same be recovered and divided among my other grandchildren."

He left fifty pounds to be divided equally among the children, grandchildren, and great grandchildren of each of his brothers and sisters. To his grandson, Benjamin Franklin Bache, he gave all his printing materials, with a thousand pounds, and a bond of unknown amount. His copy of the " History of the Academy of Sciences," in sixty or seventy quarto volumes, he bequeathed to the Philosophical Society of Philadelphia. A folio copy of " Les Arts et Les Métiers" he gave to the New England Philosophical Society, and a quarto copy of the same work to the Library Company of Philadelphia. The rest of his books he divided among Benjamin Franklin Bache, William Temple Franklin, and his cousin, Jonathan Williams ; himself marking in the catalogue the works he designed for each. He gave one hundred pounds to the managers of the Boston free schools, the interest of which was to be devoted to the purchase of silver medals for the encouragement of scholarship in the schools. Two thousand pounds of the salary still due to him as President of Pennsylvania, he bequeathed for the purpose of improving the navigation of the Schuylkill River. His old business debts he gave to the Pennsylvania Hospital : "hoping," he said, " that those debtors, and the descendants of such as are deceased, who now, as I find, make some difficulty of satisfying such antiquated demands as just debts, may, however, be induced to pay or give them as charity to that excellent institution."

Henry Hill, John Jay, Francis Hopkinson, and Edward Duffield, were named by him executors of his will. It was dated July 17th, 1788.

A year later, he added a remarkable codicil, more extensive than the will itself. Learning that the work upon the Schuylkill was not likely to be undertaken for many years, he revoked the bequest of two thousand pounds, and devoted it to the institution of a scheme of continuous benevolence, the idea of which he had caught from a French work by Mathon De La Cour. The scheme, however, was not unlike in principle that of his own continuous loan to Benjamin Webb. He explains his plan, with curious particularity, thus :

" I have considered that among artisans, good apprentices are most likely to make good citizens, and having myself been bred to a manual art, printing, in my native town, and afterwards assisted to set up my business in Philadelphia by kind loans of money from two friends there, which was the foundation of my fortune, and of all the utility in life that may be ascribed to me, I wish to be useful even after my death, if possible, in forming and advancing other young men, that may be serviceable to their country in both those towns. To this end, I devote two thousand pounds sterling, of which I give one thousand thereof to the inhabitants of the town of Boston, in Massachusetts, and the other thousand to the inhabitants of the city of Philadelphia, in trust, to and for the uses, intents, and purposes hereinafter mentioned and declared.

" The said sum of one thousand pounds sterling, if accepted by the inhabitants of the town of Boston, shall be managed under the direction of the selectmen, united with the ministers of the oldest Episcopalian, Congregational, and Presbyterian churches in that town, who are to let out the same upon interest at five per cent. per annum to such young married artificers, under the age of twenty-five years, as have served an apprenticeship in the said town, and faithfully fulfilled the duties required in their indentures, so as to obtain a good moral character from at least two respectable citizens, who are willing to become their sureties, in a bond with the applicants, for the repayment of the moneys so lent, with interest, according to the terms hereinafter prescribed ; all which bonds are to be taken for Spanish milled dollars, or the value thereof in current gold coin ; and the managers shall keep a bound book or books, wherein shall be entered the names of those who shall apply for and receive the benefits of this institution, and of their sureties, together with the sums lent, the dates, and other necessary and proper records respecting the business and concerns of this institution. And, as these loans are intended to assist young married artificers in setting up their business, they are to be proportioned, by the discretion of the managers, so as not to exceed sixty pounds sterling to one person, nor to be less than fifteen pounds ; and, if the number of appliers so entitled should be so large as that the sum will not suffice to afford to each as much as might otherwise not be improper, the proportion to each shall be diminshed so as to afford to every one some assistance. These aids may, therefore, be small at first, but, as the capital increases by the accumulated interest, they will be more ample. And, in order to serve as many as possible in their turn, as well as to make the repayment of the principal borrowed more easy, each borrower shall be obliged to pay, with the yearly interest, one tenth part of the principal, which sums of principal and interest, so paid in, shall be again let out to fresh borrowers.

" And, as it is presumed that there will always be found in Boston virtuous and benevolent citizens, willing to bestow a part of their time in doing good to the rising generation, by superintending and managing this institution gratis, it is hoped, that no part of the money will, at any time, be dead, or be diverted to other purposes, but be continually augmenting by the interest ; in which case there may, in time, be more than the occasions in Boston shall require, and then some may be spared to the neighboring or other towns in the said State of Massachusetts, who may desire to have it ; such towns engaging to pay punctually the interest and the portions of the principal, annually, to the inhabitants of the town of Boston.

" If this plan is executed, and succeeds as projected without interruption, for one hundred years, the sum will then be one hundred and thirty-one thousand pounds ; of which I would have the managers of the donation to the town of Boston then lay out, at their discretion, one hundred thousand pounds in public works, which may be judged of most general utility to the inhabitants; such as fortifications, bridges, aqueducts, public buildings, baths, pavements, or whatever may make living in the town more convenient to its people, and render it more agreeable to strangers resorting thither for health or a temporary residence. The remaining thirty-one thousand pounds I would have continued to be let out on interest, in the manner above directed, for another hundred years, as I hope it will have been found that the institution has had a good effect on the conduct of youth, and been of service to many worthy characters and useful citizens. At the end of this second term, if no unfortunate accident has prevented the operation, the sum will be four millions and sixty-one thousand pounds sterling; of which I leave one million sixty-one thousand pounds to the disposition of the inhabitants of the town of Boston, and three millions to the disposition of the government of the State, not presuming to carry my views farther.

" All the directions herein given, respecting the disposition and management of the donation to the inhabitants of Boston, I would have observed respecting that to the inhabitants of Philadelphia, only, as Philadelphia is incorporated, I request the corporation of that city to undertake the management, agreeably to the said directions; and I do hereby vest them with full and ample powers for that purpose."

Such was the scheme adopted by Franklin, for the benefit of a class he always loved—skillful, honest mechanics. We shall have to state, by and by, what success has attended the benevolent project.

Two other items of this codicil are peculiarly interesting :

" I wish to be buried by the side of my wife, if it may be, and that a marble stone, to be made by Chambers, six feet long, four feet wide, plain, with only a small molding round the upper edge, and this inscription,

BENJAMIN
AND   } FRANKLIN.
DEBORAH
178–

to be placed over us both.

" My fine crab-tree walking-stick, with a gold head, curiously wrought in the form of the cap of liberty, I give to my friend, and the friend of mankind, *General Washington.* If it were a scepter, he has merited it, and would become it. It was a present to me from that excellent woman, Madame de Forbach, the Dowager Duchess of Deux-Ponts, connected with some verses, which should go with it."*

His health improved while he was preparing for death. His friend, Brissot, destined to die by the guillotine as chief of the Girondins, was in America in 1788, and visited Franklin in September. "Thanks to God," he wrote, "Franklin still exists! This great man, for so many years the preceptor of the Americans, who so gloriously contributed to their independence—death had threatened his days ; but our fears are dissipated, and his health is restored. I have just been to see him, and enjoy his conversation, in the midst of his books, which he still calls his best friends. The pains of his cruel infirmity change not the serenity of his countenance, nor the calmness of his conversation. If these appeared so agreeable to our Frenchmen, who enjoyed his friendship in Paris, how would they seem to them here, where no diplomatic functions impose upon him that mask of reserve, which was sometimes so chilling to his guests. Franklin, surrounded by his family, appears to be one of those patriarchs, whom he has so well described, and whose language he has copied with such simple eloquence. He seems one of those ancient philosophers who, at times, descended from the sphere of his elevated genius, to instruct weak mortals, by accommodating himself to their feebleness. I have found in America a great number of enlightened politicians and virtuous men ; but I find none who appear to possess, in so high a degree as Franklin, the characteristics of a real philosopher."†

Franklin served out his third year as President of Pennsylvania, rejoicing that the Constitution of the State forbade his re-election. The only thing he would receive of the State in the way of compensation for his three years' services, was the reimbursement of the postage he had paid on official letters, which the old records inform us amounted to £77 5s. 6d. Released from office, he wrote assiduously upon his Autobiography.

One affair, which remained to be concluded, gave him much con-

---

* This cane is now among the Washington Relics, in the Patent Office, at Washington. The verses appear to have been lost.

† J. P. Brissot's Travels in America, vol. i., p. 179.

cern. His accounts with the general government were still unsettled, and the rumor was industriously circulated that he owed
Congress a large sum. His accounts, it is true, had been examined
in Paris by the commissioner appointed by Congress, and the
amount formally claimed by him, which differed from the report
of the commissioner only in the sum of seven cents, had been paid
in Paris ; but there remained certain other demands, which he
thought equally entitled to liquidation. On his return home, he
had sent to New York, to submit these demands to Congress, his
grandson, who was informed that Congress could not take them
into consideration until after the arrival of certain documents from
France. Three years passed without his receiving from Congress
any communication on the subject. Desiring to have his accounts
closed before his death, anxious, also, to leave some provision for
his grandson, who had lost the opportunity of acquiring a profession by being employed for eight years as Secretary to the French
legation, he wrote to Congress in November, 1788, and inclosed
his letter in a private one to Charles Thomson, the Secretary to
Congress. These two letters record a series of facts which may
serve to encourage public men of the present time, by showing
them, that the very greatest diplomatic services ever rendered by
one man to his country, and those services rendered by a Franklin,
services as essential to the success of the revolution as those of
General Washington, won from the Congress of the United States,
not only no word of recognition, but not even the just pecuniary
recompense. This may seem encouragement of the Hibernian description. Not so ; for it is always a solace to a faithful servant
of the public who has returned home from distant service to encounter slander instead of commendation, reproachful silence instead of public thanks, to know that the great ones of old experienced similar treatment.

Franklin now modestly recounted his claims upon the consideration of Congress. He reminded them that his services in England,
in opposing the Stamp Act and the other oppressive measures that
preceded the revolution, had rendered him so obnoxious to the
British government that he was deprived, first, of his postmaster-
ship, which yielded an income of three hundred pounds a year, and
afterward of his colonial agencies, which produced him nine hundred
pounds a year. He mentioned his services at home during the first

year of the war, when he had assisted in the fortifications of Philadelphia, had nearly lost his life in the journey to Canada, and had
invested all the money he could raise in the public funds. Then he
was sent abroad with a promise of a clear income, over all expenses,
of five hundred pounds a year, and the assistance of a secretary, at a
salary of a thousand pounds a year to include all expenses. No secretary was ever sent him, and he was compelled to retain the services
of his grandson, who had served for some time for his board only, and
afterward at a salary barely sufficient for his decent maintenance.
Meanwhile he had served Congress, not as embassador merely, but as
consul, judge of admiralty, purchasing agent, and banker. One of
the privateers sent out by him had captured, in a single year, seventy-
five prizes, upon every one of which he had been obliged to adjudi-
cate. And such was the number of the bills of exchange sent out
to him by Congress, each of which required careful and personal
inspection, that he was obliged to forego his annual journey for
exercise, and to confine himself so constantly to his office, as to
bring on a malady incurable, and one of the most painful to which
the human body is subject.

These were his services. In his private letter to Mr. Thomson,
he detailed the items of his requital :

"I must own," he wrote, "I did hope, that, as it is customary
in Europe to make some liberal provision for ministers when they
return home from foreign service, the Congress would at least have
been kind enough to have shown their approbation of my conduct
by a grant of a small tract of land in their western country, which
might have been of use and some honor to my posterity. And I
cannot but still think they will do something of the kind for me,
whenever they shall be pleased to take my services into consideration; as I see by their minutes, that they have allowed Mr. Lee
handsomely for his services in England, before his appointment to
France, in which services I and Mr. Bollan co-operated with him,
and have had no such allowance ; and, since his return, he has
been very properly rewarded with a good place, as well as my friend
Mr. Jay; though these are trifling compensations in comparison
with what was granted by the king to M. Gérard on his return
from America.

"But how different is what has happened to me. On my return
from England, in 1775, the Congress bestowed on me the office of

postmaster-general, for which I was very thankful. It was indeed an office I had some kind of right to, as having previously greatly enlarged the revenue of the post by the regulations I had contrived and established while I possessed it under the crown. When I was sent to France, I left it in the hands of my son-in-law, who was to act as my deputy. But soon after my departure it was taken from me, and given to Mr. Hazard. When the English ministry formerly thought fit to deprive me of the office, they left me, however, the privilege of receiving and sending my letters free of postage, which is the usage when a postmaster is not displaced for misconduct in the office ; but, in America, I have ever since had the postage demanded of me, which, since my return from France, has amounted to about fifty pounds, much of it occasioned by my having acted as minister there.

" When I took my grandson, William Temple Franklin, with me to France, I purposed, after giving him the French language, to educate him in the study and practice of the law. But, by the repeated expectations given me of a secretary, and constant disappointments, I was induced, and indeed obliged, to retain him with me to assist in the secretary's office, which disappointments continued till my return, by which time so many years of the opportunity of his studying the law were lost, and his habits of life become so different, that it appeared no longer advisable ; and I then, considering him as brought up in the diplomatic line, and well qualified by his knowledge in that branch for the employ of a secretary at least, (in which opinion I was not alone, for three of my colleagues, without the smallest solicitation from me, chose him secretary of the negotiation for treaties, which they had been empowered to do), took the liberty of recommending him to the Congress for their protection. This was the only favor I ever asked of them ; and the only answer I received was, a resolution superseding him, and appointing Colonel Humphreys in his place ; a gentleman, who, though he might have indeed a good deal of military merit, certainly had none in the diplomatic line, and had neither the French language, nor the experience, nor the address proper to qualify him for such an employment.

" This is all to yourself only, as a private friend ; for I have not, nor ever shall, make any public complaint ; and even if I could have foreseen such unkind treatment from Congress, their refusing

.me thanks would not in the least have abated my zeal for the cause, and ardor in support of it.   I know something of the nature of such changeable assemblies, and how little successors know of the services that have been rendered to the corps before their admission, or feel themselves obliged by such services; and what effect in obliterating a sense of them, during the absence of the servant in a distant country, the artful and reiterated malevolent insinuations of one or two envious and malicious persons may have on the minds of members, even of the most equitable, candid, and honorable dispositions; and therefore I will pass these reflections into oblivion."

The application of Dr. Franklin for a final settlement never reached the ear of Congress.   It was four months after these letters were dispatched before a quorum of that body was assembled, and, during the interval, Franklin may have withdrawn his application.   There is, at least, no allusion to the subject in the journals of Congress. Dr. Sparks surmises that some explanation of the apparent insensibility of Congress to the merits of Dr. Franklin is to be found in the fact, that his evil genius, Arthur Lee, was then one of the Commissioners of the Treasury, by whom his accounts would have been first examined.   Under the subsequent reign of federalism, the descendants of Franklin were, of course, on the side of the republican minority, and that reign lasted until 1801, when the matter had long been forgotten.   Hence, the curious fact that, to this day, the United States owes money to Benjamin Franklin, for work and labor done.   The chief item in his account was the unpaid portion of the thousand pounds a year which his secretary was to have received—about five thousand pounds in all, a sum which might have been, if well used, a compensation to his grandson for the loss of a profession.

There appears to have been a strong prejudice in the minds of the Lee and Adams party against William Temple Franklin.   Lafayette, who had seen him much at the French court, had so favorable an opinion of his character, that he wrote to General Washington expressly in his behalf: "This letter, my dear General, goes with our old friend Dr. Franklin, who, I hope, will be received with that respect he so much deserves.   It will be forwarded by his grandson, a very deserving young man, who wishes being introduced by me to you; and I beg leave to recommend him to your attentions. He has been much employed in public; got nothing by it; and, as the Doctor loves him better than any thing in the world, I think he ought to have the satisfaction to see him noticed by Congress. You will oblige me to let them know that I spoke to you my mind about it."*

It was of no avail. We have seen that even the desire of the young man to be employed as secretary to the Convention of 1787 was not gratified. The defection of his father, his own long residence abroad, the stain upon the birth of both, the malevolence of Arthur Lee, and the more urgent claims of men distinguished in the field, were the causes of his failure to obtain from Congress the employment which his grandfather desired for him. I have not been able to ascertain that there was any thing in his own conduct or character that justified this neglect, except that his abilities were not extraordinary. The manner in which he edited the works of his grandfather shows that he inherited little of Franklin's genius or acuteness. Tradition reports him a lively, agreeable young gentleman, well skilled in the arts and graces which were requisite in a secretary of legation in the last century. The drawings with which he illustrated Franklin's humorous letters and philosophical writings were sufficiently good for their purpose.

Mrs. Bache presented Franklin with another grandchild in 1788, which called from Mrs. Mecom one of her characteristic gushes of sisterly affection. "I can with sincerity say," wrote the good old soul, when she had heard of her brother's fall and the birth of this child, "that I should have been glad to have borne part of your pain, to have eased my dear brother. They tell me you are much better: may God continue you so! I rejoice with you and the happy parents in the increase of your family. It is said Mr. Bache is remarkable for having the finest children in Philadelphia. How much pleasure must they give you when you have ease to enjoy it! I long to have every one to kiss and play with that I see pass the street, that looks clean and healthy. You did not give me the name. I think this is the seventh. Mrs. Bache may make up my number, twelve, though she did not begin so young. My love to them all. God bless them, says their affectionate aunt and your affectionate and grateful sister."

* "Letters to Washington." Sparks, iv., 110.

And, later : " Oh, that I could mitigate your ·pains or griofs ! but instead of being able to do that, I and mine have always been a great cause of grief and trouble to you, though, blessed be God, you have never discovered any thing but the pleasure of doing good, and Heaven has blessed you in the deed ; though you suffer what is the lot of all men, in a greater or less degree, pain and sickness, the consciousness of the rectitude of all your actions, both for public and private benefit, will support your hope for a more blessed state to all eternity, where, my dear brother, we shall meet ; though may it be yet many years before you are called off this stage, in favor to the inhabitants, who will greatly miss you whenever that time comes. * * * I suppose you see our newspapers, where you see how fond our people are to say something of Dr. Franklin, I believe mostly to do him honor, but some choose to embellish the language to their own fancy."

CHAPTER IV.

LAST LABORS.

THE labors of Dr. Franklin's last year were sufficient of themselves to give any one a great and lasting fame as a man of humor and public spirit. Yet, during a great part of the time, he lay upon his bed a prey to the most excruciating anguish. As he approached the close of his life, the paroxysms of his disease became more and more violent, and the intervals of relief were of shorter duration. No one, however, could ever perceive the slightest diminution either of the force or of the brilliancy of his mind. Except when he was totally prostrated by the long endurance of pain, he was the same joyous, witty, story-telling, benevolent Franklin, his friends had ever known him ; happy still in the society of his philosophical brethren, happiest when surrounded by his many grandchildren. Mrs. Duane, wife of the Honorable William J. Duane, of General Jackson's cabinet, was one of those grandchildren who played about the bed of this patient, suffering old man. She was a school-girl, eight years old, during Franklin's last year, and she lingered among us until the spring of 1863, retaining almost to the last an extraordinary vigor of mind and body. I have heard her say that her most vivid recollection of that year was the interest which her grandfather took in her having her lesson duly learned for the next day. Every evening after tea, she was accustomed to go to his bedside, hand him her Webster's spelling-book, and say her lesson to him. She could remember little else, but this alone was worth going to Philadelphia to hear.

His affectionate old friend Mrs. Hewson, who had removed to Philadelphia upon his advice, records, that during the last two years of his life he had not two months in all of freedom from pain. No repining, no peevish expression, she says, ever escaped him. " When the pain was not too violent to be amused, he employed himself with his books, his pen, or in conversation with his friends; and upon every occasion displayed the clearness of his intellect and the cheerfulness of his temper. Even when the intervals from pain were so short, that his words were frequently interrupted, I have known him to hold a discourse in a sublime strain of piety. I never shall forget one day that I passed with our friend last summer (1789). I found him in bed in great agony; but, when that agony abated a little, I asked him if I should read to him. He said, Yes; and the first book I met with was ' Johnson's Lives of the Poets.' I read the Life of Watts, who was a favorite author with Dr. Franklin; and, instead of lulling him to sleep, it roused him to a display of the powers of his memory and his reason. He repeated several of Watts's ' Lyric Poems,' and descanted upon their sublimity in a strain worthy of them and of their pious author."

The warmest, the tenderest love cheered the last days of one who, if God is love, was as like God as any man then alive.

It is touching to read in the correspondence between Franklin and his sister, that one of the last topics on which they wrote was the one in which they had, perhaps, taken most interest when they were children together at the old home in Boston—namely, *Soap*. Mrs. Mecom had saved some of her father's recipes for making the more choice varieties of this article, in the hope that they might be useful to her descendants; and so they proved. She used to send her brother boxes of the soap made by her grandson, and he, to the very end of his life, interested himself in getting the soap sold in Philadelphia to advantage, often admonishing the young man to be sure and send a good article. The reader may smile if I confess, that as often as I have read these soap letters, I have been reminded of Wordsworth's little poem, which stands first in his collected works, and upon which Coleridge so fondly comments in the Friend :

> " My heart leaps up when I behold
> A Rainbow in the sky ;
> So was it when my life began ;
> So is it now I am a Man :
> So be it when I shall grow old,
> Or let me die !
> The Child is Father of the Man ;
> And I could wish my days to be
> Bound each to each by natural piety."

Smile, reader, if you will ; but I believe that Wordsworth and Coleridge would both have admitted the aptness of the poem, and agreed that a cake of soap becomes as poetical as a rainbow, when a Franklin, who began life by making it, occupies some of his last hours in selling it for his sister.

The French revolution, in 1789, had assumed its terrific aspect. In 1787, as we have seen, Dr. Franklin hailed the Assembly of the Notables as a good omen for France. To some friends surrounding his bedside who had been expressing their astonishment at the course of events in France, he is reported to have said : " Why, I see nothing singular in all this, but, on the contrary, what might naturally be expected. The French have served an apprenticeship to Liberty in this country, and now that they are out of their time, they have set up for themselves."* The queen, Marie Antoinette, recognized the same truth when she said, in the same year, in one of her letters to Madame de Polignac : " The time of illusions is past, and to-day we pay dear for our infatuation and enthusiasm for the American war."

In 1789, the year of the Bastile and the *Lanterne*, Franklin, too, began to tremble for his old friends, and for France. The chief actors in that fearful scene, Lafayette, Mirabeau, Necker, Brissot, the King, the Queen, de Vergennes, and others, he had been in the habit of meeting for nine years, entertaining and entertained ; and for many of them he cherished the warmest regard. The news of

* Gazette of the United States, Sept. 4, 1790.

the dissensions in the States-general, of the famine, of the fall of the Bastile, the march upon Versailles, the lamp-post executions, the confinement of the King and Queen in their palace, filled him with anxiety. He could say with Charles Fox, " I wish the French were like our old friends, the Americans, and I should scarcely be afraid for them." But they were men of a different stamp, and had inherited far different circumstances. Franklin feared for his friends more than he hoped for France. His last year, however, was solaced by the amazing prosperity of his own country, which gained advantage from the very commotions that appalled and impoverished Europe.

His writings, during the year 1789, when we consider his great age and his bodily condition, are nothing short of wonderful. His famous protest against Latin and Greek as a means of education, of which some account has been given in a previous chapter, was written this year. It is done with all his ancient spirit and humor. In conversation at his own house, he would introduce the same subject, and use the illustrations which he employs so happily in his pamphlet. He is reported to have said, one evening, while talking on the subject : " When the custom of wearing broad cuffs with buttons first began, there was a reason for it ; the cuffs might be brought down over the hands, and thus guard them from wet and cold. But gloves came into use, and the broad cuffs were unnecessary ; yet the custom was still retained. So likewise with cocked hats. The wide brim, when let down, afforded a protection from the rain and sun. Umbrellas were introduced, yet fashion prevailed to keep cocked hats in vogue, although they were rather cumbersome than useful. Thus with the Latin language. When nearly all the books in Europe were written in that language, the study of it was essential in every system of education ; but it is now scarcely needed, except as an accomplishment, since it has everywhere given place, as a vehicle of thought and knowledge, to some one of the modern tongues."*

How strange that, to this hour, in all the most famous schools of Christendom, those languages, which record but the prattle of infant Man, should be preferred, as a means of forming the mind of youth, to those glorious tongues in which a Goethe, a Schiller,

---

* Dr. Sparks, i., 526.

Chadron State College Library

Chadron. Nebr...

a Montaigne, a Cervantes, a Shakspeare, a Franklin, utter the thoughts of Man coming of age !

One of Franklin's wittiest performances of this year, worthy of his best days, was an essay on the abuse of the liberty of the press in attacking private character. It was his boast, that his own newspaper, the *Pennsylvania Gazette*, during an existence of nearly sixty years, under his own management and that of his successors, had never assailed the character of a private individual, nor indecently criticised the conduct of a public man. During the revolutionary war, the newspapers of the United States, provoked, it must be owned, by the outrageous vituperation of the tory organs in New York and elsewhere, had lapsed into habitual indecorum, and the habit remained when the provocation had ceased. The dissensions preceding and following the adoption of the new Constitution were bitter in the extreme, and the newspapers were the vehicles of violent recrimination. Franklin humorously advised the legislature to do one of two things, either to restrain the liberty of the press, or restore the liberty of the cudgel. He said, that if the liberty of the press meant merely the liberty of defaming private character, he, for his part, was willing to exchange his *liberty* of abusing for the *privilege* of not being abused. He was willing, however, to leave the liberty of the press untouched, provided the liberty of the cudgel went with it *pari passu*.

"Thus, my fellow-citizens," said he, "if an impudent writer attacks your reputation, dearer to you perhaps than your life, and puts his name to the charge, you may go to him as openly and break his head. If he conceals himself behind the printer, and you can nevertheless discover who he is, you may in like manner way-lay him in the night, attack him behind, and give him a good drubbing. Thus far goes my project as to *private* resentment and retribution. But if the public should ever happen to be affronted, *as it ought to be*, with the conduct of such writers, I would not advise proceeding immediately to these extremities ; but that we should in moderation content ourselves with tarring and feathering, and tossing them in a blanket. If, however, it should be thought that this proposal of mine may disturb the public peace, I would then humbly recommend to our legislators to take up the consideration of both liberties, that of the *press*, and that of the *cudgel*, and by an explicit law mark their extent and limits ; and, at the same time that they secure the person of a citizen from *assaults*, they would likewise provide for the security of his *reputation*." This article is wit and gayety from the beginning to the end.

In August, 1789, was laid the corner-stone of a new building designed for the Library founded by the Junto, half a century before. The edifice thus begun was the handsome and commodious one in Fifth Street, opposite the State House, in which the Library has ever since been deposited. It is still an ornament to the neighborhood, and exhibits in a niche in front of the building a marble statue of Franklin, presented by William Bingham. Dr. Franklin, whose infirmities prevented his attending the ceremony, wrote an inscription for the corner-stone, but omitted the mention of his own name. The Committee supplied the omission, and the inscription, as amended by them, reads thus:

" Be it remembered
In honor of the Philadelphia Youth,
(then chiefly artificers)
that in MDCCXXXI.,
they cheerfully,
at the instance of Benjamin Franklin,
one of their number,
instituted the Philadelphia Library,
which, though small at first,
is become highly valuable and extensively useful
and which the walls of this edifice
are now destined to contain and preserve,
the first stone of whose foundation
was here placed,
the thirty-first day of August, 1789."

The artisans of Philadelphia manifested great interest in the construction of the new building. A number of apprentices, we are told, were allowed to give enough labor to it to purchase a share in the Library. The designers of the building must have been gentlemen rich in faith, for though the Library then numbered little more than six thousand volumes, they provided an edifice which is only full now that it contains seventy thousand. There are a few larger libraries than this in the United States, but it is doubtful if there is one which contains so large a proportion of valuable matter. It has the best of all the works which have appeared since it was founded, with as little of the trash as could be expected in an institution managed by and working for fallible beings. A fund is now (1862) forming for the purpose of erecting a still larger building, that shall have the advantage of being fire-proof, which the present structure does not possess. There is no question that Philadelphia, so liberal in works of real utility, will enable the managers to carry out their scheme on a scale as ample for the present time as the building in Fifth Street was for 1789.

The abolition of slavery and the care of emancipated negroes were the last public objects which engaged the attention and employed the pen of Franklin. As president of "The Pennsylvania Society for Promoting the Abolition of Slavery, and the Relief of free Negroes unlawfully held in bondage," he wrote a Plan for improving the condition of the free blacks. He advised a committee of twenty-four members, to be divided into four sub-committees; one, to superintend the general conduct of the free negroes, and give advice, protection, and aid to ·such as needed them: another, to place out young negroes as apprentices: another, to provide schools for the free blacks: and another, to provide employ ment for adults. He wrote, also, an eloquent address to the public, asking pecuniary aid to carry out his plan. "Slavery," said he, "is such an atrocious debasement of human nature, that its very extirpation, if not performed with solicitous care, may sometimes open a source of serious evils. The unhappy man, who has long been treated as a brute animal, too frequently sinks beneath the common standard of the human species. The galling chains, that bind his body, do also fetter his intellectual faculties, and impair the social affections of his heart. Accustomed to move like a mere machine, by the will of a master, reflection is suspended; he has not the power of choice; and reason and conscience have but little influence over his conduct, because he is chiefly governed by the passion of fear. He is poor and friendless; perhaps worn out by extreme labor, age, and disease." And hence, he argued, the duty which devolved upon the community to receive these poor creatures coming from the house of bondage, with cordiality, and to give them the assistance, the advice, the instruction, the protection of which they stood in need.

Among Franklin's private letters of this year, there is one, written in December, to Noah Webster, which must have filled four or five sheets of letter paper, full of interesting gossip upon words and phrases, corruptions of language, recollections of his old printing days, and the art preservative of arts. Webster was then a young man just married, but he had already published the Spelling-Book, upon which he lived while he wrote his great dictionary, and which still sells a million copies a year.

He wrote to General Washington to congratulate him upon his recovery from the illness which had so much alarmed the country. "For my own personal ease," he wrote, "I should have died two years ago; but, though those years have been spent in excruciating pain, I am pleased that I have lived them, since they have brought me to see our present situation. I am now finishing my eighty-fourth year, and probably with it my career in this life; but in whatever state of existence I am placed in hereafter, if I retain any memory of what has passed here, I shall with it retain the esteem, respect, and affection, with which I have long been, my dear friend, yours most sincerely."

"Would to God, my dear sir," replied Washington, "that I could congratulate you upon the removal of that excruciating pain under which you labor, and that your existence might close with as much ease to yourself, as its continuance has been beneficial to our country and useful to mankind; or, if the united wishes of a free people, joined with the earnest prayers of every friend to science and humanity, could relieve the body from pains or infirmities, that you could claim an exemption on this score. But this cannot be, and you have within yourself the only resource to which we can confidently apply for relief, a philosophic mind.

"If to be venerated for benevolence, if to be admired for talents, if to be esteemed for patriotism, if to be beloved for philanthropy, can gratify the human mind, you must have the pleasing consolation to know that you have not lived in vain. And I flatter myself that it will not be ranked among the least grateful occurrences of your life to be assured that, so long as I retain my memory, you will be recollected with respect, veneration, and affection by your sincere friend."

CHAPTER V.

BENJAMIN FRANKLIN'S LAST PUBLIC ACT.

It will be seen more clearly by posterity than it can be by us, that the Declaration of Independence of 1776 was the knell of American slavery.

"We hold these truths to be self-evident, that all men are created equal; that they are endowed by their Creator with certain inalienable rights; that among these are life, liberty, and the pursuit of happiness."

These words were followed by victory so marvelous, that such cool heads as Washington and Franklin could not help regarding it as the visible sanction and indorsement of an Omnipotent God. The victory secure, the first thought of free America was to apply the Declaration to the case of the negro slaves. From that hour began the struggle between Interest and Conscience, or between erroneous and enlightened views of Interest, which has been well named the Irrepressible Conflict, and which, continuing without cessation for seventy-five years, sought, at length, the final arbitrament of arms. The very compromises of the Constitution, which seemed to give a kind of national sanction to slavery, were admitted only because the majority of the Convention took it for granted that an anomaly so palpably absurd and inconsistent as slavery, would not, could not stand its ground against the new spirit of the age. They felt, as Mr. Mill has recently expressed it, that slavery had been "completely judged and decided;"* the only question that remained was, the most convenient mode of ending it, and that was the concern of the States.

There was, however, one branch of the system which lay within the province of Congress, and that was the importation of slaves from Africa. Hence, while the Northern States were maturing plans for the abolition of slavery within their own borders, and Virginia was indulging the sentimentalities of the question, admitting the wrong, but persisting in it, Congress discussed propositions for suppressing the slave-trade. There was a great debate on this subject in the spring of 1789, which attracted universal atten-

* "Political Economy," i., 319, Am. Ed.

tion, and was read with the deepest interest by the aged Franklin. The debate arose on the motion to lay a tax of ten dollars on each slave imported.

The leader of the opposition to all measures tending to the abolition of slavery or the slave-trade, was Mr. James Jackson, of Georgia, an active and influential member. He spoke on the subject in the manner and in the spirit since, so familiar to the people of the United States. Take a few sentences from Mr. Benton's " Abridgment of the Debates :"

" Mr. Jackson said it was the fashion of the day to favor the liberty of slaves. He would not go into a discussion of the subject ; but he believed it was capable of demonstration that they were better off in their present situation than they would be if they were manumitted. What are they to do if they are discharged ? Work for a living ? Experience has shown us they will not. Examine what has become of those in Maryland ; many of them have been set free in that State. Did they turn themselves to industry and useful pursuits ? No, they turn out common pickpockets, petty larceny villains. And is this mercy, forsooth, to turn them into a way in which they must lose their lives ? for when they are thrown upon the world, void of property and connections, they cannot get their living but by pilfering. What is to be done for compensation ? Will Virginia set all her negroes free ? Will they give up the money they cost them, and to whom ? When this practice comes to be tried there, the sound of liberty will lose those charms which make it grateful to the ravished ear. But our slaves are not in a worse situation than they were on the coast of Africa It is not uncommon there for the parents to sell their children in peace ; and in war the whole are taken and made slaves together. In these cases it is only a change of one slavery for another ; and are they not better here, where they have a master, bound by the ties of interest and law to provide for their support and comfort in old age or infirmity, in which, if they were free, they would sink under the pressure of woe for want of assistance ?"*

After much debate the motion was withdrawn, on the understanding that the proposition should be revived in the form of a separate bill. The House sat until late in the summer, but the promised bill does not appear to have been introduced.

* " Benton's Abridgment," i.. 74.

Congress met again on the fourth of January, 1790. Early in the session, the Friends' Meeting of Pennsylvania, New Jersey, New York, West Maryland, and West Virginia, sent a petition to the House, asking the suppression of the slave-trade, which led to a most animated debate. Mr. Jackson again distinguished himself as the champion of slavery. He said, very truly, that the suppression of the slave-trade by the general government would convey to "our Southern brethren" an impression that the government desired the abolition of slavery, which impression would give them a feeling of insecurity; and even the discussion of the subject in Congress would have the same effect. He then proceeded in the usual impudent style of the chivalry:

"I would beg to ask those, then, who are desirous of freeing the negroes, if they have funds sufficient to pay for them? If they have, they may come forward on that business with some propriety; but, if they have not, they should keep themselves quiet, and not interfere with a business in which they are not interested. They may as well come forward and solicit Congress to interdict the West India trade, because it is injurious to the morals of mankind; from thence we import rum, which has a debasing influence upon the consumer. But, sir, is the whole morality of the United States confined to the Quakers? Are they the only people whose feelings are to be consulted on this occasion? Is it to them we owe our present happiness? Was it they who formed the constitution? Did they, by their arms or contributions, establish our independence? I believe they were generally opposed to that measure; why, then, on their application, should we injure men who, at the risk of their lives and fortunes, secured to the community their liberty and property? If Congress pay any uncommon degree of attention to their petition, it will furnish just ground of alarm to the Southern States. But why do these men set themselves up in such a particular manner against slavery? Do they understand the rights of mankind, and the disposition of Providence, better than others? If they were to consult that book which claims our regard, they will find that slavery is not only allowed but commended. Their Saviour, who possessed more benevolence and commiseration than they pretend to, has allowed of it; and if they fully examine the subject, they will find that slavery has been no novel doctrine since the days of Cain; but be these things as they may, I hope the House will order the petition to lie on the table, in order to prevent an alarm to our Southern brethren."

This was on the eleventh of February. On the day following a memorial was presented to the House from men who were not open to the taunt that they had opposed the revolutionary war. The Abolition Society, of which Dr. Franklin was president, addressed the House on this occasion. Their memorial, signed by him, was as follows :

"The memorial respectfully showeth,

"That, from a regard for the happiness of mankind, an association was formed several years since in this State, by a number of her citizens, of various religious denominations, for promoting the abolition of slavery, and for the relief of those unlawfully held in bondage. A just and acute conception of the true principles of liberty, as it spread through the land, produced accessions to their numbers, many friends to their cause, and a Legislative co-operation with their views, which, by the blessing of Divine Providence, have been successfully directed to the relieving from bondage a large number of their fellow-creatures of the African race. They have also the satisfaction to observe, that in consequence of that spirit of philanthropy and genuine liberty which is generally diffusing its beneficial influence, similar institutions are forming at home and abroad.

" That mankind are all formed by the same Almighty Being, alike objects of his care, and equally designed for the enjoyment of happiness, the Christian religion teaches us to believe, and the political creed of Americans fully coincides with the position. Your memorialists, particularly engaged in attending to the distresses arising from slavery, believe it their indispensable duty to present this subject to your notice. They have observed, with real satisfaction, that many important and salutary powers are vested in you for 'promoting the welfare and securing the blessings of liberty to the people of the United States;' and as they conceive that these blessings ought rightfully to be administered, without distinction of color, to all descriptions of people, so they indulge themselves in the pleasing expectation, that nothing which can be done for the relief of the unhappy objects of their care will be either omitted or delayed.

*

" From a persuasion that equal liberty was originally the portion, and is still the birthright of all men; and influenced by the strong ties of humanity, andt he principles of their institution, your memorialists conceive themselves bound to use all justifiable endeavors to loosen the bands of slavery, and promote a general enjoyment of the blessings of freedom. Under these impressions, they earnestly entreat your serious attention to the subject of slavery; that you will be pleased to countenance the restoration of liberty to those unhappy men, who alone, in this land of freedom, are degraded into perpetual bondage, and who, amidst the general joy of surrounding freemen, are groaning in servile subjection; that you will devise means for removing this inconsistency from the character of the American people; that you will promote mercy and justice towards this distressed race, and that you will step to the very verge of the power vested in you for discouraging every species of traffic in the persons of our fellow-men.

" BENJAMIN FRANKLIN, President.

" PHILADELPHIA, <i>February</i> 3, 1790."*

Another long debote: the question being, Shall the petition lie on the table, or be referred to a committee for consideration? Mr. Jackson again led the opposition.

Religion, he said, was <i>not</i> against slavery. Search the Bible from Genesis to Revelation, and " you will find the current setting strong the other way. There never was a government on the face of the earth, but what permitted slavery. The purest sons of freedom in the Grecian Republics, the citizens of Athens and Lacedæmon, all held slaves. On this principle the nations of Europe are associated; it is the basis of the feudal system. But suppose all this to have been wrong, let me ask the gentleman if it is good policy to bring forward a business at this moment, likely to light up the flame of civil discord; for the people of the Southern States will resist one tyranny as soon as another? The other parts of the continent may bear them down by force of arms, but they will never suffer themselves to be divested of their property without a struggle. The gentleman says, if he was a Federal judge, he does not know to what length he would go in emancipating these people; but I believe his judgment would be of short

* " Benton's Abridgment," i., 208.

duration in Georgia, *perhaps even the existence of such a judge might be in danger.*"

Slavery, we perceive, is the same to-day, yesterday, and forever. So are the advocates of slavery. The closing sentence about the danger to the existence of " such a judge" contains the entire argument for slavery. The debates of seventy years have added nothing to that sole position : Oppose slavery, and I will kill you if I can catch you.

The petition, despite the outcry of the Georgia and South Carolina members, was triumphantly committed—forty-three to fourteen.

The shallow arrogance of Jackson stirred the dying Franklin to the last exertion on earth of his great powers. He wrote a satirical piece, in his finest vein of humor, for one of the newspapers : in which the arguments of Jackson were inimitably parodied. This remarkable production bears date, March 23d, 1790, twenty-four days before the death of its author. I know not if any other man of eighty-four has given such evidence as this piece affords of undiminished powers of mind. I give it place here entire as a great biographical fact :

"TO THE EDITOR OF THE FEDERAL GAZETTE.

" *March* 23d, 1790.

" SIR :—Reading last night in your excellent paper the speech of Mr. Jackson in Congress, against their meddling with the affair of slavery, or attempting to mend the condition of the slaves, it put me in mind of a similar one made about one hundred years since by Sidi Mehemet Ibrahim, a member of the Divan of Algiers, which may be seen in Martin's Account of his Consulship, anno 1687. It was against granting the petition of the sect called *Erika*, or Purists, who prayed for the abolition of piracy and slavery as being unjust. Mr. Jackson does not quote it; perhaps he has not seen it. If, therefore, some of its reasonings are to be found in his eloquent speech, it may only show that men's interests and intellects operate and are operated on with surprising similarity in all countries and climates, whenever they are under similar circumstances. The African's speech, as translated, is as follows :

" '*Allah Bismillah*, &c.   *God is great, and Mahomet is his Prophet.*

" ' Have these *Erika* considered the consequences of granting their petition ?   If we cease our cruises against the Christians, how shall we be furnished with the commodities their countries produce, and which are so necessary for us ?   If we forbear to make slaves of their people, who in this hot climate are to culti- vate our lands ?   Who are to perform the common labors of our city, and in our families ?   Must we not then be our own slaves ?   And is there not more compassion and more favor due to us as Mussulmen, than to these Christian dogs ?   We have now above fifty thousand slaves in and near Algiers.   This number, if not kept up by fresh supplies, will soon diminish, and be gradually an- nihilated.   If we then cease taking and plundering the infidel ships, and making slaves of the seamen and passengers, our lands will become of no value for want of cultivation ; the rents of houses in the city will sink one-half ; and the revenue of govern- ment arising from its share of prizes be totally destroyed !   And for what ?   To gratify the whims of a whimsical sect, who would have us not only forbear making more slaves, but even manumit those we have.

" ' But who is to indemnify their masters for the loss ?   Will the state do it ?   Is our treasury sufficient ?   Will the *Erika* do it ?   Can they do it ?   Or would they, to do what they think justice to the slaves, do a greater injustice to the owners ?   And if we set our slaves free, what is to be done with them ?   Few of them will re- turn to their countries ; they know too well the greater hardships they must there be subject to ; they will not embrace our holy re ligion ; they will not adopt our manners ; our people will not pol- lute themselves by intermarrying with them.   Must we maintain them as beggars in our streets, or suffer our properties to be the prey of their pillage ?   For men accustomed to slavery will not work for a livelihood when not compelled.   And what is there so pitiable in their present condition ?   Were they not slaves in their own countries ?

" ' Are not Spain, Portugal, France, and the Italian states govern- ed by despots, who hold all their subjects in slavery, without ex- ception ?   Even England treats its sailors as slaves ; for they are, whenever the government pleases, seized, and confined in ships-of-war, condemned not only to work, but to fight, for small wages, or a mere subsistence, not better than our slaves are allowed by us. Is their condition then made worse by their falling into our hands? No; they have only exchanged one slavery for another, and I may say a better; for here they are brought into a land where the sun of Islamism gives forth its light, and shines in full splendor, and they have an opportunity of making themselves acquainted with the true doctrine, and thereby saving their immortal souls. Those who remain at home have not that happiness. Sending the slaves home, then, would be sending them out of light into darkness.

"'I repeat the question, What is to be done with them? I have heard it suggested, that they may be planted in the wilderness, where there is plenty of land for them to subsist on, and where they may flourish as a free state; but they are, I doubt, too little disposed to labor without compulsion, as well as too ignorant to establish a good government, and the wild Arabs would soon molest and destroy or again enslave them. While serving us, we take care to provide them with every thing, and they are treated with humanity. The laborers in their own country are, as I am well informed, worse fed, lodged, and clothed. The condition of most of them is therefore already mended, and requires no further improvement. Here their lives are in safety. They are not liable to be impressed for soldiers, and forced to cut one another's Christian throats, as in the wars of their own countries. If some of the religious mad bigots, who now tease us with their silly petitions, have in a fit of blind zeal freed their slaves, it was not generosity, it was not humanity, that moved them to the action; it was from the conscious burden of a load of sins, and a hope, from the supposed merits of so good a work, to be excused from damnation.

"'How grossly are they mistaken to suppose slavery to be disallowed by the Alcoran! Are not the two precepts, to quote no more, '*Masters, treat your slaves with kindness: Slaves, serve your masters with cheerfulness and fidelity,*' clear proofs to the contrary? Nor can the plundering of infidels be in that sacred book forbidden, since it is well known from it, that God has given the world, and all that it contains, to his faithful Mussulmen, who are to enjoy it of right as fast as they conquer it. Let us then hear no more of this detestable proposition, the manumission of Christian slaves, the adoption of which would, by depreciating our lands and houses, and thereby depriving so many good citizens of their properties, create universal discontent, and provoke insurrections, to the endangering of government and producing general confusion. I have therefore no doubt, but this wise council will prefer the comfort and happiness of a whole nation of true believers to the whim of a few *Erika*, and dismiss their petition.

"The result was, as Martin tells us, that the Divan came to this resolution: 'The doctrine, that plundering and enslaving the Christians is unjust, is at best *problematical ;* but that it is the interest of this state to continue the practice, is clear ; therefore, let the petition be rejected.'

"And it was rejected accordingly.

"And since like motives are apt to produce in the minds of men like opinions and resolutions, may we not, Mr. Brown, venture to predict, from this account, that the petitions to the Parliament of England for abolishing the slave-trade, to say nothing of other legislatures, and the debates upon them, will have a similar conclusion? I am, sir, your constant reader, and humble servant,

"HISTORICUS."

The effect of this satire upon the public mind was the greater, from the fact, that, at that time, vast numbers of Christians were actually held in bondage by the Algerines. By the sea-faring men of that day, and their relations on shore, the horrors of the Algerine bondage were vividly realized ; they were the frequent theme of the forecastle, the fireside, the newspaper, and the novel. There were few people in a seaport town, in 1790, who were not acquainted with some one who had been chased by the pirates of the Mediterranean, or held in captivity by them. Dr. Stuber, a distinguished Philadelphian of that day, mentions that many persons searched the bookstores and libraries of the town for " Martin's Account of his Consulship, anno 1687," from which the speech of Sidi Mehemet Ibrahim was said to have been taken.

CHAPTER VI.

CLOSING SCENES.

WHEN Dr. Franklin wrote this parody upon Mr. Jackson, he was nearer the end of his life than his most observant friends could have. supposed. He wrote it in an interval of ease, that lasted four weeks, during which he was so free from pain that he could discontinue the use of opium, to which he had been often compelled to resort, to relieve the intolerable anguish of his complaint. Such was the vigor of his constitution, that his appetite at once returned, his strength increased, and he was able to exert all the force of his genius.

During this interval, he received an interesting letter from his old friend, Dr. Ezra Stiles, President of Yale College, asking him to give his portrait for the college library, if he had one to spare. Having made his request, the good president proceeded to ask him a question. He said that, as long he had known Dr. Franklin, he had never learned his sentiments respecting religion. "I wish," he added "to know the opinion of my venerable friend concerning Jesus of Nazareth. He will not impute this to impertinence or improper curiosity, in one, who, for so many years has continued to love, estimate, and reverence his abilities and literary character, with an ardor and affection bordering on adoration."

Dr. Franklin replied, that, with regard to the portrait, he had not one in his possession worthy of a place in the library of Yale, but that an excellent artist had lately arrived, and, if he would undertake the work, he would cheerfully pay the expense. "But," said he, "he must not delay setting about it, or I may slip through his fingers, for I am now in my eighty-fifth year, and very infirm." He then answered the question with respect to his religious opinions, remarking that this was the first time he had ever been questioned on the subject :

"Here is my creed. I believe in one God, the Creator of the universe. That he governs it by his Providence. That he ought to be worshipped. That the most acceptable service we render to him is doing good to his other children. That the soul of man is immortal, and will be treated with justice in another life respecting its conduct in this.   These I take to be the fundamental points in all sound religion, and I regard them as you do in whatever sect I meet with them.

"As to Jesus of Nazareth, my opinion of whom you particularly desire, I think his system of morals and his religion, as he left them to us, the best the world ever saw, or is like to see ; but I apprehend it has received various corrupting changes, and I have, with most of the present Dissenters in England, some doubts as to his Divinity; though it is a question I do not dogmatize upon, having never studied it, and think it needless to busy myself with it now, when I expect soon an opportunity of knowing the truth with less trouble.   I see no harm, however, in its being believed, if that belief has the good consequence, as probably it has, of making his doctrines more respected and more observed ; especially as I do not perceive that the Supreme takes it amiss, by distinguishing the unbelievers in his government of the world with any peculiar marks of his displeasure.

"I shall only add, respecting myself, that, having experienced the goodness of that Being in conducting me prosperously through a long life, I have no doubt of its continuance in the next, though without the smallest conceit of meriting such goodness.

"P. S. I confide, that you will not expose me to criticisms and censures by publishing any part of this communication to you.   I have ever let others enjoy their religious sentiments, without reflecting on them for those that appeared to me unsupportable or even absurd.   All sects here, and we have a great variety, have experienced my good will in assisting them with subscriptions for the building their new places of worship ; and, as I have never opposed any of their doctrines, I hope to go out of the world in peace with them all."

On one of the last days of this respite from suffering, he wrote a brief, last letter to his sister, apologizing for the crookedness of the lines, which, he said, was owing to the awkwardness of writing in bed.

Mr. Jefferson, who had recently returned from France, passed through Philadelphia, in March, 1790, on his way to join the government at New York as Secretary of State.   He has left us an interesting, but too brief, account of his interview with Dr. Franklin on this occasion.

"I called," he says, "on the venerable and beloved Franklin. He was then on the bed of sickness from which he never rose. My recent return from a country in which he had left so many friends, and the perilous convulsions to which they had been exposed, revived all his anxieties to know what part they had taken, and what had been their course, and what their fate. He went over all in succession, with a rapidity and animation almost too much for his strength. When all his inquiries were satisfied, and a pause took place, I told him I had learned with much pleasure that since his return to America, he had been occupied in preparing for the world the history of his own life. 'I cannot say much of that,' said he, 'but I will give you a sample of what I shall leave,' and he directed his little grandson (William Bache), who was standing by the bedside, to hand him a paper from the table, to which he pointed. He did so, and the Doctor putting it into my hands, desired me to take it and read it at my leisure. It was about a quire of folio paper, written in a large and running hand, very like his own. I looked into it slightly, then shut it, and said I would accept his permission to read it, and would carefully return it. He said, 'No, keep it.' Not certain of his meaning, I again looked into it, folded it for my pocket, and said again, I would certainly return it. 'No,' said he, 'keep it.' I put it into my pocket, and shortly after took leave of him."*

The manuscript proved to be Franklin's narrative of his negotiation with Lord Howe and Mrs. Howe, in London, in 1774. It had been well if Mr. Jefferson had complied with Dr. Franklin's charge to "keep it." We should then have had a perfect copy. He thought it his duty, however, to give up the paper to William Temple Franklin, to whom Dr. Franklin had bequeathed all his papers.

Elsewhere, Mr. Jefferson says of this interview: "I found our friend, Doctor Franklin, in his bed—cheerful and free from pain, but still in his bed. He took a lively interest in the details I gave him of your revolution. I observed his face often flushed in the course of it. He is much emaciated."†

No important change appeared in his condition until about sixteen days before his death, when he became feverish, though he was

---

* Works of Jefferson, i., 108.   † Ibid., iii. 184.

still free from severe pain. Three or four days after, he complained of pain in the left side of the chest, which increased until it became acute, and was attended by cough and difficulty of breathing. The manner in which his attack of pleurisy had broken up, nearly sixty years before, was prophetic of the issue of his present disorder. The pleurisy terminated in an abscess of the lungs, which finally broke, and he was almost suffocated by the abundance and suddenness of the discharge. A few years after, a second attack ended in a similar manner. It was an abscess of the lungs which now gave him so much distress. His anguish was such, at times, that a groan escaped him, for which he would offer a kind of apology to those who stood round his bed. He said he feared he did not bear his pain as he ought, and that, no doubt, his present sufferings were designed to wean him from a world in which he was no longer competent to act his part. To a clerical friend who witnessed one of his paroxysms, and was about to retire, he said, " Oh, no; don't go away. These pains will soon be over. They are for my good ; and, besides, what are the pains of a moment in comparison with the pleasures of eternity ?" He had a picture of Christ on the cross placed so that he could conveniently look at it as he lay in bed. " That," he would say, " is the picture of one who came into the world to teach men to love one another."*

. His anguish was not continuous ; there were hours in which he conversed cheerfully with his friends, and attended to the requests of visitors. Nine days before he died, he wrote a letter of some length to Mr. Jefferson, in which he gave certain information desired by Jefferson respecting our northeastern boundary, as defined in the negotiations at Paris in 1783. This letter is written with all his wonted clearness and obliging fullness of detail, showing memory and other faculties of mind still unimpaired.

Five days before his death, the pain in the chest, the cough, and the difficulty of breathing suddenly ceased. His family hoped now that the crisis was passed and that he would recover ; but he was not himself deceived. He insisted on getting up that his bed might be made, in order, as he said, that he might " die in a decent manner." His daughter said that she hoped he would get well, and live many years. " I hope not," he replied. When he had

* Weems, p. 237.

again been removed to his bed, the abscess burst, and he discharged a great quantity of matter; but before he could clear his lungs, his strength failed, the organs of respiration became oppressed, and he breathed with great difficulty. Some one advising him to change his position so that he might breathe easier, he said, "A dying man can do nothing easy." These were the last of his words that have been recorded. He soon sunk into a lethargy from which he never revived. At eleven o'clock at night, April 17th, 1790, surrounded by his family and nearest friends, he quietly expired, aged eighty-four years, three months, and eleven days.

His last look, it is recorded, was cast upon the picture of Christ. He died with his eyes fixed upon it. His countenance recovered, at once, all its wonted serenity and benignity, and he lay like a good old man in a gentle slumber. To use the ancient language, he had fallen asleep in Jesus, and rested in hope of a blessed immortality.

Four days after, his body was borne to the tomb, and laid by the side of his wife. Philadelphia followed him to his last resting-place. The newspapers which, a month before, had given the world the last effusion of his genius, tell us how the city honored the remains of " our late learned and illustrious citizen." The following was the order of the procession:

" All the Clergy of the city, before the Corpse.
The Corpse,
carried by Citizens.
The Pall, supported by the President of the State,
the Chief-Justice, the President of the Bank,
Samuel Powell, William Bingham, and
David Rittenhouse, Esquires.
Mourners,
Consisting of the family of the deceased, with a
number of particular friends.
The Secretary and Members of the Supreme
Executive Council.
The Speaker and Members of the General Assembly,
Judges of the Supreme Court,
And other Officers of Government.
The Gentlemen of the Bar.

The Mayor and Corporation of the City of
Philadelphia.
The Printers of the city, with their Journeymen
and Apprentices.
The Philosophical Society.
The College of Physicians.
The Cincinnati.
The College of Philadelphia.
Sundry other Societies—together with a numerous and respectable
body of Citizens.

" The concourse of spectators was greater than ever was known
on a like occasion. It is computed that not less than 20,000 persons
attended and witnessed the funeral. The order and silence which
prevailed, during the Procession, deeply evinced the heartfelt sense,
entertained by all classes of citizens, of the unparralleled virtues,
talents, and services of the deceased."*

The mourning for the departure of Franklin does not appear to
have been quite unanimous even in the Council of Philadelphia :
two members of which signified their intention *not* to wear crape on
their arms in his honor.   Whether, however, this was a Quakerly
scruple or a dislike of the man, does not appear in the record.

Congress, then in session at New York, having been formally
notified of his death, Mr. James Madison addressed the House of
Representatives, April 22 :

" Mr. SPEAKER : As we have been informed, not only through
the channel of the newspapers, but by a more direct communication,
of the decease of an illustrious character, whose native genius has
rendered distinguished services to the cause of science and of mankind in general ; and whose patriotic exertions have contributed in
a high degree to the independence and prosperity of this country
in particular ; the occasion seems to call upon us to pay some tribute to his memory expressive of the tender veneration his country
feels for such distinguished merit.   I therefore move the following
resolution :

" The House being informed of the decease of BENJAMIN FRANK-
LIN, a citizen whose native genius was not more an ornament to
human nature than his various exertions of it have been precious

* Gazette of the United States, April 28, 1790.

to science, to freedom, and to his country, do resolve, as a mark of the veneration due to his memory, that the members wear the customary badge of mourning for one month.'

The resolution was unanimously passed, without further remark. The brevity and decency of these proceedings present a pleasing contrast to the lavish and prolonged eulogium of later times.

Among the public addresses delivered at the time upon Dr. Franklin, was one by Dr. Ezra Stiles to the professors and students of Yale College, who was not prevented by Franklin's heterodox letter from doing ample justice to his eminent qualities of heart and mind. The Philosophical Society, which had met so often of late years in Dr. Franklin's new library, appointed one of their number, Dr. William Smith, to pronounce a eulogy of his character and services, which was delivered and published.

It was to be expected that the France of 1790 would receive the tidings of Franklin's death with emotion. Honors rendered to *him*, the great Plebeian, the sage of the new Republic, were so much dishonor put upon hereditary rank. Mirabeau, whom Franklin had known in Paris as a wild man about town, writing for his maintenance, was then the foremost man of France, riding in the whirlwind and directing the storm of revolution. June 11th, Mirabeau rose, at the opening of the National Legislature, and spoke as follows :

" Franklin is dead !. The genius, that freed America and poured a flood of light over Europe, has returned to the bosom of the Divinity.

" The sage whom two worlds claim as their own, the man for whom the history of science and the history of empires contend with each other, held, without doubt, a high rank in the human race.

" Too long have political cabinets taken formal note of the death of those who were great only in their funeral panegyrics. Too long has the etiquette of courts prescribed hypocritical mourning. Nations should wear mourning only for their benefactors. The representatives of nations should recommend to their homage none but the heroes of humanity.

" The Congress has ordained, throughout the United States, a mourning of one month for the death of Franklin ; and, at this moment, America is paying this tribute of veneration and gratitude to one of the fathers of her Constitution.

" Would it not become us, gentlemen, to join in this religious act, to bear a part in this homage, rendered, in the face of the world, both to the rights of man, and to the philosopher who has most contributed to extend their sway over the whole earth ? Antiquity would have raised altars to this mighty genius, who, to the advantage of mankind, compassing in his mind the heavens and the earth, was able to restrain alike thunderbolts and tyrants. Europe, enlightened and free, owes at least a token of remembrance and regret to one of the greatest men who have ever been engaged in the service of philosophy and of liberty.

"I propose that it be decreed, that the National Assembly, during three days, shall wear mourning for Benjamin Franklin."

Rochefoucauld and Lafayette both sprang to their feet to second the proposal, but there was no need of seconding it; it was carried by acclamation. The Assembly further decreed, that the address of Mirabeau should be printed, and that the president, M. Siéyes, should communicate to the Congress of the United States the resolution which the National Assembly had passed. M. Siéyes performed the duty assigned him by addressing a letter to the President of the United States, which was full of the feeling of the hour.

" The National Assembly," he wrote, " have not been stopped in their decree by the consideration that Franklin was a stranger. Great men are the fathers of universal humanity; their loss ought to be felt, as a common misfortune, by all the tribes of the great human family; and it belongs without doubt to a nation still affected by all the sentiments which accompany the achievement of their liberty, and which owes its enfranchisement essentially to the progress of the public reason, to be the first to give the example of the filial gratitude of the people towards their true benefactors. * * * It will be remembered, that every success which he obtained in his important negotiation, was applauded and celebrated (so to express it) all over France, as so many crowns conferred on genius and virtue.

" Even then the sentiment of our rights existed in the bottom of our souls. It was easily perceived that it feelingly mingled in the interest which we took in behalf of America, and in the public vows which we preferred for your liberty.

" At last the hour of the French has arrived; we love to think, that the citizens of the United States have not regarded with indifference our steps towards liberty. Twenty-six millions of men breaking their chains, and seriously occupied in giving themselves a durable constitution, are not unworthy of the esteem of a generous people, who have preceded them in that noble career.

"We hope they will learn with interest the funeral homage which we have rendered to the Nestor of America. May this solemn act of fraternal friendship serve more and more to bind the tie, which ought to unite two free nations! May the common enjoyment of liberty shed itself over the whole globe, and become an indissoluble chain of connection among all the people of the earth! For ought they not to perceive, that they will march more steadfastly and more certainly to their true happiness, in understanding and loving each other, than in being jealous and fighting?

"May the Congress of the United States and the National Assembly of France be the first to furnish this fine spectacle to the world! And may the individuals of the two nations connect themselves by a mutual affection, worthy of the friendship which unites the two men, at this day most illustrious by their exertions for liberty, WASHINGTON and LAFAYETTE!"

Washington, in obedience to a resolution of Congress, communicated to the National Assembly "the peculiar sensibility of Congress to the tribute paid to the memory of Franklin by the enlightened and free representatives of a great nation."

The city of Paris, the revolutionary clubs, and the Academy of Sciences, each held a ceremonial in honor of the departed patriot. On the day of the municipal celebration, almost every one who appeared in the streets wore some badge of mourning, and the great rotunda of the Grain Market, where the orator of the day delivered his address, was hung with black, and the whole audience were clad in mourning. The Society of Printers of Paris, on the same day, paid peculiar honors to the memory of their illustrious craftsman. A bust of Franklin, crowned with a wreath, was placed upon a column in a spacious hall. Around the base of the column were arranged cases of type and a printing press. While one of their number was pronouncing an oration in honor of Franklin, others were employed in setting it in type; and when it was done, impressions were struck off and distributed among the crowd.

One of the club celebrations, on the same occasion, attracted particular notice. "The Friends of the Revolution and Humanity, we are told, "assembled at the *Café Procope*, and wishing to render all the honors to the memory of the celebrated Franklin, which are so justly due to it, ordered all the glasses to be covered with crape, and the inner apartment to be hung with black. On the door towards the street, was the following inscription:

"FRANKLIN EST MORT!*

"At one end of the apartment was placed his bust, crowned with oak-leaves; and at the foot of the pedestal was engraven the word

"VIR.†

"Two cypresses elevated their melancholy branches above it; on the two sides of it were the celestial and terrestial globes, charts, etc.; and under it, a serpent biting his tail, as an emblem of immortality.

"An orator read a simple but pathetic discourse, in which he recounted the benefits this illustrious Philosopher had conferred upon mankind; and, in order to honor his *manes* in a manner still more worthy of him, on the following day, a quantity of bread bought by subscription, in which every one was eager to concur, was distributed among the people."

Such honors were paid in France to the memory of Franklin. One tear of Jane Mecom, sorrowing at her house in Boston for the loss of the best of brothers, was worth them all. "Who that know and love you," she had written to him in her last letter, "can bear the thought of surviving you in this gloomy world?" She rejoined him four years after, aged eighty-two.

CHAPTER VII.

SINCE.

I WOULD fain continue my story by following this vivid Intelligence into the land of spirits. Would that I could tell the reader where the great soul of Franklin went, at eleven o'clock in the evening of April 17th, 1790, when it glided so silently from its

---

* Franklin is dead.

† A Latin word meaning, one who is eminently a MAN.

ruined tenement of clay! Where is it now? What is it now? How is it now employed? If his early dream of the inferior gods has in it any thing of truth, happy the region governed by so large, so wise, so tolerant, so benevolent a mind! One thing only we may certainly know : that, in a universe ordered with such strict economy, wherein not a leaf of the forest nor a drop of the ocean is ever destroyed or wasted, from which no most insignificant atom can ever be separated or permanently diverted from its use, this supreme creation, a great, regenerated human soul, cannot, in any sense of the word, be lost.* *Somewhere,* the soul of Franklin is happy, blest, and busy. Death cannot have changed its essential character, nor diminished its power. It was the same wise, just, and benevolent soul the day after it left the body, as it was on the day it reveled in mockery of the Georgian's mad defense of slavery.

These are vain speculations ; but we cannot help sometimes peering *at* the vail which no eye of mortal can penetrate. Curiosity will conjecture when knowledge is impossible. It remains only for me to satisfy the curiosity of the reader respecting some of the re-sults of Franklin's schemes to do good, which continued to operate after his death, and respecting the subsequent career of the persons who were dearest to him in his life.

Some readers may care to know how it has fared with the little library presented to the town of Franklin in 1784.† Mr. S. Fiske, postmaster of the town in 1862, obligingly furnishes them with the information. The books, presented by Dr. Franklin, numbering one hundred and sixteen volumes, reached the town in 1786. During the lifetime of Dr. Emmons, then the pastor of the church,

---

* This idea, I have since observed, was the ground of Franklin's expectation of a life beyond the grave. In one of his letters of 1785, there is the following passage :

"When I observe, that there is great frugality, as well as wisdom, in God's works, since he has been evidently sparing both of labor and materials; for by the various wonderful inventions of propagation, he has provided for the continual peopling his world with plants and animals, without being at the trouble of repeated new creations; and by the natural reduction of compound substances to their original elements, capable of being employed in new compositions, he has prevented the necessity of creating new matter: so that the earth, water, air, and perhaps fire, which being compounded, form wood, do, when the wood is dissolved, return, and again become air, earth, fire, and water; I say, that, when I see nothing annihilated, and not even a drop of water wasted, I cannot suspect the annihilation of souls, or believe, that he will suffer the daily waste of millions of minds ready made that now exist, and put himself to the continual trouble of making new ones. Thus finding myself to exist in the world, I believe I shall, in some shape or other, lways exist; and, with all the inconveniences human life is liable to, I shall not object to a new edition of mine; hoping, however, that the *errata* of the last may be corrected."

† Mentioned on p. 526 of this volume.

the books were taken excellent care of, but after his death some of
them were lost through the dishonesty of those to whom they were
lent, and the neglect of persons who had charge of them. A considerable number of the books remain to this day, which, by a vote
of the town in 1859, are in the custody of the Franklin Library
Association, formed three or four years since, and now possessing
a library of a thousand volumes. The original stock of books was
increased to two hundred and forty-one by the addition to it of the
" Social Library" of the town of Franklin. This occurred about
the year 1800. The change in the public taste is marked by the
large proportion of works of instruction and entertainment which
were in the Social Library, compared with the list selected by Dr.
Price in 1784. Dr. Price's catalogue shows 69 theological volumes
in 116. The Social Library had but 20 theological in 125. The
catalogue of the present library would, doubtless, show a still further decrease in the proportion of theological works. It must be
owned that the proprietors of the Social Library made a far more
enlightened selection of books for a country town than Dr. Price.
It contained history by Robertson, Rollin, Josephus, and Montesquieu, several works of travel, biographies of Pitt, Charles XII.,
Peter the Great, and Putnam, and one novel, the Vicar of Wake-
field. Franklin's gift was a permanent benefit to the town, since
it promoted, perhaps suggested, the formation of the present
flourishing Library Association. There is only one thing more
important in the United States than town and village libraries. I
hope to live to see the day when every village of a hundred inhabitants will have one, on the admirable plan devised by Franklin for
the library at Philadelphia.*

The hundred pounds left by Dr. Franklin to the Boston Free
Schools for the purchase of medals, has accomplished its purpose.
Having stimulated and rewarded application for seventy-three
years, it is stimulating application to-day. Many of the most eminent citizens of Boston boast of possessing the Franklin medal.
The fund now amounts to one thousand dollars, which produces
sixty dollars a year for the object designated in Dr. Franklin's will.

Mrs. Bache obeyed her father's injunction with regard to the

* The plan is fully detailed, with all the rules and regulations, in the Catalogue of the Philadelphia Library, which is for sale at the Library. The catalogue itself would be a valuable aid
in the selection of books.

diamonds which adorned the miniature of Louis XVI. The outer circles of diamonds she caused to be removed and sold, and on the proceeds of the sale she and her husband made the tour of Europe. The miniature now appears with only one circle of stones, set close together, numbering about a hundred and fifty. It is (1862) in the custody of the Honorable W. J. Duane, of Philadelphia.

The bequest of the old debts to the Pennsylvania Hospital was productive of nothing but trouble to the managers of that institution. Seven years after the death of Franklin a meeting of the directors was called expressly to consider how the Hospital should be delivered from this source of perplexity. At this meeting, we are told, "an extract from the last will and testament of Dr. Benjamin Franklin was produced by the managers, and read. The minutes of the managers respecting this case were then read, and likewise the report of the committee appointed by them to adjust the balances of the said ledger, and the answers they received from a number of persons to whom they have applied, and who appear to be in debt. An alphabetical list of the debts taken by the same committee was also inspected, and a general view of the ledger taken by the contributors, from which it appears that many of the debts are small; numbers of them are due from persons unknown, and all of them from thirty to sixty years old, which precludes every hope of recovering as much as will answer the demands exhibited against the decedent. It is, therefore, the unanimous opinion of the contributors present, that the legacy cannot with safety be accepted. Under these impressions it is agreed that the managers should return the ledger to Dr. Franklin's executors, with a copy of this minute."*

Even the sedan-chair which Dr. Franklin bequeathed to the Hospital, the managers have not taken care to preserve. No trace of it can now be discovered. His armonica is still possessed by one of his descendants, though in a sadly damaged plight.

The house in which he died stood until the year 1812, when it was torn down. The carriage-way which led to it is now Franklin Court.

The bequest of a thousand pounds sterling to Boston and to Philadelphia for loans to young mechanics, has not been as useful as Dr. Franklin hoped it would be. For several years after his

* Works of William Cobbett, viii., 191.

death the trust appears to have been carelessly administered in both cities. The sums lent were, in many instances, not repaid, and the trustees neglected to exact payment from the borrower or his sureties. In later years, the trustees of the Boston fund were more rigorous in compelling repayment, and it then appeared that the sureties as often had to pay as the borrower. The consequence of this was, that sureties were obtained with so much difficulty that the number of loans averaged only one in a year. In truth, Franklin, when he made his bequest, had in mind his old Junto days; when the loan of forty or fifty pounds gave a mechanic his Opportunity. In these times, when operations are carried on upon such a prodigious scale, a loan of two hundred dollars is insufficient. A good mechanic, unmarried, can save such a sum from the wages of a single year. Would it not be obeying the *spirit* of Dr. Franklin's directions to increase the amount of the loans from two hundred dollars to two thousand? The fund in both cities has increased to an amount which would warrant loans of two thousand dollars. The Philadelphia fund, I believe, is now more than thirty thousand dollars; the Boston fund nearly fifty thousand. If Dr. Franklin could have foreseen the change destined to be made in all human labors by the steam-engine, would he not have adapted his legacy to the coming order of things? Should his benevolent intentions be totally frustrated by a too close observance of the letter of his will?[*]

A few words respecting the subsequent career of Franklin's relations and descendants may be in place here.

Governor William Franklin lived in London to the age of eighty-two. After the revolution he married again, but, I believe, left no issue by his second marriage. Aaron Burr, when he was in London, in 1807, renewed his acquaintance with the former governor of his native province. He died in 1813.

William Temple Franklin rejoined his father in England, after the death of Dr. Franklin, and never again resided in America. Little is known of his career in England, except that he edited an edition of his grandfather's works, in which appeared, for the first time, many of his most interesting papers. He died at Paris in 1823.

Mr. William Duane, of Philadelphia, great grandson of Dr.

[*] See "Mill's Political Economy," American Edition, i., 283, on the limitations of the power of bequest.

Franklin, favors the reader with some particulars respecting the descendants of Dr. Franklin's only daughter, Mrs. Bache:

"The children of Benjamin and Deborah Franklin were Francis Folger and Sarah.

"*Francis Folger Franklin* was born June 20, 1732, and died November 21, 1736. His father, in a letter written many years after his death, speaks of him as having been the finest child that he had ever seen, of whom he could not then think without a sigh. I have his likeness.

"*Sarah Franklin* was born September 11, 1744; married October 29, 1767, Richard Bache, a native of Settle, Yorkshire, England, and died October 5, 1808.

"Mr. Bache was born September 12, 1739, being the eighteenth child of William Bache. His mother's maiden name was Mary Blechynden. She was the second wife. Richard Bache died July 29, 1811.

"Richard and Sarah Bache had eight children: (1) Benjamin Franklin, (2) William, (3) Sarah, (4) Elizabeth Franklin, (5) Louis, (6) Deborah, (7) Richard, and (8) Sarah.

"(1) Benjamin Franklin Bache, born August 12, 1769, was educated in France and Geneva, under the supervision of his grandfather. He was the first publisher and editor of the Aurora newspaper. He married Margaret Hartman Markoe, a native of Santa Cruz, W. L, of a Danish family, and died in Philadelphia, of the yellow fever, September 10, 1798. They had four children: Franklin, Richard, Benjamin, and Hartman; of whom the second and third died unmarried.

"Franklin Bache is a physician, and Professor of Chemistry in Jefferson Medical College. He married Aglaë Dotàdiè, a native of Philadelphia, of French origin, and has had a large family. Dr. Bache is one of the authors of the American Pharmacopœia.

"His brother Richard died a captain of ordnance, in the United States Army. He was the author of a volume of Travels in South America.

"Hartman Bache was educated at West Point, was appointed to the corps of Topographical Engineers, and is now colonel of engineers in the corps, as lately consolidated. He married Maria Meade, a sister of General George Meade, and has a family.

"(2) William Bache, born May 31, 1773, was a physician, and at one time Surveyor of the Port of Philadelphia. In November,

1797, he married Catharine Wistar, a sister of the distinguished Dr. Caspar Wistar, of Philadelphia. He died in 1818. They had three children: Sarah, Benjamin Franklin, Emma Mary, and Catharine Wistar. Sarah, the eldest, married the Rev. Charles Hodge, a professor in the Princeton Theological Seminary. She died in December, 1849, leaving a large family. Three of her sons are clergymen in the Presbyterian Church.

"Emma Mary died young. The other two children are living. Benjamin F. Bache is a physician and surgeon in the United States Navy. He has been twice married, and has a large family.

"(3) Sarah Bache, born December 1, 1775, died August 17, 1776.

"(4) Elizabeth Franklin Bache, born September 10, 1777, was married on January 9, 1800, to John Edwin Harwood, a native of England. She died in the year 1820. Of her four children, three died young. The survivor is Andrew Aken Harwood, at present a Commodore in the United States Navy, in command of the Navy Yard at Washington City. He has been twice married, and has a family.

"(5) Louis Bache, born October 7, 1779, was twice married. (His wives were Marianne Swift and Esther Ege, both of Bucks county, Pennsylvania.) He had three children by his first wife, and one by the second. Of these, William, son of the first wife, and Theophylact, son of the second, are living. Louis died in 1819. He was called after Louis XVI.

"(6) Deborah Bache, born October 1, 1781, was married December 31, 1805, to William John Duane, and died February 12, 1863. She had nine children, of whom five died before her, three of them single, and two married, who each left a son.

"(7) Richard Bache (2d), born March 11, 1784, was married in April, 1805, to Sophia Dallas, daughter of Alexander James Dallas. He was a lawyer, and died in 1848, at Galveston, Texas. He was a member of the Senate of Texas, and gave the sole negative vote in that body against its union with the United States.

"He had nine children, the eldest of whom is Alexander Dallas Bache, the Superintendent of the Coast Survey. The eldest daughter, Mary Blechynden Bache, was married to the Hon. Robert J. Walker. Two sons, George N. and Richard, were officers of the

United States Navy, and were drowned whilst engaged in the coast survey.

"(8) Sarah Bache, born September 12, 1788, was married, in 1813, to Francis Sergeant, Esq., afterwards one of the Judges of the Supreme Court of Pennsylvania. She died October 6, 1863. They had four children : three sons and a daughter. One of the sons died young, and another died unmarried in 1858. The daughter, Frances, married Dr. Christopher Grant Perry, son of the first Commodore Perry, of Newport, R. I., and has a family.

"The present number of Dr. Franklin's descendants (1863) is one hundred and ten."

Ten of whom, as before mentioned, are in the military or naval service of the United States.

Of the numerous descendants of Dr. Franklin, one, at least, inherits a share of his humor. It is Mr. William Duane, of Philadelphia, formerly the editor of that quaint and amusing periodical, *Bizarre*. Several of Mr. Duane's satirical pieces have had universal currency.*

---

* The following *jeu d'esprit*, by Mr. Duane, published at the beginning of the rebellion, and designed to ridicule the extravagance of Southern newspapers, is much in Franklin's manner. It completely " took in" several of the Northern editors, who published it as a genuine effusion of Southern journalism :

"Extracts from very late New Orleans Papers, just received in this city,

" By the Pigeon Express.

" 'All the New England troops now in Washington city are negroes, excepting three or four drummer boys. Gen. B. F. Butler, who commands them, is a native of Liberia. Our elderly readers must recollect " Old Ben," the barber, who kept his shop for so many years in Poydras street, and then emigrated to Africa with a small competency. This General Butler, of Lowell, is his son.'—*N. O. Picayune.*

" 'Several of our most eminent lawyers have united in an opinion that the ex-members of President Buchanan's cabinet have power to issue treasury notes in the name of the (late) United States. The American Bank Note Company, of New York and Philadelphia, are now preparing the plates. These notes are to be issued to our merchants at ten cents on the dollar, and their creditors in the Northern cities are to receive them at par. Since the announcement of this arrangement things wear a bright and cheerful air in our business circles.'—*N. O. Delta.*

" 'Our readers will probably remember that we last week informed them that General Scott had left the service of Mr. A. Lincoln, and joined the Confederate States : indeed, they must remember it, for the noise of the one hundred guns which they fired is still booming in our ears. We have just learned that his salary will be one hundred and twenty thousand dollars a year, payable in post notes. As the General left Washington city so suddenly as not to take a change of linen with him, the City of Richmond has advanced him his first month's salary, in the new and beautiful notes of twenty-five cents, issued by that community.'—*N. O. True Delta.*

" 'Our mint is now running night and day with a double set of hands. It is most fortunate—nay, most providential, that the old dies were all preserved. The mint is now engaged in coining half and quarter dollars of the years 1840 to 1850. The alloy is twenty-five per cent. of copper, which gives these coins a rich appearance. They are to be circulated at the North by such of our citizens as visit Newport and Saratoga this summer. Judge Brown is to take on a large amount of them to the latter place.'—*N. O. True Delta.*

Great as was the fame of Franklin in his lifetime, it cannot be said to have diminished since his death. Posterity has ratified the estimation in which he was held by contemporaries. As there are few counties in the Union which have not a town named Franklin, so there are few towns of any magnitude, which do not possess a Franklin street or a Franklin square, a Franklin hotel, a Franklin bank, a Franklin fire-engine, a Franklin lyceum, a Franklin lodge, or a Franklin charitable association. His bust and his portrait are only less universal than those of Washington, and most large cities contain something of the nature of a monument to Franklin. The familiarity of every one with his form and countenance has rendered it difficult to procure for these volumes any likeness of him which should have the interest of novelty. Mr. Charles Sumner has recently informed the public, that in the imperial library of Paris he counted himself more than one hundred portraits of Franklin.* And even this collection is exceeded, as I have already stated, by that of one of his descendants in Philadelphia, which numbers one hundred and fifty.

The typographical societies of the United States, of which there is one in most of our large cities, have long been accustomed to celebrate the anniversary of Dr. Franklin's birth by a dinner or a ball, or by assembling to listen to an address upon a topic appropriate to the occasion. In New York, this anniversary is the great festival of the year to the printers and their families. It was celebrated in the year 1864 with unusual splendor and enthusiasm.

"'Our readers have been already apprised by us that Mr. Lincoln is the victim of the dreadful demon of intemperance. We have since learned that all of his cabinet tread in his steps in this particular. An amusing anecdote will illustrate this. A clerk having occasion to procure the signature of Secretary —— (we will give his name in our evening edition), found that worthy fast asleep in his chair, with *documents* in the shape of empty champagne bottles all round him. He was so sound asleep that he could not be awakened, so placing a pen in his hand, he placed his own hand over it, and traced his signature in the proper place. This young man is a white nephew of Gov. Floyd, of Virginia, and the Governor is so indignant, that he has threatened to leave his name out of his will.'—*N. O. True Delta.*

"'A leading merchant, in Grand Gulf, Mississippi, whilst walking the streets, thinking of having a Southern Commercial Convention in that city, picked up a piece of printed paper, which proved to be a leaf of Shakspeare's Dramatic Works, a writer of whom he had never heard. The first words that struck his eye were: "Base is the slave that pays!" The vigor of this expression so pleased him, that he intends, as soon as the direct trade with England is opened, to send out for a copy of Shakspeare's works, regardless of expense.'—*Crescent City.*"

Philadelphia Press, Nov. 7, 1861.

* Atlantic Monthly for November, 1863.

Boston has shown a peculiar appreciation of the merits of its most illustrious citizen. As early as .1793, a new square in that city was named Franklin, and Mr. Charles Bulfinch, one of the first of Americans, if not the first, who made architecture his profession, erected the urn in honor of Franklin which still adorns the square. In 1827, the inscription on the stone that covered the remains of Franklin's parents, having become almost illegible, several of the public spirited citizens of Boston caused a monument of granite to be erected in its stead, on which the original inscription was deeply engraved, with this addition :

" The marble tablet,
Bearing the above inscription,
Having been dilapidated by the ravages of time,
A number of citizens,
Entertaining the most profound veneration
For the memory of the illustrious
Benjamin Franklin,
And desirous of reminding succeeding generations,
That he was born in Boston, A. D. MDCCVL,
Erected this
Obelisk
Over the graves of his parents.
MDCCCXXVII."

But of all the honors paid to the memory of a man by his native city, nothing has ever equaled the homage rendered to the character of Franklin by the citizens of Boston, in 1856, when the statue by Horatio Greenough, which stands in front of the City Hall, was inaugurated. The project, suggested by Mr. Robert C. Winthrop, in a lecture before the Massachusetts Charitable Mechanics' Association, in 1853, was taken up by that society with enthusiasm, and carried out with a promptitude truly Bostonian. Two thousand persons subscribed the requisite fund, in sums varying from a few cents to three hundred dollars. September 17th, 1856, was the day named for the inauguration. It was a universal holiday, ushered in by the ringing of bells and the discharge of cannon. For several weeks previous, the people had been preparing for the occasion, and when the day arrived, Boston was hung with decorations that spoke of Franklin and of the Nation he had assisted to call into being. The grave of his parents was covered with evergreens and beautiful wreaths of flowers. The place where he was born, the church in which he was christened, the site of his brother James's printing-office and of his father's soap and candle shop, the urn in Franklin Square, the site of the residence of his Uncle Benjamin, and of the house of Mrs. Mecom, were all appropriately marked and decorated. Sentences from Poor Richard fluttered in every street, of which the most frequently quoted were such as these : " He that hath a trade, hath an estate." " One to-day is worth two to-morrow." " Worth makes the man." " Knowledge is power." " A stitch in time saves nine." " Don't give too much for the whistle." " It is hard for an empty sack to stand upright." " Time is money." The public buildings, the theaters, the hotels, the stores, and an immense number of private houses, were profusely hung with flags, banners, streamers, and transparencies. Mr. Stephen Emmons, a lineal descendant of Uncle Benjamin, exhibited an ancient portrait of Dr. Franklin, bearing this inscription: " This picture was sent from London, July, 17, 1767, by Dr. Franklin, to my grandfather, Samuel Franklin, and has been in our family ever since." One house was adorned with a sentence from Franklin's private liturgy : " Help me to be faithful to my country, careful for its good, valiant for its defence, and obedient to its laws." Kites of every size and pattern brought to mind the sublime experiment in the fields of Philadelphia, and paintings of a wheel-barrow loaded with paper told of the time when Franklin had wheeled home the paper for his new printing-office.

The procession was marvelous.   It was five miles in length. First, marched the uniformed militia of Boston : two regiments of infantry, a battalion of dragoons, and a battery of artillery.   Then, the firemen, brilliant with red flannel and glazed helmets, with their engines gay with ribbons and wreaths ; next, the official personages of state and town, the orator and chaplain of the day, and distinguished guests in carriages.   These having passed by, the specialty of the procession appeared : cars contributed and adorned by the mechanics of Boston, headed by the members of the Association under whose auspices the statue had been erected.

A car of the school-furniture makers, covered with a canopy of flags, contained sixteen children, ranged round their teacher, as in a village school.   The car of the Ames Manufacturing Company of Chicopee, at which the statue had been cast, exhibited pyramids of weapons and silver-ware, and some of the men bore on their shoulders busts in bronze of Washington and Franklin, cast at the Manufactory. In the car of the bakers, twelve men of that craft labored at their vocation in sight of the multitude, and scattered cakes and biscuit hot from the oven among the people. The sugar-refiners, two hundred of them, all in white aprons, followed a car drawn by eight horses, heaped high with barrels of sugar. An enterprising maker of furniture-polish, not unwilling to advertise his product, contributed a giant bottle, ten feet high, on a car drawn by four horses. The workers in iron, dressed in uniform and decorated with badges, exhibited massive cannon, heaps of shells, and a great coil of cable drawn by sixteen horses. The engine-builders had a superb locomotive drawn by twenty-four horses, a load of car-wheels by twelve, another locomotive by ten, and a sugar-mill by eight. The piano-makers, five hundred in number, contributed several magnificent cars, one of which was as interesting as it was gorgeous. It contained two pianos, one made a hundred and eighty-seven years before, and the other one hundred and fifty years after, the birth of Franklin; each attended by a man in the costume of the age in which it was constructed. Another car exhibited a barber-shop in full activity; another, a cooper-shop, with men at work. The printers, as was inevitable, came out in great force. One of their cars presented a printing-office of the time of Franklin's apprenticeship, with ancient printing-press, type-case, and black balls, with printers in the dress of the period; striking off and throwing among the crowd fac-simile copies of that number of the *Boston Courant* which first contained the name of Benjamin Franklin as publisher. Another car was a modern printing-office, from the press of which copies of a comic poem upon Franklin by Mr. Shillaber, the chronicler of Mrs. Partington's conversations with her promising son, Isaac, were scattered on every side. The car of the copper-plate printers threw showers of miniature portraits of Franklin among the people. Electricity was represented by cars containing some of the apparatus employed by Franklin and Priestley, telegraphic apparatus in operation, lightning-rods, an electrotyping machine, and a modern electrical machine which gave a shock to as many as chose to touch the dangling knobs. Forty-three loaded express wagons were part of the procession.

Carlyle speaks of the opera as an " explosion of all the upholsteries. This was an explosion of all the industries. No trade carried on in Boston was unrepresented.*

The trades were followed by the Masonic Orders and the Odd Fellows, with their glittering insignia; and these by the literary, philosophic, and charitable societies. At the end of the long line were the children of the public schools, thousands in number, the boys all in their Sunday best, the girls in white adorned with blue ribbons and badges, bouquets, and wreaths of flowers.

At two in the afternoon, the procession having passed by, a vast concourse of people gathered about the statue to listen to the oration of Mr. Winthrop and to behold the uncovering of the work. Noble justice was done by the orator to the character of Franklin, except in one particular. Mr. Winthrop regretted that "Franklin had not been a more earnest student of the Gospel of Christ." No man of his time studied it more earnestly. No man of his time exhibited in his conduct so complete, so uniform, so lovely a realization of the Christian ideal. He was the consummate Christian of his day.

At the appointed moment, the orator exclaimed, pointing to the monument:

"Let it be unvailed! Let the stars and stripes no longer conceal the form of one who was always faithful to his country's flag, and who did so much to promote the glorious cause in which it was first unfurled!"

The draping flags were removed, and the statue, in all the brightness of untarnished bronze, was exposed to view, amid the cheers of the people.

* The following is the list of them, as officially reported: "Agricultural implement makers, bell founders, box makers, belt makers, brick makers, boat builders, boot and shoe makers, book binders, bakers, brush makers, brass founders, brass finishers, carpenters, carriage makers, cork cutters, confectioners, clock makers, contractors, coppersmiths, coopers, die sinkers, engine builders (steam), engine builders (fire), furniture manufacturers, flour manufacturers, gas fixture manufacturers, gas meter manufacturers, gold beaters, gilders, hair dressers and wig makers, harness makers, hat makers and finishers, house carvers, house painters, iron founders, iron furniture makers, iron manufacturers, iron safe makers, jewelers, last makers, locksmiths, life preserver makers, masons, marble workers, musical instrument makers, organ builders, paper rulers, paper hanging makers, papier maché makers, printing press makers, piano-forte makers, picture frame makers, plumbers, rope makers, riggers, sail makers, shipwrights, ship builders, saw manufacturers, ship carvers, stove and furnace makers, sheet iron workers, sign painters, silversmiths, school furniture makers, sewing machine makers, stone cutters, sugar manufacturers, soapstone manufacturers, tailors, tinsmiths, trunk makers, type founders, turners, upholsterers, window shade manufacturers, wrought iron pipe manufacturers, wooden ware manufacturers."

" And now behold him," continued the orator, " by the magic power of native genius, once more restored to our sight ! Behold him in the enjoyment of his cherished wish,—' revisiting his native town and the grounds he used to frequent when a boy !' Behold him, re-appearing on the old school-house Green, which was the play-place of his early days,—henceforth to fulfill, in some degree, to the eye of every passer-by, the charming vision of the Faëry Queen—

" ' A spacious court they see,
Both plain and pleasant to be walked in,
Where them does meet a FRANKLIN fair and free.'

Behold him, with the fur collar and linings which were the habitual badge of the master printers of the olden times, and which many an ancient portrait exhibits as the chosen decorations of not a few of the old philosophers, too,—Galileo, Copernicus, and Kepler,— who held, like him, familiar commerce with the skies ! Behold him, with the scalloped pockets and looped buttons and long Quaker-like vest and breeches, in which he stood arraigned and reviled before the council of one monarch, and in which he proudly signed the treaty of alliance with another ! Behold him, with the ' fine crab-tree walking-stick' which he bequeathed to ' his friend and the friend of mankind, General Washington,'—saying so justly, that ' if it were a scepter, he has merited it, and would become it !' "

*   *   *   *   *   *   *   *   *   *

After a happy allusion to Franklin's remark upon the picture of the sun in the hall of the Convention of 1787,* Mr. Winthrop concluded :

" Yes, venerated sage, privileged to live on

" ' Till old experience did attain
To something like prophetic strain,'—

yes, that was, indeed, a rising sun, ' coming forth as a bridegroom out of his chamber, and rejoicing as a giant to run his course.' And a glorious course he has run, enlightening and illuminating, not our own land only, but every land on the wide surface of the earth—' and there is nothing hid from the heat thereof.' God, in

* See page 581 of this volume.

his infinite mercy, grant that by no failure of his blessing or of our prayers, of his grace or of our gratitude, of his protection or of our patriotism, that sun may be seen, while it has yet hardly entered on its meridian pathway, shooting madly from its sphere and hastening to go down in blackness or in blood, leaving the world in darkness and freedom in despair! And may the visible presence of the GREAT BOSTONIAN, restored once more to our sight, by something more than a fortunate coincidence, in this hour of our country's peril, serve not merely to ornament our streets, or to commemorate his services, or even to signalize our own gratitude,—but to impress afresh, day by day, and hour by hour, upon the hearts of every man and woman and child who shall gaze upon it, a deeper sense of the value of that Liberty, that Independence, that Union, and that Constitution, for all of which he was so early, so constant, and so successful a laborer!"

The ceremonies being ended, the people dispersed to enjoy the festivities of the occasion. Boston kept open house that day. The various societies, the several bodies of mechanics, and numberless private parties, dined together, and the noise of banqueting was everywhere heard. The firemen competed for silver trumpets on the common. In the evening, the city was illuminated, and there was a display of fire-works, ending with a representation, in fire and thunder, of the storming of Sevastopol.

Such were the honors paid to the memory of Benjamin Franklin, by his native city, sixty-six years after his death. The record of the proceedings, printed by authority of the city council, is an octavo volume of 412 pages.*

" Long life to Franklin's memory!" wrote Thomas Carlyle from his retreat on the banks of the Thames. " We add our little shout to that of the Bostoners in inaugurating their monument for him. ' Long life to the memory of all brave men,' to which prayer, if we could add only, ' speedy death to the memory of all who were not so,' it would be a comprehensive petition, and of salutary tendencies, in the epoch Barnum and Hudson!"

The elder D'Israeli used to say, that " the best monument to an author is a good edition of his works." Such a monument has been erected to the memory of Dr. Franklin by the pious fidelity and

---

* " Memorial of the Inauguration of the Statue of Franklin," Boston, 1857.

zeal of a Bostonian, Dr. Jared Sparks. The libraries, the public records, and the private collections of England, France, and the United States, were so diligently searched by Dr. Sparks, that, though seven previous editions of the works of Franklin had appeared, he was able to add to his publication the astonishing number of six hundred and fifty pieces of Dr. Franklin's composition never before collected, of which four hundred and fifty had never before appeared in print. To unwearied diligence in collecting, Dr. Sparks added an admirable tact in elucidating. His notes are always such as an intelligent reader would naturally desire; and they usually contain all the information needed for a perfect understanding of the matter in hand. Dr. Sparks's edition is a monument, at once, to the memory of Benjamin Franklin, and to his own diligence, tact, and faithfulness. In forming village libraries, those ten fascinating volumes should be among the very first selected. They contain more wit, humor, knowledge, and good sense, and these presented in a more engaging and popular style, than any other set of equal extent yet published in America.

CHAPTER VIII.

REFLECTIONS.

A LIFE like Franklin's solves the problem stated in the Faust of Goethe; which is, How shall a man become satisfied with his life? Neither self-culture, nor any less worthy kind of self-indulgence satisfies. Franklin would have said to the ennuied scholar, that which his life says to all cultivated men: *Communicate!* The Public Weal—it is an object great enough for the greatest intellect, difficult enough for the most eager spirit, interesting enough for the most ennuied soul.

One of the most surprising things ever said by Franklin occurs at the beginning of his Autobiography, where he declares, that if it were left to his choice, he should have no objection to live his life over again, even if he were not allowed the author's privilege of correcting in a second edition the faults of the first. He was sixty-five years of age when he penned this observation, which, he tells us, he had often uttered in conversation with his friends. I apprehend, that there have lived few men, even of the most fortunate, who, at the age of sixty-five, could have sincerely uttered such a sentiment as this. But even Franklin could only say, that he " should have no objection" to live his life over again —Franklin, who enjoyed, perhaps, as great a sum-total of happiness as was ever enjoyed in the compass of one human life. Such is the troubled lot of man on earth!

As he contemplated his own career with such unusual compla-cency, so contemporaries regarded it with an unusual unanimity of approval. He lived almost universally admired, and died almost universally lamented. If he enjoyed more than any other man of his time, it can also be said with truth, that he contributed as much as any man of his time to the enjoyment of others. These two are great facts: he achieved a sustained happiness for himself, and added greatly to the happiness of his fellow men. Of such a man we can say with the utmost confidence, that he must have complied, in a remarkable degree, with the essential conditions of human wel-fare; or, in other words, that he must have been an eminently wise and virtuous person ; since there is no such thing possible as con-tinuous well-being, apart from intelligent goodness.

This is taken for granted. We have a right to say, after so long a recorded residence of man on earth, that no one has ever been able to cheat the Universe out of a welfare. The price must have been paid; the conditions must have been complied with. Nor can there be, in modern times, such a thing as a lastingly unjust fame. One who lived in the view of mankind as Franklin did, and has retained the cordial approval of five generations, and is loved the more the more intimately he is known, must have been, in very truth, the friend and benefactor of his race. The soul of goodness must have dwelt in that man. He must have done nobly, as well as correctly.

Franklin, then, let us simply say, *lived well ;* and enjoyed, in con-sequence, the joyous and lasting welfare which follows, neces-sarily, from a compliance with the eternal laws. Surely, then, it is well for us, at the close of our labors, to consider what are those conditions of welfare with which he so signally complied, and to in-quire how much of his happiness was due to circumstances beyond his control, and how much to circumstances within his control.

Why he alone of seventeen children should have been greatly

endowed, is a preliminary question to which science has not yet enabled us to give any kind of answer. We only know the fact. His brothers and sisters all led ordinary lives in ordinary spheres; only his youngest sister seemed, in any sense, his peer, and she only by virtue of her loving heart. And even she, dearly as she loved her brother, was awed by his presence, and dared not, as she said, utter her thoughts freely in his hearing, but sat worshiping him in silence. Baffling mystery! that in one of the humblest homes of a colonial town, there should have been born sixteen children of only average understanding, and one who grew up to teach and cheer the whole civilized world. Yet the stuff of which Franklin was made was all in that family. It was the veritable father of Franklin, whose voice at the close of the day, accompanied by his violin, was "extremely agreeable to hear." It was his true grandfather who sung an early song of toleration. And we see bits of him in Uncle Benjamin, in his great-uncle Thomas, in his sister Jane, in his runaway brother Josiah, and even in his churlish brother James. But only he was a FRANKLIN in full measure. He was the one great, round, sound apple on the tree. In our great ignorance of nature's most hidden laws, we can only say, that Benjamin Franklin inherited from his ancestors great powers of mind, and a most happy constitution of body.

When ordinary parents produce an extraordinary child, it is as though one eagle's egg had been placed in a hen's nest, and hatched with the rest of the brood; they know not what to do with their strange offspring. But nature takes care of her darling. The spark of intelligence, kindled by Uncle Benjamin's doggerel, was nourished by the few crumbs of knowledge in his father's little library; and soon the mettlesome, inquisitive boy forced his way, against much opposition, to the only university in America that was fit for him—his brother's printing-office. The Harvard of that day would have choked or expelled him. The office of the *New England Courant* put him in connection with the free thought of Boston, such as it was, and with the free thought of England, such as it was. He thus escaped the second great peril of his life. The first was, the danger of his following the example of Josiah and running away to sea; the second was the more imminent peril of embracing the theology of terror, and remaining all his life a spiritual bondman.

Such a fate actually befell the only New-Englander of his time who approached him in natural gifts—Jonathan Edwards, of whom Benjamin Franklin was the great colonial antidote. They might have been co-operators. Instead of writing that most hideous of all the productions of a virtuous mind, that saddest perversion of God's truth ever composed, " Sinners in the hands of an angry God," Edwards might have done as much for one branch of science as Franklin did for many. But he fell under the dominion of terror. " It pleased God," he impiously says, " to seize me with a pleurisy, in which he brought me nigh to the grave, and shook me over the pit of hell." He should rather have said this : I, Jonathan Edwrds, in my great ignorance, violated so grossly God's holy laws in relation to my body, that it rose in revolt against me, and such was the violence of the contest between the vital principle and the diseased organs, that I was laid prostrate until the disease was expelled.

How happy was the greater Franklin in escaping the terrorism which laid waste the souls of so large a number of his contemporaries ! But it cost him dear. It was a merit in him that he pushed his early skepticism to the uttermost. He touched bottom. He was not afraid of logical consequences. The force of denial can no farther go than in his London pamphlet upon Liberty and Necessity ; for he therein arrives at the goal which resolute young skeptics must all reach at last : Nothing is but what is not. He did not escape all the moral dangers of the situation. Wandering in that great dark Babylon, without guide or chart, with foolish Ralph for his companion, and a club of witty heathen for his mentors, with young blood in his veins and the ardor of genius in his nerves, he went astray ; he was licentious and extravagant ; he forgot his true love over the sea ; he departed from the good ways of his ancestors, and was in danger of making total shipwreck of his life. He might, like Ralph, have hurried into premature production, and squandered his powers as a hackney writer and pensioner of corrupt ministries. There was danger of his setting up a swimming school, and passing his existence in floundering about in the Thames. He might have subsided into a respectable London printer, and become, like his friend Strahan, printer to the king, and a silent, insignificant member of the House of Commons. From the manifold perils of his London life, his inherited good sense and his early good habits barely sufficed to deliver him.

Most young men of ability, during the last two hundred years, have suffered an experience like this; because, on coming to years of reflection, the appointed moral instructors of their generation have not been able to win their confidence and control their understandings.

Many have never emerged from the Slough of Despond. But the chosen few have struggled through it to the firm land of belief and activity. The story of one such we find written, with all the fiery eloquence of genius, in Mr. Carlyle's "Sartor Resartus." But the author of that work is a Scotchman, and a Scotchman is the most tenacious and unchangeable of mortals. Consequently, the hero of that tale achieved regeneration only after such a dire and protracted wrestle with the Powers of Darkness, that his being was wrenched all awry, and he has never recovered either his good temper or his digestion. He briefly tells the story in conversation:

"And I had been destined by my father and my father's minister to be myself a minister of the Kirk of Scotland. But now that I had gained the years of man's estate, I was not sure that I believed the doctrines of my father's kirk; and it was needful that I should now settle it. And so I entered into my chamber, and closed the door. And around about me there came a trooping throng of phantasms dire, from the abysmal depths of nethermost perdition. Doubt, Fear, Unbelief, Mockery, and Scoffing were there; and I wrestled with them in the travail and agony of spirit. Thus was it, Sir, for weeks. Whether I ate I know not; whether I drank I know not; whether I slept I know not. But I only know that when I came forth again beneath the glimpses of the moon, it was with the direful persuasion that I was the miserable owner of a diabolical apparatus called a Stomach. And I never have been free from that knowledge from that hour to this; and I suppose that I never shall be until I am laid away in my grave."*

Thus it was that the bound and imprisoned Scottish giant attained such light and liberty as he was able to attain. It was far different with the better natured, the better educated, the English Franklin. He took to regeneration more kindly. It was a process more gentle, more gradual, and more complete. It was, at first, more an affair

* Harper's Magazine, January, 1863. Article, "Carlyle's Table Talk."

of the heart than of the head; for he tells us that, though he felt there must be a flaw somewhere in the argument of his pamphlet, he could not even then discover what it was. He was only clear that virtue was altogether lovely, beneficent, and safe, and that vice was entirely foolish and base; and he was able deliberately and finally to choose the better part, and address himself, with all his might, to the conquest of himself and the cheerful performance of his work. How comprehensive the liturgy which he composed for himself! How touching his ceaseless strivings, to subdue what was unruly in him, and to develop what was human and improving! How admirable the success that rewarded his efforts! How consoling to mortals less gifted to perceive, that a Franklin could not dispense with systematic efforts to keep his baser part in subjection, and that, in the very enthusiasm of his first resolves, he was not able to avoid lapses into error. But, stumble as he might, his face was *set* toward Jerusalem. He avoided, also, the fatal error of confining his efforts to the regulation of his moral conduct. He read, he observed, he studied, he gained knowledge, he acquired the substance of all the knowledge then possessed by mankind. He became the best educated man of his time.*

Regeneration, perhaps, ought not to be necessary. It is possible to conceive of a civilization which should so nurture and train the young soul that it would grow up to noble and intelligent manhood without experiencing the throes of a second birth. But no such civilization exists. A man who attains self-control, insight, knowledge, and an entireness of devotion to a worthy task, generally does so by unlearning much that he has been taught, and by learning much that no one can teach him. Usually he has to tread the wine-press alone. He has to grope his way, with little aid and no encouragement, to the true faith. No one helped Franklin or Carlyle. On the

* " How stupid," says Theodore Parker, " is the New England notion of what makes an educated man! A little Latin, a little Greek, a little of speculative mathematics, and knowledge of a few books—but the understanding, the imagination, the reason, may be a howling wilderness, and the conscience be as unproductive and lifeless as the Dead Sea. Talk with Rev. Dr. Choker; you say he is an ' educated man,' though he has not mind and conscience enough to know that it is a *Devil*, not a *God*, who could create men to damn them eternally. Talk with Captain Goodwin, and you say ' he is not educated,' though he has all his intellectual and moral faculties in the most healthful activity; can build a ship, sail her round the world, selling one cargo well and profitably, and buying another; can amputate a leg, and make a wooden one to take its place; and manage the affairs of any town in Plymouth county."— *Weiss's Life and Correspondence of Theodore Parker*, ii., 419.

contrary, the parental fowls flutter in affright, as the young eagle soars away toward the sun. Because he has flown beyond their gaze, they can only conclude that he is " lost."

It is difficult to define such a misused word as regeneration. But most men perceive something of the loveliness of a regenerated soul, and all men participate in the fruits of their labors. Many of us have been reading lately the instructive works of Mr. Herbert Spencer. There must have been a time when this great author, now so serenely wise, so variously learned, so free from the vanities, prejudices, and small ambitions of his race, time, and country, so calm and moderate in statement, so clear in reasoning and just in conclusion, so tenderly and far-reachingly thoughtful for human welfare,—there must have been a time when he, too, was a vain, ignorant, restless, foolish youth, with all the appetites and passions of youth clamoring for gratification—an inhabitant of a nation that had almost forgotten that there is any thing better for a man on earth than to be exempt from the necessity of labor, and live in ignoble ease upon the labor of others. Perhaps, he could tell us, if he would, that there was a time, a day, an hour, when the mean nothingness of a life not devoted to heroic effort in the service of mankind, flashes upon his mind. Then, he reckoned up his powers and opportunities, selected his work, and bent himself, with all his means and talents, to the performance of the chosen task. Thenceforward, no waste, no unworthy self-indulgence; but all time, all means, all chances, all talents, economized for the business of his life. This is regeneration. Nor is it necessary to be a great author to taste its sweetness. A cobbler in his stall may enter as heartily and nobly into his work of clothing the feet of mankind, as the philosopher into informing their heads. Happy they, who have escaped from the bondage of self to the glorious liberty of disinterested toil ! Miserable they, who remain in bondage, slaves to hunger and ambition !

Franklin, then, was one of those who have achieved regeneration, and in circumstances that would have repelled a common mind from attempting it; for he was surrounded by people who passed their lives in making virtue hideous ; clothing it in uncouth garments, and recommending it in speech more uncouth. It was taken for granted, at that period, that to be a man of spirit and knowledge, it was necessary to be, also, flippant and immoral. Franklin showed Philadelphia that it was possible to be virtuous without the stimulus of terror; that a man could be a Christian without lapsing into the pagan superstitions from which his youthful genius had recoiled; that a man could be religious without having any thing to do with theology.

I have ventured to call Franklin the consummate Christian of his time. Indeed, I know not who, of any time, has exhibited more of the spirit of Christ. Like Christ, he lived among a host of narrow and intolerant sects without quarreling with any of them. Like Christ, he subordinated opinions and observances to conduct and feelings. He was tolerant of every thing but intolerance, and made some charitable allowance even for that. At poor Polly Baker, he had not a stone to throw. We see him, at different periods of his life, associating on friendly terms, with Quakers, Tunkers, Moravians, Methodists, Presbyterians, Catholics, Deists, and Atheists; with Mandeville, Samuel Cooper, Ezra Stiles, Whitefield, Priestley, Price, Chatham, John Carroll, Voltaire, and the Papal Nuncio; meeting them all on the common ground of human fellowship, making light of their theoretical opinions, valuing them only for their human worth. This was because he did not over-estimate the intellect of man, nor undervalue his heart. He knew well what a blind, mad little creature man is, when he essays to know the "Unknowable," and explain the unexplainable; and that differences of mere opinion on *such* subjects have no importance, except so far as they tend to divide men who are naturally brothers. He was also aware, that the strong-holds of superstition are never to be carried by direct assault, but gradually undermined by the rising tide of knowledge and good feeling. His whole life was a calm, good-natured protest against narrowness, intolerance, and bigotry, and a moving comment upon the fundamental doctrine of the Christian religion, that "THE ACCEPTABLE WAY OF SERVING GOD IS TO DO GOOD TO HIS OTHER CREATURES." He went about the world doing good.

This doctrine of the nothingness of theological opinion compared with right conduct and right feeling, seems to be of the essence of Franklin's religion. Opinion divides; feeling unites. If the church is to continue to be an institution of modern communities, I know not how it is to do so except by permitting the utmost conceivable latitude of opinion, and concerning itself only with the conduct and feelings of men. Goethe, Schiller, Voltaire, Hume,

Franklin, Jefferson, we know from their own avowals, would have gladly belonged to such a church.

The subsequent career of Franklin presents this peculiarity: he lived three lives in one; he was a man of business, a man of science, and a statesman; and in each of these careers, he accomplished as much as could be expected of a man wholly devoted to it.

The advantage which a rich man has over a poor man is, that, while a poor man is compelled to do whatever work he can find to do, a rich man is at liberty to select his task. This inestimable liberty of choice being desired by all men, by the noble and the base alike, the competition for the prize is so keen, that it is usually all a man can do, in an average lifetime, to win it. Accordingly we find that often the father earns the leisure which the son employs. One Sir Robert Peel accumulates twelve hundred thousand pounds, and another Sir Robert Peel governs the British empire. One Pitt gets the Pitt diamond, and another makes it the basis of a career in politics. Old Zachary Macaulay brought home the gold-dust from Africa which established Thomas Babington Macaulay in literature. Judge Prescott saved and invested his fees, with which his son bought the chance to write Ferdinand and Isabella. Nobility itself, according to Lord Burleigh, is nothing but ancient wealth. Sometimes an heiress is good enough to bestow upon her husband this priceless opportunity to achieve; and indeed, an heiress should regard that as her " mission," unless she has a task of her own to perform. A University or a Cathedral has occasionally done this. Newton had his professorship; so had Kepler—such as it was. Galileo, Leibnitz, Goethe, Bentham, Ricardo, Mill, Byron, Scott, Shelley, Carlyle, Farraday, Wilberforce, Adam Smith, Alison, Tennyson, Grote, Washington, Jefferson, Madison, Monroe, John Quincy Adams, all inherited estates, incomes, or places, or had incomes bestowed upon them. It is fortunate that affairs are so ordered as to admit of the occasional bestowment of leisure upon able men; for there is now, and always will be, a great deal of work to be done in the world, which can only be well done by persons who need not make it pay.

Franklin was one of those who had the force to earn his own leisure and the grace to use it well. At the age of forty-two he was a free man; i. e., he had an estate of seven hundred pounds a year. He became, successively, the servant of Philadelphia, Pennsylvania, the colonies, England, France, the United States, and mankind. It was a proof of unusual ability that he should have fairly won his leisure at forty-two; it was an evidence of his goodness and good sense, that he should have made a free gift of it to the public. If nothing is more demoralizing than philanthropy pursued as a vocation, for money, nothing is nobler than the devotion to it of well-earned leisure. Howard inherited an estate, Franklin earned one, and the Master of both had an equivalent in being able to dispense with a place wherein to lay his head.

"It is incredible," wrote Franklin once, "the quantity of good that may be done in a country by a single man, who will *make a business* of it, and not suffer himself to be diverted from that purpose by different avocations, studies, or amusements."

As a commentary upon this remark, I will present here a catalogue of the good deeds of Franklin himself, beginning at the time of his regeneration.

He established and inspired the Junto, the most sensible, useful, and pleasant club of which we have any knowledge.

He founded the Philadelphia Library, parent of a thousand libraries, an immense and endless good to the whole of the civilized portion of the United States, the States not barbarized by slavery.

He edited the best newspaper in the colonies, one which published no libels and fomented no quarrels, which quickened the intelligence of Pennsylvania, and gave the onward impulse to the press of America.

He was the first who turned to great account the engine of advertising, an indispensable element in modern business.

He published Poor Richard, by means of which so much of the wit and wisdom of all ages as its readers could appropriate and enjoy, was brought home to their minds, in such words as they could understand and remember forever.

He created the post-office system of America; and forbore to avail himself, as postmaster, of privileges from which he had formerly suffered.

It was he who caused Philadelphia to be paved, lighted, and cleaned.

As fuel became scarce in the vicinity of the colonial towns, he invented the Franklin Stove, which economized it, and suggested the subsequent warming inventions, in which America beats the world. Besides making a free gift of this invention to the public, he generously wrote an extensive pamphlet explaining its construction and utility.

He delivered civilized mankind from the nuisance, once universal, of smoky chimneys.

He was the first effective preacher of the blessed gospel of ventilation. He spoke, and the windows of hospitals were lowered; consumption ceased to gasp, and fever to inhale poison.

He devoted the leisure of seven years, and all the energy of his genius, to the science of electricity, which gave a stronger impulse to scientific inquiry than any other event of that century. He taught Goethe to experiment in electricity, and set all students to making electrical machines. He robbed thunder of its terrors and lightning of its power to destroy.

He was chiefly instrumental in founding the first high school of Pennsylvania, and died protesting against the abuse of the funds of that institution in teaching American youth the languages of Greece and Rome, while French, Spanish, and German were spoken in the streets and were required in the commerce of the wharves.

He founded the American Philosophical Society, the first organization in America of the friends of science.

He suggested the use of mineral manures, introduced the basket willow, and promoted the early culture of silk.

He lent the indispensable assistance of his name and tact to the founding of the Philadelphia Hospital.

Entering into politics, he broke the spell of Quakerism, and woke Pennsylvania from the dream of unarmed safety.

He led Pennsylvania in its thirty years' struggle with the mean tyranny of the Penns, a rehearsal of the subsequent contest with the King of Great Britain.

When the Indians were ravaging and scalping within eighty miles of Philadelphia, General Benjamin Franklin led the troops of the city against them.

He was the author of the first scheme of uniting the colonies, a scheme so suitable that it was adopted, in its essential features, in the union of the States, and binds us together to this day.

He assisted England to keep Canada, when there was danger of its falling back into the hands of a reactionary race.

More than any other man, he was instrumental in causing the

repeal of the Stamp Act, which deferred the inevitable struggle until the colonies were strong enough to triumph.

More than any other man, he educated the colonies up to independence, and secured for them in England the sympathy and support of the Brights, the Cobdens, the Spencers, and Mills of that day. His examination before the House of Commons struck both countries as the speeches of Henry Ward Beecher (a genuine brother of Franklin) did in the autumn of 1863. As the eloquent preacher set England right upon the questions of to-day, so did Franklin upon those of 1765. And Franklin would have kept her right but for the impenetrable stupidity of George III.

He discovered the temperature of the Gulf stream.

He discovered that Northeast storms begin in the Southwest.

He invented the invaluable contrivance by which a fire consumes its own smoke.

He made important discoveries respecting the causes of the most universal of all diseases—colds.

He pointed out the advantage of building ships in water-tight compartments, taking the hint from the Chinese.

He expounded the theory of navigation which is now universally adopted by intelligent seamen, and of which a charlatan and a traitor has received the credit.

At the beginning of the revolution, he was the soul of the party whose sentiments Thomas Paine spoke in "Common Sense."

In Paris, as the antidote to the restless distrust of Arthur Lee, and the restless vanity of John Adams, he saved the alliance over and over again, and brought the negotiations for peace to a successful close. His mere presence in Europe was a moving plea for the rights of man.

In the Convention of 1787, his indomitable good humor was, probably, the uniting element, wanting which the Convention would have dissolved without having done its work.

His last labors were for the abolition of slavery and the aid of its emancipated victims.

Having, during a very long life, instructed, stimulated, cheered, amused and elevated his countrymen and all mankind, he was faithful to them to the end, and added to his other services the edifying spectacle of a calm, cheerful, and triumphant death ; leaving behind him a mass of writings, full of his own kindness, humor, and wisdom, to perpetuate his influence, and sweeten the life of coming generations.

Such is the brief record of the more conspicuous actions of Benjamin Franklin. What is the shade to this bright picture of a well-spent life ?

It is common to say, that great merits imply great defects. This may be true in the case of great, unregenerate men, such as Napoleon, Mirabeau, Voltaire, and Byron. But we are now speaking of a man, who, before his propensities had hardened into unchangeable habits, *discovered* his weakness, his incompleteness, his latent baseness, his possible moral ruin, and who deliberately set himself the task of correcting his faults, enlightening his ignorance, and cultivating his better nature. Franklin, the "natural man," was a disorderly man of genius, fond of pleasure, not averse to the grosser pleasures of sense, capable of pushing his way in the world, and of becoming Sir Benjamin Franklin, baronet, a common-place, good-natured, self-indulgent, successful man of business. He chose the better part ; he sided against the Penns and the King, and dedicated his leisure to the public good. It was natural that he should have been puffed up by his great celebrity, and his great places ; on the contrary he retained his modesty and his simplicity, his love of homely old friends, relations, and places. To parody Falstaff's words, he was always Ben to his old friends, Benjamin to his brothers and sisters, and Dr. Franklin "to the rest of Europe." Except Shakspeare, no great writer has shown so little of the vanity of authorship. He does not appear ever to have suggested the collection of his writings, or to have concerned himself in their republication except as an act of friendship to an editor. When they had accomplished their immediate purpose, he appears to have thought of them no more. And as to his Autobiography, when he had written the few pages which recorded the favorite, oft-told anecdotes of his youthful days, he had no heart in the work, and could not force himself to complete it. He had made, indeed, as complete a conquest of self-love as it is desirable a man should.

Nevertheless, there must have been some shade to the picture, else Franklin had not been human. He did not wholly escape the grossness of the age in which he lived, and a little of the vulgarity of the shop always clung to him. In later years, at London and Paris, he may have been, at times, something more of a *bon vivant* than became the man who had demonstrated, at nineteen, the futility of beer. All men were clubbists then, and the uniting element of clubs was wine. I think, too, that his political opinions were, in some degree, unfavorably affected by his long residence among Quakers. If all men could be Quakers, then Franklin's dream of unbought public service might be realized; but, as the world is, if the public require the service of talent, it must be paid for at the market price. As a rule, a lawyer in great practice, *i. e.*, a great lawyer, will not accept, and, generally, ought not to accept, a precarious judgeship or cabinet place, at a salary barely equal to his necessary expenses. Franklin, perhaps, cannot justly be pronounced a great "thinker." He was a humorist. He had immense common sense; but not so much insight into the deeper questions that concern mankind. The art of living was his forte; but the place of his residence was the earth.

Vice has been defined as "virtue in excess." A man of great daring and executive force errs on the side of rashness and want of consideration of opposing wills and interests. The danger of a man, like Franklin, of quick sympathies and great understanding, is to be *too* tolerant of error. Franklin's remark to Dr. Stiles that, perhaps, the popular belief in the divinity of Christ was a beneficial error, seems to be a case in point. There are no beneficial errors. If Jesus Christ is God, it is important for all men to be acquainted with the fact. If he is not, a belief that he is cannot really enhance the good influence of his example and his words. Truth and virtue are akin; one cannot be promoted by the sacrifice of the other. Franklin occasionally carried his philosophic indifference with regard to popular beliefs to an extreme, and, sometimes, was over-cautious in giving expression to his own. For various amiable reasons, he forbore to give complete utterance to some of his negative opinions, as, for example, in his letter to Dr. Stiles.

Franklin's amazing tolerance of the most diverse and painful creeds has given pause to many who love the man. Judging him by the standard of Herbert Spencer, who has stated the doctrine of toleration more clearly than any one else, he is justified in the main. Three cardinal facts, observes Mr. Spencer, are the ground of toleration:

First, " The existence of a fundamental verity under all forms of religion, however degraded. In each of them there is a soul of truth. Through the gross body of dogmas, traditions, and rites which contain it, it is always visible, dimly or clearly, as the case may be. This it is which gives vitality even to the rudest creed; this it is which survives every modification; and this it is which we must not forget when condemning the forms under which it is presented."

Secondly, " While those concrete elements in which each creed embodies this soul of truth are bad as measured by an absolute standard, they are good as measured by a relative standard. Though from higher perceptions they hide the abstract verity within them; yet to lower perceptions they render this verity more appreciable than it otherwise would be. They serve to make real and influential over men that which would else be unreal and uninfluential. Or we may call them the protective envelopes, without which the contained truth would die."

Thirdly, " These various beliefs are parts of the constituted order of things, and not accidental, but necessary parts. Seeing how one or the other of them is everywhere present, is of perennial growth; and, when cut down, redevelops in a form but slightly modified; we cannot avoid the inference that they are needful accompaniments of human life, severally fitted to the societies in which they are indigenous."

" Our toleration, therefore, should be the widest possible; or, rather, we should aim at something beyond toleration, as commonly understood. In dealing with alien beliefs, our endeavor must be, not simply to refrain from injustice of word or deed; but, also, to do justice by an open recognition of positive worth. We must qualify our disagreement with as much as may be of sympathy."

So far, Dr. Franklin's practice and Mr. Spencer's theory are in accord. But, adds Mr. Spencer,

" Whoever hesitates to utter that which he thinks the highest truth, lest it should be too much in advance of the time, may reassure himself by looking at his acts from an unpersonal point of view. Let him duly realize the fact that opinion is the agency through which character adapts external arrangements to itself— that his opinion rightly forms part of this agency—is a unit of force, constituting, with other such units, the general power which works out social changes ; and he will perceive that he may properly give full utterance to his innermost conviction, leaving it to produce what effect it may.　It is not for nothing that he has those sympathies with some principles and repugnance to others.　He, with all his capacities, and aspirations, and beliefs, is not an accident, but a product of the time.　He must remember that while he is a descendant of the past, he is a parent of the future ; and that his thoughts are as children born to him, whom he may not carelessly let die. He, like every other man, may properly consider himself as one of the myriad agencies through whom works the Unknown Cause ; and when the Unknown Cause produces in him a certain belief, he is thereby anthorized to profess and act out that belief.　For to render, in their highest sense, the words of the poet :

> "——'Nature is made better by no mean,
> But nature makes that mean : over that art
> Which you say adds to nature, is an art
> That nature makes.'

"Not as adventitious, therefore, will the wise man regard the faith which is in him.　The highest truth he sees he will fearlessly utter ; knowing that, let what may come of it, he is thus playing his right part in the world—knowing that if he can effect the change he aims at—well ; if not—well also : though not *so* well."[*]

In the spirit of this passage, we could wish Franklin had written when he wrote to the unknown person who asked his advice as to the publication of a treatise containing unpopular doctrines.

But to conclude.　We find that several fortunate circumstances in the lot of Franklin were not due to any act of his own ; such as his great gifts, his birth in a pure and virtuous family, his birth in large America, in an age of free inquiry, and his early opportunities of mental culture.　But we have observed that the enjoyment of all these advantages did not make him a happy or a virtuous man, or an orderly, useful member of society.　The great event in his life was his deliberate and final choice to dedicate himself to virtue and the public good.　*This* was his own act.　In this the person of humblest endowments may imitate him.　From that act dates the part of his career which yielded him substantial welfare,

---

[*] Herbert Spencer's "First Principles," p. 123.

and which his countrymen now contemplate with pleasure and gratitude. It made a MAN of him. It gave him the command of his powers and his resources. It enabled him to extract from life all its latent good, and to make his life a vast addition to the sum of good in the world.

Men have lived who were more magnificently endowed than Franklin. Men have lived whose lives were more splendid and heroic than his. If the inhabitants of the earth were required to select, to represent them in some celestial congress composed of the various orders of intelligent beings, a specimen of the human race, and we should send a Shakspeare, the celestials would say, He is one of *us ;* or a Napoleon, the fallen angels might claim him. But if we desired to select a man who could present in his own character the largest amount of human worth with the least of human frailty, and in his own lot on earth the largest amount of enjoyment with the least of suffering; one whose character was estimable without being too exceptionally good, and his lot happy without being too generally unattainable ; one who could bear in his letter of credence, with the greatest truth,

This is a Man, and his life on earth was such as good men may live,

I know not who, of the renowned of all ages, we could more fitly choose to represent us in that high court of the universe, than Benjamin Franklin, printer, of Philadelphia.

APPENDIX.

APPENDIX.

I.

BY LORD JEFFREY.—1806.

" THIS self-taught American is the most rational, perhaps, of all philosophers. He never loses sight of common sense in any of his speculations; and when his philosophy does not consist entirely in its fair and vigorous application, it is always regulated and controlled by it in its application and result. No individual, perhaps, ever possessed a juster understanding, or was so seldom obstructed in the use of it by indolence, enthusiasm, or authority. Dr. Franklin received no regular education; and he spent the greater part of his life in a society where there was no relish, and no encouragement for literature. On an ordinary mind, these circumstances would have produced their usual effects, of repressing all sorts of intellectual ambition or activity, and perpetuating a generation of incurious mechanics: but to an understanding like Franklin's, we cannot help considering them as peculiarly propitious, and imagine that we can trace back to them distinctly, almost all the peculiarities of his intellectual character. Regular education, we think, is unfavorable to vigor or originality of understanding. Like civilization, it makes society more intelligent and agreeable; but it levels the distinctions of nature. It strengthens and assists the feeble; but it deprives the strong of his triumph, and casts down the hopes of the aspiring. It accomplishes this, not only by training up the mind in an habitual veneration for authorities, but by leading us to bestow a disproportionate degree of attention upon studies that are only valuable as keys or instruments for the understanding, they come at last to be regarded as ultimate objects of pursuit; and the means of education are absurdly mistaken for its end. How many powerful understandings have been lost in the Dialectics of Aristotle! And of how much good philosophy are we daily defrauded, by the preposterous error of taking a knowledge of prosody for useful learning! The mind of a man, who has escaped this training, will at least have fair play. Whatever other errors he may fall into, he will be safe at least from these infatuations. If he thinks proper, after he grows up, to study Greek, it will be for some better purpose than to become acquainted with its dialects. His prejudices will be those of a man, and not of a school-boy; and his speculations and conclusions will be independent of the maxims of tutors, and the oracles of literary patrons. The consequences of living in a refined and literary community, are nearly of the same kind with those of a regular education. There are so many critics to be satisfied—so many qualifications to be established—so many rivals to encounter, and so much derision to be hazarded, that a young man is apt to be deterred from so perilous an enterprise, and led to seek for distinction in some safer line of exertion. He is discouraged by the fame and perfection of certain models and favorites, who are always in the mouths of his judges, and, 'under them his genius is rebuked,' and his originality repressed, till he sinks into a paltry copyist, or aims at distinction by extravagance and affectation. In such a state of society, he feels that mediocrity has no chance of distinction; and what beginner can expect to rise at once into excellence? He imagines that mere good sense will attract no attention; and that the manner is of much more importance than the matter, in a candidate for public admiration. In his attention to the manner, the matter is apt to be neglected; and, in his solicitude to please those who require elegance of diction, brilliancy of wit, or harmony of periods, he is in some danger of forgetting that strength of reason, and accuracy of observation, by which he first proposed to recommend himself. His attention, when extended to so many collateral objects, is no longer vigorous or collected,— the stream, divided into so many channels, ceases to flow either deep or strong;—he becomes an unsuccessful pretender to fine writing, and is satisfied with the frivolous praise of elegance or vivacity. We are disposed to ascribe so much power to these obstructions to intellectual originality, that we cannot help fancying. that, if Franklin had been bred in a college, he would have contented himself with expounding the meters of Pindar, and mixing argument with his port in the common room; and that if Boston had abounded with men of letters, he would never have ventured to come forth from his printing-house, or been driven back to it, at any rate, by the sneers of the critics, after the first publication of his essays in the 'Busy-body.' This will probably be thought exaggerated; but it cannot be denied, we think, that the contrary circumstances in his history had a powerful effect in determining the character of his understanding, and in producing those peculiar habits of reasoning and investigation by which his writings are distinguished. He was encouraged to publish, because there was scarcely any one around him whom he could not easily excel. He wrote with great brevity, because he had not leisure for more voluminous compositions, and because he knew that the readers to whom he addressed himself were, for the most part, as busy as himself. For the same reason, he studied great perspicuity and simplicity of statement; his countrymen had no relish for fine writing, and could not easily be made to understand a deduction depending on a long or elaborate process of reasoning. He was forced, therefore, to concentrate what he had to say; and since he had no chance of being admired for the beauty of his composition, it was natural for him to aim at making an impression by the force and the clearness of his statements. His conclusions were often rash and inaccurate, from the same circumstances which rendered his productions concise. Philosophy and speculation did not form the business of his life; nor did he dedicate himself to any particular study, with a view to exhaust and complete the investigation of it in all its parts, and under all its relations. He engaged in every interesting inquiry that suggested itself to him, rather as the necessary exercise of a powerful and active mind, than as a task which he had bound himself to perform. He cast a quick and penetrating glance over the facts and the data that were presented to him; and drew his conclusions with a rapidity and precision that have not often been equaled; but he did not stop to examine the completeness of the data upon which he proceeded, nor to consider the ultimate effect or application of the principles to which he had been conducted. In all questions, therefore, where the facts upon which he was to determine, and the materials from which his judgment was to be formed, were either few in number, or of such a nature as not to be overlooked, his reasons are for the most part perfectly just and conclusive, and his decisions unexceptionably sound; but where the elements of the calculation were more numerous and widely scattered, it appears to us that he has often been precipitate, and that he has either been misled by a partial apprehension of the conditions of the problem, or has discovered only a portion of the truth which lay before him. In all physical inquiries; in almost all questions of particular and immediate policy; and in much of what relates to the practical wisdom and the happiness of private life, his views will be found to be admirable, and the reasoning by which they are supported most masterly and convincing. But upon subjects of general politics, of abstract morality, and political economy, his notions appear to be more unsatisfactory and incomplete. He seems to have wanted leisure, and perhaps inclination also, to spread out before him the whole vast premises of these extensive sciences, and scarcely to have had patience to hunt for his conclusions through so wide and intricate a region as that upon which they invited him to enter. He has been satisfied, therefore, on every occasion, with reasoning from a very limited view of the facts, and often from a particular instance: he has done all that sagacity and sound sense could do with such materials; but it cannot excite wonder, if he has sometimes overlooked an essential part of the argument, and often advanced a particular truth into the place of a general principle. He seldom reasoned upon these subjects at all, we believe, without having some practical application of them immediately in view; and as he began the investigation rather to determine a particular case, than to establish a general maxim, so he probably desisted as soon as he had relieved himself of the present difficulty. There are not many among the thorough-bred scholars and philosophers of Europe, who can lay claim to distinction in more than one or two departments of science or literature. The uneducated tradesman of America has left writings that call for our attention, in natural philosophy—in politics,—in political economy,—and in general literature and morality."

* * * * * * * * * *

" As a writer on morality and general literature, the merits of Dr. Franklin cannot be estimated properly, without taking into consideration the peculiarities that have been already alluded to, in his early history and situation. He never had the benefit of any academical instruction, nor of the society of men of letters;—his style was formed entirely by his own judgment and occasional reading; and most of his moral pieces were written while he was a tradesman, addressing himself to the tradesmen of his native city. We cannot expect, therefore, either that he should write with extraordinary eloquence or grace; or that he should treat of the accomplishments, follies, and occupations of polite life. He had no great occasion, as a moralist, to expose the guilt and the folly of gaming or seduction; or to point a poignant and playful ridicule against the higher immoralities of fashionable life. To the mechanics and traders of Boston and Philadelphia, such warnings were altogether unnecessary; and he endeavored, therefore, with more appropriate eloquence to impress upon them the importance of industry, sobriety, and economy, and to direct their wise and humble ambition to the attainment of useful knowledge and honorable independence. That morality, after all, is certainly the most valuable, which is adapted to the circumstances of the greater part of mankind; and that eloquence is the most meritorious, that is calculated to convince and persuade the multitude to virtue. Nothing can be more perfectly and beautifully adapted to its object, than most of Dr. Franklin's compositions of this sort. The tone of familiarity, of good will, and homely jocularity,—the plain and pointed illustrations—the short sentences, made up of short words— and the strong sense, clear information, and obvious conviction of the author himself, make most of his moral exhortations perfect models of popular eloquence; and afford the finest specimens of a style which has been but too little cultivated in a country which numbers perhaps more than 100,000 readers among its tradesmen and artificers. In writings which possess such solid and unusual merit, it is of no great consequence that the fastidious eye of a critic can discover many blemishes. There is a good deal of vulgarity in the practical writings of Dr. Franklin; and more vulgarity than was any way necessary for the object he had in view. There is something childish, too, in some of his attempts at pleasantry: his story of the whistle, and his Parisian letter, announcing the discovery that the sun gives light as soon as he rises, are instances of this. The Soliloquy of an Ephemeris, however, is much better; and both it, and the Dialogue with the Gout, are executed with the lightness and spirit of genuine French compositions. The speech in the Divan of Algiers, composed as a parody on those of the defenders of the Slave-trade, and the Scriptural parable against persecution, are inimitable ;—they have all the point and facility of the fine pleasantries of Swift and Arbuthnot, with something more of directness and apparent sincerity. The style of his letters, in general, is excellent. They are chiefly remarkable for great simplicity of language, admirable good sense and ingenuity, and an amiable and inoffensive cheerfulness, that is never overclouded or eclipsed."

*   *   *   *   *   *   *   *   *   *

"Upon the whole, we look upon the life and writings of Dr. Franklin as affording a striking illustration of the incalculable value of a sound and well directed understanding, and of the comparative uselessness of learning and laborious accomplishments. Without the slightest pretensions to the character of a scholar or a man of science, he has extended the bounds of human knowledge on a variety of subjects, which scholars and men of science had previously investigated without success; and has only been found deficient in those studies which the learned have generally turned from in disdain. We would not be understood to say any thing in disparagement of scholarship and science; but the value of these instruments is apt to be overrated by their possessors; and it is a wholesome mortification to show them that the work may be done without them. We have long known that their employment does not insure its success."*

II.

BY SIR JAMES MACKINTOSH.—1812.

"The cause of the Americans in France owed part of its success to the peculiar character, as well as extraordinary talents, of their agent at Paris, Benjamin Franklin. Bred a printer, at Boston, he had raised himself to a respectable station by the most ingenious industry and frugality ; and, having acquired celebrity by his philosophical discourses, he had occupied a considerable office in the colonies at the commencement of the disturbance. This singular man long labored to avert a rupture; and, notwithstanding his cold and cautious character, he shed tears at the prospect of separation; but he was too wise to deliberate after decision. Having once made his determination, he adhered to it with a firmness which neither the advances of England nor the adversity of America could shake. He considered a return to the ancient friendship as impossible, and every conciliatory proposal as a snare to divide America and to betray her into absolute

* "Edinburgh Review," No. 16, July, 1806.

submission. At Paris he was preceded and aided by his philosophical fame. His steady and downright character was a singularity which the accomplished diplomatists of France had not learned how to conquer. The simplicity of a Republican, a Presbyterian, and a printer, transported at the age of seventy to the most polished court of Europe, by amusing the frivolous and interesting the romantic, excited a disposition at Versailles, favorable to his cause.

"Early accustomed to contemplate infant societies and uncultivated nature, his mind was original and independent. He derived neither aid nor incumbrance from learning, which enslaves every mind not powerful to master and govern it. He was, therefore, exempt from those prejudices of nation and age which every learned education fosters. Reared in colonies struggling into existence, where necessity so often calls out ingenious contrivance, he adapted even philosophical experiment to the direct convenience of mankind. The same spirit is still more conspicuous in his moral and political writings. An independence of thought, a constant and direct reference to utility, a consequent abstinence from whatever is merely curious and ornamental, or even remotely useful, a talent for ingeniously betraying vice and prejudice into an admission of reason, and for exhibiting their sophisms in that state of undisguised absurdity in which they are ludicrous, with a singular power of striking illustration from homely objects, would justify us in calling Franklin the American Socrates."[*]

III.

BY JOHN FOSTER.—1818.

" THE character displayed by Franklin's correspondence is an unusual combination of elements. The main substance of the intellectual part of it is a superlative good sense, evinced and acting in all the modes of that high endowment ; such as an intuitively prompt and perfect, and steadily continuing apprehension ; a sagacity which with admirable ease strikes through all superficial and delusive appearances of things to the essence and true relations ; a faculty of reasoning in a manner marvelously simple, direct, and decisive ; a power of reducing a subject or question to its plainest principles ; an unaffected daring to meet whatever is to be opposed, in an explicit, direct manner, and in the point of its main strength ; a facility of applying familiar truth and self-evident propositions for resolving the most uncommon difficulties ; and a happy adroitness of illustration by parallel cases, supposed or real, the real ones being copiously supplied by a large and most observant acquaintance with the world. • It is

---

[*] Sketched for a History of England. See " Life of Mackintosh," by his Son, ii., 202.

obvious how much this same accurate observation of the world would contribute to that power of interpreting the involuntary indications of character, and of detecting motives and designs in all sorts of persons he had to deal with, and to that foresight of consequences in all practical concerns, in which he was probably never surpassed. It is gratifying to observe how soon he would see to the very bottom of the characters and schemes of plausible hypocrites and veteran statesmen, proud as they might be of the recollected number of their stratagems and their dupes, and so confident of their talents for undermining and overreaching, that it took some of them a considerable time to become fully aware of the hazard of attempting their practice upon the Republican. Not one of their inadvertencies, or of their overdone professions, or of the inconsistencies into which the most systematic craft is liable to be sometimes betrayed, was ever lost upon him. There are in the course of these letters curious and striking instances of personages of great pretension, and of other personages seeking to effect their purposes under the guise of making no pretension, putting him in full possession of their principles and designs, by means of circumstances which they little suspected to be betraying them, and for which he, if it was necessary, could be discreet enough to appear never the wiser. In process of time, however, courtiers, ministers, intriguers, and the diplomatic gentry, had the mist cleared from their faculties sufficiently to understand what kind of man they had to do with. There is one thing deficient in this collection for the perfect illustration of Dr. Franklin's judgment. He resided a long course of years in France, in the exercise of the most important official functions for the American States, both during and after the war; and a great majority of the letters are dated at Passy, near Paris. As the French government was a most efficient friend to America in that momentous and perilous season, and her minister at the French Court experienced there all manner of respect and complaisance, it was natural enough he should speak in terms of considerable favor of that people and their governors,—of favor to certain extent— *quoad hoc.* But we are in vain curious to know whether this complacency was any thing like limited by justice. We are compelled to doubt it, from observing the many unqualified expressions of partiality to the French and their rulers, and from nowhere finding any terms appropriate to the frivolity of the nation, and the despotism and ambition of the government. Why do we find none such? Are there no preserved letters manifesting that the Republican philosopher maintained a clear perception and a condemnatory judgment of such things, in spite of the Parisian adulation to himself, and the aid given to the rising republic by a tyrannic monarchy? And as to that aid itself, it would be one of the most memorable examples of the weakness of strong minds, if Franklin could ever for a moment mistake, or estimate, otherwise than with contempt, the motive that prompted it: a motive which, in any case in which he had not been interested, would have placed the whole affair of this alliance and assistance in quite a different light from that in which he seemed so gratified to regard it. A profligate and tyrannical court a disinterested friend to a people asserting their freedom, and in the form of a republic! And could the American embassador, though gratified of course by the fact of powerful assistance, affect to accept from that court, without a great struggle with his rising indignant scorn, the hypocritical cant and cajolery about co-operation against oppression, respect for the virtuous and interesting patriots of the New World, and the like, as expressive of its true principles, in seizing so favorable an occasion, for giving effect to its hatred against England? And could he, into the bargain, contemplate an enslaved and debased people, pass in front of the Bastile, and behold the ruinous extravagance and monstrous depravity of that court, with feelings which required nothing to keep them in the indulgent tone but the recollection of French troops and French money employed in America?

"If the editor had in his possession any letters or other manuscripts tending to prove that no such beguilement took effect upon a judgment, on which so many other kinds of persons and things attempted in vain to impose, it was due to Franklin's reputation for independence of judgment, to have given them, even though they should have brought some impeachment upon his sincerity, in the grateful and laudatory expressions repeatedly here employed respecting France and its interference in the contest. In a general moral estimate of his qualities, insincerity would seem to find very little place. His principles appear to have borne a striking correspondence, in simplicity, directness, and decision, to the character of his understanding. Credit may be given him for having through life very rarely prosecuted any purpose which he did not deliberately approve; and his manner of prosecution was distinguished, as far as appears, by a plain honesty in the choice of means, by a contempt of artifice and petty devices, by a calm inflexibility, and by a greater confidence of success than is usually combined with so clear and extended a foresight of the difficulties; but indeed that foresight of the difficulties might justify his confidence of the adaptation of his measures for encountering them. He appears to have possessed an almost invincible self-command, which bore him through all the negotiations, strifes with ignorance, obstinacy, duplicity, and opposing interest, and through tiresome delays and untoward incidents, with a sustained firmness which preserved to him in all cases the most advantageous exercise of his faculties, and with a prudence of deportment beyond the attainment of the most disciplined adepts in mere political intrigue and court-practice. He was capable, indeed, of feeling an intense indignation, which comes out in full expression in some of his letters, relating to the character of the English government, as displayed in its policy towards

America. This bitter detestation is most unreservedly disclosed in some of his confidential correspondence with David Hartley, an English member of Parliament, a personal friend of Dr. Franklin, without costing the ministers the condescension of official intercourse and inquiry. These vituperative passages have a corrosive energy, by virtue of force of mind and of justice, which perfectly precludes all appearance of littleness and mere temper in the indignation. It is the dignified character of Cato or Aristides. And if a manifestation of it in similar terms ever took place in personal conference with such men as were its objects, it must have appeared any thing rather than an ungoverned irritability : nor would it have been possible to despise the indignant tone in which contempt was mingled with anger, as far as the two sentiments are compatible. Believing that the men who provoked these caustic sentences did for the most part deserve them, we confess we have read them with that sort of pleasure which is felt in seeing justice made to strike, by vindictive power of mind, on the characters of men whose stations defended their persons and fortunes from the most direct modes of retribution. When at length all was accomplished that with long and earnest expostulation he had predicted, and been ridiculed for predicting to the English statesmen, as certain consequences of persisting in their infatuated course, we find no rancorous recollection, no language of extravagant triumph at the splendid result, nor of excessive self-complacency in the retrospect of his own important share in conducting the great undertaking above to such a consummation. His feelings do not seem to have been elated above the pitch of a calm satisfaction at having materially contributed to the success of a righteous cause, a success in which he was convinced he saw not simply the vindication of American rights, but the prospect of unlimited benefit to mankind. And here it may be remarked, that his predominant passion appears to have been a love of the useful. The useful was to him the *summum bonum*, the supreme fair, the sublime and beautiful, which it may not perhaps be extravagant to believe he was in quest of every week for half a century, in whatever place, or study, or practical undertaking. No department was too plain or humble for him to occupy himself in for this purpose; and in affairs of the most ambitious order this was still systematically his object. Whether in directing the constructing of chimneys or of constitutions, lecturing on the saving of candles or on the economy of national revenues, he was still intent on the same end, the question always being how to obtain the most of solid tangible advantage by the plainest and easiest means. There has rarely been a mortal, of high intelligence and flattering fame, on whom the pomps of life were so powerless. On him were completely thrown away the oratorical and poetical heroics about glory, of which heroics it was enough that he easily perceived the intention or effect to be, to explode all sober truth and substantial good, and to impel men, at the very best of the matter, through some career of vanity, but commonly through mischief, slaughter, and devastation, in mad pursuit of what amounts at last, if attained, to some certain quantity of noise and empty show, and intoxicated transient elation.   He was so far an admirable spirit for acting the Mentor to a young republic.   It will not be his fault if the citizens of America shall ever become so servile to European example as to think a multitude of supernumerary places, enormous salaries, and a fastidious economy of society, a necessary security or decoration of that political liberty which they enjoy in pre-eminence above every nation on earth.   In these letters of their patriarch and philosopher they will be amply warned, by repeated and emphatical representations, of the desperate mischief of a political system in which the public resources shall be expended in a way to give the government both the interest and the means to corrupt the people.

"The political portion (the larger portion) of this correspondence will be a valuable addition to the mass of lessons and documents which might have been supposed long since sufficient to disenchant all thinking men of their awful reverence for state mystery and cabinet wisdom, and ministerial integrity and senatorial independence.   We would hope, in spite of all appearances, that the times may not be very far off when the infatuation of accepting the will of the persons that happen to be in power, as the evidence of wisdom and right, will no longer bereave nations of their sense, and their peace, and the fruits of their industry and improvements,— no longer render worse than useless, for the public interests, the very consciences of men whose conduct relative to their individual concerns bears a fair appearance of sound principle and understanding.   We will hope for a time when no secret history of important events will display the odious spectacle of a great nation's energies and resources, and the quiet of the world, surrendered without reserve to the mercy, and that mercy 'cruel,' of such men as Franklin had to warn, in vain, of the consequences of their policy respecting America.   The correspondence gives an exhibition of almost every thing that ought to enforce on a nation the duty of exercising a constitutional jealousy of the executive.   English readers may here see how worthily were confided the public interests of their forefathers, involving to an incalculable extent their own.   They may see how, while those forefathers looked on, many of them for a great while too infatuated with what they called loyalty to dare even a thought of disapprobation, those interests were sported with and sacrificed by men who cared not *what* they sacrificed, so long as their own pride and resentment and emolument could stand exempted.   They may see how fatally too late those forefathers were in discovering that their public managers had begun their career in the madness of presumption ; and that warning, and time, and disastrous experiments, and national suffering, had done nothing towards curing it. They will see how, while a show of dignity, and a talk of justice, national honor, and so forth, were kept up before the people, there were no expedients and tricks too mean, no corruptions too gross, no cabals and compromises of disagreeing selfishness too degrading to have their share in the state machinery which was working behind this state exhibition. What is the instruction resulting from all this, but the very reverse of what we have so often heard inculcated on the one hand by interested and corrupt advocates, and on the other by good men, of the quietest school? What should it be but that nations ought to maintain a systematic habitual jealousy and examination relative to the principles and schemes of their rulers; that especially all movements toward a *war* should excite a ten-fold vigilance of this distrust, it being always a strong probability that the measure is wrong, but a perfect certainty that an infinity of delusions will be poured out on the people to persuade them that it is right. But to return to an *honest* politician. Great admiration is due to the firm, explicit and manly tone with which he meets the inquiries, the insidious propositions, or the hinted menaces, of the hostile government and its agents; to the patience with which he encounters the same overtures and attempted impositions, in a succession of varied forms ; to the coolness and clearness with which he sometimes discusses and the dignified contempt with which he sometimes spurns." * * * * * * *

"The most entertaining, however, and by no means uninstructive division of his letters, will be the first part, called 'Miscellaneous,' and consisting chiefly of letters of friendship, abounding in tokens of benevolence, sparkling not unfrequently with satiric pleasantry, but of a bland, good-natured kind, arising in the most easy, natural manner, and thrown off with admirable simplicity and brevity of expression. There are short discussions relating to various arts and conveniences of life, plain instructions for persons deficient in cultivation, and the means for it ; condolences on the death of friends, and frequent references, in an advanced stage of the correspondence, to his old age and approaching death. Moral principles and questions are sometimes considered and simplified ; and American affairs are often brought in view, though not set forth in the diplomatic style. It is unnecessary to remark that Franklin was not so much a man of books as of affairs ; but he was not the less for that a speculative man. Every concern became an intellectual subject to a mind so acutely and perpetually attentive to the relation of cause and effect. For enlargement of his sphere of speculation, his deficiency of literature, in the usual sense of the term, was excellently compensated by so wide an acquaintance with the world and with distinguished individuals of all ranks, professions and attainments. It may be, however, that a more bookish and contemplative employment of some portion of his life would have left one deficiency of his mental character less palpable. There appears to have been but little in that character of the element of sublimity. We do not meet with many bright elevations of thought, or powerful, enchanting impulses of sentiment, or brilliant, transient glimpses of ideal worlds. Strong, independent, comprehensive, never remitting intelligence, proceeding on the plain ground of things, and acting in a manner always equal to, and never appearing at moments to surpass itself, constituted his mental power. In its operation it has no risings and fallings, no disturbance into eloquence or poetry, no cloudiness of smoke indeed, but no darting of flames. A consequence of this perfect uniformity is, that all subjects treated, appear to be on a level, the loftiest and most insignificant being commented on in the same unalterable strain of calm, plain sense, which brings all things to its own standard, insomuch that a great subject shall sometimes seem to become less while it is elucidated, and less commanding while it is enforced. In discoursing of serious subjects, Franklin imposes gravity on the reader, but does not excite solemnity, and on grand ones he never displays or inspires enthusiasm." *   *   *   *   *   *   *

" But the most remarkable letter in the volume is one written in his eighty-fifth year to Dr. Ezra Stiles, President of Yale College, who had in a very friendly and respectful manner solicited some information respecting the aged philosopher's opinion of the Christian religion. Franklin's reply to an inquiry, which he says had never been made to him before, is written with kindness and seriousness, but nevertheless in terms not a little evasive. But perhaps it would in effect have as much explicitness as his venerable correspondent could wish, for it would too clearly inform the good man, as it does its present readers, that this philosopher and patriot, and as in many points of view he may most justly be regarded, philanthropist, was content and prepared to venture into another world without any hold upon the Christian faith. In many former letters, as well as in this last, he constantly professes his firm belief in an Almighty Being, wise and good, and exercising a providential government over the world : and in a future state of conscious existence, rendered probable by the nature of the human soul, and by the analogies presented in the renovations and reproductions in other classes of being, and rendered necessary by the unsatisfactory state of allotment and retribution on earth. On the ground of such a faith, so sustained, he appears always to anticipate with complacency the appointed removal to another scene, confident that he should continue to experience in another life the goodness of that Being who had been so favorable to him in this, ' though without the smallest conceit,' he says, ' of meriting such goodness.' The merely philosophic language uniformly employed in his repeated anticipations of an immortal life, taken together with two or three profane passages* in these letters (there are but few

" * One of the most prominent and offensive is in a very short letter (p. 115, 4to.) written when past eighty, on the occasion of the death of a person whom he calls ' Our poor friend Ben. Kent.' We were going to transcribe it, but it is better to leave such vile stuff where it is."

such passages), and with the manner in which he equivocates on the question respectfully pressed upon him by the worthy President of Yale College, respecting his opinion of Christ, leave no room to doubt that whatever he did really think of the Divine Teacher, he substantially rejected Christianity—that he refused to acknowledge it in any thing like the character of a peculiar economy for the illumination and redemption of a fallen and guilty race. Nothing, probably, that he believed, was believed on the authority of its declarations, and nothing that he assumed to hope after death, was expected on the ground of its redeeming efficacy and promises. And this state of opinions it appears that he self-complacently maintained without variation during the long course of his activities and speculations on the great scale ; for in this letter to Dr. Stiles, of the date of 1790, he inclosed, as expressive of his latest opinions, one written nearly forty years before, in answer to some religious admonitions addressed to him by George Whitefield. So that, throughout a period much surpassing the average duration of the life of man, spent in a vigorous and diversified exercise of an eminently acute and independent intellect, with all the lights of the world around him, he failed to attain the one grand simple apprehension how man is to be accepted with God. There is even cause to doubt whether he ever made the inquiry with any real solicitude to meet impartially the claims of that religion which avows itself to be on evidence, a declaration of the mind of the Almighty on the momentous subject. On any question of physics, or mechanics, or policy, or temporal utility of any kind, or morals as detached from religion, he could bend the whole force of his spirit, and the result was often a gratifying proof of the greatness of that force; but the religion of Christ it would appear that he could pass by with an easy assumption that whatever might be the truth concerning it, he could perfectly well do without it. To us this appears a mournful and awful spectacle; and the more so from that entire, unaffected tranquillity with which he regarded the whole concern in the conscious near approach of death. Some of the great Christian topics it was needless to busy himself about then, because he should soon learn the 'truth with less trouble.' "*

IV.

BY LORD BROUGHAM.—1839.

" ONE of the most remarkable men, certainly, of our times, as a politician, or of any age, as a philosopher, was Franklin, who also stands alone in combining together these two characters, the greatest that man can sustain, and in this, that having borne the first part in enlarging science, by one of

* "Contributions of John Foster to the Eclectic Review," vol. ii., 1818.

the greatest discoveries ever made, he bore the second part in founding one of the greatest empires in the world.

"In this truly great man every thing seems to concur that goes towards the constitution of exalted merit. First, he was the architect of his own fortune. Born in the humblest station, he raised himself by his talents and his industry, first to the place in society which may be attained with the help only of ordinary abilities, great application, and good luck; but next to the loftier hights which a daring and happy genius alone can scale; and the poor printer's boy who, at one period of his life, had no covering to shelter his head from the dews of night, rent in twain the proud dominion of England, and lived to be the embassador of a Commonwealth which he had formed, at the court of the haughty monarchs of France, who had been his allies.

"Then, he had been tried by prosperity as well as adverse fortune, and had passed unhurt through the perils of both. No ordinary apprentice, no common-place journeyman, ever laid the foundations of his independence in habits of industry and temperance more deep than he did, whose genius was afterward to rank him with the Galileos and Newtons of the old world. No patrician, born to shine in courts, or assist at the councils of monarchs, ever bore his honors in a lofty station more easily, or was less spoiled by the enjoyment of them, than this common workman did when negotiating with royal representatives, or caressed by all the beauty and fashion of the most brilliant court in Europe.

"Again, he was self-taught in all he knew. His hours of study were stolen from those of sleep and of meals, or gained by some ingenious contrivance for reading while the work of daily calling went on. Assisted by none of the helps which affluence tenders to the studies of the rich, he had to supply the place of tutors by redoubled diligence, and of commentaries by repeated perusal. Nay, the possession of books was to be obtained by copying what the art, which he himself exercised, furnished easily to others.

"Next, the circumstances under which others succumb he made to yield, and bend to his own purposes—a successful leader of a revolt that ended in complete triumph, after appearing desperate for years; a great discoverer in philosophy, without the ordinary helps to knowledge; a writer, famed for his chaste style, without a classical education; a skillful negotiator, though never bred to politics; ending as a favorite, nay, a pattern of fashion, when the guest of frivolous courts, the life which he had begun in garrets and in workshops.

"Lastly, combinations of faculties, in others deemed impossible, appeared easy and natural to him. The philosopher, delighted in speculation, was also eminently a man of action. Ingenious reasoning, refined and subtle consultation, were in him combined with prompt resolution and inflexible firmness of purpose. To a lively fancy, he joined a learned and deep reflection; his original and inventive genius stooped to the convenient alliance of the most ordinary prudence in every-day affairs; the mind that soared above the clouds, and was conversant with the loftiest of human contemplations, disdained not to make proverbs and feign parables for the guidance of apprenticed youths and servile maidens; and the hands that sketched a free constitution for a whole continent, or drew down the lightning from heaven, easily and cheerfully lent themselves to simplify the apparatus by which truths were to be illustrated, or discoveries pursued.

"His whole course, both in acting and in speculation, was simple and plain, ever preferring the easiest and the shortest road, nor ever having recourse to any but the simplest means to compass his ends. His policy rejected all refinements, and aimed at accomplishing its purposes by the most rational and obvious expedients. His language was unadorned, and used as a medium of communicating his thoughts, not of raising admiration, but it was pure, expressive, racy. His manner of reasoning was manly and cogent, the address of a rational being to others of the same order, and so concise that, preferring decision to discussion, he never exceeded a quarter of an hour in any public address. His correspondence upon business, whether private or on state affairs, is a model of clearness and compendious shortness, nor can any state papers surpass in dignity and impression those of which he is believed to have been the author in the earlier part of the American revolutionary war. His mode of philosophizing was the purest application of the inductive principle, so eminently adapted to his nature, and so clearly dictated by common sense, that we can have little doubt it would have been suggested by Franklin, if it had not been unfolded by Bacon, though it is as clear that, in this esse, it would have been expounded in far more simple terms. But of all this great man's scientific excellencies, the most remarkable is the smallness, the simplicity, the apparent inadequacy, of the means which he employed in his experimental researches. His discoveries were made with hardly any apparatus at all, and if, at any time, he had been led to employ instruments of a somewhat less ordinary description, he never rested satisfied until he had, as it were, afterward translated the process, by resolving the problem with such simple machinery, that you might say he had done it wholly unaided by apparatus. The experiments by which the identity of lightning and electricity was demonstrated, were made with a sheet of brown paper, a bit of twine, a silk thread, and an iron key.

"Upon the integrity of this great man, whether in public or in private life, there rests no stain. Strictly honest, and even scrupulously punctual in all his dealings, he preserved in the highest fortune that regularity which he had practiced as well as inculcated in the lowest. The phrase which he once used when interrupted in his proceedings upon the most arduous and important affairs, by a demand of some petty item in a long account-- . 'Thou shalt not muzzle the ox that treads out the corn '—has been cited against him as proving the laxity of his dealings when in trust of public money; it plainly proves the reverse, for he well knew, in a country abounding in discussion, and full of bitter personal animosities, nothing could be gained of immunity by refusing to produce his vouchers at the fitting time; and his venturing to use such language demonstrates that he knew his conduct to be really above all suspicion.

"In domestic life he was faultless, and in the intercourse of society, delightful. There was a constant good humor and a playful wit, easy, and of high relish, without any ambition to shine, the natural fruit of his lively fancy, his solid, natural good sense, and his cheerful temper, that gave his conversation an unspeakable charm, and alike suited every circle, from the humblest to the most elevated. With all his strong opinions, so often solemnly declared, so imperishably recorded in his deeds, he retained a tolerance for those who differed with him, which could not be surpassed in men whose principles hang so loosely about them as to be taken up for a convenient cloak, and laid down when found to impede their progress. In his family he was every thing that worth, warm affections, and sound prudence could contribute to make a man both useful and amiable, respected and beloved. In religion, he would by many be reckoned a latitudinarian; yet it is certain that his mind was imbued with a deep sense of the Divine perfections, a constant impression of our accountable nature, and a lively hope of future enjoyment. Accordingly, his death-bed, the test of both faith and works, was easy and placid, resigned and devout, and indicated at once an unflinching retrospect of the past, and a comfortable assurance of the future."

" If we turn from the truly great man whom we have been contemplating, to his celebrated contemporary in the old world, Frederick II., who only affected the philosophy that Franklin possessed, and employed his talents for civil and military affairs, in extinguishing that independence which Franklin's life was consecrated to establish, the contrast is marvelous indeed, between the Monarch and the Printer."*

V.

BY DR. JARED SPARKS.—1840.

"THE strong and distinguishing features of his mind were sagacity, quickness of perception, and soundness of judgment. His imagination was lively, without being extravagant. In short, he possessed a perfect mas-

* Lord Brougham's "Sketches of Statesmen of the Time of George III."

tery over the faculties of his understanding and over his passions. Having this power always at command, and never being turned aside either by vanity or selfishness, he was enabled to pursue his objects with a directness and constancy, that rarely failed to insure success. It was as fortunate for the world, as it was for his own fame, that the benevolence of such a man was limited only by his means and opportunities of doing good, and that, in every sphere of action through a long course of years, his single aim was to promote the happiness of his fellow-men by enlarging their knowledge, improving their condition, teaching them practical lessons of wisdom and prudence, and inculcating the principles of rectitude and the habits of a virtuous life."*

VI.

BY GEORGE BANCROFT.—1844.

With placid tranquillity, Benjamin Franklin looked quietly and deeply into the secrets of nature. His clear understanding was never perverted by passion, or corrupted by the pride of theory. The son of a rigid Calvinist, the grandson of a tolerant Quaker, he had from boyhood been familiar not only with theological subtilties, but with a catholic respect for freedom of mind. Skeptical of tradition as the basis of faith, he respected reason, rather than authority; and, after a momentary lapse into fatalism, escaping from the mazes of fixed decrees and free will, he gained, with increasing years, an increasing trust in the overruling providence of God. Adhering to none 'of all the religions' in the colonies, he yet devoutly, though without form, adhered to religion. But though famous as disputant, and having a natural aptitude for metaphysics, he obeyed the tendency of his age, and sought by observation to win an insight into the mysteries of being. Loving truth, without prejudice and without bias, he discovered intuitively the identity of the laws of nature with those of which humanity is conscious; so that his mind was like a mirror, in which the universe as it reflected itself, revealed her laws. He was free from mysticism, even to a fault. His morality, repudiating ascetic severities, and the system which enjoins them, was indulgent to appetites of which he abhorred the sway; but his affections were of a calm intensity; in all his career, the love of man gained the mastery over personal interest. He had not the imagination which inspires the bard or kindles the orator; but an exquisite propriety, parsimonious of ornament, gave ease of expression and graceful simplicity even to his most careless writings. In life, also, his tastes were delicate. Indifferent to the pleasures of the table, he relished the delights of music and harmony, of which he enlarged the instruments. His blandness of temper, his modesty, the benignity of his man-

* "Life and Works of Franklin," i., 584."

ners, made him the favorite of intelligent society; and, with healthy cheerfulness, he derived pleasure from books, from philosophy, from conversation, —now calmly administering consolation to the sorrower, now indulging in the expression of light-hearted gayety. In his intercourse, the universality of his perceptions bore, perhaps, the character of humor; but, while he clearly discerned the contrast between the grandeur of the universe and the feebleness of man, a serene benevolence saved him from contempt of his race, or disgust at its toils. To superficial observers, he might have seemed as an alien from speculative truth, limiting himself to the world of the senses; and yet, in study, and among men, his mind always sought, with unaffected simplicity, to discover and apply the general principles by which nature and affairs are controlled,—now deducing from the theory of caloric improvements in fireplaces and lanterns, and now advancing human freedom by firm inductions from the inalienable rights of man. Never professing enthusiasm, never making a parade of sentiment, his practical wisdom was sometimes mistaken for the offspring of selfish prudence; yet his hope was steadfast, like that hope which rests on the Rock of Ages, and his conduct was as unerring as though the light that led him was a light from heaven. He ever anticipated action by theories of self-sacrificing virtue; and yet, in the moments of intense activity, he, from the highest abodes of ideal truth, brought down and applied to the affairs of life the sublimest principles of goodness, as noiselessly and unostentatiously as became the man who, with a kite and hempen string, drew the lightning from the skies. He separated himself so little from his age, that he has been called the representative of materialism; and yet, when he thought on religion, his mind passed beyond reliance on sects to faith in God; when he wrote on politics, he founded the freedom of his country on principles that know no change; when he turned an observing eye on nature, he passed always from the effect to the cause, from individual appearances to universal laws; when he reflected on history, his philosophic mind found gladness and repose in the clear anticipation of the progress of humanity."*

VII.

BY ROBERT C. WINTHROP.—1856.

"Certainly, if any man of his age, or of almost any other age, ever earned the reputation of a doer of good, and of having lived usefully, it was Benjamin Franklin. No life was ever more eminently and practically a useful life than his. Capable of the greatest things, he condescended to the humblest. He never sat down to make himself famous. He never secluded himself from the common walks and duties of society in order to accomplish a great

* "Bancroft's History of the United States," iii., 378.

reputation, much less to accumulate a great fortune. He wrote no elaborate histories, or learned treatises, or stately tomes. Short essays or tracts, thrown off at a heat to answer an immediate end,—letters to his associates in science or politics,—letters to his family and friends,—these make up the great bull of his literary productions; and, under the admirable editorship of Mr Sparks, nine noble volumes do they fill,—abounding in evidences of a wisdom, sagacity, ingenuity, diligence, freshness of thought, fullness of information, comprehensiveness of reach, and devotedness of purpose, such as are rarely to be found associated in any single man. Wherever he found any thing to be done, he did it; any thing to be investigated, he investigated it; any thing to be invented or discovered, he forthwith tried to invent or discover it, and almost always succeeded. He did every thing as if his whole attention in life had been given to that one thing. And thus, while he did enough in literature to be classed among the great writers of his day; enough in invention and science to secure him the reputation of a great philosopher; enough in domestic politics to win the title of a great statesman; enough in foreign negotiations to merit the designation of a great diplomatist; he found time to do enough, also, in works of general utility, humanity, and benevolence, to insure him a perpetual memory as a great philanthropist.

"No form of personal suffering or social evil escaped his attention, or appealed in vain for such relief or remedy as his prudence could suggest or his purse supply. From that day of his early youth, when, a wanderer from his home and friends in a strange place, he was seen sharing his rolls with a poor woman and child, to the last act of his public life, when he signed that well-known memorial to Congress, as President of the Anti-Slavery Society of Pennsylvania, a spirit of earnest and practical benevolence runs like a golden thread along his whole career. Would to Heaven that he could have looked earlier at that great evil at which he looked at last, and that the practical resources and marvelous sagacity of his mighty intellect could have been brought seasonably to bear upon the solution of a problem, now almost too intricate for any human faculties! Would to Heaven that he could have tasked his invention for a mode of drawing the fires safely from that portentous cloud,—in his day, indeed, hardly bigger than a man's hand,—but which is now blackening the whole sky, and threatening to rend asunder that noble fabric of union, of which he himself proposed the earliest model!"*

VIII.

BY HORACE GREELEY.—1862.

"OF the men whom the world currently terms *Self-Made*—that is, who severally fought their life-battles without the aid of inherited wealth, or

* "Address at the Inauguration of the Franklin Statue at Boston."

family honors, or educational advantages, perhaps our American FRANKLIN stands highest in the civilized world's regard. The salient feature of his career is its uniformity. In an age of wars, he never led an army, nor set a squadron in the field. He never performed any dazzling achievement. Though an admired writer and one of the greatest of scientific discoverers, he was not a genius. His progress from the mean tallow-chandler's shop of his Boston father, crammed full of hungry brothers and sisters, to the gilded saloons of Versailles, where he stood the 'observed of all observers,' —in fact, more a king than the gentle Louis, was marked by no abrupt transition, no break, no bound—he seems not so much to have risen as to have grown. You cannot say when he ceased to be poor, or unknown, or powerless; he steps into each new and higher position as if he had been born for just that; you know that his newspaper, his almanac, his electrical researches, his parliamentary service, his diplomacy, were the best of their time; but who can say that he was more admirable in one field of useful effort than another? An embassador, it has been smartly said, is one 'sent abroad to lie for his country;' yet you feel that this man could eminently serve his country in perfect truth—that his frank sincerity and heartfelt appreciation of the best points in the French character, in Parisian life, served her better than the most artful dissimulation, the most plausible hypocrisy. The French Alliance was worth more to us than Saratoga—for it gave us Yorktown—and it was not Gates's victory, as is commonly asserted, but Franklin's power and popularity, alike in the *salons* and at Court, that gained us the French alliance.

"We cannot help asking, Were poverty and obstacle among the causes, or only the incidents, of this man's greatness? Had he been cradled in affluence and dandled in the lap of luxury, had he been crammed by tutors and learnedly boxed by professors—had Harvard or Yale conferred degrees upon him at twenty, as they both rather superfluously did when he was nearly fifty—had his youth been devoted to Latin conjugations and Greek hexameters rather than to candle-dipping and type-setting—would he have been the usefully great man he indisputably was? Admit that these queries can never be conclusively answered, they may yet be profitably pondered.

*   *   *   *   *   *   *   *   *   *

"I think I adequately appreciate the greatness of Washington; yet I must place Franklin above him as the consummate type and flowering of human nature under the skies of colonial America. Not that Washington was born to competence and all needful facilities for instruction, so that he began responsible life on vantage-ground that Franklin toiled twenty arduous, precious years to reach—I cannot feel that this fact has undue weight with me. I realize that there are elements of dignity, of grandeur, in the character of Washington for which that of Franklin affords no parallel. But when I contemplate the immense variety and versatility of Franklin's services to his country and to mankind—when I think of him as a writer whose first effusions commanded attention in his early boyhood—as the monitor and teacher of his fellow-journeymen in a London printing-office—as almost from the outset a prosperous and influential editor when journalism had never before been a source of power—as taking his place naturally at the head of the postal service in America and of the earliest attempts to form a practical confederation of the Colonies—when I see him, never an enthusiast, and now nearly threescore-and-ten, renouncing office, hazarding fame, fortune, every thing, to struggle for the independence of his country—he having most to lose by failure of any American—his only son a bitter Loyalist—he cheerfully and repeatedly braving the dangers of an ocean swarming with enemies, to render his country the service as embassador which no other man could perform—and finally, when more than eighty years old, crowning a life of duty and honor by helping to frame that immortal Constitution which made us one nation forever—I cannot place Franklin second to any other American. He could not have done the work of Washington—no other man could—but then he did so many admirable things which Washington had too sound a judgment even to attempt. And, great as Washington was, he was not great enough to write and print, after he had achieved power and world-wide fame, a frank, ingenuous confession of his youthful follies and sins for the instruction and admonition of others. Many a man can look calmly down the throats of roaring cannon who lacks the courage and true philanthropy essential to those called to render this service to mankind."*

* From an unpublished Lecture on Self-Made Men.

INDEX.

Chadron State College Library
Chadron, Nebraska